The Candid Idylls of a State Representative

Byrne Corbin

Copyright © 2024 by Byrne L. Corbin.

ISBN 978-1-961358-98-0 (softcover)
ISBN 978-1-961358-88-1 (eBook)

All rights reserved. No part of this book may be reproduced or transmitted in any form or by any means, electronic or mechanical, including photocopying, recording, or by any information storage and retrieval system without express written permission from the author, except in the case of brief quotations embodied in critical reviews and certain other noncommercial uses permitted by copyright law.

Printed in the United States of America.

Contents

Byrne L. Corbin, U. Mass/Boston 11
Announcing Candidacy For The 1966 Election 12
Your Vote Makes A Difference League Of Women Voters 13
Elizabeth N. Metayer, Representative 14
Mrs. Metayer Closes Campaign On Weekend Note Of Optimism 15
9-8-74 16
Candidate's Night Set 16
Rep Races Will Highlight Tuesday's Primary Election Service
    In More Meaningful Way Pledged By Elizabeth Metayer 8-25-74 17
Dignan Accuses Mrs. Metayer Of Campaign Law Infringement Braintree Forum, ... 19
200 Pack Candidates Night In Braintree 20
Illegality Charged 20
Allegation Denied 21
Questions 21
Urges Crackdown 21
Favors Pay Raise 22
Candidate For State Representative 22
I Feel Like A Winner Already, Candidate Tells Throng At Fete 24
The Braintree Observer And Sunday Forum 25
Around Circlesby Olive Laing 25
Metayer Proposes Planning Not Gimmicks 25
Coffee Hours Held For Elizabeth Metayer Star 27
Metayer Urges All To Register & Vote 28
To The Editor 29
Mrs. Metayer, Rep. Dignan Seek 7th Norfolk Seat 30
20 Years Of Service 31
My Speech At Candidate's Night 33
Dear Friend, ... 34
We're Number One 35
Braintree Picks First Woman To Post As State Representative 35
The Braintree Observer And Sunday Forum
    Sunday, September 15, 1974 Editorial 37
9-15-74 39
Family Affair 41
"Victory" 41
The Patriot Ledger, Thursday, Jan. 2, 1975 41
Citation For Distinguished Public Service 43

The Patriot Ledger, Wed., March 26, 1975	44
Local Rep Carries 'No Station' To Decisive Victory In House	44
Guest Editorial 8-3-75	46
South Quincy Mbta Station	46
Freshman Rep Is 'A Doer By Nature" By Pamela Blevins	47
House Seat 102	50
Selected Columns From The First Year Of State Representative Elizabeth N. Metayer	55
"Swearing In"	57
"More From The State House"	59
"Orientation"	61
"Busy! Busy!	62
"Committee Assignments"	63
Lady Of The House (The Observer-Forum)	65
4-6-75	67
4-13-75	69
4-20-75	71
4-27-75	73
5-4-75	74
5-11-75	76
5-18-75	77
5-25-75	79
6-1-75	81
June 8, 1975	83
June 15, 1975	85
June 22, 1975	87
June 29, 1975	89
July 6, 1975	90
July 13, 1975	93
August 3, 1975	95
August 10, 1975	97
August 17, 1975	99
August 24, 1975	101
September 14, 1975	103
September 21, 1975	105
September 28, 1975	106
October 5, 1975	108
October 12, 1975	110
October 19, 1975	112
October 26, 1975	114
November 2, 1975	116

December 7, 1975...118
December 14, 1975...119
January 4, 1976...121
January 11, 1976...123
January 18, 1976...125
January 25, 1976...127
February 15, 1976...128
February 22, 1976...130
February 29, 1976...132
April 4, 1976...134
May 2, 1976..136
May 9, 1976..138
May 30, 1976..141
July 18, 1976..143
July 25, 1976..145
August 15, 1976..147
August 29, 1976..149
September 26, 1976 151
October 3, 1976..153
October 10, 1976..156
October 17, 1976..158
October 24, 1976..160
November 21, 1976 162
December 12, 1976...164
December 19, 1976...166
December 26, 1976...168
January 2, 1977...171
January 9, 1977...173
January 16, 1977...175
January 30, 1977...177
February 27, 1977...180
March 6, 1977 182
March 13, 1977 184
April 17, 1977...186
May 1, 1977..188
May 8, 1977..190
May 29, 1977..192
June 26, 1977...197
July 10, 1977..198
July 24, 1977..201
July 31, 1977..202

August 8, 1977	205
August 21, 1977	207
October 30, 1977	209
November 20, 1977	211
December 11, 1977	213
December 18, 1977	215
January 8, 1978	218
January 15, 1978	220
February 19, 1978	222
February 26, 1978	224
4-30-78	226
2-18-78	228
7-9-78	230
7-16-78	232
8-6-78	234
8-13-78	237
9-10-78	239
The Braintree Observer And Sunday Forum-Page Twelve Sunday, September 17, 1978	241
9-21-78	243
9-28-78	244
10-5-78	245
11-9-78	247
11-16-78	248
12-14-78	250
12-21-78	251
1-18-79	253
1-4-79	254
1-11-79	256
2-1-79	258
3-1-79	259
3-15-79	261
4-19-79	262
5-7-79	264
The Pearl Tree Crossing	265
Aircraft Noise	265
Bottle Bill	266
Tax Cap	266
The National Conference Of State Legislatures	267
7-19-79	267
7-26-79	269

8-2-79	270
8-16-79	271
8-30-79	273
9-13-79	274
10-4-79	276
10-11-79	277
11-15-79	279
11-22-79	280
12-13-79	281
1-3-80	282
1-10-80	283
January 17, 1980	285
January 24, 1980	286
February 21, 1980	287
April 3, 1980	289
April 24, 1980	290
May 1, 1980	292
May 8, 1980	293
May 29, 1980	295
6-12-80	296
7-10-80	297
7-17-80	300
8-21-80	301
8-28-80	302
9-18-80	304
9-25-80	305
10-2-80	307
10-23-80	308
10-30-80	310
11-13-80	311
11-27-80	313
12-11-80	314
1-8-81	316
1-15-81	317
1-22-81	318
February 5, 1981	319
February 12, 1981	321
March 26, 1981	322
April 2, 1981	324
April 9, 1981	325
4-16-81	327

4-30-81	328
5-21-81	330
6-11-81	331
7-2-81	332
7-9-81	334
7-16-81	335
7-23-81	336
8-13-81	338
9-3-81	339
10-2-81	341
10-9-81	342
10-16-81	343
10-30-81	345
12-4-81	346
12-11-81	347
12-18-81	348
1-15-82	350
1-29-82	351
9-1-82	353
3-12-82	354
3-19-82	355
4-23-82	357
5-7-82	358
5-14-82	360
The Braintree Star May 28, 1982	361
The Braintree Star May 28, 1982	362
The Braintree Star May 28, 1982	362
5-21-82	362
6-4-82	364
7-2-82	366
7-9-82	367
July 16, 1982	368
July 23, 1982	370
August 13, 1982	371
September 20, 1982	373
September 17, 1982	374
November 26, 1982	375
August 27, 1982	377
September 24,1982	379
October 1st, 1982	380
October 8, 1982	381

October 29, 1982	382
November 12, 1982	384
January 14	385
January 21, 1983	386
February 4, 1983	388
January 28, 1983	389
February 25, 1983	391
March 18th, 1983	392
March 25, 1983	394
April 8, 1983	395
April 22, 1983	397
June 17, 1983	398
July 8, 1983	400
July 22, 1983	401
October 7, 1983	403
November 11, 1983	404
November 25, 1983	406
December 9, 1983	407
December 16, 1983	409
February 3, 1984	410
March 10, 1984	412
March 16, 1984	413
March 23, 1984	415
April 13, 1984	416
April 27, 1984	418
June 8, 1984	419
July 13, 1984 July 6th Column	420
July 13th Column	422
July 27, 1984	423
Braintree Forum And Observer	426
"Bibs" Loved Every Minute Of 40 Years' Service	430
Braintree Gazette	433
Braintree Star	435
Local The Patriot Ledger, Saturday, December 1, 1984	437
State Representative Elizabeth N. Metayer Tribute	438
My Speech At My Testimonial Dinner At Sheraton Tara, 11-29-84	439
The Massachusetts Political Almanac	441
Key Votes Of 1981-1982 Sessions:	442
Patriot Ledger	443
The Braintree Forum	443
Braintree Forum And Observer	445

The Commonwealth Of Massachusetts	448
Beacon Hill By Renee Loth	450
Braintree Forum And Observer	450
The Boston Globe Magazine	452
Bibs Feels A Warm Glow About The Reunion Of Braintree-Ites	452
Philergians-90 Years Old And Still Going Strong	454
Braintree Forum And Observer	456
Wednesday, December 21, 1988	457
You Are The Best! Wednesday, January 9, 1985	460
Heritage Week	460
Delights In Forum's Honor	461
Challenges Of 1985	462
The Braintree Star Lady Of The House	463
The Braintree Star Lady Of The House	465
The Braintree Star Lady Of The House	466
The Braintree Star Lady Of The House	468
The Braintree Star Lady Of The House	469
The Braintree Star Lady Of The House	471
The Braintree Star Lady Of The House	472
1-04-85	474

BYRNE L. CORBIN   U. MASS/BOSTON

The State Representative

A State Representative's job is one which requires very hard work, long hours, as well as first-hand knowledge of our government, past, present and future. Whether he or she is battling for a bill on Beacon Hill, listening to a constituent's gripes, or trying to balance our budget, a State Representative's job is a twenty-four hour a day deal.

Aside from Beacon Hill a State Representative's job calls for attending social events, fund raisers and public meetings of all kinds. It is also not uncommon for a State Representative to receive calls at any time of the day, or on any day for that matter. Be it during Sunday dinner or on Christmas morning, the call comes in if someone needs his street plowed so he can get the car out or anything else.

But the bottom line is that the State Representative has to know his or her people and their needs, and must carry those needs through. Remarkable as it may seem, my State Representative in Braintree does meet the needs of everyone in our town, and still has time to be an excellent cook. I should know because I've been eating Sunday dinner with my family at her home since I've been old enough to sit up in a chair.

As well as being an extraordinary State Representative, she happens to be my grandmother. Having a grandmother as a State Representative one might ask if she still has time to be with her grandchildren and family. The answer to that is definitely yes because if she isn't busy cooking dinner, with as many vegetables as God created, she is sewing on buttons or editing and typing my papers. Even better, she is always there when I just need someone to talk to when the going gets rough. Be it school, work, family or girl friends, she has this incredible ability, although she is a half century my senior, to put herself in my shoes and tell me in her wise way what she thinks I should do. When she talks to me as I hold her hand, and she looks at me, I know she is speaking from the bottom of her heart; and when she says she'll do anything to help me, she means it.

My grandmother, State Representative Elizabeth N. Metayer is not only one of the finest grandmothers anyone could ever ask for, she is one of the most highly respected people in the State House. Just ask any of her colleagues, even the Republicans. (She's a Democrat.) As well as dedicating herself to her family, she also dedicates herself to public service. Her mother once told her "If you cast your bread upon the water it will come back as cake." For my grandmother the icing on the cake of a life in public service has been five terms as State Representative from Braintree. Her election in 1974 capped 36 years of volunteer work in Braintree, ranging from settling up a story hour for preschoolers at Watson Park Library to sponsoring a girls softball team, to serving as a town meeting member as well as presiding over the Braintree Point Woman's Club and the Democratic Town Committee.

Along the way she traveled all 50 states and 24 foreign countries with my grandfather who is just as wonderful as my grandmother. While she is on Beacon Hill, he is busy at home keeping their gorgeous house and landscape looking good. He even finds time to help me with my car when it is not running well (which is often), or just to talk with me about the good ole days.

Right here we have a simple solution to a lot of our world problems. With my grandmother as President in the White House we'd have it made. She'd invite all the heads of state over for dinner, listen to their troubles, sew on their buttons, and by the end of the evening everyone would be calling each other "Lambchop" and "Honey" and be kissing each other goodbye as they left. My grandfather, of course, could take care of the White House grounds.

People are her political philosophy
Elizabeth Metayer
for State Representative

ANNOUNCING CANDIDACY FOR THE 1966 ELECTION

Events have unfolded over the past months, which have shocked me as they have shocked all of America, have led me to this moment of decision.

Because I believe that the people should control their government, rather than that politicians should control people, I am announcing my candidacy for the office of State Representative of the 7th Norfolk District.

It was not an easy decision to make. It represents a great sacrifice on my part in that I shall have to curtail other activities, have less time to spend with my family, and give up my usual summer vacation travel.

But I feel that my commitment to the concept of good government BY the people is more important at this time, when it has been shown so clearly to all of us that bad government has the most damaging effect upon a country, or a state than any other single influence.

I feel that I have served my community well during the more than 15 years that I have been involved with its civic affairs, and I believe that I can take that past experience with me to the State House as an informed, concerned State Representative.

Government should be comprised of all facets of the community, from the 18 year old to the grandparent, in order to represent all of the people it is designed to serve. Certain professions and interest groups are overly represented at present, and it is my desire to represent all of the people, rather than to be an elected lobbyist for any group.

As my young grandsons have grown older each year, I have become increasingly concerned about what lies ahead for them in the areas of education, natural resources, income security and other factors that make for a secure and comfortable future. I could stay at home and enjoy their company today, but it is my concern for their tomorrows that prompts my quest for public office. I am aware that being concerned about them is not good enough, that demonstrating my concern for them and all the residents of my community through positive, constructive action is the best avenue to follow in demonstrating that concern.

My candidacy will concern itself with the issues that face our state government and with my stands on those issues. I intend to work vigorously to earn through my own efforts the votes of the community I hope to serve. If elected, I will act in office independently rather than as a rubber stamp for any special interest group.

My record as a Town Meeting member, Chairman of the Town's Technical Advisory Committee on Transportation, and in serving in several other capacities stands as proof of my dedication to the people of Braintree. It is the foundation upon which I hope to build as a representative of the town in state government.

I am no politician. I realize that I am not a politician, but politics has never been a good substitute for good government. And good government is what I hope to participate in as State Representative.

YOUR VOTE MAKES A DIFFERENCE LEAGUE OF WOMEN VOTERS

Elizabeth N. Metayer (D)

Education: Hickox Secretarial School; Executive Secretarial; Courses at Harvard University.

Qualifications: Seventeen years Town Meeting Member, Chairman, Technical Advisory Committee on Transportation; Legislative Chairman, Council on Aging, Founding and First President Braintree League of Women Voters; Co-founder Northeast Braintree Civic Ass'n.; Secretary Dump Site Selection Committee (Braintree); Established "Friends of Thayer Public Library".

Other: Listed in - Two Thousand Women of Achievement.

Answer: "I shall serve as a full-time representative, attend committee hearings on all important bills and, on important issues, hold public hearings and invite towns people to attend. I shall be available on a regular basis, one day each week, at my home or in a town office, for people with problems, opinions or concerns to communicate directly with me.

I will speak out for those unable to speak for themselves; support legislation for consumer protection, conservation of natural resources, reform in campaign spending and increased political accountability.

I will work with others who are truly concerned with fiscal reform to demand economy in state tax relief for the homeowner and revamping of the antiquated state budgeting system spending, that funds may be available for essential human services."

NOTE: If you vote at the following polling places; The 8th Norfolk is your district; Town Hall, Morrison School, Liberty School, highland School, any polling place in Holbrook.

ELIZABETH N. METAYER   REPRESENTATIVE

May I present my qualifications?

As a past president of the Braintree League of Women Voters, I have studied in considerable depth many key issues which will be facing the State Legislature during the next few years - the implementation of provisions of the Willis Harrington Report, and their possible effect on public education; the tax structure; civil service updating; the implementation of the Home Rule Amendment; to name a few.

As a Town Meeting member, a local legislator, of ten years standing, I feel sufficiently well acquainted with the interrelationship between our town and state governments to legislate intelligently.

I can and will devote full time to an office which I firmly believe requires full time legislators.

I see the Commonwealth as a chain of homes and families, where a woman who has budgeted the family income, been mindful of raising tax rates, and cared for and educated a family, can legislate effectively, particularly in the areas of health, education and welfare - the natural concerns of a woman.

I stand on a record of concern with and involvement in civic affairs that spans more than fifteen years.

My platform is based upon a deep concern for fiscal responsibility; I would support, with knowledge, legislation involving consumer protection, the alleviation of water and air pollution, the conservation of our natural resources, and constitutional effectiveness.

As a legislator, I would be empowered to play a more meaningful role in seeking for the district an MBTA rapid transit extension which will be both acceptable to possible commuters, and practical from the taxpayers standpoint, keeping in mind at all times not only the needs but the physical effects on this suburban district.

A peoples' candidate, I would attempt to legislate with courage and responsibility with regard for the constituents who placed me in office, my only concern.

9-8-74   MRS. METAYER CLOSES CAMPAIGN ON WEEKEND NOTE OF OPTIMISM

Mrs. Elizabeth Metayer closed her campaign for State Representative on an optimistic note this weekend.

"I have worked long and hard these past months, bringing my quest for office directly to the people," she said, "and the people have responded with an enthusiasm that is truly heartening." "Mine has been an issue-centered campaign, in which I have reminded the people of Braintree of my long-time dedicated unpaid service to the town, my record of accomplishment, and leadership, hope to serve them even more fully as their State Representative." she said.

"It is difficult to run against in incumbent, particularly one I respect personally," Mrs. Metayer said, "but personal feelings must be put aside when dealing with public issues. A public official has a voting record which must be examined fully before he is returned to office, just as my own record of accomplishment must be scrutinized."

"During this campaign, I have brought out instances where my stands on important issues differ from those recorded as votes by my opponent, citing roll call votes on record at the State House," she said, "and many of our views on issues that concern people differ sharply, giving the voters a clear choice next Tuesday.

"House to house canvassing is a stimulating experience, it means a direct encounter with people at every door, with questions on matters of great concern to the individual citizen being brought fourth dozens of times per day," Mrs. Metayer added. "It is a great challenge, but the challenge of people, and hearing their concerns, is, to me, the most important part of how I plan to work as their representative, for theirs are the voices that I will respond to, rather than to the cries of the special interest lobbyists."

"I would like to thank the thousands of citizens I have met during my canvassing, and at my coffee hours, for the encouragement and the warmth they have exhibited. They have made this campaign worthwhile, regardless of the outcome," the long-time civic leader stated.

"I only hope that they will all vote in the Primary Election on Tuesday," she added, "because people are what government should be all about, as we have learned all-too-clearly in recent months as we watched the events that have unfolded in Washington. The results of Tuesday's election now depend upon the necessity for the individual voter to exercise his or her responsibility as a true American to be heard where it counts - at the polls – regardless of the outcome," Mrs. Metayer concluded.

9-8-74

We support Elizabeth Metayer for State Representative because we believe the time has come

When Braintree needs a full-time Representative. We need someone who will be on the job every day, all day, and Mrs. Metayer has pledged that she will. We have known Elizabeth Metayer for many years, and over the past 12 of those years have worked closely with her on many town committees.

We know she is qualified!

Olive and Don Laing
82 Standish Avenue

8-20-74   CANDIDATE'S NIGHT SET

Joseph M. Tierney, last minute challenger for the U.S. Congressional seat now held by James A. Burke, has agreed to appear at the townwide Candidates' Night to be held September 5. Congressman Burke has not yet either accepted or declined an invitation to appear.

The "Night" will be held at the East Junior High School at 7:15 p.m., five days before the September 10 primaries.

Five of the six contenders for State Representative will also be present. Both of the candidates for the new 7th Norfolk seat (Braintree) and three of the four candidates for the 8th Norfolk seat (Braintree precincts 2,9,10 and 12, plus all of Holbrook) have accepted. They are: William J. Dignan and Elizabeth N. Metayer of the 7th District, and Robert E. Frazier, Andrew H. Card, Jr., and Frank W. McGaughey of the 8th District, James G. Keefe of the 8th District has not yet replied to his invitation.

Also scheduled to appear on the platform are County Commissioner candidate James J. Heggie, Jr. of Canton, and candidates for County Sheriff, including the incumbent, Charles W. Hedges of Dedham, and Charles H. Marshall of Quincy.

REP RACES WILL HIGHLIGHT TUESDAY'S PRIMARY ELECTION SERVICE IN MORE MEANINGFUL WAY PLEDGED BY ELIZABETH METAYER 8-25-74

A desire to serve her community in a more meaningful way led her into the race for State Representative, Democratic Candidate Elizabeth Metayer told a large coffee hour gathering this past week (the most recent of which was held at the home of Mrs. Timothy Cronin of Alida Road.) During the several years she served as Chairman of the Technical Advisory on Transportation (TAC), she learned how state authorities, through legislation, have gained monumental power over communities such as Braintree, including the right to take property by eminent domain.

"There is no such thing as home rule when state laws tie the hands of local officials and private citizens," Mrs. Metayer said. Participating in local civic groups and in the Town Meeting has been educational and rewarding, the candidate said, but she has come to realize how great the need is for civic-minded, non-political people to represent the homeowner and taxpayer at the state level, where the laws that govern their lives are made. "We have too many politicians in government," she noted, "and not enough representation by those who have no vested interest or profession to protect when they vote on proposed legislation." "It is time for the average citizen and his entire family to have a voice, not only at our Town Hall, but under the golden dome of the State House as well," she added. "The average worker has much of his hard-earned salary taken away from him in taxes, but what is he receiving in return? As an example, he has to pay the bill for the MBTA to rumble along behind his home, when he did not want it there in the first pace," Mrs. Metayer said.

Voicing her concern about young people and their general distrust of government, Mrs. Metayer noted that the professional politicians who made up the now-defunct Nixon administration were well-educated men, many of whom were attorneys "who should have set the best of examples for our young. Instead," she said, "most of them are now either in jail or under indictment. The young people can have their faith in government restored only by having an opportunity to participate in it, to become part of it through the voting process, and, most importantly, by being encouraged to look at government as a possible career. That is why I conducted a voter registration drive in Braintree recently, and why I propose an intern program for high school students at the State House," she said.

My registration drive will benefit all candidates in the primary election, and the intern program will benefit whoever is elected, so these programs have not been offered selfishly, to further my own candidacy," she added.

Working as liaison for the Council on Aging, she has learned first-hand of the problems faced by the elderly who are living on fixed incomes. "Our senior citizens should not be forced to live without sufficient nourishment, clothing or housing facilities because the politicians do not consider them as a strong voting bloc," Mrs. Metayer said. "They have paid taxes for decades, and many of them brought up their children during the lean years of the Depression, which left them little to put aside for themselves. The legislature has not provided them with proper tax relief, and something must be done about that. To me, they are as important as the young, and I intend to become their advocate at the State House as well," she said.

"We have seen what politicians at every level have done to government, and to people in recent years," Mrs. Metayer said, "but I want to prove what people like myself, who are not politicians, can do FOR government. I have worked on civic and governmental committees and projects for my town for the past 20 years, and I would like to take my proven record of concern for the people of Braintree one step further, by being allowed the privilege of serving all of them as their State Representative."

"And I will never quit on my responsibility," Mrs. Metayer emphasized. "No matter what the heat, I will stay in the kitchen."

The race for State Representative from the Seventh Norfolk District will highlight the Democratic primary election this coming Tuesday. In this contest incumbent William J. Dignan will be opposed by Elizabeth Metayer. The Seventh Norfolk District includes precincts 1, 3, 4, 5, 6, 7, 8 and 11 in Braintree.

In the Eighth Norfolk District Robert E. Frazier will be contested by James G. Keefe and Frank W. McGaughey, both of Holbrook.

Present Attorney General Robert H. Quinn will be opposed in the Democratic primary race for Governor by former State Representative Michael S. Dukakis.

The race for Lieutenant Governor will find a five man field: Eva B. Hester, Christoper A. Iannella, former State Representative and present Boston City Councillor; John Pierce Lynch, former State Representative and present Registrar of Deeds; and Thomas Martin Sullivan, present Selectman from Randolph. The largest field on the democratic ballot will be for Attorney General.

We honorably endorse Elizabeth "Bibs" Metayer for State Representative

May we ask you, our friends, to do the same. Thank you.

Harold and Mary Furlani, 79 Richard Road.

9-8-74 — DIGNAN ACCUSES MRS. METAYER OF CAMPAIGN LAW INFRINGEMENT BRAINTREE FORUM,

Representative William J. Dignan accused his Democratic primary opponent Elizabeth N. Metayer of violating the election law at a Candidates Night Thursday at East Junior High.

Mr. Dignan said Mrs. Metayer failed to file proper documents with the state in regard to her organization committee as provided for under the Campaign Reform Act of 1973. He referred specifically to a commercial on radio station WJDA which Mr. Dignan said was paid for by Jay Hedlund whereas Mrs. Gael Corbin was listed as treasurer.

Mr. Dignan concluded his opening attack by stating "it takes a lot of brass to want to make laws stricter, when she can't comply with the present laws." He pointed out that the penalty for violation of campaign laws is punishable by a $1,000.00 fine or one year in prison.

Mrs. Metayer replied that she was "taken aback" by the charges and apologized for her committee if they did indeed commit any wrong. She added that she would "hate to be in prison when I am elected representative.

Jay Hedlund asked Mr. Dignan if he knew for a fact that he (Mr. Hedlund) had signed the check. Mr. Dignan replied he received the information from Win Bettinson of WJDA. Mr. Hedlund then informed Mr. Dignan that the check had, in fact, been signed by the Committee's advertising agent, Mediareps. This was confirmed Friday by WJDA officials and a spokesman for Mediareps.

Mr. Hudlund asked Mr. Dignan when he learned of the alleged violation and when Mr. Dignan replied he did notknow, he was asked by Mr. Hedlund why he waited until the "11th hour" to reveal it. Mr. Dignan did not respond. He also asked Mr. Dignan if his financial report to the election committee two years ago was not in fact returned twice for more detailed information. When Mr. Dignan replied "no," Mr. Hedlund advised that he had seen the records at the Secretary of State's office indicating that this was so.

In other questions from the floor, the two candidates differed in several areas: Pension Offset Bill: Mr. Dignan did not think it right to collect simultaneously a pension and unemployment. Mrs. Metayer said she had a real concern for the elderly and they could use all the help they could get.

Gun Control: Mrs. Metayer said she favors strong gun control laws, while Mr. Dignan stated that only "good people" would register guns and dishonest people would not.

Full-time Representation and Legislative Pay Raise: Mr. Dignan said he does and will devote all the time necessary to do the job, but it was not a full-time position. He also favored a pay raise. Mrs. Metayer stated she could not envision the office of representative as being a part-time job and would devote full-time representation at the State House if elected. She added that she was against a pay raise for legislators.

200 PACK CANDIDATES NIGHT IN BRAINTREE

Braintree At least 200 people jammed East Junior High School last night to hear candidates Tuesday's primary elections.for Congress, state representative, and sheriff of Norfolk County make political appeals before Congressional candidates U.S. Rep. James A. Burke, D-Milton, and Republican Joseph M. Tierney; candidates for state representative in the seventh and eighth District, Elizabeth N. Metayer, Rep. William J. Dignan of Braintree, Rep. Robert E. Frazier of Braintree, James G. Keefe, Frank W. McDonald, all Democrats, and Republican Andrew H. Card; and candidates for sheriff of Norolk County, Alan J. Boyd, Clifford H. Marshall, George B. McDonald, all Democrats, Republican Sheriff Charles W. Hedges, attended the candidates night sponsored by the Braintree Jaycees and League of Women Voters to air their political views.

Two other candidates for sheriff, Paul E. Barry and John H. Brownell, did not appear at session.

ILLEGALITY CHARGED

Despite lengthy discussion, there was little heated debate until the later hours when incumbent State Rep. Dignan accused his opponent in the race for state representative from the seventh Norfolk District Mrs. Elizabeth N. Metayer of illegal campaign activities.

Rep. Dignan charged the Committee to Elect Mrs. Metayer with failure to organize within the legal deadline and alleged that radio time was purchased by campaign manager Jay. H. Hedlund when Mrs. Gael Corbin is legally listed as treasurer.

He charged Mrs. Metayer "beats the drums for tighter campaign laws" but does not conform herself.

He stated the alleged violation carries a penalty of fine and imprisonment.

Mrs. Metayer apologized for any possible nonconforming actions of the committee.

ALLEGATION DENIED

However, Mr. Hedlund denied any wrongdoing on the part of the committee to elect Mrs. Metayer and said he had not paid for any radio time on station WJDA. He explained radio time was purchased by Media Representatives, 25 Elm St., retained by the committee to promote Mrs. Metayer's campaign. He said the advertising agency was reimbursed by committee treasurer Mrs. Corbin.

A spokesman for Media Representatives later clarified that Mr. Hedlund's name appeared on a written request for radio time according to a new law requiring such requests be made as an initial step in purchasing political advertising time.

However, he said the radio time was paid for by Media Representatives and that the agency was reimbursed by the treasurer, Mrs. Corbin, on a check drawn on a bank account for the Committee to Elect Mrs. Metayer.

QUESTIONS

The charges were interspersed with questions from the audience which ranged from the candidates' views on child support to Mrs. Metayer's idea of "little city halls."

The candidates differed mainly in their opinions over handgun legislation, fulltime representative, and child support of working mothers.

Mrs. Metayer said she would be consistently against unregistered guns and unlimited sales. She advocated registration of all handguns and rifles with stiff sentences for abusers.

URGES CRACKDOWN

But Rep. Dignan countered that the registration of guns will not solve the problem of gun abuse. He felt judges are not giving "firm enough sentences" to discourage gun abuses and advocated a "crackdown on the wrongdoer."

He also felt that as representative, he had devoted enough time to the job as was necessary and that the position doesn't require fulltime effort. But Mrs. Metayer replied that she "can't envision running the multimillion dollar business of government on a part-time basis." She also stated she was not "all that concerned about salary" and would oppose a pay raise for legislators.

FAVORS PAY RAISE

Rep. Dignan favored the increase to reflect the rising cost of living. He felt legislators should be compensated for the spiraling cost of living.

He also felt a move for child support for working mothers was "a first step" but felt the economy does not allow great expansion of the idea.

But Mrs. Metayer fully supported the measure. "I support any benefits for working mothers," she declared. He felt savings could be reflected in reduced welfare payments.

On a local level, the two candidates stood opposed to the location for the proposed MBTA station for Braintree.

Rep. Dignan claimed the dump site favored by Mrs. Metayer would cause additional congestion in the Union Street area and suggested locating the facility in South Quincy.

CANDIDATE FOR STATE REPRESENTATIVE

Elizabeth N. Metayer of 33 Arthur Street, East Braintree has formally announced her candidacy for the Democratic nomination for State Representative from the new 7th Norfolk District.

Mrs. Metayer, known to many as "Bibs", is married to Edward A. Metayer and has been active for the past 20 years in political, civic and social affairs in Braintree. She narrowly missed gaining the Democratic nomination for State Representative in 1966 when the district included all of Braintree and Quincy Point. The present district, for the first time this year due to re-districting, is composed only of Precincts one, three, four, five, six seven, eight and eleven from Braintree. One person will be elected to represent that district.

In making her announcement Mrs. Metayer said that three questions about her run for public office invariably arise. "People ask me why I am running, what are my qualifications and what do I hope to accomplish," she said.

"I am running because I, along with many others, see the need for full-time active and dedicated representation for Braintree at the State House. As Chairman of the Technical Advisory Committee on Transportation in dealing with the MBTA and as legislative liaison for the Council on Aging, I have been in close and continuing contact with state agencies and officials. As a fighter for Braintree's interests in these and other matters I have come to realize how important it is for citizens to have strong representatives who will provide leadership and vocal support on important issues. I am running to offer the people of Braintree a choice between continuation of the old problems - rising taxes, increased power of state agencies and deteriorating services to the people - or the development of new solutions based on what is needed rather than on political expediency. I am running because I feel that I, and others dedicated to public service, can make a difference," Mrs. Metayer said. Mrs. Metayer rested her qualification for the office on her 20 year record of public service. She has been a Town Meeting Member for 17 years, in addition to her service on the Technical Advisory Committee and the Council on Aging. She has served on the Dump Site Selection Committee, the Northeast Braintree Civic Association and is presently Secretary of the Precinct Seven Association. She was the Founding and First President of the Braintree League of Women Voters; President of the Archbishop Williams Guild; President, Quincy Deanery, Archdiocesan Council of Catholic Women; two term President of the Braintree Point Woman's Club and Federation Secretary of the Philergians. She has also held statewide office as Chairman of International Affairs and Chairman of Drama of the Massachusetts State Federation of Women's Clubs. In addition Mrs. Metayer has been involved with many fundraising drives including positions as Town Chairman of the Cancer Crusade, Co- chairman of the Mothers March for the March of Dimes and Public Relations Chairman for the united Fund.

"I feel that my primary qualification for serving in the House of Representatives is a record of service which I believe gives strong evidence of my effectiveness and my commitment to the total community," Mrs. Metayer added..

Mrs. Metayer said that she had some definite objectives both for her campaign and for when she takes office. "I will have a campaign that will rely on personal contact so that the people may question me and give me their thinking about state affairs. I will canvass house to house and will attend as many Coffee Hours and other functions as we can schedule. I want the people to see that the energy and dedication I put into campaigning will go to work for them once I am elected," she said.

"When I take office I will work for and speak out on the right to a full and decent life that the undereducated, the poor, the handicapped and the as yet unborn should be able to expect. I will support, as I have done in the past, legislation for consumer protection, conservation of our natural resources, reforms in campaign spending and increased political accountability. Fundamentally, however, I will work with those others who are truly concerned with fiscal reform to demand budgeting system," Mrs. Metayer pledged. economy in state spending, tax relief for the homeowner and a revamping of the antiquated state stand on any and all pertinent issues as they arise. I have, I hope during my service to Braintree built a reputation of active and honest commitment to the community. In summary Mrs. Metayer said, "I expect as a legislator, as well as during my campaign, to take a I want to further that commitment in the sensitive position of State Representative and I would act in such a way as to protect and enhance that reputation for service to the community.

7-7-74   I FEEL LIKE A WINNER ALREADY, CANDIDATE TELLS THRONG AT FETE

More than 300 people turned out last Saturday night to honor State Representative candidate Elizabeth N. Metayer at a reception at the Knights of Columbus Hall in South Braintree.

Mrs. Metayer is running in the Democratic primary for the nomination for state representative from the Seventh Norfolk District, which includes Braintree precincts one, three, four, five, six, seven, eight and eleven. In welcoming those who attended the affair, Mrs. Metayer said, "I feel like a winner already because of the wonderful people I have attracted to my candidacy." She emphasized that it is extremely important in this period of American politics that people take an active part in campaigns and in their government so that the system will be revitalized. She vowed to take steps as a legislator to encourage participation by all groups and individual citizens into the governmental process. "When I am a representative I intend to initiate what I call 'little town meetings.' When there is an important issue under scrutiny at the State House, I will arrange for a hall here in Braintree and call a 'little town meeting.' I will invite experts who would share their expertise on the matter - whether it be education, law enforcement or consumer protection or any other vital issue. I will encourage private citizens who will be directly affected by the proposed legislation to give me their thoughts. Then when I vote on the issue at the State House I will be intelligently informed about how my district views the matter," Mrs. Metayer said.

Mrs. Metayer, who narrowly lost a nomination for Representative in 1966, said that the position she seeks would be a culmination of more than 20 years in service to Braintree. She said, "I will go to the State House to serve the people of Braintree and the state. I will seek no higher office, and I desire no appointment such as a judgeship. I will be able to vote independently and free from any selfish motive or personal ambition." She later said that she felt that this was an important consideration in light of how low in esteem professional politicians are presently held by the electorate. Following Mrs. Metayer's remarks, she was surprised by the performance of a song written especially for her campaign, which featured Mrs. Metayer's long history of political and civic involvement and her dedication to her community. It was written and performed by the professional singing group, "The Happy Hearts." The performance by Rosemary McCarthy, and Jane Cronin of Braintree and Pat Marcotte and Ginny DiTullio of Weymouth with accompaniment by Mary Burns Reilly, brought a standing ovation from the audience. Other entertainment was provided by master of ceremonies Bill Flanagan and "The Versatiles" of Braintree.

7-4-74 THE BRAINTREE OBSERVER AND SUNDAY FORUM

WHEN FRIENDS MEET

Mrs. Elizabeth N. Metayer, candidate for Representative from the seventh Norfolk district (Braintree Precincts 1,3,4,5,6,7,8 and 11) is greeted warmly by Ernest Sheehan at the recent reception in her honor at K of C Hall. Some 300 enthusiastic supporters gave Mrs. Metayer a standing ovation following her brief talk during which she outlined some of her goals and pledged to be a full-time Representative. A buffet, dancing and entertainment were included in the evening.

AROUND CIRCLESBY OLIVE LAING

It was Bibs Metayer Night at K of C Hall last Saturday evening when more than 300 admirers turned out for a reception, buffet and dance in her honor...Radiant, and obviously moved by the "Hello Bibs" greeting sung by the throng of well-wishers, the guest of honor and her husband, Ted, stood for a moment smiling and nodding as the standing crowd applauded...She was wearing a full-length bright red gown which set off her youthful figure perfectly...The hall was festooned in red, white and blue, and the blue covers on the tables-for-ten complemented the centerpieces of fresh garden flowers...One of the highlights of the evening was the medley of songs sung by "The Happy Hearts," all chosen especially for Bibs Metayer and climaxed with an original, written by Rosemary McCarthy, one of the members of the popular singing group...It was titled, "It Takes a Woman," and there was no mistaking its fun message...It brought the house down...The Frank Marinelli Orchestra provided great music for the dancing and a mid-evening buffet was enjoyed.

METAYER PROPOSES PLANNING NOT GIMMICKS

"The homeowner must not be misled into thinking that gimmicks, games and political promises will deliver real tax relief. What is needed is a serious minded legislature that will take the time and make the difficult decisions necessary to cut waste from the budget, establish realistic fiscal priorities and reform the budget making process."

With those words Elizabeth N. Metayer, candidate for the Democratic nomination for state representative from the Seventh Norfolk District (Braintree precincts one, three, four, five, six, seven, eight and eleven) outlined her views on the state's economy and tax picture to a group of businessmen in Braintree this week.

"The state's economy is in seriously bad shape and the state legislature is fiddling while the tax-pressed homeowner burns." Mrs. Metayer said. She pointed out that a study by the First National Bank of Boston has shown that Massachusetts is one of the only two states in the country that will have a budget deficit this year. The study also indicates that Massachusetts is the only state in the nation faced with a tax increase for the next year.

"The legislature is providing band-aids for the state's fiscal operations when major surgery is necessary," Mrs. Metayer said. "For a good example, my opponent has called for an increase in legalized gambling to solve our tax ills. We have been promised such miracle drugs before. The sales tax was to have provided instant relief for the homeowner. The lottery was to have kept taxes down. But, as the bank's study has shown, our state - already one of the most heavily taxed in the country - faces still another tax increase. We need fewer promises and gimmicks from politicians, more hard work by people dedicated to a cut in wasteful state programs and real budget making reform." Mrs. Metayer pledged to vote against any new taxes until real tax reform is undertaken by the legislature. "We need to institute 'planned, programmed budgeting' at once - at least in the major budget departments such as welfare, education, corrections and human services. The bulk of our state tax dollars is going into these areas and the present/budget system does not provide any realistic review of the effectiveness of programs, does not indicate areas of duplication and encourages the perpetuation of programs that have met their original goals. It would take some time to fully implement "PPBS" but it would be a move into modern budget development and would provide an effective tool for those who will be watchdogs on state spending," the businesswoman added. Mrs. Metayer also said that the state legislature must move beyond providing everything for everyone. "We must establish priorities and stick to those priorities. Some programs just cannot be passed if there is no money to pay for it. In recent years the legislature has often passed bills and yet not provide funding for the new programs. Typically, the burden then falls on the local property tax and the towns become responsible for paying the legislature's bills. Even when town meetings try to be fiscally responsible, the legislature forces new obligations onto the towns. This must stop. Each bill should have a 'price tag' and if the legislature is not going to pay that cost the towns and their officials should be informed in advance that they will be expected to on the need for the new programs." pick up the check. That way they can lobby their representatives and senators on the towns' views fundamental to the issue of tax reform is a cut in wasteful state spending, Mrs. Metayer stressed. "The state house should not be a high paying refuge for former legislators who have been defeated in elections.

The people have become fed up with a patronage system that provides jobs like the one former Senator Joe Ward was promised when he was defeated two years ago. When you walk through the State House and see the number of former elected officials with high paying appointed jobs you realize that example is the rule rather than the exception," Mrs. Metayer added. Mrs. Metayer called for major reforms of the antiquated and wasteful county system of government and urged an aggressive attempt by the state to encourage businesses to come to and remain in Massachusetts. She is also for more effective employment training and job placement programs by the state.

"Fiscal reform requires legislators who are committed to long and hard hours at the State House. If elected I will not offer the empty promise that betting on professional or college football games will solve our tax problems. Instead I will spend these hours at the State House helping to develop real tax relief for the homeowners of Braintree, through sound budget formation, hardened opposition to wasteful spending and establishment of realistic priorities for state spending," Mrs. Metayer pledged.

7-31-74 COFFEE HOURS HELD FOR ELIZABETH METAYER STAR

In a series of coffee hours held this past week for Elizabeth N. Metayer who is running for state representative from the new Seventh Norfolk District (precincts one, three, four, five, six, seven, eight and eleven), the Democratic candidate has pledged to "request from the leadership that I be placed on the legislature's Transportation Committee to protect Braintree's interests during theExpansion of the MBTA."

Answering a direct question on the subject of a coffee hour hosted by Mary Beaver of 51 Emerald Avenue, Mrs. Metayer said, "The extension of the MBTA to Braintree is one of the most critical areas where state action will affect the town in the next decade. We need to have an active representative at the State House to protect the town's interests. A position on the Transportation Committee would give me the exposure and the leverage the town will need with the MBTA and the State Department Transportation to insure that rapid transit will serve our town's best interests."

Mrs. Metayer served as the chairman of the town's Technical Advisory Committee on Transportation (TAC), and in that role had continuous contact with the MBTA and state agencies involved with extension of rapid transit to Braintree. She spearheaded the drive against an elevated rail system that was proposed for the town in the 1960's and was active in citizen opposition to the location of a subway station at the traffic snarled Capen's Circle area of North Braintree.

"As chairman of the TAC Committee I fought the MBTA when it was difficult for towns to have Input to how the expansion would take place. Our Committee action stopped the elevated structure and bought us some time so that now the town does have some say and can exercise some options and influence on the MBTA plans. For those plans to represent the best interest of Braintree we need a representative who is willing to spend full time at the state house, who will speak out at hearings and on the floor of the House for Braintree's interests, and who will keep our local officials informed Mrs. Metayer said. of the MBTA and state plans for every step of the way. I pledge to do just that as a representative," Mrs. Metayer said that the overall transportation plans for Braintree must also include swift and effective solution of other traffic problems in Braintree. She specifically mentioned the long standing problem of congestion at Five Corners and the underpass at the Expressway at River Street. She pointed out that these problems are under the authority of the state, but the problems facing residents in these areas are not being dealt with properly.

7-28-74 METAYER URGES ALL TO REGISTER & VOTE

Elizabeth N. Metayer, candidate for the Democratic nomination for the state representative from the new Seventh Norfolk District (Braintree precincts one, three, four, five, six, seven, eight and eleven) announced this week that her campaign has undertaken a major voter registration drive because she feels, "One person can make a difference-whether that one person is running for office or is casting a vote at the ballot box."

Mrs. Metayer said that she mailed out 3,000 notices to residents of the Seventh Norfolk District who have not yet registered, reminding them that special hours have been established to make it easier for people to register to vote in the September 10 Primary Election. To vote in that election people must register by August 13. To do so, unregistered citizens may go to Town Hall any business day between 8:30 a.m. and 4:30 p.m. Special hours have also been scheduled to make it easier for residents to register. Those hours are: Monday, August 5, from 7-9 p.m. at Town Hall; Wednesday, August 7, from 7-9 p.m. at the East Braintree Fire Station; Saturday August 10, from noon to 10 p.m. at Town Hall; and Tuesday, August 13, from 9 a.m. to 10 p.m. at Town Hall.

Mrs. Metayer urged unregistered citizens to register and vote. She said, "I am running for office because I believe one person can make a difference. The only way to improve our government is to get good people elected. Each good person who goes to the State House can join with a growing band of others dedicated to service, not power. The same way that I feel one person can make a difference at the State House, I also feel that one person can make a difference at the ballot box." Mrs. Metayer emphasized that although she would love to have all the newly registered voters for her, she felt the most important consideration is for all the townspeople to take an active interest in political campaigns currently underway. She said, "I am more than willing to have all voters carefully examine my record and that of my opponent, to listen to our stands on the issues and to question our positions - and then have them vote intelligently for whomever they feel would be the better representative. It is essential to the quality of our government, however, that voters take an active interest in political campaigns. If they do then we can feel more confident that the better candidate will win and that we can start to improve our government. For good people to do nothing would only lead to a continuation of mediocre service and high taxes that we are getting from our state legislature."

To vote in the Democratic Primary on September 10, voters must be registered either as a Democrat or Independent by August 13. If the voter is an Independent, he or she may vote in the Democratic Primary merely by asking for a Democratic ballot at the polling booth on Primary Day. Cards will be available at each voting location on that day so that voters may change their registration back to Independent immediately after voting, if they so choose.

Mrs. Metayer has been frequently asked by Republicans about what they must do to be able to vote in the Democratic Primary, since there is no Republican candidate running for state representative in her district this year. To vote in the Democratic Primary, Republicans must change their registration to Independent or Democrat by August 13. They may do so at the town clerk's office in Town Hall or at the special registration sessions that have been scheduled. After they cast their ballot in the Democratic Primary, these voters may fill out the cards available at the polling and change their registration back to Republican, if they so choose.

7-28-74 TO THE EDITOR

"POLITICAL RHETORIC" CRITICIZED BY CANDIDATE

To the Editor.

I am interested to see Mr. Dignan, my opponent for State Representative from the 7th Norfolk District (Braintree) asking the Department of Public Works that "at least half" of the Quincy Avenue Bridge be open to traffic during the bridge reconstruction.

I am disappointed, however, that this effort by him is coming at such a late hour. We in the Precinct Seven Association foresaw last winter the difficulties that this reconstruction would generate for businesses and residents of the area. We held two meetings devoted to the problem, neither of which Mr. Dignan attended.

In these two meetings, one of which was attended by two D.P.W. engineers, one of whom was Primo Parola, District Project Engineer for the D.P.W., these problems were discussed in detail.

It was explained to us that the present drawbridge and the type of construction necessary for the new bridge did not render feasible the proposal by Selectman Laing that half of the bridge remain open to traffic during construction. At his suggestion therefore, and with the support of the Precinct Seven Association a shuttle bus service was instituted to aid the residents during the difficulties of the construction period.

This past Monday a group of residents from the area attended the Selectmen's Meeting and presented their case for one way traffic on Shaw and Allen Streets. This would cut down traffic congestion and lessen the safety hazard created by the detoured traffic from Quincy Avenue. We are sorry that Mr. Dignan could not be at that meeting either.

We trust that citizen action at the right time will be more effective than political rhetoric at a "convenient" time during a campaign.

Elizabeth N. Metayer
33 Arthur Street
Braintree

MRS. METAYER, REP. DIGNAN SEEK 7TH NORFOLK SEAT

Two candidates are seeking the Democratic nomination for state representative from the new Seventh Norfolk District, which includes in Braintree precincts 1, 3, 4, 5, 6, 7, 8 and 11. They are Elizabeth N. Metayer and Rep. William J. Dignan. There are no Republican candidates in the race.

Elizabeth N. Metayer

Elizabeth N. Metayer, 62, of 33 Arthur St., Braintree, is making her first bid for state representative for the 7th Norfolk District.

Mrs. Metayer, a graduate of Hickox Secretarial School, said she would like to make a fulltime job of being state representative and would attend committee meetings on all important bills and hold public hearings to bring speakers and invite townspeople to participate "on all important bills that will effect their lives."

"I will speak out for others, support legislation for consumer protection, conservation of natural resources and reform in campaign spending," she said.

To Demand Economy" "I will work with others concerned with fiscal reform to demand economy in state spending," she continued, "and work towards revamping of the antiquated state budgeting system to provide Money for essential human services. Mrs. Metayer has been a town meeting member for the past 17 years, chairman of the technical advisory committee on transportation; legislative chairman of the Council on Aging; secretary of the Precinct Seven Assn.; co-founder of the Northeast Braintree Civic Assn.; founder and first President of the Braintree League of Women Voters; past president of the Archbishop Williams Mothers Guild and a member of numerous other organizations.

Mrs. Metayer has been named in "Two Thousand Women of Achievement" in 1969, the "National Register of Prominent Americans" in 1969 and "Who's Who in American Politics," in 1969.

William J. Dignan

William J. Dignan, 47, of 48 Celia Road, Braintree, is a candidate for a third term as a Democratic state representative.

An attorney, he is a graduate of Suffolk University and Suffolk University Law School.

He is a town meeting member, and special town counsel for the Municipal Light Board.

Mr. Dignan favors a hard line approach on the MBTA extension to Braintree as a top priority issue.

"Braintree shall not become a parking lot for Weymouth commuters," he states.

He believes the Supreme Court erred in allowing abortion on demand. He also believes tougher penalties are needed for lawbreakers and opposes furloughs for hardened criminals.

20 YEARS OF SERVICE

Why am I Running?

Will hamburger be $2.50 a pound when my grandson is bringing up his family? Will young people continue to shudder at the word "politician"? Will the elderly soon not be able to afford carfare to visit their children? Questions like these have motivated me to run for state representative. I believe one person can make a difference. One person dedicated to service, not power, dedicated to need, not expediency; dedicated to people, not special interests.

There is a vital need for active, fulltime representation for Braintree at the State House. I have seen it personally. As Chairman of the Technical Advisory Committee on Transportation in dealing with the MBTA, and as legislative liaison for the Council on Aging, I have been in close contact with state agencies and officials. As a fighter for Braintree in these matters, I have seen firsthand how imperative it is for citizens to have strong representatives who will provide leadership and who will speak out on important issues.

I am running to offer the people of Braintree a choice. Do you want the continuation of skyrocketing taxes? Do you want state agencies to tighten their stranglehold even further, as services deteriorate? Do you want political expediency to rule every decision?

Or do you want to help me find new solutions?

What Are My Qualifications?

I feel my primary qualification for serving in the House of Representatives is my record of 20 years of service to the community of Braintree.

This work has transcended political lines and cut across generation gaps. I have worked with the very young, teen-agers, my peers and the elderly. I have founded, chaired and served on numerous committees ranging from transportation to conservation, from dump site selection to the problems of the local libraries.

This work has included the chairmanship of several charity drives over the years such as the Cancer Crusade, the United Fund and the Mothers' March Against Polio. I have also held elected offices in several political and social organizations, including the Founding and First Presidency of the Braintree League of Women Voters.

During this time I have, I hope, built a reputation of active, honest, independent commitment to the community. I see service in the House of Representatives -- not as a stepping stone to higher office - but as an end in itself, a vitally sensitive position where I could continue to work for the community of Braintree.

What Do I Hope To Accomplish?

I have definite objectives both for my campaign and for my years in office. My campaign relies on a vigorous schedule of personal contact, so that people may question me and share with me their thinking on state affairs. It is this same type of energy, dedication and voter contact that I will bring to the office of State Representative.

When I am in office I will speak out for those who cannot speak for themselves -- the under- educate, the poor, the handicapped, the elderly, the yet unborn.

I will support legislation for consumer protection, conservation of natural resources, reform in campaign spending and increased political accountability.

Fundamentally I will work with others who are truly concerned with fiscal reform to demand budgeting system. economy in state spending, tax relief for the homeowner and a revamping of the antiquated state budgeting system. I would like to work with others dedicated to public service to show that politics and politicians can represent the best of the American Spirit.

Elizabeth Metayer for Representative

Mary Wybieracki
23 Anderson Road
Ernest D. Frawley
80 Monatiquot Avenue
James and Mary Morrissey
28 Adams Street
S. Alan and Noreen Curtis
16 Deborah Land
Joe and Elaine Lally
56 Arthur Street
Jay and Carel Hedlund
263 Elm Street
Paul and Claire McGaffigan
9 Woodledge Lane

9-5-74 MY SPEECH AT CANDIDATE'S NIGHT

My most sincere thanks to the Jaycees and the League of Women Voters...

My campaign these past weeks has been a vigorous one, geared to the issues that face you – the people -- in the next two years.

- A state budget that has more than doubled in the past six years.
- Young people who shudder at the word "politician".
- The elderly, who can barely afford to eat on their fixed incomes.

Concern for people such as these has motivated me to seek the office of State Representative, because I believe that one person CAN make a difference, if that person is dedicated to service, not power; sensitive to need rather than expediency; and committed to people, not special interests. There is a vital need for Braintree to have active, full-time representation at the State House. I have seen this need personally as Chairman of the Town's Transportation Advisory Committee in dealing with the MBTA; and as legislative liaison for the Council on Aging.

As a fighter for Braintree in these and other areas-dealing with state agencies and officials, I have seen first-hand how imperative it is for our town to have strong representatives who will provide leadership and will speak out on important issues.

I offer the people of Braintree a choice.

Do you want state agencies to tighten their stranglehold on communities even as services deteriorate?

Do you want political expediency to color every decision; or do you feel that you - as citizens - are more important?

Or do you want to help me find solutions to our mutual problems?

Every citizen has the right to run for office, and I feel that I have EARNED the right to be elected. My prime qualification for seeking office is my 20 years of service to Braintree. This service has transcended political lines, and bridged generation gaps.

I have worked with the very young, teen-agers, my peers and the elderly. I have chaired and served on countless committees; and chaired charity drives. In my 17 years as a Town Meeting Member and my work as founding and first president of our League of Women Voters, I have proved my effectiveness in leadership roles.

Through the years I have, I hope, built a reputation for active, honest, independent commitment to my community; and I see service as your State Representative not as a stepping stone to higher office, but as an end in itself, an extension of that commitment.

My campaign has relied upon a vigorous schedule of personal contact, sharing people's thinking on state issues. I am in my tenth week of going house to house; and yesterday held my 31st Coffee Hour (with five to go.) It is this type of energy, dedication and voter contact I intend to bring to the office of State Representative.

When elected, my first priority will be to work with others who are deeply concerned about fiscal reform, to demand economy in state spending, tax relief for the homeowner and the elderly, and a revamping of the outdated state budget system.

I will support legislation for consumer protection; conservation of natural resources; reform in campaign practices; and increased accountability by public officials; and will work with others dedicated to public service, to prove that public officials CAN represent the best of the American spirit. You can give me that chance by voting for me next Tuesday. Thank you.

DEAR FRIEND,

I want to thank you for signing my nomination papers for State Representative. Because you and many others were kind enough to sign my papers, my name will be on the ballot on September 10 Primary Day as I seek the Democratic nomination for State Representative from eight of Braintree Precincts (One, Three, Four, Five, Six, Seven, Eight and Eleven.) I thank you for giving me that chance.

Your act of signing my nomination paper in no way obligates you to vote for me. I would hope, however, that as my campaign progresses you will have the chance to study the issues, question my positions and carefully consider my candidacy.

State and national politics are presently in a condition that does not engender great confidence from the people. The only way to improve our government, I believe, is for good people to take an active role in holding office holders accountable.

I would urge you, and others, to take an active part in the political campaigns presently underway to insure that a person who reflects what you want from your government will be elected. Whom you support - whether it be me, my opponent, or any candidate for other elective office - is not the most important thing. What is important is that good people become actively involved in the political process so that we can once again have a government that we can respect and trust. If you do feel that I would help bring the State House an honesty and active dedication that has long been needed, I would welcome any help you may be able to lend.

Sincerely,
Elizabeth N. Metayer
Candidate for State Representative
33 Arthur Street
East Braintree, Mass.
02184
Tel. 843-5159

WE'RE NUMBER ONE

Mr. and Mrs. Edward A Metayer, Ted and Bibs to their countless friends, pose for their first photo after hearing the total vote in Mrs. Metayer's stunning upset victory over incumbent William J. Dignan in the Democratic primary race for State Representative in the Seventh Norfolk District. Mrs. Metayer's win virtually assures her a seat in the house as there was no Republican running. She took a clear win in seven of the eight precincts comprising her district, including her opponent's (352-303) and a whopping vote of confidence in her home precinct 7 (672-210). Her door-to-door canvass of the district was a key to the success of Braintree's first "Lady of the House."

BRAINTREE PICKS FIRST WOMAN TO POST AS STATE REPRESENTATIVE

Talking to The Patriot Ledger at a victory celebration at the Braintree Yacht Club following last night's election, Mrs. Metayer said although she and her husband Edward of 33 Arthur St.; their son Richard of Mystic, Conn. and their daughter Gail, Mrs. James Corbin Jr. of Braintree, were "almost too happy and excited over the results to think of the future," she added. "I have given thought to how I will serve as the first woman state representative from Braintree."

"I would like to be placed on the transportation committee so that from my experience as a member of TAC, (Technical Advisory Committee) on transportation I could be of benefit to the committee particularly since the MBTA's Red Line is planning to be extended into Braintree. This will change the entire character of the town so I would like to be there to be of any service I can.

"I will not be a representative who attends sessions just for roll calls. I will be a participant and an active participant."

Mrs. Metayer, "Bibs," as she is known to club women, town meeting members, library personnel, the elderly, is an author and professional book reviewer, having been listed in "Who's Who in American Politics," the 1972 International "Who's Who in Community Service" and "Who's Who among Authors and Journalists," said one of her main and steadfast rules as a representative will be "accountability."

Views and Opinions

"I feel it is high time politicians be accountable for their actions. I know no legislator can be an expert on all matters that are to be voted upon but before voting on an issue I plan to seek views and opinions of those who are knowledgeable in a specific area. "If we are voting on an educational issue I will first talk to the superintendent of schools, the school committee members, officials of the Braintree Education Association, students, parents and teachers. I will call meetings of these educators and after receiving their expertise on an educational issue I will then vote. I will maintain the same policy on a law enforcement matter or on any other matter before being recorded for or against.

"I feel that this new honor which I humbly accept because of the confidence people of Braintree have shown in me, is an awesome responsibility, perhaps the biggest responsibility I have ever faced. This responsibility calls for me representing people at the state level where I will be dealing with laws which constantly affect the quality of our lives."

Asked what she felt helped her most in winning the election Mrs. Metayer said, "My victory was brought about by the hundreds of dedicated people; people who are concerned about good government as I am. Many people whom I never knew before came and asked how they could help, many, too, changed their party affiliation from Republican to Democrat so they could work and vote for me.

"Even though I have lived in Braintree for 27 years I feel I really got to know people and to know some of their problems by my door to door canvassing. Being a woman may have made a difference because as one man said "we men haven't done too good a job so I will vote for you."

Young people, Mrs. Metayer said, were very enthusiastic about this election and they too "helped me in my campaign."

Mrs. Metayer plans to publish all her campaign donations. She said she was "committed to no one."

Throughout the campaign her campaign managers Jay Hedlund and Frank Wilhelm said "Bibs" had no periods of depression or concern. WE worried but she didn't, Mr. Hedlund said.

Mrs. Metayer is a slightly graying lady, 5 ft. 3 inches tall wearing a size 5, makes and designs all of her clothes. Her son Richard is a seventh generation engineer in the family. He is married to the former Dolores Creehan of Braintree. They have two sons Richard Jr. 15, Franklin John 11. Her daughter Gael and her husband Jim of the Modernfold Co. in Wellesley live at 65 Alexander Road. They have three sons, all students at Sacred Heart school; James M. II, 13; Byrne Laurence, 12 and Gregory Scott, 7. A past president of the Braintree Point Women's Club Mrs. Metayer has served as 17 years as a town meeting member; chairman, technical advisory committee on transportation; legislative chairman Braintree Council on Aging, supported the Circuit Breaker concept of property tax, relief for the elderly and served on the dump site selection committee. She is presently secretary of the Precinct Seven Association, is the founding and first president Braintree League of Women Voters, past president Archbishop Williams Guild, past president Quincy Deanery, Archdiocesan Council of Catholic Women; two term president Braintree Point Women's Club; town chairman of Cancer Crusade, co-chairman Mothers' March Against Polio and public relations chairman of the United Way.

THE BRAINTREE OBSERVER AND SUNDAY FORUM
SUNDAY, SEPTEMBER 15, 1974
EDITORIAL

Elizabeth Metayer has done more than win elections as Braintree's first woman legislator, although she deserves that distinction for the tireless work she has done for her community.

Elizabeth Metayer has infused a spirit of love and understanding among people representing different approaches to politics. Her candidacy and campaign brought together individuals of every political, philosophical and religious persuasion.

Elizabeth Metayer was not the liberal candidate for the office of State Rep., although we are aware that some very nasty things were said along that line behind closed doors. Every leading conservative in town backed her, and worked diligently for her election.

Elizabeth Metayer was not the conservative candidate, either. Every leading liberal in town backed her, and worked diligently for her election. We do not like using labels such as "liberal" and "conservative" but sometimes no other description will do when explaining basic political philosophies.

Elizabeth Metayer's victory was due, in large measure, to her own tireless efforts in canvassing from door to door among the people who are to become her constituency. It was an example for her campaign workers to follow. And she was like a Pied Piper, gathering more and more followers as she trekked along the campaign trail. People remembered her fights for them against the incinerator in East Braintree, against an elevated MBTA track through town, and for such things as buses to handle walkers and school children during the reconstruction of the Quincy Avenue Bridge. Elizabeth Metayer has been a diligent worker for the Sacred Heart Church, the Braintree Philergians and her beloved Braintree Point Woman's Club, and a leader in promoting their charitable causes. She has led drives to collect money to fight mankind's insidious diseases. In short, she has worked for people for a long, long time. And the people remembered that on Tuesday, and voted with confidence that she would continue to work for them at the State House.

Elizabeth Metayer made only one demand of her campaign workers: that they keep the campaign at a high level, confined to the issues, and they did. Undoubtedly, they would have done so without her admonition, because they are that kind of people, people who would never stoop to conquer. In the pragmatic world of politics, a campaign is a cut and dried affair, with charts and polls and clichés as its hallmarks. But the Metayer campaign was different. The coalition of people who supported her was unique, and the spirit of camaraderie that developed among people who had never agreed on politics, much less on a candidate, was unprecedented in this town.

Elizabeth Metayer's campaign was a big "love-in", imbued with spirit, begun by a charismatic candidate, which spread contagiously among the dozens of workers and hundreds of supporters who wanted that same spirit to be taken to the State House by the lady from Arthur Street.

Elizabeth Metayer set the tone of her campaign, and her workers played in harmony during the past months. Elizabeth Metayer was told on Tuesday by the people of Braintree, "We trust you to do the right thing." And she will.

It was 2 a.m., the votes had been tallied, and it was time for a winner to surface Metayer, Democratic nominee for State Representative, flashes her winning smile shared by Selectman Donald J. Laing, and another long-time friend, Elizabeth Metayer polled a smashing upset victory over incumbent William J. Dignan election for the Seventh Norfolk District seat.

"The tumult and shouting dies; the Captains and the Kings depart…"

Now AWE has filled my quiet soul, and JOY is flooding full my heart

For life's great dream I'll soon fulfill - I'LL SPEAK FOR YOU ON BEACON HILL, YOU BEAUTIFUL PEOPLE OF BRAINTREE!

***

The Commonwealth of Massachusetts
Office of the Secretary
State House, Boston 02133
John F.X. Davoren

Secretary of the Commonwealth
Elizabeth N. Metayer
33 Arthur St.
Braintree, Mass.

September 23, 1974

Dear Sir:
    You are hereby notified that it appears by the returns made to this office as required by law that you were nominated at the Primaries held September 10, 1974 as Candidate for the Office of Representative Seventh Norfolk District, under the political designation of Democrat to be voted for at the State Election November 5, 1974.

Very Respectfully,
John F.X. Davoren
Secretary of the Commonwealth

9-15-74

    My Thanks; My Love and My Gratitude...
    To the beautiful people of Braintree who helped to plan and run my issue-oriented campaign; whose magnificent commitment and dedication helped to bring that campaign to a successful conclusion; and who - from all corners of this beloved town of ours went to the polls and placed their trust in me by giving me that most prized possession - their vote. Thank you and God love you, every beautiful one of you! I will not betray your trust. And as for those two great adopted sons of mine - my Campaign Managers, Jay and Frank, Wow! I'll luv ya forever!!!

Elizabeth N. Metayer
Democratic Nominee for State Representative

***

United States Senate Washington, D.C. 20510

November 8, 1974

Hon. Elizabeth N. Metayer
33 Arthur Street
Braintree, Massachusetts 02185

Dear Mrs. Metayer:

The splendid Democratic victory throughout our state as well as the nation is a source of great pride and I want to take this opportunity to express my warmest congratulations to you for your contribution to this victory.

Working together, I am confident that we can attain the high goals and accomplish the important programs for Massachusetts.

I look forward to seeing you soon.

With all good wishes.

Sincerely,
Edward M. Kennedy

***

Michael S. Dukakis

November 15, 1974

Representative Elizabeth N. Metayer
33 Arthur Street
Braintree, Massachusetts

Dear Representative:

Congratulations on your victory. I look forward to meeting with you in the near future to discuss the many problems facing the state and our opportunity to work together for their solution.

Please feel free to contact my office at any time. I hope that the legislative and executive branches, while maintaining their independence from one another, will be able to function cooperatively, and that we can place Massachusetts in the forefront of state governments.

Sincerely yours,
Michael S. Dukakis
MSD/las
"Hope we'll have a chance to meet and talk soon"

Dwarfed by the size of the State House, newly-sworn Representative Elizabeth N. Metayer has her first picture taken under the golden dome. Mrs. Metayer represents eight precincts in Braintree, and Andrew H. Card, Jr., also a freshman legislator represents the other four.

FAMILY AFFAIR

After just having left swearing in ceremonies in the State House on Wednesday morning, the family of newly-sworn Representative Elizabeth N. Metayer poses on the steps for a family photo. In front, from left are Edward A. Metayer, her husband; grandson Gregory Corbin and Rep. Metayer. At the rear are grandsons James and Byrne Corbin, daughter Gael and her husband James M. Corbin of 65 Alexander. Son Richard's family, who live in Connecticut, were unable to attend the ceremonies due to the hospitalization of young Richard.

"VICTORY"

"The tumult and shouting dies; the Captains and the Kings depart..."
Now AWE has filled my quiet soul, and JOY is flooding full my heart
For life's great dream I'll soon fulfill - I'LL SPEAK FOR YOU ON BEACON HILL, YOU BEAUTIFUL PEOPLE OF BRAINTREE!

THE PATRIOT LEDGER, THURSDAY, JAN. 2, 1975

'GRAMMA' METAYER SOURCE OF PRIDE FOR HER FAMILY
BY VERA S. CASEY

Braintree - "WE are so proud of Gramma and we are happy we could attend her inauguration at the State House in Boston."

"We loved seeing her raise her hand and be sworn into office and we are so happy for her." So said three grandsons of the towns' first woman state representative, Mrs. Elizabeth Metayer of 33 Arthur St., Mrs. Metayer, accepted her oath of office at formal ceremonies in the state house at 11:30 yesterday. The oath was administered by outgoing Gov. Francis W. Sargent.

Mrs. Metayer's grandsons are James M. Corbin, II, 13, Byrne, 12, and Gregory, 7, All of whom attend Sacred Heart School in Weymouth.

James said, "It's different to have your grandmother in politics. You usually think, that grandmothers don't take such an interest in politics. You always think of grandmothers as being at home." James said he loved being at the ceremonies but he said, "I didn't like the side jokes made by the speaker of the House to the committee members he appointed. I don't think that on such a special day there should be jokes between themselves when others there don't know what they are joking about."

James also said, at a post-inaugural open house at his grandmother's and grandfather's home, that he didn't see the need for everyone clapping when "most of us didn't know why we were clapping." (James referred to the guests applauding at each motion made relative either to appointments or committees to escort officials to the speakers rostrum or to routine matters on the agenda.) Byrne said, "It was a very exciting day and a special day for the family. I was so happy when Gramma was sworn in but I thought everyone voted too fast. They didn't seem to take enough time to think about what they were voting on."

"Youngest grandson Gregory said he felt like his brothers that "it was a big day for me to be there and a very special day for Gramma. I am very proud of her.

James said that he had been very interested in his grandmother's campaign. "I felt especially proud when friends would ask if it was my grandmother who was running for office. I sure was happy to say yes but I am even happier to have been at her inaugural." Byrne, who had to rush to finish his paper route before the family could leave to go into the State House said, "It was worth the rushing." Seated in the gallery with their parents, Mr. and Mrs. James Corbin Jr. of 65 Alexander Road, and their grandfather, Edward Metayer, the boys kept Grampa busy answering such questions as "Who's that man," or "Who is that woman," or "Who is that man in the tall silk hat," (referring to the sergeant at arms.)

Mrs. Metayer's son, Richard and his family from Mystic, Conn., were unable to attend one of their children was ill.

Mrs. Metayer said, at her home, after the ceremonies, "Today is certainly a high moment in my life. Never has the dawning of a New Year provided me with such vast opportunities for service for others."

"I am alternately awed by the responsibility I've accepted, that of representing my beloved townspeople on Beacon Hill and thus affecting, in so many ways, the quality of their lives." Mrs. Metayer said she is "eager to light her one small candle and to serve her townspeople to the best of her ability."

Mrs. Metayer said she wishes to stay close to the people she represents and that she will welcome residents communications when they are concerned about pending issues. "I shall need and want input from them."

"A legislator does not automatically become knowledgeable about all the issues. I shall seek the counsel and ask for the expertise of those whose fields of endeavor I shall be invading by my action in the House of Representatives."

***

Otis B. Oakman Jr.

February 19, 1975

Rep. Elizabeth N. Metayer
7th Northfolk District
House of Representatives

Dear Elizabeth -

    May I take this opportunity to thank you most sincerely for arranging to have me give the invocation prayer before your Legislative body last Tuesday. It was an experience I shall always treasure.
    However, I was more impressed by your gracious reception, your "bubbling" energy that seemed to bring a bit of happiness to all around you - I was tremendously proud to realize that you were our representative. Keep up your good work-your efforts are appreciated here in Braintree -again, my deep and genuine thanks.

Otis B. Oakman Jr.
"Oakie"

P.S. Please try to save Saturday afternoon on March 15th for our super-duper production "Braintree fights for Liberty."

CITATION FOR DISTINGUISHED PUBLIC SERVICE

To the Citizens of Massachusetts
Common Wealth of Massachusetts

Elizabeth N. Metayer

Years of Stewardship in the Massachusetts General Court Commencing 1975 In recognition of those who accept the responsibility to shape the character of government institutions to meet the social needs of our time-location in the relentless quest for human dignity and opportunity through self-government.

THE PATRIOT LEDGER, WED., MARCH 26, 1975

Braintree's Famous Sons - Robert N. Bruynell, town clerk, left, displays a poster depicting four famous natives of Braintree including John Adams, John Quincy Adams, John Hancock and Gen. Sylvanus Thayer together with replicas of their original birth records which are part of Braintree's archives, prior to presenting the poster to governor Michael Dukakis, as Rep. Elizabeth N. Metayer, D-Braintree, looks on.

That presentation took place in Doric Hall at the State House recently when a memorial to John Adams, one of the town's first representatives to the General Court was unveiled. The memorial, consists of a number of modernistic blocks of varying heights and bearing famous statements made by Adams, is surmounted by a portrait of John Adams.

5-11-75 LOCAL REP CARRIES 'NO STATION' TO DECISIVE VICTORY IN HOUSE

Carried by Representative Elizabeth N. Metayer for the Joint Committee on Transportation, Commonwealth of Massachusetts, House Bill 511, An Act Prohibiting the Massachusetts Bay Transportation Authority From Constructing a Rapid Transit Station in the Southern Area of the City of Quincy won overwhelming support in the House of Representatives on Wednesday. Representative Metayer is a member of the Transportation Committee.

An effort by Representative W. Paul White (D. Dorchester) to secure postponement of consideration of the bill was soundly defeated by a vote of 189 to 33. "The motion, made by Representative White, sought to postpone consideration of the bill for two weeks, which I vehemently opposed," Representative Metayer said. "Thus a 'NAY' vote, as indicated in the Roll Call Record found elsewhere on this page, is a vote in favor of the bill."

It was to all intents and purposes Representative Metayer's "Maiden Speech." She had spoken previously but briefly in support of a Health Care measure. "I was saving my steam for the BIG one, however," said Representative Metayer, "the bill to prohibit the M.B.T.A. from building the same rapid transit station previously proposed for North Braintree, with a horrendous ramp system a couple of hundred yards down the track in South Quincy, with the same set of problems for all of us attendant upon the thing," she said. "Incidentally," she added, "I was delighted when my Transportation Committee

Chairman selected me, a Freshman Representative, to carry such a vital bill - when I realized they trusted me to that extent, the Representative said. The bill has been sent to the Committee on Bills in the Third Reading, and will return to the House to be engrossed, the Representative said.

"It should be noted," she added, "that the margin of the vote in favor of House 511 is sufficient to sustain its passage should the Governor see fit to veto it." The representative indicated that Fred Salvucci, the Governor's Secretary of Transportation, is in favor of the South Quincy Station. "By tradition the Speaker of the House does not vote except to break a tie," Representative Metayer said. "Happily this was NO tie," she added. "It was a big win…a decided win…"

Testifying also in support of the bill were representatives Brett, Thomas F. Brownell, Robert A. Cerasoli and William D. Delahunt of Quincy and Andrew H. Card, Jr., of Holbrook.

***

The Commonwealth of Massachusetts
House of Representatives
Committee on Rules
State House, Boston

Thomas W. McGee
Speaker
"I voted for Speaker McGee"

July 1, 1975

Dear Representative Metayer–Elizabeth,

Thank you for making today the happiest day in my life. I'll always remember and appreciate your vote.

I will try as hard as I possibly can to make you always proud of that vote.

Sincerely,
Tom
Thomas W. McGee
SPEAKER OF THE HOUSE
TWM: hs

P.S. - I really appreciate your kindness and support. Thanks so much.

GUEST EDITORIAL 8-3-75

No one who reads this paper can fail to be aware of the magnitude of the fiscal crisis that currently faces the Commonwealth of Massachusetts. With a bankrupt New York City serving as a horrible example of what could conceivably happen to this great State of ours if we do not all - each and every one of us - "bite the bullet," to use that most unhappy popular phrase, tighten our belts, pull in our reigns and concentrate on what amounts to SURVIVAL! Yes, it IS as bad as all that. With a $700 Million dollar tax increase proposal in the offing - for which legislators cannot possibly vote because taxpayers cannot possibly absorb it - it becomes clear that EVERYONE is going to be affected in some way or another by the decisions we shall have to make in the weeks ahead.

The House Ways and Means Committee - reluctantly, I am certain - MUST, as it is doing, take a firm stand and demand cuts everywhere they can be made. The difficult decisions the members of this committee are making will serve as a prelude to the even more difficult decisions we members of the General Court, serving you, the wonderful people who elected us, will ultimately be forced to make. For the House of Ways and Means Committee merely RECOMMENDS; we must VOTE the final package into law. It's a horrendous responsibility.

Accordingly, elsewhere in this paper you will find an advertisement, privately paid for, I might add, in which you, my constituents, will be given an opportunity to air your views, to let me know how YOU feel about budget cuts and cuts in human services and elsewhere...about the whole sad budget and tax picture. Your recommendations will influence my vote on these critical issues; here is your chance to speak out. I'll be listening! Help me to serve you!

Elizabeth N. Metayer
State Representative.

7-3-75   SOUTH QUINCY MBTA STATION

Braintree and Quincy State Representative and representatives of civic associations within the two communities were denied, at least temporarily, the opportunity to bring their case against the proposed South Quincy MBTA Station to the attention of Frank Herringer, Administrator of the Urban Mass Transit Administration in Washington this Friday, Representative Elizabeth Metayer revealed this weekend.

She has received no response to a letter seeking an appointment for the Boston group to meet with the UMTA officials on the 27th; nor were her telephone calls to Mr. Herringer's Washington office returned, the Representative said.

After a series of persistent attempts to reach Mr. Herringer personally, she received a call from the regional UMTA office in Cambridge. Her letter had been forwarded to them to handle, she was told. The Washington trip was apparently off, Representative Metayer said. An attempt to set up an immediate appointment with Mr. Peter Stowell, Regional Director of UMTA, also failed, the Representative said. Mr. Stowell was not to be available until next week, she was told.

Representative Metayer and Andrew Card of Braintree as well as Representative Joseph Brett, Thomas Brownell and Robert Cerasoli of Quincy had planned the trip to Washington. They were to be accompanied by Joseph Hernon, president of the Northeast Braintree Civic Association, Pasquale DiStefano, President of the South Quincy group and a number of other interested citizens of both communities.

Representative Metayer was also informed that Mr. Herringer will terminate his association with UMTA as of July 1, she said. "We shall keep our appointment with the Cambridge group," the representative said; "and as soon as Mr. Herringer's successor is named, we shall resume our efforts to take our case directly to the nation's capitol. There are federal funds involved; and we still feel the people MUST have a voice in the kinds of facilities proposed for their communities when federal funds are involved. We're going to fight for that voice in our destiny," she said.

11-9-75 FRESHMAN REP IS 'A DOER BY NATURE" BY PAMELA BLEVINS

State Representatives Andrew H. Card, Jr. and Elizabeth N. Metayer were elected to office just a year ago. They joined the legislative body during one of the most crisis-ridden times in the Commonwealth's history.

In the first of a two part series, Mrs. Metayer discusses her freshman year on Beacon Hill. It is a little after 9 a.m. on a balmy November morning and the thick crowd of rush hour commuters streams out of the Park Street subway station on Boston Common. Some walk off toward the shopping district along Washington Street while others head toward the banks and insurance companies hidden in the long shadows of the financial district down off Post Office Square.

One woman carrying a bulging brown brief case turns left and falls into step with another group walking up a tree-lined path through the historic Common, where cows once grazed, toward the sun-tipped gold dome of the State House.

She proceeds under the the arch where State officials park their cars, enters the building, picks up a stack of mail at the State House post office and takes an elevator to her office on the fourth floor, where she begins another hectic day as one of Braintree's two Representatives sitting on Beacon Hill.

"Normally, I take the MBTA to work - the 8 a.m. bus from East Braintree," explains Representative Elizabeth N. Metayer. "I come and go during the rush hour, and traffic on the expressway is so terrible it is much easier to commute this way. If it's good enough for the Governor," she says with a quick smile, "it's good enough for me."

Representative Metayer, the first woman from Braintree to sit on Beacon Hill, won election in the newly-formed Seventh Norfolk District last year when she defeated two-term incumbent William J. Dignan in the State Primary. She ran unopposed in the November ballot.

"I ran because of my frustration with government as a result of Watergate, and an increasing awareness of the role government plays in the lives of people. I was also very unhappy with a lot of the legislation that was being filed," she explained. "You know, you can sit back and carry on, or you can do something about it if you don't like a situation. I'm a doer by nature and a believer in the Christopher's' motto - 'It is better to light one small candle than curse the darkness.'"

"I am also people-oriented," she continued, "and I saw this public service as an opportunity to help people. I think it's very sad that people need political help to right injustice and get things accomplished by the government. People should be heard directly without having to use political muscle. But, given political reality, everyone on occasion does need help and that's where I come in. The most rewarding part of this job is knowing I have the ability to help people."

There are a couple of students here to see you from Massasoit Community College," announces the receptionist in the large, blue-walled office Mrs. Metayer shares with eleven other reps. A young man and woman walk over to the desk and introduce themselves.

"I didn't know it was so easy to talk to people like you," he says shaking his head in disbelief. They've come to ask her if there is anything she can do to stop proposed budget cuts affecting community colleges. Three more students join the group, and Mrs. Metayer carefully and realistically explains that it is too late to do anything now because the budget is ready for approval. The students are "torn to pieces" because they fear their education is in jeopardy.

By the time they leave the office, probably to attend a large rally of other students outside in front of the State House, they have learned that their plight isn't as bad as the rumors they'd heard had led them to believe. They understand, too, why the cuts are necessary if the Commonwealth is to avoid default. And while they may not agree with what has happened, at least now they know the why behind it, and they also know what they can do in the months ahead to make the system work for them.

"I'm frequently asked, 'Don't you get tired of having people come to you with problems?' I answer, 'No, when you seek elective office, you become a public servant. Nobody pounds you into running for office.'"

There is no such thing as a "typical day at the State House."

Mrs. Metayer is a member of the Transportation Committee, which handles the entire transportation budget and anything to do with transportation - from the MBTA to the DPW to the MDC: and the Health Care Committee, which deals "with everything and anything that affects the health of the Commonwealth."

One day might find her schedule full of hearings on Health Care bills. "These hearings are often interrupted by roll calls, so I have to drop everything, race down and vote on a bill I may not have heard debate on," she explains. "It calls for a snap judgment and I freely admit that I can make mistakes in voting, especially when I'm hearing thousands of bills I cannot possibly be acquainted with. Typically, you are conversant with the bills that come before your own committee, but often you cannot get to other committee meetings because there are scheduling conflicts." Another day might find her sitting behind her desk answering letters and discussing problems over the phone. Then there are meetings in Braintree, her weekly Monday night sessions for constituents at Town Hall, ribbon-cutting ceremonies and a host of other social and political commitments. "This is a wonderfully effective level of government to work at," observed Mrs. Metayer. "There are many ways I can help the town from here."

Mrs. Metayer is no newcomer to government. She has been a Town Meeting Member for 18 years and has served as chairman of the Technical Advisory Committee on Transportation. She was active in preventing the MBTA from building a controversial rapid transit station at North Braintree. Her interest in government extended from local to state to national when she became founding and first President of the Braintree League of Women Voters.

"I was asked to run for office this time," she said. "I ran once in 1966 and almost passed the primary. I really had little hope of winning last year, but I thought it would afford a good opportunity to voice the frustrations of a lot of the people I was meeting via coffee hours, candidate's nights and meetings, and spotlight the role government plays in people's lives.

This is the most exciting thing I've ever done in my life, and my life has been very exciting. I think you have to love this kind of work to do well at it," she continued. "It is a demanding job, and I don't' know how anyone can do it part time. Maybe they aren't as close to their constituents as I Am."

Although she enjoys being a legislator, she misses seeing her family and grandchildren and being able to go away for a weekend now and then. "I have very little family life now," she said. "I'm lucky if I get to see my grandchildren (she has five grandsons) once a week."

Would she run for a second term?

"I'll run for the next twenty years as long as I'm healthy and able to do the job," she said

HOUSE SEAT 102

1981 - 82	Elizabeth N. Metayer
1980 - 81	"
1979 - 80	"
1977-78	Alfred Saggese, Jr.
1973-76	Paul H. Guzzi
1971 - 72	James F. Hart
1969 - 70	John J. Janas
1967-68	"
1965-66	"
1963 - 64	Philip A. Quinn
1961 - 62	"
1959 - 60	"
1957 - 58	"
1955 - 56	"
1953 - 54	"
1351 - 52	"
1949 - 50	"
1947-48	Charles E. Ferguson
1945 - 46	Russel P. Brown
1943-44	Charles F. Holman
1941-42	Francis W. Nyhan
1939 - 40	Jeremiah J. Sullivan
1937 - 38	Thomas A. Flaherty
1935 - 36	William C. Lunney
1933 - 34	Timothy J. McDonough
1931 - 32	Phillip H. Stacey
1929 - 30	Joseph J. Borgatti
1927 – 28	Maynard E. S. Clemens
1925 - 26	"
1923 - 24	John T. Farrell Bristol
1921	Vernon W. Evans (Essex'
1920	Daniel J. Hayden (Essex)

Byrne L. Corbin

1919	Frank Putnam (Lowell)
1918	John Cronin Flamoden'
1917	Arthur bower (Essex
1916	John N. Osborne (Essex)
1915	Thomas J. Giblin (Suffolk)
1914	Henry H. Sears (Barnstaple)
1913	James J. Bacigalupo (Suffolk)
1912	Clarence A. Barnes (Bristol)
1911	Louis R. Kiernan (Suffolk)
1910	George swann Plymouth)
1909	Albert Blaisdell (Middlesex)
1908	Edward Collins (Boston)
1907	William Learned Worcester)
1906	Thomas Priscoll (Chelsea)
1905	William A. Bailey (Northamoton)
1904	Julius Gates (Asby)
1903	Edwin J. Mills (Fall River)
1902	Michael Mahonev (Lowell
1901	Peter Sullivan (Worcester)
1900	Henry Chase (Westborough)
1899	William Pike (Groveland)
1898	Francis Leland (Otter River
1897	William Porter (Agawam)
1896	Charles Monroe (Southbridge)
1895	Thomas Donahue (Bristol)
1894	Alfred S. Roe (Worcester)
1893	Anthony Smalley (Nantucket)
1892	George W. Perkins (Middlesex)
1891	Timothy Howard (Worcester)
1890	William Mahanna (Lenox)
1889	Clarence Lovell (Boston)
1888	J. Henry Robinson (Southborough)
1887	Samuel C. Darling (Middlesex)
1886	Dudley P. Bailey (Middlesex)
1885	Augustus P. Gorman (Fall River)

1884	Edmund Snow (Suffolk)
1883	Sprague S. Stetson (Plymouth)
1882	Alfred Ziegler (Boston)
1881	Gilbert A. Japley (Danvers)
1880	Stephen Flanders (Chilmark)
1879	William Ingraham (Watertown)
1878	Solon Walton (Wakefield)
1877	Sydney Whitehouse (Boston)
1876	Thomas Barity (Lowell)
1875	Philo Keith (Bridgewater)
1874	Porter Nutting (Northampton)
1873	William Creesy (Salem)
1872	William Osborne (E. Bridgewater)
1871	Robert Bower (Lawrence)
1870	James L. Harriman (Hudson)
1869	Avery J. Denison (Franklin)
1868	Joel B. Williams (Hampden)
1867	John V. Barker (Berkshire)
1866	William Searer (Norfolk)
1865	Sylvester S. May (Berkshire)
1864	George W. Copeland (Middlesex)
1863	Thomas Pierce (Plymouth)
1862	Oliver Loud (Norfolk)
1861	Benjamin Otis (Worcester)
1860	Thomas Hills (Suffolk)
1859	Ezra Brownell (Bristol)
1858	Abraham G. Wyman (Suffolk)
1857	Madison Sweetser (S. Reading)
1856	Jonathan Jones (Chicopee)
1855	not available
1854	H. G. Parker (Greenfield)
1853	
1852	Thomas Kempton (New Bedford)
1851	George White (Peterson)
1850	Ira Broad (Holden)

1849	Philo Sanford (Boston)
1848	William Rose (Suffolk)
1847	Samuel rumam (Franklin
1846	Esek Saunders (Worcester)
1845	William D. Bullock (Pawtucket)
1844	John Leland (Middlesex)
1843	Nathaniel Townsend (Berkley)
1842	Henry C. Perkins (Essex)
1841	George Hood (Lynn)
1840	John Carpenter (Wilbraham)
1839	Oliver Dickinson (Amherst
1838	not available
1837	not available
1836	Cranston Howe (Boston)
1835	Jason Janes (E. Hampton)
1834	Horace W. Taft (Sunderland)
1833	Stephen Sargent, Jr. (Amesbury)
1832	Josiah Caldwell (Ipswch)
1831	John Wheelwright (Boston)
1830	Samuel Bement (Ashfield)
1829	not available
1827-28	Warren Lovering (Norfolk)
1826	John Muzzy (Middlesex)
1825	Esek Pitts (Worcester)
1824	Thomas Payson (essex)

The listings of the House of Representatives in the manual of the General Court prior to 1822 do not include the seat number with each representative

Selected Columns from the First Year of State Representative Elizabeth N. Metayer

Elected to represent the Town of Braintree, Mass. Served from 1974 – 1984

10-5-75   "SWEARING IN"

It was a day to remember…a day toward which all the other days of her exciting life seem to have pointed like so many arrows. It was climbing Mt. Everest…and crossing the Atlantic in a rowboat…and scaling the Grand Convon wall all rolled into one…"I, Elizabeth Metayer, do solemnly swear…" I was actually standing there within the half moon of that most historic Chamber…the HOUSE OF REPRESENTATIVES…I and 239 other "legislators"…I was one of the group; I BELONGED!

It was to be Governor Sargent's "Last Hurrah", this swearing in of the members of the General Court: and I, a winner, found myself looking toward the defeated Governor with compassionate eyes.

The words of the Oath were finding a warm response within my soul. "Do solemnly swear", I thought; do SOLEMNLY swear…Solemn indeed, this oath and this moment in my life; and now the Governor was echoing thoughts that have been mine for oh, so many years. "A Nation's worth," he was saying, "is measured by the concern it has for its people." A Nation's worth indeed, I thought; a legislator's worth, as well…

Our arrival in the House Chamber had been preceded by a Democratic Caucus where we gathered to nominate our Candidate for Speaker of the House; and where I had the opportunity of meeting oh, so many FRIENDLY colleagues. They're a great group, I can already tell! The Hon. David M. Bartley having been selected as our Candidate; and our business having been concluded, how exciting it was now to find ourselves pushing our way through crowds of people…legislators families and friends, we were to learn, all of whom stood patiently by the Chamber doors, hoping to be admitted finally and permitted to STAND for the 2½ hour "Sitting" of the House.

I found my heart hammering with excitement. I was now about to enter the historic Chamber for the very first time…to take my place within that august circle…to open another wonderful chapter in my life.

I entered the House Chamber, my eyes rising quickly to the Gallery above where hopefully I should find the people I love. I do! There is Ted, my wonderful husband; and my beautiful children, Gael and Jim along with their small boys, Jim and Byrne and Greg, my adored grandsons. Son Richard and his dear Dolores and their two great boys, Richard and Franklin have been prevented from coming by young Richard's sudden hospitalization, but I can feel their thoughts about me There is Jay, my great Campaign Manager and my "adopted" son; Barbara, my terrific Precinct Seven Captain: Bernice. that much loved State House VI.P. whose sterling worth and unmatched brilliance as the Executive Secretary to the House Counsel will be spread upon the record a short while later by none other than Abingtons own John Buckley, retiring as a "Rep" to assume a Cabinet position in the new administration…Bernice, the treasured friend who has so smoothed my pathway to the "House" that now I feel I quite belong. Rosemary and Vera, my very dear friends…find them all.

They're there, their "nods and becks and wreathed smiles" matching my own

The day was to be easily the most exciting of my life. I was to find my seat - H-141, the seat once occupied for sixteen golden years by our Herb Hollis; and then for two by our Don Laing, and then for two by our Bob Frazier…the "Braintree Seat", it has been called, and now 'tis mine…

I was to watch, enchanted, all the protocol, the pomp and circumstance that is a facet of our government by the General Court, the oldest bicameral legislature in these great United States, incidentally; dating as it does back to 1630 when the membership meetings of the Massachusetts Bay Colony bore that selfsame name - the "General Court!"

In the early 17th century, I was to learn, it had been called the House of Deputies. Not until 1692 did it adopt the name, "House of Representatives", becoming then the world's first governing body of that name.

Yes, I was to find myself seated in H-141, looking back over the centuries… wondering who in all those years have occupied this place…what great distinguished Massachusetts men. Is there way to find this out, I ask myself? Must check this bright detail with my Bernice…

The Speaker was to be elected by Roll Call vote – my first! And the Hon. Mr. Bartley was to win; and then the Senators and the Governor to be formally informed of the election; and by a House Committee appointed to perform the happy task… and, incidentally, to be led between the Chambers by no less a personage than the tall Sergeant-at-Arms, a gentleman resplendent in top hat and handsome staff which I am certain has a name, however I've not yet learned it…

The Clerk of the Court, the much loved Wallace Mills, was not to be appointed and to read aloud the Orders of the Day…I was to find delight in all the protocol; to thrill at sight of my own name upon the Roll Call board, if that is what 'tis called (Must ask Bernice that one, as well; what would I do without her??? to feel somehow that I indeed BELONG within this hallowed place.

The awesomeness of the task I've undertaken stirs my soul. I'm PROUD and HUMBLE each in turn. The knowledge that what I shall do or fail to do within my term will now affect the quality of life for all the people of the Commonwealth sweeps over me like some great surging wave…" I, Elizabeth Metayer, do solemnly swear…" My eyes rise high as now take this oath…high above the bright gold wings that frame the great House clock; high above the handsome murals that depict those grave historic moments on the walls; high above even the Bullfinch State House dome; high above the bright blue sky that lies without this lovely day; high above all else, it seems, to where the loving Father of us all can hear the prayer within my heart. "Dear God," I ask, "Help me to measure up; help me to justify their faith in me - those wonderful people on my team; and those wonderful people who have voted for me - help me ever to remember that this legislator's worth will e'er be measured by the deep concern she has for all people she will serve…help me, I fnd myself praying; and I ask you wonderful people who have elected me to join me in that prayer that I SHALL measure up…that I SHALL justify your faith in me…

And now, a Happy and a Blessed New Year to one and all. May you have LOVE and PEACE and JOY and HEALTH and family and friends - for if you have all of these, THEN YOU HAVE EVERYTHING! I do!

1-12-75 "MORE FROM THE STATE HOUSE"

Life, with a capital "L" goes on on Beacon Hill; and what joy to be right there in the thick of things!

Every day seems to bring to light another exciting facet of the life of a "legislator." This week, for instance, began with a bang. I was actually appointed to the TRANSPORTATION COMMITTEE!

AND to the HEALTH CARE COMMITTEE! Two challenging and great appointments, both offering what I envision as unlimited opportunity for service to the people of our Town and of our Commonwealth.

The events of January 1 were the subject of my last week's "Cabbage…and…in view of the favorable response I'm receiving to that bit of reported History, may we continue with January 2, another Red Letter Day at the State House? We had assembled in the magnificent House Chamber, we Representatives. We had come to watch a brand new Governor sworn in. He had stood there, Michael S. Dukakis, young of face and form, idealistic, eager to tackle the great task that lay before him; bright of eye; confident of manner…and I had thrilled at sight of him.

His arrival in the House had been preceded by all the pomp and circumstance I have come to expect (and to enjoy) when the House "sits"…the Opening Prayer by Monsignor Kerr, the House Chaplain; the Salute to Old Glory; and the singing of our National Anthem as it was never sung before, or so it seemed. I stood there throughout the rendition; and it was as though I were hearing it for the very first time; this stirring hymn that has been woven so deeply into the fabric of our lives.

The Chief Justices had been admitted; and a Committee appointed from among the members of both Houses to inform the Governor and the Lieutenant Governor Elect that we this columnist actually included in that "we"…) awaited their arrival.

This was to be a joint session, presided over by Senate President Kevin Harrington who from his lofty 6'9" of height had warmly welcomed his fellow Senators, along with former Governors Saltonstall, Furcolo and Peabody and a number of visiting Congressmen, including "Tip" O'Neill, the "Father of the Lt. Governor" as he was to be later introduced. And now - the arrival of the Governor and lieutenant Governor Elect and the swearing in ceremony itself. the swearing in of a Governor who in a political sense was born, raised and nurtured in this Chamber to quote him.

"One who has served in the General Court will become the Chief Executive for the first time in two decades," he was to tell the assembled legislators; and "it will not be the last" he was to add.

Governor Dukakis speech was to be a simple straightforward one, with emphasis on the life of none other than our own Sam Adams. What a proud moment for a legislator from Braintree whose historic Town hall houses the birth records of the two Adams Presidents! "This State is richer and more attractive than any other in the nation," he would add. "We have mountains and river valleys, and beaches along our coast without equal in any of the other 49 states." How many times Ted and 1 had reminded one another of these facts as we sped back and forth across this wonderful country of ours.

We have brainpower and talent unmatched anywhere in the world" he would boast: "So our standards must be high; our commitments must call for the best that is in us. And our goals must be lofty ones." "Amen, I found myself saying softly

This swearing in our brand new Governor and Tom O'Neill, his Lieutenant Governor was to mark the beginning of a wonderful day, a day that would not end until the wee small hours…a day that would include our attendance, in the company of so many of those we love, at the Governor's Inaugural Gala. (Where, we might add, we had persuaded Ted to arrive in a tuxedo, only to find the Governor in a business suit…Oh no, he wasn't alone; there were a great many other formally attired gentlemen on hand, and a host of formally attired ladies.)

We were to thrill to the incomparable music of Arthur Fiedler and our own Boston Pops; to the Voices of Black Persuasion; the New England Conservatory Ragtime Ensemble (Memories of wonderful New Orleans as they played the "Blues") and the Afro American Artists Dance Company It was to be an evening wherein we would find ourselves walking as though in a dream through a brand new world we never had hoped to inhabit.

We're still walking through that dream world incidentally; and every day the walking gets better…

Take today, for instance, and that appointment to the TRANSPORTATION COMMITTEE; and to that brand new COMMITTEE ON HEALTH CARE as well. What a challenge awaits us! And what an exciting experience it all was! The appointments had been dealt with alphabetically, you see; and your columnists name had been included with those named under the letter "H" to the Committee on HEALTH CARE. Initially disappointed, I had promptly applied my own brand of philosophy to the situation. "You really HAD set your sights too high in asking for the Transportation Committee, I had told myself firmly. "After all, you ARE a Freshman legislator…And Health Care will be very interesting. It's a brand new Committee and a mighty important issue."

And then, in the midst of all this philosophizing, the incredible happened. Speaker Bartley had managed to reach the letter T and was announcing his appointments to the prized "TRANSPORTATION COMMITTEE" and he was saying my name… "Metayer of Braintree." He was actually saying it, I all but cheered!

Two weeks of Orientation now and I shall come to know in more detail the workings of the Great and General Court; and to actually be a part of it. How exciting and beautiful my life has ever been! And this new turn of events is easily the most exciting time of all… Thank you, Braintree, you Beautitul town, You!

2-2-75 "ORIENTATION"

We've been evolving into "Legislators," we Freshmen members of the House of Representatives…and with the most impressive set of educators the world of politics has probably ever known…The Joint Committee on Rules; assisted by the Clerk of the House of Representatives; the Program for Legislative Improvement: the Legislative Research Council and Bureau and the Legislative Service Bureau. The Institute for Government Services of the University of Massachusetts…The Institute for Politics J. F. Kennedy School of Government; Harvard University…and the Bureau of Adult Education of the Department of Education.

The Orientation program for the entering class of 1975, 169th Biennial Session of the Massachusetts Great and General Court was to be done up Brown; and it was! We were even to hold Commencement Exercises and to be awarded a Certificate issued by the Department of Education, attesting to the fact that we had completed a course in Legislative Procedures.

Our Orientation program had begun with a welcome by the Legislative Leaders and a panel Discussion with Senators Anna Buckley and John F. Parker along with Representatives George Kavarian and Anthony Gallugi, all fellow legislators with their own particular philosophies and points of view were to attend seminars on the Massachusetts Economy (its dismal!); to learn how the Media views the Legislator and the Legislature, to meet our Attorney General and Secretary of State, our State Treasurer and State Auditor; and to learn a bit about the functions of each of these; to become informed about the budget, revenue and taxes in a seminar that was to be conducted by key figures in each of those three areas. We were to learn much of the needs and aspirations of the Judiciary; and meanwhile, at the hands of a superb instructor, Clerk of the House of Representatives Wallace C. Mills, to become reasonably well-acquainted (we students falling short of our teacher) with the intricacies of legislative procedure. And - at last - we were to really participate in a true "sitting" of that most august body, the HOUSE OF REPRESENTATIVES! The experience was awe-inspinng. Beneath the Speaker's rostrum a plaque bearing the words of a martyred President… "John Fitzgerald Kennedy spoke trom this rostrum to the Massachusetts General Court on January 9, 1961," we read. "I carry with me from this State to that high and lonely office to which I now succeed," he had said, "the fond memories of firm friendships. The enduring qualities of Massachusetts…will not be and could not be forgotten in this nation's executive mansion. Courage-integrity-judgment-dedication- these are the historic qualities of the Bay Colony and the Bay State - the qualities which this state has consistently sent to this Chamber on Beacon Hill here in Boston and to Capitol Hill back in Washington. And these are the qualities which with God's help this son of Massachusetts hopes will characterize our government's conduct in the four stormy years that lie ahead. "Courage-integrity-judgment-dedication."The words seeped deep into my soul; may they remain there for all the years I shall serve the people of the town I hold dear and the State I treasure.

Other quotes were to come to my mind as I looked back over the two weeks of indoctrination just passed. "The role of the legislator is using concern to push for economic stability...Economic development must be established as a town problem, not a state problem; the State and Federal governments should play only supportive and guidance roles...(I m a Home Ruler, so I'll agree to that. businessmen need an Ombudsman to guide them through State and local governments...The Legislature is a very human kind of institution. The business of this Chamber is to make decisions and there will be many times when you will have to vote aye or nay and will wish you might vote "MAYBE"...Now we belong to the people and the public is a hard taskmaster...You are a politican and it is an honorable and ancient profession...You can't fool anybody; your colleagues are professionals...You must temper the flame of idealism with the realities of life...Your representative owes you not only industry but his intellect...Success is never final...Employ sincerity, simplicity and directness: use a ten cent word rather than a dollar one...A bill's importance is judged by the number of people it affects." Wonderful quotes, all of them; I shall try to remember each and every one.

We have been assured by our Governor, Michael Dukakis, that because he came from the Legislature he hopes to work closely with us; and by Lieutenant-Governor Tom O'Neill that we are "the best prepared Freshman Class the State has ever seen." We have been advised, when speaking to an issue. to "be good: be brief: be gone!"

Why are we all there, I ask myself wonderingly as I look about me at the diverse group of individuals who have elected to take upon themselves the business of governing??? Essentially, I decide, our motivation is pretty much the same. We are there because each one of us in his (or her) own way is committed to improving the quality of life for the people of his town and of his State; and when it comes to improving the quality of life for our Massachusetts citizens it's here on Beacon Hill where the action is!

Every day brings a new State House adventure for this happy columnist. It's beautiful on Beacon Hill! love it love it love it!

2-9-75 "BUSY! BUSY!

No time to have my hair done or to shop for pretty clothes;
Thank goodness for the pantsuit that will hide my running hose;
Seems the workload for this legislator grows and grows and grows,
And where that rascal time goes, golly, goodness only knows..
No time for phoning brightly all the friends I love to know;
Now that there's a Friday "Sitting" even STORY HOUR must go.
I could use a pair of roller skates for dashing to and fro
Through the myriad State agencies, constituents in tow..

No time for social gatherings; my days are spent instead
At those great Committee Hearings where so many things are said
That affect the lives of people, or that keep out of the red
This poor troubled Massachusetts whose economy seems dead...
~ I'm off to our House "Sittings" where the State's business is done;
And although we suffer keenly on occasion, it's sure fun:
And where all the wise lawmaking has in earnest now begun...
Shall I ever get to know my revered colleagues every one???
The circles that are growing, I observe with some chagrin
Neath my eyes (though THEY'RE still shining), now come almost to my chin;
And I find at each weeks end that it invariably has been
Six or seven hectic days since have greeted kith and kin..
Yes, I'm madly, wildly busy - the proverbial busy bee
As I wrestle with the problems of the State's economy
Versus all the crucial needs of an oppressed humanity;
How to reconcile the whole contrives to haunt poor troubled me....
My phone now rings from morn till night! The freshening gold of morning light
Has barely crossed the Braintree sky - betokening the day - when I
Am off by bus and train to where my world grows every day more fair;
That wondrous place called Beacon Hill...still approach it with a thrill)..
The STATE HOUSE...Neath its Golden Dome, WHAT JOY TO KNOW
    I'M NOW AT HOME

2-16-75   "COMMITTEE ASSIGNMENTS"

"I was surprised to find so few Representatives in the Chamber," said my friend of long standing.

Lieutenant Commander Otis B. Oakman, as he offered an absolutely beautiful prayer to open the morning session of our House of Representatives on February 18...

Where are all the OTHER Representatives? asked my young friend Danny Clark as he, alone with his nice Mom, Joanne and fifty-three other young Cub Scouts from Braintree's Pack 196 rose to be acknowledged by the Speaker of the House on the occasion of their visit to Beacon Hill a few days back...

So - where ARE all the other members of the General Court as sessions open on Beacon Hill...those fortunate men and women who are being paid to represent and to protect the best interests of their constituents and their Commonwealth??? The answer is simple! Take it from one of them one who happened to be on hand when both of my good friends were asking this question simply because in each delighttul instance it was a Tuesday and she has no Committee Hearings Scheduled that day.

The remaining members of the General Court...those Representatives whose empty seats scream loudly for explanation were, in all probability, sitting quietly in Committee Hearings, listening intently to the pros and cons of issues that are being addressed in the various bills that are to be heard before their group...

Later on in executive session (now open to the public by virtue of our new open meeting laws) those Committee members will discuss the pros and cons and vote finally either favorably or adversely upon each and every issue. It's a slow and time-consuming process!

It is actually in Committee that the mettle of a bill is tested, we have learned; for there is little chance actually of overturning by debate on the House floor that sad "ought not to pass" verdict of a Joint Legislative Committe

This Representative happens to be a member of TWO Committees...the Health Care and the Transportation Committees...and two decidedly heavy committees they happen to be, each one handling countless bills. My Committee Hearings are scheduled to begin at 10:30 a.m. and to end goodness know knows when (close to 10:00 p.m. in Health Care one day last week...) This Committee activity is scheduled for two and sometimes three days a week. Compounding the problem, of course, are those controversial issues like the Optometrists versus the Ophthalmologists bills, about which I have received 371 pieces of mail and it's still coming; or the local Pharmacists versus those cut-rate drug chains; or the patients' rights legislation or a dozen others. These come within the province of my Health Care Committee, which incidentally I LOVE! That exciting facet of my legislative labors must however vie with the activities and the Hearings that are being scheduled by my Transportation Committee. Actually I am still struggling to work out these two assignments since Committee Hearings for both are scheduled for the same two days each week - Mondays and Wednesdays...

There are times - especially when "Roll Call in the House" is ringing out off and on all afternoon when I have all the earmarks of a "Yo-Yo," bouncing as I must back and forth between the two Committee Hearing Rooms in a frantic effort not to miss the best of two worlds. "There," you are saying; (I can HEAR you!) "Isn't that just like the State to schedule TWO Committee Hearings at the same time for the same Representative on the selfsame days? Poor management, as usual..."

Well, it really isn't the fault of the State at all. There just simply aren't enough hearing rooms. We all have to take turns using them. Later on when our new State Building is finished, they tell me, things will be different. Until that time, however - the Yo-Yo!

It's a wonderful WHIRL, however; and if only you knew how much I am learning! Compulsive note taker that I am, I find myself accumulating monumental quantities of information which I hope later on when only twelve or sixteen of each day's hours are called for by my legislative obligations - to peruse and to digest so that I shall be able to crop up with all sorts of useful (and useless) information at the drop of the proverbial chapeau. Greetings to all of you from beautiful and busy Beacon Hill.

3-30-75 LADY OF THE HOUSE
(THE OBSERVER-FORUM)

"Lady of the House" will replace the longtime "Cabbages and Kings" of your columnist, 99 percent of whose time, awake or sleeping, seems to be geared toward life 'neath the golden dome on Beacon Hill, in the most fascinating house on earth, the HOUSE OF REPRESENTATIVES! "Just how many bills HAVE you filed or co-sponsored anyhow?" asked a colleague one day last week as, included in the stack of mail he had deposited on my desk he spied several of the "green cards" that serve to remind legislators of the hearing dates of bills with which they are personally involved. "You get half a dozen of these things daily," he added. A slight exaggeration, that half a dozen daily bit; but there HAVE been a bunch of them. So- having embarked on this column change from "Cabbages and Kings" to "Lady of the House," I decided to look back and report on some of those bills I have indeed filed or co-sponsored…like S-716, which supported the concept of a combination of rapid transit and rail commuting; and S-334, which sought to establish a manpower training program. We simply have to get people off the Welfare rolls and into productive employment…And S-336, which was a petition to authorize the Consumers Council to prohibit the raising of prices on certain foods and other items once they have been placed on shelves and offered for sale. Incidentally, I had filed a similar bill for Braintree's own Fred Hanson.

And S-375, which provided for the biennial payment of County taxes by the cities and towns. I had also filed a petition similar to this one at the request of our own terrific Town Accountant, Walter Kirkland, and was happy to join Senator Arthur Tobin in a reinforcing bill. Now that our taxes are to be collected twice yearly, our County taxes should be paid twice yearly. And - speaking of the County, would you have believed that the rate of interest charged by this branch of our government on overdue accounts is currently 12 percent?? S-376, which I co-sponsored, seeks to reduce this interest rate to 8 percent. Braintree, I learned from Mr. Kirkland, always has paid its county assessment on time. It represents a soaring figure, however - from $125, 423,.39 in 1964 to $537, 352. 46 in 1974. Just think of the interest we would be paying if one year we FAILED to pay our county tax on time.

Next comes 3-380. I did not co-sponsor that one. I opposed it, for it would have authorized the County Commissioners of Norfolk County to continue an expensive study relative to the establishment of REGIONAL solid waste disposal and collection districts within this county. Alerted to its intent just in time, I had contacted our Braintree Selectmen who promptly expressed their opposition to any legislation which would take control of the Braintree incinerator away from the Town of Braintree. I hastily added their opposition to my own before the Committee involved. Besides, S-380 had been filed in conjunction with S-381, which would have given these Norfolk County Commissioners authority to "establish, operate, maintain and control facilities for the collection, transfer, processing and disposal of solid wastes." Can't you picture what could happen to the Town of Braintree and its incinerator if that little old bill sailed through the Legislature? I opposed it vehemently. Incidentally, needless to say, I DID NOT file or I did, however, co-sponsor S-680, which was a petition to require a reduced rate of 50 percent by gas, electric and telephone companies for service to the elderly. They are in dire straights, those wonderful Senior Citizens who, having contributed so heavily to the economy during the course of their lifetimes, now find themselves facing the bleak task of coping with inflation of pensions that are geared to yesteryear's low wages…And I co-sponsored S-631, which would exempt from state regulations those famous Beano games staged in our Housing for the Elderly complexes.

I also co-sponsored S-752, which petitioned that "no increase in payments made to the aged person under the provisions of the federal Social Security Act shall be deemed to be income of such aged person"…and S-957, which would provide penalties for those violating the provisions of the Food Stamp program.

Then there was S-1141, which would provide that the Registry of Motor Vehicles shall issue ID cards to persons who do not possess licenses (at a token amount, merely to make the program self-sustaining).

Ever mindful of the nightmare situation attendant upon the upcoming 100 percent valuation situation, I co-sponsored S-1480, which would provide real estate tax relief for low and middle income persons through a "circuit breaker" system of credits or refunds on state income tax. And, incidentally, how delighted I was as I sat in Gardner Auditorium, awaiting my turn at the mike, to hear our Taxation Committee Co-Chairman announce the committee's endorsement of the circuit breaker concept…And now comes S-1476, which I co-sponsored eagerly, for it called for a legislative amendment to the Constitution, authorizing the classification of property according to its USE for the purpose of taxation. What a triumph it would represent for those of us who are struggling against this nightmare that threatens our town if the Taxation Committee were to report THAT ONE out favorably!

I was equally happy to be listed as co-sponsor of S-1479, which would increase the exemption on income taxes for elderly taxpayers. The elderly have their backs against the wall. I know because so many of them have called me and written to me of their fears and anxieties in this inflation-ridden time. There was S-1481, as well; I co-sponsored that one. It would increase exemptions from property tax for widows, veterans and the elderly in those cities and towns which have gone to 100 percent valuation.

Now on a lighter note - I co-sponsored S-1534, which would provide for the establishment of footpaths and bicycle trails wherever a highway, road or street is being constructed, reconstructed or relocated. I kept remembering as I did so the European countries I had visited, where alongside every set of railroad tracks as well as along just about every highway bicycle paths ran merrily; and people cycled to and fro as we roared along in those marvelous European trains, a pretty sight - and, with the energy shortage, inflation and the rest, a practical solution to commuting and to recreation…

Incidentally, I had the pleasure of sitting in with Senator Burke, our Transportation Committee Co-Chairman, on a subcommittee which came up with a great redraft of this bicycle bill. It just might pass!

S-1535, also co-sponsored by this legislator, would provide minibus service throughout the Town for the duration of the Bicentennial celebration, and beyond, for use by our elderly and handicapped citizens. This bill is currently in Limbo, being explored for both federal funds and Bicentennial Commission cooperation (once those federal funds are assured…). And then there was S-1537, which sought legislation to prohibit on new "minibikes" a sound pressure level of more than 73. decibels. What a sop for sore ears that particular piece of legislation would be!

Gosh, I haven't begun to scratch the surface, I can see that; and here I am filling up page after page with the doings of this "Lady of the House."

It's all YOUR fault, however, you wonderful readers! You've been telling me for weeks what fun it is to share in the doings, the comings and the goings on Beacon Hill… So there'll be loads more to follow…

And, oh yes, next week I'll tell you how I came to co-sponsor so many SENATE bills in addition to all the House bills that would normally be mine…Should have told you that bit way back in the beginning!

4-6-75

How did it happen that I, a member of the House of Representatives, served as co-sponsor of so many SENATE bills, you undoubtedly wondered as you read my column last week…Well, quite simply, one cold December day just previous to the filing deadline date for legislation, I received a call from the office of our own State Senator Arthur H. Tobin.

"The Senator," said a warm and friendly voice, "invites you to drop by and examine the bills he intends to file, to see if you'd care to co-sponsor any of them." I lost no time in heading for the State House and examining a sheaf of bills from which I extracted a sizeable number with the contents of which I was in accord. Incidentally, Senator Tobin has been graciousness itself to this columnist since her arrival on Beacon Hill.

Now, what does it involve, this co-sponsorship of bills? Well, I was soon to learn the answer to that one. It requires keeping track of them; securing background information on them; speaking to them before the appropriate committee in Committee Hearings, and being prepared to defend them from the onslaughts of the twenty-one or so members of the committees involved.

The job was not to be easily handled, believe me - especially when hearings on said bills were scheduled for precisely the same time as hearings on both of my State Committees, which also had been scheduled simultaneously…and I would find myself having to be present in three or four places at once…There was to be a slightly silver lining, however. Legislators, I learned, are permitted to speak out of turn; and so one IS able to dash madly from one room to another, managing somehow.

To tuck everything nicely in…And it's all marvelously interesting…And by dint of this little old column of mine I hope to make you, my readers and constituents, so conversant with what goes on under that magnificent Golden Dome of ours that at least ten or twenty of you will be ready to challenge me two years from now when I aspire to serve a second term, representing the wonderful people of Braintree. Now a bit about those committees on which I serve, before we go on to discuss the many remaining bills I have sponsored, co-sponsored or been involved in supporting actively. First of all, the newly formed Committee on Health Care. Here we will have initial review and oversight of all legislation that is public health related, with the exception of health insurance. Within this area of public health we shall be dealing with a wide variety of programs and activities, ranging from the Medicaid program to the various regulatory activities to health protection and treatment programs. Included among these will be general guidelines for the licensing and regulation of hospitals, clinics and long term care facilities. The Department of Health must, of course, license and approve these health facilities; and individual health practitioners like physicians, psychologists, nurses, chiropractors, dentists, druggists, optometrists and podiatrists as well as nursing home administrators must be certified; while psychiatrists and physical therapists have to be licensed by the Board of Registration in Medicine.

Our Health Care Committee will be involved with the Rate Setting Commission in the Executive Office of Human Services, I was surprised to learn; and with Health Reorganization, primarily HSRA, the proposal to reorganize the health regulatory functions so as to facilitate coordinated planning and policy implementation; and with the state Medical Assistance Program or Medicaid as it is called; and with the Certificate of Need Program, whose intent is to regulate capital investment in facilities and equipment for health care by deterring unnecessary construction and expansion, the costs of which would be passed on to the consumer.

What an amazing collection of facts and fancies I would manage to amass on this fascinating committee! And what exciting issues I was to hear debated and discussed by the experts in their particular fields…like patients' rights; and fluoridation; and optometrists versus ophthalmologists; and pharmacists versus the cut-rate chains.

It's all challenging and exciting indeed…But more on those Senate bills I have been co-sponsoring with our own State Senator. S. 335, which would require employers to list job vacancies with the Division of Unemployment Security. How timely this one, with the state unemployment funds in jeopardy, and unemployment increasing in leaps and bounds! And S. 632, which would establish a basic rate structure for gas and electric service…And S. 1536, which would direct the MBTA to provide modifications of bus steps for the disabled and the elderly. How often we've witnessed an elderly or disabled person struggling to negotiate the steps of an MBTA bus while the driver looked on impatiently (or patiently)…And S. 1538, which would direct the MBTA to charge all persons 65 years of age and older no fee on its rapid transit and surface lines. Why not? I had asked myself as I examined that one. Haven't we all ridden on all but empty cars and trains during off peak hours??? We are obligated to pay the operators of those vehicles for an eight-hour shift regardless of how few passengers they tote… so why not let our elderly citizens fill up those empty seats? They'll not travel on peak hours, take my word for it.

4-13-75

A bit about my second committee assignment; and the one toward which I just naturally gravitated the moment I announced my candidacy for State Representative… membership of the all-important to Braintree right now that we're back dealing with the M.B.T.A. once more – TRANSPORTATION COMMITTEE!

The public hearings before this committee, I was soon to learn, cover a wide variety of matters, ranging from petitions which direct the State Department of Public Works to name a bridge after a veteran or after some very prominent official - deceased, of course - to petitions which would authorize the D.P.W. or the M.B.T.A. to increase its bonded indebtedness by massive amounts for highway or mass transit improvements.

We might be hearing petitions directing said department to construct specific highways; or to maintain specific roads; or to acquire land by eminent domain; or to investigate the feasibility of erecting pedestrian overpasses over a highway or a railroad crossing…We might be dealing with the restriction of night flying or the reduction of the noise level at Logan Airport; or with petitions that would provide incentives to commuters to car-pool it. There could be petitions that relate to the acquisition of railroad rights-of-way; or to improved transportation facilities; or to reduced fare for the elderly and the handicapped. We might be dealing with the provision of increased state aid to the M.B.T.A. or with increased local highway aid outside the M.B.T.A. district; or with the reorganization of the several state agencies within the transportation area; or with the maintenance of local service within the M.B.T.A. district, and outside the district.

Now, how in the world was I to familiarize myself with all the many aspects of this wide variety of issues, I wondered wildly as - a brand new legislator - I approached my first committee hearing with as close to fear and trembling as I have been known to come. A briefing session on committee procedures was to set my mind somewhat at rest- that and the realization that "challenge" seemed ever to have been my middle name…

At any rate, I was to learn the following: That bills would be grouped according to subject matter; and that prior to the committee hearing on individual bills or petitions, the joint research staff would prepare a report for the committee membership. This report would contain a summary of each of the bills…a summary which would reflect the present law which the proposed legislation was attempting to amend; and what that proposed change was designed to do and what changes it would make in the present statute. Now, should state funds be involved in the legislation, cost factors would hopefully be included in the initial presentation - "ball park figures," our legislative friends were to call them - and they would be sought religiously by committee members in this period of bullet biting.

I was to sit entranced through my initial transportation committee hearings, astounded at the extensive knowledge of our Committee Chairmen and Vice Chairman… And, incidentally, I was to learn from our distinguished Vice Chairman, Representative Nickinello, that as a Freshman legislator he had been appointed committee clerk; and that, after a mere two years in that role, he had been named Vice-Chairman. The reason was apparent!

Every bill or petition that has been heard before the Committee will be voted on afterwards in executive session, I was to learn. It will be voted favorably, or carry an "ought not to pass" recommendation. And it will go next to the House for consideration and voting.

The House meets at eleven o'clock each day; and awaiting each legislator is a copy of the Calendar which will list each of the bills to be considered, along with the committee recommendation. The Speaker proceeds then to take the day's Calendar, bill by bill, and read each item aloud. If the bill has received an "Ought not to pass" verdict from committee, and as the Speaker identifies it by page and calendar number, no representative present calls "Pass!", the "ought not to pass" decision stands, and the report of the committee on that bill is accepted. Should a House member wish to challenge the committee decision and debate the bill, he (or she) will call "Pass." The Speaker will say, "The Chair hears pass" and go on to the next listed item.

The morning session has begun with a prayer by the House Chaplain, Monsignor Kerr; and a salute to the flag; and with the reading of each item on the Calendar it is brought to a close…temporarily…for at one o'clock that same afternoon the House members will gather in the Chamber and the business of the Commonwealth will begin in earnest.

There now, so many of you have asked just how bills ARE handled in the House, I felt that you all might be interested in the procedure. It's a wonderfully efficient procedure, incidentally…And by now you must have realized that it is before Committee that your bill must be defended; it is the committee vote you must seek to obtain; and it is difficult indeed to overturn on the floor of the Chamber a decision of the committee which has heard and evaluated the merits of your bill. A committee member will be assigned to "carry" the bill, which means that he must defend the committee decision should it be challenged in the House; and hopefully muster enough support to maintain his committee's position all along the line. He will have assistance in handling this assignment, needless to say. The committee's research staff will prepare a Bill history folder for him, with all the necessary and vital information he will need; how well he handles that information, however, will be up to him! Why do I keep saying "he?" And "him?" I have not volunteered to carry a bill so far, but I have been tempted to offer to do just that once or twice along the way. And -oh, yes - a member may "dissent" from a committee decision, and the fact is noted in the House Calendar. It is usually one of the dissenters who challenges the committee decision and debates it on the floor of the House. Doesn't it all sound exciting and wonderful? It is!

4-20-75

Being the first woman State Representative from this wonderful little old town of ours, I have a thing about "firsts."

I was particularly interested, therefore, in this "First in the Nation" compendium for our wonderful little old state:

In 1630, the first session of the Massachusetts General Court was held on October 17.

1644, and for the first time the House of Deputies separated from the House of Magistrates.

1676, and we passed the first legislation for the care of the "insane."

1692, and the House of Deputies was renamed the House of Representatives; this was the first time this name was used.

1764, and the First Official Census was authorized by the General Court.

1780, and the First General Court adopted the new Constitution in use in the entire world and was the prototype for the Federal Constitution framed in 1787.

1788, and ours was the first state to outlaw the African Slave Trade.

1820, and the first amendment to the constitution was accepted, which granted voting privileges to all male citizens over twenty-one years of age. (No Woman's Lib in those days…)

1821, and the First Public High Schools were established.

1836, and ours was the first state to regulate investments by insurance companies.

1837, and we established the first State Board of Education in the United States, with Horace Mann, who was a former member of the Massachusetts House, appointed as its first Chairman.

1841, and ours was the first state to adopt a probation system.

1842, and Massachusetts was the first state to enact laws regulating child labor.

1843, and we were pioneers in the treatment of the mentally retarded, thanks to the efforts of Dorothea Dix and Dr. Samuel Woodward.

1847, and our cities and towns were authorized to provide for adult education.

1852, and we passed the first mandatory school attendance law.

1855, and we established the first Department of Insurance in the nation. That same year the first Bill was passed, prohibiting discrimination based on race, creed, color or religious opinion in establishing qualifications for admission into public schools.

1864, and ours was the first state to establish a Board of Health

1865, and we were the first state to create a law enforcement agency with police powers everywhere in the state - a Department of Public Safety.

1869, and we were first to establish a Bureau of Labor Statistics to gather and compile information on the wage earners of the state.

1885, and a Constitutional Amendment was ratified granting the General Court the power to regulate elections.

1888, and the first use of the Reform-oriented "Australian Ballot" was authorized by the General Court.

1893, and we created the first State Highway department in the nation.

1900, and we were responsible for proposing the first motor vehicle legislation. It requires that automobiles be equipped with bumpers!

1912, and Massachusetts was the first state in the nation to establish a retirement system for Public employees. And in that same year, the nation's first minimum wage law was enacted on June 4.

1913, and we enacted the first law in the United States to require examination by two appointed psychiatrists for people accused of capital or repeated offenses. It was the Briggs Law.

1918, and we established the first State Board of Housing. In that same year, the first public housing project in the nation was completed in Lowell.

1919, and in an effort to modernize our state government, we designated responsibility for preparation of the budget to the Governor.

1923, and THE FIRST WOMAN WERE ELECTED TO THE MASSACHUSETTS HOUSE OF REPRESENTATIVES!

You will pardon me if I cut off the list of Massachusetts "firsts" at precisely this point. There's more, you know. According to political scientist Jack L. Walker of the University of Michigan, who compiled these marvelous statistics, Massachusetts ranks as the "second most innovative" state in the nation, trailing only the state of New York! Small wonder I am consumed with a special kind of awe as I walk the marble halls of our magnificent State House and realize that I belong there! More "firsts" next week, and I sincerely hope that reading them all, you will be as proud of our great State as I am!

4-27-75

Being the first woman State Representative from this great town of Braintree, small wonder I am persuaded to continue my litany of "firsts" for the sovereign State of Massachusetts...which litany we ended last week with the year 1923 when the first WOMEN were elected to the Massachusetts House of Representatives. We continue with 1926, when the first woman was appointed to serve as Speaker Pro Tempore of the House; her name - M. Sylvia Donaldson; and 1928, when the first shellfish purification plant was built...The litany continues...1930, and Massachusetts was the first state in the union to employ females as Police Officers.

- 1948, and we were the first state to tie public assistance grants to the cost of living index.
- 1955, and our state established the first contributory program of group insurance combining life and health insurance for state employees.
- 1957, and we adopted the farm-labor minimum wage act.
- 1962, and Massachusetts established the first statewide program for the detection of Phenlyketenuria in babies...(And I couldn't even find that word in my Webster's Dictionary!)
- 1963, and we were first to establish the Consumer's Council.
- 1965, and Massachusetts passed the first Racial Imbalance Law in the nation.
- 1966, and we established the Massachusetts Housing Finance Agency.
- 1967, and our state passed the Truth-in-Advertising Act. That same year, we were first with a Truth-in-Lending act.
- 1968, and we were first with a Department of Community Affairs...And first with a Gun Control Act.
- 1968, and Consumer Protection Laws were uppermost in the minds of our legislators. We came through with the first Insurance Policy Discrimination Act; Auto Insurance Cancellation Act; and First Insurance Cancellation Act.
- 1969, and Massachusetts was first in the nation to adopt an "Anti-Snob Zoning Law" to aid the construction of public housing. That same year, we came through with the Massachusetts Medicaid Act.
- 1970, and our state passed the first state Unit Pricing Law. We were also first to establish No Fault Insurance...a first in the national proposal concerning automobile accident claims. During this year of "firsts," we also passed the well-known "Shea Bill," which attempted to clarify the war-time. powers of the President of Congress.
- 1971, an equally important year of "firsts"...We were first in the nation to adopt a Bi-Lingual Education Law; and to adopt a Lead Paint-Poisoning Law; and to pass a comprehensive revision of the laws relating to alcoholism and public drunkenness.
- 1972, and an especially innovative General Court was responsible for a series of truly vital "firsts"

The Candid Idylls of a State Representative

...It included the establishment of an Environmental Protection Division under the Attorney General, which carried the strict requirement that Environmental Impact Reports be filed before the start of all major public projects. (Man's relationship to his environment and his dependence on same had finally been recognized...) And a new office of Children's Affairs was created. A community based corrections system was instituted, with the potential to be the most unique and extensive in the nation, surpassing even that of the State of California. And - most far-reaching of all in its potential effects - a national model law on "Special Education" was passed. It guaranteed equal educational opportunity to physically and emotionally handicapped youngsters formerly considered "uneducable."

5-4-75

An exciting week, this one, on Beacon Hill! Not only because we are dealing with vital and controversial legislation - which we are - but because wonderful fringe benefits are coming the way of those legislators who, like myself, love to be learning new and interesting things...programs like the series of "Energy Dialogues" which were scheduled for Monday, Tuesday, Wednesday and Thursday under the Aegis of that splendid source of information, the Science Resource Network of the General Court.

Monday's dialogue between the experts and our legislators included a discussion of "offshore oil drilling, refinery siting and the impact of all development designed to outline the implications of raw oil, policies for Massachusetts and legislative options which are emerging." It included a discussion of the economic and environmental impact of offshore oil drilling; and was fascinating indeed.

Tuesday, however, turned out to be one of the most exciting days of this year, for the subject under discussion was Nuclear Energy; and oh! What amazing facts I accumulated about this frequently challenged energy source!

There were the comments of Dr. Manson Benedict, for instance - Professor Emeritus, Mass. Institute of Technology and first Chairman of that school's Dept. of Nuclear Engineering. "Although nuclear plants cost more to build than conventional plants, the fueling costs are so much less that the overall cost of nuclear electricity is much lower," he said; and he compared the daily nuclear fuel bill of $47, 000 to one of $130, 000 in a similarly sized 350 megawatt plant burning coal at $20 a ton, and $315,000 in a plant burning oil.

Once charged with fuel, a nuclear plant can run for a year without refueling, so that it can't be shut down by mine or rail strikes, or lack of available oil, the good Doctor told us. And he described the elaborate precautions taken to protect the general public from radioactivity, viz. the three barriers; the metal cladding surrounding the fuel; the eight-inch thick reactor pressure vessel that holds the fuel; the cooling water to which it transfers its heat; and the air-tight steel and concrete building housing the reactor.

"Nowhere in the world has any member of the general public been injured, much less killed, by operation of more than 60 power plants now operating, some for more than 15 years," Dr. Benedict said - a record "unique in the world's experience". All of which sounded just great, we might add.

Then along came Dr. Kent Hansen, Professor, Dept. of Nuclear Engineering, M.I.T. who quoted the environmental costs of alternatives to nuclear plants...like land use - the mining of coal, which occasions the destruction of 100,000 acres annually to supply 100 plants, as opposed to 1600 acres for nuclear plants; 20 million tons of coal waste as opposed to 200 tons of nuclear waste. There were the occupational hazards quoted-264 deaths annually in open pit mining; 400 in conventional mining; 15 in nuclear activity. The nightmare of black lung disease was stressed. It was all marvelously convincing.

Marson Pratt, Senior Vice President of Adams, Harkness and Hill, Inc. and former Chairman, Governor's Public Power Study Commission added an economic facet. Oil burning costs of 50 mills per kilowatt hour as opposed to nuclear cost of 36 mills per kilowatt hour. "The government should aid nuclear power rather than slow it down." he said. I was all set to write letters to my Congressman when along came Dr. George Kistiakowsky, Professor Emeritus Harvard University, Former Vice President, National Academy of Sciences. (I THINK he said at one point he was one of those who made the first atom bomb...)

Dr. K. admitted there were SOME safety aspects; and the cost factors were there... but when a nuclear plant is in trouble, it's BAD! he said. Radio-active waste, thrown in the water, could be dangerous for thousands of years, representing a threat to future generations, he said. Legislators like myself appeared to sit entranced as the the delightful professor outlined the many dangers implicit in the scattering of nuclear facilities about the country - plants that so many of us have looked upon as the Panacea for all of our energy ills.

He stressed the threat of the hijacking of radioactive waste material on our highways; of terrorists occupying and threatening to blow up the plants themselves; of the necessity for madly expanding counter intelligence...With a thousand plants scattered about the country we'd have to have armed guards everywhere, he said. I envisioned a form of police state as he talked.

The handling of nuclear waste came in for animated discussion. We learned that 110 shipments of this radioactive material pass through the Commonwealth each year; and that there appear to be far too few restrictions to assure its safe passage. Currently the waste would appear to be transferred to E.R.G.A. where a long term solution would be to convert it to solid form and bury it thousands of feet under the earth in geologically suitable areas; in the Kansas Salt Mines, for instance; or in above ground storage facilities where the containers would be cooled by water and air, and carefully supervised.

There are two kinds of nuclear waste, we learned. There is high level waste with a small quantity of plutonium and radioactive fission products; and low level waste, viz. floor sweepings, uniforms, etc.

Plutonium lasts for 500,000 years, incidentally; and fission products for 600 years. Your representative found herself listening spellbound as one interesting fact after another came to light, like the matter of the storage of huge quantities of nerve gas after World War II, with the Pentagon LOSING THE RECORDS of just where they stored it.

Do you know what??? I shall take a whole lot more comfort now in the knowledge that those "Concerned Scientists" about which we read tidbits now and then keep piping about and keeping an eye on things nuclear, than I ever have before; how about it???

5-11-75

Another exciting week on Beacon Hill-with the days blending into the other in a flurry of activity and accomplishment…with an Annual Meeting of the Massachusetts Legislators Association made marvelous by the astounding realization that I, Elizabeth N. Metayer really BELONGED there…along with a few other considerations like the nice fact that our neighboring Colleague and good friend, Representative Joe Brett, had been installed that very afternoon as Vice-President of the group and was there to be congratulated by all of us; that my dinner companions were delightful and the dinner superb; that Senator "Billy" Bulger rivaled Bob Hope as M.C. for the evening; and that it was topped off by a film on James Michael Curley that literally brought that colorful character to life forcing countless of his peers to share unbelievably amusing reminiscences with the rest of us…And oh, yes, in addition, by the fact that all the great political figures - past and present – whose faces we have witnessed in the newspapers and whose voices we have heard on TV paraded about with a great show of handshaking, back slapping and the rest, in true political style. It was "HURRAH" all the way; and, happily, not the LAST one!

Then came my first go at a Constitutional Convention, or "Con Con" as it is termed affectionately hereabouts…a Joint Senate and House Convention, at which I was expected to testify on my bill to assess real property on the basis of "USE" rather than the "FAIR MARKET VALUE" we're having to live with so unhappily - and I think unfairly- here in Braintree. Action on this issue was postponed until Wednesday next, incidentally.

There was also my really "MaidenSpeech" on the floor of the House Chamber. Actually I had spoken before - on a Health Care Committee issue-but not to such lengths as I was permitted to go with this one, as I carried for the Transportation Committee our famous House Bill 511 which seeks to prevent the building of a rapid transit station in South Quincy. That's really like having it in North Braintree, you know, so closely are they situated…

Incidentally I loved watching several of my very good friends as they sat in the Chamber beaming while I testified, quite like a group of proud parents with a small child on display. What a truly great group of human beings these Legislators are! I've grown to love just about every one of them. And, of course, what joy to have proven effective as your legislator by securing a 189 to 33 favorable vote!

Meanwhile, we were to be addressing such controversial subjects as the use of "dum dum" bullets by our police force; and of course - since last columning, meeting with the Governor and seething over the proposed tax increases for his bonding program. Cigarette tax-O.K! But NOT gasoline tax! More on that in subsequent columns however - and there WILL be more…

It is Spring on Beacon Hill these days, despite those grim gray skies we've been "enjoying" of late. The benches on the Common are all filled; jonquils are abloom and squirrels romp about the lawns; and strolling young musicians by the score are entertaining there along the walks. There even seem to be SOME slumberers beneath the trees…Outfits are MARVELOUS! I can't believe one-tenth of what I see! Carnaby Street and Harvard Square all rolled into one…

I've really never been in Boston when Spring was springing…can't recall now ever having strolled the walks of Boston Common with a lingering look back on now MY Beacon Hill; or finding there the green grass greening wildly day by day. It's all quite wonderful, of course.

I'm having great response to those evening Office Hours at Braintree's Town Hall on Monday nights. There seem to be wall to wall people. This past Monday evening's hours had to be cancelled, as will be next Monday evening's hours, of course, by virtue of Town Meeting. Holidays and Town Meeting days on Mondays must be out. But there'll be other Mondays; and I'll be right on hand from seven to nine o'clock and frequently beyond. So if you've problems I can help to solve; if you've opinions to be shared or bills that I must face - why, drop by and say "Hello!"…That's what I'm there for!

****

5-18-75

It was quite a week on Beacon Hill!

An amendment to H-5867 provided for voluntary "No Smoking" places in public buildings; H- 5353, a bill to create a Public Power Authority, went down to defeat, 179-46; the M.B.T.A. was cited as a glaring example of what a nightmare an Authority can become. H-5869 lost decisively. It was a bill to give public service employees (excluding Civil Service employees) the right to strike…And then there was H-2679, a bill to enroll children in kindergarten in the calendar year of their age; this bill failed miserably with a vote of 188 to 40.

Closer in vote was a bill to establish a local school committee screening committee on sex education, which failed initially but later won in a reconsidered vote. H-5930 came about as a result of a recent court decision relative to the right of a citizen to defend himself within his home. It called for the appointment of a special committee of the House to make an investigation and study of the impact of this decision on the safety of the citizens of the Commonwealth. A vote of 170 to 58 assured the establishment of such a committee; and legislation will promptly be filed on this matter as well. An attempt to amend the controlled substance act by revising the penalty for the possession of marijuana went down to defeat, 173 to 51; and a graduated income tax was voted, 186-39. Victorious was a bill - with a vote of 159 to 70-providing that no child shall be assigned or denied to school on the basis of sex, race, color or national origin.

H-588, a bill to return the administration of the "Welfare program to Cities and Towns went through the House quite handily, 154 to 71 (and thence to Ways and Means); and a bill to pay 10 percent of the money recovered in Welfare fraud to the person reporting the fraud failed, 177 to 49.

The Legislators indeed have a grave concern for detecting fraudulent welfare cases, however the thought of setting citizen against citizen was a bit too much.

On a close vote of 111 to 108 the House voted suspension of Joint Rule 12 which would then give subpoena power to the Legislative Food Commission. The proposal, on the face of things, seemed alarming. It was explained, however that the Food Commission had held hearings on the responsibility of the huge supermarket chains to keep down escalating food prices and to justify huge profits. The simplest of questionnaires went answered. The Attorney General has stated he has not the time nor the staff to investigate escalating food prices; and so this hard working committee seeks subpoena power as a last resort….

Failing by a vote of 156 to 69 was a bill to include "passive euthanasia" in the items under study by a special Commission investigating human clinical investigation and experimental therapy. Prevailing however was a bill that would provide a right to counsel for certain teachers - with 194 AYES and but 28 NAYS; as well as a bill requiring prompt transmission of dues deductions to associations of teachers. The vote-182 to 41…

A bill to ban the use of non-returnable bottles failed, 148 to 63. And then - in a Joint Constitutional Convention of the Senate and the House it was voted to place the Equal Rights Amendment on the Ballot so that the people of the Commonwealth may indicate to their duly elected representatives their preference in the matter…And down to defeat went a proposed Constitutional Amendment to abolish the Governors Council.

Had you any idea of the scope and variety of the kinds of bills we deal with daily in the State Legislature? I confess I hadn't realized the half of it. And, incidentally, how your representative agonizes over some of the votes she is called upon to cast…the decisions she if forced to make on truly crucial issues that will affect the quality of life for her constituents…It's an awesome responsibility, this representation of the people I love on Beacon Hill.

But to return to this particular week's legislation - the most exciting vote of all…and it came about bright and early on the very first day…House Bill 511, our bill to prevent the building of a rapid transit station in South Quincy, (which is the same as building it in North Braintree) went to be exgrossed WITHOUT DEBATE!

It was bound to happen, I had been assured by my colleagues in the know! "With a vote of 189 to 133," they said, "who would take a chance on challenging it again?" They were right; and so all of the ammunition I had stocked up and toted to the House in preparation for further debate went unused - Hallelujah! - And now it is up to the Senate…Our own Senator Arthur Tobin has assured me he sees no difficulty for it there; it would be great, however, if you, my readers - those of you who don't want that station - would put a note in the mail to Senator Arthur Tobin, in care of the State House, Boston 02133. We'd appreciate it - those of us who have worked so hard for this all- important bill…and you'd be supporting our claim of the importance of the issue to the people of Braintree.

Yes sir (and madam), it was quite a week on Beacon Hill…How do YOU feel about any of these issues? Do let me know.

****

5-25-75

One of my Colleagues put it so well on Wednesday afternoon as we failed in our attempt to override the Governor's veto of H-511- that bill that seeks to prevent the building of the South Quincy MBTA Station. "Elizabeth," he said sagely, "We covered parts 1, 2 and 3 in our Political Science courses; we never got to part 4." Part 4, we had discovered to our dismay, represents raw, naked political power.

The Governor had vetoed the bill the previous evening after it had passed the Senate. I wasn't too surprised. I had seen the Secretary of Transportation flying about as I waited by the elevator at day's end. What I failed to anticipate, however, was the fact that three-quarters of an hour before the one o'clock session was to begin, I would learn that the veto "Message from His Excellency, the Governor" was to be voted on that very afternoon.

There was little or no time to plan strategy. I tried madly to reach everyone by phone and succeeded only in reaching Representative Cerasoli; then I quickly drafted a letter of thanks to those of our Colleagues who had voted with us before, asking their continued support; and raced to have the missive re-produced…only to learn from reproduced… only to learn from the Speaker's Office that the distribution of any communication of this sort within the Chamber is prohibited. There was, needless to say, no time to have it delivered to the various offices; and so that avenue of communication was blocked. And now it was off to the Chamber at one; and here we were in for a bleak surprise, for lobbyists by the dozens were waiting there to meet and greet those 240 members of the

House of Representatives, 160 of whose votes we would need to override the Governor's veto. "Elizabeth," friends kept saying, "For goodness sake get out of there and lobby for your bill!" I couldn't. I was too busy mentally addressing the "10 reasons for building the station" which had been listed in a South Shore Chamber of Commerce handout that had been circulated around the State House throughout the morning.

The debate began. It had been preceded by a veritable crusade of newspaper propaganda. Braintree's own representative to the Metropolitan Area Planning Council, Joe Magaldi (if his appointment is still in force) had castigated the Quincy and Braintree representatives in the Patriot Ledger a few days previously, stating that we had not attended a meeting because there were no television cameras or reporters present, knowing full well that had we Representatives been invited or been notified of the meeting by the "Chamber," we'd have been there with bells…He had also limited the station opposition to an "elite corps" of 25 or so people…

But to return to the debate. Our principal opponent, we learned, was to be Barney Frank, a powerful debater and a Boston Representative who very naturally thought it would be a jim dandy idea to have a rapid transit station, complete with ramps, in far-off Braintree. Barney was to "filibuster" until the hour of 2:99 p.m. when a scheduled Constitutional Convention was to begin and we had to interrupt debate until its conclusion.

Now we know we should have asked for a roll-call vote then and there; I do believe we would have had the vote. We didn't however; we wanted to dispute his statements; to debate the issues. We were wrong, for during the next ninety minutes while the Joint Convention debated, the most unbelievable display of raw, naked political power went on just beyond the Chamber doors.

The Governor was there; the Governor's Secretary, Mr. Johnson was there; the Secretary of Transportation was there, along with every labor leader from here to Arkansas, including former Secretary of State Davoren, now a labor leader himself. The M.B.T.A. had its most popular "guns" in force; and former "reps" who had found a berth within that hallowed group were busily reminding their 'Buddies" of past friendships. There were representatives from each of the countless supporting groups; and even some Senators pipped about to join the parade.

"A vote for the bill and against the station is an ANTI-LABOR vote," Representatives were told, including THIS Representative, who had been called from the Chamber to be lobbied by the labor crew. The passage of the Bill over the Governor's veto was branded as an affront to organized Labor. It was quite a scene, that Chamber Lobby. "The GOVERNOR himself was there?" someone said incredulously. "In all the years I have been in the State House, I never heard of the Governor lobbying." "He was there," I said. "As a matter of fact I was so stunned to see him as I went to meet with the summoning labor lobbyists that I came to an abrupt halt at sight of him. "Elizabeth," said a Colleague, "I see you looking at the Governor; haven't you MET him yet???" As a matter of fact, I had met him an hour or so before when I had gone with Senator Tobin to be photographed with him as he signed the Braintree Air Rights (over any South Braintree Station) Bill. I had said sweetly to him, "We love you, Governor, but we're going to have to fight you on your veto this afternoon." He had merely smiled. He was aware of the scope and magnitude of the troops he had lined up against us.

And now the Constitutional Convention was ended and the debate on H-511 resumed; but by now every Representative in the Chamber had been lobbied and pressured by everyone in sight...So how do you feel now, you Freshman Representative from Braintree - known on Beacon Hill for those starry-eyed expressions of faith and delight in the General Court??? Embittered???

Discouraged??? Not really. Disappointed, to be sure; and a little heartsick at thought of the fact that the people of Braintree may have to live with a facility they do not want, in an area unsuited to it; and with all the problems that will be generated by its being there...But THE CARDS WERE STACKED AGAINST US - and we hadn't ever gotten to part 4 of that Political Science Course; we never dreamed what raw, naked, political power can produce in the way of pressure in that "Court of Last Resort" on Beacon Hill.

H-511 was a classic example of people vs. the Bureaucracy as this Representative had pointed out to her Colleagues...If only the PEOPLE had won - what a case would have been made for that much maligned General Court of ours as the Court of Last Resort - in fact - for the people of the Commonwealth!

Well, there's still that meeting on May 28; and U.M.T.A. DOES hold the Federal purse strings; and it's my understanding STILL that the people of a community have to accept a facility before Federal funds may be spent. So let's FLOCK to the Quincy Masonic Temple on May 28! Let's let U.M.T.A. know that the final power should and does rest with the PEOPLE in this great Democracy of ours. We'll be looking for all of you...

****

6-1-75

Life goes on on Beacon Hill.

We lost another battle on House 511. The labor leaders and other lobbyists had wasted no time in furthering their ends with our Colleagues; and it was apparent that the influence of the gentleman in the corner office was also paying off...So though we may have won reconsideration on that controversial piece of legislation that would prevent the building of an MBTA facility, complete with those horrendous ramps, in South Quincy (which is like having it in North Braintree) - we decided not to debate the issue again.

The House climate was a poor one for debate anyhow. The climate in which a bill is being heard can be a deciding factor in any crucial issue; and the House members had just returned to the Chamber in a rather bad mood after a two hour Democratic Caucus in which the Governor's tax and bond proposal had been addressed heatedly and in depth. They were to be faced with a decision crucial to so many of their constituents - whether to accept an unpalatable and unacceptable tax increase proposal or to condemn 10, 800 people in one category and goodness knows how many in another, to payless pay days…With the proposed gas tax reduced from four cents per gallon to one cent per gallon (and how regretfully we had to concede that one cent per gallon DOES represent only twenty cents per week for the average driver); and with the meals tax exemption removed (with the approval of the Association of Older Americans as an alternative to the cutting down of S.S.I. medical coverage), an additional five cents per pack cigarette tax; and an additional liquor tax - the amount needed to float a 450 Million dollar bond issue was to be provided for.

It was passed after lengthy and heated debate. There seemed to be no alternative as the case for the bonding of past due obligations and current expenditures was presented to us. Without the bond issue, there would be no checks for Welfare recipients, and no checks for State employees, we were assured.

As House 6149 was set up, the removal of the meals tax exemption would yield 40 Million; the cigarette tax increase 35 Million; the liquor tax increase 13 Million and the gasoline tax increase 24 Million (it's a high yield tax) - a total of 112 Million dollars which would be sufficient to handle the five year bond issue for this year.

The alternative offered to us, viz. passing one huge 700 to 800 Million tax increase later on, seemed like an impossible dream. For one thing, as it was pointed out to us we would have to match dollar for dollar. With the bonding of the 450 Million, however, we could manage payment over a five year period with less impact on the poor long-suffering tax payer.

Not a pretty situation either way for Democratic legislators, who are in trouble, no matter how they vote. These days on Beacon Hill it would appear easier to be a Republican. Knowing they haven't a majority the Republicans can piously don white hats and vote with the angels every time…Ah, me…so much for politics!

There were other issues of importance this week. An Amendment to place a nineteen year old drinking law on the ballot for 1976 failed; and H-6147 went to a third reading.

The highlight of this "week that was" came, however when during Wednesday's Constitutional Convention a a proposal for a legislative amendment to the constitution authorizing classification of property according to its USE for purposes of taxation sailed through the House beautifully. It will, of course have to pass once more, and then be placed upon the ballot; but it's a start! A number of legislators debated the issue. I used as a classic example of the "unfairness" of the "fair market value" approach rather than the "use" classification, Article 54 of our own recent Braintree Town Warrant under which it was voted to place under the control of our Conservation Commission a piece of land, purchased for $6000 on November 3 last and declared unsuitable for building and suitable only for conservation purpose. The price the Town paid for it was $7500- the original purchase price of $6000 plus $1500 which was the cost of fill placed on the lot by its new owner prior to the realization that it was wetlands and he couldn't get permission to build there in a million years. Now what "fair market value" had our assessing firm placed upon this piece of property??? $28,700…

I reminded my Colleagues as well of the Farmland Assessment Act, General Law, Chapter 61-A, which was passed a year ago by the State Legislature. This law enables farmland to be assessed on the basis of its "current" use rather than on its "market value." There was good reason for this, I told them. Our Massachusetts farmers were going down the drain. Well, I said - our Massachusetts homes - our cities and town will be going down the drain under fair market value. Can you do less for THEM, I asked??

I am writing this Column here under the Golden Dome itself. It is Thursday evening and we have adjourned for an hour, to return at seven-thirty for what promises to be a long session on a deficiency budget which is presently being debated in the Senate… How exciting is this life on Beacon Hill!

JUNE 8, 1975

This has been the week that was!

Monday…It is 6:30 PM. at the State House. The day has been a busy one, with Sr. Ramon and a group of beautifully behaved young students from St. Francis School vying for my noon hour with a Health Care Executive Committee meeting on H-6092. That's a controversial Bill that seeks to freeze hospital costs. An unacceptable idea to the Health Care Committee; and we are seeking to come up with an alternative proposal that can be reasonably acceptable to all parties concerned, hospitals and patients alike.

Our afternoon Chamber session had gotten off to a good start, only to be adjourned until 4:00 P.M. When it was hoped a Senate and House Conference Committee would come in with a tax proposal for that controversial and horrendous bond issue the Governor feels he must have in order to get through the remainder of this year so as to begin the next fiscal year relatively debt free. Now why are we here at 6:30 P.M. at the State House when we should be enroute to Braintree and those elusive Office Hours we had hoped to be holding at Town Hall, this being a Monday evening??? Well, we had assembled at four, only to be recessed until seven, at which time the Conference Committee will surely have come in with a proposal for us to vote either up or down. "Either up or down" - "Aye, there's the rub," we are told…There will be no chance of amending the Bill or removing one or another of the taxes that are so difficult for me to accept, though accept them I must when faced with the only alternative- the matching of a two year deficit (this year's and next year's) dollar for dollar with a tax program, the magnitude of which we have not before seen in this, our sovereign State…With the bond issue we shall have five years to pay it back with an annual payment of $110 million dollars or so rather than the $450 million in one fell swoop.

To the Chamber now, for it is close to seven. Ho hum! "The Senate is close to agreement," we are told; but HOW close??? The clock ticks on.

It is 9:50 PM. And at last after recessing - and recessing - and recessing - we are face to face with the Conference Committee report. It's a combination of the best effort of give and take, we are told, of both branches of the Legislature. And now there is debate… and debate…and debate.

It is 11:40 PM. And the debate is still going on. We are reminded that Massachusetts, unlike the Federal Government, MUST balance its budget.

It is 12:05 A.M.-five minutes past the witching hour before the vote is finally taken. It loses 131 to 95. I have decided to vote against it. There MUST BE other taxable items, I tell myself.…but ARE there???

It is back to the Conference Committee now for another go at this tax package which must serve as a prelude to the bond issue that would appear to be crucial in straightening out the fiscal affairs of the Commonwealth for this year that is to end on June 30.

Whatever happened to Tuesday??? Obviously nothing very exciting transpired on that day, for now it is Wednesday and more exciting events are imminent on Beacon Hill.

Our story will begin at 2:00 PM with the Senate and House calling a Constitutional Convention. Item One on the Calendar is a "Proposal for a Legislative Amendment to the Constitution providing that no child shall be assigned or denied to a school on the basis of sex, race, color or national origin. "It is to be SOME item, for by 2:45 PM. strange things have begun to happen on Beacon Hill. Senator Owens, a member of the Black Caucus, has begun a filibuster that is to go on, with one Black Caucus member succeeding another, until it will be impossible to secure a Quorum of members willing to consume the quantities of aspirin that will enable their tortured heads to survive the kind of onslaught a filibuster represents. The call has gone out; the doors of the Chamber have been locked on those of my Colleagues who are unfortunate enough to have been seated in the Chamber when a Quorum Call went out.

(Ladies are NEVER locked in, I am happy to learn; and so I have escaped to my office and my constituent work while the President attempts vainly, hour in and hour out, to secure a Quorum and hence to put to a vote this controversial Amendment the Black Caucus is pledged to resist to the end.)

It is nine o'clock and I am hungry. A mix-up in dinner arrangements has brought about my failure. To dine out or have a sandwich brought in; I settle for a Colleague's extra roll and butter and a tired "Ayd" or two I have retrieved from the bottom of my handbag. And - as a safeguard against any similar future emergencies I resolve to give Colonel Tinkham a call and investigate his "K" rations (or is it "C" rations???)

The clock says 10:30 PM. and the Senate President has decided to give up. After vainly attempting to secure a Quorum over the hours, he decided to adjourn the Convention. The House is called back into session and the Calendar resumed.

And now it is Thursday and a new tax proposal having been agreed upon by the Conference Committee, we are at it again, debating the merits (and it sure is difficult to find any merits) of a proposal to increase the tax on cigarettes by five cents; on liquor by a 20 percent surcharge; on gasoline by a tax of one cent per gallon; and on meals to increase the tax from 5 percent to 8 percent; retaining the present $1.00 exemption.

How can I vote in favor of this tax package, I ask myself; and yet how can I fail to do just that?? Our nursing homes and hospitals are facing bankruptcy as a result of the vast amounts of money owed to them by the Commonwealth. There is no money for our welfare recipients and our State employees.

The only alternative to voting for a tax program would be to delay payment of this year's debts and add them to next year's debts, compounding our problem hopelessly. The question is: Do we owe the money? The answer is "Yes." And shall we pay it? The answer has to be "Yes" to that one, too.

No one LIKES taxes; we hate them with a purple passion. But we must keep open our nursing homes; we must pay our doctors and our hospitals; we must pay our debts… Putting off payment of last year's debts can't be the answer. That's how we got into this predicament in the first place, we are reminded. It's a clear case of acting in a fiscally responsible manner, we decide. And we decide not to throw obstacles in the way of a Governor who appears to be struggling to bring about fiscal reform. That's what we want more than anything else on Beacon Hill-FISCAL REFORM! We decide to give him a chance by wiping the 1975 slate clean and letting him prove himself with the 1976 budget…

The die is cast. The vote is taken. The tax package will be in force for the five years it will take to pay off the bond. The House has voted for it…It is 11:00 PM… "A WEEK THAT WAS" indeed!

JUNE 15, 1975

Another week…and the tax bill is really, in a sense, still with us; for we are about to deal with the bond issue to which the tax bill has been a dismal prelude. But that doesn't come until Tuesday…This past Monday has had a bright spot or two…It began with my appearance before the Local Affairs Committee on behalf of the Town I love; and then at noon it was off to Doric hall for the I presentation of a marvelous Bicentennial Exhibit of original Currier and Ives lithographs based on events of the American Revolution. The prints have have been loaned to us by the Travelers Insurance Company. There are 20 of them; each depicting some event in the early years of our Republic.

The famous partnership of Nathaniel Currier and James Merritt Ives was still flourishing in 1876, we learn, and to mark the Centennial of this land of ours, they have issued dozens of lithographs depicting scenes from the American Revolution. These are, needless to say, collectors' items today. We view with delight the twenty lithographs the Travelers Insurance Company has permitted our Bicentennial Committee to place on exhibit in Doric Hall.

There's the "Story of the Revolution", with an old man and a small boy sharing in the telling: and the Minute-Men of the Revolution"; and Washington, Appointed Commander in Chief", "The Battle of Bunker Hill", "Washington taking Command of the American Army - July 3, 1775"; "The Declaration of Independence"; "The Declaration Committee"; with Thomas Jefferson at their head, Hancock's Defiance"; "Independence Hall, Philadelphia 1776"; "Heroes of "76 June 11, 1776; "John marching to the Right"; "Washington Crossing the Delaware"; "Washington at Princeton January 3, 1777". What was he doing there, I wanted to know. After the victory at Trenton, it developed he out-maneuvered the British and defeated them at Princeton and went into winter quarters at Morristown. "The First Meeting of Washington and Lafayette"; "Surrender of General Burgo Burgoyne at Saratoga, N.Y. October 17, 1777"; "Capture of Andre 1780"; "Surrender of Lord Cornwallis at Yorktown Va., October 19, 1781"; "Cornwallis is Taken!"; "Washington's Entry into New York"; "Washington's Reception on the Bridge at Trenton"; and "The Inauguration of Washington." The lithographs are incredibly beautiful; and how I wish they were to be left in Doric Hall for longer than this one week so that many of you may be able to see them…It is on to other parts of the State for them, however…have never known the meaning of indigestion, have had it since voting for that wretched bit of legislation I was forced to digest last week…and now here it is before us again…only now it's the bond!

We had repaired, during one of our recesses, to the Senate Chamber to hear the debate. It had become pretty much of a partisan issue, of course, with the same arguments being advanced in the Senate as in the House. Why do we need SO MUCH money? Why do we really NEED the money? So and so says we can manage with a hundred million less…It goes on and on…The simple truth appears, however to be that we must have a vote on the bond in order to use available funds for the emergency situations that are already with us. It is indeed "Government by crisis"; however where can the people turn for solutions to their problems except to the Government; and where can the Government turn for the wherewith to solve the problems of its people but to the people? It seems to boil down to just that. The employees of nursing homes in the western part of the state are on strike today, we learn; our nursing homes are going bankrupt; so are our hospitals. We are in a bind. As I see it, we have no alternative but to vote for the bond. The Senate has voted affirmatively on it; now it has come to us. Time is running out. We follow their example.

Your legislator reaches once more for those Rolaids she turned to after voting in support of the tax package last week. as she reluctantly presses the light that will show up

GREEN on the Roll Call Board...Yes, we'll be back again with a bad case of indigestion, but at least the A.F.D.C. People will be able to feed their little ones; and the State employees will be paid; and those druggists and doctors whose long overdue Medicaid bills are about to be paid as a result of our action will extend credit to the needy once more...The die would appear to have been cast...

The Alternative would have been to raise close to one Billion Dollars in taxes, dollar for dollar to cover the deficits for both this year and next. We would have to double the present tax on earned and unearned income. The only way, apparently, in which we have a chance of solving the present horrendous problem, is to do what is so very unpleasant for all of us. Bonding is decidedly distasteful solution, but it would appear to be the best solution available to the plight of the Commonwealth....Yes, the die is cast!

P.S. The Senate has just failed to secure the necessary two-thirds vote...WE'RE BACK WITH THE NIGHTMARE AGAIN...

JUNE 22, 1975

The week begins in a relatively quiet way on Beacon Hill, "the tumult and the shouting" having died down with the Governor's signature on that wildly controversial bond issue; and - an informal session having been scheduled for Monday, with Tuesday a Boston holiday a majority of the "Captains and the Kings" having departed for parts unknown, we used the day as a sort of catch-up vehicle for our constituent work, which seems ever and always to require just a little bit more time than we are able to give to it.

Goodness, have I begun by saying the week began quietly????

On Monday evening, while I am holding my little old weekly office hours at Town Hall, the Governor of the Commonwealth takes to the air to announce a $687 million dollar DEFICIT for 1976! What impact will this horrendous budget deficit have on the lives of all of us. I wonder dismally as I look beyond my window on a rainy Tuesday morning that must be reflecting the mood of everyone who has heard him, especially those legislators who will be forced to vote on that incredible budget and the taxes that will have to go with it....

"I'll just vote AGAINST it," I tell myself; but will that make the deficit disappear?? Of course not....

I console myself by shelving temporarily the dreary tax picture that awaits me and by dwelling on the House of Representatives itself, and on the State House wherein it is housed. The Massachusetts State House has been the repository of three and one-half centuries of history and government, being itself one hundred and seventy years old. It was built not long after the revolution. Here in our archives we may find the historic documents on the first permanent settlement of our State. Portraits of our Massachusetts leaders adorn the walls of this historic structure.

The building itself was designed by the famous Boston architect, Charles Bulfinch, who spent many months studying the ancient Roman and Greek temples, adapting their forms for the new. State House which would feature rows of handsome columns and a stately dome. At the top of the dome the architect place a large gilt pine cone, symbolic of the pine forests that helped the early settlers to survive. Paul Revere made the copper that covered the wooden dome, which was gilded in 1861, painted gray during World War II and has been covered twice since that time with 23 karat gold.

The State House was placed on the brown of Beacon Hill in an area that once was the cow pasture of no less a personage than John Hancock. The best craftsman in Boston worked for three years, laying the bricks; building and decorating the interior. The facility was finally finished in 1798.

Excluding the two marble wings on either side of the building and the large yellow brick north annex, the State House looks pretty much today as it did when the task of building this first center of government was finished.

An interesting group of statues adorn the grounds outside. There's Anne Hutchinson with one of her nine children. Anne was banished from the Colony in the early seventeenth century for daring to question Puritan theology. And there's Mary Dyer, a martyr to her Quaker faith. There's Daniel

Webster, the spellbinding orator, and Horace Mann, a dedicated educator who fought for public education for all the children of the Commonwealth. General Thomas Hooker of Civil War fame is on horseback near the east wing of the State House; while looking toward Boston Common, one finds a bas relief monument honoring the Massachusetts 54th Regiment. This first black volunteer unit was led by Robert Gould Shaw, who lost his life in battle at Fort Wagner, South Carolina. Incidentally, the artist-sculpture Augustus St. Gaudens was commissioned to make this sculpture for the State House interior; his work was so large, however, that it had to be placed outside.

One enters the State House to find oneself in Doric Hall so named for the double row of columns with Doric capitals that architect Bulfinch employed. The Hall is rich in history. Here President Madsion was tendered a banquet upon his visit to Boston in 1817; and here a grand reception was given for General Lafayette during his American tour in 1824. Social gatherings and official ceremonies are still held here; and the huge double doors at its front entrance are opened on only two occasions; when a Governor leaves the State House for the last time after his term of office has expired and when a President of the United States visits Beacon Hill.

Excepting for the marble floor of Doric Hall, which replaced the first wooden one, the room looks much as it did when it was built. There's a bronze statue of John Hancock, our first Governor, on the west wall surrounded by portraits of Provincial Royal Governors. And on the east wall, one finds one of the only three known full-length paintings of President Lincoln. There are four cannon in the Hall, all of which were captured during the Revolutionary War and the War of 1812. There will be more on this wonderful State House of ours in subsequent weeks…I'm hoping it will whet your appetites for a real visit to Beacon Hill.

JUNE 29, 1975

With a pall of gloom-hanging over Beacon Hill as a result of the devastating budget deficit announced by our Governor for the year ahead, it seemed an appropriate moment for this distraught legislator to reproduce for her column a "fable" which was recounted by our fine Secretary of State, Paul Guzzi, for the prize winning students who were honored in the House Chamber last Saturday morning, for their contributions to a proposed publication, "A Child's Guide to the State House." Your Representative was one of four or five on hand to share in the pride of teachers and parents of five young students from St. Francis School and two fourth grade classes from Sacred Heart in Weymouth and East Braintree, all of whom were among the very proud winners. The fable was so delightful that I sought and received permission from Secretary Guzzi to pass it along to you in my column. It was written by James Reton in a column entitled "Washington," and it reads as follows:

"Once upon a time - this was way back in 1975 - the richest city in the world went broke. The mayor went to the governor of the state, but the governor was broke too. Both of them then appealed to the president of the richest nation in all history, but he was out trying to borrow $80 million topay last year's bills.

"This is a pretty pickle," said the president, who was a great phrase-maker, so he issued a proclamation summoning all the wise men and women of all generations to meet at Madison Square Gardens to analyze the problem. The Garden was vacant then because the Knicks hadn't made the playoffs.

In his opening speech, the president blamed the Congress for appropriating the money it didn't have. Then the governors blamed Washington for not voting enough money for the states, and the Congress blamed the people for living the life of Riley. Riley, who was sitting in the balcony, protested that his life had actually been miserable ever since the government took away his free liquor stamps.

Calvin Coolidge tottered to the podium and said financial deficits were the result of a shortage of money. He added that unemployment would vanish as soon as everybody had a job.

George Meany said Mr. Coolidge was entirely right, but insisted that jobs must be better paid. and that the government must prime the pump. The president intervened to say that he didn't even have a pump to prime.

Benjamin Franklin, who was back in town for the Bicentennial, then delivered the keynote speech:

"Some people seem to think," he said, "that this country can afford to fight wars, feed and police the world, send everybody to college, bring back the nickel subway fare, invade the moon, raise wages, lower prices, expand production, and stamp out inflation, pollution, cancer, and the singing commercial - all at once. But we must choose," he insisted.

"Choose! Choose!" shouted the people.

Senator Buckley of New York, speaking for the trickledowners, chose growth, business expansion, lower taxes and bigger depletion allowances.

Ronald Reagan and George Wallace, speaking for themselves, chose a new political party, "The Wallgans," that would represent "the best of the worst" or vice versa.

The conservationists chose clean air, clean water, and clean living, even, as they said, if we were clean broke.

The Pentagon chose bigger defense budgets, bigger bombers, and bigger contracts, and better retirement jobs in Big Business.

The feminists suggested equality of opportunity for all women, but George McGovern insisted that equality of opportunity was not enough and should be replaced by equality of results.

On a point of order, Mr. Franklin, obviously in exasperation, regained the microphone and asked what the hell was going on around here.

Is there no unity," he asked, "no common faith, no common body of knowledge or principle, no common moral and intellectual discipline?' But nobody answered.

MORAL: If you're broke, and really looking for the truth, never invite an old man to the celebration."

It seems to me that as we look at the deficit budget the Governor has promised to present to us within the next few days, we, too, must "Choose! Choose!" right here at the sad state level. The programs that would appear to have brought us to this sorry pass have all been great in concept- there's no denying that - but apparently no one dreamed of the fantastic costs that would accrue from implementation of these programs. Well, now we know; and unless the State is to face bankruptcy, we must indeed commence to take a cold hard look at all the fine fair programs we've proposed…and "Choose! Choose! Choose!" The choices we shall have to make will be by far the most difficult choices of my life…

JULY 6, 1975

Absolutely everything seems to be happening to the Freshmen "Reps" this year on Beacon Hill…A monumental bond issue; an even more monumental budget deficit; second and third legislative days; and this week - a brand new Speaker of the House of Representatives!

Speaker Bartley's appointment as President of Holyoke Community College had been announced on T.V. on Tuesday morning. "Well," I had said to Teddy, as I reached for the keys of the car and prepared to take off, "This will indeed be a long one. Expect me when you see me." The two-twelfths budget, you see, was facing Conference Committee action before returning to the House from the Senate where it had been debated until 2:00 A.M. that morning. We would have to remain in session until it was released by that Committee. Now - THE ELECTION OF A BRAND NEW SPEAKER AS WELL!

The resignation of Speaker of the House David M. Bartley was to prove to be a moving experience for all of us…despite the characteristic aplomb with which he was to pull it off.

"Not since Tom Dewey was elected President by the Chicago Tribune," he told those in the press gallery who had been predicting his resignation for months, "have so many been so right for so long…"

"Old Speakers never die," he added in a further attempt at merriment, "they just lose their parking space, that parking space that was loaned about seven years ago by the men and women of the House of Representatives." An attempt at flippancy, of course… But there was nothing flip about the remarks that followed it. "You chose me as your Speaker," he said. "It was a compliment for which I can never truly thank you, but for which I shall always be grateful. It is terribly important," he added, "in this trying time, that your House be in firm, sure hands." Speaker Bartley ended his remarks with the famous "Miles to go before I sleep" quotation, to applause that literally rocked the Chamber. His resignation was handed to House Clerk Wallace Mills; Minority Leader Frank Hatch presented him with an engraved Acushnet Bull's Eye Putter, and, with the gavel in the hands of Representative Michael Paul Feeney, Dean of the House (a member since 1939), the Democrats retired to Gardner Auditorium for a caucus that was to see Majority Leader, Representative Thomas W. McGee, nominated by acclamation.

"I have lived for this moment," said an obviously moved Speaker McGee. Referring to "My House," the Speaker said seriously, "I realize that every action I take and everything I do will reflect on you." And now it was back to the chamber for the election of this brand new Speaker of the House…and election on which each member of the House was to be polled. How exciting to rise as my name was called and announce brightly, "Thomas W. McGee." Our brand new Speaker was, incidentally, to receive 187 votes; with the Minority Leader receiving traditionally the Republican votes, 114 votes would have been necessary for the election of the man who was to face in the months to come perhaps the most horrendous collection of problems that state has ever known. What a responsibility for this man," I thought. "What courage he possesses!" Traditionally also a Committee is named to leave the Chamber, proceed to the Speaker's Office and escort the newly elected Speaker to the Chamber. What a thrill it was to hear my own name called as a member of that escorting Committee, and to march off with the rest; to bid a second farewell to Speaker Bartley; and then to wish so very well the man who was prepared to fill his shoes - Representative Thomas W. McGee of Lynn, Majority Leader of the House for many years…To march back with him along the marble corridors and through the Chamber doors; to enter the House of Representatives to a deafening round of applause that must have made the Sacred Cod, high up above; tremble on its moorings...

And now it was time for Speaker of the House McGee to make a special kind of "maiden speech." A tribute first to his "beautiful and charming wife" (She is!); his handsome children; a loving Mother from whom quite obviously Speaker McGee had managed to inherit his zest for public service...his brothers and his sister...all of whom were watching from the gallery with such pride...

And it was then time for the brand new Speaker of the House to speak his mind. "My philosophy hasn't changed a bit since I began," he said. "If you go out in the morning and you are able to help one person during the day, you have done something worthwhile," he said, "All of us collectively in this Chamber help more people than it is realized," the Speaker said. "I like to be a plain speaker, and like Harry Truman I'm not ashamed to be a politician," he added. "A politician," he added, "is a man who knows how to run the Government; a statesman is a politician who has been dead 10 or 15 years. The crisis we are facing this year," the Speaker said, "the crisis of getting the State back into shape is the granddaddy of them all." Predicting "a combination of new revenue and the diminished services," he told the members of HIS house, "I will need your help; I want your help." Speaker McGee outlined his aims; to strengthen the concept of the separation and balance of power, to increase the growing power and professionalism of the Legislature; (Under this aim he announced the granting of Post Audit powers to the Health Care Committee as a pilot project WHOOPEE! That's one of mine!)...to take time out in the law-making process; "It is time we started sorting out our laws," he said. "If we have laws that can't be made to work, let's get rid of them if we can." (My sentiments exactly!); to utilize in problem solving the talents of every man and woman in the Chamber... "Our words today," said Speaker McGee, "will be filed away and forgotten; it will be our ACTIONS that will be remembered."

There was a new note to the voice of the newly elected Speaker as he outlined his aims and plans for the members of HIS house. As the Chamber roared its approval of those aims he grew increasingly more eloquent, more assured...He had given full credit to all those in State Government who had had a hand in shaping the Legislative Leader he had become. He will need our prayers - yours and mine for the task that lies ahead is a horrendous one....

There now, my faithful readers, my beloved constituents, you have shared with me another rich experience from Beacon Hill: I still cannot believe that I am sharing this as well!

JULY 13, 1975

The House of Representatives has recessed until July 21…which does not mean that no one on Beacon Hill is working. The House Ways and Means Committee (our son Richard always referred to it as the "Ways to be Mean Committee" when his mother was Woman's Clubbing: the phrase would seem to be an apt one for the twenty-five House members who MUST, by sheer necessity, tear the Governor's budget to shreds and come up with additional outs in order to assure its passage…)…the House Ways and Means Committee will be working all five days of each week doing just that; this legislator spent Wednesday morning at the Department of Public Works and Friday afternoon at U.M.T.A.; all on the South Quincy rapid transit proposal. There is mail to be picked up at the State House and read for possible constituent problems; and there was fun to be had as Ted and I pipped about the Chamber and photographed it, inch by inch, because there was no one at home but the Court Officers who seemed to enjoy our little trek almost as much as we did. Oh yes, I photographed Ted at the Speaker's rostrum, and he photographed me - all in fun, you understand! So-having no legislative action to report, and having been told by a number of you that you enjoyed my first column on the State House per se, here goes with a bit more of it…

There's a narrow corridor at the rear of historic Doric Hall. It marks the beginning of the north annex addition which dates back to the 19th century; and it leads directly into the larger Senate Staircase Hall. One looks above to where a colored glass window carries the names of various: republics. In that Senate Staircase Hall there are actually two marble staircases, the one on the east side leading to the Senate and the one on the west going directly to the Governor's office. A large bronze of an army nurse attending a Civil War soldier commands one's attention; as do the three fine paintings high on the north wall, all portraying dramatic events in the history of our fair State. We find James Otis, for instance, a young Boston lawyer, arguing against the Writs of Assistance in the year 1763. How well I remember studying the history of these writs as a historically-minded school girl, and bitterly resenting the Governor's Writs that enabled the Crown's officers to enter and search any home or any warehouse….

We find, on the right, Bostonians dumping tea into the harbor as a protest against the tax imposed by the British Parliament and then, on the left, Paul Revere with that famous ride of his…And now we are in the magnificent Hall of Flags. It's a huge circular room and it's surrounded by handsome columns of marble, with the floor patterned with innumerable varieties and colors of this same marble. Built originally as a memorial to the soldiers of the Civil War, its flags now include, as well, those of the Spanish-American War and World Wars I and II. In a case on the west wall may be seen a flag that flew on the cruiser "Boston" in the waters off Vietnam. The flags, case after case of them, trace the history of war as it affected the residents of the commonwealth; and they seem especially to delight the small fry, those school children who are brought on a field trip to perhaps the most exciting destination in the Commonwealth - the State House on Beacon Hill!

There are other paintings in the Hall of Flags. We find the Pilgrims on their good ship "Mayflower;" and the battle that produced the "shot heard 'round the world," we see the Puritan minister, John Eliot, teaching the Indians; and over all we find an immense skylight of colored glass. Here will be found the seals of the thirteen original states; and our school children from Braintree, many of them, delighted in lying on their backs on the marble floor for a better view of that magnificent skylight above.

And now we are enroute to my own first love, the House of Representatives, via a huge marble stairway leading from the Hall of Flags to the historic third floor above. We pause on the landing to view a magnificent stained glass window that portrays the many seals that have been used over the centuries by the governments of our beloved state. High at the top of this beautiful window is the seal used by the first colony; it bears, appropriately enough, the figure of an Indian. The seal that is used today occupies the central place in this historic scene; it was adopted by the Constitution of 1780. The figure of a man holds in his hands the Magna Charta; that was used during the Revolution.

The seal carries a Latin motto incidentally which translated reads, "By the sword we seek peace, but peace only under liberty." Surrounding the seals are three others which were used by Provincial governors during the years from 1685 to 1775.

A brief look at the Fingold State Library located at the rear of the third floor before we proceed to the house chamber. It contains over a million volumes dealing with state and local history; as well as public documents, directories and government laws. It also contains, I am proud to report (thanks to the kind concern of legislator Herbert Hollis) a copy of "Braintree-Our Town." Permanently displayed in this beautiful library is the parchment Commission which was given to Governor Andros by King James II. We were in London, Ted and I. We were having a tour of the various palaces, the dwelling places of the royalty the English love to display. "And here," said our guide in his finest clipped British," is the home of the last American queen, the wife of King James II." I couldn't restrain an audible chuckle after the first start of surprise." She was, you know," said the guide firmly, "your Queen, I mean…" And you know, he was right, of course….

Well, it seems as though we shall not get to the House Chamber at all this week; it is so easy to ramble on about the magnificent building that crowns our Beacon Hill; and there is so very much to tell. Oh well, we'll be back with more; and may I suggest that those of you who are planning a trip to our wonderful State House tuck these columns away for future reference. You'll know precisely what to look for!

AUGUST 3, 1975

The House of Representatives continues to meet in informal sessions; the formal sessions will begin in earnest on Monday next, however, and Speaker of the House Thomas W. McGee promises to dredge up all pending legislation from the House Ways and Means Committee. His remarks suggest to the members of "His House" that a full and formidable schedule lies ahead. The thought is exciting!

He's proving to be a strong and firm Presiding Officer, our Speaker McGee, incidentally, a jealous guardian of the prestige and stature of the House of Representatives. We applaud his attitude. This particular House member was delighted to learn, for instance, that on Tuesday last, one of her colleagues was requested by the Speaker to leave the Chamber; he was, it develops, not properly attired in jacket and tie! I like that!

Despite the informality of our current sessions, however, life on the Hill continues to be exciting and rewarding. How kind and helpful we have found absolutely everyone under that Golden Dome to be! Our legislative problems and concerns disappear completely, for instance, in the marvelously skilled hands of House Counsel Joseph Schuler and that amazingly informed Braintree-ite, Bernice Delory, the counsel's executive secretary. (What would we do without them?)

And then, for this freshman legislator, there is the unending kindness of our State Senator, Arthur Tobin. It was he, for instance, who called to my attention just last week the pending approved construction project on Pond Street...called it to my attention and permitted me to bask in the publicity attendant upon its announcement. "It was one of so many of his kindnesses, incidentally...

There is, as well, the great kindness and cooperation of our office secretary, the incredibly efficient and lovely Linda Miles, who amazes me constantly by her ability to keep abreast of my unending correspondence, smiling as she does so. There are the agencies who seem so speedily to address the problems of my constituents and to come up with answers, not always to my satisfaction or theirs, but what a comfort to know we're all in there trying! And how wonderful, when the solution is a happy one, to bask in the realization that someone's load is just a wee bit lighter because of what her legislator has been able to do to lighten a burden she was unable to carry all by herself! (Or himself, of course...)

This week there were the unusual little "extras" to lighten our own particular load...A Health Care Committee meeting which opened up all sorts of future possibilities for us, its members, for instance; and bright and early on Monday morning - the launching ceremony of a Bicentennial Conastoga Wagon which was to be dispatched and sent on its way to Valley Forge by the Governor of the Commonwealth, Michael Dukakis! What fun to watch the Governor, along with the Co-Chairmen of the Bicentennial Committee, Senator Atkins and Representative Piro, climb up on that high affair and hold the reins of the gallant steeds who were to pull it, with all the aplomb of true Colonial settlers of that enchanting era! And what fun, especially, to hear one of the ladies, handsomely attired as were they all, a Mrs. Fitzpatrick, I believe, introduced as the "horseperson" of the entourage! Now really...

Well, at any rate, having not much else to report from Beacon Hill, your legislator thought she might bring you a sampling of the prayers for divine guidance with which we start each day of legislative deliberations there. These are offered by the House Chaplain, Monsignor George V. Kerr, or by a Guest Chaplain. A sampling follows:

From Monsignor Kerr.

> "Grant, O Lord, that all our actions this day will depend on high motives, good will and cheerful patience. High motives give them their value before God; good will makes them vigorous and cheerful; patience makes them peaceful, pleasant and worthwhile.
>
> Give us the wisdom this day, O Lord, ever to understand that the one who goes to one's daily toil with good will and cheerful patience, out of love for You, is a much nobler person in Your sight than the man who, from mere human motives, shines with splendid actions in the sight of the world. Amen."

And from the Reverend Bruce E. Berry, pastor of Saint James United Methodist Church in Stoneham:

"Eternal God, Who hast given to us an abundant land and who has raised up leaders across the years to found and nurture a great nation: We praise Thee for these evidences of Thy grace. May we, each one, be faithful stewards of the resources of this land, including the human resources of our several communities.

Especially bless, O lord, these here assembled, elected to govern over us. We are grateful for their commitment to this task. Give to them strength and wisdom, encourage to do the right as Thou dost enlighten them to see the right. In time of stress give them an inner peace. In time of bewilderment, give them understanding. In time of weariness, renewed energy. Even so pray we for us all. Amen."

And from Rabbi Samuel S. Kenner, Executive Director of the United Synagogue of America in Brookline:

> "We invoke Your name, Lord of Humankind, as we begin discussion of affairs of state. We pray for a clear recognition of the basic fact that the body politic exists for the benefit of the body citizen, that our deeds, not our words, are the functional proof of our purposes and goals. As we move through our legislative lives, making decisions affecting other lives, may we always have before us a statement of the rabbis of ancient

Israel - 'Pray for the peace of the city, for in the peace thereof,. you shall have peace.' May we do more than pray. Amen."

We shall need prayers such as these, for we shall desperately need divine guidance in the days ahead, we "servants of the people..." We shall need your prayers as well, my good and faithful constituents, that we may judge fairly and vote wisely, for ours will be a tremendous, a horrendous responsibility. We, your legislators will be forced to make decisions that will forever affect the lives of you, the people we are privileged to serve....

AUGUST 10, 1975

What a great response I've had to that newspaper questionnaire of mine!

I am beginning already to get the picture on how you my constituents and friends feel about budgets and cuts and taxes...the whole bit! I also find your additional comments and the nice little notes you are enclosing with your questionnaires interesting and frequently heartening. Haven't I always said you're the world's greatest, you Braintree-ites???

Occasional amusing as well as "interesting" and "heartening" things are happening as a result of that little old "ad" however...There are the telephone calls I find myself receiving. "Mrs. Metayer," said a nice pleasant female voice on Monday evening last, for instance, "Tell me, please, what do you mean by 'this advertisement privately paid for' in your newspaper questionnaire?" "Why," I said, and there must have been a note of puzzlement in my voice, It means that I, myself, am paying for it. Why???" "There," said the lady to someone in the background, "I told you so. It DOES mean that Mrs. Metayer is paying for it." "Tell me." i, "Why do you ask? What did you THINK it meant?" "Well," she said apologetically, one of my friends said it was probably paid for out of some SLUSH FUND you have at the State House for that purpose; and another one thought that maybe some LOBBYIST paid for it." "Good heavens," I said with a laugh, "A SLUSH FUND at the State House??? I can assure you that you couldn't get away with a BUBBLE GUM FUND on Beacon Hill these days...not with the present climate there..."

As for LOBBYISTS, I can assure you the only thing I've gotten from a LOBBYIST to date is a South Shore phone book so I might get to my constituents who have problems all the quicker..." "Who IS this, anyhow?" I asked. "Oh," said the lady, "I don't want to tell you. You'll be MAD at my friends." "Believe me I'm not mad at your friends," I said gaily; but do tell them they can make amends for their suspicions by filling out my questionnaire and sending it along tonight..."

But to return to that little old questionnaire. "It's great to see you here at Town Hall," said my friend Mr. Jenkins; he happened to be the first one to hand me his neatly

The Candid Idylls of a State Representative

filled out clipping. "I like this idea of yours - having weekly office hours," he added approvingly. Well, to date I have received 47 returns...5 on Monday evening; 23 in Tuesday's mail and 19 in Wednesday's mail. Today I had Ted pick up two large poster boards at the local picture framing establishment, onto which I shall transfer your statistics...I shall arrange it in two sections so as to provide ample room for entering the thousands of AYES and NAYS I expect to receive. (You see what an optimist I am!) And when all is said and done, I shall hopefully be in a better position to vote on the incredible tax and budget issues that lie ahead. See how IMPORTANT it is for you to take a few little minutes of your time to let me have your fiscal thinking???

By the way, there is a small but very important correction to be made on the questionnaire before you return it to me. In the column under "COST OF LIVING RAISES," Item 2, it reads, "Do you favor granting an 11 per cent Cost of Living Raise to retired STATE EMPLOYEES and retired TEACHERS?" It should have read, "Do you favor RESCINDING the 11 per cent Cost of Living Raise to retired STATE EMPLOYEES and retired TEACHERS?" The 11 per cent cost of living raise has been mandated, you see; these retired people are already receiving it. It is applied only to pensions up to $6,000 annually, or to the first $6,000 of retirees' pensions. I have been told that the average pension, including the 11 per cent cost of living increase, is in the vicinity of $5,200 annually, particularly in the case of teachers who were pensioned when salaries were relatively small. Rescinding the increase would reduce this amount to $4,983. I would ask that you correct the wording before marking your preference and returning it to me; and I thank you for doing so...It was MY mistake!

It is Wednesday evening as I write this little old column, and I am still on Beacon Hill. The House is about to wrestle with another two-twelfths budget as it was presented to us by the governor, with a redraft by Ways and Means. We have temporarily recessed twice while the Committee on Ways and Means, already tired and drawn after a month of public hearings and melees on the ENTIRE 1976 budget, struggles with its analysis of this additional two-twelfths budget, and prepares its defense.

During the first two-hour recess, I found myself dashing home to Braintree for the family car. It could be a very late session; and so I shall be reluctant to travel home via the M.B.T.A. As I usually do. (My good friend Barbara picks me up and drives me in to the State House each morning at eight - the angel!) Now we have been handed a second recess - a one-hour recess this time; the Ways and Means Committee is not yet ready for the fray. I welcome it. I can write my little old column; haven't had time for it prior to tonight; and TODAY was my deadline...What a legislator REALLY needs is a thirty-six hour day!

AUGUST 17, 1975

This was to have been an ordinary run-of-the-mill "lady of the House" column. I had written my column on Wednesday evening as I ordinarily do. It dealt rather generally with the Welfare issue which has me lying awake nights, incidentally; and then it went on to report the results of the first 100 questionnaires that have been returned to me by my constituents.

And then, along came Thursday; and an event occurred on Beacon Hill that saw me telephoning Rosemary, my Editor, and saying, "Hold that column; I'll write another tonight." The event??? A riot in the State House…within the very Chamber wherein we were debating a Bill which would enable Massachusetts to pursue the establishment of a Presidential primary.

The hour was one-thirty or thereabout, and I had found myself struggling to absorb the debate as I madly consolidated all the last minute arrangements for the trip we were to make to Washington on Friday morning…eleven of us incidentally, including both Braintree State Representatives (with the remaining "Rep" supporting our stand but unable to be with us); two members of the Quincy City Council; representatives from both Braintree and Quincy Civic Associations; and a couple of concerned citizens. We planned to make a last ditch appeal to the Urban Mass Transportation Administration to prevent the building of the South Quincy Station. They hold the federal purse strings; and in our judgment they represent our Court of Last Resort…

And then, suddenly, it was happening. A group of young white men and women, hands clasped in a tight chain, burst through the door of the Chamber and proceeded down the aisle. Their intent was apparent - to take over the rostrum. And the Court Officers, whose duty it is to protect the Speaker of the House and the Representatives themselves, sprang to stop them. The melee that followed was an incredible one. The screams and chants of the demonstrators filled the Chamber. They were joined by a group that had taken over the gallery, a group that proceeded to join in the screaming and chanting as they hurled quantities of paper down upon us in the Chamber below. The Court officers, few among whom are very young, were quickly in trouble with the rugged young men and women with whom they struggled, as were the pages who leaped above the desks to help…And so the Representatives entered the fray - some of them young, and some not so young. Some among the demonstrators seemed possessed of maniacal strength. They had obviously, to my way of thinking, come to hurt people, and to be hurt in return so that they might charge bureaucratic brutality. They spat, and hurled obscenities as they fought, I feared for our Speaker. He's a strong and fearless leader and will not easily be intimidated. He wasn't. He stood there on the rostrum, calm and cool, while I waited terrified, for the rain of paper to stop, to be replaced by a molotov cocktail perhaps or even a bomb.

Initially my reaction to what I had thought to be a Welfare Rights group demonstration had been one of compassion. "God help them," I thought. "They must indeed be hungry and desperate to be driven to take this kind of action," I thought. I had agonized over my vote to remove the 18,000 people from the General Relief rolls the previous day. I had left my dinner untouched, unable to get food past the choking in my throat as I envisioned the possibility of someone going hungry because of my vote that afternoon; I had lain awake, praying that those in the affected category, who really deserved help would be given it. There had been stories at the State House of students taking over old abandoned farmhouses and living in communes, accepting welfare, using food stamps and having their education paid for at the nearby Amherst campus…and other tales of student abuse; I found myself hoping and praying that these were primarily the people whose rape of the State treasury would have been ended by our action. Yes, initially, as the invasion of the Chamber was begun, I had viewed the demonstrators with compassion. The compassion vanished, however, as I took a closer look at the rioters; they were young and rugged and well fed. They were obviously not needy men and women with families who, through no fault of their own, had lost their jobs. These dissenters were bent on disrupting our governmental process. And they were accompanied by older men who screamed from the front row of the gallery along with the best of them.

I picked up one of the leaflets with which those in the gallery had littered the chamber floor. "Statement delivered at State House," I read, "By: People for Economic Survival" and the Northampton Coalition to Fight the Cutbacks." It was not to my way of thinking, the work of a group of students. Those involved seemed to label the afternoon melee as an attack against government, the work of outside agitators, as is so many of these "demonstrations" that grow increasingly violent and menacing. I found myself agreeing. It was a tragic afternoon that ended with one Court Officer rushed to the hospital with broken ribs and possible internal injuries, (a not so young Court Officer, incidentally); with one Representative, (also not so young and a victim of recent open heart surgery) taken to the hospital and placed under observation; with two other Representatives injured; and with scores among us shaken and frightened. I wish I had behaved bravely and with dispatch while the riot was in progress. I didn't. I hid my face in my hands and prayed.

Now I would hope and pray that if we in the State House assessed the situation correctly and it is indeed the work of outside organizers and agitators, the legitimate Welfare Rights organizations will be quick to disclaim all responsibility for the actions of this mob that invaded the Chamber…to disassociate themselves from this militant group as speedily as possible.

Incidentally, I do not feel that this kind of situation will be permitted to happen again in the House of Representatives. The militants today drifted in twos and threes, in small groups which suddenly converged and stormed the Chamber entrance. We have been forewarned, however. And Speaker McGee will see to it, I am certain, that from here on in, the members of HIS house are protected. Only two of the demonstrators were arrested, incidentally. "On what charge?" asked the Capitol Police Chief when a Colleague asked why more among the groups were not arrested. "Disturbing the peace," said my fellow "Rep." "Disturbing MY peace, if you like," he added, indicating HE would be happy to prefer charges. "We couldn't make it stick." said the Police Chief. Have we given over our State to the lawbreakers, we were asking one another? No wonder those "law and order" advocates are increasing by leaps and bounds. The Boston Police had been unable to help; The State Police had been unable to help; all were being used to deal with rioting elsewhere in the State; only the M.D.C. Police had been able to respond - late. The experience at the State House today was a harrowing one. Never dreamed when I was elected to the House of Representatives I would be facing a situation like the one we faced this afternoon. I, however, am not easily intimidated either. "Are you going to write about this in your column?" asked one of my Braintree friends as we stood about discussing the events of the afternoon. "I don't know," I said thoughtfully, "Do you think I should?" "I certainly do." he said. And so VOICI!

AUGUST 24, 1975

Another Wednesday evening; and another deadline date for this "Lady of the House." It's been a busy week on Beacon Hill…and at 33 Arthur Street, where your questionnaires continue to pour in, to be recorded and tallied and their results evaluated…to be "Oh!"d and "Ah!"d over as surprise after surprise surfaces for the legislator who is tickled to death she published the little old questionnaire, so interesting are the results, and so pleased do her constituents appear to be at having been given an opportunity to express themselves about the vital issues that confront us all on Beacon Hill. And - once more - thank you for your nice little notes and friendly comments; wish I had time to answer each and every one of you!

But now to the questionnaire itself, and to the results of an evaluation of the first one hundred received. "Do you favor substantial cuts in spending rather than new taxes?" 95 of you said "Yes"; 2 said "No"; three failed to answer the question. Whenever a discrepancy appears in the total, the inference is that the question was left unanswered in a number of questionnaires. And by the way, it isn't the least bit essential for you to sign your names to these questionnaires; the important thing is that I have your thinking on the issues of the day… "Do you favor cuts in welfare?" 90 of you said "Yes", with 8 "No"s. "In A.F.D.C.?" 57 said "Yes"; 35 "No." "In Old Age and Medical Assistance?" I should have separated those two, since though 66 of you said "Yes" and 21 said "No", many of you underlined "Old Age" and crossed out "Medical Assistance."

In the category of General Relief, the vote was 71 to 18 for cuts in spending; while in the category of Veterans' Benefits, a surprising number of you, 65 to be exact, voted for cuts, with only 24voting against them. 75 of you opted to cut the budgets of State Colleges and Universities, with 29 opposing such cuts.

81 of you favored cuts in Personnel; with 69 opting for cuts in Services. And then we come to the 11 percent Cost of Living increase. For the "Blind, Elderly and Disabled" the vote was 50 in the affirmative and 45 in the negative; for rescinding the 11 percent increase to retired State Employees and Teachers, the vote was 77 to 22 in favor of taking such action. I have since learned, however, that there is a question as to whether this can be done. As for an 11 percent increase to present State Employees, the vote was 8 for it to 91 against it….29 of you were willing to grant a 5 percent increase to the blind, elderly and disabled; 16 to retired State Employees and Teachers; and 18 to present State Employees…who came under strong opposition with a vote for "large cuts" in this area of 86 to 5 in favor.

There is not a doubt in my mind - you cannot absorb new taxes to any extent. 58 of you will accept a Sales Tax increase; and 17 an Income Tax increase; the rest of you, by your silence, are saying with the younger generations, "No Way!"

The last two items on my questionnaire literally floored me. Had I been asked to vote for "Off-Track Betting" prior to this questionnaire, I would have unequivocally stated, "No Gambling as a means of raising revenue??? How incredible!" Now I find 64 of you opting for just that off-track betting, with only 34 of you in opposition to the idea. Amazing! And equally amazing - your vote to increase tuition in State Colleges and Universities. I voted against an increase just a month or two ago. I now find you favor the tuition increase 84 to 14: See how important it is to answer that little old questionnaire??? I'll vote in favor of a tuition increase next time…

And if I follow the advice of a dozen of you, I'll certainly vote for substantial increases to out-of- state students…

There now, I've given you a small idea of how my Braintree constituents feel about a number of things. Their sentiment was reflected in my vote of yesterday on the Welfare issue…It was with a sinking heart that I flipped the switch that sent an "Aye" vote on the Roll Call board, removing from the Welfare rolls as I did so those 18,000 or so "employables" that the Governor feels must look for jobs. A sinking heart indeed; and yet I kept reminding myself that many of them are students who are collecting welfare from the State, food stamps from the State and college tuition from the State, and all at the same time; and that many of these must have parents or brothers or sisters who should. and must assume some responsibility for them. They cannot all be orphans who wish to work but cannot find employment…At least, I pray they are not; and away down deep I feel we may be opening up a brand new way of life for many of them who WILL be forced to seek new jobs where they may make new friends and form new contacts. I pray that this will be so. Yes, it's been a busy week on Beacon Hill. Tomorrow we shall face the Welfare issue again; it has gone to the Joint Conference Committee of the House and the Senate, the Senate having added. amendments to it. Friday is the very last day for this Budget; and Friday is the day on which we shall be flying to Washington to keep an appointment with one Roger Crowell, Massachusetts Administrator of the Urban Mass Transportation Administration. We shall discuss with him the proposed South Quincy M.B.T.A. Station with the huge ramp complex that goes with it. U.M.T.A. holds the federal purse strings. We are traveling to Washington, flying down on Friday morning and back on Friday evening, at our own expense (just in case any of you suspect it to be a "junket") so as to bring our concerns and objections to the highest authority there is, the man with the capital grants...By the time you read this, of course, our trip will be over, and we'll tell you all about it in next week's "Lady of the House." Keep those questionnaires coming my friends!

SEPTEMBER 14, 1975

I could write a book on what has happened on Beacon Hill this week...To begin with, there was Representative Ray Rourk's farewell speech. It was touching and meaningful. "I leave here," he said, "knowing that the House of Representatives continue to be the VOICE of the Commonwealth...a co-equal branch of Government...with a slight edge..." I heard him with a feeling of nostalgic regret. "If only," I thought "The HOUSE had overturned the Governor's veto on that anti-South Quincy MBTA station bill last spring, how truly could it be said of us that we do indeed represent the VOICE of the Commonwealth's people!!! Oh, well...

But to return to Ray Rourke's farewell to Beacon Hill. "We expected to find your POEM in Sunday's column on Ray Rourke," a number of State House people (and a few others) had said. The reference, of course, was to the farewell verse I had dashed off in the Chamber on the afternoon of Ray's testimonial dinner. (I am beginning to be referred to as the 'Poet Laureate of the Transportation Committee...') "Goodness," I said; "I just never thought of it; I'll put it in next Sunday if you wish.

So here goes:

"He's quite a guy. He's debonair,
With just a soupcon of devil-may care...
He's dapper as "Dan": a warm, friendly man,
With a golden smile lighting a bright summer tan.
His attire ever dashing...perennially smart...
He's a guy with a flair; and a guy with a heart...
A truly great CHAIRMAN; a real fine and fair man;
Our Ray will be kissed; and quite sorely missed
As he leaves for this post that he just can't resist...
We expect, under Ray, e'en the MBTA
Should receive a new look; turn a leaf in its book;
And that all of the facets of State Transportation
Should rapidly change to be first in the Nation.
Though tonight we feel blue as we bid him adieu,

May we wish - one and all - skies perennially blue
For a fabulous Colleague we'll not soon forget…
May this new post with "Fred" be his best venture yet!"

Incidentally, the irrepressible Representative Rourke had managed to add a delightful touch to his farewell remarks… "Today is Louis Nickinello's 35th birthday" he had said; (Louis has served with distinction as Vice chairman of Ray's Committee) "I understand. Mr. Speaker, that you have a present for him;" he added; "I would like to stay here and witness the presentation of the present." The "present" to which he referred, was, of course, Chairmanship of the Transportation Committee. Well, we're happy to report that Speaker of the House Thomas W. McGee rose beautifully to the occasion. "The Chair would like to make the following appointment," he said. You guessed it! Louis Nickinello is our brand new Chairman! It's a great choice, needless to say - one wonderful guy replacing another…

So now what else has been happening this week? Well, another of Massachusetts' favorite sons has left our hallowed halls to seek his fortune elsewhere. This time it was to be Quincy Representative William D. Delahunt who departed to fill the post of Norfolk County's District Attorney. He, too, will be sorely missed by his Colleagues, this handsome young man with his unfailing smile and charming manner. We were, needless to say, on hand to witness his swearing in by the Governor of the Commonwealth. He will occupy a position that "requires great courage, integrity and ability," the Governor told his family and friends. "It is a great privilege to swear him in. He is going to do us proud!" He said. And, speaking of pride, I found myself studying the proud faces of Bill Delahunt's family his lovely wife and children and Mother and Dad, as their fine young man was solemnly repeating the words of commitment to "faithfully and impartially discharge and perform, etc, etc." How very much of history we are watching these days in the House of Representatives, I thought fondly. And speaking of history, Representative Antone S. Aguiar, my Chamber neighbor, was to add a bit more of it that very afternoon. A lieutenant-Colonel in the Civil Affairs Brigade, Army Reserve, "Tony" had spent the weekend at Fort Indian Town Gap in Pennsylvania where 7500 Vietnamese refugees are still being processed at the rate of about 100 per day. (There were 15,000 refugees originally.) "Their morale is good," he told us. "For the most part they are very highly skilled people - doctors, engineers, lawyers, police; there is very little crime or violence there;" he said. "There are a lot of families a husband and wife and grandparents and children; and some single men, soldiers or paratroopers who were several hundred miles from their families and had to flee for their lives. Colonel Aguiar spoke of attending Mass in the Vietnamese language, celebrated by a Vietnamese priest; and of evening sessions under the trees with groups of three Americans meeting on a common ground with dozens of Vietnamese men, women and children… "The kids especially gathered about us," said Representative Aguiar, "and we talked to them. They are handsome and so resourceful. The five year olds take care of the three year olds. I had a bag of peanuts," he said, "I gave the peanuts to them. One of them dashed off to return with a gift for me in return - a book on how to play tennis."

They're marvelously interesting, these Colleagues of mine in the House of Representatives, diversified as they are in background and interests…

Now I have one more matter of importance to bring to the attention of my wonderful readers. It's the quest for an apartment for two lovely young nuns who would like to live in Braintree. They can afford to pay no more than $200.00 monthly for a HEATED apartment. One of the ladies is a brilliant State House staff member; and wouldn't I just love to have her as a Constituent! Is there anyone out there among my readers with an apartment suitable for these two beautiful people? Do let me hear from you! See, I told you I could write a book on what is happening on Beacon Hill this week; I've almost done just that! And I haven't even touched on what we've tackled legislatively…Oh well, we'll get to all that next week…

SEPTEMBER 21, 1975

Here it is Wednesday of another week on Beacon Hill. Not very much has happened to date. We voted to better compensate those District Attorneys who will be forced to give up private practice, and work full time in this demanding position. This mandating of full time service represents in my opinion, a giant step forward; I can envision so many areas of conflict in prosecuting a case as District Attorney; and then perhaps defending the defendant on a later criminal charge.

And oh yes, we forced Governor Dukakis to resubmit his $2.8 million supplemental budget for Boston school desegregation costs; and then, by persuading him to withdraw the National Guard from the desegregation scene by Friday of this week - and other diverse means - we were able to reduce the $2.8 million figure to a mere??? $1.1 million. It's astounding to me to note how those million dollar figures are tossed about on Beacon Hill. You will be happy to know, however, the legislators are becoming more economy-minded by the minute as we view the horrendous budget and tax package that it is proposed to bring before us within a few short days…Yes, we are indeed about to receive House One, THE budget for which we have been waiting since the happy New Year's Day on which your legislator was sworn into the Freshman Class on Beacon Hill…

Tomorrow looms as a most exciting kind of day. Along with a number of other "Reps," I shall be meeting with Senator Birch Bayh, one of our Presidential hopefuls at 10:30 A.M. at the Parker House. At 12:30 P.M. it will be off to the McCormack Building for a meeting with Peter Metz in the 16th floor Transportation Headquarters. Here we shall be discussing the costing out of expenses of rail freight, as well as the economic impact of terminating rail service - freight service, of course -especially in this and the Cape Cod areas. I'm a member of the Railroads Sub-Committee along with Representative Richard Kendall, and so this will be vitally interesting to both of us.

From the office of Peter Metz, I shall proceed to the office of Raymond Rourke, the State's new Assistant Secretary of Transportation; Ray is on the 16th floor at the same address; that's a definite plus, time-wise; and of course, he is the former Chairman of our Joint Transportation Committee. I propose to discuss with him a number of additional aspects of our campaign to prevent the building of that eternal and infernal South Quincy Station. Somehow I feel much more comfortable about having a friend in the State's Transportation Secretariat…

Today's chamber session was a little longer than usual. The Senate was wrestling with the amended school desegregation costs Bill which we had sent their way earlier; and we in the House patiently awaited its return for enactment. It came back, finally. You know, there are truly wonderful safeguards in the State Constitution that is our own; safeguards that should indeed serve to prevent the passage of much harmful as unnecessary legislation. So many opportunities are given to us to challenge or amend, to recommit or hold and indeed to pass the legislation that comes before us e'er it takes it final plunge into the Executive Branch for the governor's signature…

One more week and I'll probably be knee-deep in House One, that frightening to contemplate Budget that is at last coming our way. Where to cut, I shall be wondering; what to pass; what programs to eliminate, or curtail…You have given me a truly fine insight into the kinds of cuts you can live with; and the taxes you might be able to absorb, you wonderful constituents. I shall publish those findings; and I thank each and every one of you who took the time and trouble to return my questionnaire. And, incidentally, if you haven't manage to return those questionnaires; or indeed have lost sight of them, I've copies available for you, and it's not too late, even now, to get your fiscal thinking across to your legislator.

Copies may be picked up at my home or at my weekly Office Hours at Braintree Town Hall on Monday evenings from seven to nine. Those Office Hours are simply marvelous, by the way; I seem to have wall-to-wall people drop by to see me and I welcome each and every one of them…Some of my constituents come by with problems; and some are merely seeking information; and some of you just drop over enroute to another meeting in Town Hall simply to say, "Hello." I'm there in the foyer, you know… Each and every Monday evening. I'll be seeing you, I hope….

SEPTEMBER 28, 1975

This will undoubtedly be the most disturbing week of my life on Beacon Hill; for the combined budget-tax package will come before the House on Thursday, and its passage cannot fail to bring misery and heartache to countless of our Commonwealth's citizens. And yet - what is the alternative to these horrendous and massive cuts that are being proposed by the Committee on Ways and Means? A tax program that the working poor cannot possibly assimilate…those enormous numbers of people who are holding two jobs now to keep a roof over the heads of their families; and that food that is ever spiraling in price - on the table to feed them.

Yes, it's an horrendous problem that faces the Commonwealth of Massachusetts; a multi-faceted one, born of years of overspending on programs that were wonderful in concept but beyond the financial reach of the taxpayers; and of robbing Peter to pay you-know-whom; and of putting off until tomorrow that which should have been faced financially today.

So how DO we react to this awful task that lies before us, we legislators who will be forced to VOTE the cuts; to VOTE the taxes that must be paid despite those cuts; to evaluate the relative merits of one proposed budget cut against the other; and to try to take the action least harmful to the greatest number of people??? How do we react??? Speaking for myself, I agonize and fret; lie sleepless and unseeing; and I pray as one lobbying group after another bombards me with letters, and with phone calls, with pleas and complaints, until my compassionate soul is ill.

For how DOES one respond to the cry for continued help of a distraught young mother of THREE retarded children? To the sweet young couple who say. "My child is doing so well; she'll be able to go to the Weymouth Memorial School next year and it's all because of the care she received. in the home stimulation program… And now they're going to eliminate it…" To the volunteer workers from that vitally important Special Needs Adoption service center? To the sad-eyed mother of a child in the Omega program for "severely handicapped autistic adolescents?" To the parents and grandparents of deaf, blind children whose world will soon be plunged into disruption with the termination of their program? To the proponents of the Survival program? To those who feel that with drug rehabilitation, PREVENTION is almost more important than CURE? (And the prevention funds are cut…) To the little ones at the Boston School for the Deaf? To the beautiful young parents of the small cerebral palsy child who, if she had "but ONE year more with the Preschool Nursery School for Cerebral Palsy children would be able to enter the Weymouth Public Schools with her brother???" To those for whom the Day Care Centers mean the difference between holding a job and seeking public assistance? To the residents of "Sunlight House" in Scituate where deaf, blind AND retarded children are living in a residential situation with as much of normalcy as they will ever be able to know??? What do you SAY to people who write of their handicapped children; their horrendous problems: their fears of leaving uncared for those exceptional children - of any and all ages - the Father of us all has sent their way??? What CAN you say?

Words, I found, just simply would not come as I sat at St. Coletta's on a Friday evening just a week ago, and listened to the litany of heartache that was brought my way - for there is little or nothing really that CAN be said with a State that is broke, its credit rating imperiled, its taxpayers' backs against the wall…with a State that is weighing the advisability of closing public health hospitals; of closing mental health facilities; of bringing to a halt, temporarily at least, even that ambitious new medical hospital facility that was intended to train countless nice young family practitioners for service within the rural areas of our State; of delaying for one year at least, the staffing and operation of an elaborate UMass Teaching hospital that could add immeasurably to the debt we should have to face, come '76...the Teaching Hospital at Worcester.

Yes, there are terrible decisions that must be made on Beacon Hill during this weekend that lies ahead. There are students from our State colleges and such to be met and dealt with as they promenade about the place; to have to persuade that EVERYONE must bite the bullet and make sacrifices if our Commonwealth is to survive; to have to convince that if a choice is to be made between feeding the hungry and caring for the handicapped...and placing greater numbers of faculty members in the classrooms of our colleges...they must expect just what our choice will be. All in all, this will be quite a week on Beacon Hill! Our Speaker of the House, the Honorable Thomas W. McGee, has indicated we may spend the weekend there. "We must have that budget and tax package," he says; and understandably...For with the passing of each day, projected tax revenues will shrink...We've lost a couple of months already... And so the need for action is quite dire....And, if you're looking for ACTION, Beacon Hill's the place to be these days...The funny thing is, though, most of us are far too busy to observe it. "Did you see the demonstrators from the Citizens for Concerted Cooperation, the COCC group?" Teddy will say to me come evening...Or "How about that group of enraged adolescents that picketed the State House this morning - what did you think of them???" I have to smile and shrug and say concernedly, "What did they want???" And then I must admit I invariably add a sigh or two. "I hope SOME of my Colleagues observed their demonstration; or accepted their petitions; or heard their grievances..." I say sadly.

As for THIS legislator, I'm so totally concerned with all the grim, grey, ghastly implications of this horror of a budget, I've not time to look without. Demonstrations, I'm afeared, are par for the course; and the course - it sure is ROUGH these days on Beacon Hill!

OCTOBER 5, 1975

Another Wednesday, and another newspaper deadline. It is close to 12 midnight. The House of Representatives has been "sitting" since 1:00 this afternoon and in all probability will be "sitting" until 3 A.M. tomorrow morning just as they have "sat" until 2:30 A.M. on Monday and 3 A.M. on Tuesday...You didn't know that the House "sits," I warrant, I didn't. The Senate, incidentally, "meets"....

It must be clear to my readers what lies behind these unbelievable hours we are being forced to keep on Beacon Hill - It's the horrendous Budget and Tax program we are having to deal with "Horrendous" - I keep using that word again and again in my columns, for there is indeed an element of horror in being forced to vote on the curtailment of human services and higher education; of having to turn one's back on such things as cost-of-living increases for those dear retired teachers and others whose influence upon our lives has been so great...Yes, HORRENDOUS IS INDEED THE WORD!

Caucuses (or is it Cauci) are the order of the day on Beacon Hill; and from them emerges a pattern of statements and claims, of statistics and sophistries, of proposals and portents that finds this legislator "bewitched, bothered and bewildered" in dealing with the whole complex problem... "We have cut down the Secretariat to bare bones.... and gone on from there..." we have been told by the capable, informed and articulate Chairman of the Ways and Means Committee, Representative John Finnegan. "We started with a zero based budget and asked of each department, "Why it exists? Is there a duplication? Is it doing the job? Could it be done better? Could it be done cheaper?" We never before have cut a Budget-just reduced the amount requested." The Chairman's reasoning appeals indeed to this freshman legislator whose commitment to planned "Sub-committees have been established," he tell us. "We have set a time-table...to get the budget to the Senate by October 1. The Senate needs three weeks time." He says as he outlines the necessity for a Conference Committee; and states his goal - to have the Governor's signature on the bill by November 1... "The spectra of hungry children and snake pit conditions is so much rhetoric in order to stampede us," this articulate, informed young man is to tell his colleagues.

Of the 1,000 Main Accounts with their 16 subsidiaries, he is to say: "We went through Account by Account. There was input from Hearings, from sub-committees, from staff people and from budget people."

"Decisions are difficult," he would add. "None of us likes what we have had to do." I believe him.

Chairman Finnegan would deplore the enormous energy expense involved in the administration of our State buildings. "Many of our newer colleges and buildings are electrically heated," he would tell us, "That is the most expensive kind. In some of the new institutions you can't open the window and so they must be air conditioned," He would say, "and so the Bureau of Building Construction is being asked to look into the possibility of getting the windows open and the electric heat out." In several of the Agencies, Representative Finnegan was to report that he has found "too much duplication; with too much money being spent on the administrative level and too little services being offered." Of the higher education budget, the Ways and Means Chairman was to say, "Schools don't have to turn away students; only Deans," and he would remind his colleagues, "that the State Colleges do indeed have fiscal autonomy and it is up to the administration of these state colleges to determine where the cuts can best be made."

"The curriculum should not suffer," he would say, "but the days of wine and roses are over."

"Welfare will be fully funded," Representative Finnegan was to tell his colleagues; "A.F.D.C. will be fully funded; and there will be no diminution in the size of S.S.I. checks," he was to add. Terming Massachusetts "the most generous state in the nation to the elderly," Representative Finnegan would state, "The average family of four on A.F.D.C. takes home just under $7,000 a year, tax free; and that includes medical assistance. The average State employee makes $10,000 and takes home $7,000."

These statements of the Chairman of the Ways and Means Committee race, one after another, through my mind as I sit here at midnight of a Wednesday evening on Beacon Hill and listen to an endless stream of debate on a budget that should have come our way in January last, but has come our way instead on a mild October evening which bids fair to become a mild October morning in this "beautiful bastion of democracy" up here on Beacon Hill. And the worst – Voting on this horrendous budget and tax package lies dead ahead!

OCTOBER 12, 1975

Should you pick up a paper these days, and observe a picture of "Lady of the House" participating in a ribbon-cutting ceremony, her hair disheveled; her overblouse descending unstylishly a full inch below her decidedly stylish jacket, (whose bottom button, incidentally, lies glaringly open) - forgive and forget! She just hadn't time to consult a mirror…Sartorial elegance at ten A.M. on the morning after the last evening??? (It was morning actually) of the "Week that Was" could not be expected to be par for the course for any member of the House of Representatives. We were sleepwalking.

As a matter of fact, speaking of that "Week that Was" never did I dream I could function on fifteen hours' sleep in a five day period…

House sessions, however, ran into the two, three, and four A.M. area night after night, picking up at the usual time next morning…and so sleep seemed somehow to fall quite naturally into the category of a luxury item to be indulged in only if and when business as usual was out of the way.

Occasioning the "Week that Was," of course, was the combined Budget and Tax package which should have come our way long months before, but had finally made it to the House! And adding to the element of haste was the grim realization that each day's delay in passing a tax bill would cost the State a million dollars in lost tax revenue. No wonder we were at it day and night on Beacon Hill!

The "bare bones" budget of Representative John Finnegan's Ways and Means Committee was, of course, being attacked with amendment after amendment, some to effect further cuts in agency budgets; and some to restore cuts in programs. There was to be considerable see-sawing back and forth on our roll call votes as more information on an issue would come to light during reconsideration of a vote…reconsideration which was being sought either by the leadership or by a "gung ho" legislator who felt that a second time around could prove more fruitful…

Have I said it before in one of my columns? (If so, please excuse the repetition), I never cease to marvel at the genius of our founding fathers as I realize how many times a Bill may be debated before finally becoming law. I find quite frequently that it is possible to be persuaded of an error in judgment on a first vote, which can be corrected by a differing vote on the second try. This is especially true when one has been called from a Committee Hearing to a "roll call in two minutes" situation where one has not heard the debate and must make a snap judgment.…which is not an easy thing to do…

There was, for instance, the 143 to 81 initial vote to substantially reduce the Executive Office of Human Services. I was among the "ayes". The idea seemed in keeping with the general austerity we were demanding of all state offices. But then came the startling announcement that by our action we had succeeded in eliminating the office entirely as of October 31, the proposed budget figure having been all but spent to date. Reconsideration was to prevail; and I and many others were to find ourselves voting against the cut next time around. There is already enough chaos in the Human Services area, we had decided…There were amendments to close some of our newer state hospitals including Shattuck and the Massachusetts Medical School. Those of us on the Health Care Committee, however those of us who had sat through hours of testimony on the condition of many of our antiquated public and mental health facilities; and were involved in evaluating the possibility of transferring certain aspects of mental health and correctional programs to the newer building - could not in good conscience vote in favor of these attempts to eliminate the new and therefore found ourselves in the position. of having to keep the old…the old crumbling structures that will any day now constitute prime targets for condemnation by a federal government that, once it pokes its large fiscal nose into State affairs, has a great deal to say about how State programs are administered (or not administered). I found myself agonizing over some of the decisions I felt obliged to make for a State that is broke; that cannot pay its bills; that - it would appear - has overspent and over programmed for the past several years and now has to face up to a fiscal crisis that - if it is not faced up to - could result in another New York City nightmare…

We are dealing, however, with a number of strange quirks in this difficult situation… strange to this freshman legislator, that is…There are, for instance, the legislators who lead the battle to restore those Human Services cuts which all of us deplore AND THEN VOTE AGAINST THE TAX PACKAGE TO PAY FOR ALL HUMAN SERVICES. They can't "take the heat", we are told. That's irresponsibility with a capital "I" to my way of thinking. We MUST unfortunately vote new taxes. The only alternative would be to let the state go down the drain and join New York City…in Bankruptcy in which case, incidentally, the cities and towns - you and I, the taxpayers - would have to foot the state's bills.

As I see the situation on Beacon Hill, we are like a family with a $100 a week income that has purchased a $50,000 home, a Cadillac car, and the very finest and latest of appliances, and comes face to face with paying the bills. It can't be done...

All of the programs that have been implemented within the State during the past few progressive years are WONDERFUL in concept; but with the failing economy, and inflation, and an ever increasing demand for goods and services to be provided by the State, some of these programs will simply have to be provided by the State, some of these programs will simply have to be curtailed. We agonize over the fact, but we fear that it IS a fact.

We can keep reminding people that it is entirely up to the agency administration, or the program head, to determine where the demanded budget cuts are to be made. I join with many of my colleagues in praying that these cuts will be made wherever possible at the top, in administration rather than in the services themselves, for only then will the least number of our deserving constituents be affected...will the hurt be felt the least... These are SAD days on Beacon Hill - sad days for the Commonwealth's lawmakers; and for the Commonwealth's citizens; and for the Commonwealth itself, which, as I see it, is struggling for survival...And yet - how wonderful to be there!

OCTOBER 19, 1975

How to bring home to you, my readers, the TRAUMA of that "Week that Was" that was touched on briefly by your columnist in her last "lady of the You-Know-What? The feeling almost akin to despair with which caring, compassionate legislators found themselves having to vote AGAINST the restoration of human services cuts and FOR additional taxes when they were persuaded by a very forthright Ways and Means Committee Chairman that the Commonwealth's back is fiscally against the wall; and that simply postponing the day of fiscal reckoning for another in a series of decidedly fiscally irresponsible years will contribute nothing toward the health of a state that has over-spent and over-programmed and must face the issue squarely and DO SOMETHING ABOUT IT before it is too late.

And what to DECIDE to do about it-in THAT lay the trauma of the "Week that Was" - where to hold the line; and where to stand pat against the unbelievable pressures that were coming our way from each and every one of the myriad agencies, programs, departments, boards, categories and organizations...how to reckon with the calls and letters of distraught and fearful parents of children whose needs are currently being met and now are threatened; the calls and letters and pleas of the elderly and the handicapped; of the welfare rights organizations and the taxpayers groups; of the demonstrators from the state college and universities and from the ranks of the crippled and the retarded; of the students - the belligerent ones who seek eagerly for a cause; and the fearful ones who have been persuaded by their administrators (who, incidentally have the authority to decide where the cuts shall be made, but you'd never know that fact when listening to the students)…who have been persuaded by their administrators that the quality of their education is totally at stake. The picture was to prove incredibly, hopelessly Sad because we were to be dealing with a situation where the poor were pitted against the poor; the deserving against the deserving; while standing in the wings, his hands clasped in pleading, we would have to note the presence of the overburdened taxpayer. His load has grown heavier with the years; and so he, himself has reached the point where he, too, has begun to pressure those unhappy legislators who find themselves caught in the middle of it all.

It's not easy to face the fact that the state is broke - that this bottomless pit of the green stuff the state has been tossing about so generously for years is emptied out - and it's distressing to face the fact that many of the legislators who seek dramatically to restore cuts that each and every one of us would like to see restored…who make the appealing speeches on the Chamber floor and find themselves lauded in the local press as the White Knights of Beacon Hill THEN FAIL TO VOTE FOR TAXES THAT WILL PAY FOR ANY of the programs, cut or uncut, whose restoration they espouse gallantly.

"There now," I can hear some of you saying, "she is getting disillusioned; she is losing her enthusiasm; she is slightly less starry-eyed than she was nine months ago…" Slightly less starry- eyed, to be sure; but she's a woman, you see, with a sense of fiscal responsibility as well as a compassionate heart; a woman who has budgeted all her life; who hasn't spent what she didn't have; who DIDN'T get in over her head financially… and in that she feels she's like ninety-nine out of a hundred other of the Commonwealth's citizens who have been footing the bills for the running of this great state of ours; but who must see now that the day of reckoning is at hand.

She'd love to restore everything that has been taken out of the state budget; she knows, however, that's unrealistic; that there's a limit to what the people in the middle-income wise - and the WORKING poor can pay…and she feels that limit has been reached. "How do you feel," she has been asked again and again, "when a threatened parent of a needy child calls? Or a truly deserving Medicaid recipient appeals for help?" How does she feel? She grieves; she must admit she tosses and she turns these nights that follow days on Beacon Hill. All she can do, however, is pray that when we've sorted out the needy and the greedy; and evaluated the programs that are ours; and eliminated the duplication that indeed exists; and skimmed off the salaries of some of those "fat cats" we're reading about at the administrative level and restored the funds to where they rightfully belong to the services that are being offered to the needy and the helpless…when we've truly implemented some form of planned program budgeting on Beacon Hill, so that agencies will have to JUSTIFY their budget requests; and JUSTIFY their programs…THEN THERE WILL BE SUFFICIENT FUNDING FOR THE SERVICES WE CAN AFFORD TO OFFER to the needy of our state.

This, as I see it, must be our aim on Beacon Hill if we're to manage to escape New York City's tragic fate...a fate that incidentally-should New York City default - could well have a ripple effect upon our own ability to survive.

It's a marvelous situation, incidentally, this hearing from those great constituents of mine...on any issue...and on every issue. People, you see, MUST CARE if they're to get the kind of government they deserve. Which brings me to another point before I bring this column to a close. There's no better way to indicate caring than to keep informed...about your state, and about your town. Now, the town's civic associations are all committed to that one end to keeping you informed. It's a great place to go for an answer to your problem, you know - a meeting of your neighborhood civic association. Your "Lady of the House" is planning to do just that and to be on hand with an answer or two perhaps, at one of these civic association meetings in the very near future; she hopes you'll be on hand with the questions...The date is Thursday October 23; the time 8 P.M.; the place Braintree Town Hall; and the sponsoring organization? Why, that live wire Northeast Civic Association of ours!

You're all urged to attend this timely meeting, needless to say. We're hoping you'll pack the hall; you'll turn off that TV set and show you CARE about the problems that face your community by showing up. We've plenty of hot issues in this town of ours, goodness knows! Well, here's a platform for their airing...Shall we see you there? We hope so.

OCTOBER 26, 1975

With the budget and tax bill in the limbo of the Senate, we seem to be marking time on Beacon Hill these days. To be sure we have our daily quota of controversial bills. The leghold trap bill is back again 8 in a modified form, so to speak. This time it's for the establishment of a study commission to determine IF the use of the leghold trap is cruel - a scientific study, you understand.

We have had to deal with the home rule issue of providing tenure to one James Kelly, the incumbent coordinating safety officer in the school department of the City of Boston. I'm leery of tenure, but apparently Mr. Kelly is doing a bang-up job, and this is a home rule bill, and since it has the consent of the Mayor and the powers that be in its home city, it was not surprising to find it go sailing through despite a certain amount of debate on philosophic grounds.

A bill to remove the Mayor of a city as the sole licensing authority for cable T.V. and to make his decision subject to the approval of the City Council has gone down to defeat; in our case, the appointing authority would be our Board of Selectmen, so this bill presented no real problem for Braintree anyway.

Within the Transportation Committee, of which I am a member, we are hard at work coming to grips - section by section and, in effect item by item - with the immense

Transportation budget. We must sit for hours in the executive sessions that follows hearings with Transportation Secretary Salvucci, and D.P.W. Commissioner Carroll and MBTA General Manager Kiley. and if you think they have not been on the griddle, and didn't have to respond to some very searching inquiries, you're wrong! This is a year of fiscal crisis; and the legislature's Transportation committee has no alternatives but to scrutinize every aspect of a transportation budget that has soared to Mt. Everest during the past few years.

There are one hundred issues to be faced…What of rail services? With thousands of jobs at stake and the economy in a slump, can we do aught but purchase and restore to some semblance of order those abandoned FREIGHT lines on the South Shore and elsewhere? What about passenger service to the Cape-shall we restore it??? And what about AMTRAK??? Shall we have a go at service from New York to Cape Cod via Worcester and Springfield; and will it pay? (It never has paid - Amtrak, I mean; at least not to my knowledge.) The questions are to be faced, and faced squarely before a final draft of the immense transportation bill is in readiness for voting. Decisions, however, are difficult to make. But then, aren't ALL decisions difficult to make these days on Beacon Hill? It must have been so easy when nobody worried about where the wherewith was coming from as they voted for every living thing in sight! Well, as our Ways and Means Chairman has pointed out to us, "the days of wine and roses" are over. Constituent letters, like everything else in our legislative lives these days, have centered around budget and tax decisions. Our retired teachers deplore the House decision to make their "automatic" cost of living increase SUBJECT TO APPROPRIATION. We wonder if they understand that they will NOT lose the 11 per cent increase they were given this year; that, in fact, they will keep it until the end of December, 1976, after which any additional cost of living increase will be granted subject to appropriation…meaning that if the economy improves and the state can afford it, they will get it. Incidentally, in this situation our retired teachers are the ONLY group that has received the 11 percent cost of living increase all year and will receive it next year. There is no more deserving group of people on earth than these wonderful retired teachers of ours; and all hearts in the State House leaned toward granting them an ADDITIONAL cost of living increase in January. But Ways and Means assured us that should we grant an additional cost of living increase to our teachers, every group in the state would lobby madly for the 11 per cent they had failed to receive THIS year…and the state simply doesn't have the wherewith to pay it. The state - as I keep repeating -is BROKE! It was pointed out to this legislator, incidentally, that the removal of 25A from the Bill would simply have placed our teachers, who, it is thought, will ALWAYS be looked upon with an especially fond eye, in the same category as all other groups under the state budget. I hope this clears up the apprehension some of our retired teachers may have about what we have done this fall on Beacon Hill. Judging from the letters I am receiving, many of them fear that they will LOSE the 11 per cent cost of living increase they've enjoyed this year. "Taint so! I have rechecked my facts with no less an authority than Ways and Means Chairman John

Finnegan this very afternoon - for the letters I was receiving had left me in doubt about the action we actually did take during the traumatic "Week that Was" on Beacon Hill.

Temporarily now, within the Chamber of the House of Representatives, "the tumult and the shouting" have all died; and the "Captains and the Kings" within the Senate now hold sway. The budget and the tax bill are THEIR grave concern. We wait within the wings while they're on stage. We know that finally it will return, this controversial budget and tax package we must face; it will return, to be sent to a Conference Committee, and thence to come our way for one more time ere it becomes the law by which we all must live in '76.

"When will you prorogue?" people keep asking… "Well," I say quite merrily, "As I see things up here on Beacon Hill, we just might not prorogue at all. Could be we'll be celebrating New Year's Eve in the Chamber; grabbing a catnap or two at our desks; and then going right into 1976 without ever leaving this beautiful facility that nestles so serenely??? under the Golden Dome…THAT would sure make history," I add.

And history, they tell me, is what we've been managing to make all year on Beacon Hill.

NOVEMBER 2, 1975

By now you must all have learned that the unsigned letter appearing at the bottom of last week's LADY OF THE HOUSE was not sent by your representative. Someone in the vast recesses of the printing office inadvertently cut off the signature of Selectman Tony Mollica; a fact which I am certain will today have been duly noted elsewhere in the "Forum." And incidentally it was quite awhile before I understood the comments I was hearing on Sunday morning, isn't it nice to know that our readers do indeed read our letters, Braintree-ites???

This past week on Beacon Hill (it is always Wednesday when my column goes to press) started off with a bang. With a Joint Conference Committee having to struggle with a Senate budget and tax bill that according to the latest figures, wound up sporting no less than FIVE HUNDRED amendments, was apparent that no possible compromise could be worked out in time to have the Governor's signature on a bill by November 1. Accordingly, once again we were to face the necessity of passing another one-twelfth budget so that the business of the state could proceed. There appeared to be general consternation within the House of Representatives. One more one-twelfth budget and an additional loss of one million dollars daily in tax revenues…both prospects were decidedly distasteful to all of us. We were telling each other, "C'est la guerre." however; take my word for it, la guerre is still going on on Beacon Hill.

There were to be a few lighter moments before the blow for a one-twelfth budget was struck. Lloyd Bucher, (if that is how you spell his name), the Commander of the ill-fated "Pueblo" of not too recent fame, came to visit Boston and was presented in the Chamber. That was on Monday. And today, the Marine Corps League celebrated with pomp and beauty the 200th Monday Anniversary of those "semper fidelis" United States Marine!

It was a colorful and beautiful ceremony, with Marines wearing the traditional uniforms dating from revolutionary times to today's gorgeous Bicentennial regalia. Speaker of the House Thomas McGee, a Marine veteran of the tragic battle of Iwo Jima, presented a stirring Resolution voted upon in the House and our Senator Arthur H. Tobin presented a second stirring Resolution voted upon in the Senate. Governor Michael S. Dukakis was on hand with a Proclamation; and Secretary of State Paul Guzzi, another ex-Marine was there…and with the word "Once a Marine, always a Marine" woven like a strong thread through the tapestry of the occasion, should we dare to say an "EX" Marine??? The colorful flags and uniforms of the different periods in Marine Corps history blended with the dramatic beauty of their Hall of Flags setting to form a unique and moving panorama for a ceremonial occasion that would be difficult to surpass in patriotic splendor.

Goodness I almost forgot the Tuesday happening that provided a lighter moment or two in the lives of legislators. It was the SOME DAY SHE'LL BE GOVERNOR exhibit of the role women have played in the history of the country and of the Commonwealth. We women legislators were pictured in one corner of the exhibit. We had been asked to produce an ACTION SHOT and I had toted in a few I had salvaged from campaign days, among them a picture of some of our handsome neighborhood teenagers chatting with me on the front steps of the family menage…It's among my very favorite pictures, and it made an instant hit with charming young lady who was arranging the exhibit… and so voila! It hangs there. The exhibit will be up all week and all this legislator needs is time to really look it over and absorb it. "She's up front at the speaker's platform, she's in the smoke-filled rooms. She's voting and legislating, campaigning and lobbying, working and winning," I read with a feeling akin to delight. "Am I really doing all those marvelous things" I asked myself, still a bit on the incredulous side…Is this really I??? And then I laughed aloud as I read what followed on our sharp yellow handout. "Back in 1825, the only place for women at the State House was in the ladies' spectators' gallery watching. A woman's major civil liberty was the right to remain silent."

Oh well, so much for SOME DAY SHE'LL BE GOVERNOR! It really IS a most delightful exhibit; do hope some of you will drop by to see it….Now-back to that wretched on-twelfth budget once more. It was passed today after the personal plea of the very popular Speaker of the House; and went winging its way to the Senate…WHERE IT STALLED! Speaker McGee had recessed the House, subject to the call of the Chair - for "an hour or so…" that seemed like ample time for the Senate to rush the Bill through and return it to us for enactment. It wasn't! And so here it is Wednesday evening and tomorrow we must wait once more for its return…hopefully early in the afternoon…though we are meeting IN FULL FORMAL SESSION at eleven! As you can see, we do indeed have our LIGHTER moments on Beacon Hill; at any rate, THIS WEEK some of those moments have been on the light side…But the business of conducting GOVERNMENT BY CRISIS under the Golden Dome seems to grow heavier and darker and more ponderous with every passing day. And there is so very much at stake…Our COMMONWEALTH'S at stake…Pray God that we shall manage to steer our Ship of State through all these troubled waters.

DECEMBER 7, 1975

Wednesday again, and another week has managed to fly by on Beacon Hill…

This particular Wednesday has proved to be an especially hectic one. The first Wednesday in December, you see, is the deadline date for filing legislation for the coming year; and so from all corners of the State House the legislators scurried, bills in hand, facing the inexorably racing clock as they were contending with an unusually heavy, debate-laden and roll-call rife session of the House.

As I witnessed the petitions piling up on Beacon Hill, I reflected anew upon the legislative process itself, and upon the wisdom and forethought of those framers of our early constitution…How astute they were! what IS to happen to those thousands of petitions the members of the General Court, particularly of the House of Representatives, have been filing up to and including Wednesday, the third of December…this very Day??? Well, to begin with, we are reminded that any citizen of Massachusetts may, under the right of free petition, request his or her representative to file a legislative document. Said petition, once it is filed, will be referred by the House (or Senate if it originates there) Clerk to an appropriate legislative committee. It will be assigned a number and sent to the printer.

A public hearing must be held by the joint legislative committee on each and every petition. The petitioner is notified of the hearing date in advance so that he (or she - mustn't lose sight of Women's Lib…) may be on hand to defend the bill.

An executive committee will follow the public hearing; this will also be open to the public; and here the bill may be given a favorable vote or an "ought not to pass" verdict. Those committee members, incidentally, who disagree strongly with the committee decision may be listed as "dissenters." A bill may be amended by the committee; or it may referred to another committee; in each case, needless to say, by vote of the committee members.

So now the bill has been reported out of committee and it reaches the House! Here it is to be subjected to a first, second and third reading before being engrossed. An "ought not to pass" will either be accepted, or an attempt made to substitute the bill for the committee report. The bill dies if the adverse vote of the committee is accepted; and as a general rule these adverse committee reports are upheld. (All of which means that if one has a bill to defend, the place to defend it is really before the legislative committee at that public hearing…)

Debate, of course, can be expected on any and all controversial measures; AND a lot of seemingly uncontroversial ones as well. And we have some powerful and delightfully articulate debaters in the House of Representatives…

Motions to lay on the table; (we've not had one to date, but they tell me they're in order); to postpone action; to recommit to the appropriate committee or to refer to another committee, are all in order prior to ordering the bill to a third reading. And, incidentally, a bill is not given a third reading until such time as the committee on Bills in the Third Reading has examined it and corrected it if correction is indicated; has insured accuracy both in the text and those statutes to which the bill refers; as well as consistency in the language of the bill.

Any changes that are made by the committee on Bills in the Third Reading are reported back on the floor as amendments.

There are three methods of voting: the voice vote, the standing vote, or calling of the Yeas and Nays. Non-controversial matters are usually handled with a voice vote; or a standing vote. Controversial matters can usually be expected to result in a roll-call vote, with "Roll call in three minutes; (or 2 minutes; or even 1 minute) the Court Officers will summon the members!" ringing out over the squawk boxes and echoing in the House lobby.

At the engrossing stage which follows the third reading of a bill or resolve debate and new motions are still in order. With a vote to engross, however, the bill goes to the other branch, to repeat the process before returning to the first branch for enactment. There is enactment in the House, then in the Senate; and finally the bill goes to the Governor for his signature.

The Governor is allowed ten days for action on any matter placed before him; and unless an emergency preamble has been added to the bill, it becomes law within ninety days. With an emergency preamble, it becomes law immediately; and, incidentally, an emergency preamble may be added either by the General Court or by the Governor. The Governor may veto a bill, in which case the veto may be overturned by a two-thirds majority vote of each branch. He may also return the bill with amendments which are placed before the General court for consideration.

If the Governor has taken no action on a bill or resolve within ten days, it becomes law automatically. Should the legislative session end, however, before the ten day period has passed, the bill is dead. Much comment has been made on the differing aspects of the morning and afternoon sessions in the House Chamber. Next week I'll attempt to differentiate between them for your information so that should you drop by for a session at the State House (and I hope you will) you will better understand what is going on as your legislators conduct the business of this state that is our own…

DECEMBER 14, 1975

It is eleven A.M. on Beacon Hill; and from all corners of the State House legislators race toward the historic House Chamber for a "Full formal session" of the House of Representatives. Speaker Thomas W. McGee is on the rostrum; and House Clerk Wallace Mills and his assistants are at the ready; Monsignor George Kerr is on hand to deliver one of the beautiful and inspiring prayers for divine guidance with which each session of the House begins.

A prayer; a salute to the flag of the United States of America; and the Speaker is asking, "Is there objection to proceeding with the Orders of the day?" There is none. And so another day in the life of your state representative and her colleagues is about to begin.

A copy of the House Calendar has been placed at the desk of each of the 240 legislators. Hopefully they have perused it in advance and so are at least partly familiar with the business at hand. And Now the Chair reads the Calendar as follows: "Page 1, Item 1234…."

The legislators eyes and ears are attuned to the bills which are to come before them in the day that lies ahead. If a particular member plans to challenge or debate a bill; or has reservations about it; or is desirous of learning more about it, he or she says, "Pass" as the item is reached on the Calendar. At that point the item is slated for the second call of the calendar, normally scheduled for 1 P.M. There is no debate on the first call of an item. Frequently bills that have been ordered to a third reading and are being held by the Committee on Bills in the Third Reading for approval and possible correction are "held;" and the Chair states so as the items are reached on the day's Calendar.

On items that are not "passed," the membership disposes of them in turn. Bills may be advanced to their next reading; orders may be adopted; and committee reports may be accepted at that time. The afternoon session, scheduled usually for 1 P.M. houses the debate on controversial and sometimes not in the least controversial issues. It is there that the articulate and the non-articulate members of General Court present their facts and refute one another's arguments and generally discuss any and all facets of the legislation that, if passed (or for that matter, if NOT passed) will affect the lives of every citizen in the Commonwealth.

Bills are "carried" by the chairman (if they are particularly controversial) or by any member of the Committee before which they have been heard; and the legislator who carries a bill hopefully is equipped to handle the questions and to deal with the reservations of his colleagues in the House. It is fascinating, incidentally, to observe the styles of the various House members. Some are actors; and some are smooth as silk; while others tend a bit toward belligerency; some are articulate while others grope for words; some are dramatic in their every gesture while others are as simple as schoolboys. All have one thing in common - however they are fighting for what they feel is the good of their constituents and of the Commonwealth as a whole.

They're sincere and dedicated people, these members of the House of Representative, make no mistake about that. Their work load is heavy; the problems they are called upon to address and to attempt to solve are complex and difficult. There is constituent mail to be answered; and there are lobbyists unnumbered to be dealt with; there are the phone calls that consistently erode the hours of their leisure time…and frequently call them from the Chamber at critical moments of debate. There are constituent problems to be solved; and local issues to be faced; there is the inter-Relationship between the government of the towns in which they live and the state upon whose government they must leave their mark…and inter-relationship which, if they are to function properly, they must recognize and address. There are the countless meetings…the Committee Hearings; the "Executive Committee" meetings; the information meetings; the seminars; the caucuses. And they're perhaps the most exciting and rewarding days of their lives…"How do you

DO it?" asked my friend "Ibby" this evening as, after a very long day on Beacon Hill (where we are rushing to prorogue in time to afford us a two weeks' Christmas holiday), your legislator arrived - late by virtue of a late House session - for the third in a series of evenings that housed our Special Town Meeting. I frequently ask myself that very same question. "How DO I do it?" Well, the answer is simple. When one loves the things one is doing; when one ends every day with a feeling of accomplishment…of having left one's mark on someone's life…of having helped another human; or solved another problem; or set in motion the wheels that will lift an insurmountable burden from the heart of a constituent…then the workload one carries is light. Did I say "a two weeks' CHRISTMAS holiday??" Where on earth did my first year go on Beacon Hill??? I scarcely noticed its passing.

JANUARY 4, 1976

1975 is coming to a close on Beacon Hill. Another year lies dead ahead, its legislative issues as yet unmet - indeed, for the most part, unknown. And so, unable to look ahead, we find ourselves looking back…back upon many of the more important acts that were signed into law in '75. Like Chapter 61, which provided for the payment of unemployment compensation checks every two weeks, rather than weekly.

And Chapter 151, the CAMPAIGN CONTRIBUTION LAW which clarifies conflicting laws and established an Independent Director of Campaign Finance…and "expanded 'media' definition regarding campaign expense limits; and provides for first-in-nation vendor responsibility to report purchase of goods and services by candidates," and sets a minimum of $50 on those receipts and disbursements which must be accounted for by checks.

Under Chapter 200, a certain amount of FUEL SWITCHING will be allowed when atmospheric conditions permit - high sulfur fuel being allowed to be burned by utilities-industry providing it conforms to Federal and State air quality standards.

Under Chapter 363, MEDICAL MALPRACTICE problems were addressed. A two year risk pool will be established to provide insurance coverage for those doctors unable to secure insurance on the open market. A special tribunal, including a Superior Court judge, a doctor and a lawyer, will be empowered to screen out nuisance malpractice claims prior to trial. A $2,000 bond will be required of the individual making the malpractice claim, which bond will be forfeited if the suit is adjudged to be merely a nuisance claim.

In an attempt to control rising hospital costs, Chapter 424 was to be extended. Under it, hospitals will be required to justify their charges on the basis of increased and unavoidable hospital costs. In deference to non-smokers, Chapter 465, a SMOKING BAN was passed. Under it smoking is prohibited in such public places as supermarkets, elevators, MBTA vehicles, etc...with smoking permitted only in specified areas in hospitals, libraries, museums, etc.

Chapter 698 provided for NO FAULT DIVORCE, with "irretrievable breakdown" between the parties acceptable as a ground for divorce. In the case of an uncontested divorce, the decree becomes final in 10 months; with a contested divorce, the decree becomes final in 24 months. (Statistics indicate that in Massachusetts 80 to 85 percent of divorces are uncontested.)

Under Chapter 728, an INSURANCE RATING BUREAU was established to provide an independent analysis of auto insurance rate requests, with the costs to be assessed against the insurance companies.

Solar energy (one of my pet subjects) was given a boost with the provision of a 10 year property tax exemption on solar heating-hot water systems as an encouragement for the installation of these potentially vital new energy devices. How productive WAS the legislative year of 1975 on Beacon Hill???

There are those who say that NOTHING really was done legislatively in comparison to other years...and there are those who say that our preoccupation with the budget and the fiscal crisis that was ours caused legislation to be shelved...and there are others who remind us of the statements of our Speaker, the Honorable Thomas W. McGee who stated in his "maiden" speech that we had far too many laws that never were enforced and he would hopefully address this problem in the years that lay ahead.

Your representative is reminded forcibly of a day some months ago when first she learned that Civil Service employees, sadly needed in some of our facilities, could not be transferred from others where a decided surplus exists. "What a foolish law," I had stated to a Colleague in the House. "Well," he had replied, "WE VOTED IT: WE'RE RESPONSIBLE." "I can't believe it," I had said; "but that's why we're in the fiscal fix, we're in. Laws were passed with no regard for the consequences!" My fellow representative had laughed aloud. "NOT THIS YEAR." he had said, shaking his head. "NOTHING has been passed this year!" "Well." I replied firmly, "Amen to that. If we're not doing all the good you'd like done, we're not doing any more HARM!"

Yes, a great deal of legislation failed in passage during 1975. Perhaps it WAS our preoccupation with the budget, as had been said. I prefer to think, however, that it was due to the fact that "the days of wine and roses are over" in Massachusetts; and we're facing reality head-on. We're firmly planting the realization that the State is no longer the bottomless financial pit it was once thought to be; that economy must be the watchword from now on. And if you should ask this representative - it's high time we did just that.

A Happy 1976, everybody! May it be a happier one for poor old fiscally harried Massachusetts. We'll try our best to make it one, we members of the General Court - YOU MAY DEPEND ON THAT!

JANUARY 11, 1976

It's a different kind of Wednesday on Beacon Hill where the second year of my legislative adventure is about to begin with all the pomp and circumstance that has obviously come to us directly from that Great Britain upon whose way of doing things our own was partly patterned a couple of centuries back. I am reminded indeed of the pomp of England's parliamentary sessions as I wend my way, along with the other members of a Committee appointed by Speaker McGee, to advise the "members of the Honorable Senate" that the House is in session and awaits their arrival.

It is to be a joint session of the House and Senate; and the Governor is to deliver his "State of the State" message. It has opened with a particularly beautiful prayer in which divine guidance is asked in our deliberations and actions during the year ahead…and if ever divine guidance was needed, it is here on Beacon Hill where the fate of so many rests within our hands.

We stride down the marble corridors to the Senate where we are greeted with much pleasantry; and where witty exchanges between Senate President Harrington and our Majority Leader Maclean lend a note of gaiety to the proceedings.

The Honorable Thomas W. McGee, our House Speaker, is to make "a few brief remarks." His intense love "for this Chamber and the people I serve with," as well as "for this State and for this Country" shines through every word that is uttered by this dedicated leader who somehow manages to find time for everyone and everything - with a resultant work week that can run to seven days and evenings…His statement that he "tries to compromise with the other branches of government.

But not with his principles" draws loud applause from the House members who grow more loyal to Speaker McGee, it seems, every day on Beacon Hill.

The Minority Leader, Francis Hatch, follows the House Speaker with a decidedly pessimistic view of our state problems. "The job of being a legislator has never been more traumatic and more demanding," he tells his Colleagues. (We have found this out…)

A second House committee has been sent to escort the "Honorable Members of the Senate"; and they return with same. Senate President Harrington takes over the rostrum and a joint committee is appointed to "wait upon His Excellency the Governor, and inform him that the two House are assembled."

Now the Governor, along with the joint committee members, the Lieutenant Governor and several of the cabinet members and friends, arrives upon the scene. He begins his address by assuring the members of the Great and General Court that "making decisions is difficult for those members of the legislature who are committed to Social Justice. The hard measures we took, I took faced with the worst fiscal crisis in the history of the State." he says, "Look at New York," says the Governor, "that was the fate that would have befallen the State had we not taken the steps we did in the year behind us. The central question before us in January of "76 is whether we have learned the lessons of 75…" The Governor's speech is somber and uninterrupted by applause. I look about me at the faces of my Colleagues; they are, for the most part, solemn and even grim.

We have had an extremely difficult year; and a second difficult year lies ahead; we are already mentally gearing up for it….

To have had to vote a budget that brought hardship to so many, and a tax package that brought hardship to so many more - all in one legislative session - has been a traumatic experience indeed for the predominantly Democratic House membership who, having the majority vote, had no alternative but to vote for both…or accept responsibility for the fiscal chaos that would have followed their failure to do so - the inevitability of default.

The Governor in his speech has blamed the Federal Government for its "failure to provide a job for everyone who wants to work; and decent medical care for every citizen," a situation that he claims is "driving the states to bankruptcy." "Our most important single goal in 1976 is to continue and broaden the tough fiscal policies begun in '75," he states. We perhaps accept the validity of his statement - even as we deplore the necessity for making further inroads upon the well-being and financial security of the people we love.

Indeed, that prayer for divine guidance that opened the 1976 session of the House of Representatives MUST BE HEARD by the loving Father of us all, I tell myself; and divine guidance must be forthcoming for all of us as we face another traumatic year on Beacon Hill.

The Convention is dissolved; the members of the Senate return to their Chamber; the Governor to the Executive Office… "The House will be in a brief recess," the Speaker says, as dozens of "mikes" are removed from the rostrum area, and members of the media strive madly to record the Speaker's reaction to the Governor's speech. Prominent among the group we find, quite naturally, the incomparable and delightful Dick Flavin, whose bits of satire and news broadcasting we find so entertaining….

A rather sad note is to be added to the session as Representative Henry O'Donnell now proceeds to the rostrum to make a farewell speech to his colleagues; he has been appointed by the Governor as his legislative liaison with the House members. We wish him the very best…

And now another legislative year has begun on Beacon Hill, a year which your lady of the House hopes to face with courage and dedication, and a deep and abiding commitment to the "romance of public service."

Perhaps you, my readers, will send your own little "Prayers for divine guidance" heavenward, that she will use this second year on Beacon Hill wisely and well; and in a manner that will protect to the utmost the best interests of the constituents she truly loves…

JANUARY 18, 1976

The House of Representatives is in recess until January 26...The situation is necessitated, of course, by the fact that - the 1975 bills and petitions having required endless attention, legal and otherwise, right up to the last day of the session - 1976's bills and petitions had to take a back seat in preparation, placing in legal language, printing and assignment to appropriate committees. On Monday of this past week, however, here's one legislator who was mighty thankful not to have had to brave the elements and head for Beacon Hill. Other than on that particular day, however, I find myself either missing the place at home, or heading for the Golden Dome on general principles. At any rate, with the current legislative stalemate, so to speak, at the State House, I find myself free to take a more detailed look at what is happening politically here in Braintree; and what a joy it is to find so many of our wonderful citizens filing papers that could lead to the joys of public service, an area which I, personally, find so amazingly rewarding! And then, of course, there's the current hoopla of the Presidential Primaries.

Campaigns and elections always have fascinated this columnist; and, in my spare moments I seem to have accumulated little bits and pieces of America's political history that perhaps warrant sharing...like the origin of the famous hand-painted banner of Thomas Jefferson that may be found in the Smithsonian Institution.

It was during the 1800 campaign for the Presidency Thomas Jefferson was making speeches here and there that called for stronger State governments. The fact appeared to have angered Alexander Hamilton, who was a Federalist and who favored a centralized and strong Federal Government. Jefferson's federalist opponents were Braintree's own John Adams and Charles C. Pinckney; and Hamilton, although he himself was not a Presidential candidate, rode horseback through all the streets of New York to stump for Jefferson's Federalist opponents.

The election results showed a tie of the electoral votes between Mr. Jefferson and Aaron Burr, both of whom at that time bore the designation of Democratic Republicans. The Constitution provided that, in this circumstance, the election would be referred to the House of Representatives for resolution. The House selected Jefferson as President and Aaron Burr as Vice President.

In that period of our history, Presidential and Vice Presidential candidates were not balloted together. The Presidential candidate who came in with the second largest number of electoral votes automatically became Vice President.

Jefferson's victory was celebrated duly with parades; and the hand-painted banner to which I had reference earlier, was made to be carried in these parades.

There's an Andrew Jackson Poster in the Smithsonian Institution Collection as well...and therein lies another tale. The incomparable "Andy" ran for President for the first time in 1824; he lost the race to Braintree's John Quincy Adams. He had won the popular vote actually, he failed however to win the majority of electoral votes that was, at that time, required by the Constitution.

Jackson's supporters were irate. They claimed that the election had been stolen by Adams who, they stated, had made a deal with the then Speaker of the House, Henry Clay, also a candidate for the presidency.

A campaign to win the 1828 election was immediately begun; and the Jackson supporters formed a brand new party for their purpose. It was called the DEMOCRATIC PARTY - and the beginning of the Democratic Party as we know it today.

In his second attempt, Jackson ran for President labeled as the "Hero of New Orleans;" and his campaign saw the origin of all the organization, excitement and gaiety we have come to look for in most political campaigns. As history tells us, Andy Jackson was elected, and then re-elected in 1832. He has been designated as America's first "log-cabin President," incidentally.

In 1836, Martin Van Buren was elected to the Presidency to serve but one term at the end of which he was seen by many to have been ineffective, extremely unpopular, and the butt of a host of uncomplimentary slogans - which, for the benefit of his descendants I shall refrain from listing here.

By now another new party had emerged the Whig Party. Its two principal contenders were Henry Clay, the Kentuckian, and William Henry Harrison. The Whigs appear to have been a scrappy group. The supporters of Clay attacked Harrison with a vengeance. "Give him a barrel of hard cider and a pension of $2,000 a year, and he'll sit the rest of his days in his log cabin and study philosophy." they chanted. Harrison turned the tables on them, however; and won the nomination. A new slogan had emerged from all the in-fighting within the Whig Party. It was "Log Cabin and Hard Cider," and the Whigs with their man Harrison, who had styled himself as a "man of the people" while seeking nomination, went on to win the election.

His had been an emotional appeal to the voters; the technique had been used earlier by Andrew Jackson.

In all American history, so it is claimed, there has never been a wilder, more colorful and exciting campaign than this election of William Henry Harrison. The slogans had been turned to advantage by having been put to music; and rallies and parades became an accepted aspect of every campaign from that day on.

Oh yes, there's a banner in the Smithsonian on this one as well…It reads, "E PLURIBUSUNUM for HARRISON & TYLER. And no reduction of the prices of labor…The LOG CABIN, The house OUR FATHERS lived in. STONEHAM July 4, 1840."

Incidentally, these bits and pieces of information came my way via a marvelous series of cards, "Recalling Our Heritage" that were published by Congdon & Carpenter of Providence and Fall River as a Bicentennial tribute. I loved receiving and reading them; and hope you will enjoy sharing them with me.

JANUARY 25, 1976

A further glimpse or two into America's political history, as in Massachusetts we await resumption of the 1976 session of the House of Representatives where we shall be making a bit of history ourselves...

Appeal to the ethnic vote has been used, we read, during the campaign of 1848, by both Zachary Taylor and Winfield Scott...And by 1860, Abraham Lincoln was courting the ethnic vote to a very great degree. As a matter of fact, we may find in the Smithsonian Institution a handsome three-sided handmade transparency which was used in a political parade during Lincoln's time; and which employs both the English and German languages in its campaign appeal. There's a likeness of my favorite President which was obviously illuminated from within by a three-burner torch. It reads, "OLD ABE....ICH MEIN. PRINCE OF RAILS," meaning, of course, "OLD ABE is our man." And the reference to the "PRINCE OF RAILS" as a designation for Lincoln, the rail splitter" is thought to have tied the candidate to the Prince of Wales, who was constantly in the news at that period in our history. We are all aware of the log cabin background of the man who is so universally loved; and the "Prince of Rails" slogan was employed to highlight the humble beginnings from which the Man of Peace had sprung...

The campaign of 1880 continued to generate appeal to the ethnic vote; and we find within the Smithsonian another banner which was planned for use in the Pennsylvania Dutch country. James a Garfield and Chester A. Arthur were the Republican candidates; and Garfield was an ordained minister in the Disciples of Christ Church. He obviously appealed strongly to the deeply religious people of this Pennsylvania Dutch region; and he was elected President, with Arthur elected as Vice-President.

Garfield was to be the last of our "log cabin Presidents;" and his term of office was to be terminated tragically by an assassin shortly after his inauguration. Garfield was to be succeeded by the Vice President, Chester A. Arthur, who is remembered for having headed an Administration which rid itself of political corruption and machine politics; and reformed Civil Service...

By 1884, the Democrats were to be back in power with the election of Grover Cleveland. They were to successfully lick the Republicans with the slogan, "Blaine! Blaine! James G. Blaine, The continental liar from the State of Maine." Cleveland was to have a rather unique experience in American politics, elected in 1884, he was to be defeated by Benjamin Harrison in 1888 and then returned to the White House in 1892.

1896 was to see one of the most colorful political campaigns in American history. William McKinley was to be the victor; and the principal issue had evolved around the "gold vs the silver standard of coinage." McKinley, a native of Ohio, was to remain at home and conduct a "front porch campaign" while his Democratic opponent, who was no less than William Jennings Bryan, was to crisscross the entire country in a railroad car, making speeches in every hamlet he passed. The political speeches of Bryan were to be fiery and eloquent. He had made no less than twenty-seven of them by nightfall of the day before the election, collapsing with fatigue as the night was ended. One of Bryan's quotes has been used by other politicians over the years. "You shall not press down upon the brow of labor this crown of thorns; you shall not crucify mankind upon a cross of gold."

1912 was to see another exciting Presidential campaign. It was, we read, one of personalities - the incumbent President Taft; the scholarly Woodrow Wilson; and the incomparable "Teddy" Roosevelt all competing for the office of Chief Executive. Wilson, then Governor of New Jersey, was to be nominated on the 46th ballot at the Democratic Convention. Roosevelt had challenged President Taft at the Republican Convention; and having lost out, then had formed the "Progressive Party" at the Bull Moose Convention.

It was all to no avail. Wilson was to be the victor; and to be re-elected in 1916 with his appealing slogan, "He kept us out of war!" It was not long, however, before we were to join the Allies in World War I.

Theodore Roosevelt had campaigned successfully as a Republican in 1904 having succeeded the assassinated President Mckinley in 1901. His mottoes are marvelous to read. "Don't flinch, don't foul, hit the line hard," was among the most famous of them. Roosevelt's charge up San Juan Hill during the Spanish-American War was to tie him politically to the "Rough Rider" image; and then there were the "teddybear" and the "bull moose" stories with which that rugged early American was to be identified.

It was November of 1902, we read, while "Teddy" was on a hunting expedition in Mississippi. A small bear had been captured and brought to him to shoot. This ardent conservationist and humanitarian promptly refused to end the life of the little animal; it was "cruel' and "unsportsmanlike," he said firmly. Washington Post cartoonist Clifford R. Berryman, picked up the story in his cartoon; and from one end of the country to the other "teddy bears" were the "in thing."… And then while campaigning as a Progressive Party candidate, Theodore Roosevelt was questioned about his tremendous energy and asked how he felt; he replied, "I feel like a bull moose!" Well, that reply was to become the symbol of the 1912 unsuccessful effort that was made to regain the Presidency by "Teddy" Roosevelt; and did you know he was really the first ardent conservationist the country had ever known???

FEBRUARY 15, 1976

Perhaps it is because I found a small spring bulb poking its little green nose up through the cold winter ground in my garden last Sunday like a sign of hope…Or perhaps it is because that horrendous State Budget I've been grappling with for the past two weekends seems to include provisions for "monitoring" in setting up state agency budgets; AND a section on "Program Budgets" (a pet of mine)…At any rate, a feeling of optimism seems to be setting in; a hope that the year that lies ahead on Beacon Hill may not be quite so bad as the last one…budget and tax-wise, that is.

The proposed budget which was submitted by Governor Dukakis on January 28 is detailed and readable. There are some aspects of the proposals that are decidedly disturbing, needless to say - like the cuts in state aid, for instance; which cuts would have a profound effect on the property tax Massachusetts residents will be asked to pay. For poor, harassed Braintree residents, still bowed down under the added burdens imposed by the recent 100 percent valuation nightmare, this is bad news indeed; and it is hoped that the Massachusetts League of Citizens and Towns will fight it to the last ditch. There must be other, better ways...But, to return initially to the "monitoring" provisions to which we had reference and to what I see as an awareness of fiscal responsibility, may I present a few quotes from the Governor's budget to indicate he IS on the right track in those area. "This year," he writes, "the budget document sets forth more than the traditional budgetary requests and recommendation. It is a factual recitation of where the Commonwealth has been in the last few years and where it was heading. It is a statement of the direction that this Administration has chosen for the Commonwealth for the 1977 fiscal year- toward striking an appropriate balance between fiscal stability and sound management practices and social responsibility. Coupled with the events of the 1976 fiscal year, this goal can be reached through the exercise of fiscal restraint; effective personnel and program management; reasonable and factual revenue estimates; and through the realization that programs and services, other than those which are absolutely essential, are curtailed." that the Commonwealth can provide programs and services for its less fortunate only to the degree In the area of Personnel, we are informed by the Governor that the number of authorized positions increased by 45.9 percent during the past ten years, with a personnel total of 63,583 as of October, year, with 2,635 positions to be eliminated in 1977. Another ray of hope...1975; however through the process of attrition some 2,630 permanent positions were estimated last.

We should by now be aware of the enormous impact of welfare costs on the swollen state budget. Quite obviously the Governor is not oblivious to the fact, for we read, in the Human Services areas of the budget, "FY 1977 is a year when services and costs will be closely monitored and evaluated...A caseload growth, the Department plans caseload management reforms, including a vigorous computer matching and client response system. Computer matching will help identify ineligible cases, and the client response system will obtain more accurate information volunteered by clients. those cases with a high possibility of error." Both of these systems will contribute to the Department's overall goal of selectively redetermining.

This is good news indeed, for the ineligible must be denied public assistance if funds are to be available for the eligible; and the withholding of federal funds as a result of our chronically high percentage of errors could prove to be the straw that breaks the proverbial back...

Incidentally, may your columnist flash back briefly to the LADY OF THE HOUSE she submitted last week. A constituent, of whom she happens to be very fond, appeared at the State House, holding the column tightly in her hand. "How COULD you convey

The Candid Idylls of a State Representative | 129

the impression that every one in the Great and General Court is 100 percent solid gold?" she asked with ire. "And that there is no FAT in the state budget?" Well, in the discussion that followed, I trust that I convinced the lady that I had in no way intended to suggest that there is no fat in the STATE BUDGET - only that the representatives to whom I am close don't seem to be enjoying any of it. This was not a complaint, just a statement of fact. AND that the eleven representatives in my office, all of whom come from different parts of the state and appear to represent decidedly differing segments of the citizenry ARE indeed conscientious and hard working and untouched or unaided by the proverbial FAT in the budget we keep reading about. Which brings me to a specific point.

There well may be FAT in the state budget, however a general statement of that effect is really of little value. We legislators, dealing as we are with hundreds of bills and constituent problems and requests and the like, have no real way of identifying that fat. AND HERE IS WHERE YOU, MY READERS, MY CONSTITUENTS COME IN. If, indeed, you know of any area or any agency in state government where FAT is present, please let me hear from you, identifying the area and-or the agency. I assure you that I am as anxious to separate the wheat from the chaff as any one of you; and I give you my solemn promise that I shall bring the specific instance of FAT to the attention of those whose responsibility it is to review and make recommendations on the budget- the Secretary of Administration and Finance; and the House and Senate Chairmen of Ways and Means. Incidentally, I wonder how many of you are aware that last year saw the first time in history that the House of Representatives cut the Governor's budget - and by 350 million dollars, NO SMALL AMOUNT…And that the House of Representatives cut its own legislative budget by one million dollars…

Believe me, we're trying on Beacon Hill; but YOU can help. Let me hear from you on that FAT we read about; I'll track it down. Citizen input is a vital ingredient in government; and this legislator welcomes it with open arms! By the way, have you ever before read direct quotations from a state budget??? We're trying!

FEBRUARY 22, 1976

Lots of activity on Beacon Hill this past week despite the fact that not too many bills have actually reached the chamber for consideration and voting - certainly no controversial legislation has come our way since last your Lady of the House reported to her favorite people….

Our Transportation Committee Hearings have begun, with Agency Bills heard first. Mr. David Gunn, representing the M.B.T.A. came before us to explain away??? some of the problems encountered by the Authority during those recent snowstorms that sent it into a spin. The "T's" chief problem appears to lie with its operating equipment, new as well as old, it would appear. On the Red Line, which your legislator happens to use most days, the difficulty arose primarily from "over-sophistication" we were told. The sophisticated signal system simply did not work. "A lot of decisions made five years ago were made when technology was going to save the transit system," Mr. Gunn told the members of our committee. "The operators and the maintenance people were not involved in the decision making process when new equipment was purchased," he said, assuring legislators as he did so that the policy in that area would definitely undergo a change. "The policy of deferring maintenance on the T started away back to hide the deficit." Mr. Gunn said, adding that they are now "Fighting against a tremendous backlog of deferred maintenance."

The M.B.T.A. spokesman outlined the problems encountered during the recent storms. "Moisture in the braking system was a problem," he said, 'We are now putting alcohol into the braking system." On the Red Line the T is "analyzing the situation and trying to weed out repeaters (among the cars), to identify and correct the problems." "The much-touted Bart System in San Francisco has only 35 or 40 per cent viability," Mr. Gunn said. Mr. Mangini, also representing the T discussed problems with the power supply. "The T feels that purchasing power from Edison is best," he said. Capital improvements envisioned will include track improvements on the Green Line, Transportation committee members were told, as well as improvements in the communications system, with radio communication between the Central Control System at High Street and the operators themselves; a telephone system to communicate within the tunnels to the central system for emergencies; improvements to the police radio system; and in the area of safety, tunnel ventilation; an A.C. Lighting system for emergencies; dry standpipe mains and bullet proof collector booths. Add to this capital improvement program fleet improvement with a bus replacement program; rapid transit equipment and streetcar replacement and modernization and possibly more, and one has a slight idea of what lies ahead for an Authority that is coming more and more under fire as assessments. against the cities and towns grow ever higher, and the share of an astronomical deficit that is levied against the beleaguered State of Massachusetts soars out of sight as well. I'd sure rather be me, (to quote a line from a popular song,) than Mr. Gunn these days…or Mr. Mangini…

Spent a couple of hours at the House Ways and Means Committee Hearing on the Governor's bill on short-term debt restructuring, House Bill 4345, "An Act to Restructure the Short-Term Debt of the commonwealth and Certain Agencies and Authorities Thereof."

Short-term notes, it appears, have been rolled over repeatedly for years within our Commonwealth, a costly and untidy method of debt management. It has been likened to a situation where a home owner elects to re-mortgage his home each year, rather than to take out a mortgage for twenty or thirty years. The interest charges are excessive. Now, with the bond market all but dried up as a result of the New York City crisis and our own fiscal problems, a concerted effort is being made to transfer some of the state's short-term notes to long-term bonds.

There are safeguards within the bill that would hopefully prevent in the future the kinds of crises we have been plagued with during the past year. It's been a rough year in the area of bond and note sale, needless to say; and next month the state must re-finance $137 million in state-guaranteed local housing authority notes.

The Bill consolidates bond issuing authority in the Treasurer; and it places limitations on the buildup of short time debt on local housing authorities and the M.H.F.A. it will impose discipline in that for every one dollar of bonds sold between now and January 1, 1978, only 20 cents worth of notes will be allowed to be sold; and they only providing a bond sale is impossible. No executive session has as yet been scheduled by Ways and Means. H-4345 is a 31 page, comprehensive and technical document; and a great deal of time, we warrant, will be taken by our brilliant Chairman, Representative John Finnegan and his bright committee, before voting on the Bill is considered. Today (Thursday) was IWO JIMA DAY at the State House where we celebrated the 31st Anniversary of that historic event in the magnificent Hall of Flags. Can it possibly be that a year has passed since last we observed that moment in our history, I asked myself, as I wended my way down the long marble corridors to what must surely be one of the world's loveliest settings for such an event??? The U.S. Army Band was on hand with its Opening Fanfare; there was the Posting of Colors; and the National Anthem reverberating throughout this magnificent place, rising to the roof in a manner that set every patriotic heart racing. Monsignor Kerr's Invocation was appropriate and beautiful, as were the remarks of the state's official family as, one after another, they brought the greeting of the Commonwealth to the overflow crowd in attendance. The Speaker of our House, the Hon. Thomas W. McGee, a surviving veteran of the gallant Marine action at Iwo Jima, brought the greeting of the General Court in a manner which delighted those of his colleagues who were there in attendance. The words of Admiral Nimitz were quoted again and again, "Uncommon valor for the common good"

…It was impressive and beautiful with the incomparable "Battle Hymn of the Republic," the Marine Hymn" and the rest adding color and brilliance to the observance of a day in history the survivors of Iwo Jima (and there were many on hand) must live again and again in memory as each year the month of February rolls around.

Yes, there has been lots of activity on Beacon Hill this past week…and all of it interesting and exciting. And lots of activity lies ahead. Your Lady of the House hopes to share every bit of it with the wonderful Braintree-ites who sent her there.

FEBRUARY 29, 1976

Committee Hearings have begun in earnest on Beacon Hill. Your legislator, dedicated to the work of both of her committees - Transportation and Health Care - has begun for the second year the mad task of trying to attend legislative hearings and executive sessions scheduled simultaneously by both committees…not an easy task! The solution of bouncing back and forth between the two failed last year to work at all; the alternative - to scrutinize carefully the bills coming before both committees and decided which package will have the greatest impact and is perhaps the most complicated and therefore the most deserving of close attention - had to be decided upon during the last session and will probably have to suffice this year as well. Wish I were twins, however.... or even triplets - then I could attend both committee hearings and contend with my constituent work as well and all at the same time....

So now, what kinds of bills are coming before those two exciting committees on which I serve anyhow??? Well, in Transportation we have had a great many pieces of legislation dealing with traffic control. There was, for instance, an attempt to strike out the sentence which was added last year by Chapter 234, in which the use of flashing white WALK pedestrian traffic control signals was prohibited. It received an unfavorable report from our committee. We had had a marvelous demonstration of the dangers inherent in the use of this signal system last year, the energetic Marilyn Johnson having demonstrated with young children the confusion that can arise with this type of pedestrian signal. The Department of Public Works was petitioned to install a flashing school warning sign at a dangerous Worcester crosswalk; this bill received a FAVORABLE vote. An Act providing for the installation of emergency communications equipment on limited access highways also received a FAVORABLE vote; this should prove to be a source of comfort to those traveling our highways, particularly at night when a stopped vehicle can cause or be the victim of a serious accident. An Act repealing the authority of the State Department of Public Works in matters of traffic control within city limits or town limits also received a FAVORABLE; the intent of the bill apparently to permit local municipalities to control traffic signing and the costs related thereto. This particular bill was amended so as not to apply either to ONE WAY STREET or STOP signs. Bills establishing penalties for the fraudulent use of passes on the M.B. T.A. as well as for the evasion of fares or toll fees, received FAVORABLE votes; as did an Act authorizing the M.B.T.A. to lease air rights over its transportation facilities...AND an Act providing that the City of Somerville have first option relative to the purchase of certain land in the City of Somerville owned by the M.B.T.A.; along with a similar Act involving the City of Everett.

An Act requiring the M.B.T.A. to award contracts to the lowest bidder received a FAVORABLE This legislation not only requires competitive bidding, but it requires filed sub bids on certain items; the M.B.T.A.'s present policy is to seek bids on a complete project, having general contractors come in with a figure which covers all aspects of a job.

A legislative attempt to assign a police officer to all stations under the control of the M.B.T.A received an OUGHT NOT TO PASS. The need for police protection is a recognized one, however, with the general wave of austerity that is sweeping the State House...AND the astronomical authority deficit the state has had to face...there is slim chance of receiving a favorable vote on any legislation which would involve the expenditure of additional M.B.T.A. funds.

A move to create a special commission to investigate the management and operation of the M.B.T.A. failed to receive a FAVORABLE; it was felt that our sub-committee should be given an opportunity to handle this aspect of the transportation problem before it is brought to law.

An attempt to have the M.B.T.A. install closed circuit television cameras as protective devices in critical area subway stations also failed to receive a favorable committee report. The enormous installation cost - six or seven millions of dollars - plus the threat of vandalism and a lack of perfection in existing systems, occasioned an OUGHT NOT TO PASS vote on the part of thecommittee members.

Unfavorably reported was an Act providing for the establishment of free rest rooms at M.B.T.A. Stations. The rest rooms at M.B.T.A. Stations ARE free, we were informed; and as an anti-vandalism and anti-crime measure the key to said rest rooms are retained by the collectors, to be provided upon request. It was suggested by committee members that a notice to this effect be placed adjacent to the collectors' booths, it being generally felt that the public is unaware of the fact that this service is offered by the authority. Incidentally we had made this same request of said authority during the last session when a similar bill was filed; they had promised to handle the matter; perhaps they will get around to doing that this year. We hope so.

"Rest rooms are available at all stations for men and women," we were told by authority. "Many rest rooms have been modernized and eventually all will be done over. There is no charge for use but for security reasons, keys are held by collectors." We plan to make such a request of a collector in the very near future…and to watch for those signs!

The Transportation Committee is a marvelously interesting one; so is the Health Care Committee, about which I shall write next week. There, too, bills of the most complex and varied kinds come our way; and how very much we learn, we members of the Great and General Court! Incidentally how much easier it is for us freshmen legislators this year; we now have a background of information upon which to build. And we are able to identify so many of the speakers who come before our committees, to anticipate their pitch even before they start to speak. Have I mentioned before that it's all rather wonderful???

APRIL 4, 1976

To a history buff like your Lady of the House, the following Proclamation By the Great and General Court of the colony of Massachusetts Bay, adopted by the House of Representatives on January 23, 1776, has a special appeal. You will understand, I am sure, why - having read it I decided it must be passed along to you, my readers, with whom I would share every single exciting experience that is mine on Beacon Hill…

"The frailty of human nature, the wants of individuals, and the numerous dangers which surround them, through the source of life, have in all ages, and in every country, impelled them to form societies, and establish governments.

As the happiness of the people is the sole end of government, so the consent of the people is the only foundation of it, in reason, morality, and the natural fitness of things; And therefore every act of government, every exercise of sovereignty, against, or without, the consent of the people, is injustice, usurpation, and tyranny.

It is a maxim, that in every government, there must exist somewhere, a supreme sovereign, absolute, and uncontrollable power: But this power resides always in the body of the people; and it is a maxim, that in every government, there must exist somewhere, a supreme sovereign, never was, or can be delegated to one man, or a few; the great Creator having never given to men a right to vest others with authority over them, unlimited either in duration or degree.

When Kings, ministers, governors, or legislators therefore, instead of exercising the powers entrusted with them, according to the principles, form and proportions stated by the constitution, and established by the original compact, prostitute those powers to the purposes of oppression; - to subvert, instead of supporting a free constitution; - to destroy, instead of preserving the lives, liberties and properties of the people; - they are no longer to be deemed magistrates vested with a sacred character, but become public enemies, and ought to be resisted.

The administration of Great Britain, despising equally the justice, humanity and magnanimity of their ancestors; and the rights, liberties and courage of Americans have, for a course of years, labored to establish a sovereignty in American, not founded in the consent of the people, but in the mere will of persons a thousand leagues from us, whom we know not, and have endeavored to establish this sovereignty over us, against our consent, in all cases whatsoever.

The Colonies, during this period, have recurred to every peaceable resource in a free constitution, by Petitions and Remonstrances, to obtain justice; which have been not only denied to them, but they have been treated with unexampled indignity and contempt; and at length, open war of the most atrocious, cruel and sanguinary kind, has been commenced against them. To this, an open, manly and successful resistance has hitherto been made. Thirteen Colonies are now firmly united in the conduct of this most just and necessary war, under the wise councils of their Congress. It is the will of Providence, for wise, righteous, and gracious ends, that this Colony should have been singled out, by the enemies of America, as the first object both of their envy and their revenge; and after having been made the subject of several merciless and vindictive statutes, one of which was intended to subvert our constitution by Charter, it made the seat of war.

But as our enemies have proceeded to such barbarous extremities, commencing hostilities upon the good people of this Colony, and with unprecedented malice exerting their power to spread the calamities of fire, sword and famine through the land, and no reasonable prospect remains of a speedy reconciliation with Great Britain, the congress have resolved: "That no obedience being due to the act of parliament for altering the Chapter of the Colony of Massachusetts Bay, nor to a governor or lieutenant governor, who will not observe the directions of, but endeavor to subvert that Charter, the governor and lieutenant governor of that Colony, are to be considered as absent, and their offices vacant, and as there is no Council there, and inconvenience arising from the suspension of the powers of government are intolerable, especially at a time when General Gage hath actually levied war, and is carrying on hostilities against his Majesty's peaceable and loyal Subjects, of that Colony; that in order to conform as near as may be to the spirit and substance of the Charter, it be recommended to the Provincial Convention, to write letters to the inhabitants of the several places which are entitled to representation in assembly, requesting them, to choose such representatives; and that assembly, when chosen, do elect counselors; and that such assembly and council, exercise the powers of government until a governor of his Majesty's appointment will consent to govern the Colony according to its Charter."

In pursuance of which advice, the good people of this colony have chosen a full and free representation of themselves, who, being convened in assembly have elected a Council; who, as the executive branch of government, have constituted necessary officers through the Colony. The present generation, therefore, may be congratulated on the acquisition of a form of government more immediately in all its branches, under the influence and control of the people; and therefore more free and happy than was enjoyed by their ancestors."

This fascinating Proclamation is unfortunately too long for one column. I shall therefore, have to continue in next week's Lady of the House. Hope you're enjoying looking back with me upon the pages of yesterday's history for a bit of the wonder and excitement that is government "of the people, by the people, and for the people." as it was away back there when freedom began…

MAY 2, 1976

"Mrs. Metayer of Braintree then moved as a mark of respect to the memory of the Bernice W. Delory of Braintree Executive Secretary to the Counsel to the House and Clerk of the Committee on Bills in the Third Reading, the House adjourn, and the motion prevailed"…Thus for all time would the Journal of the House of Representatives of the Great and General Court, for the 26th day of April 1976 record the passing of a truly great lady. The House mourned the loss of a brilliant executive secretary, loved and respected by everyone; your Lady of the House mourned the passing of a treasured, and incredibly dear friend.

The day had been an infinitely sad one under the Golden Dome. The Committee on Bills in the Third Reading; which Bernice Delory had served with such distinction was "in shock" to quote the Speaker of the House, the Honorable Thomas W. McGee. Colleagues, all aware of our close friendship (we met daily by the first floor door and journeyed home together) offered condolences. "You look like Snedecker looked when Dick Landry went," said one of them, "Stricken..." Stricken indeed I was, for this beautiful and brilliant woman was a truly unique individual...her quick wit -sometimes caustic but very delightful; her smart repartee; her vivacious and sparkling personality, along with the keen intellect with which she was blessed, rendered Bernice Delory a delight to know. We shall miss her.

The week that was to mark this sad event had begun so very beautifully...with the General Sylvanus Thayer Bicentennial Concert on Friday evening at Thayer Academy. Fifty or more handsome West Point Cadets just "39 days and 12 hours" short of graduation, in a program that was stirring, beautiful and nostalgic...And then afterwards the fun "Candlelight Open House" at nearby Thayer House, our historical center.

Saturday morning had seen the largest parade in Braintree's history, a two-hour spectacle which had included militia units, our own and others; marching regiments; color guards; drum and bugle corps; marching police officers and firefighters; and floats...and floats...and floats.

I had shared slightly in the reflected glory of the parade's Grand Marshal, Congressman James Burke, riding smartly as I did in a handsome white convertible; and flanked fore and aft by four of the Congressman's Blue Knights Motorcyclists. Felt like the President! But then it was Saturday evening; and the tragedy had struck.

This week on Beacon Hill has been a hectic one indeed. All bills had to be reported out of committee by Wednesday, the 28th, or receive an adverse report; and so it was public hearings and executive sessions one atop the other as we scrambled to complete our work. On Monday next we shall begin in earnest to tackle the difficult, the controversial legislation - like the Bottle Bills and the Gun Control Bills and the Fair Share Electric Rate proposition.

Meanwhile we wrestle with the many facets of that Fair Share approach to the high cost of electricity. There are so very many ramifications to what had been presented to the general public and particularly to our elderly as a solution to one of the financial woes that beset them - the high. cost of electricity...It is NOT! For one thing, it does not address itself to the fuel charge at all; and for another, the one dollar per month that will be saved on their electric bills will be offset in spades. by the increased cost of electricity for community schools, municipal building, the M.B.T.A. and the rest- all of which will be reflected in their rent or real estate taxes.

The M.B.T.A. alone, for instance, despite the fact that much of its power is generated at its own plant, would have paid an additional $283,500 last year under the flat rate "Fair Share" plan; and as the M.B.T.A. expands and purchases its power from other utility companies, that figure will rise higher-to be further reflected in assessments, and therefore in the property tax.

The Candid Idylls of a State Representative | 137

Your L. of the H. was busy this past week turning up additional projections on the fair Share proposal. For instance, on the 16 Greater Boston hospitals, a 34 per cent increase would result, or total of $2,495,000.00 to be reflected, needless to say, in increased hospital costs for all of us; on 5 Boston area universities, the increase would be 33.4 percent, or a total of $1,500,000, which would bring about increased tuition costs. On the Commonwealth of Massachusetts the added cost would $750,000, or an increase of 25 per cent, to be raised by state taxes.

Equally disturbing is the loss of jobs, with consequent increases in our Welfare caseload. Projections from the Greater Boston Chamber of Commerce, for instance, show a $90 million increase in electric costs to business, with a consequent loss of 36,000 jobs…from the Associated Industries of Massachusetts, a $100 million increase in electric costs to industry-large users, with a loss of 41,000 jobs.

Perhaps we should be investigating alternatives like flat rates within each category of use, viz. residential, commercial, industrial, etc. The delivery of one category of supply DOES differ from another in cost, we have been persuaded. How FAIR is Fair Share anyhow, we keep wondering as we pore over statistics and peruse the many letters with their projected job losses that have come our way from concerned constituents. Incidentally, here is a classic example of the gray areas clouding what was presented as a black and white issue.

There are other considerations to be faced…like an estimated 24 per cent increase in electric power for supermarkets, which would no doubt be reflected in higher food prices. The same situation would, needless to say, prevail with Massachusetts food processing companies; and with retail store and discount houses. The discounts would undoubtedly shrink!

We want with all our might to help our elderly and low income people with their financial problems, but there must be a better way! At any rate, we shall face the problem of Fair Share on Monday; perhaps an acceptable alternative will be proposed; we hope so…

MAY 9, 1976

"Mrs. Metayer of Braintree then moved that as a mark of respect to the memory of former Representative Carl R. Johnson, Jr., a member of the House from Braintree from 1959 to 1966 inclusive, the House adjourn and the motion prevailed."…Thus for all time would the Journal of the House of Representatives of the Great and General Court, for the 3rd day of May, 1976 record the passing of the Moderator of the Town of Braintree, Carl R. Johnson, Jr. A most unique individual indeed, former State Representative Johnson - possessed of extraordinary ability; indomitable courage; unsurpassed devotion to God and Country; faith in the political system of which he had been a part for so very many years; and a meticulousness that was to include the advance, personal planning of even the smallest detail of a beautiful burial service. What a heritage this man has left to the sons and daughters, the grandsons and granddaughters who will come after him, I thought, as I walked behind the Governor of the State and the Speaker of the House of Representatives through the aisles of a Church that was filled with the people who mourned him. Carl R. Johnson, Jr., has left his mark upon his town, his state and his country; not many mortals live to say the same. Another interesting week on Beacon Hill. Friday morning, and it was off to Quincy District Court. The observance was Quincy's; but it was Braintree's Day in Court. Three distinguished service awards were to be made the first to the most outstanding Quincy attorney, who turned out to be Braintree's own Edward H. Libertine. We were remembering as this brilliant and charming man made a typically clever acceptance speech…back to the time a number of years ago when, acting as Amicus Curiae (Friend of the Court) he had come to the assistance of the people of East Braintree, investing without remuneration absolute hours of his extremely valuable time in preventing the building of a regional incinerator in Echo Lake. Edward H. Libertine, Esq. has a history of this kind of civic involvement; and we applaud the choice of the Quincy Bar Association. They know class when they see it, those Quincy attorneys, we thought with considerable pride.

The second distinguished service award was also to go to Braintree-ites. From among the gathering of Norfolk County Police Chiefs, our own John V. Polio had been selected to present awards to two of his courageous officers - Sgt. Leonard Torrey and Patrolman Robert S. Devin, both of whom had been shot in the line of duty during the past few months.

The third distinguished service award was to be presented to the South Shore Chamber of Commerce in recognition of its cooperation with a work-restitution program instituted by Judge Kramer of the Quincy Court. No one from the Chamber was present to accept the award; I had found myself smiling as I realized that had the Chamber group not been tied up elsewhere that lovely morning, Braintree's own Ron Frazier would probably have been the individual accepting the third of these distinguished service awards which will be given annually on Law Day from here on in. Sunday housed another delightful and rewarding experience for your Lady of the House as she attended the Third Annual "Eagle" Court of Honor for Troop 67, Boy Scouts of America. What a thrill it was to find St. Francis Church Parish Hall packed with the parents (and undoubtedly grandparents; believe me, I'd have been there if my grandson was attaining the rank of Eagle Scout), the relatives and the friends of the FIVE splendid young men who had achieved the distinction of reaching that high pinnacle of Scouting-the rank of EAGLE! William Edward Gately, Jr.; Christopher Thomas Mahoney; Peter Stephen Marinelli; Martin Charles Murphy, Jr.; and Paul Robert Steeves…I had watched them with pride as they stood upon the platform awaiting their fine high moment. Young manhood at its finest, I had thought; the future of our country is in their hands and truly it must be quite safe within the hands of such as these.

There were words of praise for the parents of these five young men; and for the Scoutmaster and his fine Assistants who may well take credit for the long hard hours of service in their area of Scouting that had brought out the best in these five boys, to make of them fine men. A wonderful evening it had been; another of the fringe benefits that come the way of those whose days are spent on Beacon Hill. Loved every moment of it, from the beautiful Mass that preceded the ceremony to the scrumptious, home-cooked goodies in the buffet that followed it.

Monday had been earmarked as a long hard day upon the Hill. Three controversial bills, all stemming from initiative petition activity, were to be debated. House Bill 4200, the so-called "Bottle Bill," a bill to prohibit the manufacture and sale of non-returnable bottles and cans; House Bill 4201, the "Fair Share" bill, which upon close examination proved to be anything BUT fair; and House Bill 4202, the "Gun Control" bill, which called for the confiscation of all handguns. The Bottle Bill was to be voted down, 146 to 85. The issue was to prove to be anything but a black or white situation; there were gray areas, and many of them. Was it Big Business who lobbied to kill the bill as some of our colleagues charged? Could 20,000 to 30,000 homes really be heated with the energy wasted in the manufacture of the billion and a half throwaway containers we toss upon our dumping areas? Was the Federal Reserve Bank study correct in estimating an increase of 187 to 1400 new jobs if the bill were to become law? Or would 1,000 well paid employees lose their jobs if the bill prevailed? Would stores within the border towns be forced to close their doors? Would a REGIONAL approach, with all New England participating, provide the solution to the inequity claimed by all those border towns? The questions and the claims came thick and fast. Your Lady of the House had found herself voting for the bill; secure in the knowledge, however, that the matter will be addressed as a referendum question in the fall.

It was a good deal easier to vote AGAINST the so-called "Fair Share" bill; and against the Gun Control legislation, the cost of which, incidentally, was estimated to be as high as 125 Million dollars. Confiscated guns would have to be paid for by the State, you see; and the State doesn't have a dime. Furthermore, the possibility of levying any additional taxes upon the people of our poor beleaguered Commonwealth leaves us, your legislators, as cold as it does our constituents. All three of these bills went down to defeat, incidentally!

One more week has passed on Beacon Hill. Wednesday of next week will house a Constitutional Convention, called jointly by the Senate and the House. That will be an interesting day; we'll let you know what happens.

MAY 30, 1976

It is Thursday morning; and your Lady of the House has arisen at dawn to see to it that this column reaches the Observer-Forum on time for publication…a situation necessitated by three extremely busy evenings, two of which housed Town Meeting sessions, and the third of which housed another form of legislative get-together. The days have been out of the picture entirely for any of the extracurricular activities we might like to pursue, for life on Beacon Hill represents a race against the clock from dawn to dusk.

Monday morning began bright and early with the swearing-in of the new Associate Justice of the Supreme Court of the Commonwealth, the Honorable Paul J. Liacos. The House Chamber provided the setting for this very impressive ceremony. Speaker McGee, a Boston University Law School classmate of Justice Liacos, and a friend of twenty-five years standing, presided over the event. "There is a sense of deep feeling when someone with whom you have been associated reaches the top; and he is certainly doing that today," he said of the grave, dark-eyed gentleman who shared the Speaker's platform with him. Governor Dukakis termed the swearing-in "one of the most pleasant duties in the seventeen months in office" he has "enjoyed;" labeling the new Associate Justice as an "able and public-spirited judge." One of the speakers quoted from remarks that were directed some years past to the incomparable Justice Brandeis, stating his conception of a judge's calling "nothing less than a translation of the American life into the American dream." It was very impressive, this ceremony on Beacon Hill. office, for I have never before witnessed the swearing in of a Supreme Court Justice. There was a slight sideline to the affair, however which your Lady of the House cannot keep to herself. The Chamber was crowded, and she was directed by one of the great Court Officers we have in the State House to "a seat down at the front." She promptly seated herself at the end of the second row of spectators. There was nothing unusual in the fact that all others in the area were male; it is the norm for the situation in the House where there are but 14 females out of a body of 240.

There WAS something unusual about those companions of hers, however, for the distinguished ones on the platform kept nodding to them; and the T.V. cameras kept pointing their way. With horror, your L. of the H. suddenly came to the realization that she was sharing the area with a group of judges whose presence was being acknowledged all over the place. In addition, she was being regarded periodically by the platform occupants who were obviously trying desperately to place a female "judge" who had suddenly arisen from nowhere. What to do? To rise and walk out, calling attention to oneself? Or to remain quietly where one was and rejoice in a front row seat? Your Lady of the House did the latter. "Your Honor, I must apologize to you for my intrusion into your distinguished group," I said to my neighbor as the ceremonies were concluded. "A mere State Representative I have no earthly right to be here; I did not realize you were all judges, and simply blundered in." "My dear," said the kindly gentleman, "No apology is necessary. A 'mere State Representative, as you term yourself, is ELECTED by the people; we are not!" Ah, me...Yesterday morning it was off again at dawn, for a visit to the Department of Youth Services' female detention center at the Charlestown YMCA. We had been told of the unbelievably bad conditions at this center where young girls from the ages of seven to seventeen are housed overnight, and sometimes longer, for disposition of their cases through the courts.

The report had not been exaggerated. We found seven young girls penned into a unbelievably small, dirty room with a pool table and a pack of cards to supplement the inevitable small T.V. set. (Not very uplifting forms of entertainment for girls in trouble, we thought.) Their kitchen area, dirty and unkempt, would fit nicely into the worst form of ghetto situation; their dormitory, with its cots lined up one beside the other, additional thin mattresses for the overflow guests (for whom these would be placed upon the floor) placed above the original bed mattresses for hauling out if necessary; the dingy windows; the locked doors; the entire picture so depressing that your L. of the H. was unable to recover for the remainder of the day...All this for children in trouble from the ages of SEVEN to seventeen. We were appalled. And the charges for which "Auntie T's" girls are held there? For prostitution, for armed robbery, for accessory after the fact of murder. The litany went on while the four women "reps" who had come unexpectedly to inspect the place recoiled in horror and, I am certain, joined in a prayer of thanksgiving with your own L. of the H. for the normalcy and beauty of their own well-ordered lives.

An inspection of the male juvenile quarters downstairs - palatial by contrast - provided the legislators with comparative facts for presentation to the proper authorities in the very near future. This facility in Charlestown - the only female D.Y.S. detention center in the state - must be dealt with; it must be improved, or new quarters found. We get to see another side of life on Beacon Hill, a side which does not touch the lives the people we ourselves have known...which is why we are there undoubtedly.

Wednesday's Constitutional Convention, a Joint Session of the Two Houses, was to house a number of interesting amendments concurrently assigned for consideration. A "Proposal for a Legislative Amendment to the Constitution to provide for mandatory capital punishment for certain crimes" was not to be taken up, but was to be deferred until a date late in June. A decision pending in the U.S. Supreme Court will have a bearing on the issue.

A proposal for a Legislative Amendment to "authorize the Commonwealth to take property for the beautification of highways" was voted; as was a proposal "increasing the time within which a proposed charter or charter revision shall be submitted to the city council of a city or the selectmen of a town," (from 10 to 18 months) and a proposal "relative to submitting certain information to voters;" AND "providing a four-year term for members of the House of Representatives and the Senate." (by one vote.)

Voted down was a proposal "providing for the election of judges of the supreme judicial court." The "CONCON" was adjourned at six-thirty or so, to be continued two weeks hence; an interesting and exciting afternoon lying behind us as we trouped from under the Golden Dome and headed homeward...Interesting and exciting as are all of our days on Beacon Hill.

JULY 18, 1976

The two week Recess of the Great and General Court will be ended by the time you read this column; and we shall be prepared to face on the morrow (July 19) those line items on the 1977 Budget which the Governor has seen fit to veto.

It has been a happy interlude, needless to say - with only intermittent days at the State House for tying up the loose ends your legislator was unable to handle from home - and, in the meantime, attending countless evening All Star baseball games for the purpose of cheering on three Braintree grandsons, all of whom had managed to make the All Star teams and were able thus to extend the Little League season sufficiently so that a busy grandmother might have the leisure to attend a few of those early evening games…And - NEED ONE SAY HOW PROUD WAS YOUR L. OF THE H. WHEN "METAYER'S MAURAUDERS" WON THE CHAMPIONSHIP??? And – SHE WAS ON HAND TO SEE THEM DO IT??? Much more satisfying than taking a vacation elsewhere, we decided, as we sat in Watson Park or Lakeside or the High School fields and watched our young people spending their time in a productive way while their parents and grandparents cheered them on…

But what a time to have a Recess, we thought happily, WITH THE TALL SHIPS COMING TO BOSTON, AND THE QUEEN OF ENGLAND VISITING HERE… And speaking of those TALL SHIPS, your L. of the H. was among the reportedly thirty-five members of the House and Senate who were invited aboard the "VIRGINIA C" by the Massachusetts Bay Yacht Clubs Association, Inc. to view the Tall Ships Parade in Boston Harbor on Saturday last.

The day was made to order, weather-wise, we had decided as, at eight o'clock on that exciting morning, we joined our other fortunate colleagues at Pier 1 of the Northern Avenue Bridge. We never did learn the criteria that was employed in our selections; nor did we ask; just congratulated ourselves on being present and sharing the happy experience with the House Speaker, Representative McGee, and our friends.

We had sailed merrily out into the harbor to a wonderful spot where the Tall Ships would pass majestically before us; and, amid much merriment had anchored and prepared to await their arrival. And-THEN THEY CAME!

How to describe the thrill of sighting the U.S.S. Constitution, the nation's oldest commission warship, dating back to the year 1794, we understand, as she sailed past us enroute to the harbor entrance, her masts rising toward the sky, the harbor tugs proudly speeding her on her way to greet her visiting tall friends of the sea…We had found ourselves snapping pictures ecstatically; especially when, leading the parade of ships into the harbor, we had watched her firing those antiquated guns of hers with all the zest of a modern destroyer.

Leading the parade of visitors was the "Dar Pomorza", a magnificent Polish square-rigger, 277 in length, her sails flung against a sky that housed just enough soft white clouds to form a special photographic background for this lovely lady among the Tall Ships who had been selected to be firstin line as the visitors rode the vessel past our port bow.

A number of lesser vessels and then came the second of the Tall Ships, the "Juan Sebastian de Elcano", a four masted topsail schooner from Spain, 304' in beautiful length, her sails stark against the New England sky, her country's flag flying above her.

The sight of the "Christian Radich" of Norway had brought its own special brand of delight for your L. of the H. because she had witnessed this magnificent 258' square-rigger in Oslo Harbor to greet the "Stella Maris" on its return from a trip around the Cape Horn! How well we were able to recall the bright blue day in Norway when we had watched the Stella Maris arrive; and waiting; and beheld the Norwegian cadets of the "Radich" pipe its sailors ashore and then serenade them with a program of sea chanties that floated out over the harbor and back again in a way one could never forget...

There were other Tall Ships, so many of them, to bring delight into the hearts of observers everywhere on that eventful Saturday morning. With what zest we found ourselves snapping the "Sagre", for instance, Purtugal's magnificent bark 293'-8" in length, each of her sails bearing the huge red Maltese crosses that will prove of delight to this camera fan's eyes, we are sure, when our films are developed at nearby Alves.

And - wonder of wonders, the "Sir Winston Churchill", a three-master topsail schooner, 135' in length, English as we might judge from the name - its all -GIRL crew standing at attention and strung along the yardarms and even at the topmast point upon the Main Skysail; silhouetted against the sails as gracefully as any figurehead we might ever have seen plowing its way upon a schooner's bow. Did your L. of the H. ever snap pictures of that one!!! That's where YOU'D be if you had the chance, Bibs," called colleague Jim Keefe; and we'd said "Amen" to that...

Can we possible fail to mention the "Black Pearl" a 70' American brigantine that stood out from the rest in sheer dark drama; or that lovely little Irish ship, the Bermuda ketch "Creidne"... "Hip, hip hooray," our happy little group had called as she sailed by; and Hip hip hooray" came back across the waves in answer. How merry it had all been that happy day, with the gulls and the helicopters circling each other in the soft summer sky; and the sun warm upon our faces in the open vessel; and those barks, schooners and brigantines sailing past us, echoes of another age not too long past; with a million people cheering and waving and exulting in the Bicentennial drama they were privileged to watch.

And it's all not over yet...Tomorrow is Thursday, and we'll be off again at dawn, this time to ride the "Bay State" our own Mass. Maritime Academy training ship, far out into the harbor to watch those Tall Ships sail away - homeward bound for the Plymouth, England port from which they first had sailed so many weeks ago.

What a spectacle, this coming of the Tall Ships to Boston! The words of the poet, John Masefield, in his wonderful "Sea Fever" had kept coming to mind. "I must go down to the sea again, to the lonely sea and the sky, And all I ask is a tall ship and a star to steer her by..." And now more memories...of the day when Ted and your L. of the H. had attended the funeral service of said John Masefield in London's Westminister Abbey, and had heard a Shakespearean actor recite that selfsame "Sea Fever" in that magnificent setting; and had then watched as the urn containing the ashes of England's poet laureate had been buried in the floor of the abbey, five feet from where the Metayers were seated. How wonderful are memories…And a lot of them were made the day the Tall Ships came to Boston!

JULY 25, 1976

Wednesday evening again; and another column deadline date is at hand for your legislator who has spent the evening sharing with those three remarkable grandsons of hers and their lovely mother forty absolutely beautiful slides of the incomparable Tall Ships as they paraded into Boston Harbor, the U.S.S. Constitution at their head, on Saturday the 10th of this historic Bicentennial month; your Lady of the House thrilling still to the sight of those magnificent barks and brigantines and schooners from the Age of Sail. "'Twas almost like being aboard the 'Virginia C' all over again"…This has been an eventful week to date. For one thing, the House voted to override twenty-one of the twenty-three-line items of the 1977 Budget the Governor had seen fit to veto – mostly because we were convinced that to eliminate funding in the areas proposed would merely bring about deficiencies which would have to be acted upon as the year neared its end; a situation which developed last year. The governor had defended his line item vetoes as necessary in order to balance a $15 million shortage in the Medicaid account. Our ways and Means Chairman, Representative John Finnegan stated his conviction that the money is there, and we believed him.

Line item vetoes in the areas of local aid for Chapter 70 and Chapter 766 appeared to be totally unacceptable to the members of the House; as did a veto which would have reduced the appropriation for the retarded in state schools, already threatened by virtue of their inadequacies, with the loss of federal funds. At any rate, the veto on only two of the Governor's items was sustained. The debate, incidentally, was long and intense; it was close to six o'clock when the House adjourned on Monday, the 19th.

Tuesday was to prove to be an especially interesting day for your L. of the H. for the first draft of some of the provisions of the long-awaited proposed Hospital Cost Control Bill was presented to the members of the Health Care Committee, with instructions to read and digest the admittedly rough drafts and prepare to deal with them in Executive sessions Monday and Tuesday of next week. Wish I might discuss the aspects of the proposal here in my column. We have been asked, however, we committee members to refrain from doing so until an official position is taken by the committee and since this is a Health Care Committee total plan for controlling hospital costs while maintaining high quality patient care, we willingly await committee action before sharing with a great many vitally interested individuals the legislation we propose to file in this critical area of cost control.

We had expected the Auto Insurance Bill to come our way this week; that is, a House-Senate conference committee version of the bill that is designed to overhaul the state's automobile insurance laws and come up with a workable merit system…a goal that has long been desired by those accident-free good drivers who have had to pay for the negligence of the poor drivers who have contributed to such an extent in sending Massachusetts automobile insurance rates soaring out of sight. The legislation would abolish no-fault insurance for property damage coverage's thank goodness; it would permit open competition in rating by insurance companies; and it would assess an insurance surcharge on those drivers found guilty of moving violations driving under the influence; operating to endanger, etc., the amount of the surcharge to be determined by the severity of the offense. The long sought auto body shop regulation provision was eliminated from the legislation by the conference committee, we learned, after its members were assured - or so we have been told - by Senate President Harrington that auto body shops are to be dealt with later this year by the Attorney General in a series of new rules and regulations to be promulgated by his Office. We trust the Senate President is right on this facet of the overall insurance problem. How do you feel about the proposed Auto Insurance Bill, my good constituents? To date, I have received only the kinds of letters that would support passage of the legislation as speedily as possible; these have come primarily from those in the insurance business. We welcome the comments of these knowledgeable individuals and hope they'll keep them coming as they read proposed changes and amendments in the local press.

Off-track betting is about to rear its head in the Great and General Court, we have just read; how do you feel about that? In my questionnaire of last year, it was voted on favorably by a very wide margin indeed.

Goodness, your L. of the H. has devoted lines and lines on the Parade of those Tall Ships to Boston without ever once mentioning a SECOND cruise we legislators were privileged to take out into Boston Harbor - this time to witness their departure from this historic place - a departure that would commence that last leg of that race that began in Plymouth, England, and is soon to end in that self-same place. We sailed away on the good ship "Bay State", the training ship of the Massachusetts Maritime Academy, on the day they were destined to leave. It's a wonderful old ship, this fine "Bay State". Once it was called "Empire State IV"; and once the "USNS Henry Gibbons". It was designed as a troopship, and delivered to the War Department in 1943, we were told. And from February of 1943 to December of 1945, she sailed the Atlantic and European Theatre of operations. The then "USNS Henry Gibbons" operated in the Mediterranean, the Atlantic and Pacific Theatres, making a total of 24 voyages and carrying around 3,000 troops and officers on each of the voyages. She subsequently carried home military dependents; then served as a "bride ship" and by 1951, 54 voyages had been completed by this rugged big ship that now serves as a training ship for our fine Massachusetts Maritime Academy, renamed - and hopefully for the last time - the "Bay State." The weather was not especially fair on the day the last remnants of the Tall Ships had left

Boston Harbor; but everything was sunny on that fine tall ship that was our own, with members of the General Court and members of the Academy Alumnae, their wives and children, sharing picture-taking and camaraderie, box lunches and cold drinks as the ship move gracefully along a slate grey sea, with a slate grey sky o'erhead, and a sea of ships of every size and description imaginable, spread out for all to see.

And so our Bicentennial observance celebration moves inexorably to a close; but hasn't it been fun every historic inch of the way???

AUGUST 15, 1976

Among the highlights of this week on Beacon Hill can be listed most certainly the happy experience of this Wednesday deadline evening - the observance of "Peter M. Kormann Day" in Braintree and in the State of Massachusetts - at which observance in a Testimonial Dinner tribute your Lady of the House was privileged to present to this outstanding young American a Resolution from the House of Representatives of the Great and General Court.

What a year to represent Braintree on Beacon Hill, I keep telling myself, as one historic event after another has its raison e'etre in this wonderful South Shore town of ours; and now to have numbered among my constituents the first American Olympic Medal winner in 44 years in Gymnastics…and the first American Olympic Medal winner in the history of the Olympics in the floor exercises that captured the coveted bronze…Truly, "my cup runneth over" to quote from You-Know-What. Braintree has had quite a history of first, you know. John Adams, for instance, was the first to draw up and have passed in our Town Meeting those historic "Braintree Resolutions" that led to the calling of the First Continental Congress and ultimately to freedom for this beautiful land of ours…And John Hancock, another Braintree-ite was the first governor of the Commonwealth…And General Sylvanus Thayer was the first one to recognize the importance of revitalizing our American Military Academy at West Point…And now here is our latest and perhaps most exciting first because we are here to share it -PETER M. KORMANN'S magnificent first at the XXI Olympiad in Montreal!

Truly as we witnessed the modesty and the poise of this Olympic medal winner who has brought such fame to the town we represent, our confidence in the younger generation - confidence we have never seemed to lose - soared to greater heights perhaps than ever before. Peter, the Olympic Medal winner, is an outstanding athlete; but Peter, the individual, is an outstanding and beautiful young man, the obvious product of a fine and stable family where faith in God and in one another has indeed born fruit. Peter M. Kormann, we salute you! And wish for you all the very choicest of life's blessing…A happy and productive and truly beautiful life.

So what else has happened on Beacon Hill since last we wrote??? Well, climaxing 18 months of consideration and negotiation, the Legislative Committee on Health Care has finally come to agreement on a bill to regulate and control hospital costs and charges throughout the Commonwealth.

The Bill is Senate Bill 1508, for those of you who are interested in securing a copy and it attempts to curtail the cost of health care to the consumer by the establishment of an 11-member Hospital Policy Review Board as well as a 21-member special commission to oversee and to make recommendations on the health care delivery system in the state.

The legislation is being supported by the state's major providers of health care, the Massachusetts Hospital Association; the Insurance Industry, including Blue Cross, the Rate Setting Commission, and Governor Dukakis, who was responsible for submitting the original legislation which was finally hammered out in a manner that could be acceptable to all parties concerned.

The new 11-member Hospital Policy review Board will have the authority and the power to review the promulgation of new rules governing hospital charges and rates as set by the Rate Setting Commission. The Board will have the authority to call a public hearing at the request of two board members who may then make public their reactions to the rates as set by the Rate Setting Commission.

Chapter 424 of the Acts of 1975, under which the health care delivery system has been operating, will be strengthened by authorizing the Rate Setting Commission to review and disapprove hospital budgets annually. Currently the Commission has the authority merely to review requested hospital rate increases.

The Health Care Committee is empowered to re-enter into the negotiation process between the Rate Setting Commission and the Mass. Hospital Associations, should an impasse occur in reaching agreement on proposed methodology for grouping hospitals and comparing hospital costs and charges, prior to the October 1, 1979, deadline.

A uniform cost reporting and cost allocation system would be set up to allow Rate Setting to ultimately approve any future hospital charges after a comparison of costs which would be made available to them via this uniform reporting system.

The Special Commission will include legislators, the Commissioners of Public Health and Insurance; the Rate Setting Commission Chairman; the Secretaries of Consumer Affairs and Elder Affairs; Health Maintenance Organizations; Mass. Hospital Association; the Mass. Medical Society; The Mass. Federation of Nursing Homes; the Mass. Nurses Association; the Associated Industries of Massachusetts; the General Public; the consumer and organized labor. This 21 member commission expires January 31, 1980, pending re-establishment by the General Court; and it may hold public hearing, conduct investigations and require the filing of any and all information that relates to any matter which affects the cost of all health related services.

The Commission may call witnesses and request documents, records and other papers; and it is authorized to make recommendations to the General court on any and all matters that pertain to the health care delivery system.

The Commission's charge is to "develop methods for constructing a system of uniform prospective rates for hospital services."

The Bill would eliminate Section 25A from the 1977 Fiscal Year Budget, which would have implemented a 30% decrease in doctor's fees for Medicaid patients; and in Section 27 would eliminate enforcement of a 7 per cent CAP on hospital nursing home increases; and Section 28, would eliminate the necessity of that second medical opinion by the Department of Public Welfare in all elective medical care; Section 32, which deals with the non-payment for administrating necessary days for Welfare patients. Your Lady of the House has grave reservations about those last provisions; And so she "reserved her right" instead of voting favorably for the bill- until such time as she is convinced that those concessions are vital to the acceptance of the legislation by the parties involved in the health care delivery system.

Included also in the proposed statute is an assessment formula, based on percentages which will provided the where with to finance the staffing and implementation of this 21 member Special Commission directive to conduct an on-going study of the entire health care delivery system within the commonwealth.

Hallelujah! We have the hospital cost control bill! We are not totally satisfied with all of its provision; however it is the very first time all segments of the industry have come together and hammered out acceptable means of controlling costs and any defects that surface along the way can be dealt with legislatively, for the Health Care Committee is in the picture to stay.

AUGUST 29, 1976

"Mrs. Metayer of Braintree then moved that as a mark of respect to the memory of Horace T. Cahill, former Speaker of the House, Massachusetts Lieutenant Governor and Superior Court Justice, the House adjourn and the motion prevailed…"

And thus for all time would the Journal of the House of Representatives of the great General Courts, for the 25th day of August, 1976, record the passing of another distinguished Braintree-ite…A most unique individual indeed, Judge Cahill; an outstanding member of the opposite political party to your Lady of the House, he would have, on each occasion, signed her nomination papers by way of greeting her and wishing her well.

Many years have passed since first I had the pleasure of meeting this brilliant superior court justice whose spouse was to be numbered among my very favorite people as time went by. I remember well, however, his quite gentle manner, the twinkle in his eye; the dry humor that could suddenly punctuate his conversation; the dearness of the judge whom all termed "stern but just…"

I grieved a bit as the realization swept over me that now for the third time in as many months "Mrs. Metayer of Braintree" has moved to have the House adjourn in memory of a friend…I never knew him as Speaker of the House, for that, I believe was 1937–1938, and it was 1947 before I first arrived in Braintree. I recall, however, Josephine, his marvelous wife and my friend, duly recounting reminiscences of Horace Cahill's days on Beacon Hill. Somehow I gathered the general impression that he loved the place almost as much as I do…

Wednesday, the House of Representatives recessed until after the Primary Election, so that those among our membership who have opposition, may be able to campaign. We've been far too busy to allow much time for campaigning, incidentally. And so we can only hope that those who have been responsive to their constituents and dedicated in their performance will be returned to office. Your lady of the House is keeping her fingers crossed as she storms Heaven on behalf of a rather large number of especially dear colleagues who are facing the trauma of an aggressive opponent while they are tied to their desks under a heavy schedule of essential constituent work. Never did realize how traumatic that experience can be, by the way; I find myself looking about the office and into the faces of those colleagues who have become warm friends - during the past two years; and wondering how we shall be able to adjust to an individual who has succeeded in defeating any one of them…And yet, this being a Democracy, a representative at any level has no alternative but to bow gracefully to the will of the people…Oh well, only a couple of weeks more to go….

It has been rather an interesting week as are all the weeks on Beacon Hill. It began last Friday afternoon when Ted and I accepted an invitation to ride to Rockport on the new variable-inclination multiple-unit electric train that is on loan to the M.B.T.A. from the Italian State Railways. A Fiat product, the M.B.T.A. is testing its performance, possibly with an eye to using this kind of train on our rail lines.

It's a lovely train, capable of traveling at speeds up to 82 miles per hour, we were told…only that aspect of its performance could not be tested, for from Beverly to Rockport the speed had to be held at 35 miles per hour owing to the poor condition of our railroad roadbed.

"We keep our European railbeds in good repair; in first class condition," said young Francesco Cordano, Management Assistant for Fiat, who is traveling with the train, and whom we found absolutely delightful to chat with. Ted and he began our relationship with a series of questions and answers about the engineering aspects of the train. It wasn't long, however, before we learned that Francesco Cordano is a native of Florence, our favorite Italian city; and was there in the midst of the disastrous 1966 flood that destroyed so much of the beauty of the place. We were there a few months later in 1967; and how exciting it was to exchange reminiscences of the ravaged cathedrals and museums and palaces, and to learn of the restoration attempts that have been completed and the damage that still remains.

"It is really the fault of the person who opened the dam above when the flood waters threatened to destroy it," he said, "without notifying those in the path of the torrents of water that followed. There was one flood at 2:00 A.M.; and another two hours or so later; and a third a couple of hours later; and the city was marooned…isolated…cut off completely until the Americans came with their wonderful equipment and helped to restore the city…" How many times have we heard that story repeated as we traveled across Europe, I thought… "the Americans came and helped…" Francesco's tales were marvelous, incidentally.…There was the story of a trainload of people who were totally marooned for more than a day when their train pulled into the station to be so submerged as to be unable to discharge its passengers or continue through the flooded area to high ground. The Americans helped in that area as well, said our young Italian friend.

The train itself is beautiful, we decided, Ted and I, after having taken the trip; and ridden in the cab with the engineer; and watched the roadbed rise to meet us; and chatted with friends; and sipped coffee and had fun. Only the price is prohibitive, we opined. $400,000 for the one in which we were riding. "Probably $450,000 or $475,000 by now, with inflation," to quote the M.B.T.A.'s Mila Dixon; "and, of course, they would have to be air conditioned; that would be more…"

Yes, the train is indeed beautiful, we thought; but half a million dollars per train??? No way, we fear…

So now we are in recess; but your Lady of the House will continue to be available; continue to be on hand…and she'll continue to hold Office Hours on Monday evening at Town Hall from 7:00 to 9:00. And she will want to hear from you if there's legislation in which you are interested; or a bill you wish filed next year; or any other area in which she has been able to serve you over these past two years.

And…Oh, yes…Thank you for having made that Registration Drive of mine such a success. Boby Bruynell, our own Town Clerk, tells me that Braintree has 913 additional voters as a result of this year's new registrations. That's welcome news indeed; for only by having a voice in the election of your government officials can you really have a voice in government…And what a role GOVERNMENT plays in the lives of all of us!

SEPTEMBER 26, 1976

On Monday of this past week, the House of Representatives met once again in full formal session, its temporary recess ended; and before the day was over, Prorogation Rules had been adopted and the stage set for what could conceivably be our very first experience at prorogation, we members of the Freshman Class of 1975; for last year we went from one year to the next without having prorogued at all. So what exactly does the adoption of Prorogation Rules imply???

Well, primarily it means that the normal procedural process for handling legislation is speeded up; bills will flow more quickly from the House to the Senate and vice versa;

and a sharp lookout must be kept by those among us whose bills languish in Ways and Means or elsewhere lest we suddenly find we have prorogued with no action taken and our bills defunct for the year 1976.

The Massachusetts legislative process is indeed a fascinating one. Our governmental structure had its beginning in the establishment of the Massachusetts Bay Colony as a commercial enterprise by the English, you know; and nine years after the Plymouth Colony was settled, a private English corporation was granted a charter under the name of the "Governor and Company of Massachusetts Bay in New England."

Quite obviously the charter was given with the idea of establishing a trading company here in the new world; and so in this year of 1629, the company was organized as a "corporate structure." It held four General Court sessions a year; and it annually elected a governor, a deputy-governor and a Board of Directors whose members were freemen or stockholders. They passed legislation for the governing of the colony. The General Court was moved from England to America; and John Winthrop, its governor, settled in Boston.

Actually the company's first General Court was held in 1630 here in Boston, with all members participating. It was shortly decided, however, to send instead to this General Court two representatives from each of the towns involved.

In 1644, an event occurred which led to the establishment of two branches of the legislature - the House and the Senate. A poor widow had lost her sow, and a wealthy shopkeeper had found and claimed the animal. A lower court decision having been made in favor of the shopkeeper, the widow appealed the decision to the General Court. Because there were more "freemen" than "assistants" on hand for the session, the poor widow won her appeal…and her sow…and out of this strange disagreement the two present branches of the legislature - the House and the Senate - emerged. From that day forward the two branches have deliberated separately, with concurrence of both houses essential for the adoption of a law.

In the year 1684, the charters of the Massachusetts Bay Colony and the Plymouth Colony were revoked: and it was not until seven years later that the two colonies were merged and the Province of Massachusetts Bay came into being. The new charter granted to this body removed its corporate structure, giving it a governing structure instead, with the governor, appointed by the crown, holding the power of veto…a power which our governor holds to this very day.

The Province of Massachusetts Bay was in existence from 1691 until 1774, at which time the, provincial charter ceased to exist. The province became an independent state which was governed by a provisional congress with no governor. The General Court then functioned as the executive administrative and legislative government of the province.

Actually from 1630 on, the General Court had been uninterruptedly passing laws and carrying on the business of Massachusetts. It is the oldest legislature in the country, you know; and incidentally our constitution, which is the oldest recorded constitution in its original form in the world, was drafted by Braintree's own John Adams in the year 1780.

Adams' proposal identified us as a "body politic, governed by certain laws for the common good." He proposed that the province be named the Commonwealth of Massachusetts. The word "commonwealth" stems from a group of reformers of the Cromwellian era in England who held the public good in high esteem. Massachusetts is one of four of our American Commonwealths incidentally; the remaining three being Virginia, Pennsylvania and Kentucky. With the adoption of the constitution in the year 1780, the General Court passed and changed laws year after year; and in the 1830's those laws were consolidated into a code, or the compilation general nature were put into a code which was called the Revised Statutes. of existing laws. A commission was appointed and by the year 1836, all laws of a permanent and periodic revisions or recodifications were made by special legislative commissions, in the year 1860, and in 1882, and in 1902, 1921 and 1932. All statutes of a permanent and general nature were placed in one collection or code, with the code classified by subject and given chapter numbers. The commissions had been charged with the task of examining and reassessing all of the statutes that had been passed by the legislature in the intervening years. These would be added to or removed from the code, or changed to remove extra verbiage or to restructure chapters.

The titles of the code changed from Revised Laws, to General Statutes, to Public Statutes, and finally to the present "General Laws of Massachusetts." The tercentenary edition of 1932 has been updated by two separate editions of these General Laws, editions that were published by commercial law book publishers, however, and not by the General Court. Another recodification is generally considered to be long overdue.

Well, so much for the historical aspects of the legislative process of our state. But how interesting to note that the General Court, now known as the "Great and General Court" can trace its origin all the way back to those early settlers who landed at Plymouth Rock and elected to stay here in the section of America we call our own…what a heritage is ours in Massachusetts.

OCTOBER 3, 1976

"Tis a busy busy place," this State House of ours. With a wild burst of energy and activity legislation is being rushed between the House and the Senate. The Committee on Bills in the Third Reading has accelerated an already fast pace to breakneck speed as it contends with the hundreds of bills that are stalemated there; and the Committee on Ways and Means girds to ward off the onslaught of legislator-hopefuls who still dream of getting their pet bill out of that overworked committee and on the floor of the House.

Much, needless to say, is therefore happening legislatively. We have dealt with some of the more difficult provisions of the current Lead Paint Law, for instance, exempting all single-family, owner-occupied homes from the provisions of the state's lead paint poisoning law. The current law would prevent the sale of our older homes to families with any children under six years of age unless the homes are lead paint free; or the lead painted areas are made inaccessible to small children. Inasmuch as most single family homes, (not only city apartments) whose age is 30 years or more, have lead paint on the interior surfaces; and since banks were refusing in many instances to give mortgages to prospective buyers of these older homes unless and until they had removed all lead paint from the home's interior; and since the cost of this paint removal is prohibitively high, unbelievable burdens were being placed upon buyer and seller alike as they strove to obey the lead paint poisoning law-frequently within a seven to ten day period.

Owners of these older homes are still required to notify prospective buyers of the possibility of the presence of the offensive lead paint, needless to say, but the single-family exemptions and the notifications provision were adopted as amendments to this new bill which was designed to relax some of the most difficult-to-live-with provisions of the very stringent lead paint poisoning law that was passed a year or two ago. The burden of removing lead paint from these older homes was lessened in the House-passed bill which still stipulates, however, that cracking, peeling, scaling or loose paint, plaster or any other similar material must be removed either by scraping, sanding or treating with a wire brush before being repainted; or else they must be covered. Any material which is not loose or cracking, scaling or peeling need not be removed unless it is on areas that may be readily chewed by the small fry.

The House also has passed a bill which would make it illegal for any employer to demand any portion or all of the tips that are given to employees serving food or beverages. Employers, however, may deduct business costs, workmen's compensation, and social security contributions and federal taxes from any service charges on credit card transactions.

All assistant district attorneys will be working full-time by 1979, according to another House-passed bill, with salaries set for the positions.

The House has, in addition, passed a bill establishing specific procedures pharmacists must follow in the setting up of a patient profile system, a bill necessitated by the claim that some patients are being supplied with contradictory medications.

One of the most widely supported bills to have received initial approval by the House this past week was one to exempt meals furnished to students both at public and private colleges from the eight percent meal tax which was passed last year.

The bill is directed, or course, toward those meals that are taken as part of a college room and board contract, we were told; and it would not include any meals served to a member of the public who happened to be at the college. This bill if enacted will be effective as of January 1, 1977. Without debate, the House gave its initial approval to legislation which would regulate the practice of acupuncture. This bill would require the Board of Registrations in Medicine, with the approval of the Department of Public Health and the Board of Registration of Dental Examiners, to establish rules and regulations for this relatively new science.

Most important of all, perhaps, was the legislation which would call for legislative review of all state agency rules and regulations. This bill, applicable to state agencies only and not to cities and towns, would require that any adopted or amended rule or regulation be submitted to the legislature for approval or disapproval. The legislature would be permitted to rule on whether or not the rules conform with the intent of laws that have been passed by them authorizing these rules and regulations. Existent rules and regulations will be reviewed within 60 days of the bill's being signed into law; with possible amendments reviewed annually from 1977 on.

On this particular piece of legislation, our Speaker of the House, the Honorable Thomas McGee, relinquished his place on the rostrum to go before the House membership to term the bill "vitally important." He assured us that the state's rules and regulations need straightening out; the members obviously agreed, to the tune of a 194 to 22 roll call vote. Incidentally, our House members gave close to final approval to a Senate-passed bill which would call for publication by the Secretary of State of a record of all existent rules and regulations of our state agencies. This record would be made available for purchase by the general public, which has apparently indicated an interest in such a publication and can utilize it to advantage.

We passed a bill that would create a board of pipefitter examiners; and this particular legislator is working to place before the House a Senate bill that would establish a board of registration of hearing aid dealers. It is only lately that I have learned of the lack of any formal education for the making of ear molds, a most vital component of our present hearing aids; and that there are not even minimal requirements for setting oneself up as a hearing aid dealer; nor is there any medium for disciplining a dealer whose quality of service is questionable. What a shock it was to learn of a case where a citizen, seeking advice from an ear mold specialist on the selection of a reputable hearing aid center, was told to LOOK IN THE BOSTON YELLOW PAGES AND TRY THEM ALL!

Well, a Senate Bill has been filed to create a board that would oversee this situation; and this particular legislator intends to work hard to get it to the Governor's desk for signing. Meanwhile we spend our days struggling to contend with the mound of bills that are as yet unpassed from the more than 11,000 pieces of legislation that have been filed this year. And we just might prorogue sometime in October, they're saying on Beacon Hill. I'll believe it when it happens.

We sure are busy!

OCTOBER 10, 1976

This has been a most momentous week on Beacon Hill for your Lady of the House, for we finally succeeded in getting a Hospital Cost Control Bill through our branch of the legislature. As a member of the Joint Committee on Health Care, I had labored with my colleagues through months of negotiations, testimony, evaluations, compromise and give-and-take, to bring about the kind of legislation that would constitute a first step in the containment of those hospital costs that have the citizens of Massachusetts in a stranglehold. The simple truth of today's health care situation is that the average citizen can't afford to get sick; can't afford the hospital bills that illness brings; and can't afford the cost of the kind of health insurance that will permit him or her to handle those hospital bills.

Well, we on the Health Care Committee have at last rounded the first corner in cost control- and it wasn't easy! For the first time in history we have been able to get all the state's major providers of health care together and in agreement - albeit reluctantly - with the initial provisions of House Bill 5414. H-5414 actually represents the ultimate in negotiations, to my way of thinking, for it was preceded by several other bills offered by our Health Care Committee; and it will mandate scrutiny of only those sections of the budget which hospitals have used to substantiate an application for a rate increase.

Hospital Costs HAD to be controlled; there's no doubt of that fact. A figure of $200 per day for 1977, with the possibility of further increases in the years beyond, has found every Massachusetts citizen living in mortal fear of illness; while the consequent uncontrolled medicaid costs imperil a state budget that absolutely cannot allow for additional tax increases.

So what, primarily, does House Bill 5414 do to control those soaring hospital costs which have been sending our good people into a decline and our Medicaid costs out of sight? Well, it gives the State Rate Setting Commission new controls over hospital budgets, as we have said; as well as the power to establish standards for the methods to be used for the grouping of hospitals, and the controlling of costs. In addition it gives to the Health Care Committee the authority to determine whether a third party arbitrator should be named to resolve any dispute that results in the determination of these hospital groupings or any other of the aspects of methodology that may arise.

The final House vote was 211 to 2, representing a significant win for both the Legislature and the Administration on this vital piece of legislation for the control of hospital costs.

Now it is Thursday, and the Senate having concurred, the Hospital Cost Control Bill is on its way to the Governor's desk for signing; and AMEN to that! To be sure it represents only the first step in control; the working out of the methodology will be a sticky wicket; but the recognition of the enormity of our cost problems by all those involved in the health care delivery system is a giant step in the right direction. It must carry us all forward!

There were other happenings on Beacon Hill this past week. Initial House approval was given to a bill which would permit the City of Boston to tax those commercial properties that have mushroomed during the past few years at Logan Airport - the hotels and gas stations and the like.

And Attorney General Francis X. Bellotti, at the request of the Senate, issued an advisory opinion to the effect that the state welfare department cannot spend money for medical assistance that is in excess of the appropriation for same. And initial House approval was given to legislation which would bar high school girls from participating on certain boys' contact sports teams, viz. football, basketball, ice hockey, wrestling, soccer and lacrosse. (An amendment would permit local school committees to sanction exceptions to this rule, however.)

And we checked on that House-passed bill to increase the drinking age from 18 to 19, to learn that the Senate has requested its Committee on Ways and Means to discharge it. It has been there since last spring.

Your L. of the H. has been personally involved in the fate of two Braintree bills in particular, both of which are of vital interest to this community she serves and both of which she was requested by the town to file. One bill would permit Braintree to place as a referendum question on the ballot the issue of whether or not to fluoridate the water supply. The warrant article that secured the local approval necessary for this step to be taken was placed on our town warrant last year by a group of concerned citizens who have steadfastly maintained that a previous referendum question on the issue was ambiguously phrased and so our Braintree citizens did not realize quite what was at stake. "Should the fluoridation of our water supply be CONTINUED?" townspeople were initially asked; and the vote was in the affirmative. It was afterwards maintained, however, that inasmuch as the water supply was NOT fluoridated at the time of the referendum question, it was misleading and our citizens were confused in their assessment of the effects of their vote.

The new referendum question will read, "Should the Board of Health be instructed to fluoridate the water supply?" or words to that effect. The House Committee on Bills in the Third Reading is currently in the process of re-phrasing the legislation so as to assure its legality; and I have been promised that it will come before the House for enactment on Tuesday next. I had succeeded in securing a favorable vote from our Health care Committee; and shall hopefully see it placed upon the Governor's desk before prorogation. A new vote upon this referendum question should satisfy those on both sides of this most-controversial issue; and settle the matter once and for all. My second problem bill is the one to free 360 square feet of M.D.C. land in the Blue Hills Reservation, so as to provide the footage necessary for the installation of a signalization system at the intersection of Wood Road and Route 37. You have been reading, I am certain, of the roadblocks that have been placed in our way on this issue. Rest assured, however, that knowing the vital importance of this signalization system to our community, I shall pursue it with dogged determination, leaving nothing undone to secure its passage. That bill also, House 445, will hopefully be on the Governor's desk before our legislative sessions end for this year on Beacon Hill.

Incidentally, the thought of prorogation is a rather exciting one. We have been in session for 21 straight months; ending the 1975 session at 10:45 P.M. on New Year's Eve, and heading straight into the 1976 session a couple of days later. And by the way, let me hasten to assure you that though I shall not be sitting in the House Chamber each day as is currently the case, I'll be available to you, my constituents, just as totally as though we had not prorogued at all. I'll still be on the other end of my State House phone or my home phone, waiting to be of help to you if help is needed.

OCTOBER 17, 1976

We are hurrying to prorogue in the House of Representatives - after 21 months of house sessions. Saturday would appear to be the target date as I write this column on Thursday morning; which means that by the time you read of this week's doings on Beacon Hill, we may be wending a weary way homeward on Sunday morning after the traditional all-night or longer ordeal of prorogation…Or, needless to say, we may still be there wrestling with the flood of bills that come one's way e'er the year's activities on Beacon Hill are brought to a thundering close…

Now, in the light of a number of recent phone calls regarding legislation that has been filed this past year by your Lady of the House, it would seem appropriate to explain to my constituents the relationship between a town's legislator and the town's various boards and departments.

When a town board or department has come to a decision on an issue which requires legislative action, the legislator is contacted and requested to file a bill which would bring that legislative action about. The request for legislative action must be accompanied by proof of local approval in order to receive the initial approval from the appropriate state committee that is really a requisite for getting a bill through the House. (An occasional OUGHT NOT TO PASS vote of the committee is overturned in the House; this is a rarity, however.) Once the bill has been filed - carrying the representative's name and the town board's approval - it becomes the responsibility of the representative to secure passage of the bill in the House and follow it all the way to the Governor's desk.

This same situation, needless to say, would prevail with any legislative action that is mandated by vote of the Town Meeting. All of which means that when you, my constituents, read in the local press that Representative Metayer filed a bill affecting the Town of Braintree, it does not mean that she herself has initiated the action. It means simply that she is carrying out one of the multiple duties of a public servant at any level of government; she is obeying the dictates of a particular town board or department, or of the Town Meeting itself.

There now, so much for the relationship between a town's legislator and the town itself, its boards and departments…

On the other hand, there are many bills which a legislator files of her own volition because she deems them necessary or helpful to her constituents, or to the people of her state. Falling within that category are the several bills I filed this past year, for the second consecutive year, to ease the burden for the property owners of our town, besieged as it is by the application of 100% valuation - a situation which I fought long and hard against before it became a fait accompli…

There is House Bill 429, for instance, which would have increased the real estate tax exemption of the elderly to the amount of six thousand dollars valuation or the sum of six hundred dollars, which ever would result in the abatement of the greater amount of tax due in a city or town which values real estate at one hundred per cent…

And House Bill 430, which would have brought about the same increase in real estate tax exemption for widows and children…And House Bill 431, which would have provided the same exemption from taxation on real estate owned by the handicapped and disabled… And House Bill 432, which would have provided a greater real estate tax abatement to veterans…And House Bill 433, which would have increased the income limits of elderly persons from six thousand dollars to seventy-five hundred dollars for a single person and eighty five hundred for a married couple applying for real estate tax relief.

So why have none of these absolutely critical bills passed the House??? Well, it seems that to apply these increased abatements only to those towns or cities who have gone to 100% valuation is UNCONSTITUTIONAL. Any increase in the amount of real estate tax abatement would have to apply to the entire state of Massachusetts, 100% valuation or otherwise; and the cost of such a program would be no less than 260 million dollars… Inasmuch as the state could not possibly come up with 260 million dollars, its present fiscal situation being what it is, the money would have to be raised through an additional TAX program. And I am certain that you, my constituents, know how futile it would be for any legislator to attempt to get another tax bill of that magnitude through the House of Representatives or anywhere else.

And so we continue to grieve for the people of our wonderful town who are currently facing the monumental real estate tax burdens they are being forced to carry by virtue of this 100% valuation nightmare. And we continue to exhort anyone unable to meet these real estate taxes to contact our Braintree Assessors and request all possible information on the varieties of tax relief that are available to them. There ARE some assists, of course; some of these assists are distasteful, needless to say…But in my humble opinion, any and all avenues should be explored by the elderly, the widows, the incapacitated and the veterans…By ANYONE in grave tax difficulties, before one's home is forced on a real estate market that could easily become glutted; and before one is forced to move from a community in which he has lived for many happy years.

I'll be filing those tax relief bills again next year, needless to say - in the hope that eventually something will be done constitutionally to bring about a more equitable real estate tax situation. And I am certain that the State's Joint Committee on taxation will be just as weary of hearing from me next year on the issue as they have become during the two years past. For all your sakes I keep hoping for a miracle, however the acceptance of the circuit breaker tax concept under which my bills would have to be placed, which would represent more of a miracle then even your optimistic legislator could hope to see come to pass, at least in the immediate future. Nonetheless, we'll continue to work hard, and to pray hard, for a solution to this real estate tax problem that has so many of the people I love laid low. And we are conferring with our Town Assessors on the possibility of a better approach to the problem.

And now we march steadily toward prorogation, we members of the Great and General Court…This does not mean that your Lady of the House will become unavailable to you. She'll be at home more, needless to say, but still covering her phone either from the office or from 33 Arthur Street. So - with the 1977 session lying ahead, don't forget that under the right of free petition she can file bills for YOU as well as for the Town of Braintree and for selected groups of constituents…And she can help to solve your problems if help is possible for you. She'll be on hand, serving you all the way as she has tried to serve you in the two years that will end officially one day this week.

And once again she thanks you for that special privilege - the privilege of rendering that service for the people of Braintree in the Great and General Court.

OCTOBER 24, 1976

It was a strange sort of prorogation so said the old timers on Beacon Hill. A couple of prorogation parties that we know of - one in a house committee room; and one at Republican headquarters…Can't speak for the Republicans affair, but the bi-partisan was, in my opinion, a singularly subdued bash…

Perhaps it was because we have been forced to come to grips with such a variety of problems in our state Capital during the term of office just ended…the twenty-one months of straight legislative sessions we've lived through…sobering problems that were decidedly difficult for legislators to attack responsibly.

At any rate, the relatively calm atmosphere appeared to be broken only by the steady traffic that went on between the House and the upper branch as representatives and senators worked together to bring their pet bills to final enactment before the Great and General Court prorogued.

Some of those "old timers" we have mentioned previously discussed the prorogation doings of other days and "Do you remember???" was the standard opener. We delighted in some of their tales, tall and amusing, needless to say…

There was a delightful interval of music as the Dublin Police Choir, a 50-man choral group attired in smart blue blazers invaded the Chamber for a concert. And a fun ending as Speaker McGee's voice thundered above all others in a stirring rendition of "God Bless America."

Dominating the day on a sad note however were the farewell speeches of those members of the Great and General Court who were spending their last day in the company of their legislative colleagues.

They came to the podium at the invitation of the House Speaker - the retiring and the defeated - to weep openly in turn as they bid farewell to the colleagues with whom they had served, some for a short time…and others for many years…

"Why are you retiring?" I had asked one of them, a committee chairman whom I have grown to know very well. "Well," said my friend Donald, "I feel that I MUST return to my family before it's too late. Did you know," he said, "that my baby is 19 years of age and I've never really had time to know her. I've been here 22 years. The long hours; the evening meeting and constituent demands; all the requirements of holding public office…I haven't had time for my family. I want to spend some time with them before the kids are all gone…"

That, I found, was the rationale behind most of the retirement decisions. Time for the family.…There were fun speeches, needless to say, by Representative George Keverian, the Majority Whip, whom many of you, my constituents, will remember from my last Reception. (His speech was hilarious!)

We felt he sort of saved the day for those of us who were moved to tears so frequently as our colleagues bid us farewell. Representative Keverian's unbelievably funny ad libbing never fails to send the House members into hilarity; and a spot of hilarity was surely needed to dispel the gloom that pervaded the Chamber that prorogation day.

"A paper from the Senate," the Speaker would announce; and we would settle down to hear that Ace of House Clerks, "Wally" Mills, intone the language of the latest piece of legislation to emerge from the Upper Chamber of the Great and General Court. Or "Report from Committee"; and we'd be brought to attention once again.

Meanwhile there was lobbying to be done on our most important bills; and telephone calls to be received in the lobby and dealt with in the office above. There was racing and chasing back and forth between the Senate and the House. And there was chagrin over a bill which just could not be freed from one deliberative body to the other; or rejoicing that some fortunate "rep" or senator had succeeded in getting his or her pet bill all the way to enactment before that Great and General Court should prorogue.

Well, prorogue we finally did, after a couple of all but all-night sessions in which actually not too many bills were permitted to see the legislative light. Many remained in the Committee on Ways and Means, their cost prohibitive and the fiscal situation of the Commonwealth too precarious - and we were glad they did - and many more remained in the Committees on Bills in the Third Reading…

Well, anyway, there's another legislative year ahead, we told ourselves quite philosophically, we legislators whose legislative efforts had not always been allowed to bear fruit, and perhaps next year the economy will improve, and those fiscal constraints we've placed on agencies and departments will bring about a healthier fiscal situation for poor dear Massachusetts; and we'll begin to see daylight; and we won't have to face the kinds of crises we've been forced to face in one area after another since the 1975 session commenced. But meanwhile, speaking of the next legislative session, please remember that under the right of free petition, any one of you may file a bill by simply making the request of your legislator. I've already received a few in response to my previous offer, but there's plenty of time for more. The deadline date for filing is the first Wednesday in December, but the sooner you get them to me the sooner I can get them to the House Counsel's office to put into legal language.

And meanwhile again, speaking of the legislative session just ended, may I thank you, my constituents, for all the communications I have received in regard to pending legislation; and for your generous involvement in the legislative process. Your Lady of the House is on Beacon Hill to represent YOU! She is YOUR voice; and only if your voice is heard can she truly represent you. So keep those letters and phone calls coming. Remember that government is a two-way street; and that in view of the enormous role government plays in the lives of all of us, it behooves us to keep that two-way street well traveled by the voters whose voice at the polls send their representatives to the General Court to do the kind of job they want done.

NOVEMBER 21, 1976

Prorogation would seem to be an ideal time for looking back over the legislative year 1976 and reviewing some of the major measures that were enacted during this decidedly problem-riddled session of the Great and General Court.

There was, for instance, an emergency measure to help cope with the continuing State fiscal crisis. Now Chapter 4 of the Acts of 1976, it provides for the restructuring of the State's short-term debt; and authorizes the conversion of much of the short-term debt into long-term bonds. It also establishes certain limits on additional short-term indebtedness. This new law has been described by Governor Dukakis as "an important first step toward solving the state's credit problem on a long term basis." Solving the state's credit problem on a long range basis had to be one of the most crucial issues facing your representatives on Beacon Hill.

There was legislation which became Chapter 64 of the Acts of 1976 and which provides retail gasoline dealers with certain legal rights in their dealings with suppliers. This legislation is designed to lessen the "life and death" hold major oil companies have on the service station owners by, for example, allowing station operators to set their own station hours; to accept or reject participation in premium, coupon or give-away schemes which usually cost the retailer money; and to provide more financial protection in terms of security deposits and a change in marketing agreement. Signed into law as well was legislation which allows optometrists to advertise the sale price of ophthalmic goods:

eyeglasses, contact lenses, frames. This consumer protection legislation became Chapter 91 of the Acts of 1976.

Chapter 121 protects Massachusetts corporations by providing a new set of regulations and standards governing the procedure by which an out-of-state concern could "take over" a Massachusetts-based corporation.

Chapter 150 creates a national cemetery within our state by permitting the transfer of 750 acres of state-owned land at Otis Air Force Base to the U.S. Government for use as a National Cemetery. Chapter 158 authorizes the Department of Public Works to take part in a 90 percent federally funded program to equip certain limited access highways with emergency communications equipment. We were particularly pleased with this legislation. There is a decidedly comfortable feeling about being on the road at night and glimpsing those emergency phones along the roadway a short distance apart - particularly for women traveling alone.

Chapter 192 requires the return to consumers of funds into their charge accounts in excess of the actual balance owed. It requires notification to the consumer of the existence of a balance in his favor, and imposes an 18 percent penalty for balances held beyond six months - Another consumer oriented bill!

Chapter 226 deals with the Solar Energy Research Site issue. It transfers the former Lyman School in Westborough to the control of the State Executive Office of Administration and Finance where it shall be held for possible transfer to the Federal Government as a site of the proposed Solar Energy Research Institute. This site involves 300 acres of land, and legislative action was taken in conjunction with the Solar Institute citing a proposal made on behalf of the six New England states by the New England Council.

Chapter 266, the Auto Insurance Reform Act repeals no-fault property damage coverage; creates a merit rating plan with bad drivers penalized and their surcharges going to reduce rates paid by safe drivers. It promotes competition in pricing by various insurance companies writing auto coverage in Massachusetts. We shall see how this competitive situation will affect our rates; the first figures appeared in the press this week and were eagerly absorbed by our insurers.

Chapter 298, the Anti-Arab Boycott prohibits Massachusetts companies from entering into agreements with Arab nations aimed at a boycott of Israel as a condition of doing business.

And Chapter 302, the School Building Assistance legislation provides for a continuation of the School Building Assistance program through which the State aids local communities. It also tightens fiscal controls over the program to stretch the effective use of each dollar; and sets up as well a priority schedule for approval of school projects based on immediacy and degree of need, with most critical projects given top ranking.

Chapter 303 provides for the use of District Court Judges to relieve the congestion in Superior Courts. And Chapter 304 provides for a 5 percent cost of living increase for retired state, county and municipal employees. And Chapter 327, relating to the merger of corporations, provides that unless corporate charters or bylaws provide otherwise, no two companies can merge without 51 percent approval of each class of stockholders of each company.

Chapter 347, a Dredging Disposal act, requires that the Department of Environmental Quality Engineering set up a permit system for the disposal of dredged material to prevent ecological damage to our coastal areas. And Chapter 369, the South Essex Ocean Sanctuary bill, zones the waters off the North Shore between Manchester and Lynn-Swampscott against commercial development.

There was, needless to say, much additional important legislation passed into law during the session just ended on Beacon Hill; and we shall pass these bills along to you in subsequent columns. Listing the Chapter numbers however, which incidentally came our way through the courtesy of Speaker McGee, will afford any of you who are interested in a specific law the opportunity to be able to identify that law, a copy of which may be obtained by writing to the Document Room at the State House, Boston 02133.

There now, a significant number of my readers have asked that I "dig out" and use again specific columns from my "Cabbages and Kings" days; and, since we shall not always be directing our remarks toward legislative matters in the next few weeks, I propose to do just that the moment I find time to wade through old clippings and old newspapers and come up with the columns requested. Meanwhile, my very dear readers, be patient…This is a very busy time indeed for your representative on Beacon Hill. We are in the process of preparing next year's legislation; and, by the way, for those of you who wish to file legislation under the right of free petition, unless you have your legislation couched in legal language it must be in the hands of our House Counsel's office by November 24. That's a deadline date that is fast approaching; so make haste… This representative, like Mr. Dickens' old friend Barkis (if that is how one spells his name); it's a few years since I perused that wonderful Dickens' work)…This representative-like Mr. Dickens' old friend Barkis (or is it Barcus??) is WILLIN'…Just give me a quick summary of what you want IN A LETTER, and I'll file the bill for you. And may I suggest that you bring the letter to my home just in case the post office delays the mail; it happens now and then and 'twould be too bad if you were too late for this very important legislative action…

DECEMBER 12, 1976

"It's getting to look a lot like Christmas" on Beacon Hill! The most beautiful Christmas tree imaginable is now gracing historic Doric Hall…I was made aware of its presence almost from the moment I entered the State House on Wednesday morning. Small bits and pieces of spruce still lay along the corridors, indicating the route the giant evergreen had taken in its trek toward Doric; and sending tantalizing wafts of Christmas fragrance through the halls of the historic place it was about to grace. I hastened to trace the source of it all…the twenty foot Colorado Blue Spruce caressed the handsome high dome of Doric Hall; and spread wide its arms to all but touch the central pillars of what is the original section of our State House building. Lights lay along its branches like great gleaming jewels; and Christmas ornaments were hung against the garlands of tinsel that draped the gigantic Christmas symbol from top to bottom. And - white paper snowflakes in intricate designs, along with strings of white paper dollies added a delightful touch to this Christmas symbol which will be viewed by hundreds of CHILDREN during the vacation season that lies ahead. The tree itself had been donated by the Massachusetts Christmas Tree Association, in cooperation with the Department of Environmental Management and the Massachusetts Farm Bureau, we were informed; and with the present fiscal situation within the commonwealth we were delighted to learn that fact.

"It's beautiful!" I said to the small knot of Doric Dames who were not at the moment occupied in taking our incessant stream of visitors on a tour of the State House, "Who made those pretty snowflakes and little string of paper dolls:" I asked. "I did," said Doric Dame Sylvia Stone. "Do you like them?" "I LOVE them," I said; "They add so much to the tree; and the kids will just love them."

"Well," she said, "a couple of lady visitors were terribly critical of our tree. They said the ornaments weren't hung evenly; and the tinsel was tarnished…I thought my small effort would add to it. And it's fun to cut out the snowflakes…No two of them alike and all that. And you know what they say about people who cut out strings of paper dolls; it's therapy in certain places we can name…" We laughed merrily. "If the tinsel is tarnished, I hadn't noticed it," I said; "and I think the ornaments look beautiful. Speak to some people of Jacob's ladder and they would ask HOW MANY STEPS…" I said with a laugh. At which point we began, for the hundredth time, we State House enthusiasts, to discuss the beauty and history of the place. "Do you know that this State House has an ATTIC just like any other house we know of????" said Sylvia. "It contains the most marvelous old pictures and memorabilia, and it's up on the fifth floor…Would you like to see it?" she asked, after I reacted in the precise manner one would expect of someone as dearly in love with our historic state Capitol as your L. of the H….

"Have you time right now?" Sylvia asked eagerly. "I'LL MAKE time," I said; a whole new vista of experience opening widely before me. And so it was off to the fifth floor of the State House. "You have to use the stairs because there is no way to take elevators to where the attic is located," said a young man who appeared to know whereof he spoke…

And so it was off up the grand central staircase from the second to the third floor; thence to the fourth floor and finally to the fifth floor where we were to arrive slightly winded and in a truly alien land.

"The door to the attic area is along the corridor," said my friend Sylvia confidently. It was; but it was LOCKED! We groaned. "Never mind," said my tour guide, "There's another door around the corner and further along," and we dashed merrily off for another hundred yards or so - TO FIND THE SECOND DOOR SECURELY LOCKED! "Gosh," I said disappointedly, "I had hoped to discover all sorts of marvelous treasures to share with my constituents via my column this coming week. Imagine the kinds of things that would be stored in the attic of a Capitol building that dates back to the eighteenth century..."

"Well," said my tour guide comfortingly, "They were working on this area; the doors won't always be locked. We'll come again. You try them now and then," I said, "And-if you find an open door, call me right away at the office and I'll dash up and join you," which is where we left this new potential State House venture that I trust will turn up all sorts of interesting things to share with you in future columns.

There is a more leisurely feeling about our State House activities these days. The Chamber, which I find myself visiting even briefly every two or three days, is even more impressive and beautiful in the quiet of idleness. I find myself contemplating the vast stretches of history that have been covered here in this historic place where the laws of the Commonwealth are turned out.

Good laws have been passed here; Massachusetts has a history of pathfinding, of leading the way...And bad laws have been passed here, the human element having to enter into all phases of government. Evil and corruption must have entered under the Golden Dome in the several centuries of its existence, I reflected with some regret... but the grand old Capital mansion has managed merely to grow more serene and calm, knowing full well it could outwait those who would corrupt it...lying securely as it does on the crown of a Beacon Hill that has become synonymous with Boston from one end of the world to the other.

So much for a legislator's thought on an in-between day under the Golden Dome. The bill-filing rush is over; the holiday season lies dead ahead; my constituents still have their problems which I try desperately to resolve for them; and we all march steadily toward Christmas, that favorite day of the year for most of us...How dearly I wish for all of you who have accorded me the privilege of representing you on "the Hill" the most heavenly and happy Christmas season you've ever known...

DECEMBER 19, 1976

"Let's have some of your 'Cabbages' again...the ones you wrote before you got to be Lady of the House...like the ones on Christmas and your grandchildren and not minding growing older..." We've been hearing this suggestion from a number of our readers, and so VOICI! Here's a "Cabbage" on the Christmas season, that wonderful time of year we're presently enjoying. It dates away back to December 8, 1963. Have I really been doing this little old column for all those years??? Guess I have!

Its title is "Christmas Memories." Christmastime is for remembering...for looking back...It's Christmastime again. December has arrived once more - that blessed month toward which all the other months of the year point like so many arrows. Yes, it's Christmastime again; and so we look back, and we remember....

Christmas was a wonderful day for children in our home. Every child found under the christmas tree exactly what she had asked of Santa. I smile to myself as I remember a long list of questionable articles he was committed by family tradition to bring…like knickers; and shiny rubber boots that came to the knee and enabled my sister Gladys and yours truly to wade through every puddle between our house and school; and short hair, styled by Jordan Marsh, when bobbed hair was just coming in and the mothers of correct young ladies were fighting it every inch of the way! ("You'll be sorry; mark my words, YOU'LL BE SORRY!!!" We weren't!) Oh, the wily ways of the young…Christmastime in our neighborhood (the Fellsway in Malden) was wonderful, too. There was something on every neighbor's tree for every neighbor's child - a red paper cornucopia stuffed with candy; or a chocolate Santa; or a candy cane. We'd go from house to house to "see the tree" and receive a Christmas treat.

Christmas Eve was the most fun of all. We'd bundle up against the cold and climb merrily into Dad's Hudson Super Six and head for Fitchburg. There'd be Mother and Dad, and "Gaga", the tiny gentle paternal grandmother who made her home with us; and all five of the chattering Nener children. Dad would have lit the nice long charcoal heater that kept our feet like toast in the back seat while the rest of our anatomy froze. We'd all rush to occupy the two small jump seats that were such fun (and Mother would referee the argument that always developed) and off we'd go. Dear Aunt Birdie lived in Fitchburg - Mother's oldest sister, with her great warm heart and incomparable graciousness. And, oh! Those wonderful Christmas eve journeys to her happy home. Invariably it would snow, and we'd sit fascinated as the gold of our headlights sent the tiny snow "fairies" (not flakes) as we imaginative children called them, scurrying into the black night.

We'd journey, and Fitchburg would lie before us, its Christmas lights flung like a great necklace of jewels against the black throat of night. Aunt Birdie's house at last-and out would pour the Neners, toting myriads of gaily wrapped gifts.

Grandmother Philips, our maternal grandmother, would be there; and she'd embrace "Gaga" and they'd disappear together into "Grandma's room" like two delighted schoolgirls. They'd been "best friends" in England long ago when they were children; and they were still "best friends." Dad and Uncle Harry would trim the fragrant big tree that filled the living room with magic. Oh, the joy of those Christmastime evenings, with Mother and Uncle Samuel at the piano, and Dad at the violin, and each of us saying our "Christmas piece" in turn (We all "took elocution", heaven help our audiences) or singing our Christmas song. There'd be a thousand candles on the tree, or so and spilling their gold profusely into the Christmas night…it seemed; real live candles of wax in a riot of color, fastened by small metal holders to the branches.

Other things I remember of Christmastime. Mother would term each of the little kindnesses we children performed during the Advent season a "a little piece of straw for the manger of the Christ Child, to keep Him warm against the winter snow." "How cold the little Christ Child will be on Christmas morning," she would say to us when we misbehaved…And how very hard we tried to make His manger warm…One thing more I remember - the Christmas plum pudding! It took a full day to bring life this bit of Christmas magic. There'd be piles of raisins; and piles of currants; and piles of muscats; there'd be lemon peel and citron and beef suet and spices; and there'd be our annual ceremony. Each one of us in turn, according to his age, would stir that fabulous Christmas pudding. "Gaga" would begin the ritual; and Dad and Mother would follow; and then the children down to the tiniest tot, into whose moist little palm Mother would place the great wooden spoon.

Wonderful, strange-sounding Gaelic words would issue from Mother's lips as each of us stirred the spicy mixture. She was saying an ancient Gaelic prayer, a bit of Gaelic from her Irish ancestors. Translated it would have read, "May the blessing of God descend upon our home this Christmas season and remain with us throughout the coming year…" Mother's plum pudding was always the highlight of the Christmas dinner. Dad would pour brandy over it, and Mother would tuck a sprig of real holly in its crown and then ignite it. I always fancied I saw a Christmas angel in the soft blue flame that sent the spicy fragrance of Mother's Christmas pudding through the house.

I remember other things as well - the big wax "holy candle" in the living room window. "We must light the way for the Christ Child," Mother would say; "we must let Him know there is room in our hearts and home for Him on Christmas morning."

Yes, Christmastime is for remembering, for looking back…way, way back…May the Christmas memories that I have made for those I love, my wonderful husband, and my own dear children, have the warmth and wonder, the beauty and the faith of those marvelous memories that are my own at Christmastime!

A happy and holy Christmas to each and every one of you, my wonderful readers… And may the blessing of God descent upon YOUR homes this Christmas season and remain with you all throughout the coming year…

DECEMBER 26, 1976

HAPPY NEW YEAR RESOLUTIONS to you! You're making a dozen or two, of course; I always do. The first step is naturally to convince yourself that you're anything less than perfect, and then it's easy!

I've been making New Year Resolutions for years, with interesting results. I recall vividly the year I solemnly resolved to be on time for all engagements with my dear husband – engagements where arrangements had been made to meet somewhere…Well, after two close calls at a couple of intersections, and half a nervous breakdown, I found my dear spouse begging me to return to my desultory ways.

And the year away back when the young Metayers were still in the bosom of their family, and I resolved to stay on a budget. "Casseroles???" they cried in chorus; "Hash???" Those recipes for such delicacies as "a MARVELOUS tuna casserole, red flannel hash and macaroni salad, so good and nourishing" to quote the neighbors, speedily found themselves relegated to the garbage heap along with their creations; while the food bill soared despite the New Year resolution on the budget situation.

And then there was the year I resolved to be quiet in company and let others do the talking. "Elizabeth," I told myself firmly, "it is high time you reformed. Be a good LISTENER this year instead of monopolizing the conversation as you normally do." The "new me" turned out to be a shock to the community. "Elizabeth just sat there disapproving," it was said of my debut. I received three fast telephone calls. "My dear," said my first caller, "you are doing too many things; you looked positively ILL this EVENING." "Are you bored with our program?" asked a second. "I know you didn't enjoy yourself a bit," said the third, "and I felt exactly the same way; That MARY..." It sure was a relief to toss that particular New Year resolution to the four winds...

One year I resolved not to look for the inevitable "wheels within wheels" on issues (to quote my good friend Mr. Dickens). Life was unutterably dull...And another year I would learn to say "No!" I would cease being active to the point of exhaustion in the 500 or so clubs and organization I belonged to at the time. I kept that resolution for a full year; and I did not renew it come January of the next - you may take my word for that when I found that just as my dear husband had predicted, the 500 or so organizations went along beautifully without me...

I've resolved at least a dozen times in as many years not to leave things until the very last minute; however I get my most creative thoughts at 2 A.M. of every due date. You wouldn't have me settle for anything less than my best in the interest of mere punctuality now, would you??? So...RESOLUTIONS I've made for the 1977:

1. Not to overload the electrical circuits in the house next Christmas with a thousand candles and stars and wonderful Christmas tree lights", thereby causing friend husband to clutch the fire insurance policy in one hand while he throws the electric switch with the other.

2. To start my Christmas shopping in July. (I promise I shan't buy everyone a bathing suit.)

3. Not to pray for snowstorms because they're so beautiful. (Husband is getting along in years; and snow shovelers are not as plentiful as they used to be, and I just MUST get to the State House every day, regardless of the weather...)

4. Not to boast about my grandchildren (even thought they are, without doubt, the five most remarkable children in existence.)

5. Not to prescribe a drug at the drop of a symptom. I, personally, will toss down any pill or powder on the recommendation of a friend, and it invariably comes as a bit of a shock when someone recoils from my own proffered aspirin or seventeen way cold tablet.

6. Not to be a chronic do-gooder. It can backfire. It did last week. It was one of those seemingly 40 below zero days on Tremont street in Boston, and a little

old lady was begging alms for the poor. She was a hundred! At least, she looked a hundred; but, come to think of it, so did I after the raw winter winds had pinched my face blue.

At any rate, the carolers were singing on Boston Common, and the little Christ Child's figure had warmed my heart, and the Christmas spirit was upon me 100%. I tossed a coin into her basket and then found myself saying kindly, "Would you like a nice warm cup of coffee?" The lady nodded absently. I was to realize later that it must have been an ABSENT nod; at the time, however, I was merely convinced that the dear soul was too touched by my kindness to speak. Brigham's was several blocks away, and I dashed merrily off in its direction. "May I have a cup of coffee to go?" I asked. I'll have my own cup later, I thought; I don't need it as much as that poor dear lady does. "To Go???" The clerk groaned as though the added burden of placing a cover on cardboard cup was more than she could bear, nonetheless the coffee finally came my way. I headed happily for the revolving door, only to have three teen-agers pour through it at the same time, squishing my little old carton, and all but squishing me. I looked wistfully back at the forbidding face of the coffee dispenser and decided against going back for another cup to replace the one that had sprung a leak and was to drip dolefully down the front of my coat from one end of Tremont street to the other, saturating my glove as it did so and turning the fingers that clutched it to ice. "Oh well," I told myself, "it's all for the sake of a little Christmas kindness," and finally there was the little old lady, her nose as red and her lips as blue as my own. "I'm sorry," I said as I handed her the carton, "Some of it got spilled; some boys raced through the revolving door as I was going through… "I never managed, however, to get to the end of the nice apologetic sentence I had prepared. The dear soul had snatched the coffee cup from my hand, raised it to her lips and then dashed the contents to the Tremont Street pavement. "It's COLD," she said petulantly. "Anyhow," she added, "you shouldn't have troubled yourself, I hate the stuff, NEVER DRINK IT!"

7. I've had a few additional resolutions for 1977. I resolve to be a little kinder, to invest enough of me to assure some merited measure of return; to extend the warm wide hand of friendship to those who need a friend; to find the sterling worth of just about all of the fine human beings I encounter; to live every day in this exciting world of ours as though it were my last; to stop frequently to count my blessing…to thank the loving Father of us all for a wonderful family in a wonderful home in a wonderful town, in a wonderful county, with personal "freedom from want and freedom from fear and freedom to work and freedom to pray"…And, so yes, - NOT TO BE SO LONG-WINDED in my columns next year.

8. HAPPY NEW YEAR everybody! And may health, happiness and prosperity be yours, every single wonderful one of you!

JANUARY 2, 1977

It's 1977! And the celebration of America's 200th Birthday is officially behind us. Wouldn't you like to be around in 2076 when this country of ours sets out to observe its Tricentennial, however?? Wonder what life will be like in Braintree as our 300th Birthday rolls around. And-speaking of life in Braintree our own Bicentennial observance ended with a bang a few days back…

"We're presenting a Yule gift to the Town Clerk in a final Bicentennial ceremony," said "Pat" Leonard, our town's most enthusiastic Bicentennial observance promoter, a week or so ago. "We're going to ride to Town Hall in my 1921 Buick, and present the town with a wrapped Christmas package reading 'Please Do Not Open Until December 2075.' It has been sealed to preserve its contents for the next 99 years. Will you wear your Bicentennial costume and ride with us? Mel Miller will wear his; and Otis Oakman will wear his; and I'm going to be dressed as Santa Claus and drive the car." "I'd LOVE to," I had replied (never did lose an opportunity to wear that little old hoop-skirted attire). "You do realize it will be an open car, and you'll freeze to death," said friend husband practically. "Yes, of course, but won't it be fun?" I had replied gaily. "Besides, it could turn out to be warm on Wednesday next…"

It wasn't. The temperature was around zero or less when that 'chill factor' we hear so much about was taken into consideration. Nonetheless, off we went to march to Pat's Parkside Circle home and the merriest experience ever.

"Oakie," as we know him, had already arrived and was admiring some marvelous slides of our host's exploits as I made my hoop-skirted entrance. "You'll freeze," said Rosanna, Pat's darling wife.

"You'll have to use a buffalo robe; and I've a nice warm raccoon coat that has been in the family since the twenties. You'll need everything we own to keep warm today. I know," she added, "I've had to use the buffalo robe in July. That car's cold."

Mel was to arrive next, handsome indeed in his Bicentennial costume, but showing at least four inches of exposed calf where the Bicentennial stockings failed to reach the Bicentennial breeches. "I'm the one who'll freeze," he said. Nonetheless, we were off-down the driveway and along the main streets of Braintree, amid a whirl of skirts and robes of fur and feathers, waving merrily as we rode to the cars whose horns blew happily on all sides, and to the younger generation who were braving the cold to convene on the sidewalks.

"husbands and wives will decide it was SOME OFFICE PARTY when their mates arrive home to report the sight of Santa Claus driving a party of colonists in his 1921 Buick," we told one another gaily. "If we wind up at good old Mortimer Peck's from a case of pneumonia, they'll have to add a postscript to that little old Bicentennial package," we decided. It will read: "Greater love hath no man or woman than that they should give up their lives for their town's Bicentennial."

The Candid Idylls of a State Representative

"Thank heavens the hunting season is over," I was to observe from beneath a sea of fur, "I'd be a gonner for sure."

Town Hall at last, and it was out of the buick and into that historic place for the final ceremony. The box was to be presented to Town Clerk Robert N. Bruynell beside a lighted Christmas tree in the Selectmen's office. It would contain instructions for the Town Clerk of 2076 on the opening of the marvelous time capsule that had been placed on the Town Hall grounds the previous July 4, as well as an iron cylinder containing the capsule inventory and precise directions on the opening of that Bicentennial time capsule which contains a vivid and precise description of life in Braintree as it is lived today. Mr. Leonard had proudly pointed out the "gypsy lock" on the box itself, and the code for opening it. "there isn't a nail or any other kind of fastener that you can see, he had said proudly.

The Box contains a trowel that was used by Mason Frank Deluca (on hand for the occasion), in the building of the Cairn; newspaper accounts of the time capsule dedication; correspondence relative to the dedication ceremony; a book written by Patrick J. Leonard, Jr.; Mrs. Bryce M. Lockwood's notes on the patriotic dedication song (the words for which had been written by our own Observer-Forum editor, Rosemary Newman); Armen Milton's music; a copy of Town Clerk Bruynell's remarks; and the original handwritten copy of your Lady of the House's dedication speech. (Have we said before how absolutely great it has been to represent historic Braintree in the Great and General Court during this Bicentennial year?)

Altogether it was a fun time, and as we rode back through the town at the end of the ceremony, with the car horns blowing and our "Merry Christmases" ringing on the air (and rigor mortis setting in about our persons), we decided again and again that those who extend themselves in the community…who "do things"…have the most fun, and sure do get the most out of life.

This Bicentennial year has certainly been a memorable one for every American. It can be over done, needless to say however. We laugh merrily as we recall having read a letter to dear old Ann Landers on the subject when the Bicentennial merriment was at its height…a letter of complaint about the "lunatics who live across the street" and "have made our neighborhood the laughing stock of the town." It seems they "painted their house red, white and blue; five flagpoles in the front yard fly Old Glory from dawn till dusk," and three papier mache figures adorn the lawn. There's Betsy Ross, sewing the flag; Washington crossing the Delaware, and John Hancock signing the Declaration of Independence. Lights flash the cheery message "Happy Birthday U.S.A." and a public address system blasts the "Battle Hymn of the Republic," the National Anthem and "God Bless America." Besides which, the "nut' who owns the house mows his lawn, it seems, while wearing a fake beard and a tricorner hat.

There now, and you thought that Mr. Oakman, Mr. Miller and your State Rep. were carrying patriotism to the extreme when they joined Santa Claus in his 1921 Buick touring car trek to Town Hall when it was a mere ten above zero, didn't you???

JANUARY 9, 1977

What fun we have been having over last week's column...Almost as much fun as the event that precipitated it - that bicentennial ride in an open 1921 touring car on a deep-freeze December Day in a bicentennial costume with Santa Claus at the wheel! (not of the costume...of the car!

You will all hopefully recall the fact that our own inimitable "Pat" Leonard was the Santa Claus in question; that our own inimitable "Oakie" Oakman was one of the appropriately garbed colonists (to wit: COLONEL Ebenezer Thayer...) as was your Lady of the House; and that the third Colonist "Mel" Miller, having donned a costume that had never been intended for a colonist, six foot two or so in height, was showing a shivering expanse of calf as he waved to the amazed spectators we were encountering along the line of march from Parkside Circle to Braintree Town Hall.

At any rate, fun it all was; and the fun continues to come our way...like the fun note we received from that same "Mel" Miller one day this week. "Dear Mrs. Metayer," it read, "this is to inform you that the dignity of your office is Not enhanced by your riding around in 1921 open touring cars with the temperature hovering near the zero mark. As my Representative in the Great and General Court, I expect your conduct to reflect the solemnity of your office; and you not to engage in the levity reflected in the actions of your constituents.

Furthermore you may be interested to know that my Attorney has instigated suit against one Patrick J. Leonard, charging this individual with deliberately inducing a severe case of frostbite on the lower limbs of one Melvin V. Miller, by insisting that this same Mr. Miller ride in scant Colonial attire in this same open car while the other occupants were either bundled up in Buffalo robes or dressed as Santa Claus and well able to withstand the rigors of the North Pole.

The fact that Mr. Miller doesn't have sense enough to say NO to these crazy ideas, has no bearing on this case. When it is obvious that an individual has lost control of his faculties, then it is incumbent on his peers to protect him from his folly. Since you encouraged and applauded this incident, with no attempt to prevent the terrible discomfort suffered by the plaintiff, then it is likely that you will be charged as an accomplice in this very serious case.

The moral of this story is, - Grandmothers do not do these things.

(Oops, I just remembered, GRANDFATHERS also should have more sense.)" The letter was Signed "Mel"...Mel, that intrepid third colonist and fourth member of the happy nuts who brought Braintree's Bicentennial celebration to a Christmas close which must, in any man's language, have been termed a MEMORABLE ONE.

Oh yes, this same "Mel" Miller, in a second little missive, penned along with the above, signed himself, "Mel Miller, Chairman 2076 Committee." Do you suppose he is planning to be around when that little old Time Capsule that graces our town hall lawn is OPENED??? If so, I warn him - Buffalo robe or no buffalo robe - I shan't take a second ride in that 1921 Buick! At least not on December 23 or whatever the date happened to have been…So many events are happening these days in connection with the exciting holiday season that it's difficult to keep such mundane things as DATES straight!

It is Wednesday evening as I write this column; and today, in a colorful ceremonial, we members of the House of Representatives were sworn into office once again; our families tucked proudly into the gallery and the chamber aisles…our "Happy New Years" echoing and re-echoing around the historic Chamber interior…our hearts warm and our hopes high as we begin another session of the Great and General Court. Our Speaker, the Honorable Thomas W. McGee, was overwhelmingly elected to lead us through the difficult year that lies ahead. His acceptance speech was warm and human and completely typical; the sincerity and dedication…and the intense love of HIS House and of all that it represents in government "of, by and for THE PEOPLE of the Commonwealth," and the loyalty of HIS House members clearly manifested in the shining through his every word, sustained applause that punctuated his remarks. Speaker McGee has, in the opinion of the majority of his colleagues and those close to things on Beacon Hill, restored to a remarkable degree the dignity and the prestige of the House of Representatives; and in so doing has managed to develop a rapport with his House members that is a joy to note. Incidentally, a couple of our Speaker's remarks deserve repetition. He was elected WITHOUT HAVING ASKED HIS MEMBERS TO SIGN A PLEDGE CARD! This decision of Speaker McGee's applied not only to his veteran but to his NEW House members; and he was proud of it! We trust the members of the Fourth Estate will note that very important fact in their newspaper coverage of today's events on Beacon Hill by the way. And a second statement of sufficient importance to merit repetition. HIS DOOR IS ALWAYS OPEN FIRST AND FOREMOST TO HIS HOUSE MEMBERS! We can personally attest to both of these facts. "If you can't see me at noon, come back," he said. "Come back as late as seven or eight o'clock; I'll be there!" We can attest to that fact as well. Speaker McGee is THERE! Methinks he's there twenty-four hours a day.

Well, at any rate, another session of the Great and General Court lies dead ahead. What will it bring, we wondered this morning as we looked about at our colleagues across the broad aisle of the House Chamber? What decisions shall we have to make? What crises shall we have to face? May those decisions be the right ones for the constituents we love and for the people of the Commonwealth…May those crises be handled in a way that is most equitable and fair for all of us…And may the good Lord stay close to the individuals our Massachusetts citizens have sent to Beacon Hill to represent them; we shall need HIS divine guidance…and your prayers…For I assure you - WE CARE!

JANUARY 16, 1977

"Admit His Excellency, Michael S. Dukakis, Governor of the Commonwealth," the Senate President intoned in a Joint Session of the House and Senate; and we were about to hear Our Chief Executive's "State of the State" Message. It was Wednesday morning' and the House Chamber was crowded to capacity. The galleries were filled. The 1977 session of the Great and General Court was...after a storm-occasioned delay or two - about to truly begin!

The Governor would begin by stating that the past two years had housed "The worst financial storm in the modern history of the Commonwealth." And pledging to make the next two "productive ones for Massachusetts, 1976," he said "saw a strengthening of our fiscal stability, a restoration of confidence in our economy and major improvements in the day-to-day operation of State government." Stating that we can "no longer merely grow and spend," he called for a "new creativity - a willingness to explore new and more imaginative ways to improve the quality of life of our people without massive new spending programs.'

Governor Dukakis would review the legislative accomplishments of the past year... auto insurance reform; hospital cost control; reorganization and consumer-orientation of the Department of Public Utilities; transformation of the Alcoholic Beverages Control Commission...Expanded and improved services for the mentally retarded, the mentally ill, disturbed adolescents and children. He pledged a goal of "jobs for those who need them...men and women who are looking for work, ready to work, able to work, are ENTITLED to work." "70,000 more people in the Commonwealth are working today than in January of 1975," the Governor stated.

He promised some measure of property tax relief... "A major effort to help local communities stabilize property tax increases. I am proposing a program to increase state assistance to localities and to limit expenditures imposed on local communities," he stated. Pointing to the fact that not a single bill mandating new programs for our cities and towns without providing the money to pay for them had been signed into law during the past two years, Governor Dukakis said, "The legislative leadership and I are agreed that we will not mandate additional financial responsibilities on the cities and towns without the money to pay for them." AMEN to that, we legislators say... He promised to push for Judicial Reform. "The courts of the Commonwealth today are paralyzed," he said. "People have to wait three, four, even five years for their civil cases to be heard in Superior Court. Prompt trial is guaranteed by our Constitution. Violent crimes which could be prevented happen because of intolerable delays between arrest and trial. Criminals who should be behind bars are on the street because the courts cannot schedule their trials," he said. "Democracy is rooted in the principle of justice, and today in Massachusetts justice is denied every day, every hour, in every court in the state."

On the whole, the Governor's "State of the State" message was well received. It reflected in our opinion, the concerns we legislators have been expressing over the past two years; and the concerns which our Democratic leadership have expressed repeatedly. We look forward to what could turn out to be a most productive year on Beacon Hill.

And now, in response to the request of a number of you, your L. of the H. looks back upon her "Cabbages and Kings" days to a column she wrote upon being invited, at age fifty, to become a weekly columnist for what was then "The Sunday News." It expresses her tried and true philosophy that in life every decade gets better. We quote:

"I shall hate it when I'm fifty!
I was barely twenty-two
And the world was wide with wonder,
and the sky was cobalt blue
While ahead life stretched before me
like a roadway strewn with flowers…
Oh, the blessed, breathless beauty
of those twenty-twoish hours!
I shall hate it being fifty!
I shall love my life no more,
To be FIFTY-HALF A HUNDRED-
What a dreadful, dreadful bore!

I'll just hate it when I'm fifty;
I was almost thirty-eight.
And my roots were firm and fastened;
And my children, tall and straight,
Brought their magic to my moments,
And their glory to my days.
Oh, the wise sophistication of
my thirty-eight-ish ways!
I shall hate it being fifty;
life is fleeing far too fast.
Let me cling, please, to my thirties;
let me make their magic last!
How I'll hate it when I'm fifty.
I was nearly forty-three
And my children planned quite gaily
to go sailing off from me,
And I watched with apprehension while
they blithely marched toward life;
While my daughter sought a husband,
and my son brought home a wife.
Oh, how lonely and how empty

now my days were doomed to be.
How I faced with trepidation
thoughts of being drab fifty!

How I LOVE IT, being fifty;
here I'm nearly fifty-one,
And, my children nicely married,
all my days I fill with FUN!
I may spend their golden hours
in a spree of pure delight;
With a pen beguile the morning;
with a book beguile the night.
I could maybe RUN FOR OFFICE..
plan a gift shop...write a book...
I could give this great wide world
of ours another brand new look!
Why, I LOVE it, being fifty;
I face SIXTY with a zest,
For the years that follow fifty
are decidedly the best!"

The nicest thing about life as I see it is the fact that each decade of living is an exciting prelude to the next. At twenty-two I wouldn't have had the depth, the insight to write "Cabbages and Kings"; at thirty eight, I wouldn't have had the time; at forty-three, I might not have had the interest; but at FIFTY- what FUN! Here's to being Fifty....

P.S. At sixty, life is even more fun! And have you ever noticed what a ball a group of senior citizens have when they get together. Take it from your Lady of the House, you may not quite believe it, but every decade does get better...I'm looking forward to the seventies!

JANUARY 30, 1977

All but lifted is the pall that descended over the State House last Monday morning with the news that the Speaker of the House, the Hon. Thomas W. McGee, lay critically injured at Mass. General Hospital after a skiing accident. He is out of the Intensive Care Unit as of today, Thursday; and with good luck and a lot of prayer he may be back with us within three or four weeks. Hallelujah!

The week has been a rather hectic one for this legislator. Our Transportation Committee Hearing began on Wednesday morning, with much attention focused on a number of bills that would mandate police protection at all M.B.T.A. stations. The present M.B.T.A. police force of 61 officers who must cover three shifts makes this mandate impossible to carry out, and the Authority has been requested to come up with information as to the present station coverage and projections for future increase in the law enforcement's staff. Fear of the criminal element that haunts the underground stations particularly has cut sharply into M.B.T.A. revenue, it is claimed...Our public hearings are followed immediately by the executive board hearing at which the vote of the committee is taken. We find this procedure to be an efficient and satisfactory one, since the testimony on the legislation is fresh in our minds as we consider its fate.

Today, Thursday, was a particularly hectic but interesting day for our Committee members. As chairman of the sub-committee on the Port Authority, I had responded eagerly to Massport's invitation to board its fireboat and inspect present and hear discussed proposed port facilities within our wonderful Boston Harbor. The morning cold gripped on, and the winds from the water all but swept us out to sea as we crossed a suspended sort of gangplank leading from the airport to the craft which nevertheless sped over the decidedly "choppy" sea, Captain W. Jeffrey at the helm, beautifully and smoothly. It's a marvelous fireboat, 83' long, with a capacity of 6,000 gallons at 150 lbs pressure. Set up as a communications center, it is available for rendering mutual aid for 23 communities, and is tied as well to the Aircraft Tower, the State Police and the Boston Police.

We were to inspect first the Castle Island facility, which is being operated under a long-term lease by Sea-Land, but can accommodate only a low profile crane for container handling by virtue of its location in the airport's runway area, and the fact that the island's structure could bring about problems if a crane, we learned, cannot handle containers weighing more than 27.5 tons. Moran Pier, we were told, is operating well above it capacity, with a resultant use of the expensive overtime that cuts significantly into its profit.

The place to develop the Seaport of Boston is the South Boston Naval Annex, Port Director David Davis told us. It has two dry-docks; is close to the transportation network; and Massport is cooperating with the city of Boston in planning to build a new access road to the facility. It has deep water; several cranes; a hinterland for boxes; it could have Roll on Roll off facilities, and Container facilities. It is surplused by the Navy, is technically under the supervision of the General Services Administration, and is technically being purchased by the Land Bank for the City of Boston. Air approach presents no problem, and the sea passenger trade could be accommodated at Commonwealth and the Fish Piers, we were told.

The Mystic Pier, with its two larger and higher cranes capable of lifting 46 tons and 70 tons respectively and moving from hold to hold on a ship, was extremely interesting to view. Incidentally - there have been no labor problems in Boston during the past 18 months, "a record for eastern ports, we were told. I found the inspection of our harbor marvelously interesting; and incidentally, interesting as well is the book I'm reading on the subject. It's called "Seaport Dynamics" and your legislator buried her nose in it until 2 A.M. this morning…

There is so much to be learned, however, about our exciting new assignment.

Home on the double and it was to be off to the Norfolk County Agricultural School at five o'clock for a tour of that splendid facility for that is what it turned out to be - a splendid facility…Now here we are at the typewriter madly racing to meet the early morning deadline at our own Observer-Forum.

Oh yes, we include in this week's column a third of your requests from those "Cabbages and Kings" days we've left behind us. It is called "LET IT BE SAID," and we quote:

Let it be said of me that laughter came quite freely to my lips;
That tears quite seldom found a pathway to my eyes;
That when I face the dying of a day,
And knelt beside my bedside for to pray,
I found with joy that with the setting sun
I counted one more kindness freely done.
Let it be said of me that ALWAYS I was kind;
And seldom cries of rancor left behind;
That for my fellow man I truly cared;
That those I loved were many and diverse;
That other considerations than my purse
Directed all the spending of my gold;
That to my neighbors' wants I was not cold…
Let it be said of me that I stood firm and strong
When Life's grey problems came my way along;
That every single day I smiled at life
And at the gentle man with whom, as wife
I shared much more of laughter than of tears
As, side by side, we marched down all the years…
Let it be said as Mother I was fond;
That time has served to strengthen that dear bond;
That grandsons look my way with love and joy
As I have loved their coming, each sweet boy…
Then - most importantly - let it be said of me
I walked serenely toward Eternity,
For then as woman, mother and as wife
Shall I have earned the beauty of my life.

FEBRUARY 27, 1977

Another hectic week on Beacon Hill. We obviously could ill afford the luxury of that Washington's Birthday holiday on Monday. The remainder of the week to date has passed in a mad dash to catch up on a caseload that, though marvelously interesting has been a crushing one indeed.

And speaking of that Washington's Birthday holiday, it was celebrated nicely on Tuesday morning under the Golden Dome where an overflow crowd filled historic Doric hall to hear – whom do you think??? Braintree's own Commander Otis B. Oakman, Jr. as the occasion's featured speaker! His address was a tribute indeed to the Father of our Country; we expected that; it was also a tribute to three outstanding Massachusetts citizens…(we're amazed that one of them wasn't a Braintree-ite!)George Washington, "Oakie" told his audience in his own inimitable and fascinating manner, had five great qualities. He had an innate ability to inspire us; he was impeccably honest and truthful; he was staunch in adversity; he could stand up to a tough situation and live it through. "Even the British Army admitted that he was the most capable military leader of his day, not only in America but in Europe," Commander Oakman told his audience. "and" - he added, "He had a perceptive judgment of character."

To prove this last point, our speaker informed his audience that three of Washington's greatest generals were born, lived and died in Massachusetts. Commander Oakman then proceeded to review the exploits of Massachusetts' own Henry Knox, "who learned everything he knew about artillery from a book" and performed such a feat of heroism in moving those vital cannon from Fort Ticonderoga to Boston; and General John Glover" of the Codfish Aristocracy" who saved the Continental Army at the Battle of Long Island; and General Benjamin Lincoln of Hingham, who was permitted by General Washington to accept the sword of surrender from Cornwallis "because he had previously surrendered HIS sword to a British General" in the routs at Savannah, Georgia and Charleston, South Carolina."

Our own Braintree-ite was, needless to say, a hit…and how proud was this representative to be standing in the audience (all seats having been speedily occupied) as Commander Oakman brought to life the hero of the occasion, the great American whose birthday we were there to observe. Proud also were the four Braintree Cub Scouts from Den 3, Pack 24 - Robbie McLean, John Hauber, Ralph Thibodeau and Timmy Skinner who, with their Den Mother, Mrs. McLean and her assistant, Mrs. Hauber, happened to be visiting the State House on that particular morning and so to be on hand to participate in the Commonwealth's holiday observance. And, incidentally, speaking of those four young Cub Scouts, there should have been five. Brian Foley was forced to miss the exciting visit, his mother having unhappily been rushed off to the hospital with an attack of appendicitis a day or two before. The boys really had a ball, by the way. There being so few of them we were able to arrange not only a tour of the State House and a visit to the Chamber, but a chat with the Governor as well- AND the fun of being photographed in that great tall chair they've seen so many times on T.V. when His Excellency ceremoniously signed historic pieces of legislation in the Council Chambers! "Is that because he's kind of like a king?" one of the Boys had asked, commenting on the high backed chair that dominates the center of the Chamber. "Well not really," we had laughed, but we're certain the boys felt almost royal as they ensconced themselves, two at a time, for the waiting photographer, Governor Dukakis standing happily at their side. Special Town Meeting on Tuesday evening at East Junior High School, and the day was to end as it began, in a flurry of excitement. Life has not been all fun and games this week under the Golden Dome however. Today, Wednesday, for instance, one could have used a twin or even a couple of triplets to cover all bases that had to be covered as the day progressed. Our Transportation committee hearings commenced at 10:30 A.M., for instance; and our Health Care Committee hearing at 11:00. (These were to go on from 11:00 to goodness knows when- having a meeting for 7:30 this evening, this committee member was forced to leave Gardner Auditorium at 5:45; the hearings were still going on...) Meanwhile, also at 11:00 before the Committee on Taxation, six of my own bills were being heard and would have to be defended. There was H-379, which attempts to increase the abatement of taxes on the real property of certain widows and children. And H-380, which seeks to increase the real estate tax exemption of those seventy years of age or over; and H-381 which attempts to increase the income limits of certain elderly persons for the purposes of determining eligibility for a real estate tax abatement; and H-382, which would increase the real estate tax abatement for disabled veterans; and H-383, which seeks to do the same for persons totally and permanently incapacitated for work; and H4690, a bill which was phrased at my request by an Assessor of the Town of Braintree, and which seeks to increase the whole estate which certain individuals may have to qualify for a real estate tax exemption. Some of the above bills seek to have the increased abatement amounts apply only to those communities that have gone to 100% valuation, with other communities remaining static. Some do not. How will these bills fare, we wondered, as we lined up with a dozen or so other legislators whose bills seeking help for the elderly were also being heard before Taxation -86 of them in all... Time will, of course, tell. Similar bills filed by this legislator last year and the year before managed to die in Ways and Means without ever reaching the floor of the House of Representatives...but there are considerably more bills being heard this year. We just might manage to secure some relief for those constituents of ours who are struggling under tax burdens they find impossible to bear. Incidentally, we've also filed legislation to create a commission to study the entire tax structure with a view to placing less emphasis on the real estate tax. We're trying every way we know to get help for our constituents... There now, we managed almost to overlook in our report of today's activities, another happy event. Braintree's own Jay Nuss, Regional manager of Robert Stone, Inc. arrived at the State House to be sworn in by our Secretary of State, Paul Guzzi, as a Notary Public... And there was a time out while we were photographed by Braintree's own Jack Leonard, the State House Photographer and the artist who can manage to eradicate wrinkles with a flash of his flashbulb, we tell him). Jack Leonard - always so gracious and so available when those groups of merry school children visit their seat of government on the Hill.

Taken all together it's been another exciting week to date under that Golden Dome…and gosh, shall we ever be busy tomorrow (Thursday) and the next day, as we tear around, trying madly to catch up with those constituent problems we've been forced to shelve as we raced against the clock on Beacon Hill. But what a wonderful way to live!

MARCH 6, 1977

Spring really IS winging its way to Massachusetts. We've a dozen different signs of it on Beacon Hill. There are Glee Clubs performing on the Common; and orators orating on the walkways leading to the State House. The elderly have resumed the reading of their daily papers on the winter-weary park benches while the young are mounting the State House steps two at a time as the spring sap runs. AND we are spending our days under the Golden Dome in a mad dash from committee hearing to chamber to committee hearing to chamber as the customary rash of spring roll calls come our way from a House that has begun to stir…and with a vengeance.

Spring is most definitely winging its way specifically to Braintree. The hyacinths are up in the family bulb garden! True - they're a mite curled around the edges; and they're not quite as high off the ground as they were this time last year; but they ARE up! "Last year, they were up on February 12," our own Jim Corbin III had announced when we made the fateful discovery of their presence last Sunday after donning boots and wading through a muddy back garden. (Grandson Jim is the family statistician as well as the family weatherman.) "This year I'd count myself fortunate if they had been up by March 12," I had replied gaily. "As a matter of fact, I shouldn't have been too surprised if they hadn't appeared at all. What a winter!" Well, at any rate, they ARE up and what a happy thought that is for all of us.

Life on "the Hill" continues to be a daily adventure. Monday, for instance, the Honorable Thomas W. McGee, our distinguished Speaker of the House WAS BACK ON THE ROSTRUM! What a moment when he walked unannounced down the side Chamber aisle and headed toward his normal place among us, after his tragic skiing accident, was greeted with a standing ovation that must have brought warmth to his compassionate heart and should hopefully act as a balm of sorts against the prolonged suffering that will be attendant upon his ultimate return to perfect health. "Tommy" McGee, as he is known to most of us, has been missed and sorely. Shall we ever be happy to see him back in harness, even for a limited time each day, come Monday morning next. Our bills continue to be heard before committee…those bills that we filed in such numbers last December and must now be able to defend. Today it was my Sunset legislation that had to be defended, House Bill 4523. "What IS this Sunset concept people are talking about?" I have been asked. Well, it's legislation to provide for a system of periodic legislative review, termination or re- establishment of state boards, divisions, agencies, councils and commissions - to quote the wording of the bill.

People are demanding economy and efficiency and dependability in their government services, this legislator told the Joint Committee on State Administration this morning. "How accountable are the myriad governmental units we're forced to deal with in Massachusetts?" I asked. Has the proliferation really been so great that we have all but lost track of who does what? Are those myriad units of government more responsive to the interests they serve than to the consumer they were designed to protect? Are there duplication of services?

House Bill 4523, which was designed to find the answers to these questions and others provides for a review of a specific group of our governmental units over a two-year period, beginning with a target date of July 1, 1979 for the first group, and ending with July 1, 1983 for the last group of units listed in the bill. This initial review will be repeated each six years; and new governmental units would have a life span of six years only, when they would have to come up for review before Being permitted to continue.

And the procedure for auditing the performance of the units? Well, dealing with the target date of July 1, 1979, by 18 months prior to that date, or in other words by January 1, 1978 the units listed in the bill for the first termination date will submit to the Legislative Committee on Post Audit a written statement which will include the functions performed by them; and of these functions duplicated by another governmental unit; and functions or powers deemed to be inconsistent with the requirements of the public and consequently able to be terminated; and a zero based budget review. How many people served and to what extent, etc.? A copy of this detailed report would be made available to member of the General Court.

The Post Audit Committee will have a year in which to conduct a performance audit of the governmental unit. This performance audit must be completed by January 1, 1979; with recommendations as to termination or re-establishment of the unit referred to the appropriate committee shall hold a public hearing within 30 days of receipt of these recommendations from Post Audit. And finally the legislative committee will come to a judgment on the issue of whether or not the unit is essential.

We have listed in our bill some of the criteria that would be employed in coming to that determination; the legislative committees would undoubtedly employ others. For instance, would the absence of regulation prove harmful to the public health, safety or welfare? Does the operation of the unit increase the COST of the goods or services and by how much? Does the unit protect the public, or the individuals regulated? To what extent have qualified applicants been permitted to serve the public? Are complaints handled well? And is disciplinary action taken if indicated? Are there any programs that have not been implemented during the past year, and were these needs met without these programs? These are the kinds of questions our legislative committees will hopefully be asking when they determine whether or not to terminate the governmental unit or to sanction its continued existence. A final report will be issued by the legislative committee by June 20, 1979, hitting the target date of July 1, 1979. If a unit is terminated, it will have one year to wind up its affairs; if continued, its life span will be for the next six years, at the end of which it will undergo the review process once again.

There now, that is the SUNSET concept. How will it fare, people are asking? We really have no idea. A number of similar bills have been filed, including S-1125, the Common Cause legislation on which we are also listed as a co-sponsor; and several others. We hope that perhaps the best aspects of all of them can be combined in one manageable vehicle. We'd love to see the Sunset concept given a chance to work; we'll be pushing for it!

MARCH 13, 1977

Six o'clock at the State House of a warm "suddenly spring" kind of evening with the temperature in the sixties…

We walk the State House corridors, our footsteps echoing along the empty places. Closed doors turn cold unfriendly faces where just an hour before they'd lain invitingly open; the custodians ply their mops; and a couple of mutually hard-working colleagues join us at the elevator where we find ourselves exchanging pleasantries while waiting for our lift to pick us up…

The customary exit has been locked and so we move toward where the Capitol Police stand guard upon the one front entrance now remaining open.

We've passed en route the great locked doors of our beautiful House Chamber and 'tis strange indeed, this feeling of being barred from the place we hold so dear.…And we bid the officer on duty a nice warm "good night" and open wide the huge bronze door to then descend the steps of this, our Capitol building. The warm sweet scent of evening comes our way.

Park Street wears a deserted look and so we settle for the Common walkway just across the way, where bongo drums are sending forth their music on the night; and where a "poet" of sorts will hand us oh, so proudly, his "anthology" of "verse" to quote the ragged boy. It's gibberish, we think perusing it as on the train we head for Quincy; and the paper that's been used to set it down for poor posterity has certainly seen better days; but there's an eager friendly glow within the "poet's" eyes, and so we've thanked him warmly and responded happily to his smile…

It's been a lovely day on Beacon Hill; as a matter of fact, it's been a lovely week… We've been so busy we've been dizzy. We've had Transportation Committee Hearings and Executive sessions and Health Care Committee Hearing and Executive sessions; and they've had to compete for time with House sessions and the unending coverage before the appropriate committees of those countless bills we filed and co-sponsored during December last.…AND, of course, there were the constituent problems that all have to be addressed.

There were my bills to increase the exemption on income tax for elderly taxpayers; as well as to grant to disabled persons an excise tax exemption; and to exempt elderly purchasers from excises charged on meals; and to charge all persons sixty-five years of age and older no fee on the M.B.T.A. To provide modifications of bus steps for the disabled and elderly…Had to dash from committee hearing room to committee hearing room to record support for all of those bills, a number of which were to be heard simultaneously on the very same day. "Taint easy, this dashing from place to place this time of year, but somehow it all manages to get done; and how interesting and exciting it is! Evenings have been busy affairs as well, with Monday devoted to a delightful Legislators Dinner as guest of our Savings Bankers…Had to cancel our Monday evening office hours at Town Hall for that one, but there are occasions when such a cancellation is necessary. We hope our constituents will understand that if we fail to show at seven or thereabouts come Monday evening at Town Hall it is because we've other and more pressing legislative commitments and we'll be there as usual on the following Monday. We're always available at the State House, needless to say, where our phone number is 727-5374 or at our home where it is 843-5159.

So now what else is new under the Golden Dome??? Speaker McGee is back with us again and in great form, pounding the gavel with a force that makes me wince, for it must cause great pain to his poor mending ribs; and yesterday we met, we South Shore "reps" with Fred Salvucci, Secretary of Transportation; and John Carroll, Public Works Commissioner; and Robert Kiley, M.B.T.A. General Manager of "Super Chief" as he was called some months ago. The meeting had been called by rep. Bob Ambler and Senator Allan McKinnon in an obviously futile and last ditch attempt to bring some order to the chaos that we all envision while looking down the road to EIGHT full years of bridge deck construction on the poor Southeast Expressway. And it was to come to naught, we hate to say. We all spoke in turn about the problems we must face, but no one really had the answer of the three who were on hand to hear our pleas. The bridge decks have to be rebuilt; they represent a menace to our drivers and they could conceivably collapse, we've been informed. They're thirty years in age and that's a lifetime, so we hear, for bridge decks of this sort. The work's essential, to be sure; but how we'll all contend with traffic problems while that work is being done brings graying to our hair.

Representatives Teahan of Whitman, Conway of Nantucket and your Lady of the House had prepared a late filed bill to prevent the opening of that Diamond lane on the Expressway that the D.P.W. desires. In our joint view it represents a safety hazard of extraordinary proportions. Only those with four passengers would be permitted to use the "Carpool" lane adjacent to the center strip, and can't you envision the accidents that will inevitably follow the cutting over of our drivers to the speedier lane upon the left??? And what happens if a car breaks down within that carpool lane? And how will one enforce it, this edict that none but car-poolers will be permitted to use the high speed lane??? We'd sought a ruling from the Attorney General as to the Diamond Lane. Constitutional it is, according to our distinguished A.G., but practical in the view of most of us, it is NOT…

Well, obviously Bob Teahan's announcement of the legislation we planned to file has caused the several gentlemen at the top to have second thoughts about the whole affair. We have just concluded reading this evening's Ledger. They've decided to delay the implementation of the Diamond Lane until further studies are made.

Well, so much for the past week on Beacon Hill. This is our hectic season as the thousands of bills that were filed this year come before our committees for action, action that is forthcoming in very few instances, we might add. OUGHT NOT TO PASS would seem to be the order of the day. We come to what amounts to a halt on passing legislation in the Great and General court this year. And we're in favor of this turn of events. To quote the Speaker of the House, "Let's take a look at the laws we have before we pass a lot of new ones." Amen to that, we say.

Keep your letters coming. Your rep wants and needs input from each and every one of you.

APRIL 17, 1977

A dynamite week on Beacon Hill, with a number of my legislative goals in sight or in the immediate offing. To begin with that vital legislation involving the transfer of a small portion of M.D.C. land at Wood Road and Route 37 is on the governor's desk, awaiting only his signature to serve as a go-ahead for the letting of contracts on the six-signal traffic signalization project for South Shore Plaza. The signing date as scheduled under normal circumstances would be April 23, however, this representative can't bear to wait that long. It's too important to the town. Consequently we hopefully set a few wheels in motion today that just could see the signing ceremony scheduled for Tuesday next. We'll know tomorrow when our legislative liaison, "Hank" O'Donnell gets back to us. What a happy day 'twill be when we stand beside the governor and watch as he affixes his signature to a bill we've been struggling with for the past two years.

Then there's the controversial Fluoridation legislation…legislation which would enable the town to place upon the ballot a clearly worded fluoridation question. This time it will read, "Shall the Town fluoridate its water supply?" and not "Shall fluoridation BE CONTINUED in the town?" The latter was the phrasing required by the Commonwealth at the time of the last referendum. Was it misleading, or did our townspeople know for sure what they were voting on in 1972 when a majority of our citizens voted in the affirmative? That question has torn the town asunder, so to speak…has caused a polarization on the issue that can only be removed by a conclusive vote, one way or the other, on the fluoridation issue. Whether you are "pro" or "anti" fluoridation if you believe in the democratic process, you must of necessity be pleased that, unless the governor vetoes the bill, our Board of Health members will at last be able to truly know the will of the people. Incidentally, we worked hard to get through the House legislation that would provide for the rewording of the question; this was accomplished last year, and it paved the way for what we now hope will be the resolution of the issue once and for all.

As a member of the Joint Committee on Transportation it was a distinct pleasure also this week to be able to arrange to bring to Braintree the Chairman of our committee, the Honorable Louis R. Nickinello of Natick. On Tuesday evening at Town Hall, I presented this articulate legislator in a discussion of House Bill 1739, his proposal to restructure the financing of the M.B.T.A. Six of my colleagues on the Transportation Committee were present on the platform, as were several guest legislators from the area. We had been guests of the South Shore Chamber of Commerce at a buffet supper at Thayer Academy prior to the Town Hall Meeting. The Chamber had handled publicity for the meeting, however an insufficient number of officials had apparently been reached, for attendance at this very important meeting was sparse indeed. Nonetheless it was a most productive meeting, with Chairman Nickinello ready, able and willing to answer every question that came his way…and what fun to see him on Channel Seven News upon our arrival home that evening. There appears to be some misunderstanding about the fate of my education bill, the legislation I filed in conjunction with three of my colleagues, which would direct the State Department of Education to prepare examinations for 12th Grade students. The newspaper reported our School Committee members in opposition to the bill. "Not so," said a School Committee member when the story appeared. "We didn't think it went far enough, that's all. We felt that such examinations should be given prior to students reaching Grade 12." "Hallelujah." I said happily. "Your colleague expressed that thought to me the other evening. I consulted the Chairman of our Education Committee today. We agreed to amend the bill to include exams at the 9th, 10th, 11th and 12th grade levels; giving the Department of Education a reasonable amount of time to come up with them." Here's hoping now that our Education Committee Chairman, rep. Frank Matrango, and Dr. Anrig can come to a meeting of the minds on this bill so that it will be reported out favorably. We have a feeling we'd get it through the House without too much difficulty with a favorable report. There's an awful lot of flak coming the way of the Legislature in regard to neglect of the basics in many of our school systems. We'll bank on Braintree's school system coming out on top, incidentally, should the School Committee elect to utilize the available exams. Their use is not mandatory, needless to say; there's local option…Anyhow, we understand the paper has been requested to print a retraction on the unfavorable school committee vote, and we'll get back to them with a redraft of the bill once changes have been decided upon. Today, Wednesday, was a particularly delightful day. It began at nine-thirty right here in town, with groundbreaking ceremonies for the Water Department's E.D.A. federally funded and much needed improvements in the pumping station area. Sunny were the skies as we posed for the cameramen with Water Commissioner Joe Cleggett doing duty with the shovel; may the skies continue to be sunny throughout the length and breadth of the project! Back to Resthaven at the conclusion of the ceremonies, for the awarding of a citation to Resthaven Nursing Home's 100 year old Mary Michaud. Have I said 100 year "old" Mary Michaud??? Should have made it 100 year YOUNG Mary Michaud. Attired in a pretty pink frock, her silver hair shining and her cheeks rosy with excitement the lady was having the time of her life as we arrived to do her honor. A small birdie reported later Mary Michaud joined a friend in performing an Irish Jig for her well-wishers…

Now this evening, and 'tis still Wednesday, it was off to the Precinct Seven Meeting at eight and at nine to the St. Thomas More Sodality meeting where we were privileged to participate in a panel discussion of possible careers for our young high school students. Needless to say, I recommended to the hundred or so mothers who were gathered there to receive career information that if they had a "doer" for a daughter, they recommend she set her sights on politics as a career…and find her way to Beacon Hill…(but not before this legislator is ready to retire…)

Legislation is proceeding at an accelerated pace under the Golden Dome, where we're addressing a multiplicity of issues…How do you feel about the Cox Report on Court Reform??? the Bottle Bill, Binding Arbitration, the State Budget, our legislation on Rules and Regulations??? Do let me hear from you. We welcome your input, as always…

MAY 1, 1977

There just aren't enough hours on Beacon Hill these days. Committee work has been hectic, especially for one who has had to try madly to tuck in the public hearings and executive sessions of two extremely busy committees like Transportation and Health Care - and all at the same time. I find myself arriving each morning at the State House, wishing fiercely that I might turn up a twin somewhere…climbing the broad stone steps beneath an archway of blossoming cherry trees and saying mentally, "Now, I must call so and so about such and such immediately; and I must dash right down to the House Counsel's office… and call the M.D.C. And Michael Westgate of E.S.I.C. And Dave Davis of Massport; and check the committee list and weigh the relative merits of those Transportation and Health Care Bills so as to decide where to go at eleven when both have their hearings scheduled; and I must run down to see Jack Murphy in Bills in the Third Reading about the holdup on the Braintree Fluoridation bill and drop in on Arthur Desrocher at Ways and Means; there could be more news on the Homemakers Services situation…

Despite all these comings and goings we've been able to tuck in a few bonus experiences this past week, however.

It was a fun experience, for instance, to participate in a State House Seminar held for a group of U.Mass - Boston students…and a challenge indeed to share the program with such heavies as Rep. Frank Harch, Minority Leader of the House and Rep. John Finnegan, Chairman of House Ways and Means as well as Senate President Kevin Harrington's Aide, Michael Ventresca of the Executive Office of Environmental Affairs and State House Reporter Brian McNiff. A challenge, to be sure, to speak for one-half hour on my impressions of the Legislature from the standpoint of a relatively new member and a woman…A challenge in contemplation, but it turned out to be a delightful and most rewarding experience indeed to share those impressions with the bright and beautiful group of young people who attended the Seminar with their dynamite Professor, George Goodwin, Jr. It is always a source of special joy to me to work with young people - and I seemed to feel an instant rapport with this particular group - which incidentally included Braintree's young Town Meeting Member Fred Hanson, along with young men and women from all across the state.

Had another rewarding evening as guest speaker at the Annual Meeting of the South Shore Chapter of the Mass. Federation of Nursing Homes. As a member of the Health Care Committee. I have a great concern for the problems that are facing our nursing homes, torn as they are between the necessity of implementing the many rules and regulations that are mandated by the federal and state government, (the federal government even more so than the state) and the fiscal realities of a Commonwealth forced by its troubled financial status to severely curtail payment for Medicaid and Welfare patients. These make up the bulk of the patients of many of our Massachusetts nursing homes.

One especially delightful treat we were able to sandwich in between Health Care Committee doings was the visit of Commander Jacques Cousteau to the House Chamber. Thin as the proverbial rail, his bright eyes glowed with enthusiasm and strength as this distinguished scientist outlined possible solutions to the energy crisis and warned his listeners of the "irreparable harm" they may be doing to our environment.

Fresh from a helicopter tour of the Islands, the Harbor and the Bay, he opened his remarks by commenting on the "efforts to revitalize the harbor and bay by the General Court." As Chairman of the Transportation Committee's Sub Committee currently working madly on the development of the Boston Seaport, I delighted in his remarks. "Water and life are synonymous," he told his listeners, "All the problems we have today do not exist as a result of science and technology, but only in the misuse of this. Our only recourse to improve our world is the development and the better use of science and technology."

"When building a judgment about a new technology our judgments must not be made as opportunistic judgments." he said, "We have to refer to basic criteria. When new development has the risk of endangering life on the planet it has to be abandoned. No new development should be undertaken if it damages irreparably the planet." Commander Cousteau told the members of the General Court assembled in Joint session.

"Damage done by shore drilling if improperly done, cannot be repaired. If we are to defer to the advice of specialists, we must screen potential specialists so they cannot be biased and have no vested interest."

The scientist warned of the potential danger of nuclear energy. "Nuclear wastes have to be stored somewhere for hundreds or thousands of years," he said. "If all of the nuclear programs of the world were to start according to schedule, in the year 2000 there would be in the world 1200 nuclear plants, 120 of these in the developing nations, out of any serious control. Development of nuclear energy is important to separate from nuclear weapons," he said.

The Candid Idylls of a State Representative

Commander Cousteau stressed the importance of the development of solar and thermal energy as alternatives to nuclear energy. "The biggest natural Solar concentration of the world is in the ocean," he said, "It will cost 858 Billions of dollars to develop 25-28% of our energy needs by nuclear means. The cost of developing all the energy we need by Solar and Thermal methods would be 1½ Trillion dollars. (A staggering sum, to be sure; can't even envision a billion, let alone a trillion, can you???) Cousteau turned to the matter of oil spills, stressing the menace of allowing ships run by Flags of Convenience in our waters, "These Liberian ships are American owned," he said. "A captain can secure a license to run one for $150. There is no licensing of Officers of the Watch, and the crews are picked up anywhere. No wonder so many tankers are lost and so many oil spills occur," he said.

The Commander announced his intention of advising President Carter to set a time limit after which all ships without the American Flag would be denied access to American waters. A fabulous speaker and his appearance before members of the General Court easily constituted one of the highlights of this past week on Beacon Hill.

MAY 8, 1977

With the advance of Spring, the tempo appears to be slowing down slightly on Beacon Hill. Those Public Hearings and executive sessions that have occupied the time and attention of committee members like myself, have all but come to a halt. We are now dealing in committee with only those bills that have been granted an extension of time in the interest of securing additional vital information or coming to a compromise agreement on some facet of the legislation.

The advance of Spring on Beacon Hill has brought with it other changes. We are aware of them as we dash up Park Street each morning, the Golden Dome in sight. The great bronze figures of Daniel Webster and Horace Mann, for instance, are now visible through a screen of lush and lovely lilac in full bloom; and, as freshening spring winds drift across those blossoming Japanese Cherry trees that line the walks, we find ourselves toting a sprinkling pale pink petals…petals that lie in fragrant pools beneath the bowls that cup the trees, and in soft sweet drifts upon the grey of granite. They gather in the cracks that line the handsome granite blocks, and float lazily through the open State House doorways to the halls beyond, there to lie…a fragrant, fair reminder that 'tis Spring on Beacon Hill…

So what are we doing with our mornings these days beneath the Golden Dome? Well, we're on hand come afternoon as well, there in the House…able to be on hand within the chamber at 11:00 A.M. each day rather than at Committee Hearings.

not just for roll call vote…a much more comfortable situation, to be sure, than having to contend with the "Roll call in the House in 4 minutes" interruption that haunts our committee hearings. "Tain't easy to race from Gardner Auditorium to the

Chamber in 4 brief minutes, then grope madly for information on a bill that is at stake and come to judgment on an issue all within a minute or so...to return to the Hearing Room forthwith; and once again to dive knee-deep into the matter at hand, only to be summoned back to the Chamber for another roll call.

"Doesn't it drive you crazy, the way these politicians run in and out in the middle of hearings???" One dear lady remarked within my hearing on one such occasion (Obviously for my benefit). "No wonder the state's in such a mess with those nitwits in charge," she had added. "We're answering roll calls," I had said pleasantly. "Our roll call record is very important to all of us."

"Well," said the lady, "I can find no excuse for a system that works like that - keeping the public waiting while you people run back and forth answering roll calls. I intend to discuss possible changes in the system anyhow with my friend Mike...THE GOVERNOR..." she had added patronizingly. "You do that," I had said, smothering the desire to laugh out loud at thought of the reaction of her "friend Mike" to the dear gal's criticism of that particular facet of "the system."

At any rate, our days have indeed quieted a mite; and, since as a Braintree Town Meeting Member I am facing long nights of Town Meeting debate, I must admit I welcome the less hectic days...One of which was NOT this past Wednesday when as a member of the Transportation Committee my afternoon was spent in executive session on the Bond Issue for the Department of Public Works, the M.D.C. and the M.B.T.A....a period punctuated by a number of those "rush-to-get-information-and-vote-intelligently" roll calls. This representative finds those situations extremely difficult to take; votes either for or against a bill can easily be regretted when viewed in quiet retrospect. Still-it IS the system, and we can't think really of any way to change it.

That lull we speak of is, by the way, the lull before a storm on Beacon Hill, for the Redistricting will grace??? the May 16th Calendar, we understand. This particular legislator is one of the few fortunate ones in this area. Braintree being a perfect district population-wise, I shall not have to run against a colleague, a situation I would deplore. My district, with acceptance of the plan, will include the entire Town of Braintree, a fact for which I am extremely grateful.

The Budget, when - all its myriad public hearings over - it reaches the floor of the house, will represent one more horrendous hurdle for us to overcome in our attempts to bring the dear old Ship of State into safe harbor. An examination of the huge document that came to us from the Governor a couple of months back, reveals some decidedly startling statistics about the way we are spending our Massachusetts tax dollars. An enormously large share of the Governor's budget must be used for Human Services...close to Two Billion dollars of a slightly more than Four Billion total amount The general public would appear to be convinced that the state should and can solve all the many problems that beset its citizens. Is it because families are becoming increasingly less close in their relationships that they are willing to assume no responsibility at all for the problems that beset one another, we wonder, as we face the ever mounting lobbying tactics of those seeking increased programs, increased funding, increased everything from a state whose treasury is no longer the apparent bottomless pit it once was???

Changing the subject, just in case you did not know it, this past week was Polish Week on Beacon Hill and elsewhere, and spectators by the hundreds have been coming to Doric Hall and viewing "One Thousand Years of Polish History and Culture," the most beautiful exhibit imaginable sponsored by the American Institute of Polish Culture. While awaiting the arrival of a group of visiting Kindergartners from Watson School on Wednesday morning we had a wonderful opportunity to view it…and to delight in it.

This past week has housed three nights of a Braintree Town Meeting that will go on for many more of same…We've been able to attend the first three sessions, scheduled for Monday, Tuesday and Wednesday evenings…a rare situation for our very busy month of May. Now we shall have to be absent for the three meetings scheduled for the week of May 9…all for legislative commitments. We shall be in Framingham on Monday evening with the Transportation Committee; in Boston on Tuesday evening and in Randolph on Wednesday evening. Obviously we are not going to be able to represent the great people who elected us to be their voice in Town Meeting, and so shall have to resign and in the interest of fairness to the people who elect us, permit one who CAN represent them all the way have an opportunity to do so. After twenty years as a Town Meeting Member, you may well imagine the sacrifices this represents. Oh well…

MAY 29, 1977

Redistricting of the House of Representatives is a Fait Accompli as this column goes to press; the traumatic and difficult task of reducing the size of the House from 240 to 160 members is at last over; and we rejoice with a House Speaker and a Chairman of the Redistricting Committee who must have experienced the most difficult period of their lives, and whose sleepless nights (to judge by their haggard appearance) have hopefully come to an end.

Horrendous decisions must have had to be made on where and how to apply the scalpel to the House membership. We keep wondering how any business executive or board of directors, face with the dictate to cut one-third of their employees from the ranks, would handle the decision on whom to cut and whom to keep. What criteria would be employed, we wonder? Could they cut off and float out to sea key people in their organizations? Would it be done on the basis of seniority? Or superiority? Or dispensability? (if there IS such a word) Or indispensability??? What an incredibly difficult task has been performed by those in charge of this mandated undertaking.…

Apart from the redistricting issue, the week has been an interesting one. Saturday was fun, attending as we did a Girls' Softball Game where we delighted in the playing of Metayer's Marauders," that absolutely great group of girls whose performance on the playing field we are only able to witness now and then on Saturday afternoon, arriving as we do home from the State House too late to tuck in their evening games. It was fun, as well, to watch Grandson Byrne and his Little League team on the Watson Park diamond…difficult, however, to tuck both games in, played as they were simultaneously…

Sunday was to house a series of vitally interesting events. It was off first to American Legion Hall where a group of lovely young people were to receive awards for their essays on "What the Flag Means to Me." Having three additional engagements, all scheduled from 2:00 to 4:00 P.M. we were unable to do anything but drop by and request the Chairman to convey our congratulations to these fine young people. The Flag happens to mean a very great deal to this rep, who wished heartily that she might remain to hear those prize-winning essays…

Next on our busy Sunday afternoon agenda was to be the Dedication Ceremony of the new William H. Dwyer Building at the Blue Hills Regional Vocational Institute in Canton. We were to present a citation honoring the event to the widow of the beautiful human being to whom the building was being dedicated, who would, in turn, present it to the school. Platform guests were to include Braintree High School Headmaster John Leroy, a member of the school Committee for that marvelous institution which serves to provide vocational education for so many of our surrounding towns. We knew Mr. Dwyer well; and we remember him as the embodiment of everything worthwhile in mankind…The ceremony was moving and memorable; and the huge crowd contained a sizable number of my great constituents…On next to the Highland School where its beloved retiring Principal, Mrs. Gloria Santo, was being honored with the most colorful and lovely Reception we've attended in a very long while. The room had been decorated by her fond students; and flowers, butterflies an bees in gorgeous colors vied with one another for space on the colorful walls. Arriving late by virtue of my attendance at Blue Hills, where the ceremony turned out to be a very lengthy as well as a very lovely one, we were delighted obliged to present our Citation apart from the regular program. The gracious and lovely lady was delighted with it nonetheless; and this Rep. was indeed proud and pleased to have been asked to represent the House in this manner before a lady who has earned the love and affection of parents and children alike over a 35 year period of dedicated involvement with the town and its school-children.

And then, after a Sunday evening meeting, it was Monday and the news of the Governor's veto of the Braintree Fluoridation Bill was awaiting me at the State House. The vetoing of this totally Home Rule Bill has caused a series of shock waves throughout the town, needless to say. To review for those of you who are unfamiliar with the background of H-5583, "An Act Authorizing a Referendum in the Town of Braintree on the Fluoridation of the Public Water Supply," in 1972, at the direction of the Braintree

Board of Health, a Referendum article was placed in the Town Warrant, seeking to determine if the citizens of Braintree wished their water supply to be fluoridated. The State changed the wording of the question to read "Shall the fluoridation of the public water supply for domestic use in Braintree's be CONTINUED?" Why the wording in this way when we had not at that time ever fluoridated our water supply? That's the question that has stumped a lot of people. Actually General law 111, Section 8C dictates that particular wording for some reason or other - we have not been able to determine why. The townspeople voted 8936 to 7647 to "continue" the fluoridation of their water supply. Well, immediately afterwards, the Town Clerk began to be deluged with calls from people who were declaring that they had misunderstood the question; that the Board of Health had acted deviously, etc., etc. Actually the Board of Health had not acted deviously at all; the deviousness lay in the wording of the stupid legislation passed by the state.

Well, because of the furor over whether or not the people knew what they were voting on, the Finance Committee has refused to vote favorably on the funds for fluoridating the water; and the Town Meeting has refused to do so; and this has gone on YEAR AFTER YEAR since 1972. Meanwhile the pro and anti fluoridationists have been polarized; one entire evening of each of our Town Meetings has been devoted to this one issue; and a 10 Taxpayers Suit has been filed to force the town to fluoridate the water supply, a suit in which our Town Counsel must defend the actions of the town.

So meanwhile, what has been happening to that original and strange legislative wording that has caused all the furor? Last year, in the realization of the ambiguity of the phrasing and because other communities were having the same problem, the law was changed to read - as it should have read in the beginning - "Shall the public water supply for domestic use in (this city) (this town) be fluoridated?" And now communities such as Braintree where divisiveness is a disturbing element, will be given an opportunity to face the issue fairly…and to decide fairly whether or not their water supply should be fluoridated.

An article was inserted in our Town Warrant seeking authority for a second Referendum question to be placed on our town ballot in March; and, with a favorable vote. The bill was filed with the Legislature. That bill was H-5583…and the Governor VETOED it on the grounds that he favors fluoridation. This was not a pro or anti fluoridation issue, however. Whether you are a pro or anti fluoridation, you must wish as your town officials do, that the issue would be settled once and for all, one way or another, and dispensed with. H5583 is not a PRO FLUORIDATION BILL; IT'S A PRO JUSTICE Bill. It seeks only a fair shake for the voters of Braintree. Our task now will be to overturn the Governor's veto…a monumental talk, to be sure, but we shall give it all we have. And so another week ends on Beacon Hill…Another decidedly eventful one, we might add…JUNE 12, 1977.

It was to be 7:30 A.M. on Saturday morning when your L. of the H. would turn into her driveway after the last twenty-hour session on the incredible state budget - one of several unbelievably long sessions that had gone on all week as we struggled with the largest state budget in the history of the Commonwealth...the largest and as engrossed, certainly the most complicated.

Approximately one hundred and fifty amendments would have been added to House Bill 6100 before its engrossment would be finally voted. Why so many, you are undoubtedly wondering...We who were assembled in the House Chamber to deal with our annual budget nightmare

wondered the same thing; and then a variety of reasons came gradually to mind. There is, first of all, the redistricting atmosphere that so completely permeates the House these days, and can be expected to do so for the next year. Colleagues who will be fighting for survival in 1978 are headline hunting, espousing causes, simultaneously moving every budget extra under the sun for their districts and writing press releases to prove their worth to the communities they represent. It's understandable and to be expected.

Now, the offering of one hundred and fifty amendments is all well and good, but each of those amendments just naturally manages to generate debate...very very LENGTHY debate in some instances...Hours of it...The representative with the proposal must of necessity be debated by the Chairman of Ways and Means assuming, of course, that the amendment offered is going to cost the state money and so affect the total of the budget the Ways and Means committee has been struggling with for lo, these many months. The sponsor of the amendment hopes that then some of his colleagues will join in the debate - backing his proposal, needless to say. They do, and the debate goes on, in some instances for HOURS ON END! On ONE subject, one amendment! All of which leads me to the matter of those all-night legislative sessions on Beacon Hill...

Why on earth does the Speaker DO that?" constituents were asking of their representatives on all sides. "It's ridiculous. Why doesn't he adjourn at a sensible hour and resume next day?" We've never discussed this aspect of leadership with Speaker McGee, needless to say, it's his decision. We do feel, however, that we have a pretty good idea of why he DOESN'T adjourn at a "sensible" hour and resume next day. That would give the sponsors of those 150 amendments more and more and more time to rest up from the day's doings on their amendments and return next day all set to go on for another couple of hours...on the same issue...repeating the previous day's debate and undoubtedly adding a bit more.

The Budget goes first to a Third Reading in the House, and it was at this stage that each and every one of those amendments was offered, and most of them debated at length over the first three days (and nights). The entire Budget, however, all 69 pages and a thousand items on it must be engrossed AFTER it has taken its third reading... And during the engrossment of the bill each and every one of those 150 amendments can again be challenged, changed, amended, debated and voted upon in the unbelievably time consuming legislative process. The budget debate could conceivably have gone on for weeks IF the Speaker had not decided to take matters into his own hands and keep us in session until H-6100 was engrossed which engrossment occurred finally at close to 7:00 A.M. on Saturday morning after the twenty-hour session that had served as a prelude to my turning into the family driveway at 7:30 A.M. on that particular day.

Now, just in case you feel that our contact with the 1978 state budget is behind us, let me assure you 'tis anything but so. The Budget is currently in the Senate where 150 additional amendments could conceivably be offered before it emerges from that particular branch of government. We in the House will undoubtedly then refuse to accept the Senate's myriad changes, and H-6100 will go to a Committee of Conference where negotiations will bring about a compromise on disputed issues, the Conference Committee will be composed of representatives and senators. From the Committee of Conference the bill will return to the House. Now we cannot amend it in any way. We must either vote it UP or DOWN as is…And sometimes that's the most difficult vote of all.

So many of you have commented on the legislature's way of handling the state budget, and a number of you have asked me to outline the manner in which it is handled, so "VOILA!" The multitude of amendments offered this year represents an unusual situation for those dealing with our Commonwealth's budget. In our opinion the majority of them do not properly belong in the budget, however the lowering of the state meals tax from 8% to 5% could have placed the budget in a rather different light and so opened the floodgates for the offering of everything under the sun.

Well, so much for the horrendously large state budget much of the size of which is due directly to the ever increasing demand for human services And from agencies whose appetite for funding would appear to be insatiable if we are to judge by the incessant lobbying that has gone on during the entire budget session. We keep praying for an improved economy; and perhaps a change in the attitude of our citizens who seem to feel that the state can and should handle each and every one of their problems.

Now, changing the subject, we neglected in last week's column to thank so many of you great constituents that you are for the many letters we have received in reaction to this representative's appearance on the WBZ-TV "We're 4 Boston" program. How very nice to know you all (the letter writers) seemed to enjoy the little segment of the week's events that featured your L. of the H. It was certainly a fun thing to do. The only drawback to the event would appear to have been the fact that I NEVER GOT TO SEE IT! It so happened that we were in session until 7:15 that evening (and NOT on the budget; we are frequently tied up on other matters). Our Transportation Committee had scheduled a Public Hearing in Needham on House Bill 1739, the Chairman's M.B.T.A. Restructuring legislation. The Hearing was scheduled for 8:00 P.M. so it had to be off to Needham under full sail the moment we adjourned, and on to the platform, where we supported the Chairman by our committee presence through a two-hour plus meeting in which Rep. Nickinello answered more question than we ever dreamed it possible to ask. Dinner hour that evening turned out to be 10:45 P.M…Having swallowed lunch whole at 11:30 that morning so as to tuck in a committee meeting before the one o'clock session, we came very close to devouring our colleagues before the Public Hearing adjourned. SO - NEEDLESS TO SAY - it was to be after midnight when we returned to Braintree, without ever having had the opportunity to view ourselves in action. Oh well, C'est La Guerre! And "Thank You!" You kind letter writers…

JUNE 26, 1977

'Tis said we shall recess for the month of July, we members of the General Court. Words to that effect are circulating about the State House; nothing, however, being certain but death and taxes to quote you-know-who, we shall not believe it until the Speaker wields his gavel and makes a solemn pronouncement to that effect. Shan't know what to do with me if I find I'll not be having to dash off at dawn each day, praying as I go that the good old Red Line will be functioning normally, and that I shall manage to tuck into the day that lies ahead a full day and a half's schedule of things to do on Beacon Hill. Had another interesting week under the Golden Dome. It began with the Democratic Issues Convention on Saturday morning. We departed at seven under a hazy sky that was to bring with it a veritable heat-wave…departed for Holy Cross College in Worcester where the Convention was to be held. It was the first political convention this representative had ever attended; and we must admit it wasn't much fun. It was extremely warm in the gym where close to 2,000 delegates were assembled (so they tell me); and it seemed rather interminable. Amendments to the party platform that had been soundly defeated in the morning workshops were trotted out in the Plenary session and adopted, which rather surprised a great many of us. The entire party position in support of Welfare Reform was defeated by a total of 18 votes. We had attended that particular morning workshop and the support of the Welfare Reform measure was overwhelming. BY evening, however, delegates having departed in droves and the issue having been placed before what to us represented a stacked house (or a reasonable facsimile), the entire Welfare Reform package was voted down. We feel that Welfare Reform has to be one of the most vital issues facing the Commonwealth of Massachusetts; and we were, therefore, most disappointed. It represented another experience, nonetheless. Incidentally, they tell me there's nothing new about this situation. All Conventions are rather stacked, so THEY say…They also tell me I'm a "great representative but a terrible POLITICIAN;" "if that weren't so, I'd have EXPECTED the Convention to be stacked." "That's POLITICS," THEY say…Oh, well, The Governor's WORKFARE program, and the entire concept of workfare seemed particularly distasteful to those delegates who were working so hard to defeat the welfare reform package. We think the idea of Workfare for AFDC fathers is a sound one. We happen not to feel that good honest work is degrading; and that putting welfare fathers to work is "punitive." We were outvoted however, by our fellow delegates…Oh, well, "You can't win them all," THEY also say… Wasn't the weekend Lovely??? We gardened, and painted a bit; attended a lovely little Sunday evening gathering in honor of her "Dad" at Gael's home, Sunday being "Father's

Day," and Gael being a particularly fond daughter. Alexander Road, like the rest of Braintree, was ablaze with spring flowers, and its lawns were lush and green. Gael's pool never looked more inviting, but though we arrived in the appropriate garb for swimming - would you believe it??? - we hadn't the courage to dive in. The water, after all the rain we've been subjected to, was COLD! Next Sunday, perhaps!

We're still taking bows over our 174 to 52 House vote to overturn the governor's veto of Braintree's Home Rule bill on the fluoridation issues. It is, however, running into difficulty in the Senate. we're sorry to report. Senator Tobin is working furiously to secure the 26 Senate votes necessary to overturn the veto in the upper branch, and we're trying to help.

The Governor has been having a rather rough time with his vetoes of late. There was also this week the overturning of his veto of a bill requiring teachers to lead all public school students in daily recitation of the Pledge of Allegiance. The Governor had questioned the constitutionality of the bill on the basis of the fact that it is in violation of the First Amendment of the U.S. Constitution. Obviously the House of Representatives was not prepared to accept that reasoning. Only 27 votes in support of his position could be mustered. And what a lark as the entire House membership burst into song with a stirring "God Bless America" as the vote was tallied. It must be the full moon, as the Speaker said afterwards…

Summer is advancing rapidly these days on Beacon Hill. The street singers are out in force, seated on the cement sidewalks and about the Park Street Station…some with small babies in their arms; all with guitars, and strange attire and stranger friends…The vendors are about; and fruit stands are set up and merrily dispensing wares. Tourist are training cameras upon the Golden Dome from every corner of the place; and pouring up the steps; and visiting the chamber; and asking the inevitable question, "Where is the chandelier Paul Revere made???" (They're FASCINATED by the chandelier and seem surprised when told he also was responsible for the Golden Dome they've photographed enroute.) Garden flowers are everywhere in all the vases on the desks of all the gals…roses and snapdragons; pansies and peonies…Ah, yes, 'tis summer on the Hill! The sprinklers on the lawns are keeping all things green…and wetting down unwary passersby, this rep included, who can't seem to remember to avoid their misty paths…Ah, yes, 'tis summer on the Hill, and because 'tis summer on the Hill, 'tis great to be alive and THERE…

JULY 10, 1977

The House of Representatives is in recess…until August 1, when we shall return in an informal session; and thence until August 4, when we shall return in another informal session; and then until August 8, when we shall return in full formal session to deal with the controversial issue that has been responsible for the prolonged delay in getting the State Budget to the Governor's desk…and has been responsible for those long nightly sessions under the Golden Dome…the legislation that would prevent the use of state welfare money for abortions other than therapeutic ones. The order to recess was formally adopted and placed in effect at 2:00A.M. this morning (Wednesday). This representative must return to the State House by 9:00 tomorrow morning, nonetheless. There's a vital meeting with Commissioner of Mental Health Okin and Education Commissioner Anrig scheduled for that hour. It deals with the problem of transferring retarded little ones from clinical nursery school into a collaborative public school system. We hope that some compromises can be worked out on the issue. Representative Sheets of Quincy, as a member of the State Committee on Education, has arranged the meeting and we trust it will be a productive one.

So many nice events have occurred during the past week to counteract the difficulties of dealing with the unending series of filibusters, acknowledged and otherwise, that have accompanied the progress of the 1978 state budget through the House. First of all there was the exciting knowledge that "Metayer's Marauders," that intrepid and delightful Girls' Softball team we're privileged to sponsor, had won the 1977 Championship in the East Braintree Girls' League. What fun to be present at the crucial game and to hand the winning trophies to each and every one of these beautiful young athletes. Couldn't have happened if the game hadn't been scheduled for the weekend. It was! And so we were able to attend and to be in on the exciting finish of what was a great season for the "Marauders" and for all other bright young girls who participated in this relatively new league. We hope to award a Citation to our outstanding team…and a second Citation to its great young coach, our good friend, Betty Barton. Betty's first attempt at coaching sure paid off. She's terrific at the art of getting the best from her cute young charges.

Changing the subject, one more fourth of July has been celebrated in this town we love so well…and with the charm and aplomb we've come to expect from that dedicated group of young men and women to whom we've entrusted this project for the past few years.

We hated to miss the Chicken Fry and Strawberry Festival on Friday evening. We were tied up at the State House, watching the clock eagerly in the hope that by some miracle we'd manage to make both. The miracle failed to happen. We hear, however, that both were wonderfully successful, the food great and the music delightful.

We did manage to make the Field Day on Saturday afternoon, however we had to leave early as we were due back into session at six P.M. It was fun, however, while it lasted; and the youngsters of the town appeared to be enjoying the entertainment no end…

Having turned the family car into the driveway at 4:45 A.M. On Sunday morning after an all-night session on the Budget…a session which included a filibuster that threatened to keep us there for 24-48 hours, according to its participants…we were unable to tuck in attendance at Church and the Knights of Columbus Pancake Breakfast which we always enjoy so much…especially in view of the fact that we faced as one of the Grand Marshalls the Holiday Parade that was scheduled for 5:00 PM. THAT DAY!

What fun it was to perform that exciting chore while riding in the smartest little surrey with the fringe on top we've seen in many years…behind a handsome young horse named Tony, who seemed to take to his first parade like a duck to you-know-what! It was also fun to participate in the awarding of the trophies for participating Floats… five in all, one of which was deservedly awarded to our good friend "Pat" Junior, and was purchased in Canada, we learned. And where do you suppose its original owner was traced to??? Believe it or not-to Braintree! This kind of coincidence could only happen in the Leonard family, we warrant.

Our Fourth of July celebration was not to end with the Braintree Parade, however. Monday was to house another exciting event to which Ted and I had been invited - the annual turnaround of Old Ironsides, grande dame of the nations' fleet! As guests of the Mass. Bay Yacht Clubs Association, we boarded the Vietnam gunboat, "Marathon" now owned by the Massachusetts Maritime Academy, for a marvelous view of the Constitution as she sailed up Boston Harbor, two fireboats saluting her all the way; to be followed by a parade of decorated boats from all the yacht clubs of the Commonwealth…A delightful sight indeed; and what fun to share the happy occasion with our good friends and organization officials "Ed" Mazzuchelli and "Dan" Richardi, along with their charming wives and family…AND with Braintree's "Bob" Cunningham…How handsome these three gentlemen looked in their smart Association uniforms!

The 180 year old frigate which we know as U.S.S. Constitution, was towed from her Charlestown berth to Castle Island where the guns at Ft. Independence answered her 21-gun salute quite smartly. The yearly turnaround of Old Ironsides is scheduled in order that her masts and timbers will weather evenly while she is moored at the dock. Her position is changed each year so that the wild winter winds of New England may weather her evenly on both sides. It is inconceivable that this all-wooden ship could have withstood the pounding of a naval battle; and what little protection was offered for the brave crews of close to two centuries ago who manned her…

Back in session yesterday (Tuesday) where we are happy to report that both a 1978 State Budget and an Insurance Bill were finally enacted and placed on the Governor's desk. We have deliberately refrained from discussing these controversial pieces of legislation as the newspapers and television programs have devoted much of their time and space to keeping you informed of the progress of both issues along the line. Suffice to say, we're glad they're over and done with. The State simply had to have a budget; and our overcharged drivers had to have a rebate; and so a Budget and an Insurance Bill had to be passed! The anti-abortion issue remains to be faced in August, separate and apart from the Budget…Our Health Care Committee will meanwhile schedule a Public Committee hearing on the bill; and we look for more fireworks in Gardner Auditorium that day than we observed on the fourth of July weekend! Oh well, "C'est la Guerre!"

JULY 24, 1977

We are in Recess, and we find ourselves perambulating from the State House to the pool and thence to the local ball field for that series of All Star Championship games in which grandson Byrne is playing up a storm these days...a triple and a home run both in one game, for instance...the 1st game, which his team won handily, 13 to 3, or thereabouts. (We lose track of some of those scores, we're so intent on the plays themselves...AND the players...)

It's a pleasant change, and especially welcome during this wild spell of heat when, we believe it or not, our State House office air conditioner is having difficulties and giving us occupants of a windowless fourth-floor office a sauna-type setting in which to function. Oh, well...We've managed to survive so far, and the heat wave may break within a week or two, they tell us...

Despite the recess, a certain air of activity permeates the State House; and it's rather nice to be able to spare time for corridor chatting with our colleagues; and to enjoy a leisurely sandwich at what passes for a restaurant under the Golden Dome - our Snack Bar!

With leisure, we managed to learn a few interesting facts about this and that during these corridor chats with staff people from our various committees as well. We learned, for instance, a bit about today's pacemaker; and as a member of the Health Care Committee we were delighted to add this information to our ever-increasing knowledge about that most vital of subjects, the Commonwealth's health. We wonder how many of you are aware of the fact that when a pacemaker gets to the end of its batteries, it must be replaced. We weren't We discussed this medical marvel with someone who wears one. As we understand it, if his heart misses a beat, the pacemaker gives one electronically, which we feel is marvelous to begin with. However - and this, we opine, is even more marvelous the appurtenance has an electronic monitor; and the wearer of the pacemaker may call a number in Texas, toll free, from any place in the world. He places the telephone receiver on this little instrument which incidentally is smaller than a package of cigarettes. An electrocardiogram is then taken in Texas and is then informed as to whether it's time to change the pacemaker. If so, an appointment is made for him at the hospital and a report sent to the family doctor. What an age we live in, we thought as we walked away from the pacemaker's wearer. Can all this possibly be true??? It must be...

We've had time to look into some extra-curricular activities as well these slightly more leisurely days...and to read some of the personal problemless mail that has come our way over the past few months...and to look through some of the mailings that are slightly less than crucial to a bill or to an issue or to a sphere of activity and so were set aside...In the course of which we came upon a couple of what we felt were interesting quotes, worth sharing with you, my readers.

There was, for instance, that famous quote of Henry Clay: "Government is a trust, and the officers of the government are trustees; and both the trust and the trustees are created for the benefit of the people." A splendid thought and one which we shall try always to remember in our dealing with you wonderful people who have sent to this L. of the H. and then there is always that oft-quoted line, "No man's life, liberty or property is safe while the legislature is in session…" Wow! We particularly wish to thank our dear friend Frances for her lovely note and the flattering writing she enclosed. We thought this, too, was deserving of sharing with you, my constituents. "A Class Candidate…A class official.." We hear the phrase constantly under the Golden Dome. So what DOES constitute a CLASS public official, we've wondered more than once. The following definition of "CLASS' puts the quality beautifully into words…We quote: you can meet life head on and handle whatever comes along.

"What is CLASS?" Class never runs scared. It is sure-footed and confident in the knowledge that Jacob had it Esau didn't

Symbolically, we can look to Jacob's wrestling match with the angel. Those who have class have wrestled with their own personal "angel" and won a victory that marks them thereafter.

Class never makes excuses. It takes its lumps and learns from past mistakes.

Class is considerate of others. It knows that good manners are nothing more than a series of petty sacrifices.

Class bespeaks an aristocracy that has nothing to do with ancestors or money. The most affluent blue blood can be totally without class while the descendant of a Welsh miner may ooze class from every pore.

Class never tries to build itself up by tearing others down. Class is ALREADY up and need not strive to look better by making others look worse.

Class can "walk with kings and keep its virtue and talk with crowds and keep the common touch." Everyone is comfortable with the person who has class - because he is comfortable with himself. If you have class you don't need much of anything else. If you don't have it, no matter what else you have - it doesn't make much difference."

Haven't succeeded in reaching my friend Frances by phone as yet; however we know she reads the "Forum" and feel confident she will approve of my sharing this lovely definition of CLASS with my CLASS constituents…And, THANKS, Fran!

JULY 31, 1977

We are in the final week of our legislative recess…How speedily it has flown! The atmosphere under the Golden Dome has been an easy restful one. We've had our constituent work, but no legislative sessions: no committee hearings; no racing from the heights or the depths for roll-calls…And so the days have melted away, and we'll return to normal rested and relaxed.

The flow of mail to members of the Great and General Court is one aspect of life that maintains a business-as-usual tempo. And the letters we lawmakers receive are indeed many and varied. Like the one that graced this representative's mail last week. It came from a student many miles from Braintree. "Dear Representative," it read. "My aunt said you are always nice to students and she reads your paper. I am taking a summer course and we have a class project we're working on. I am enclosing a copy; and I would like to have your views on all the issues. Please take care of it promptly as it must be in by next Monday. Thank you. I am depending on you, and I'll tell my aunt. She votes for you." Signed "Lisa." (The missive contained 10 issues; we hope our letter reached the young lady "By next Monday...")

Not many of our letters are written in that vein, needless to say. As bureaucracy grows within the state government, an increasingly large number of matters are mishandled, and it is to their lawmakers that frustrated citizens turn for help…And frequently lawmakers are the only ones who can manage to unsnarl their problems. This particular aspect of public service is the one this lawmaker especially enjoys. A problem-solver by nature, your representative takes enormous satisfaction in being able to ease a constituent's life by helping to solve his problem. We don't always succeed in doing so; however we certainly try hard in every instance. And need we say what a happy feeling it gives one to know that one or two people in the community are sleeping easier of a night because of what we were able to do…So don't hesitate to ask for help from your L. of the H. To serve the residents of Braintree is what she was elected to do.

Incidentally, there's quite a contrast between the legislator one learns about in the textbooks and the real flesh-and-blood legislator; we learned that fact quite speedily. Within the textbooks, and ideally, the legislator studies all of the bills in depth (9,000 of them annually); she reads all the promotional material that is available on each one; seeks an expert opinion from scientists and educators; weighs the pros and cons; decides on a position and then votes that way. And to be candid, that is how we envisioned things prior to our election. Actually, if the issue is one which is discussed in public hearing before our particular committees, we are (if we attend all possible committee hearings and we do) sufficiently conversant with the bill to have come up with a judgment before the committee position is taken at an executive session…Or ramifications may surface during the executive session…At any rate, one knows enough about the issue to discuss it with inquiring colleagues. If, however, the issue has been heard before another committee, one is faced with the necessity of discussing it with the committee chairman or a committee member whose opinion one values; reading all possible material on the subject; and listening to the debate that is presented during the session. And THEN coming to a judgment on whether to press that red light or green light on the roll call record…And if you don't think we agonize over some of our votes, let me enlighten you. WE DO! It's an awesome responsibility, the making of laws that will affect for all time and in many ways the wonderful people who sent us there to represent them…But - how very much we learn about so many different subjects in the university that is the HILL! Something or some things new every single day of our lives. One of the more exciting aspects of public service in the opinion of this fortunate legislator…Always did LOVE school! As a matter of fact, love EVERYTHING about life under the beautiful Golden Dome.

Have another lovely little bit of writing to share with you, my readers. This beautiful piece was culled from a delightful publication, "Praying Hands," which I receive periodically, thanks to the generosity of my good friend, Ted, who must have known what pleasure I'd derive from it. It is called "Green Boughs and Singing Birds" and was written by William Arthur Ward. It reads" "Here are five 'green boughs' we should strive to keep in our hearts:

The green bough of ENTHUSIASM. Enthusiasm is not only contagious…it is attractive. The singing bird of success is drawn toward the green bough of enthusiasm. Where there is enthusiasm, there is excitement, and where there is positive excitement, there is more joy in the job, more sparkle in the eye, and more zest in our living.

The green bough of KINDNESS. Kindness is the Golden Rule in action. Surely what the world needs now is more kindness. The green boughs of kindness grow from the tree of love, and when we truly love others, kindness is natural and instinctive. We should remember the little girl's prayer: 'God, help the bad people to be good; and please help the good people to be nice.'

The green bough of GENEROSITY. Our lives sing with joy when we generously share ourselves, our talents and resources in loving service to others. Generosity is the secret of happiness; it is the golden key that unlocks the gates to joy, fulfillment and life more abundant.

The green bough of HUMOR. It has been said that if we learn to laugh at ourselves, we will always be amused. The green bough of humor helps us to laugh at ourselves even when we make a faux pas, when we goof up, when we trip over our tongues, or when we write something similar to this brief advertisement: "Good used typewriter for sale by secretary with wide carriage."

The green bough of GRATITUDE. Green boughs of gratitude provide the perfect home for the bluebirds of happiness. With gratitude in our hearts, there can be no room for self-pity, resentment or bitterness. Gratitude attracts more blessings - especially when we humbly and joyfully express our thanksgiving to our God and to those who have encouraged and inspired us."

Just LOVED that delightful article and hope that you, my readers, derive satisfaction and inspiration from the reading of it…Incidentally, in regard to the green bough of ENTHUSIASM, we recall the fact once a beloved clergyman stated that the word "enthusiasm" translated from its derivation, means "God within." And on that green bough of KINDNESS, we've a sign on the door of Room 446 at the State House which reads, "It's nice to be IMPORTANT, but it's more important to be NICE." Don't you love that one???? We don't know whether the sign has anything to do with it or not, but the nicest people in the world - legislators and employees- - are housed in our Room446 at the State House…

AUGUST 8, 1977

It was back to the Chamber on Monday August 1- to an informal session, to be sure - but a number of "messages from His Excellency, the Governor" and a few Resolutions and vetoed items came before us…And it was good to be back again…

Tomorrow the work of the House will begin again in earnest, for on that date a bill to end state-aided abortions for Welfare Recipients will be debated…certainly the most emotional issue we've faced in a long while. Will there be a repetition of the filibustering we were forced to endure a month back as the anti-abortion forces attempted to scuttle the state budget? We hope not. Debate on an issue is extremely interesting and most useful in enabling a legislator to come to a judgment on legislation; but filibustering…reading from the Congressional Record, for instance; or repeating over and over again for hours on end the same phrases, can be tiresome indeed. Oh well, we shall see.

We've a lot of unfinished business, we members of the General Court, as well we know. There's Court Reform, for instance. We've had the Cox Committee Report for several months now; and with the state budget and the auto insurance legislation out of the way, we'll hopefully have time to address this major issue. Few people can fail to see the necessity for the reforming of our Court System. The drafting of a proposal for the comprehensive reform of our state's judicial system will be a difficult task indeed, requiring the cooperation of both our legislative leadership and the executive branch. We trust all hands will join forces in this vitally needed area of reform; and that some action on the issue will be taken during this session.

As a member of the Health Care Committee, this legislator is extremely interested in a series of bills now pending, which affect the Certificate of Need process under which a hospital's or nursing home's proposal to increase medical facilities and equipment must have state approval…including legislation drafted by Human Services Secretary Jerald Stevens' ad hoc committee that would make some concessions to health care providers but give the state "a handle" on any major equipment purchases proposed by physicians. Health care costs must be controlled as well we know; but it's a controversial and multi-faceted issue, this requirement of a Certificate of Need for any hospital or nursing home expansion or change.

We've a $17 million supplementary budget to address. It was sent to the legislature by the Governor last week; and covers the additional salary costs that were arrived at through the recent collective bargaining action. And we've a second supplementary budget pending, they tell me – one to cover Metco funding, and MBTA debt service and that controversial mandatory school breakfast program.

The Legislative Process is an interesting one; and we've been asked to describe it every now and then by someone who wishes to file a bill or is merely curious as to the course a bill takes once it is filed. So - VOICI! We legislators receive a printed House Calendar each morning in the Chamber at the eleven o'clock session. We have been given a partial list of bills the previous day; and we may have secured a copy of the House Calendar for our earlier perusal by applying for it at the Document Room. The printed House Calendar contains all bills that have had a public hearing before the appropriate joint legislative committee. These bills have received either a favorable or an adverse report. The items on the House Calendar are read in turn by the House Clerk, and they are not debated unless a member disagrees with the report of the committee; in which event he will call "Pass!" That bill will then be debated in the one P.M. Session, the morning sessions being reserved to process matters that are not controversial.

Bills that have received favorable reports by legislative committees will appear on the House Calendar for a second reading, after which second reading a bill is open for debate or amendments before it is ordered to a third reading. The legislation must then be approved by House Counsel, whose responsibility it is to check the bill to assure its being in proper legal form before it is read a third time. The bill is read a third time when it is again open for debate or amendments. The question then comes on passing the bill to be engrossed. Legislation that has received an adverse or OUGHT NOT TO PASS report by a legislative committee appears on the House Calendar. The question is then on accepting the adverse report; and any member who disagrees with the adverse committee report can move to amend the report by substitution of a bill.

In most instances questions before the House are settled by a voice vote or by a standing vote. If a member, however, further doubts the vote, and 29 other members are willing to stand with him, a call of the ayes and nays…in other words, a Roll Call is in order. Then it is that the voices of the Court Officers can be heard calling out "Roll Call in the House in 4 minutes!" Or "3 minutes!" Or even, on occasion, if the Speaker is fairly confident we are all on hand, "2 minutes!" That is the point at which we may be seen racing from committee hearings or offices or snack bar (if we've missed lunch, being far too busy to bother with such mundane activities where we are madly tucking something in to keep body and soul together…to the House Chamber so as not to spoil that vital Roll Call record that's so important to each one of us. And, incidentally, if you are familiar with the distance between Gardner Auditorium and the House Chamber, you may well imagine the breathless state at which we frequently arrive - to inquire madly as to the content of the bill and what it entails and what the debate revealed about it, and then to come to a judgment and press the red or green light…all in the 4 or even 3 minutes we've been provided with for such action. We'd be in Gardner Auditorium for a committee hearing, of course. Whenever a large crowd is expected to testify on a bill the committee books Gardner auditorium for its public hearing. We frequently use it on our Health Committee hearings; seldom on Transportation.

If a bill has been passed to be engrossed in the House, it goes to the Senate where it must receive the same number of readings as it is given in the House. When a bill is passed to be engrossed by both branches, it is sent to the Governor for signing…or vetoing…

Legislative procedure is a thorough and time-consuming process, wouldn't you agree? And we really do have ample opportunity to consider the ramifications of all bills before they become law…

Thank Heavens!

AUGUST 21, 1977

Another interesting week on Beacon Hill, Having a deep concern for the problems of our Massachusetts fishermen, menaced as they are by foreign fishing vessels and the rest, we availed ourselves of an opportunity on Friday last, to "see what lobstering is all about" and acquaint ourselves with problems that are faced by this particular group of fishermen. Accordingly, we arranged - Ted and I-to spend a day on a lobster boat with Nathaniel "Laddie" Dexter, a lobsterman with fifteen years of experience, so we were told, and the current President of the South shore Lobster Fishermen's Association. "I like to know what we're dealing with when we have legislation on a particular subject," I had replied to my dear husband's query as to "why in the world" I was interested in lobstering…hadn't I enough issues to worry about already?"

"How long do you wish to stay out?' I had been asked. "Oh," I had replied airily, not having the foggiest notion of what lobstering is all about, "All day probably." And all day it was to be…

We were to meet "Laddie" at Green Harbor and take off on the "new fiberglass craft, 'Happy Days.'" "How early can you leave?" the lobsterman wanted to know. "As early as you wish," I had replied, thinking in terms of nine or ten. "Good," he had said sweetly, "Then supposing we say seven o'clock from the Town Pier." I was able to gasp inaudibly, happily, as I mentally made plans for arising at five, leaving Braintree at six and turning in at the town Pier on time…

The day was to provide an adventure we shall not soon forget…And never again shall the Metayers fuss about the high cost of lobster! But to begin at the beginning - Lobsters, we were to learn, hibernate so to speak, a bit like bears…In cold weather they may lie dormant in the sea. They can live for as long as two years without eating, our lobsterman told us…surviving on the plankton in the water. They come into warm water to moult…to shed their shells; and they swim in schools like fish.

Very little is known about lobsters, Laddie told us. Biologists form Massachusetts disagree with biologists from Maine; and biologists from Maine disagree with biologists from Canada…Laddie had brought no lunch along though he was planning to check 400 traps, a chore which would take him at least until 3:30 that afternoon. "I just won't have time to eat," he had said. "you'll see why shortly."

The lobster boat had a broad deck with an outer rim a foot or so in width. "We should have brought chairs," I had whispered to Ted as, stepping aboard, I observed there wasn't a place to sit anywhere. It was soon apparent to us both that there wasn't a spot to place chairs or anything else on this utilitarian and functional craft…Anything but lobstering equipment, that is.

Each trap does not have a buoy attached to it, contrary to our expectations. There is one buoy for each ten traps; and the traps are separated by 100' of rope. The fisherman would normally start at the end of his traps, we were told. The day being a bit on the foggy side however, with the sun struggling valiantly to break through, he had decided to begin at the beginning of his lines instead.

We approached the first buoy which he hauled up with a boat hook and placed on a flat surface that held three huge plastic barrels of nauseatingly odiferous bait. He then attached the line to a winch and commenced to haul the ten traps aboard, one at a time, kicking the line aside where it coiled like a great dripping snake on the deck. Laddie would open the trap, remove a lobster if one was within, replace the bait on a metal stake; (the bait would be gone even if there was NO lobster) pick up and carry to the outer rim of the boat each and every one of those 95 pound dripping traps; ride on for a bit then work the winch to reset the whole, to drop the first trap and then in turn each one of the ten per set, with 100' of rope separating them, then drop the buoy…then on to the next buoy and the next set of 10 traps…

We had expected each trap to be bulging with lobsters. They weren't. Most of them were empty. One or two contained "shorts"…lobsters not sufficiently sized for fishing. These had to be thrown back into the sea. Incidentally, each lobster had to be measured by hand with a gauge, since the taking of a short lobster can result in a $50 fine and the loss of a license. The first ten traps yielded three lobsters, each one of which had to undergo a process by which the claw were banded with an elastic, "They don't use pegs anymore," Laddie had said. "They cause the lobsters to bleed." A female lobster carrying a supply of eggs must also be thrown back into the water. And, incidentally, we were astounded to learn that they carry these eggs for 18 months and that it takes six or seven years before a lobster is sufficiently large for lobstering…

Our next stop, at 55' depth, yielded two lobsters. They, like their predecessors, were laid in a sectional tray, banded and then placed in a tank into which sea water ebbed and flowed.

The buoys are easily identifiable, we learned. Each lobsterman has a registered color and the last four digits of his Social Security Number must be placed on the buoy for additional information. "You don't have to register your particular area," Laddie told us. "The sea is open to everyone." The morning wore on. Our lobsterman, Ted and I were all tucked in together in the forward end of the boat; beside the odiferous barrels of bait. Luckily for us, we're never seasick. "If you stepped into the rear of the boat when the traps were going over, you'd be swept overboard and that would be the end of you," our "host" had said. We understood what he meant as we saw this great coil of rope race over the rear of the boat, carrying the lobster traps, one after another, into the sea behind us. We never did get to check Laddie's 400 traps. We'd only managed to check 110 of them, with a yield of about 45 to 50 lobsters, when the sun that had struggled so valiantly to break through the clouds managed to disappear completely. Fog then "crept in on little cat feet," to quote the poet; and we were lost in a sea of white that swirled about the windshield of our craft and hid everything from sight. Laddies's craft is equipped with radar, thank heavens; and so we were guided back to shore by that marvelous screen upon which he kept his eyes glued…but not until we had rendezvoused with a fellow lobsterman whose craft was not equipped with radar and who followed us in…at about eleven A.M. rather than the 3:30 P.M. originally envisioned.

Have I said I'll never complain about the price of lobsters? Laddie Dexter worked harder that day than just about anyone we've ever watched do a day's work…And thanks to him we'll know a lot more about lobstering legislation when it comes our way.

One very important thing more. If you're interested in our Braintree bus service, do make a point of attending the MBTA meeting devoted to that issue, which has been scheduled for next Tuesday, August 23, at 7:30 at the Thayer Public Library. Your input is invaluable to MBTA and to Braintree.

OCTOBER 30, 1977

A very difficult week indeed on Beacon Hill. You will undoubtedly be reading of the action of a group of "dissident" House members who have been tying up legislative business by offering motions for discharge from the Committee on Bills in the Third Reading and the Committee on Ways and Means of hundreds of bills that have been held in these two House Committees. Incidentally, we inquired and found they had not previously asked to have these bills discharged and been refused.

So that you may better understand what is happening, perhaps it might be in order to review the role of both of these committees and the relationship of that role to the bills we file.

All legislation to be filed goes primarily to the office of the House Counsel, where it is placed in legal language and researched thoroughly so that all statutes which may be affected in any way by the proposed law are spelled out within the body of the bill. The bill goes first to the appropriate committee for a public hearing; it is then voted on by committee members in executive session and given either a favorable report on an OUGHT NOT TO PASS. It goes next to the House for a second reading. If the OUGHT NOT TO PASS is to be challenged and debated by the sponsor of the bill, it is done at that time. If, however, a favorably reported bill is given a third reading, it goes then to the Committee on Bills in the Third Reading for a final check before returning to the House to be engrossed and sent to the Senate for a similar course of action. It that Committee in its final check finds that a legal or technical change is necessary, the matter must be handled before it returns to the House for engrossment. Occasionally, a bill will be returned to the House with an amendment offered by Third reading. The amendment will read that "the committee on bills in the third reading wishes to be discharged from further consideration of the bill." This means that they are not fully satisfied with the bill, but have been pressured into getting it out. I am always uneasy when this situation develops for I wonder then if the law (if the bill becomes law) will be challenged in the courts. That's costly business for the Commonwealth.

Incidentally, several of the bills in the dissidents group are my own, and I, personally, would prefer to have them judged to be 100% perfect by Third Reading before I work to make them the law of the Commonwealth. We have too many unenforceable laws already on our books, to my way of thinking.

Well now, so much for the Committee on Bills in the Third Reading. Let's look at the House Committee on Ways and Means. It is to this committee that all money bills are sent, and if the amount involved is a substantial one, that cost must be listed on the bill when it is returned to the House. Under the right of free petition here in the Commonwealth, anyone may file any legislation he wishes to file regardless of the impact on the tax situation or anything else. Many bills that are filed by our colleagues for perfectly good reason, viz. to solve existent and recognized problems, cost a great deal of money. The problem may be one that every one of us recognizes as a legitimate one, but the cost of solving that problem may be decidedly prohibitive. It could require additional state taxes in this state of ours where we are taxed to the hilt. On the other hand, it may be the kind of bill one could not in conscience vote against, a so-called "Motherhood" bill, and so it could easily become law and complicate our already overburdened tax situation. We read recently that our state's Human Services budget for 1978, for instance, will seek an increase of some 240M dollars, bringing the total to over 2 billion dollars. This representative simply could not vote for one more additional tax package for Massachusetts. And the saddest aspect of this situation is the fact that too many of our colleagues employ the irresponsible tactic of voting FOR all the goodies, regardless of cost, and AGAINST the Budget and Tax package. Well, here in the Committee on Ways and Means can be found, to our way of thinking a safety valve for the general over-taxed public. We are frequently thankful that some bills are lost there, especially in the light of complicating facts revealed in committee hearings or in debate.

Incidentally, this representative has personally experienced nothing but cooperation when the Chairman of Ways and Means is approached in regard to a bill held there. Either the bill comes out of committee, or an explanation of why it is being held is forthcoming. Other reps appear to have been less successful.

Changing the subject, we continue to be concerned about a number of vital issues that have yet be faced. There is Court Reform, for instance, which is expected to emerge next week, and the possible solution to the Binding Arbitration issue for our police and firefighters. We have yet to deal with "An act providing for the establishment of a joint labor-management committee to oversee municipal police and firefighter collective bargaining and arbitration proceedings." As we analyze this particular bill, we find it calls for a committee of 12 members: 3 from the police, 3 from the firefighters and 6 members appointed by the Governor, but selected by a coalition including representatives from the League of Cities and Towns, Mayors Association, City and Town Manager Association, and Association of Finance Committees, i.e. Local Government Advisory Committee. This coalition will meet regularly with the Governor and submit a list of 6 members which he must appoint. The panel of 12 then select an outside Chairman. The Chairman will be paid per diem; and the remaining members receive expenses only. The committee will be placed in the Department of Industry and Labor for administrative purposes, but will not be subject to it. They will provide clerical help, and the committee will endeavor to resolve issues in dispute. They will decide what matters (if any) will go to final and binding arbitration, and appoint the neutral arbiter if this is necessary. The 3-man panel then appointed has the option of taking either the final offer of each or a position in between, and their decision is binding.

Wish we had room to discuss the matter of the state employees pay raise; will do so in our next column. It should be worthy of note, however, to state here that the supplemental budget when it left the House was set at 19 million; when it left the Senate, however with 40 additional costly amendments added to it, the total cost of the budget had risen to over 73 million. It will, of course, go to a Committee of Conference, where hopefully, most of these amendments will be lost.

NOVEMBER 20, 1977

Thursday in the House of Representatives, and it was to be back to the issue of the Code of Ethics which promises to dominate House action for some time to come. Amendments that would reduce the amount of gifts, dinners, passes to theatres, museums, baseball games from $100 yearly to $35 yearly; and to extend the "gift" classification to include just about every kind of pass we may be offered; and to interpret that word "gift" as including any and all "dinners, beverages, etc." were to be debated and in most instances to be adopted.

Most interesting of all, perhaps, in the deliberations on our Ethics Code, was the rejection of an amendment that would have prevented the soliciting of campaign funds by House leaders of both the Democratic and Republican parties, specifically the "Committee to Re-elect a Democratic House," which is controlled by House Speaker Thomas W. McGee and "SAVE" and "START", the two campaign funds that are controlled by the House Minority leader, Republican Representative Francis W. Hatch, Jr.

Both parties were solidly united against that particular amendment, and in our judgment, rightly so. It becomes increasingly more difficult to raise the kind of campaign funds necessary now to run for public office, and if we dry up campaign funds of that nature we must accept the premise that only the very wealthy can run and win...in which case, we could very easily wind up with the kinds of laws that are designed to protect primarily the interest of the very wealthy…perhaps at the expense of the rest of us. Representative government, in our opinion, would be just that government that is representative of all the people of the Commonwealth. At any rate, the vote against that particular amendment was, we are happy to report, overwhelming.

There are so many gray areas in this Code of Ethics issue we're dealing with, as there are in so many of the issues we face in the General Court. Very few issues are really clear-cut unfortunately. It did not take us very long to discover that disturbing fact.

Friday evening, and here we were, Ted and I, at the D.A.V. Hall, participating in a wonderful Veterans Day Dinner Party for our surviving Braintree World War I Veterans and their ladies and the widows of World War I Veterans. The Affair had been beautifully staged by Legionnaire "Ted" Sweeney, whose beaming smile quickly set the stage for the happy mood of the guests he was greeting so cordially. And a young and smart looking group of veterans and ladies they were, incidentally!

There were a few speakers on hand to highlight the meaning of Veterans Day itself, Past State Commander of the American Legion John "Jake" Colmer among them; and what a dynamic speaker he turned out to be! But mostly it was a fun time, with music to dance to and to sing to by Braintree's own inimitable John Sullivan, entertainment that brought back memories of last year's great Legion Show; and a beaming Bob Bruynell to do the M.C.-ing in his own particular and easy style…an unbeatable set of ingredients for a happy occasion, wouldn't you say??? And it was just that…Monday and it was to be back again to the Code of Ethics. Rumor had tagged this an all-night session; as it turned out, however, we adjourned at six P.M. Allowing time for this rep to dash home to Braintree and arrive but a few minutes late at her Town Hall Office Hours. And, speaking of those Monday evening office hours of mine at Town Hall, since from here until December we shall be facing the distinct possibility of having late sessions, (This is Wednesday, my deadline date, and our session lasted again until seven P.M.) it might be advisable for my constituents to phone my home before journeying to Town Hall. Ted is always kept apprised of possible late night developments, and so can alert any inquirer as to the current status of the situation.

Monday was to be totally devoted to Ethics, and a Code, acceptable to even the most G.I. among us, was at last voted affirmatively and over-whelmingly by the House…not the entire Code, needless to say, but those aspects of the Code that deal with financial disclosure. The rest is yet to come. Tuesday was to be an especially delightful day. With the thornier aspects of the Ethics issue behind us, we were to set off at dawn and with a light heart indeed on a visit to the General Dynamics Shipyard in Quincy. The occasion was to be the departure on sea trials of the L.N.G. Tanker, "Aries," and members of the General Court - particularly our South Shore colleagues had been invited to watch the progress of the giant vessel through the Fore River Bridge. The idea, of course, was to impress upon us all the necessity for replacing the bridge which is proving inadequate to the demands of the shipyard. Watching from a launch on the other side the progress of the tanker through the bridge proved to be a bit on the scary side. The enormous "Aries" had but a fifteen foot clearance on both sides for its hull, and but two feet clearance for its superstructure. We were anything but envious of the pilot whose function it was to maneuver the giant to safety; he did so, however, and we sure applauded him for his skill.

The morning turned out to be a wintry one indeed, and so much of our tanker-watching had to be done through the launch window…while, however, we were wishing ardently we were brave enough to be viewing the historic event from the upper deck.

The "Aries," we were told, is the largest vessel General Dynamics is able currently to get through the bridge. It is 936' in length and 143' wide; and what a thrill it was to see her propellers come gradually to life, her wonderful wide hull slip almost silently from her bay; and the magnificent vessel head majestically out to sea…her great bulk silhouetted against a gray autumn sky that had the look of winter about it…her crew moving like toy figures high on the superstructure; the tugs that preceded and followed her looking in comparison with the tanker itself like the small bathtub toys of infant grandsons.

We were absolutely enchanted with the changes in the shipyard itself, the results, we were told, of a 60 million dollar investment by General Dynamics; and - if we were not running out of space we would discuss those changes, and the anticipated future of this vital yard that has developed from the brainchild of Braintree's own Thomas Watson. That will have to wait for next week's column, however; and it's such an exciting story we'll see to it that we shan't forget to include it in our next week's offering. We're thrilled to death with the story, that was beautifully demonstrated for us in a slide program in which we saw Fore River as it was in 1964 when G.D. took it over, and as it looks now. It's some story!

DECEMBER 11, 1977

It's winter on the hill. For the first time this year, the Park Square outdoor thermometer registered two degrees below freezing on Monday morning; and by Monday evening we were descending the hill amid a blinding snowstorm. Winter had arrived!

It was a pretty storm. The flakes were huge and heavy and they zinged against our umbrella as we sloshed along the pavement, wet from previous rain, staying close to the sidewalk's edge for it was well after rush hour when we left the Capitol building. This is Boston, you see, and we have been warned in our crime prevention seminars that purse snatchers can lurk in darkened doorways or in alleyways. "Always walk close to the sidewalk's edge," we have been told; and especially when our sessions are late we do just that.

We find ourselves mentally humming that little old Christmas song, "Walking in a Winter Wonderland" as enroute to the MBTA station we view Boston Common under the lights, with the snow-furred tree branches dancing in the wind as if set to music. It was a wild night actually; even the salvation army troubadours had taken cover and we missed the sound of their little bell at the subway entrance.

The snow had changed to rain by the time we reached Quincy Square, but enough of it remained to have changed that Christmas-decorated place into a veritable fairyland. Ted had a cold and so we had prevented him from picking up his spouse at the MBTA station, and we rode the bus past the gorgeously lighted trees and the snow-topped Christmas crèche, we were happy we did so. Ted would have driven home the back way and we'd not have seen Quincy Square at its Christmas best..

You will forgive me, I trust, if I wax a bit poetic in my column this week. Christmas, you see, is my very favorite time of the year, and - like the younger generation - I LOVE snow! We've been waiting for it for weeks. "It feels like snow" we've said to husband Ted on a dozen different days. "That's wishful thinking," he had assured with a grin. He does not share my enthusiasm for the white stuff...

Tuesday morning, and the thermometer at Park Square had dropped to 30 degrees. The wind whistled us up Park Street to the top of the hill where its fury reached a peak and we mounted the State House steps breathless and tousled. It is 9:00 A.M. as we enter the Capitol building, not to leave it until 10:45 that evening. The Court Reform bill will by that time have been debated to the bitter end, to be passed finally at 10:30 P.M. By a vote of 170 to 27.

It will have proved to be quite a day. Somewhere along the line leadership will have reported that a total of 79 amendments to the bill have been added to date. Many of these amendments had occasioned hours of debate, and still they came...

We had recessed for an hour or so for dinner. Outside the storm was raging and so we gals were reluctant to leave the State House; our great Chief Court Officer, Louis, had consequently volunteered to brave the icy sidewalks and the snow and pick up dinners for us at nearby Primo's. It was then fun to dine in a group around the huge lobby table, watching as we did the intermittent snow squalls launching their futile attacks against the huge Capitol windows.

Back to the Chamber for an 8:30 amendment Roll Call and by 10:30 it was to be all over. The House version of Court Reform would be headed for a Conference Committee where a compromise would be reached between our version and that of the Senate. So wherein lies the difference between the two versions as it now stands?? Both branches are in favor of a state takeover of court costs; the two agree on the issue of holding de novo trials in the District Courts as a means of relieving overcrowding at the Superior Court levels. Both bills call for a single, unified court budget. (There are currently 400 separate court budgets prepared each year.) Both bills favor a strong central administration of the court system; both would grant sweeping powers to the Chief Administrative Justice...

The branches differ on the selection process for that Chief Administrative Justice. The House version would have the Supreme Judicial Court select the Chief from a list of three nominees submitted by each of the seven court systems: the Senate version would permit the Supreme Judicial Court to select the Chief from the state's 258 judges. We can live with either version. There is some dispute on the transferability of the judges from District to Superior Court. The Senate bill would require all judges to agree on their transfer as a condition of receiving the pay increases included in both versions; the House bill would exempt some 40 judges of specialized courts from unlimited transfer.

Both bills set up personnel standards. The Senate version would permit the Chief Administrative Justice to set the standards; the House Version would primarily involve the administrative judges of each court division in the standard-setting process. And the pay increases for court personnel differ in both versions. In the House bill some clerks of court could receive as much as $9,000 in pay increase; in the Senate version the ceiling in most instances is set at $5,000.

So now it will be up to the Committee of Conference to come up with a compromise package on Court Reform which we may not amend but must vote either up or down.

We worry more than a little about the cost of Court Reform. We shall find it difficult indeed to vote for additional state taxes should this be deemed necessary for the state takeover of court costs; and we are concerned about the distribution formula for the state funding. We want Braintree to benefit property tax-wise on that distribution formula; we pray that situation will prevail.

Wednesday evening, and our session had adjourned early for our Women's Caucus Christmas Dinner Party. House Speaker Thomas W. McGee and Caucus Aide Ruth Ferguson are to be our Women's Caucus dinner guests at "T.G.L.Friday's," an exotic and delightful new restaurant on Newbury Street. "What in the world does T.G.I. stand for?" I had asked; and I'd laughed aloud when given the answer. It is none other than "Thank God it's Friday!" Isn't that original and delightful? So was our evening. The food was super; the fellowship great; and "Tommy" McGee a fascinating, fun, story-telling guest, happily expansive in this away-from-the-state- House setting....SO-here I am back in Braintree at 2:00 A.M. Of a Thursday morning dashing off my column for tomorrow's deadline…after a hectic day which included the filing date deadline for those countless bills we've managed to file - AGAIN! We'll discuss those bills in next week's column and undoubtedly a few subsequent ones. This column is too long as it is…Why do I always have so much to write about??

DECEMBER 18, 1977

For years we've been obliged to tuck in a Christmastime visit to Boston Common to see the lights; now as we leave the Capitol building each night the Common's holiday magic all lies beautifully before us - the wonderful dancing trees with their wealth of gold and blue and orange and red; the silent Christmas crèche that holds the meaning of the blessed season; the Christmas carolers; the Salvation Army troubadours; the lot…

We have watched the march of winter up the hill, and it has now led us to the highlight of the passing year- the Christmas season!

We've not yet had time to count the bills we've filed or co-sponsored for the coming session; we've been too busy filing them; but there appears to be, as always, a raft of them, many of which we'll discuss in future columns or press releases.

The weekend that preceded this week on Beacon Hill had been another happy one in Braintree. It had begun on Friday evening with attendance at the Town employees' Christmas Party, at which, thanks in large part to our delightful table companions and with the added pleasure of seeing so many of our seldom encountered Town Hall friends, we had a ball! And it was with infinite regret, we might add, that the Metayers were persuaded by rumors of icing roads to leave the party early; Ted dislikes driving on ice…

Saturday had housed for your L. of the H. the happiest chore of the year-decorating for Christmas; setting up the lights; the myriad Christmas trees, large and small; the wreaths and the candles that are a part of this wonderful Christmas season and then the outdoor spots to highlight the whole holiday performance. And then it was Sunday and we had dashed off to the fabulous "Yesteryear Yuletide Tour" of the town's oldest house, now proudly in the possession of Braintree's Mrs. Carl R. Johnson, Jr.

Mrs. Johnson is a member of our Braintree Gardeners Guild, that wonderful group that has come a mighty long way in the two years of its existence, a fact that was evidenced by the enormity of the talent displayed in the "Yesteryear Yuletide" decorations that graced the lovely old 1665 home. Words are truly inadequate to describe the Christmas magic we witnessed as we crossed the road to face a Christmas home that had stepped right out of a century long gone. From its beautifully decorated front door to the immense laurel wreaths that adorned each of the many windows, to the antique sleigh piled high with Christmas tree and gifts, the message of a seventeenth century Christmas welcome went forth for all to see. And the interior of the house from its stunning Colonially gowned hostesses to the bread baking in the oven and the chestnuts roasting on the fire represented sheer Christmas poetry.

Everything in the house had been hand-crafted by the "Gardeners"…the marvelously fashioned wreaths, no two alike; the garlands and table centerpieces; the kissing balls and appropriately trimmed Christmas trees; and the assortment of Christmas gifts that were offered for sale…We are happy to find a lovely hemp macrame hanging plant holder for a pair of treasured friends we find difficult to shop for. We pounced on it and the find provided a crowning touch to an afternoon visit that represented pure Christmas enchantment for this gal. If you missed it, folks, you lost a golden opportunity to enjoy a date with history! Congratulations, Braintree Gardeners Guild-ers! Monday morning and we had donned our thermals and set out for Beacon Hill, thinking not too happily of the walk up Park Street to the State House. The eight degree temperature registered on the Park Street thermometer did little to lift our spirits, nor did the knowledge that the chill factor had been reported at well below zero. Nonetheless we had survived…and had arrived…to face a rather uneventful day, none the worse for wear, incidentally, with the single exception of a nose that stayed frosted for the remainder of the day. When WILL some enterprising entrepreneur invent a reasonably becoming kind of nose warmer?

Monday evening, and we had again found ourselves trotting down Park Street at six-fifteen (another late night session on the Hill) amid a wild little old snowstorm, our eyes riveted to the enchantment of the Common's Christmas lights as seen through a curtain of snowflakes…with more of the same for Tuesday evening, and by the look of the night skies, we'll be going it all again tomorrow (Wednesday)…How many times in years gone by had we wished that husband Ted was adventurous enough to schedule our annual Boston Common Christmas night during a blizzard, we mused as we walked along. (He's far too sensible for such way out nonsense…but we're not…). Now here it was happening night after night without our even trying to make it happen.

The week on the Hill has been a rather uneventful one to date. We're all scrambling madly to get live bills out of whatever hiding place they've gotten into; and we're mentally endeavoring to line up procedures for defending the countless complicated bills we've filed for next year, wondering as we do so, how we shall ever be able to tuck these defenses into a schedule that will call for attendance at the myriad committee hearings that accompany membership in two extremely busy and active committees, Health Care and Transportation. Incidentally, apropos of the filing of those countless complicated bills, we had an opportunity to discuss filing procedures with one of the old-timers from the House Counsel's office, a gentleman who was busily engaged in steering a staff of lawyers through the intricacies of bill drafting in a committee room that is adjacent to our office. And-how very proud was this Braintree-ite and close personal friend of a still sadly missed Bernice Delory when he termed this distinguished Braintree resident "the greatest, most learned among other things, of the bill drafters in the Commonwealth." Bernice Delory's untimely passing is still spoken of with infinite sorrow on Beacon Hill; and this representative misses her shining, delightful, brilliant presence perhaps more than anyone there.

Well, now, it will be back to Beacon Hill tomorrow for what will undoubtedly be another uneventful day. There is so little time now to get anything of consequence to the governor's desk for signing. When a legislative session lasts all year as this has done, there is considerable confusion as the two sessions overlap. Our live bills must be filed again in order to assure any chance they might have for passage…at least, that was our private assessment and so, in addition to our new bills we had found ourselves re-filing all important old bills. A governor has ten days (exclusive of Sundays and holidays) to sign or veto a bill, you see; all bills not acted upon by him after the legislature is out of session, however, which date this year will be January 3, are POCKET VETOED. Which is undoubtedly why action on the Hill this week is frenzied but little of consequence is accomplished.

JANUARY 8, 1978

One legislative year ended and another began during this past week on Beacon Hill. Tuesday, the last day of the 1977 session, saw the Court Reform legislation go down to defeat amid a display of pyrotechnics on both sides of the aisle - only to rise again from the ashes on Wednesday morning, with the Governor's announcement that he had filed another bill which reduced the judicial pay raises to a more palatable level. Those enormous salary increases, as high as $11,000 in some cases, had figured largely in the defeat of what was seen other wise as a good bill. At any rate, the Governor's bill along with two similar Court Reform measures, went to the Judiciary committee on Wednesday, the first day of the 1978 session. A public hearing on all three bills will be held on January 11, and leadership has promised that the bill will become law by early February. We shall be happy to see that happen. Court reform is essential. The back log of cases in many of our courts finds criminals walking the streets and committing additional crimes. The speedy administration of justice is their right and ours. So, here's hoping we have that bill on the Governor's desk by early February.

1977 has been a long year for the members of the general Court. It's been an "often contentious" year, to quote from the Speaker of the House. It has, however, been a productive year in many respects. For the first time in a quarter of a century, for instance, the Legislature has voted a TAX CUT. As of January 1 of last year, the meals tax had been reduced from 8% to 6%, with a net result of $40 million dollars savings to the people of the Commonwealth.

We voted an additional $30 million in local aid, thus hopefully reducing real estate taxes for our citizens; and we've begun the State assumption of county court costs, an action which is seen as providing at least $80 million in savings to property tax payers.

We've passed a $290 million balanced transportation aid package which is projected to generate 40,000 construction jobs during the duration of the projects, which are state-wide in scope.

We were instrumental in securing $55 million in rebates for Massachusetts motorists, grossly overcharged this past year; and we've eliminated the arbitrary assignment of good drivers to the high risk pool simply on a geographical basis.

We revised our unemployment compensation program, cracking down on fraud by either party, and saving an estimated $270 million in Federal credits for Massachusetts employers.

We've initiated a pilot Jury Reform program designed to provide a better "mix" on juries, with shorter jury service time; and we've amended the Blue Laws to provide for pre-Christmas retail sales for our merchants, while protecting store employees rights at the same time, and we've abolished mandatory age 70 retirement for most public employees, allowing us to keep our productive people working.

We passed a law which reformed the taxation of Massachusetts-based life insurance companies, a change which is designed to promote home-based insurance companies and to create a special $100 million industry fund for job-creating or job-sustaining investments in Massachusetts business. This action is expected to favorably affect up to 4,000 jobs.

We have passed legislation which provides tax breaks to farmers, thus enabling them to resist selling their property for development, keeping the land in agricultural use; and we've moved to make the collective bargaining and binding arbitration process more equitable to all involved by the creation of a new screening process for disputes; we've also modernized the no fault divorce process, halving the waiting time for certain divorces, and modernizing the alimony laws to provide payment to either spouse.

A shelter for women in transition, for battered women and children, has been established; and we've moved to protect the civil rights of persons called before Grand Juries by allowing them to have counsel.

We have reorganized the State Alcoholic Beverages Control Commission; and have required insurance companies to provide easy-to-read policies for consumers (we love that one; never could understand insurance policies…); and we've abolished the archaic "Fair Trade Laws" which have set minimum retail sale price floors on so many items.

We have passed a number of bills designed to streamline the permitting process required by our many environmental protection laws so as to keep allowable development from being strangled in red tape.

We've passed an acceptable Code of Ethics; and handled the redistricting issue; and promoted a new climate that is favorable to economic development and the expansion of Massachusetts industry and business, the kind of climate which will save present jobs and create new ones…and let's face it, JOBS are the most important issue facing all of us these days in Massachusetts. Incidentally, we're happy to report that the state's close to 12% unemployment rate of two years ago has dropped to 5.8%. We wished it were lower. The loss of jobs means an increase in Welfare and Unemployment Compensation, in the many categories of Human Services which add so enormously to our state budget; the loss of jobs means human suffering as well.

Two years ago our state budget was more than $800 million out of balance, we were informed; today fiscal experts are predicting a budget surplus of $200 million or more for 1978. We've cut corners on all sides financially. The number of state employees has been reduced by several thousands, primarily by attrition. As people retire, they are not replaced.

Like all of my colleagues, Democrats and Republicans working together, I take pride in what we have been able to do and regret what we were unable to accomplish in 1977. And I look forward to what will hopefully be a year of greater achievement in 1978.

Ours is one of only four year-long sessions in the history of Massachusetts, we have been told. We've answered close to 800 Roll Calls. We now look forward to facing in the year ahead the 7,000 bills that have been filed this year and are currently in the process of being catalogued and printed. Many of them were filed by your L. of the H. She'll keep you informed on their progress as the year develops. And may the year that lies ahead be a Happy, Healthy & Prosperous one for all of you!

JANUARY 15, 1978

It is quiet on Beacon Hill these days, legislatively speaking. The several thousands of bills that have been filed are not as yet in print; our committee hearings, therefore, still lie ahead; and so we are in Informal Sessions. It's the lull before the proverbial storm, needless to say. Accordingly, interspersing our Constituent work, we've been hard at work on the family filing system, bringing things up to date; and discarding the old to make way for the new material that will come our way in such enormous quantities now that it's '78…It's not a very exciting way to spend time on Beacon Hill; it's an essential one, however, if room is to be found for the pros and cons of the myriad controversial issues that lie before us.

Today (Wednesday, my deadline date) has been VERY exciting, however. It was to begin with a beautiful event, "A Tribute to the Memory of the Braintree Senior Citizens Who Gave of their Utmost for the Progress of our Country." Chaired and planned handsomely by Senior Citizens' President "Joe" Magaldi, the services at Sons of Italy Hall were memorable in every respect. There was the celebration of a beautiful Mass by Father Berube, St. Francis' beloved Pastor, the theme of its Liturgy, LOVE. There was the music of that truly great choral group, our own "Mellow-Tones." There was a delicious breakfast, with entertaining table companions. And, to top it all off, a splendid guest speaker, Dr. James J. Callaghan, the Secretary of the Executive Office of Elder Affairs, Comm. Of Mass. Could anyone have asked for more???

Dr. Callaghan, with whom I later drove to the State House in time to hear the Governor's "State of the State Address," announced that there are 700,000 Massachusetts citizens over 65 years of age. Terming the creation of his Secretariat the result of action by the elderly who got together and petitioned the Legislature, he stated as his goal the pulling together of Federal, State and local resources for the benefit of the elderly, on whom 35 Million dollars have been spent this year, 22 Million on Home Care; 7 Million on Meals; and 3 Million on a variety of other service programs. Dr. Callaghan pledged to work toward independence and dignity for the elderly, and he reviewed legislative accomplishments on their behalf during the past year. Regarding the banning of mandatory retirement at age 70, he stated that pensions have to be at a high enough level for people to live on; that more jobs must be available for older people who wish to work; and that those who wish to work beyond retirement age should be able to do so.

The speaker cited the 100 Million housing bond which will add between 4,000 and 5,000 units for the elderly. The Governor signed that particular bill last week. He also informed us that the Governor intended to sign that long-sought bill to provide property tax relief for our elderly...House Bill 6600, on which this representative, a co-sponsor, has worked hard and persistently for the past three years. H-6600 provides relief to those over 70 years of age by eliminating the value of their domicile from their total estate value. In a community at 100% valuation, such as our own, the $40,000 estate level has excluded countless of our elderly citizens whose homes are valued at close to that amount, and frequently in excess of it. Since the value of a bank account, stocks, bonds, a car etc. must be included in estate value, the value of the domicile precluded many of our most deserving citizens from qualifying. The top estate figure has now, under H-6600, been lowered to $17,000; this, however, will not include the assessed valuation of the home, and so many more of our elderly will be entitled to the abatement, which, under this legislation has been increased from $350 to $500. Wish it might have been a greater abatement amount, however it does represent a break through and we're mighty pleased to have sponsored it...

Dr. Callaghan's immediate goals will be to establish a good strong Secretariat; to get all Senior groups together, to do a better job of Advocacy for the elderly; to try to get more elderly people involved in decision making; to monitor the spending of money and to secure more resources. A worthy group of goals, we opined as we listened to this most sincere and dedicated young man. An interesting trip to the State House where we arrived in time to see His Excellency escorted into the Joint session of the House and Senate for that "State of the State Speech"...and where we fumed to hear his admission that there IS a surplus of $200 Million dollars which he proposes to return to the cities and towns in Local Aid. Great! But was there - or was there not - a $200 Million surplus??? We'd been asking that question ever since Secretary Buckley pulled that "bottom drawer" boner a few months back. We'd been assured that no such surplus existed. Now here was our Governor proposing the spending of it...We who had voted for additional taxes at his urging, and who had wanted additional money returned to the cities and towns all year long, found ourselves deeply resentful of the Governor's election year maneuver...Oh well, so long as our own Town of Braintree profits well from the proposed formula, should we really feel so aggrieved??? Perhaps not. As a representative from Braintree, however, we shall keep close watch on the distribution formula and we pray that Braintree will indeed benefit handsomely from this unexpected surplus we find ourselves about to enjoy.

We'd another interesting experience today. Having taken a trip to the Supply Room, and having found the place locked, with a "Back in 10 Min." sign on the door, we had availed ourselves of that ten minute break to dash down the corridor to the State Archives, where we found some perfectly delightful old documents. One was entitled, "Indians 1811." "This is a petition to Governor Elbridge Gerry and the General Court from the Indians of Gay Head," we read... "The Indians are asking the Governor not to appoint a guardian to look over them. They wish to remain independent. The Indians tell the Governor that they have supported our own poor and schools and have not been chargeable to any town. There is no tribe or people of colour in the Commonwealth that live so well as we do." The manuscript is written in beautiful copperplate, and signed by "Abraham Cooper, Jean Cooper and Abigail Nevers (his mark)," We also found Paul Revere's bill for the Commonwealth seal. "Revere engraved the first seal of the Commonwealth," we read, "and charged 600 pounds for his work. His fee may seem high, but notice below this figure that the real worth of 600 inflated pounds was only 8 pounds hard money."

Sooooo-There's nothing new about inflation....

FEBRUARY 19, 1978

Life came to a standstill on Beacon Hill this past week just as it did in all parts of our storm-tossed, blizzard-battered Commonwealth.

Although we had arrived at the State House on Monday morning all set to resume our formal sessions, Speaker McGee, with an eye to the weather, had adjourned the House shortly after 2:00 P.M., we're happy to report, giving us a fighting chance to reach our homes before the full impact of the blizzard would hit.

The last act of this representative, e'er she slid down Park Street to the MBTA station, was to finalize with the Governor's office some very special plans for a very special event she is currently setting up in Doric Hall for February 21- and therein lies a tale...

A few weeks back, my friend Malcom had sent me a couple of early photographs of the State House, with a request that they be correctly dated. Well, in the course of dealing with the state Archivist, my path happily crossed that of a delightful young history buff with whom I have managed to form an instant friendship...and from whom I was to hear a fascinating tale.

The first woman ever to speak at the Massachusetts State House, she said, was one Angelina Grimke who, on February 21, 1838, addressed the General Court on the abolition of slavery. Angelina, a Southern lady of Charleston's aristocracy, was thought to have been motivated by her natural, uncorrupted feelings of kinship and love for the slave children on her family's estate. Well, according to my informant, when she spoke at the State House on that memorable occasion, Angelina had to fight a double battle. Not only the subject of her speech, which was ABOLITION, but also the idea of a woman's delivering the speech were unprecedented. Never before had a woman dared to "break through the confines of her home and attempt to reconstruct the male realm of public policy," wrote my friend Anne; and the crowd that filled the floors and balconies of the State House hissed and scoffed at this woman whom the press had branded as a "freak" referring to her not as "Angelina" but as "Develina," and attacking her "unwomanliness" and her appearance "in brazen defiance of public opinion."

Well, as has often happened in life, Angelina Grimke's audience sat spellbound as she began to speak; and as this magnetic and powerful Southern aristocrat presented to the legislators a petition signed by 20,000 Massachusetts women, demanding the liberation of black people, many borderline abolitionists were reported to have been "easily converted." I stand before you as a citizen," she said. "These petitions relate to the great and solemn subject of slavery...And because it is a political subject, it has been often tauntingly been said that women had nothing to do with it. Are we aliens because we are women?" she asked. "Are we bereft of citizenship because we are mothers, wives and daughters of a mighty people? Have women no country no interests staked in public weal - no liabilities in common peril - no partnership in a nation's guilt and shame?"

Needless to say, Your L. of the H. sat spellbound before this story of the very first woman ever to have addressed the General Court. "Let's do something about this," she had found herself saying to her new found friend. "Let's observe the occasion on February 21. I'll have a Resolution passed in the House and we'll have a celebration in Doric Hall and invite everyone in the State House - or, better still, let's see if the Governor will issue a Proclamation and have February 21 designated as "Angelina Grimke day!" Which is how it all began…

Well, the Governor's Secretary, Mary Ann, we are happy to report, had found the whole idea "neat" and was delighted to cooperate; this representative phased the Proclamation over last weekend; and the wheels began to turn. As so often happens, however, those wheels were not only to turn but to take off, for Monday morning had found my friend Anne not only rejoicing with me over the Proclamation, but coming up with some startling new developments in the Angelina Grimke Story.

Other sources had obviously been made aware of the lady's unique contribution to Massachusetts history for a play entitled "Freedom and Angelina" was scheduled to be presented at the Church of All Nations on February 23; and the director of the drama had learned of our plans and requested permission to present excerpts from the life of Angelina as part of our day's observance. Also February 20 was Angelina's birthday, it turned out, and so came another question: Could we have a birthday cake and serve cake and punch in honor of the occasion???

Needless to say, this representative was delighted to fall in with all of the additional proposals; to contact the Women's Caucus and the Black Caucus for financial help with the birthday cake and punch aspect of the program, and to propose to the Governor's Secretary, Mary Ann, that Mr. Dukakis sign the Proclamation in Doric Hall as part of the ceremony…all of which constituted the chain of circumstances that had found me braving the fates by delaying my departure from the State House on Monday afternoon while I met with Mary Ann and tied down as many as possible of the details of the Proclamation arrangement that will now form the highlight of the day's exciting events.

We'll certainly be looking forward with pleasure to that February 21 happening on Beacon Hill…And to an acquaintance with other bits and pieces of our Massachusetts history that will now develop as a result of our friendship with a new State House history buff. And doesn't this little old tale reinforce our oft-repeated philosophic observations that when one casts his bread upon the water it frequently comes back cake??? Thank you, friend Malcom, for opening one more exciting door on Beacon Hill for the representative to whom you made a simple request. And, incidentally, we hope to share other resultant tales with our Braintree readers, so many of whom have expressed approval of the fact that we intersperse reports of our legislative doings on Beacon Hill with historic tidbits which we hope they will find as interesting as we do.

P.S. This column was to have appeared in last week's "Observer-Forum." It was ready, however we had no way to get it to the staff; we learned on Sunday that the staff would have had no way of getting it to the publisher had we gotten it to our local people. There's another storm forecast for Tuesday. We're not taking any chances of having a recurrence of this past week's problem; so we're sending everything over on Monday morning as is - just in case...Hope you understand...

FEBRUARY 26, 1978

Thanks to a gentleman named George whose birthday was being observed two days early on Monday, this past week would begin on Tuesday on Beacon Hill as elsewhere in the Commonwealth...A beautiful morning, Tuesday! The 8:45 A.M. carillon on the Park Street church was filling the air with its incomparable sound as your L. of the H. left the MBTA station to wend her way up Park Street. The air on this 21 degree day was brisk and beautiful. The "Warning - Ice falling from the roof" signs had been removed from the sidewalks, we noted...sidewalks that are now devoid of the snow that had lain so heavily on them such a short time ago.

I was to find myself smiling as I recalled the first day of another week on Beacon Hill, that week on which we had returned to Boston after the Storm of the You-know-what...Though the roadway was bare and sidewalk icy, we had followed our normal route up Park Street, chatting the while with a State House employee we'd encountered on the train. We had reached the top of Park Street to learn that lying between us and Beacon Street...and consequently between us and the State House was a veritable mountain of snow. What to do to surmount that formidable obstacle??? The $64 question! Incidentally, it was now suddenly apparent to us both why everyone else had taken the roadway route up the hill. "now what?" we had asked of each other. Shall we prance down Park Street and walk back up the roadway?" "no way." we had decided in the vernacular of the YOUNG, into which category, incidentally, neither of us fitted even remotely. Thank Heavens none of my constituents were on hand to witness the alternative route we finally took...which was to climb up one side of the mountain and slide down the other on our derrieres... "you never thought you'd be taking a slide like that at YOUR age, I'll warrant," said my companion in crime. "Know I never expected to," he added merrily.

But - to return to Tuesday morning of this past week on Beacon Hill. It was to house a number of interesting events. To begin with, notification of my appointment to the Special Committee on House Chamber Design, a committee to deal with those Chamber changes which will result from the 1979 reduction in the size of the House from 240 to 160 members.

At 10:15 it was to be off to the Governor's Chambers for the swearing-in of one of my constituents, Mr. James F. Scanlan, an Executive appointee to a blue ribbon committee to study the health of the state's racing industry. Mr. Scanlan, whom I had not had the pleasure of meeting previously, proved to be a splendid choice. A lawyer, and a member of the F.B.I. for almost 27 years, he had retired in December after having distinguished himself as supervisor of the organized crime squad which covered Rhode Island, Massachusetts, New Hampshire and Maine.

The Governor announced that it is the first time that citizens, legislators and the Executive have united to tackle what is a very complicated issue. The committee will be charged with coming up with recommendations for a tax policy for racing, he said. Its chairman, David Roseman pledged to present the Governor with a report supported by "substantial evidence." The committee will observe the Open Meeting Law throughout its deliberations, he said.

Back to the Governor's office at 11:00 AM. For the signing of a Proclamation naming February 21 "Angelina Grimke Day" in Massachusetts, Angelina Grimke being the first woman ever to have addressed a legislative committee of the Massachusetts House of Representatives. It happened 140 years ago on February 21, 1838 having started the ball rolling on the lady in question, and phrased and made arrangements with the Governor for the Proclamation, it was presented to your L. of the H. who promptly turned it over to the cast members of a play on the life of Angelina Grimke, entitled "Angelina and Freedom" which will open Thursday evening at the Church of All Nations in Boston. The cast members, with the exception of Angelina herself, were all on hand for the proclamation's signing and were absolutely delighted with the occasion. Also on hand were several members of the Women's Caucus.

We're having a wonderful time with this little old Angelina Grimke story, incidentally. On Tuesday next, Gwen Mason, who is the Angelina of "Angelina and Freedom," will give the lady's original speech on the abolition of slavery within the House Chamber, being presented by this representative. She was unable to be on hand for the signing on Tuesday as she was part of the "Woman 78" Program for that day.

Thursday evening of this past week was to find your representative honored by being a special guest at the opening performance of the play…and so the Angelina Grimke story goes on…And oh yes, we introduced a Resolution honoring the lady in the House of Representatives, and that resolution will be part of next Tuesday's events as well. Well, so much for the fun and games, and, incidentally, all of these delightful events were able to be tucked in on Tuesday for one reason only. Although we were in informal sessions all week long so that a crash program of committee hearings could be held, our Transportation Committee hearings did not commence until Wednesday, leaving Tuesday free for constituent work and the special events we've elaborated upon above. A rare circumstance for your L. of the H., needless to say.

So WHY the crash program on committee hearings, you may be wondering. Well, inasmuch as we never did prorogue last year, but went immediately into the New Year, those bills we filed in such profusion last December could not be processed and printed in 1977 preparatory to being heard and dealt with early in 1978. Accordingly, we have been unable to vote on the many issues that face us. Each bill that is filed must have a public hearing before a legislative committee. It then comes to the floor with either a favorable or an adverse committee report; and only then can we take action on the legislative issue. Literally hundreds of bills, ready at last, were being heard before committees during this past week, consequently the action will begin in earnest during the week that faces us.

One more thing about that Chamber redesign, we held our first committee meeting on Wednesday morning, and one fact emerged from our deliberations… Whatever changes are necessary in the rearrangement of our menage, the watchword will be ECONOMY…It must be beautiful, of course, this Chamber of the House of Representatives. The Commonwealth's citizens must be able to take pride in it. And the historic aspects of the room must be protected and maintained. But, we must not go overboard financially in the process. I don't think we shall; too many of us are watching our pennies these days on Beacon Hill. Well, we shall see…

4-30-78

Since by virtue of our Forum deadline our week must end on Wednesday, we shall commence this week's column with Thursday's happenings, the highlight of which was to prove to be participation in the 55th Anniversary Luncheon meeting of the Braintree Rotary Club.

We had been pleased to have passed in the House of Representatives a Resolution in observance of the contribution of this great community organization to the Town of Braintree during those fifty-five years; and it was a pleasure indeed to present that Resolution to the distinguished gathering on hand. Our attendance at any Thursday luncheon meeting must always be an "iffy" affair. "If" formal session is scheduled for that day…That information will not come our way until we adjourn on the Wednesday evening. Quite obviously the fact is determined by the importance of the issues facing us the next day. If any of them are considered potentially controversial, a FORMAL session is scheduled on a Thursday; if not, our presence at the State House for a roll call at 1 p.m. is not a must. There are no roll calls in an informal session, and so if it turns out to be later than 1 p.m. when we return to the State House after a luncheon meeting similar to last Thursday's, no harm is done….But - to return to the events of that Rotary Luncheon…Patrick J. Leonard, Jr. had compiled and edited a marvelous volume - "The History of the Braintree Rotary Club - The Founding Years -1923-28," and it was this rep's good fortune to have been presented with a copy of the fascinating publication (Incidentally one of only 15 copies made…) Copies were also presented to Mrs. Gustav A. Bergfors, the widow of the Club's Charter President; to Mrs. Carroll D. Welch, to whom the book is dedicated; and to the District Governor, Charles A. Powers, Jr.

Presentation of the book was to be followed by the most delightful of slide presentations - also at the hand of "Pat" Leonard, Jr. - a history of life in Braintree during those formative years. And what fun it was to see our town as once it looked long years ago…My thanks to Rotary President Raymond F. Duffy for a wonderful hour and a half.

Friday morning and it was to be off at dawn for an 8 o'clock meeting of the Braintree Business Council where I would discuss that bill I have filed to prevent the opening of the MBTA stations in South Quincy and South Braintree until the access roads are completed. I was to present the same arguments I had used before the Joint Committee on Transportation…arguments that had won for it a unanimously favorable committee vote. One of the most compelling arguments on our South Braintree station concerns lay, in my opinion, in an MBTA handout I was able to produce (I have a happy habit of saving everything). It was passed out at a public hearing in our Town Hall in September of 1971 and it contains a statement to the effect that the station will be opened concurrent with the construction of Ivory Street….

Saturday was to house, my Kickoff Reception as a candidate for re-election to a third term in the House of Representatives. Incidentally this time I shall be seeking to represent the entire Town of Braintree and not just eight of the 12 precincts, as at present. The new situation comes about as a result of the Redistricting of the Commonwealth to implement the House cut from 240 to 160 members.

The day dawned beautifully and the party was a smash with wall-to-wall wonderful people in attendance and the happiest atmosphere we've encountered in years. Having oversold by more than 60 tickets before we had a chance to call any of them in, however, the hall was badly crowded, and we apologize for the fact. We were, however, delighted to know that we have so many friends and supporters and pray that their presence at our party indicates their approval of the manner in which they are being represented these days in the Great and General Court.

Our Heartfelt thanks, needless to say, goes out to all dear people who planned the affair and handled everything so beautifully…and who, along with their spouses, wound up devoid of a seat at the crowded reception, and who consequently had to take advantage of the absence of a dancing couple somewhere to rest their weary limbs. As a matter of fact, even the candidate had no seat…but an awful lot of fun.

And by the way, if the mark of a party's success is the reluctance of the party goers to see it end, last Saturday's affair was topnotch. The dancers having shown no signs of giving up when midnight came, we engaged the band for an additional hour. We had invited a great many people to our home at the party's end, and they arrived en masse, with the last guests to leave the after- the-party gathering at 4:45 a.m., with the day already dawned, and the birds "saying their morning prayers," to quote our dear departed Mother.

It wasn't easy, therefore, to be on hand, bright and breezy at 12 noon for the opening exercises of the Braintree Babe Ruth League, but we made it and it was a fun affair, with our boys in their colorful uniforms, their managers, coaches and parents alike all on hand, beaming prideful approval. Incidentally, the highlight of that annual occasion always manages to be, in our opinion, the singing of the "Star Spangled Banner," our National Anthem by Braintree's own Lee Cox. It comes over like a hymn, leaving us moved and rather shaken, so beautifully is it sung.

On the whole, it's been quite a week on Beacon Hill. We've had a couple of distinguished visitors to the Chamber, Rene Levesque, the Prime Minister of Quebec for one; and our own Marathon winner for the past two years, Bill Rogers, for another. We've had public hearings on that most controversial of all subjects, Laetrile with legislation filed to legalize the sale of it in Massachusetts…and we executed and sent to the House that long-awaited bill of our Transportation Committee Chairman, Rep. Louis Nickinello, which would restructure and refinance the MBTA. All bills had to be reported out of the committee by Wednesday; and it was a mad scramble indeed to get all remaining items executed and sent on their way…We'll be busy beavers from here in as hundreds of them were finally dealt with during the past three days. Aren't these spring days delightful? The thermometer registers in the fifties these nice bright mornings, and as we walk up Park Street, we find the Boston Common benches beginning to fill up with retirees. And - wonder of wonders…as we drove up Beacon Street forced to take the car in town, we found the huge MAGNOLIA trees before the Women's City Club on one morning we were in full and fragrant bloom! It's here! Spring, we mean…

2-18-78

The past week was off to a beautiful start with a series of most memorable weekend events. Friday morning, and it was off to perform one of the happiest tasks of the year for your L. of the H., the awarding of certificates to the little ones at the Watson Park Library Story Hour, or "Library School" as it is still called…a name it received while under the leadership of sister Gladys, almost ten years back. How beautiful and bright are today's 3½ to 5 year olds! It was real easy to identify once more with all thirty five or so, the graduates of the 10:30 class at Watson; to sing their songs with them; to salute their flag with them; and to look back in memory to the days when "Lady of the House" was "Cabbages and Kings," and Friday morning's "Library School" was routine procedure…as routine as, that is as dealing with 65 or 70 animated angels ever can be. At any rate, it was a fun experience; and we thank our good friend Ethel, now the gal in charge, for our annual invitation to participate in festivities.

Sunday morning, and with the sun still shining away, it was to be off to attend a Memorial Service for our deceased Braintree Firefighters…those gallant men who have "answered the last alarm," to quote one of the speakers…an especially poignant ceremony this year because of the loss of Father Jeremiah Cullinane, their former Catholic Chaplain, and the loss this week of their courageous Deputy Chief Earle Prario. Monday morning and another key House session was to await us…the Issue-Capital Punishment! House Bill 820, which was filed jointly by Rep. Michael Flaherty and Senator Arthur Lewis would provide for the death penalty for murder in the first degree unless the jury in a jury trial, or the court in a court trial recommends against the death sentence, in which case the defendant would receive a sentence of life imprisonment.

In all cases where a death penalty may be imposed, however, a subsequent pre-sentence hearing would have to be held, during which the only issue would be the determination of the punishment. Mitigating circumstances and additional relevant evidence may be presented by the defendant or his attorney during this hearing.

The death sentence may be imposed when the murder was committed in connection with rape; or when the victim was performing his duties as a police officer, firefighter or correctional officer; or during the commission of a breaking and entering; or kidnapping or attempted kidnapping; or for a second murder offense; or when the murder involved "torture, depravity of mind or an aggravated battery to the victim;" or murder for hire; or during the commission of an armed robbery; or when the murderer created a great risk of death to individuals in a specific place; or in the course of hijacking or attempted hijacking of an airplane or school bus.

H-820 details mitigating circumstances; and the bill provides that whenever the death penalty is imposed, the sentence must be reviewed by the Supreme Judicial Court, which shall consider punishment as well as the crime.

Well, so much for the details of this controversial bill which would appear to be unconstitutional in the light of a Supreme Court decision anyhow, unless and until we change the state constitution. This will undoubtedly be done in two consecutive constitutional conventions with subsequent vote of the people of the Commonwealth if we are to judge by the calls and letters we legislators have been receiving from our people. So what little surprise would the bill's opponents have had up their sleeves for Monday's session? A FILIBUSTER, which would go on for five hours and see this rep and a number of her colleagues locked in the House of Chamber for hours on end so as to assist with the matter of obtaining a quorum when the presence of a quorum was doubted again and again by the "filibuster." It wasn't easy, you see, to persuade 121 busy legislators to answer a quorum call when the response could involve being part of a captive audience for a colleague whose filibustering included the incessant repetition of a series of phrases, facts, fancies, clichés and miscellaneous statements that definitely began to grate on one's nervous system after the first 25 to 50 times. Oh well, it was to be 7:00 p.m. before the filibuster would end, and the matter carried over to Tuesday - when finally the bill would be sent to third reading and the matter disposed of- for the time being, anyhow…A new flurry of Health Care Committee activity this week was to find us hearing a bill that would provide for the immediate protection of abused or abandoned children in need of medical service. There is understandably currently a violent reaction to the problem of abused children. We had supported a bill creating the department of family and children's services last week when it was heard before the Committee on Ways and Means; and we feel certain that legislative action will deal substantially with the problem of our abused children before we adjourn the session.

And now we get to Proposition 2½, which was introduced in the House yesterday. It's Massachusetts's version of California's Proposition 13. It's a scene stealer, to be sure. Even the photographers from "Time" Magazine were to be on hand at the State House to photograph its sponsors. We all want property tax relief, to be sure. We must have property tax relief as well we know; but is proposition 2½ the answer??? California has a $7 Billion surplus to absorb some of the costs of implementing Proposition 13, a surplus which the state was hoarding even as it permitted the property tax to soar out of sight. Massachusetts has a mere $150 Million, which is earmarked for about $500 worth of programs. The issue seems to come down to the question of whether or not we want to lay off our teachers, our police and firefighters and municipal employees, and scrap our programs for the poor, the handicapped, the Chapter 766 children, the sick and the needy…Should we perhaps not wait awhile and see how California fares under Proposition 13 before Massachusetts takes the plunge??? That's the question we were asking of ourselves this past week. Actually this rep has been filing tax relief legislation for the past two years, all of which has gone nowhere…legislation to put a cap on state spending; and to prevent the implementation of state mandated programs; and recipients…and bills to otherwise curb government spending, and so curb government taxation. We all recognize the problem…but is Proposition 2½ the solution??? We're still wondering.

7-9-78

Prorogation time and the Fourth of July came together this past week-and with fireworks on both counts. At stake on Beacon Hill was, of course the State Budget, with the Committee of Conference at an impasse and seemingly unwilling or unable to resolve its differences…the differences, that is, between the House and the Senate versions of how the state should spend its money during the coming year.

We've been working late hours on the Hill while the controversy raged…burning the midnight oil on a couple of nights; and participating in an unusual Saturday House session… and even resigning ourselves to the possibility of spending the nation's birthday under the Golden Dome if it became possible to bring the budget to the floor. It is Tuesday, however, as I write this column; and that eventuality did not materialize. Tomorrow is now being slated for that threatened all-night session…

So now what did happen on July 4, the 202nd birthday of our beloved nation??? Well, we missed the threatened House session and so were able to enjoy the holiday.

Unfortunately the Committee of Conference would appear to be no nearer to a solution of its problems; or so we've been informed tonight on the 6 p.m. news; and so anything can happen tomorrow as we arrive on the Hill for an 11 a.m. roll call and another go at passing a capital outlay budget; a deficiency budget that hit a snag last week when it turned up from the Conference Committee with an outside section that placed a 5 percent cap on municipal spending and virtually repealed fiscal autonomy for our school committees; and House 1, the state budget with the abortion and local aid complications that are the root of its problem.

It's been a happy holiday, all things considered. We had hoped to throw out the ball for that fun softball game between the League of Women Voters and the town officials; however, at 5:30 on Monday evening, which was the time for the game, we were still at the State House. Being unable to park anywhere when we did finally reach the high school on Monday evening, we had to be content with watching the fireworks from afar and foregoing the fun at the high school field. We had, however, been able to share in Sunday's doings…to thoroughly enjoy the annual pancake breakfast of those great chefs among Braintree Knights of Columbus; and to participate in the annual rededication of Braintree's Tri-Centennial Time Capsule at Town Hall…A delightful experience, incidentally, and we turned out to be the featured speaker and loved looking back at our involvement with that exciting Bicentennial achievement, the only above-the-ground time capsule in history. The rainy Fourth itself had promised little or no enjoyment. We had learned from our local weatherman that the rain was to last all day, and the skies to remain dark and gloomy. It didn't turn out that way, however. The gloom was beautifully dispersed by a visit from constituent and dear friend, Paul Kennedy, who was visiting nearby and decided to "drop by to wish his representative a happy Fourth of July." The decision was a happy one for L. of the H. Instead of Fourth of July politics…and business…and legislation…and ideas…dozens of ideas that spilled forth from that gifted and imaginative businessman to find fertile ground in a representative who serves as the Transportation Committee's Chairman of the Subcommittee on the Port Authority and is committed 100 per cent to the development of our wonderful but hopelessly neglected Boston Harbor. If only prorogation wasn't quite so near! We'll not be bidding goodbye to the State House, however, even if we have prorogued; and so we'll be pursuing several of those ideas in the weeks ahead. Incidentally, late sessions under the Golden Dome are rather fun for your L. of the H. who is a night person anyhow, and so on the whole, impervious to the late hours. With a number of Metayer bills at the wire, and prorogation perilously close, we had dashed madly along the deserted State House corridors between the House Chamber and the Senate's Counsel's office in an attempt to enlist the aid of Senator Tobin in springing those bills from Senate Third Reading or Ways and Means, which, incidentally, we are pleased to report he was able to do. He even enlisted the help of the Senate President. And what a moment of triumph it was for this rep to hear President Harrington promise our state senator that our vital MBTA Board of Directors' bill would be brought out of Ways and Means on Monday. We had all but given up on that one, but had decided to pursue it up to the last gasp anyhow, just in case...all of which only goes to prove that persistence pays...We can't believe that the Governor will actually, in the final analysis, veto that bill which is so obviously equitable for our South Shore and the North Shore as well. Well, we'll see....

We're much more certain of the fate of our Driver Education bill which was enacted in the House on Monday. That legislation had also been the subject of our late night visit to Senator Tobin. The bill had been filed at the request of our School Superintendent and School Committee. It will, however, prevent the mandating of the behind-the-wheel segment of driver training during the regular school day, and at no cost whatsoever to the student. Under the provisions of the bill, those communities which feel they can provide behind-the-wheel training during the regular school day and at no cost to the students may continue to do so. Those communities, however, which feel they cannot afford to do so, will not be forced to. They may schedule the behind-the-wheel segment after school and charge the students for part or all of the cost at will. This representative has consistently voted against mandated state programs; and has indeed filed legislation to prevent this. It was, therefore, not difficult to follow the will of the Braintree school authorities right down to the end, and to see to it that the bill reached the governor's desk for signing. By the way, we were informed by the Mass. Teachers Association that everyone, including the principal signer of the original Braintree petition, had agreed to support the final amended version of the bill. It should, therefore, have no difficulty in leaving the Governor's desk all signed and sealed. We'll drop by the office of his legislative staff tomorrow, however, just in case they have questions on it; we want the bill to become law...

By the time you read this column, the General Court may be in prorogation, its work all done for the current year. It will be the first early prorogation for your L. of the H. since her election four years ago. We have invariably ended one year's business to go directly into the next. What shall I ever write about when there are no bills to be discussed or events to be reported??? We'll have to think hard about that one...

7-16-78

Prorogation time...Once upon a time it was the highlight of the year, we're told by the old timers in the House of Representatives. That was, of course, when House sessions lasted half a year. That hasn't been the case since this rep was elected. Our sessions have managed to run from one year to another with little or no interruption. This year, however, things were to be different. Because of the House cut from 240 to 160 members, the Chamber would have to be rearranged. 80 desks and chairs must be removed; also-and this represents a more difficult and time consuming process – the Chamber, having been inspected and found to be structurally unsound, must be reinforced from underneath.

The contractor who will be handling the rearrangement, has announced that in order to have everything ready for the January session, he must have the contract by July. There is a reason for this. The State House being a historic building of enormous importance, every step along the way in the Chamber reconstruction will have to be approved by a list of historic boards and commissions a mile long. Well, we have finally prorogued; and the contractor will now be able to have it with the house chamber...But what about the climate in which we moved toward that all-important prorogation???

Well, for one thing, we've had the feeling we were living on Beacon Hill. Sessions went on day and night. We found ourselves saying "Good Night" as we wended our way out of the State House at 5:15 of a morning, and "Good Morning" as we returned at 2 p.m. on the same day. And that 5:15 departure after an all-night House session happened three times during this past week...along with a 1 a.m. departure and a couple of 12 midnights.

Actually we found we rather enjoyed driving home over the Expressway at that early morning hour, finding it all but deserted excepting for a number of our South Shore colleagues. We also found those hardy joggers out in force in our own little town. "That must have been quite a party," one of them called out as we slowed down to pass him on Elm Street.

The world is especially beautiful of an early summer morning, we decided as we drove toward Braintree, the sky turning gradually grey to blue as we drove along; and the sun commencing to hurl its mauve and crimson before it prior to bursting into scarlet song at the end of our journey; the air fresh with a host of soft summer scents...

But now - what issues have we been facing on Beacon Hill as prorogation neared? We've had, of course, to deal with the budgets in their final phases, all three of them... the Deficiency, the Capital Outlay, and House 1. The governor had not as yet signed the Deficiency Budget as we left the Hill, but he was expected to do so shortly...when we prorogued, according to Secretary Buckley of Administration and Finance, whom we had questioned on this issue at 2 a.m. or so on one of the mornings, bringing home to him as we did so the plight of our nursing homes which are awaiting vital Medicaid payments, long overdue. "The governor will sign it when you prorogue," he had said firmly.

We had a number of interesting prorogation experiences, needless to say. We'd watched, for instance, as Senator Mary Fonseca filibustered for hours on end on the Court Reform Bill, reading line by line and page by page from the close to 200 page document. And we had heard the farewell speeches of countless of our colleagues who will not be seeking higher office, or returning to the Full-time pursuits they'd left behind to become state reps. A sad experience indeed...

Most exciting, however, of course, was the triumph we had enjoyed in getting out of the Senate and onto the Governor's desk for signing, that bill of ours to increase the membership of the Board of Directors of the MBTA by adding one from the South Shore and one from the North Shore. Now it was obvious to all that that bill was in grave difficulty in the "Upper Branch." Senator Kelley Obviously the word was out… "Put a hold on the bill."…was holding it in Senate Ways and Means, and each of our efforts to spring it had come to naught.

You may recall my having reported last week that Senator Arthur Tobin had taken me to meet the Senate President and had secured from him a promise to get the bill out of Senate Ways and Means this past week. Well, it hadn't happened. Despite a daily barrage of pressure on the part of your L of the H. the bill was not forthcoming…And here it was Prorogation Night, and in the last hours of prorogation night at that. Well, we are happy to report that the White Knight came to the rescue of the damsel in distress in true storybook fashion, the White Knight being, of course, the selfsame Senator Tobin, who is of course a co-sponsor of the bill.

And getting that bill through the Senate and onto the Governor's desk which he finally did, was to provide a powerful heap of drama for your representative to the Great and General Court. The Senator had to use every ounce of the clout he enjoys as Chairman of the Committee on Bills in the Third Reading…but use it he did… dashing back and forth from Senate to House, trailed by your L. of the H….fighting for the bill inch by inch despite the pessimism of his colleagues, one or two of whom had assured this rep that he Senate President wouldn't in a million years interrupt the prorogation proceedings at the last minute to enact another bill. He did, however. The bill was hurriedly enacted in the Senate just moments before that body assembled for the prorogation march to the House Chamber…And its signing was the last official act of the President of the Senate, Kevin B. Harrington, who was presiding over his last Senate session on Beacon Hill. Strangely enough, it was also the last bill to be enacted in the House of Representatives by a 240 member House. An historic document indeed, that bill to increase the membership of the "T"…Senator Tobin and I agreed…historic on both counts.

It had been a long night; and we'd spent a good part of it babysitting our bill in the Senate; but the mood of the rising sun as it turned the Hancock Building to gold on that beautiful prorogation day, was a wonderful match for my own. We'd done it! It sure hadn't been easy, but as you read this column, our bill is on the governor's desk for signing. We pray he'll do just that…sign it and make it the law of the Commonwealth….

8-6-78

Another eventful week on Beacon Hill. It was to include attendance at a Quincy session on airplane noise on Thursday evening; and, on Saturday afternoon and evening, participation in a delightful Block Party in East Braintree. This had been scheduled as a farewell affair for Lloyd and Ida Toye, the wonderful parents of our good friend Mickey. They are retiring and heading for Vermont; and this very dear couple will be sorely missed.

Lloyd Toye's farm has been for years providing delectable produce for a host of his grateful neighbors. The Metayers can now attest to the quality of those farm products since they are currently enjoying Ralph's gift of a variety of homemade jellies that had their origin in his garden. (There's more than one farmer in the Toye family obviously).

The departure of a special family from a neighborhood cannot help but diminish that neighborhood, we decided as we participated in the events and presented a Citation from the House of Representatives to the departing couple. We shall all miss Lloyd and Ida Toye.

God go with them!

Sunday morning and we were on hand at Valle's for breakfast with Governor Michael S. Dukakis…a very well attended affair…And on Monday it was off to the State House where we were to face that all important Bill of Address on Robert M. Bonin, Chief Justice of the Superior Court.

It was a solemn question we faced as we entered the chamber at 11:00 a.m. to address the Governor and the Council for the removal of the Chief Justice of the Superior Court of the Commonwealth. We had checked our state Constitution to learn that it provides that "it is the right of every citizen to be tried by judges as free, impartial and independent as the lot of humanity will admit." We also learned that justices of the Supreme Judicial court may hold office "as long as they behave themselves well" for other judges it is "during good behavior."

Judges, we found, do not hold office for life or until they are 70; they hold office during their good behavior. Now, a judge whose behavior falls below the standard to which the people of the Commonwealth are entitled may be removed by address of both the House and the Senate to the Governor and Council. This address we were to be considering on Monday morning. Incidentally, removal by address applies only to the judiciary. An elected member of the legislative and executive branches may be removed only by the impeachment process.

The power to address is needless to say, to be exercised only with enormous restraint. It is based not upon charges and allegations but only upon facts after a fair hearing. We were to remain mindful of these facts during the entire day. So what action had preceded our deliberations in the case of Robert Bonin?? Well, hearings had been held by the Supreme Judicial Court…The Chief Justice had been afforded every procedural protection. He had been given every opportunity to refute the charges that were made against him.

A number of his statements made under oath during his deposition were found contrary to the findings of the Court, and it had been their unanimous opinion that Judge Robert M. Bonin violated the Code of Judicial Conduct. They had ruled that his behavior was improper. He had been afforded a public opportunity to contest those findings in a public hearing before the Judiciary Committee. He did not do so. His defense was simply that the violations and the improper behavior were not sufficient gravity to justify his removal from office. Your L. of the H. was present at that public hearing. She heard the testimony of the justice and his attorney. Judge Bonin apologized for the first time since the proceedings began, but he did not contest the findings of the SJC.

In a unanimous opinion, the SJC had declared that the judge "was negligent almost to the point of willfulness in ignoring or brusquely dismissing information brought to his attention." The information, of course, was the fact that the proceeds from the Gore Vidal lecture were to be used in part for the defense of individuals accused of conducting a homosexual ring…individuals whose cases would be tried in the Superior Court over which the judge would preside, as its chief Justice. To quote one of the five justices on the bench (two were absent) Judge Bonin treated "friendly attempts to warn him as invasions of his privacy, reacting with the kind of stubborn resistance that produces self-inflicting wounds."

Was Judge Bonin telling the truth when he stated that he did not discuss the use of the proceeds when purchasing his tickets to the Gore Vidal lecture? Was he telling the truth when he claimed that his aide did not, as he stated initially, warn him of the lecture's implications after having received such a warning from Attorney Homans, one of the lawyers handling the defense of the members of the Revere ring? Was Judge Bonin telling the truth when he stated that he failed to hear any of the advance speakers at the lecture when they discussed the use of the funds and the "Revere Caper" (the homosexual ring)? Did he fail to HEAR or did he fail to LISTEN, we wondered, as we waded through pages of testimony and listened to hours of debate. In a judge, would not the failure to LISTEN constitute a fatal flaw, we asked.

Now, we have discussed questions that related to the Vidal Lecture only. There were many other issues involved in the case, i.e., the free rental car; the $1000 per month fee for handling outside legal work while serving as Assistant District Attorney; the reception and swearing in parties - all of the above financed by the Conboy Corporation.

It is a scant 18 months since Judge Bonin was sworn in at the State House, we reflected. And for nine of those months, the judgment of the Chief Justice has been in question; he has been involved in controversy. What assurances have we that similar instances of improper behavior would not occur again if Judge Bonin were to be permitted to remain in his exalted position, we wondered…We sat for hours in the House Chamber which was initially arctic cold, but became with passing of hours of debate, unbearably warm. We agonized over the decision we knew we must make…the decision to endorse the address to the Governor and the Council for the removal of the Chief Justice of our Superior Court. We were not alone when finally our decision was reached. The vote was 206 to 17. We wished ardently that Mr. B had had the grace to resign after censure by the SJC. The horrendous responsibility that was ours would not have had to be faced. Seems like everything under the sun has happened since your L. of the H. was elected a member of the General Court…even the address of a Superior Court Chief Justice…What next, we wonder????

8-13-78

A second Prorogation in a single legislative year…it hasn't happened often, they tell me…Not within the memory of any State House regulars I talked with, at any rate…Almost never has the governor called the legislature back into session to deal with an emergency situation. He did this year, however. We were called back into session to deal with the unhappy question of whether or not to engross the Bill of Address on Chief Justice Bonin. We dealt with the issue. We brought that sad assignment to a conclusion; and then, lo! And behold! - we found ourselves facing a second Prorogation on a lovely Tuesday evening after two days of debate and deliberation on the "emergency" issue before us.

A 207 to 17 vote to request that the Bill of Address be forwarded to the Governor and the Council had occurred the previous day, and it had been thought that the proceedings might be wrapped up in a late night session that same day. One of our colleagues had, however, moved reconsideration of the vote, and so we had found ourselves back in session on the Tuesday in question.

The Prorogation proceedings are steeped in tradition. We can recall our delight in the pomp and circumstance surrounding the functioning of Britain's parliament on the occasion of our visit there some ten years ago. At that time we had no idea that much of the same went on in our own seat of government on Beacon Hill. Nor, naturally, had we dreamed that one day we would be part of it. Here we were, however, and we were about to prorogue for the second time with your L. of the H., a participant in the proceedings. The first step in the protocol is to have the Speaker of the House (and the President of the Senate) appoint a committee whose function it is to proceed to the Governor of the Commonwealth and inform him that the business of the House had been concluded. This rep was appointed one of the ten or so members who were assigned this happy task.

We proceeded to the aisle of the House Chamber to the applause of our colleagues; marched down the State House corridors led by our Majority Leader, Rep. George Keverian, and entered the Governor's office - only to come to an abrupt stop. The Governor, it seemed, wasn't at home! Dialogue began promptly to flow like water about the confines of the gubernatorial foyer. Was he on the "T"? Had it broken down as usual, calling a halt to the legislative process? And finally, after a call from the Speaker, they tell me, "Would someone send a car for the gentleman wherever he happened to be????" Someone did. And we waited, and waited, AND WAITED, to be joined gradually by a half dozen of our colleagues who had come or been sent to ask, "What gives???" Back at the ranch meanwhile, the ranch being the House Chamber, speculation was rife about the untoward delay in the Prorogation proceedings. We should have returned promptly, and we hadn't. The Senate committee had, of course, also been derailed so to speak, and we milled about in the executive foyer, some of us studying the portraits of former governors; all of us waiting, watching and wondering…We're certain you are relieved to know that Mr. D. did indeed arrive eventually, and we all proceeded into the handsome Chamber of the Governor's Council where we found that august body also assembled and waiting.

Both committees had been preceded by their Sergeants-at-Arms, complete with staff, tall hat and tails - also reminiscent of the English Parliament, we might add.

The Governor had seated himself rather hastily, we noted, at the Head of the Council. He proceeded to accept the notification of the fact that both branches of the legislature had finished the year's business and desired to prorogue. The Secretary of State was then requested to prorogue the House and Senate; we returned to the Chamber amid cries of "Where on earth have you been?" "What kept you?" "We'll not send YOU again on an errand for the House!" etc. etc. AND finally, the Secretary of State arrived and our second prorogation was a fait accompli.

Well so much for the business of the legislature in session… "So what is going on in the Common these days?" we're being asked. "You haven't reported on that of late." Well, with the ending of the monsoon, Boston Common, we are happy to report, has become once more a veritable beehive. The park benches are bursting at the seams with Bostonians, proper and otherwise; and tourists clutching their brochures to their bosoms and pipping about viewing the frogpond, reading the inscriptions on the myriad bronzes that grace the Common green; and tossing coins to the myriad entertainers who vie with one another for the public's attention as they sing, dance emote, ride weird contraptions like unicycles and the like, and perform feats of magic on the mall and thereabouts.

Camera fans and sidewalk artists are at work on the State House from every conceivable angle on Beacon and Park Streets. And-speaking of Park Street-something new has been added since last we looked. "Ann's" the little tea shop where occasionally we stopped for a spot of coffee on cold winter mornings, has reopened under new management and is sporting a delightful new name, "The Fill-a-Buster"…How's that for a legislative gimmick???

Meanwhile, downstairs at Park Street as we await the arrival of the Quincy train, we are entertained by a different artist each day - and artists they are, these gifted young men and women whose playing moves us as well as entertains us. Is there anything more moving than a violin, beautifully and sensitively played, we found ourself wondering as we enjoyed a series of solos while awaiting our train on Wednesday evening…We are invariably reminded, and pleasantly, of Europe, where one always managed to find a struggling young entertainer or two in the local subway. It's nice to have this happening as a regular occurrence here in Boston. We find we don't mind waiting for the train at all - even when four or five ASHMONT trains pull into the station to every ONE for Quincy…a situation that invariably prevails at rush hour…

Well, so now we have prorogued once again, this time for good, we're sure. And so, if you cannot reach your L. of the H. at the State House to which we shall only be going two or three days a week, do contact her at home. Your concerns and your problems are equally important, in session or out of session.

9-10-78

Campaigns and Coffee Hours…They go hand in hand, and both are great…Braintree friends and neighbors have been giving me a great many Coffee Hours these past few weeks; we've loved every one of them. They have provided an opportunity to learn what the people of the Fifth Norfolk District, the town of Braintree, are thinking about the issues of the day and about the performance of their state representative. Are we truly representing them??? Those are the questions we're asking as we make the rounds, and we're getting the answers to them. It's a rewarding experience. "What do you feel are the most important issues in the minds of our constituents?" was a question asked by a reporter this past week. Well, our many coffee hours had provided the answer. "Most people are concerned with bread and butter issues," I had replied. "How to pay their taxes…and to see to it that tax reform is attempted…how to handle the high property taxes that have resulted from Braintree's 100% valuation situation…how to feed and clothe and educate and keep their families warm with the high fuel costs…They're concerned with the inflation that is eating into their incomes. They want jobs, and a limitation on government spending, and productivity for the tax dollars they're being forced to pay." Those are the issues that appear to be uppermost in the minds of the people I'm encountering at my coffee hours. They're also the issues that are uppermost in my mind. Incidentally, we're deeply grateful to the wonderful people who have been hosting those coffee hours and to the great people who've been willing to give up lovely summer mornings and evenings to attend them… to hear a candidate report on her past two years on Beacon Hill. Now for a change of subject entirely, much emphasis is being placed on Roll Call records of late, and I've been requested by my good friend Elaine to discuss roll calls in this column so as to provide a better picture of what a roll call truly represents. Elaine was laboring under the delusion that missing a roll call meant missing a legislative session. It isn't so. Missing a roll call does NOT mean that one has missed a session. It could mean that one was unable to get to the Chamber within the allotted THREE or FOUR or even TWO minutes allowed before it is called; or it could mean that one was forced to miss a tiny segment of a session that could have housed several roll calls.

The request for a roll call vote, or what is known as a "call of the Ayes and Nays," may be made by a legislator on a particular bill, or it may be made by the Speaker because "Under the Constitution, a roll call is required." It may be used by the Speaker to bring all members to the chamber for a specific reason when many of them are in committee hearings or busy with constituent work in their offices where they may be making essential calls for constituents while following at the same time the debate in the House Chamber via what we call the "squawk box," the sound system that relays to each of the State House offices of all the happenings in the House chamber.

"Why does a legislator move for a Roll call vote anyhow?" my friend Elaine wanted to know. Well, it may be because one wishes to have on record a vote on an issue of real importance to one's community; or it may be because the legislator is deeply committed to a point of view and hopes to ascertain the extent of support or opposition to his or her cause. Or-as in the past year with the House cut forcing colleagues to run against one another, it may be because one legislator wishes to force another into a vote which will be difficult to justify during the next election. Or, of course it may be because the issue to be addressed is a highly controversial one which has been heavily lobbied, and the bill's sponsors have been assured by the lobbyists that the vote is there.

Incidentally, may I repeat the fact that a missed roll call or two does not mean a missed House session. We have some sessions that include 10,20 or even 30 roll calls (in one day) while othersinclude none...

I, for instance, missed seven roll calls this past year. Four of them came on the evening when, during the "We're 4 Braintree" week on Channel 4, arrangements had been made by the television station to cover my Monday evening office hours at Town Hall. I had not expected a late session that Monday evening. I almost never have an advance warning on late sessions; they just happen. And it had happened on that particular Monday evening. I was forced to leave the Chamber and race to Braintree at the last minute to be on hand for the arrival of the T.V. team at Town Hall. Had I known in advance, I would have cancelled that T.V. sequence. I felt that my failure to be on hand, however, when Jerry Liddell and his crew arrived at Town Hall would have embarrassed our town officials and so I elected to take a chance and leave the Chamber. Those of you who saw that "We're 4 Braintree" week feature heard Jerry Liddell state that I had spoiled my 100% roll call record to be on hand. The fact that the issues at stake in the Chamber were minor ones, of course, had also influenced your rep's decision to sacrifice those roll calls.

The remainder of my missed roll calls came on an evening when I had promised our Park department Director to be on hand to present a citation to Bill Brooks during the dedication ceremony. Once again, an unexpected late session precipitated a situation where I had to place the town's obligations ahead of the state's.

Incidentally, I offer the above explanation of missed roll calls not to justify my 98% plus roll call record, but to clear up any possible misapprehensions among my constituents.

Now to carry the explanation of missed roll calls a bit further, one can call for a plethora of roll calls on the same issue during the same session...on sending a bill to third reading; or reconsideration of the vote for or against that step; on a reconsidered vote, if favorable; with the same process repeated at the next step along the way, the Engrossment stage...amendments to the bill may be offered en route, with each of those amendments treated similarly, causing the roll calls to pile up endlessly...all of which will hopefully explain this rep's original statement that as many as 30 roll calls can happen during what could be just a portion of a legislative day. We hope this explanation clarifies the issue somewhat for our friend Elaine and for many others who have not quite understood it.

THE BRAINTREE OBSERVER AND SUNDAY FORUM-PAGE TWELVE
SUNDAY, SEPTEMBER 17, 1978

Well, it's now official. It has been duly confirmed in the local press. The "Braintree Observer and Sunday Forum" has been sold! And so we reach the end of another era in the life of a weekly paper that has been so much a part of our own life…

Was it really as long as sixteen years ago that John Donahue, the "Forum's" first editor phoned to ask this Braintree-ite to write a weekly column for his paper? "Goodness," I remember thinking, "How shall I ever find a subject for a newspaper column every week??" It was a challenge, however.

I decided to "have a go" at it…

And- what was to be the first discovery of this fledging journalist?? She was to learn that the problem lay not with finding a suitable subject each week, but with managing to tuck into her allotted space all the things she wanted to say. "Cabbages and King" which was what we decided to call our column in those early days, began to grow longer and longer and longer. Thank Heaven for a tolerant and understanding editor…

Well, "Cabbages and Kings" managed to follow the adventures of our typical Braintree family down through the years…through the myriad happenings in a woman's life…as a wife and mother and a grandmother and a globetrotter and a clubwoman and all the other facets of her existence….There was the new grandchild to be written about, and the new puppy, and the new car…and then. later on, the adventures the acquisition of that new trailer were to bring about as the Metayers meandered for months at a time over this bright beautiful country that is ours AND over the lush lands of our neighbor to the north.

"Cabbages and Kings" was to go on for twelve long years…until four years ago when its author managed to get elected to the great and General court. It then became "Lady of the House." A cute title, everyone thought. It was the brainchild of the Forum's editor, Rosemary Newman, and we've been identified as the "Lady of the House" ever since.

We've loved both the title and the opportunity the column has provided to bring to the people of Braintree a weekly account of our doings on Beacon Hill. Well, this will be the very last column to be dropped off at the office of the Braintree Observer and Sunday Forum. It's a lonely, empty thought….

"We never knew what went on in the House of Representatives until you began to write about it," people have stated on all sides during these past four years. "We knew nothing really about the governmental process and the bills and the other doings of the General court…and what Boston common brings to light in summer, and what it's like to ride the "T" and how the view from the Hill really looks…" Well, passing along these bits and pieces of our State House existence has proved to be the happiest of chores for your Lady of the House. She's loved sharing the excitement of her life with her readers. And as she writes this last lonely column she is intensely grateful for the fact that it will continue to live in the "Braintree Star."

At any rate, we must now bid a final, fond and incredibly sad farewell to our Forum colleagues…to Rosemary, our editor; to Eleanor, our advertising manager; to Olive, our Social editor…to Laurie and Jack and Eileen and John and the rest…They're a wonderful crew, these members of the fabled Fourth Estate. They'll all be missed. And may God go with them, each and every one of them…So now, having handled one of the saddest tasks we've faced in years - the saying of farewell-what burning issue shall we address in this, the Observer's last little old Lady of the House weekly column?? Well, with the Primary election dead ahead-on next Tuesday, September 19 - what could be more appropriate than to remind our friends and neighbors of the importance of voting in this vital state election? It will be the more vital of the two elections for many of those seeking to hold public office, this representative included. For if she is victorious on Tuesday, having no known opponent in the November election, she'll be representing Braintree in the Great and General Court for yet another two years. She'll continue to serve the people FULL TIME. And during those next two years, by virtue of the House cut from 240 to 160 members and the redistricting that House cut brought about, she'll be representing the ENTIRE town of Braintree and not just eight out of the twelve town precincts.

Your L. of the H. is not the only candidate, however, to whom victory on Tuesday is of vital importance. It's a Red Letter Day for a lot of good people who are seeking to serve.

And if you feel that your particular vote isn't all that important, let me remind you that less than one vote per precinct elected JFK to the presidency. It has made the difference between victory and defeat for candidates again and again over the years. YOUR VOTE DOES COUNT! And here's hoping our tellers will be counting ALL of your votes in the wee small hours of Wednesday morning. Here's hoping also, needless to say, that the very best individual wins in each and every contest we're facing, for if ever there was a time for integrity and fiscal responsibility in government, it is now. The soaring tax rate must be curbed; the confidence of the people in their government must be restored; and government at all levels must begin a soul-searching with a view to aiming at productivity rather than expansion…

PLEASE vote on Tuesday, my very dear friends and readers. It's not only your civic duty; it's your very special privilege, a privilege for which people are fighting and dying across this storm-tossed globe on which we live.

And so, having first shed a tear or two for a paper we've grown to love, and then reminded our wonderful readers of their obligation to VOTE on Tuesday, we close another exciting chapter in what has certainly turned out to be a most exciting life. Farewell, good old "Braintree Observer and Sunday Forum!" Farewell, dear friends and colleagues on that good old B.O. & S.F. We'll be missing you all…

9-21-78

It is the last Sunday evening before the Primary election as your L. of the H. sits down to write her weekly column. Tomorrow's morning deadline lies dead ahead. Under normal circumstances It would have been written this morning. The last Sunday before the Primary can be a very hectic day, however. This particular Sunday had been all of that.

There were last minute notes to be delivered; and bases to be touched; there was a spot of fall gardening to be done; and the Metayer ménage to be slicked up a bit for the Primary Night Open House to be held here on Tuesday evening.

Well now, what were our thoughts anyhow as we piped about the family yard, snipping off the rose hips that had accumulated since last Sunday, and tucking the withered petunia blossoms under their green ground cover in the hope they'd turn to seed for next year???

"This time next week, much of the political hoopla will be over," we opined. "Those political handouts that have swept our way in a veritable torrent (our own included) will lie snugly within the piles of newsprint we'll have placed at the curb for recycling. Political careers will have withered on the vines. The People will have rightfully decided the fate of those who would represent them in the halls of government. There will be the winners and the losers and the pattern to be taken by our government in the immediate future will have begun to emerge. Some pieces of the mosaic that is that government will have fallen into place. The picture will have begun to take shape. As always, we find ourself praying that we shall wind up with the kind of "government of the people, by the people and for the people" that was envisioned by our founding fathers so long ago.

Running for re-election to a third term in the House of Representatives, this time to represent all of Braintree, has been an especially happy experience for your L. of the H. So many of the great people of the town's great people have given up their mornings and evenings to come to hear a candidate speak. You're all quite wonderful! Coffee Hours have turned out to be veritable parties, and we've enjoyed each and every one of them.

Well, by the time you read this little old weekly column, the "tumult and the shouting" will have died, the "captains and the kings" will have departed to plan for the November battle that now lies ahead, and the governmental process as we know it will once more have prevailed…our democratic form of government will have continued to work.

May our winners be generous and forgiving in their victory, and our losers be equally generous and forgiving in their defeat. May fences be mended…for no political loss is ever a total loss. One will be forever known as "John who ran for Governor," or "Joe, who almost made it for State Treasurer," or "Mary, who added a bit more class to the Congressional race".

You will never be the same, those of you who run for public office. Your life, win or lose, will have been enriched. You will have "made friends and influenced people." Not quite enough people to insure election for you losers, but a lot of people needless.

No, it wasn't a total loss for you losers at all. You'll find it difficult to be consoled by that bit of philosophy now, but in time you'll come to see its worth. You've acquired a bit more poise, a bit more confidence, (a slightly inflated ego, but that's not all bad…), a clearer understanding of people and their problems and a lot more knowledge about the office you were seeking to hold, as well as a new awareness of the enormous role that government plays in the lives of all of us. You've grown!

9-28-78

It was a primary election full of surprises. Indeed, of shocks in some instances…and it's over. Just a week ago this candidate was bringing to close a series of Coffee Hours that had been enlightening and rewarding. Other candidates must have been doing the same. I was availing myself of the opportunity to ascertain the reaction of the people I have been representing on Beacon Hill for the past four years, to the manner in which I had been representing them. Hoping to be re-elected, I was seeking guidance as to the kinds of issues I should be addressing during the next two years; I was seeking to know their concerns, their hopes and their aspirations for their state government and for the quality of their lives. Was I on the right track in representing the great people of Braintree I wanted to know; and the delightful Coffee Hours that were being held for me by friends throughout the town were providing me with a lot of answers. The people were angry with their government in general. That anger was to be translated into action at the polls on September 19.

So what about that Primary election day anyhow? Well, first of all, let me say how very proud I was of the voters of Braintree for turning out in such large numbers on that all-important day. The 50.7 percent participation of our people exceeded the statewide average by several points. It was obvious that the good people of Braintree cared. They had a stake in the election, and that stake brought them to the polls in greater numbers on September 19 than ever before. We congratulate them, and we thank them.

The day itself had dawned bright and beautiful despite the weatherman's dire predictions. Rain had been forecast all around. "Please do not allow anyone to stand for me at the polls if the weather is bad," I had cautioned my Precinct Captains. "I want no one to catch cold because of me," I had said, remembering back to the days when I had flirted with pneumonia for other candidates for public office. The concern proved unnecessary. The day was a beauty. The candidates and the voters were to profit from the fact.

There were to be a few mishaps along the Primary day route. A couple of our Metayer signs had to be rescued from the local incinerator for one thing. They'd been picked up by the Highway Department for having been left unattended for a bit. We'd reacted with horror when our good friend, Helen, had reported the fact by phone. We'd raced off to the Highway Department office to retrieve them, and then reacted with absolute delight to find that selfsame Helen bearing aloft a home-made sign proclaiming our candidacy.

"These are hard times," she had said merrily, planting a kiss as she said it upon the head of the beautiful small baby she was holding at the same time. People, we had decided then and there for the millionth time, are wonderful! At any rate, despite the inauspiciousness of its beginning, the day had ended quite beautifully for this fortunate representative who was able to celebrate happily into the wee small hours a victory that would lead to two more years on the Hill representing the world's greatest constituency.

The post-primary week had housed another couple of exciting events, we're happy to say. There was the Open House at Braintree Savings Bank where the beautifully expanded facility was publicly unveiled. A merry occasion with hosts Lindsay and Evelyn presenting their usual class performance.

And on that same evening there was the annual Awards Night of the Braintree Police Club where three of Braintree's finest were to be recognized for distinguished service above and beyond the call. Officer James Young was to be recognized for his valor in having climbed to the top of a 115,000 volt high tension tower to rescue the victim of an explosion; and Officer James Bradley for his valor in disarming and apprehending and armed hard-core narcotics user during a drugstore holdup; and Animal Control Officer Robert Dawes, who "professionalism" (to quote Chief John Polio) in handling the day-to-day problems of the town's animals and their owners, has marked him as an uniquely dedicated individual. What an exciting and eventful week this last one was for your L. of the H.

10-5-78

It was a strange sort of week on Beacon Hill. The primary election appears to have found the governor of the Commonwealth totally unprepared for the political defeat he was to suffer at the polls; and the depression that seems to have gripped him, if we are to judge by recent newspaper pictures, appears also to have extended to those in his entourage.

The corridors of the State House are almost unnaturally quiet. The governor's aides converse in subdued tones in the little lunchroom where we meet them at noon. Gone are the merry quips with which they normally greeted one another. The future is uncertain for them and it shows.

"Did you make it?" is the question of the hour as those in the State House encounter one another in the hallways. It's sad when the answer is "No!", and great, of course, when we're able to accept those "Congratulations! We knew you'd make it..."

"I can't understand what happened!" We're hearing that statement this time even as we heard it at the last election. "I didn't think I had a problem." Foolish public officials, we opine. One never can tell whether or not there's a problem...which is why this rep tucked in so many Coffee Hours during the past weeks.

Generally speaking, there's a sad kind of feeling on Beacon Hill. One grows fond of one's colleagues in the great, friendly, give-and-take atmosphere of the House. We shall miss many good friends in the session that lies ahead. We rejoice, however, and are humble in the knowledge that we've been fortunate enough to have been sent back for two more years to represent the wonderful people of Braintree in the Great and General Court.

Especially grim and solemn is the atmosphere where the committee concerned with child abuse is meeting in the wake of the horror story that occurred in our town last week- the brutal murder of little Dianne. Those of us with small children and grandchildren mentally hold them close and suffer silently as we dwell upon the horrifying fate of a small defenseless child and mourn our inability to have done anything to prevent it. "Please God," we find ourself praying, "Let the result of these committee hearings be the establishment of a mechanism that will prevent this kind of tragedy from ever happening again."

The young and the elderly are so very defenseless, we opine...and-speaking of the elderly, and thinking of happier things, we were delighted to have been invited this past week to a 100th birthday party at Braintree Manor. It was held for Frances Mahoney, 100 years young, and my friend Edith, the party's M.C., certainly did herself proud. Frances, who loves things Irish (and why not with the name "Mahoney") was to be entertained with a program of lovely Irish ballads sung by our good friend, Jack. There would be an Irish Sing-along, and a beautiful birthday cake, made in the Manor Kitchen; and a fun time for all of us. There were to be handsome Irish green centerpiece which your L. of the H. found she matched perfectly - she was wearing Irish green as well!

It was to prove to be fun visiting with the partygoers as well as with the Guest of Honor. Among them we were to find 93 year old Alice, whose "neighbors were surprised to see me mowing the family lawn last summer, and dancing all evening at the last Manor party." And we were to hear a delightful tale from one of the volunteers, my good friend Agnes. The Senior Citizens, it seems had arranged a trip for Primary Day. Well, a group of them were returning from a very happy day in New Hampshire when they realized they had not performed their civic duty. They had not voted. Well, our Seniors vote, as every public official knows. So- what to do??? The answer was simple. They just sweet-talked the bus driver into toting them to St. Thom's School and waiting for them while each and every one of them placed the appropriate X's next to their candidates' names before driving off with them to Independence Manor where they all happened to reside. Nice guy, that bus driver! As one of the candidates who hopefully received some of those X's, we salute him.

11-9-78

By the time you read this column we shall have elected a new Governor. The Gubernatorial race has been, to our way of thinking, a particularly vituperative one. Our prayers would seem to be in order for the winner that, when the voters of he Commonwealth have spoken, all vituperation may be left behind him as he assumes this high office, and that all levels of government will unite to provide for our people the very best leadership the state has ever known. For - if ever there was a time for unity and cooperation among our governmental forces, it is now. Tax relief must be provided for our people in the most equitable and palatable form possible, in a manner that will cause the least harm to the greatest number of those people. And regardless of how strongly we felt about the candidate of our choice, we must not lose sight of the fact that the people will have chosen their governor and he will need our prayers.

As a winner myself, may I take this opportunity to thank you great Braintreeites again for voting to send your L. of the H. back to Beacon Hill for another two years. You're wonderful. And I promise to continue to be responsive to your needs and your dictates, to continue to be available, and to try with all my heart to truly represent you. It is a source of real delight to me to know that I shall now be representing the entire town of Braintree and not just eight of our twelve precincts as before. I'm everybody's rep now. (Actually, I've always felt like everybody's rep, but now it is official.)

The Chamber of the House of Representatives is currently in the throes of the renovations that have been necessitated by this year's House Cut, plus the shoring up of the underpinning of the House Chamber. We were fortunate apparently not to have fallen through the defective, more than 100 year old, Chamber flooring which must now be replaced. Also to be undertaken are the adjustments for handicapped persons that are now being mandated by the federal government whenever renovations beyond a certain monetary figure are proposed. Altogether it represents an extensive renovation project, and it's currently underway. I invariably find myself checking on things in the Chamber each day I go to the State House.

It seemed strange indeed initially to see the great center door of the Chamber flung wide open. Normally this door is opened only to "Admit the Honorable Senate" or "admit His Excellency, the Govenor, "etc. A message from the Speaker of the House, placed conspicuously before the roped off lobby area explains what is happening within. "The House of Representatives regrets that the House Chamber and Gallery must be closed to the public while restoration work is in progress," it reads. "You are cordially invited to visit us when the work is completed in January." It is signed by "Thomas W. McGee, Speaker."

We have witnessed once or twice the acute disappointment of visitors to Beacon Hill upon finding our beautiful House chamber dismantled. "We'll never get back here, you know," wailed one gentleman from Thailand last week. I knew just how he felt. A few years back while Ted and I were in Hawaii we had found the beautiful Iolnai Palace in the throes in renovation. As a matter of fact as we walked across the grounds there were the exquisite Throne Chairs that had known so many colorful Hawaiian rulers set side by side upon the portico awaiting transfer to the restoration area. We have a slide of that unusual sight. But we were deeply disappointed at the state of the palace itself.

What is happening inside the House Chamber is, of course, interesting to one who is about to occupy the "new" seat of government. Carpenters race about like so many ants, their hammers and other appurtenances ringing along the State House halls. The Speaker's area is completely draped with protective coverings. The magnificent hand carving, dating back more than a century, is being carefully protected, we're happy to note. We plan to request our same House seat. Seat No. 141 has been Braintree's for close to a quarter century, and we'd like to keep it ours for the next hundred years.

Well now, so much for Beacon Hill. We've a different matter to discuss. This rep is the proud possessor of a significant number of Braintree Town Reports. They date back to 1926 and the set is very nearly complete. We've ceased to collect them ourself and shall be happy to give them to anyone in Braintree who is currently doing just that. Give us a call at home or at the State House and we'll make arrangements to turn them over to you promptly…and happily.

11-16-78

The "tumult and the shouting" have died - thank goodness! And the "Captains and the Kings" have departed, most of them off to vacation - to recover…Campaigning is hard work, regardless of how much one may enjoy it.

Needless to say, the recent election was a wonderful experience for this particular "politician." Your overwhelming vote of confidence sends me back to Beacon Hill in a warmer glow than ever. And speaking of Beacon Hill, things have begun to warm up there, as we all commence to file our legislation for the coming session. The office of the House Counsel is beginning to have that "beehive" look. Nonetheless it will be wearing its customary madhouse mien as the first Wednesday in December deadline nears. And, don't forget, all of you have the right of free petition. If there's a bill you want filed, just contact me.

And needless to say, The Golden Dome is all but lifting off the State House with the weight of the rumors that are circulating there. The departing Governor, fresh from his Washington trip, is being merrily tucked into one federal slot after another, while the members of his entourage are the subjects of much speculation (and gossip) as they seek to avoid being numbered among the unemployed. It's a bit like a soap opera, we decide as we eavesdrop in the lunchroom or chat with friends in the State House Corridors. "Will Ed King keep him? Will he go back with Mayor White? Will Paul Guzzi recommend a liberal for that slot? Can the tax cut be made?" It must be made, we decide, even as we attend meetings where ever-increasing proposals for state expenditures are being made right and left. Incidentally, have you ever encountered an election with more acrimony and vituperation attached to it? We never have. We pray that this disturbing pattern of behavior is not going to be set in Massachusetts.

It has been a busy week for your L. of the H. with one evening meeting after another. We attended another T.A.C. meeting on the monumental problems we're still having with the M.B.T.A. stations and their ramifications…the unsolved access roads for the South Braintree station and the Walkway from Independence avenue to the South Quincy station. Both issues seem to be almost as far from solution now as they were a year ago…despite the dedication and concern and the hard work of those T.A.C. members of ours. Dealing with an autonomous State agency is apparently as difficult today as it was a dozen years ago when this rep was following the same route as the town's T.A.C. chairman.

The week also housed a vitally important Precinct Seven meeting where Detective Kevin Collins, our town's Crime Prevention Officer, presented films of the crime of Breaking and Entering. It is vital, he said, for neighbors to remain alert to any sign of impending crime in their area. "Call us," he said. "We'd rather come 100 times on a false alarm than miss one opportunity to catch a criminal in the act." Protecting one's home from breaking and entering was also discussed at length and the Metayers were undoubtedly first in line at the Police Station next morning to borrow the engraving tool they offer for marking one's most valuable possessions. It can be borrowed; and it sure acts as a deterrent to a would-be housebreaker to see upon the doors of his victim a seal indicating that everything of value has been marked with the owner's Social security number, we were assured. Such an easy course to follow, we decided as we merrily marked everything we could think of. Saturday being "Veteran's Day", we were on hand at Blue Hill Cemetery's beautiful "Garden of Honor" for a Veterans Day ceremony that was indeed a moving and memorable experience. The day was a typically November one with a somber sky and the feel of rain in the air, and we pray that it was the weather that kept our townspeople away, for, other than the participants and their families there were not a dozen Braintree-ites on hand to honor the brave Braintree Veterans who are still with us and those who sleep beneath our Braintree soil. Can we have forgotten the sacrifices our brave young men were willing to make to keep us free, we wondered sadly as we viewed the sparsity of the "crowd" on the lawns beneath the platform on which we stood. Our veterans were there, needless to say. They marched, regardless of their age, to and from West Street, their colors flying…But where were the people who are so heavily in their debt? Incidentally, the Speaker, our own War Hero Moderator, Gerald Walsh was stupendous.

12-14-78

The Metayers had long dreamed of vacationing in Egypt. The House of Representatives having prorogued early this year, that dream was to become a reality.

We were to leave Braintree on December 1 and fly half way around the world to a land of pure enchantment. Our Tour Escort, a delightful young man named Michael Hollingsworth, was to meet us in New York where we were to find ourselves in the company of the most friendly and fascinating group of people to be found anywhere. There were to be 6 from Canada; 2 from Maryland; 6 from New York, 3 from Ohio, 3 from California, 2 from Virginia, with only 3 of us from Massachusetts. At Kennedy Airport we would board a huge 747 for the second leg of our flight, a journey to Brussels where we would change to a 707 for the last part of a journey that would take us back in time more than 5000 years.

How to describe our first view of Cairo Airport - the Egyptian men with their burnooses (headgear) and the gaelabeas (robes), the fascinating attire we were to find all over Egypt; the black robed women; the sheiks; the color and the excitement of a place that represented the crossroads of the Middle East. We were to look askance at the armed guards at the gate; to delight in the date palms surrounding the airport; and then to board the conveyance that awaited us and to drive through the teeming streets of Cairo to our destination, the Mena House Hotel. The Mena House Hotel…Formerly a palace, it was here that Roosevelt, Stalin and Churchill met during World War II for the famed Cairo Conference; and it was here more recently that Sadat and Begin met to resume peace negotiations. Now it is a hotel of opulence and splendor. "Some of the balconies of its rooms offer a splendid view of the Pyramids," we had read in the current issue of "Town and Country." What if ours were one of them, we thought as we drove across the teeming city that is Cairo. But-to return to that journey across Cairo…What an experience it proved to be! Along the broad avenue of the suburban "City of Sun," with its magnificent villas lining both sides, its center section a parkway graced with towering banyan trees, whose roots, we were told, have not been allowed to spread as is the way with banyans. Each month they are cut and collected and the trees pruned to shapes of conformity and beauty.

There was no one to be seen in that exclusive and elegant section of town, and we were to delight in the elaborate fencing about the villas, the fountains that splashed and the lights that sparkled, the sheer unashamed opulence of the villas that represented such a contrast to the poverty to be found within the city itself. And now the City of Sun was behind us and we were driving across the teeming streets of Giza. There were colored lights strung along the way, Sadat's picture in their midst. Bus stops were crowded with Egyptians in their colorful garb. The people streamed along the sidewalks and the roadways or sat in the coffee shops or squatted on curbstones which, incidentally were painted in alternating blocks of black and white.

We were to view ancient arched walls while a crescent moon hung appropriately above the narrow streets with their masses of people. It was the Moslem New Year, our guide informed us, hence the colored lights and the holiday atmosphere.

Giza- the city of Pharaohs - One's heart pounded with the realization that we were about to tour this ancient place, to explore at last the great pyramids that represent one of the Seven Wonders of the World.

There are close to 10 million people in Cairo, we were told, and the population increases by 1 million yearly. There is naturally a housing shortage. "Do you have a flat?" the family of marriageable daughter asks a young man seeking her hand. If he has no flat, the wedding is off.

And now we had dined and settled down for the night amid the splendor of the Mena House. It had been dark when we arrived, but would we be one of the fortunate ones with a view of the pyramids from our balcony, we wondered as we looked out upon the black of an Egyptian night. and secretly resented the intrusion of the sleeptime that lay ahead.

Morning on the Nile - We awoke to the blue and gold of the sky and sand that was to fill our souls with delight for ten full days to come. We dashed from the kingsize bed in which we had slumbered but little, drew back the wide heavy drapes that separated us from the world beyond, and voila! Filling our window with history of the ages was the great pyramid of Giza! We had truly arrived in Egypt, and the history of the ages was about to unfold, a history we plan to share with you in the weeks ahead.

12-21-78

Our first morning in Cairo, Egypt...Having found the Great Pyramid of Giza framed in our hotel window; you may well imagine how impatient I was to take the camel ride we had been promised and, via this rather different mode of travel, to reach the magnificent monument. It was not be until later in the day however. Nadia our beautiful Egyptologist guide, arrived to escort the "Treasures of Egypt Discovery" tourists first to Memphis, the Metropolis of the Old Kingdom and then to Sakkara, its Acropolis.

We drove down Pyramid Road, a highway which was built to celebrate the opening of the Suez Canal. It was a picturesque drive indeed. Eucalyptus trees lined both sides of the canal that ran beside it. Grass-roofed med houses of the Egyptian poor dotted its banks, with people and animals spread upon the walkways before them. Fifty percent of the Egyptians are peasants, we were told. Total ignorance and ill health was their lot prior to the revolution of 1952. Now, however, they have schools and hospitals, we were informed. Education, including the university, is free, our guide said. We were to be told later that said education is compulsory only to the age of twelve, and that a child of twelve who does not learn readily is forced to leave public school and if his family is unable to afford private school, the child goes to work. This could explain the many young children begging for "Baksheesh" (money) we were to encounter in our travels.

Memphis and Sakkara lie 20 kilometers south of the Pyramid Road, with Memphis on the east bank of the Nile and Sakkara on the west bank. We delighted in the drive there, the sight of the black-robed Egyptian women with immense water jars balanced on their heads, reminiscent of the biblical scenes we love. Incidentally, Egyptian peasant women wear the beautiful colored cottons for which Egypt is famous while in their homes. Outside of those homes, however, the black shapeless garments must be worn. "Husbands are jealous…!" Their faces are not veiled. Moslem women's faces are veiled, however, with the number of coins on those veils indicating the extent of their wealth.

But to return to Memphis, Egypt's first capitol. It was built as a fortress to protect its people from invasion via the Nile. (Thebes, which is now Luxor, replaced it as the capitol.) Here at Memphis we were to visit the Temple of the god, Ptah, with its immense 18th century alabaster sphinx of the great Pharaoh Ramses II. A sphinx portrays the strength of a lion and the wisdom of man, our guide informed us; and the word "Pharaoh" means "Great House." It derived from the fact that the rulers of the ancient tribes built their homes on high hills. The houses, and then the rulers were called Pharaohs. In time, the word came to mean "the living god."

The Ramses II sphinx at Memphis is portrayed wearing the Nemes, the royal head cover, with the cobra on his forehead indicating royalty and the false beard, also an emblem of rank. It, like all sphinxes, faces east and wears the trace of a smile on its face. The god, Ptah, was the protector of artists, and each Pharaoh as he returned from war added a statue and cartouche to his temple. Ptah was the only god to be represented with a round bonnet and a false beard.

Although this was to be our first encounter with Ramses II, we were soon to learn that statues of his particular pharaoh abound in Egypt. He was known as "Ramses, the Great." One of our guides however (not Nadia), referred to him as "Ramses, the Chiseler" since wherever he found a statue of another king, he had the owner's name removed and substituted his own.

At Sakkara we were to visit the famous Step Pyramid of King Zoser, the oldest pyramid in existence (about 4800 years old). It, unlike Giza, was composed of six rectangular mastabas, placed one upon the other. Beneath it was the burial chamber of the king, a pit hewn into the rock and graced with exquisite tiles and drawings. The immensity of the tombs in the acropolis at Sakkara left us breathless, some of them hewn so deeply into the mountains we were unable to see the bottom of the tomb from above. Here we were to encounter the history of the Old Kingdom which extended from the 6th to the 11th Dynasty. The Middle Kingdom which followed extended from the 12th to the 18th Dynasty, and the New Kingdom followed. Now the tombs of the Pharaohs were to increase in opulence and design, and columns were to be used for the first time in the temples of the gods. Pharaohs were to vie with one another in erecting temples within temples to the gods of Egypt, and the great monuments of limestone and sandstone and granite would soar toward the heavens, the technological skill and know-how of their creators to record for all time the advancement of the civilization and culture that was theirs. Next our visit via camel to the Great Pyramids of Giza.

1-18-79

The storied Temple of Karnak...We had seen it in the movie "Murder on the Nile", much of which was filmed there...Now we were about to ride there in an open Caleche (carriage) for the performance of SOUND AND LIGHT within the temple ruins. The Temple of Karnak, 60 acres of pylons, pillars, obelisks and colossi, ramparts and colonnades, with the 134 columns that make up its Hypostyle Chamber alone... The Great Temple of the god Amon...Much of it credited to the Pharaoh Amonhotep III in the 18th Dynasty, the massive granite blocks are held together without benefit of mortar. How did the ancient Egyptians accomplish this unbelievable feat?? The question goes unanswered today.

Approached via the "Avenue of the Sphinxes," gigantic figures with the body of a lion and the head of a ram, symbolic of both strength and fertility, the massive temple houses countless lesser temples within it, each successive Pharaoh having added a monumental structure of its own as a tribute to the god whom he owed success in battle...and otherwise...

But-to return to the performance of SOUND AND LIGHT which represented our first introduction to Karnak. The night was warm. A million stars shone down so close our inclination was to touch them. We settled ourselves in the amphitheatre provided for the event. The solemnity of our surroundings flowed from the towering ruins about us. There was music to set the scene...and then the beautiful voice came our way... "I have measured these crumbling ruins, these tumbling esplanades, these terraces, these sanctuaries, the pylons, these pillars on a gigantic scale, honeycombed with interior stairways leading to the ramparts of the Heavens...This land of Upper Egypt upon which the most grandiose structure of the world rises is said to have been the first to have risen from the primeval waters...a City of God to the glory of his creation...Do not be overwhelmed by the sheer size of these ruins. The Citadel was not designed on the scale of men but on the grand scale of God from Whom all things flowed...dreams and power, life and death...all the pomp and magnificence of the Pharaohs is at Karnak. No other ancient people conceived the art of architecture on so grandiose a scale. Who art thous, Amon??? The answer would seep from these walls, these lintels, these sacred chambers, these ruins. The answer is written everywhere in a thousand different hieroglyphics....My right eye is the day; my left eye is the night and the waters of the Nile sport from my sandals. We were to hear wafted on the desert night the history of an ancient people and their rulers and their faith in a Supreme Being. Later we were to view the Karnak by day, to wander in and out of the seemingly endless avenues of temples and monuments…to steep ourselves in the past…It would prove to be an unparalleled adventure.

So, too, would be our visit to Abu Simbel, our flight there above the vast expanse of the Sahara, and the first breathtaking sight of this Temple of Ramses II from the air above it. Abu Simbel…Here was the Temple the civilized world joined forces to move from the path of the Nile to the top of an adjacent mountain when the Great Aswan Dam was in the making. 1200 sections had to be carefully cut and moved, each weighing from 10 to 30 tons. Even the façade of the hill behind it had to be moved; to be replaced identically along with the Temple itself, in its new high location safe from the flood waters. The cost $17 Million. It was, in our opinion, well worth the investments.

A magnificent Temple. In the forefront the Great Colossi of Ramses II with the terrace before them. Next the great Hypostyle Hall with its eight statues of Ramses, four on either side. Next the Hall with its four gigantic and beautiful pillars and finally the Sanctuary itself. We were to delight in the paintings of the sun disc and the cobra, the far horizon, the clouds and the air above: the figures of the Asian and Libyan prisoners in chains; the vultures that were to provide protection for the soul of the departed Pharaoh who claimed not only to be a king but a god.

Nearby the beautiful temple of Nefertari, his favorite Queen. Four statues of Ramses and only two of Nefertari on the great terrace, needless to say. And pillars of its Hypostyle Hall portraying the King killing a Nubian, being crowned before the gods Horus and Seth: offering wine to Re-Harakhte. An occasional glimpse of the Queen before Anuket and again before Hathor. But ABU SIMBEL is there to assure the immortality of Ramses II. And immortal he must be unless and until Mother Nile decrees otherwise…Mother Nile who always has and apparently always will rule the fate of the land she created in the heart of the great sprawling desert that covers the face of her world.

1-4-79

The Pyramids of Giza…We had seen them framed in the window of our room at the Mena House Hotel and now we were about to mount our friends the camels and head for the desert area that housed them…Ted to be photographed wearing the attire of his camel driver and I not quite so dashingly garbed…both of us looking wonderfully at our ease on the huge ungainly beasts…We were to visit first the great Tomb of Cheops, "The Great Pyramid". Built 5,000 years ago, this greatest of the three monuments in 146 meters high. It is composed of 2,3000,000 to 3 million blocks of granite, each weighing from 2½ to 15 tons. The ceiling blocks are 18' × 14' in size and weigh 30 tons each. The entrance we were to use to ascend half way to the top of the pyramid's interior had been made by the tomb's ancient grave robbers, and it was no easy task to negotiate the 45° climb up a steep slope with only ladder-like steps. It was no easy task, but what a feeling to find oneself in the center of the great tomb, marveling among other things, at the two ancient air chutes that ventilated the enormous monument. The pyramid contains two Chambers and the Pharaoh Cheops was buried in the first one, we were told.

The Pyramid of Chephren was next, slightly smaller than that of his father Cheops. Chephren is the one, however, whose face has come down to us there in the desert for it is he who is represented in the guise of the Sphinx.

The tomb of Mycerinus completes Giza, that most impressive place. We were told that having built it, "the workmen came down and laying down their tools, looked up in wonderment at the magnificence they had wrought. Here now three Pharaohs were to reign…Wearing the double crown of Upper and Lower Egypt. Nearby would be the smaller tombs of their queens. This was to become a royal palace of the dead and neither wind nor sand nor remorseless time would silence the voices that would cry out wordlessly from the desert, telling for all time the story of a land and its ancient rulers.

We were to stand in awe before the mighty Sphinx with its half smile and mysterious mien, viewing it from the Temple of Chephren adjacent to it. It is carved of one block of granite and it rises, immense and awe-inspiring among the tombs that surround it. There is controversy about the destruction of the face of this guardian of the dead. Could its royal nose have been destroyed by fanatical Moslems??? Could the act of vandalism have been perpetrated by Napoleon during his invasion of Egypt??? It is not generally thought he was responsible since Napoleon brought with him scientists and astrologers to study the history of ancient Egypt. He is reputed to have said to his troops. "From the top of these pyramids, forty centuries are watching you…" The mighty monument is 4800 years old and annually during sandstorms that plague the Land of Pharaohs 2½ centimeters of erosion takes place. The weakest point of the great granite monument which incidentally was carved in one piece directly from the mountain, happens to be its nose where the damage is most evident. In 1300 years from now, according to scientists, the entire Sphinx will have eroded into dust. Its front paws were rebuilt 2000 years ago according to records found nearby. As we gazed upon this magnificent monument we found ourself pondering on the irreparable loss that would be represented by that 1300 year erosion that is foretold.

The Sphinx was built as an adjunct to the magnificent adjacent Temple of Chephren whose stones are cut to fit so well that not a pin will fit between them…whose corners are carved in one huge block whose floors are alabaster and whose pillars stand 13 meters in height…

Highlighting our involvement with the Great Pyramids of Giza was our attendance ata performance of "Sound and Light" on the evening before we were to leave the enchanting land that is Egypt. The night is dark…We sit outdoors before the three great Pyramids, the Sphinx in their midst. The music of the London Philharmonic Orchestra sets the scene for the narration of the History of Ancient Egypt, handled beautifully by the Royal Shakespeare Company. The desert is bathed in soft white light…Overhead a million stars reach down so low one can all but touch them.

"You have come tonight to the most fabulous and celebrated place in the world. Here on the plains of Giza we have the mightiest of human achievements…Gasp in awe…" The beautiful voice moves across the desert night. "We have been involved and forever present since the dawn of history, pitched stubbornly against sand and wind since the dawn of civilization. With each new dawn, I saw the sun god rise on the far bank of the Nile. For 5000 years I have seen all the suns man can remember come up in the sky." The voice is the voice of the Sphinx. It is about to recount the history of an age long gone… "I am the faithful warden at the foot of his lord. I am a Pharaoh's companion and I am he…the Pharaoh…Lord of the Desert…Lord of the Heavens…sovereign of eternity. Heroditus, the Greek called me Sphinx…"

1-11-79

We shall, of course, continue with the account of our visit to Egypt…So many of you seem to be enjoying it and we love reliving our experiences as we write of them. First, however, since a new administration has begun on Beacon Hill, we feel called upon to fill you in on some of the pomp and circumstance surrounding the Inauguration of our new Governor, Edward J. King.

The day was to begin with an extremely beautiful Inaugural Mass to which three or four hundred of us were invited. Held in St. Joseph's, the Bicentennial Church in Boston's West End, it was concelebrated by Bishop Joseph F. Maguire, a special friend to many of us, including the Governor, and a dozen or so other distinguished clergymen. The mood was prayerful. We were, as a body seeking Divine help - in the finest tradition of our Founding Fathers - in providing for our State a government "of the people, by the people and for the people" in the truest sense of the phrase. The music was magnificent, the organ and trumpets sending forth their glorious sounds to fill the lovely Church and inspire us all to raise our voices in song to the Almighty…

There was breakfast afterwards; and then we were off to the State House for the Inaugural Ceremony. The pomp and circumstance that had been eliminated to a great degree by Mr. King's predecessor, was to be restored, and we delighted in the fact. It was a moving experience for your L. of the H. to be named as one of the House Committee members to proceed to the Executive Office and inform the Governor Elect that the House was assembled and ready for the swearing in. How exciting it was to march down the State House corridor to the Executive Office through a Guard of Honor…our uniformed State Police lining both sides of the hall, standing at attention in a manner we thought befitting to the historic occasion.

Governor King was to arrive in the House Chamber, and before a Joint Session of the House and Senate to be administered the Oath of Office. His Inaugural Address would please most of us…And a new and thoroughly different, we are sure, Administration will now take over the reigns of our great state.

It was, for me, especially appealing to note his 84-year-old Mother present at the ceremony. How very often we've wished our own parents had lived to see their daughter seated in the historic House of Representatives, representing the very same town in the very same capacity as a Braintree-ite who rose to the Presidency of the United States… Braintree's own John Adams.

Well, a new era has begun for our beloved Commonwealth. We pray that Governor King will reach the goals he set for himself…that he will prove to be among our very best Chief Executives…for if he fails, not only he but the people of Massachusetts will be the losers; and if he succeeds we shall all win handsomely…the Governor himself and the people who have placed him in the corner office of Beacon Hill. Our prayers for that success will continue to rise…

Well, now to return to Egypt and our doings there…We've but a small amount of column space left so we shall forego our original intention to write of the Storied Temple of Karnak and tackle the Aswan High Dam instead. So much has been written about this engineering marvel that it was especially exciting to be standing on the "Speedway" above it, looking down on Lake Naser where 50 million cubic yards of rock and desert sand were used to create a 1.544 square mile artificial lake that we were told is six times the size of our Hoover Dam's Lake Mead. It was designed to bring irrigation to some 1.7 Million acres, and was built at a cost of One Billion Dollars. It's estimated output is 10 Billion kilo-watt hours a year, or about 2.5 times the energy currently being consumed in Egypt, we were told.

Aswan itself is numbered among the world's loveliest places. Here the Edwardians and Victorians summered in the famous old Cataract Hotel. We stayed in the New Cataract from which we could view the Old Hotel, currently being rebuilt. It's a resort for Cairo's wealthy.

Egypt itself is referred to as a "gift of the Nile." The lives of its people depend on its lifegiving water. With the building of the new dam, the entire course of the river has been changed. It is vital to the Egyptians, and is well guarded indeed. No cameras…no picture taking on the Speedway, where we stood delighting in the Egyptian blue of the Nile with the fold of the Sahara beyond…the Sahara (the word means "desert") that stretches for 6,000 miles to the Atlantic. We almost lost sight of the newts with their explosives that we noted strung along the entrance to the dam area…

Incidentally we were not quite certain we should be able to FLY to Abu Simbel from Aswan, which is 600 miles south of Cairo. "Sometimes shifting sands cover the roadway there and the airport had to be closed until the roads are shoveled out," we were told. We had laughed. "We have it with SNOW," we had said. No shifting sands had prevented our flight, however. We had seen the Aswan Lower Dam and the High Dam

The Candid Idylls of a State Representative | 257

and the storied Cataracts, and we were about now to fly to Abu Simbel to the great tomb of Ramses II which was moved from the bottom to the top of the mountain and about which we shall also write in our next column.

2-1-79

The tempo had begun to accelerate on Beacon Hill, with what could be a wildly busy year ahead. More than 5700 bills have been filed with the House Clerk alone. He reports it to be the second highest total in Commonwealth history…an average of 36 bills per member. "The average for our 240 member House was 24," our incomparable House Clerk, 'Wally' Mills said.

We derive some comfort from the fact that so many of those bills are already in print and that committee hearings have already begun in earnest. This is, of course, due to our early Prorogation last year. When our House sessions flow almost uninterruptedly from one year to the next as they have done during the past several years, the activities of our House Counsel and House Clerk and their staffs is tied to the current year, and it can be a couple of months or more before bills are in print and our public hearings have commenced.

By the time this column is in print, Bills to phase out and to abolish County government will have been heard before the Committee on Counties, as well as bills to require County advisory Boards to approve county budgets. How do you feel about county government? The cry for tax relief is obviously permeating the air of government at ALL levels.

Braintree will have had a hearing on its bill to authorize our Town forest Committee to transfer a parcel of land to the Tedeschi Realty Corporation in exchange for other land owned by "said corporation." And a hearing on a number of bills requiring owners of vacant business property to maintain it will have been heard before the Committee on Local affairs. And - speaking of that committee - we feel certain you will be interested in the fact that under a House Rule change bills that would impose a financial burden on our cities and towns will be sent to the committee on Local Affairs by our Committee on Ways and Means before action is taken…a good step forward in the opinion of this representative who has once more filed two different bills calling for full state funding for all state-mandated programs.

Under our House Rules, every bill must receive a public hearing at which the bill's sponsor and any interested citizen may offer testimony. It is then voted upon by the committee members in executive session which is also open to the public. We do indeed have open government on Beacon Hill. Incidentally there's a splendid new pamphlet entitled "Access to Law-making" now available at the State House. If you'd like a copy, a phone call to my home or office will speed it on its way to you.

Our Transportation Committee hearings are scheduled to begin on January 31, and our Health Care Committee hearings should follow shortly after. Incidentally your representative was most pleased to have been returned to the Transportation and Health Care Committees on which she has spent the past four years. They're mighty important committee assignments, and this year with a legislative aide to cover one or other of the committee hearings when both are scheduled at the same, we'll be in excellent shape, attending one and having comprehensive notes taken on the other.

We shouldn't have to miss a thing that goes on in either committees.

An extremely busy year certainly lies ahead for this rep. Who has contributed to the 5700 plus bill total by filing more than 60 bills herself. These will have to be defended before committee. They will, therefore, call for an appearance before committee and extensive prepared testimony geared to the questions committee members can be guaranteed to ask. They deal with a variety of problems, and in today's climate we are extremely optimistic about the passage of many of them. A number of our proposals were prompted by the concerns voiced by our constituents during our recent Coffee Hours, our bills to raise the legal drinking age for one…ours and the other similar bills which are scheduled to be heard on Tuesday, February 6 at 10:30 a.m. in Room 468 at the State House. So - if you feel strongly on this issue…if you are in agreement with so many parents, educators and law enforcement officials that lowering the drinking age constituted a monstrous error - do pluck up courage and come to the State House and speak out before the Committee on Government Regulations. A Simple statement will do. And you will find that our colleagues are very kind to the Commonwealth's concerned citizenry, especially if they appear nervous.

We'll be discussing the outcome of these bills and other bills and other bills we've filed in subsequent columns, as well as the other doings on Beacon Hill.

3-1-79

An exciting week on the Hill…and such a Busy one! A bill to prohibit the MBTA from constructing the controversial Walkway from Independence Avenue to the Quincy Adams Station was among those heard before our Committee on Transportation, for one thing. At the direction of our town. officials, we spoke AGAINST it and FOR the Walkway; and those officials who happened to be present in significant numbers in support of another bill - the one we'd filed at their request, which would prohibit the opening of the MBTA stations until the access roads were completed - joined us in opposition to the prohibition of the Walkway. The MBTA was, incidentally, on OUR side of the issue. A complete re-redesign of the structure would have to follow prohibition, they said; and the contract now in progress would have to be stopped pending that redesign. The "T" opposed the bill.

Our efforts at determining whether or not the town has any rights at all in the matter of the presence of Recycling Industries in our midst continued unabated. We now anxiously await the interpretation of our Town Counsel, Arthur Smith, on Section

150A of Chapter 111 of the General Laws, which we feel applies to the hazardous waste disposal facility that has us so concerned. We've requested the Commissioner of the Department of Environmental Engineering to take water and air samples in the area of the plant to determine whether any toxic materials are posing a threat to the health of the community residents. We have also asked for a stack test, there being two incinerators in the facility. The state was right there stack testing our municipal incinerator right and left. Their reports cost us thousands of dollars…and we don't burn hazardous wastes. Shouldn't a similar stack test be part of the so-called hazardous waste "inspection" process of the state, we wonder…We saw to it, incidentally, that our letter was hand delivered to E.E.Q.E. Commissioner Cortese on Tuesday and we marked it "PERSONAL".

Having filed our perennial bill to secure rapid transit service on the Red Line to and from Columbia Station, we were comforted by the knowledge that the project now has high priority status and that from all indications UMTA is looking favorably toward it. We'd pushed that hard last year through our Transportation Committee and we're delighted at that news.

The governor's tax cap plan easily stole the headlines. Although just about everyone in the state is in agreement that something must be done speedily to control local property taxes, there is concern among many that the Governor's plan will erode Home Rule. Many also find the idea of a Governor-appointed Appeals Board difficult to take; and the issues of local fiscal autonomy, collective bargaining and state-mandated programs kept surfacing during the close to all-day session on the tax cap held recently. Well, we shall see what we shall see…We, meanwhile, anxiously await the Governor's budget which we understand, in effect, places a cap on state spending as well. Changing the subject, we were interested to learn the Civil Service Commission plans to release the results of that disputed October 1978 examination for the rank of police sergeant, despite the fact that a man is currently being charged with attempting to sell a copy of the test before it was given. Apparently more than 500 police officers in 27 communities took the test. There appears to be sentiment for and against making the exam count. How SAD it is that corruption seems to surface in so many areas in these strange days of changing values and diminishing integrity. The 21 year old drinking law is still in limbo. We were shocked to read recently that the costs of mental health and alcoholism treatment which are now covered by Blue Cross/Blue Shield under the Master Medical Plan, have soared from $7 Million in 1976 to $24 Million in 1978, with $30 Million anticipated for 1979. What a sad commentary on this wonderful old world in which we live. What was it the poet wrote so long ago??? "The world is so filled with beautiful things, I'm sure we should all be as happy as kings…" We agree, and speaking of being happy, your Lady of the House was sure made happy this past week when it was pointed out to her by friend Ron that she received the second highest total of votes among the 160 members of the House of Representatives in the recent election. Thank you again, you SUPER Branitree-itres!

3-15-79

Monday morning, and the thermometer on Tremont Street registers 54 degrees as we walk up Park Street, with the golden chimes of the Park Street Church sounding, and the Golden Dome of the State House shining, and everything whispering of Spring... At home, three full inches of happy little would-be hyacinths are in evidence in the family garden, and the tulip fronds are growing tall enough to wave a bit, and March is marching towards April, and doesn't it make a difference in the hearts of all of us???

An eventful day is to lie ahead, with the drinking age issue finally resolved at age 20 with a House vote of 118 to 31. Our appearance is indicated before the Taxation Committee in defense of our bill to mandate that criteria be furnished by the Board of Assessors of a City or Town when property is revalued...We spend hours in our Health Care Committee public hearing which is dealing with such controversial issues as Denturism and Fluoridation...And come evening we hold our Office Hours at Town Hall where we learn of a further development of two Hazardous Waste Disposal facility situation. Our town Counsel, Arthur Smith announces agree with our oft-repeated claim that state law requires local Board of Health involvement and local permits before a Hazardous Waste Disposal facility can be landed in a town's midst as has happened here in Braintree. "What do you feel is the most interesting part of your work?" handsome young U.Mass/Boston student Timothy Reardon had asked of your L of the H. that particular afternoon in an interview on Women in Politics." All of it," I had answered promptly. "Everything about this University that is the Hill is challenging, exciting and rewarding." Incidentally, these interviews with our young college students are great. They provide an opportunity to get across to our young people the other side of the rather bleak picture that's given them of the people in charge of their government. My good friend, Mary Newman teaches a Government Class at U.Mass/Boston; and she sends a great many of her pupils to me. I love it...

Action in the House itself was rather negligible this past week. In the various committee hearings that found the State House hearing rooms bulging at the seams, however, action was intense. In our Health Care Committee on another day we heard bills dealing with the problems generated by the use of D.E.S. among pregnant women during the past few decades, with legislation filed to establish a central area for record-keeping on those Mothers whose offspring, both male and female, appear to be now vulnerable to cancer - a horrifying thought.

The ever-present bills to provide free restrooms in shopping centers and businesses of all kinds came before us, and it appears that a comprehensive bill will be put out favorably on the issue this year.

Defending my own bills took a great deal of my time, among them one to protect the interests of a guarantor of loan. I was appalled to learn that under existing laws, where the guaranty is not limited to a sum certain, the amount of the loan may be increased without any notification to the guarantor. My bill would provide that the guarantor would have to be notified at least 10 days in advance of any increase in liability. "It does seem that a guarantor is entitled to at least that degree of financial protection," I told members of the Judiciary Committee. "A guarantor should not, in my opinion, be held responsible for an open-ended situation which could provide liability for an amount not ever envisioned in his original guaranty of a loan," I said, asking, of course, for a FAVORABLE committee vote on the bill.

Evening events have added several other dimensions to our days as your Rep. For one thing, we attended "Guest Night" at our Braintree Woman's Club where we delighted in the Drama Committee's presentation of a wonderfully done and hilarious One-Act Play. And, in a change of pace, we participated in a Channel 4 T.V. NEW ACTION 4 program which dealt with Braintree's concerns with its unwelcome Hazardous Waste facility, located as it is close to our people and surrounded by such potentially explosive entities as the Citgo Refinery, General dynamics and our municipal Light Plant. Our town officials, state officials and concerned citizens aired their concerns. We wish there might have been more time, however we did manage to highlight the problem in a program which will be aired on WBZ-TV's Channel 4 at eight o'clock on Thursday evening, March 15. We hope you'll all be watching…

4-19-79

The Tax Cap understandably maintained its position as the Number one issue on Beacon Hill this past week, providing for all of us a difficult and soul-searching choice. For one thing, the King proposal differed greatly from the Tax Cap proposal the citizens of Massachusetts had addressed on the November referendum ballot. The tax cap provided that all state and local taxes when combined would take no larger a percentage of the total Mass personal income than the average percentage in the previous three year period.

The Governor's Tax Cap mandated a zero increase on municipal budgets regardless of the 11 percent inflation rate forecast for the coming year in short, it would actually have called for an 11 percent budget reduction on all municipal budgets across the state whether or not a community was experiencing a stable growth, like our own town, or was rapidly growing and consequently requiring additional municipal services - like Plymouth and other South Shore towns.

You may rest assured that this representative agonized over the decision she would be obliged to make on this issue. We had met with members of our Ways and Means and Taxation Committees several times and discussed the many ramifications of a zero tax cap, along with the real impact. of the 4 percent compromise that had been contained in the Taxation Committee bill. Meanwhile, incidentally, your L. of the H. was hearing from almost no one in FAVOR of the zero increase. Those calls were to come later after the issue had been voted upon. On the other hand, she was being deluged with more than 100 letters and calls OPPOSING ANY tax cap.

We honestly feel that what we did in voting for a 4 percent tax cap has been misunderstood by many. We have not in any way endorsed the idea of a 4 percent cap. I personally see no reason why Braintree for instance, would have to increase its budget by 4 percent if it does not wish to do so. Our Town Meeting members can follow the Finance Committee recommendations to the letter and vote down any expansion of services that are proposed in the Town Warrant. One fact that has been overlooked as we see it is that we have not disallowed our cities and towns individually from voting a zero based budget. This is their perogative and a privilege which they currently have without any vote of the Legislature and any move on the part of the Governor. So they have not been disallowed from going to zero increase. What we have done is to say that if they feel compelled to do so, they can go to 4 percent of last year's budget, but NO HIGHER without a 2:3 vote of the town's governing body.

It is important to remember that 80 percent of a municipal budget goes for salaries and so if a community has already negotiated contracts which are greater than an amount provided for in a 4 percent budget cap, there would be no alternative for them but to fire numbers of their employees. If people are fired by a municipality, that city or town must absorb the cost of unemployment benefits for those people, and if their families are large, the amount involved can be almost as large as the salaries they would have paid to them, with the town deprived of their services. That was another angle we had to consider in voting on this issue.

In Braintree's case, with the new MBTA station scheduled to be opened this year, and with all of the resultant problems that station opening will generate for our Police department, i.e. increased traffic and increased crime. This representative fears the effects of a reduction in the numbers of our law enforcement people. As for our firefighters, with Arson as ever growing menace in the lives of all of us, should we be considering cutting down on the number of firefighters??? We feared to accept that proposal. Hopefully our School Committee and School Administration will in the light of a decreasing pupil enrollment concentrate this year and every year on cutting corners wherever and whenever possible to keep our school costs under control.

In our opinion, the issue of keeping our Braintree property tax rate down rests with the Town officials and Town Meeting Members who today as always should be expected to "Cut their cloth according to their measure," to quote a fine old English saying. If everyone involved in the budgetary process keeps the best interests of our homeowners in mind as they prepare and review Braintree's budget requests, we can see no reason why a close to zero tax cap would not be within the realm of possibility for our town to whom a 4 percent tax cap really represents no more than a ceiling of what CAN be spent by the town without a 4:5 vote of its governing body.

5-7-79

So many happenings at the state House this past week...For one thing, much to the surprise of many of us, the governor's veto of a bill that would ban charges for directory assistance telephone calls was initially sustained in the House. We feel, however, that by the time you read this column, that vote will have been reversed. The bill's sponsor promptly moved reconsideration, and will have had a weekend to work in to secure the mere four votes necessary to overturn that veto. Our elderly people particularly would have severe financial problems with such a change in their service. The printing on telephone books has become increasingly smaller and more difficult to read of late. Additionally during recent years we have not been given telephone books for areas other than our own. It has, therefore become necessary to dial 411 on many an occasion when having the appropriate phone book would have prevented that necessity. Well, we shall see what Monday will bring on this issue.

The Governor was also in the news for his acceptance of the 4 percent tax cap. It will, he claims, reduce the amount of his promised property tax relief from $500 million to $400 million; and he will try next year for that zero cap he wants so desperately and so many of our citizens appear to want along with him.

Again on Executive action, many of us were appalled to read that a lowering of environmental standards and a reduction in local and state controls on development were recommended in a report submitted to the Governor this week by a "blue ribbon task force" of business leaders and cabinet secretaries. We've requested a copy of this report so that we may examine it in depth. The goal of the task force is, of course, to improve the business climate in Massachusetts, and that goal we may applaud, but we must also assess the cost....

On our Health care Committee this past week we took another look at a bill which had originally received an OUGHT NOT TO PASS, and which would provide funding for a state inspection agency for meat and poultry in the Commonwealth. This agency has not been funded for the past several years since it was alleged that federal inspectors were handling the same chore. It constituted a duplication of effort, we were told. Well, apparently a further investigation has substantiated the need for this "duplication of effort." The bill will now go out favorably from our committee. We've been asked to include in our Column a few tips to help in the fight to curb energy costs, so here goes: Tight storm windows are an absolute necessity; and all outside doors should be weather-stripped, and weather-stripped storm doors added. Cellar windows should also be weather-stripped; and try applying a clear plastic on the inside of them. Seal the fireplace well; and weather-strip that attic door of yours. An electric blanket can be used instead of a heated bedroom; and doors to unused or seldom used rooms can be kept closed..

Our "extra curricular legislative appearances continued unabated during the past week. Monday evening, and it was off first to the Norfolk County Hospital for the dedication of the newly renovated "Thomas K. McManus" Wing; and then to Hanover for the delightful Annual Meeting and Dinner of the Sacred Heart Mothers Club. Tuesday found us dashing down to the Parker House at noon for the Legislative Luncheon of the Mass. Association of School Business Officials; and come evening. attending the "37th Annual Get-Together of the Mass. Legislators Association", also at the Parker House - a fun evening in every respect as former reps and senators regaled the "newcomers" with tales of the way it used to be on Beacon Hill.

Sunday provided a pair of particularly rewarding experiences for your L. of the H. - first in our Braintree American Legion Hall for the presentation of Citations to the winners of the annual school children's Flag Essay Contest; and then secondly as a member of the Honorary Committee for the Aleppo Temple Shrine Activities Inc. "Spring Garden Festival", at a "High Tea" at the Shriners Burns Institute as a guest of the Festival chairman, Braintreeite Arthur L. MacDonald, Jr. A marvelous afternoon, which included a tour of that fabulous hospital where badly burned children are daily restored to health, thanks to the unceasing generosity of this fine Shriners Organization.

5-24-79 THE PEARL TREE CROSSING

Guess what??? Four years of persistent effort have paid off. The Pearl Street Crossing is at last about to be rebuilt and rebuilt handsomely at that - employing the same technique that has made crossing the tracks on Quincy Avenue (by the Shipyard) and on Elm Street such an easy experience. The complexity of the problem has stemmed from the division of responsibility between the DPW, the MBTA, Conrail and the Penn R.R. This rep had had so many conversations with Penn's headquarters in Philadelphia, she feels like a member of their staff. At any rate, the Pre-Construction Conference has been scheduled for next week; the damages suits against the town will cease; and all will hopefully be well when the crossing work is completed and one more headache removed from our community..

AIRCRAFT NOISE

With summer approaching, the problem of possible additional aircraft noise came once more for solution before our Transportation Committee this past week. I spoke in support of a bill directing the Port authority to construct a noise monitoring station in Squantum. Planes that bothered the people of Squantum in previous years have caused certain of our Braintree residents some difficulty as well, and so a Squantum monitoring station at that point seemed like a good idea. Unfortunately the bill went into a Study package, which will address a number of petitions involving Logan airport, and so we shall have to wait until the results of that study are brought back to us to learn what, if any, steps the Port Authority will take to alleviate the problem that is caused each summer when the prevailing west wind calls for the heavy use of Runway 22. Unfortunately in Airport decisions the F.A.A. holds the controlling authority; Logan can recommend only. The decision rests with the Federal authorities. We shall keep our eyes and ears open on that issue, however.

BOTTLE BILL

The Bottle Bill which had received an OUGHT NOT TO PASS from committee was fast gaveled into temporary oblivion recently, which does not mean that it is dead for the session. Reconsideration was promptly moved and we shall be addressing that vital issue again on Monday.

TAX CAP

The tax cap philosophy appears to have colored the thinking of our Town Meeting members. We were able to sit through Monday's meeting, (the first free T.M. evening we've had). And incidentally to realize how very much we miss being part of these proceedings. Thanks to that changed May scheduling, we're unable to produce the free evenings necessary for it. At any rate, it was interesting and it must have been gratifying to our hardworking Finance Committee members to note how closely the Town Meeting members followed their recommendations. This is no year to ask for anything but bare bones necessities. Braintree's real estate tax, thanks to 100 percent valuation, coupled with soaring energy costs, have a lot of peoples' backs against the wall. By the way, the 4 percent tax cap applies to all sums of money voted by a community such as our own which has the authority to levy directly a property tax to be raised from the tax levy, from free cash, from other available funds or from federal revenue sharing funds. Not included when determining the appropriation are "debt service; pension costs and retirement allowances; federal or state grant local matching requirements, revenue producing enterprises to the extent that the sums are paid from fees and charges; unemployment compensation and increases in the rates charged for special education children enrolled in institutional placements on or before the effective date of the Act."

THE NATIONAL CONFERENCE OF STATE LEGISLATURES

The National conference of State Legislatures to which I was appointed this year met in Washington D.C. this weekend. Our Transportation Committee chairman, who is the other delegate to this most prestigious organization, will attend. Your L. of the H. will not however, and we await with eagerness a report of the proceedings from an agenda which will include a discussion of the proposed Federal Deregulation of the Freight Rail Industry and consideration of the Highway Beautification act. Incidentally on our own Transportation Committee we are currently struggling with the issue of the Transportation Bond Issue for the Commonwealth. The Highway Fund which is funded by part of the gasoline tax is badly depleted. This particular fund having been used in recent years for mass transportation rather than for our highways. We are therefore, bringing the various Agency heads before our committee for a detailed explanation of their budget requests; and we plan, wherever possible, to cut their budget demands. It's a tax cap atmosphere on Beacon Hill as well as in Braintree, and high time…

7-19-79

Massachusetts has a state budget! As I write this column, House One reposes on the governor's desk awaiting his signature. It has not been easy to steer it there. The House has been in and out of recess by day and by night, for weeks on end. So, we presume, has the Senate. The leadership in both branches has met publicly and privately; has wrangled and temporized and reached one impasse after another…The Governor has had to make like a Solomon. Now, however, the budget which begun its long march toward enactment away back on March 1, is at last a fait accompli or will be when the gentleman in the corner office affixes his signature to the historic document as he is expected to do. Incidentally, the budget was approved in the House by a 131 to 22 vote, and in the Senate by a 24 to 4 vote.

So what are the highlights of this record $5.4 Billion state budget anyhow? Well, for one thing that $500 Million in local aid that was promised by the Governor has been whittled down to $166 Million, which we anticipate will be distributed to our cities and towns half through the Lottery formula. According to a chart I consulted, Braintree will receive an additional $516,746 in local aid over last year's figure as a result of this distribution formula.

There will be some income tax reductions. This issue was faced in a separate bill, by the way. Under it exemptions for dependents and persons over 65 will be increased from $600 to $700; for blind individuals from $2000 to $2200, and for a non-working spouse from $600 to $700 this year and from $700 to $800 next year. Now to return to the budget itself, it includes a 6 percent cost of living increase for AFDC recipients and a 5 percent cost of living increase for recipients of General Relief, most of whom are elderly. The biggest item is the Medicaid appropriation of $840 Million, with a $475 Million appropriation for AFDC next in line.

The Commonwealth's elderly home care program will be funded to the tune of $42 Million; $17 Million will be allocated to pay municipal hospitals for services to General Relief recipients; and $5.3 Million to the new Department of Social services. Human Services accounts, as you can see, for a very large portion of the state budget -40 percent of it, in fact. In the area of Higher Education U. of Mass is allocated $84.7 Million, with U. Mass, Boston, receiving $24.2 Million and Southeastern Mass. U. $13.85 Million. At any rate, all's well that ends well, to quote our friend Mr. Shakespeare, and although few were wholly satisfied with House One as it addresses the state's fiscal problems for 1980, there was naught but a feeble attempt to shoot it down when it emerged at last from the Committee of Conference as the vote would indicate; and, on the whole, I suppose it's a pretty good budget as budgets go. Here's hoping, however, for an adequate tax yield and a reasonably stable economy, or House One will fall far short of achieving the level of state financing it sets out to achieve.

Well, so much for the state budget...The Bottle Bill also awaits the Governor's signature; the death penalty bill is stalled in the Senate; and with intermittent rumors of early prorogation we've begun efforts in earnest to free our crucial bills from the clutches of the Committee on Bills in the Third Reading and the Committee on Ways and Means, both of which committees have been virtually paralyzed since action on the budget began.

Things appear to be winding down on the home front these summer months. It was a delightful experience, however, to share the only aspect of the town's 4th of July celebration we were on hand to enjoy, spending our holiday time as we were under the Golden Dome. I refer, of course, to the Annual Inspection of the Time Capsule when, in bicentennial costume, I had the pleasure of marching on the arm of Captain Gordon Campbell of our Braintree Militia, from the Knights of Columbus Hall to Braintree Town Hall, and then participating with Chairman Mel Miller and the incomparable Otis B. Oakman, Jr. in the inspection ceremony itself. AFTER a perfectly magnificent concert by our own superb Madrigal singers. It kind of made up for the night before the 4th events that we were envisioning from Room 446 at the State House as we recessed and recessed - only to be sent home finally, subject to the call of the Chair...which meant we were also to be tied to the family ménage and within hearing of the family telephone for the Independence Day holiday itself. Oh well, we DO have a budget now - and that's what really counts.

7-26-79

The Budget, it seems, is still with us. Though the governor has signed it, he has vetoed eight items which we shall have to deal with when we return from a week's recess on July 30. As signed, the Budget included $166 Million in additional local aid within excess of $500,000 due to come to Braintree, and $27.2 Million in income tax reductions along with a first-time state assumption of $61 Million in court costs as a result of last year's Court Reform action.

The eight sections vetoed included $34 Million in retroactive cost of living increases for AFDC recipients; however, the Governor has promised to come in with new legislation for its funding. It also includes $17 Million for the reimbursement of hospitals for general relief medical services. Also vetoed were the increase in MBTA Advisory Board expenses from $40,000 to $75,000 annually; and the retroactive aspects of the State's Chief Probation Officers' pay increases - only the retroactivity, not the increases…The Governor also vetoed some decreases in salaries of administrators in the state college system. The 1980 Budget is, on the whole, a good one in our opinion. It is, needless to say, difficult to keep down our state's expenses when the Human Services and Education budgets take such a large slice of it. The Medicaid budget alone has increased by 20 percent from last year's $700 Million to $840 Million; and we finance our educational program to the tune of $633 Million, which is more than any state in the U.S. excepting Hawaii. Well, so much for the state budget….The governor's veto of the Bottle Bill will also lie before us to be dealt with on the 30th, with little or no expectation of its being overturned either in the house or in the Senate. It is difficult indeed to secure a ⅔ vote on a controversial issue such as this one.

We were interested to read, as I am sure you were, that more and more people are turning to public transportation during this energy crises; but apprehensive indeed when we read that the Authority's Advisory Board cut in the T's deficit will lead to cuts in service. We need more service, not less…

Changing the subject, it represents the happy conclusion to a long-standing drive on the part of your L. Of the H. to learn that the Pearl Street Crossing is now in the process of being repaired – and handsomely. It represents one more proof of the old adage that persistence does pay off…

Now for another change of subject, it was indeed a happy experience for this representative to don her Bicentennial gown and join Otis Oakman, the town historian, and Captain Campbell and his Braintree Militia at the State House for "The Washingtons Belong in Boston" ceremony this past week as the Governor issued a Proclamation to that effect and in support of a drive to raise funds to keep our first President and his Lady in the Bay State where we feel they belong.

It was also fun to be part of a bit of history when, as a member of the state's Transportation Committee we sat on the platform as in a pleasing ceremony Brock Adams, Nation's Secretary of Transportation presented to the State's Secretary of

Transportation Barry Locke a check in the amount of $187.5 Million to fund the Red Line extension. "Adams showed independence', we read in the Globe story that followed his appearance at Harvard Square. We had certainly done just that. In his remarks before our assembly, he had outlined the terms under which he would remain in his cabinet post. The Administration must have a commitment to mass transportation, he said. Detroit must produce a more fuel efficient car; the President must be more accessible, along with those with increased authority among the White House staff who must be more responsive to the Congress and to the American People…It all sounded great. Mr. Adams received a tumultuous round of applause…

Well, it may have seemed like good news to the people of Massachusetts. It would appear, however, to have sounded like bad news to Mr. Carter's staffers in the nations capitol. Now, you know what usually happens to bad news…It travels fast…This particular item apparently did just that for we have since learned that upon Mr. Adams return to Washington he was in for a surprise…He is now the FORMER Secretary of Transportation. Oh, well.

8-2-79

The House has been in recess for the past week. Many of our legislators have been conventioning in San Francisco with the National Conference of State Legislatures. As one of the two House delegates to that organization from our Transportation Committee, this legislator could have been among them. It seemed preferable, however, to remain in Braintree and pick up the happenings second-hand from the materials that will undoubtedly be brought back to Boston by our second Transportation Committee delegate, our Chairman.

The week has not been without activity, however. I was able lend a hand to our Braintree Housing Authority in expediting its proposed Braintree Highlands elderly housing complex, which has been bogged down in the red tape that originated in their dealings with the state department of Community Affairs. With Senator Harold I appeared in support of the plan submitted on Thursday afternoon by our architect, and we appear to have exacted a promise from the head of that agency to expedite the project. A November date for groundbreaking was even agreed to, albeit hesitantly, by the powers that be, who incidentally expressed pleasure at our involvement in the issue. It was also possible to tuck in attendance at a meeting of the Sub-Committee on Education of the state committee appointed to observe the 200th anniversary of the Massachusetts Constitution. Speaking of that historic event, our good friend Otis Oakman, having learned of our appointment to the subcommittee on Special Events for the observance, promptly sent me a pamphlet on the Mass. Constitution which delights my patriotic soul. Shortly after the turn of the century, we read the great American political scientist, Andrew C. McLaughlin, in his presidential address before the American Historical Association said; "If I were called upon to select a single fact or enterprise which more nearly than any other thing embraced the significance of the American Revolution, I should select not Saratoga of the French Alliance, or even the Declaration of Independence - I should choose the Formation of the Massachusetts Constitution of 1780; and I should do so because the constitution rested upon the fully developed Convention, the greatest institution of government which America has produced, the institution which answered, in itself, the problem of how men could make governments of their own free will…"

How remarkable it really was that the revolutionary radicals of 1776, should have demonstrated such genius in political science. "It is easy enough to destroy a government when it had become obsolete and ineffective," we read in this very informative pamphlet, "but very difficult to re-establish the reign of law and order on a new foundation. How many nations in the present century have won their independence; how few have really secured their liberty!" We shall discuss further in our future columns the specifics of the Commonwealth's Constitution which incidentally, served as a model for the federal constitution. With the 200 observance scheduled for 1980, we're sure that many of you would like to face the festivities better informed as to what they're all about. We're learning in depth what they're all about as we read from "The Formation of the Massachusetts Constitution, "this very engaging pamphlet which contains "an address on the occasion of the 175th Anniversary of the Constitution, October 25th, 1955," by Samuel Eliot Morison. We must admit he was mite long-winded, but mighty interesting.

It was a pleasure and a privilege indeed to present a Citation from the House of Representatives on Saturday evening for this past week to our dear friends Rose and Fred Finocchi, whose 50th Wedding Anniversary was observed in a gala party at the Ridder Country Club…where, incidentally, Olive Laing, another dear friend, performed handsomely as M.C. for the evening, providing not only the anniversary couple but their two hundred guests with an entertainment we shall long remember. One more 50th Wedding Anniversary House of Representatives/Citation was in order for Mr. And Mrs. Russell E. Clark, Sr., whose planned celebration had unfortunately be cancelled because of illness…

We return to Beacon Hill in formal session on Monday morning, with a lot of unsolved problems before us…We shall be addressing those problems in next week's column.

8-16-79

The General Court is in recess. "Business as usual" within both the House and the Senate has come to a halt. It was thought for a time that not recess but prorogation lay ahead for the lawmakers. It didn't turn out that way however. Too many vital issues remain to be faced before our legislative year may end. There's the Capital Outlay budget, for one thing. No one expects the Senate to go along with our House version on that one and so Committee of Conference action, which is time consuming and complicated, would undoubtedly have followed Senate action.

The Senate had in fact adopted prorogation rules. The House, however, never did reach that point. Adopting prorogation rules means that instead of working from a daily calendar as is the normal way of doing things, legislators work directly with the Committee on Ways and Means and Bills in the Third Reading. A hectic turn of events, we might add, since all 200 of us would be lobbying like mad to effect the release of our pet bills for floor action. Well, that situation won't prevail in the House at any rate, since regardless of the incessant prorogation rumors that permeated the place, prorogation rules never were adopted, and upon our return in September we shall be proceeding as though no recess had ever intervened.

Incidentally and most importantly, although we are in recess, this legislator will naturally still be available to deal with your constituent problems. We'll be reachable either through our State House office or at home.

Well, so much for the State House activities of the past week. As a matter of fact we might say we were all at sea anyhow until Thursday evening when the speaker announced the impending recess. Come to think of it, this legislator was at sea in more ways than one this past week. What fun it was for one thing, on one of those lovely summer evenings (before the monsoon season arrived) to climb aboard and enjoy a three hour sail on a magnificent sailing craft whose mast rose fifty feet into a dark night sky where the moon emerged periodically, rising like a great golden coin from a slot to flood the sea with silver. And then, next morning, to be at sea again aboard the exciting new Hovercraft that sails each day between Hingham and Boston. What fun it was to share with the pilot of this swish boat the sight of our great Boston Harbor as it unfolded before us…Well, so much for our nautical adventures.

Now for a spot of news about our last-minute legislative doings under the Golden Dome. Our presumptive sentencing legislation made its debut with a bill aimed at imposing stiff sentences on hard-core drug pushers, we're delighted to report. An individual found guilty will serve time, and that time must fall within a narrow range. The seriousness of the types of drugs involved will be graded and coupled with sentencing; and the possession of more than forty grams of heroin will constitute a major dealer who will serve thirteen to sixteen years in state prison unless there are mitigating circumstances. Persons convicted three times on a Class A or Class B drug pushing charge will receive a life sentence…Somewhere we have read that certainty of sentence acts as more of a deterrent to crime than length of sentence; we believe that, and we're delighted that a first attempt at signing into law our presumptive sentencing bill is being attempted. Incidentally it received an overwhelming vote in the House which hopefully will guarantee its serious consideration in the Senate; and we're reasonably certain that should it reach the Governor's desk he will sign it. The bill resulted from a study of the entire issue by our judiciary committee, and my bill is part of it, we're proud to say…

Changing the subject, this representative was on hand as a member of the Transportation Committee on Friday morning as the Governor signed the $243 million transportation bond legislation which will permit construction on state highways, mass transit and aviation projects. This $243 million will be matched by $619 million in federal funds and should fund 40,000 new and existent jobs. They're vitally needed in the Commonwealth where our failing economy is of vital concern to all those entrusted with governing of the state. No new taxes had to be imposed and a sigh of relief was breathed by a lot of us who could not in conscience vote for an increase in the gas tax your L. of the H included.

8-30-79

There's an air of quiet about the State House these days. With the General court in recess, only those of us who really feel the need to appear under the Golden Dome now and then - despite the faithful coverage of our competent Aides can be found in the marble corridors and in the quiet offices. It's a nice kind of quiet, needless to say. It affords us an opportunity to track down bills in which we have had an interest and which we managed to lose sight of in the hectic days preceding our summer recess. And it also offers us an opportunity to turn our thoughts toward bills we propose to file for next year's session. And while we're on the subject of next year's bills, may we remind you of your right under Free Petition. Any one of you may file a bill simply by contacting your legislator, and December 5 is the deadline date for filing. Please don't leave it until December 1, however. This legislator is a rather organized individual. She likes all bills to be filed well ahead of the hectic deadline date. They receive better attention that way.

One very important State House meeting this past week produced an exciting update on plans for our Constitution Bicentennial celebration next year. As a member of the Sub-committee on Special Events this legislator was on hand to delight in the progress that has been made since our last meeting a couple of weeks back. We shall be sending a Traveling Train Museum across the Commonwealth, for one thing, an adaptation of the train museum that traveled throughout the state during 1976 Bicentennial celebration. It will provide a 20' glass case for the exhibit of pertinent artifacts; and the 50' x 9' train may even wind up as a permanent Boston Museum since Conrail goes directly in the Children's Museum, and that sounds like a logical place for it. A slide show dealing with the drafting of our State Constitution will be part of the exhibit, as well as a live reenactment of the event. We were treated to a sample slide show with the presentation of a marvelous item on Abe Lincoln. It was a hit! This slide show, incidentally, will be made available to our school children via filmstrips and video tapes.

Braintree's own historian H. Hobart Holly was on hand to report on Quincy's coming celebration which will last for four exciting days and sounds like a humdinger. Mr. Holly serves as our committee's liaison with the state's historical societies, and announced that in a recent Bay State Historical League publication it was suggested that all societies present a program on the constitution. Incidentally your L. of the H. will be a participant in that exciting Quincy program, we're happy to report, thanks to our good friend "Oakie" Oakman…We are mindful as we attend these meetings, and consider the matter at hand, of the amazing development of our American Revolution. Those early patriots had broken the ties with Britain, and the thirteen states had remained united. Republican government was established, and at the end of the war, eleven of those thirteen had adopted new constitutions, The Massachusetts constitution must have been the finest however, for it was chosen as a model for the national constitution that has survived so well to this very day. Actually those revolutionary leaders of ours, John Adams and Thomas Jefferson must have been students of history and politics. John Adams, writing to George Wythe who had asked his advice about the framing of the Virginia constitution put their philosophy so well. "How few of the human race have ever enjoyed an opportunity of making an election of government…for themselves or their children!" He wrote. "When, before the present epocha, had three millions of people full power and a fair opportunity to form and establish the wisest and happiest government that human wisdom can contrive" Yes thus wrote Braintree's revolutionary, John Adams, who within four years was to be granted the opportunity to draft a constitution for his own state of Massachusetts, the birthday of which constitution we shall be celebrating next year…and in Quincy, next month…

9-13-79

It's been quite a week for this representative to the General Court…Although the House will be in recess until September 17, our legislative duties have gone on. Wednesday, for instance housed a meeting with Jeff Simon, head of the Mass. Land Bank, and Brian Dacey, the new head of Boston's E.D.I.C. The object of the meeting??? To obtain a briefing on the current status of that second Massport Containerport in Boston Harbor. As Chairman of our Transportation Committee's Sub-Committee on the Port Authority, your L. Of the H. has played an exciting and significant role in bringing this second containerport about, and we have every intention of seeing to it that it becomes a reality. We discussed the issue with Governor King on Friday, and we're happy to report that we were assured of his total support of our efforts to speed the project to a satisfactory conclusion. There are, however, a number of difficulties to be overcome. A large section of the Naval Annex land that has been given to Massport for the container facility is under water and will have to be filled in. The fill will have to be transported to the site, and the well being of the people of South Boston will have to be considered carefully in setting up the traffic pattern involved in transporting that fill. That will have to be dealt with, along with the issue of securing the fill itself, hopefully from the MBTA's Southwest Corridor project. Well, these are matters in the solution of which our sub committee may be able to play an additional role.

And returning to Friday's conversation with the Governor, it occurred while we were on hand at South Station, along with a host of other federal, state and local officials for a ceremony involving the transfer of the South Station property to the MBTA, marking the beginning of the building of the first inter-modal transportation facility in the country. The ceremony was impressive. Once upon a time this train station building served over 38 million passengers annually. This situation could reoccur in the light of today's energy situation. The ceremony was followed by a bus trip to inspect the MBTAS Cabot Yard in South Boston, along with the Everett shops; and here in both places we were to observe literally hundreds of buses immobilized, awaiting repairs. With nine of the eleven hoists out of commission at the Cabot garage, it was easy to see why the T's bus service is having problems. Incidentally, we were shocked to learn that these hoists never did work, and that despite that fact the garage was accepted by the MBTA and no recourse sought. Several of these hoists are now being replaced, we're happy to report, but the work will take a certain amount of time. Mr. Foster certainly appears to have inherited a rocky system, a bus system that has for the past 4½ years been devoid of preventive maintenance in an attempt to keep the T's deficit under control. The idea is frightening. We all know what neglecting preventive maintenance could do to the family car in 4½ years: and the family car, unlike an MBTA, does not pile up mileage at the rate of 50,000 miles a year. We don't envy Mr. Foster as he tries to deal with the many problems he has inherited on the "T". And we must admit we await our daily Red Line trek to Boston with a spot of apprehension as we face the winter weather that lies ahead…

Addressing happier things, what a delightful experience it has been to participate with our Quincy neighbors in the many festivities they scheduled during the past few days in observance of the 200th Anniversary of the drafting of our Massachusetts Constitution by John Adams. Since Quincy was part of Old Braintree when the state constitution was written, your L. of the H. was vitally interested in every aspect of the Bicentennial celebration. First off, of course, back to the law office of John Adams where it was written, came the magnificent document itself, the Constitution of the Commonwealth which has lain undisturbed within the State House Archives for the past two hundred years. What a moving experience it was to stand in that very law office where it was drafted, and view the yellowed but still legible pages of the finest document of its kind in the history of government. And how exciting it was to follow the evolution of that Constitution from the original Magna Carta through a great lecture at the Quincy Historical Society Open House…AND to explore their magnificent library with no less an authority than Braintree's own historian, H. Hobart Holly. Much of the findings of that memorable experience will be shared with you in future columns. What a pity we always manage to run out of space in writing these weekly accounts of our doings…

10-4-79

The week began bright and early on Monday morning with three M.D.C. Deputy Commissioners in regard to and at the M.D.C. intersector road from Wood Road to Chickatawbut. Although the work of completing this 1/13 of a mile of roadway has already gone out to bid, we were startled to learn that the Commissioners had suddenly on a 3 to 2 vote decided AGAINST the project. It seemed advisable to bring them to Braintree to see precisely what they were voting against…The building of the intersector road had become a clear-cut necessity when the extensive island that it was decided had to be a part of the Wood Road signalization system, prevented northbound traffic on Route 37 from entering the Blue Hills Reservation without making an illegal turn on the highway or using one of the area business establishments to do so.

We hope we were able to persuade at least one of the two M.D.C. Commissioners who had voted against the road to change that vote at the next meeting of the group. We tried hard. We shall now await the outcome of that early morning meeting in Braintree.

THE FIVE CORNERS traffic situation was in the news again when in response to a request for information from Selectman Tony Mollica, we contacted the powers-that-be to learn that a contract with the consulting engineering firm of Storch Engineers has been submitted to the Federal Highway Administration. It must first be put on a list for funding under the Transportation Improvement Program at an October 2nd meeting, according to Mr. Gustafson, the project manager. Following approval, a public meeting will be held to discuss alternative solutions to the situation, including Armstrong's signalization plan.

There are so many issues to be dealt with these days on the Hill. As Chairman of the Transportation Committee's Sub-Committee on the Port Authority, I thoroughly enjoyed being brought up to date this week by representatives of Massport on the status of their second Containerport, which it is proposed to locate in the South Boston Naval Annex. It was exciting to learn of the logistics involved in the filling of the 37½ acres that now lie under water, interspersed by rotting finger piers, but which, when filled with three million cubic yards of fill, will provide - along with the ten acre jetty involved the wherewith to place a much needed containerport in this perfect locality, adjacent to the shipping lane. Having participated in the negotiations that led up to this exciting prospect, your L. of the H. is mighty interested in any and all aspects of its progress.

How will this amazing feat be accomplished, I wanted to know. There are, it appears, a couple of alternatives. They can build a coffer dam and fill caissons with gravel, filling behind it progressively as they go or they can create a dike, working from both ends… What an age we live in!!!

Changing the subject, and on a lighter but no less important note, it was a pleasure and a privilege indeed to present on behalf of the House of Representatives, a Citation to Daniel DeGregorio on the occasion of a most unique Testimonial Dinner which was given to this distinguished Braintree citizen last week in acknowledgement of his outstanding support of the South Shore Center for Brain Injured Children since its beginnings in Braintree five years ago.

It was Dan's beautiful wife Jean who first alerted him to the daily miracles that take place at the Center where Elizabeth Connors, its Director and her volunteers are literally devoting their lives to bringing hope and help to little ones suffering from brain damage. Jean, who was described by my dear friend "Liz" Connors as being "as beautiful within as she is without" serves as one of these wonderful volunteers. Dan, who owns Plaza Olds, was presented an engraved plaque on behalf of the Center. His return gift was a check for $12,000 for the Center's Building Fund. He had raised the money himself through the sale of ads in the program book for his own testimonial. Incidentally the behind-the-scene story in this…When Dan was informed that a Testimonial Dinner was in the offering for him on the basis of new honors that had come his way as an Oldsmobile Dealer, he insisted that the event be planned to highlight the work of the Center, and that its proceeds must benefit the Center's Building Fund…All of which goes to support my contention that the coin is yet to be minted which will pay for VOLUNTEERISM… Wouldn't you agree???

10-11-79

The past week was to be a momentous one on Beacon Hill as elsewhere in the United States. It would begin on a dark and dismal Monday with the arrival of Pope John Paul II on his pastoral visit to our country. For perhaps the thousandth time, rejoicing was in order for this representative to the General Court, who-by virtue of the office - had been invited to attend a Civic Reception at the Airport in honor of the arriving Pontiff.

We assembled at the State House to leave as a body in special buses, with a police car at our head and motorcycle officers everywhere else, to ride over strangely empty highways and city streets. A buffet luncheon awaited us at the Airport where we hurriedly downed a sandwich, then headed for the corridor leading to the airfield. Secret service men were everywhere, easily identifiable by the buttons on their lapels and the appurtenances in their ears. I happily settled myself in a front row seat close to the entranceway through which the dignitaries would arrive, and the family camera appeared. Subjects flowed endlessly within its range…Governor Peabody kissing Ann Landers; Governor Dukakis embracing Connecticut Governor Ella Grasso; Maine Governor Muskie in a craggy profile shot with a black beret over one eye; Congressman Brian Donnelly and Ginny and all of the other New England Congressmen and Senators…The Kennedys, and Governor King and House Speaker McGee and Senate President Bulger and Rosalyn Carter and the Princes of the Church in their scarlet and purple…And then at last the great green Aer Lingus 747, the "St. Patrick", and it filled the camera lens, to come to rest behind the platform that had been set up for the Pontiff's speech. The door was to open, and Pope John Paul II to emerge from the interior of the plane to the roar of the waiting crowd. Our camera was still at the ready. It was to be at the ready also for the address of the Pontiff himself. There was to be a final shot of his Holiness as he drove away in the motorcade that would wind its way through the streets of Boston, winding up eventually on Boston Common for the celebration of Mass. An historic film, we had found ourself thinking…A wonderful film…We envisioned setting up the family screen and reliving the arrival of Pope John Paul II for months to come…A delightful prospect…

And now it was back to the State House over a totally deserted highway, with police sirens clearing the way through the now busy Boston streets behind the State House. We were to march down Beacon Street to the Common, escorted by a contingent of State Police. There we would be shown to a section that had been reserved for us. A wonderful happening lay ahead of us, however having a full-blown cold (the first real bad one in five years), and having sat for two full hours in the cold and rain at the Airport, where an umbrella would have restricted the view of those behind us, we decided, in the light of the heavy showers that had been forecast, to pass up attendance of the Mass, and instead to return to Braintree.

The crowd before the State House and along Park Street was enormous. The Pope's cavalcade was to circle the Common en route to the altar where Mass would be said. We should, of course, have selected Beacon Street rather than Park Street for our exit from this crowded area. We didn't, however. With a friend breaking the path for us, we succeeded in making our way through the crowds. It turned out, however, to be a tragic mistake for your L. of the H., for when we reached the bottom of the hill we found to our dismay that the camera case that had been slung over our shoulders so happily had been emptied enroute. The zipper was open and the camera was gone…the camera that had traveled over much of the world with the Metayers and had taken those fantastic slides we've been able to share with others…It wasn't the camera, however, that we truly mourned. It was the film inside the camera…a film which we shall never have an opportunity to replace, and which undoubtedly the thief will carelessly discard as of no value. The film is gone. The experience, however, needless to say, will remain with us forever…

There were to be other happenings on the Hill as the week progressed…and in Braintree. We were to share a beautiful evening at Sons of Italy Hall where our American Legion Post No. 86 entertained the town's Senior Citizens with a fabulous party. Our good friend Ted Sweeney was in charge of this annual affair which is always topnotch, and which was thoroughly enjoyed as usual by several hundreds of the town's "Special Citizens". As they were affectionately termed by my good friend, Legion Commander Hugh Opie.

11-15-79

In response to a number of your requests, I shall commence my column by stating that I voted AGAINST the legislative pay raise; and though the Senate failed to stand for a roll call, the House did indeed stand, and so our vote on this issue is a public record for all to see.

The Great and General Court surprised many of us by proroguing this past week. It began to be apparent about midweek when we were plugged into a series of late night sessions, beginning in the early afternoon and ending with a return home at 4:30 a.m., 5:30 a.m., 1:30 a.m. and finally, as prorogation became a reality at 8:30a.m. on four successive days. Incidentally, it's a very different world one encounters as one drives home in the dim dark hours before dawn. There's the kind of quiet where even the rustle of the leaves on the trees invades the open car windows. The air is clear and clean, and there's a feeling that all's well.

But to return to the subject of Prorogation…What does it actually mean "to adopt prorogation rules", we keep being asked. Well, primarily it means that we must work no longer solely from a daily House calendar. Bills come to us directly from the Committee on Bills in Third Reading or the Committee on Ways and Means. The die is cast; and legislators who are anxious to see pet bills on the Governor's desk begin to exert the kind of pressure that is necessary to spring them from one or other of the two committees; and then to steer them through the House and Senate and back to the House for final enactment before the session ends.

It's an interesting time. It's a time for getting together in groups with the House elders, to hear tales of how things once were at prorogation time (and tall tales some of them are…) And with "recesses" abounding while we wait the return of bills from the Senate, it's a time for getting to know one's colleagues a little better…Hours and even days pass slowly until the final moment of prorogation is at hand. The last bill is on its way to the Governor's desk. This year those "last vital bills" included the Capital Outlay Bill and the Hazardous Waste Bill, the Energy Reorganization bill and the Auto Emissions bill, all of which, though they had gone through the House long before, had been stymied in the Senate. Leadership breathes a sigh of relief, in which they are joined by the rank and file. And a committee is appointed to inform the Governor and the members of the Governor's Council who have been summoned to the State House earlier, that the work of the legislature is ended.

Now, as a member of the appointed committee, your L. of the H. marched down the marble corridors to join the Senate committee before the executive office, and thence to proceed to the Governor's Council Chamber. The report of the year's work is to be made. 677 bills have reached the Governor for signing, it is said, along with 21 Resolves.

We file past the Governor to shake his hand and greet the Governor's Councillors. We then return to the House Chamber. We are led on these marches by the Chief Court Officer, complete with silk hat, formal attire and the rod of his office. And now, after a short wait, the Secretary of State is admitted with "A Message from his Excellency, the Governor". It is he who will put the final touch to the ceremony and we are now all in a festive mood as the Speaker uses his gavel for the last time in '79. We bid one another a Chamber farewell, for though our constituent work will go on, and we shall be hard at work preparing our bills for the coming year, we shall no longer join one another in the House Chamber for a legislative session each morning, that is, in essence, prorogation and since so many of you have been curious about it, it seemed advisable to discuss it in my column.

It's been a productive year on Beacon Hill, incidentally. The 1980 budget contained $166 million in additional state aid for our cities and towns. A state Division of Hazardous Wastes was created and given broad powers to deal with the tracking, transporting and disposal of hazardous wastes. The problem of the state's threatened water supplies has begun to be addressed with $10 million allocated to a rehabilitation study, and $2.5 million to a groundwater supply study. The drinking age has been increased from 18 to 20; and capital punishment has, on a very limited basis, been restored. Arsonists will now be required to serve ⅔ of their sentences before being eligible for parole; and in that same area of concern, smoke detectors may be required by our local authorities in all residential buildings. A patient's rights bill has been signed into law; and appropriations have been made for fuel assistance for elderly, poor and welfare families. A 4 percent cap on local spending has been imposed; and state income tax exemptions increased. The telephone company has been prohibited by law from charging for directory assistance; and the State Energy Director has been elevated to the level of cabinet secretary, with all of the state's energy and conservation responsibilities centered in his department. Yes, it's been a productive year...

11-22-79

(Editor's Note: The staff and management of the "Star" wish to extend a speedy recovery and pleasant holiday to Mrs. Metayer, Braintree's own "First Lady".)

More than 300 years ago our Pilgrim Fathers, having survived the cold and hardship of their first winter in a new land, met with their Indian friends to give thanks to their Heavenly Father for their deliverance.

A great many Novembers have come and gone since that eventful day-a great many "Thanksgiving Days". We have thanked the Lord in times of peace, and in times of war, in times of plenty and in times of privation. But always we have paused to offer thanks to the Almighty on this very special say. Someone once said, "Thanksgiving is not just a day-it is a way of life".

It is also a day for bringing families together. For renewing the familiar "ties that bind"...for stopping for a moment to count one's blessings.

As I pause on this Thanksgiving Day to look heavenward, and review all my own many reasons for giving thanks, you may be sure that I shall include among them- and it will be very high on the list- my special thanks for having been granted the privilege of representing you, the wonderful people of Braintree, in the Great and General Court.

A Happy, Happy Thanksgiving to you all!

P.S. You may undoubtedly have heard that I have had an accident and will be incapacitated for a couple of weeks. My office will still be staffed, however, by my very capable administrative aide, Ms. Suzanne Bump, with whom I shall remain in close daily contact. Please phone her directly if you have a problem or a concern will be promptly addressed as always.

12-13-79

For just one more time…Your constituent problems and concerns are currently being beautifully handled despite the fact that my recent accident prevents my daily presence at the State House.

Mrs. Suzanne Bump, my Administrative Aide, is covering my State House office and can be reached daily by telephone at 727-5374. She and I maintain a close contact and we're just as ready and willing to respond to your concerns as though we were seated side by side as usual in Room 446. So keep calling if you need our help…

Now, as a five year member of the Joint Committee on Health Care, a review of that committee's actions during the 1979 session seemed to be in order, and a number of the new health care laws that resulted appeared to be worth sharing with you. My constituents - health care being of special interest to this most impatient of patients during these long days of convalescence.

One law, Chapter 206, creates an exception to the application of the open bidding law for municipal hospitals, in order that they may wherever possible, purchase goods at a discount through private purchasing cooperatives. Two of these collectives are now servicing a majority of our private hospitals with 12 percent to 18 percent savings resulting. With soaring hospital costs, any avenue for cost containment is a welcome one.

Chapter 211 permits our cities and towns to recover the costs of maintaining and operating ambulance service by charging users for the service.

Chapter 211 addresses the issue of patients' rights in private and state hospitals, nursing homes, clinics, alcoholism and drug rehab programs, H.M.O's and mental health facilities. Upon admission to any one of these facilities that patient must now be informed of the following rights: 1. To select a facility or physician except in an emergency or in the case of a state mental health facility; 2. To a copy of an itemized bill; 3. To the names and specialty of the person responsible for the patient's care; 4. To confidentiality of records; 5. To have reasonable requests responded to promptly; 6. To know if the facility is a teaching institution; 7. To obtain a copy of any rules or regulations of the facility which apply to his or her conduct as a patient; 8. To information regarding available financial assistance and free care; 9. To inspect his or her medical records; 10. To refuse examination and treatment by a medical student or other member of the house staff. 11. To refuse to serve as a research subject; 12. To privacy during treatment; 13. To prompt life saving treatment in an emergency; 14. To informed consent; and 15. To a copy of the bill submitted to the patient's insurer, Medicaid or Medicare. Incidentally, in addition to furnishing the patient with a copy of this patients' rights information, it must be posted conspicuously in the facility.

My friend Barbara, who has been associated with hospitals during most of her adult life, expressed such approval of this new Patients' Rights legislation that it seemed like a good idea to pass its provisions along to you my constituents, via this weekly column.

Now here's hoping you're all "Happy Holiday-ing" during this beautiful Christmas Season. We're missing it all, needless to say - so much so that it was an out-and-out treat to even secure a glimpse of our beautiful South shore Plaza on TV tonight. Oh well, just you wait until next Christmas.

1-3-80

And so the "Eighties" have begun! A brand new decade lies ahead…May it be a decade of progress and accomplishment for the land we love, needless to say but may it, above all, be a decade of PEACE…

As you receive your first 1980 edition of the "Star", your L. of the H. will be back in session on Beacon Hill, cane, walker and all, in what we have been assured will be an all-day opening session of the House of Representatives. And will it ever be good to be back in the swim again! So now what has been happening during the past week for this temporarily down but by no means out legislator??? Well, certainly the most dramatic happening was the outdoors planting of the beautiful "living Christmas Tree" that was a gift of our great Braintree Rotary Club. It was planted with much ceremony by the owner and operator of the Mento Landscaping and Garden Center, John Mento himself; and after having brightened my living room and my life over the holidays it will adorn my front lawn where it will forever serve as an unending reminder of my dear Rotary Club friends; and where I'll have the fun of decorating it with Christmas lights from here on in. Now to return to Beacon Hill, which thanks to my great Administrative Aide Suzanne, has remained close throughout my convalescence. To begin with, this past week housed a momentous Commonwealth happening with the signing of two lease agreements between the Massachusetts Port Authority and the Economic Development Industrial Corporation which will pave the way for the development of a second Containerport in Boston Harbor. This marine terminal will be located in the South Boston Naval Annex and costing $80M to develop, will provide several thousand new jobs when complete, and hopefully boost our economy by $10 Million annually. Well now, why does this incident seem so super important to your L. of the H? The answer - because as Chairman of our Transportation Committee's Sub Committee on the Port Authority I played a significant role in getting the parties together and steering the issue toward a successful conclusion. Which undoubtedly explains my utter delight when Massport's Executive Director David W. Davis phoned to invite me to the lease-signing ceremony and my chagrin at not being able to be present. Oh, well the important aspect of the situation is the boon to the economy of the Commonwealth that is represented by this commitment upgrading our beautiful Boston Harbor.

Now to return to consideration of the brand new decade that lies ahead. "The Eighties of our Discontent" they are already being labeled by the pundits. We pray they're wrong. The Seventies were supposed to be fantastic. For me, they were just that. They housed wonderful years during which I was awarded the supreme privilege of representing you, the great people of Braintree, in the House of Representatives. On the whole, however, they "weren't such a much" to use that tired old quote. We lost a war; a President was forced to resign in disgrace; we've had to contend with a recession and rampant inflation; energy shortages; crass materialism and international crises. We were forced to look on helplessly while a Muslim nation held the American people at bay, hostages in an alien land. We've faced a crisis of confidence. Yes indeed the "Cynical Seventies" have left much to be desired for the American People. We did, however celebrate our 200th Birthday with "pomp and circumstance", all problems forgotten; and this particular legislator, as she faces this brand new decade, prefers to concentrate on the great good side of life in the U.S.A., and to pray with you all that despite all predictions we are facing the "Elegant Eighties" or even just the "Encouraging Eighties" as we tear the last tired page off our 1979 calendar and place a new and shining 1980 edition in its place.

1-10-80

January 2nd…the first Wednesday in January and the day on which the Legislature would meet to reconvene for the 1980 session…With my little old walker and my sturdy cane for the couple of stairways I would have to negotiate I felt considerably like Grandma Moses…but not for long…As it turned out it was more like visiting royalty, the kind of treatment I received from my own great Transportation Committee members and staff and from my Colleagues in the Chamber.

Suzanne, my trusty Administrative Aide and dear young friend must have found it woefully tiresome to dog my faltering footsteps. She managed to do so without complaining, however, lovely young woman that she is. She had driven my car to the State House and back or I'd have had to be marooned in Braintree for a while longer. At any rate, we ambled together down to the Chamber for the 11 o'clock session.

In the traditional order of the day a Committee was appointed by the Speaker and sent to summon the Senators to a joint meeting of the Legislature; and then, when that august body had joined us the committee dismissed, a second Committee was appointed by the Speaker to be sent to inform the Governor that we had reconvened. The Speaker's appointment of "Metayer of Braintree" to that second committee was greeted with considerable amusement. He had obviously forgotten that Metayer of Braintree was temporarily not her bustling self. "Now, let me see," I said merrily to my colleagues, "Shall I lead the parade with my CANE or with my WALKER??? And speaking of the first little transportation asset, "Who picked up that CANE for you?" a colleague had asked. "It's several inches too long;" the pronouncement of which verdict was followed by the summoning of a page for a trip to the State House carpenter shop for my new appendage, which is now much more satisfactory to operate.

The session having ended with a voice vote to reconsider the legislative pay raise which incidentally I had voted AGAINST last Halloween evening, we return to Room 446 where guess what awaited your L. of the H.??? A surprise "Welcome back" luncheon with pizza and champagne for the toasting of my return to the fold and the wishing of a Happy New Year all around…A gift of course from the members and staff of our Super Transportation Committee.

By the way, have you been able to guess how wonderful it was for me to be back under the Golden

Dome??? How beautiful the Chamber looked to me; and how shining were the halls and corridors, and the several gleaming star-topped Christmas trees that soared against the vaulted ceilings??? It would appear that a difficult year lies ahead for the members of the General Court however. A national recession is bound to adversely affect the Commonwealth's fiscal situation. There were rumors of a shortfall of as much as $400 million in the state budget for 1980. Under that kind of circumstance, there will be little likelihood of financing the expanded programs that are being demanded - especially in the areas of Home Care and Day Care. It could even prove difficult to maintain the present level of financing in these and other Human Services areas. And with a 4 percent cap mandated on municipal spending we will be hard put to justify anything less restrictive on state spending - despite the added burdens a recession will place upon the state in increased Welfare and Medicaid costs. We forecast a tightening of the belt all around this year, and that's a painful situation for a legislature to deal with. We keep praying that the economists are wrong even as we worry about how our elderly and our working poor AND OUR MIDDLE CLASS constituents will manage to meet their fuel bills this winter…and as we pray for at least a continuation of the good weather we've been enjoying to date.

JANUARY 17, 1980

So many issues surfacing under the Golden Dome these days, and how great it is to be back in session and in circulation getting caught up in all that is happening locally and on a statewide level.

Locally it was a step in the right direction to be present at Town Hall along with Senator Paul Harold Thursday last for the signing ceremony of a DPW contract with Storch Engineers of Boston for a $208,000 study of the Five Corners traffic nightmare. It's the SIXTH…or is it the SEVENTH such study over the past several years, however it represents one of the requirements for obtaining federal funding, so we can only hope that this will turn out to be the LAST such costly prelude to coming up with a plan that will solve the Five Corners situation once and for all.

Incidentally it was interesting to note that the New York Times on New Year's Day, carried a picture of this intersection taken at its horrendous worst.

It was also heartening to learn from the MBTA that our town officials continue to be actively involved in the issue of providing bus service to the new station when it opens. I had personally requested the "T" officials to pursue this route and not to come in with a "fait accompli" and expect the officials to accept it. It was therefore heartening to be informed by Many MacInnes, the "T"s Manager of Service Planning that after meeting with representatives of all town departments involved, she had requested of our Town Fathers "specific prioritized recommendations for bus service", (Her quote). Ridership potential and the MBTA's limited resources will have to be taken into account, needless to say, however.

On the state level, and as a member of the Health Care Committee, I was pleased to learn that Human Services Secretary Charles F. Mahoney is planning a panel discussion of the impact of the cost of those Administratively Necessary Days people are spending in expensive hospital settings because of lack of nursing home space for the patients. Also that he has appointed a Task Force to study and evaluate the Determination of Need program.

And that a 3½ year demonstration project is underway to measure the quality and cost benefits of a "case management" approach to primary care for Medicaid patients. Under this approach Medicaid patients are cared for as a family unit at one site, where the treatment is undertaken by a project team composed of physicians and nurses. The Department of Public Welfare project is operating under a federal grant. If successful it could eliminate the practice of "skipping from provider to provider". There appears, nation-wide, to be a surge toward the return of "Family Medicine", or preventative medicine. This new experimental program would appear to be in line with that trend.

Also in the Health Care area, deinstitutionalization of our mentally ill patients is having a dramatic effect on the Commonwealth's community hospitals where 1 in every 4 is now operating psych units. I was astounded to learn that in the past decade deinstitutionalization reduced the number of patients in our mental institutions from

17,500 to 2,500; also that last month our mental health commissioner called for the State to totally get out of the operating of mental health facilities. I find myself worrying considerably about the whereabouts and the well-being of these thousands of mentally ill individuals. We pray that the State knows what it is doing; that unfortunately hasn't always been so. Well, so much for a catch on our Health Care situation, excepting to add how pleasing it was to learn that the Governor proclaimed January 1980 as EYE HEALTH MONTH throughout the Commonwealth. Now for our Transportation Committee activities. It was great to participate last Tuesday as Chairman of the Sub-Committee on Aviation in our Transportation Commission meeting and to receive firsthand from Massport Director David W. Davis a current report on the proposed second containerport at the South Boston Naval Annex, which is apparently going well; along with a pledge from DPW Commission Dean Amidou that the Department will conduct a careful overview of the confusing Right Turn on Red situation throughout the Commonwealth. It's sure great to be back in the swim, or have I said that once or twice before???

JANUARY 24, 1980

We are observing the 274th birthday of John Hancock, the first Governor of the Commonwealth as I write my column; and may I say how delighted I was to learn that our present governor has selected the portrait of this distinguished Braintree-ite to adorn the wall behind his desk in the executive office.

It's been another interesting week on Beacon Hill; and how easy it has been pick up the pieces and get back into the middle of thing. It's as though I hadn't been away....

Locally the week contained some memorable events. The dedication of the Selectmens Chambers and the unveiling of a magnificent plaque in memory of the late distinguished Carl R. Johnson Jr. was a moving and beautiful occasion; and the awarding of a Citation to Archie Oberstein, the delightful fourth grader whose painting was selected from among thousands of entries to be used on the American Lung Association's 1980 Christmas Seal Stamp for our state was a happy experience indeed.

In the State House, the week's highlight was of course, Governor Edward j. King's State of the State address which was delivered to a joint session of the Legislature on Monday evening. The Governor set forth his goals for the year that lies ahead, among them a reform of the Commonwealth's civil service system; (we've long awaited that one.) an energy conservation program that would mandate energy audits of all homes and assist middle income families in the financing of recommended energy saving improvements; a proposal for revamping the MBTA so that service will be improved at the lowest possible cost; the selection of sites for hazardous waste disposal; curb on existent agency regulations and control of proposed regulations; a job training program for the unemployed and underemployed; and changes in the state and local tax structures.

On the whole it was an excellent address, well delivered and received; and we hope that the gentleman in the corner office will reach every one of the goals he has set for himself.

The month of January has been proclaimed by our Governor as "Eye Health Month" throughout the Commonwealth…As stated in the Proclamation, its purpose is to increase the individual citizens knowledge and understanding of the eyes, their functions and the appropriate care to protect them…to "better understand the importance of eyecare and eye health-the protecting of one of our most precious gifts, our vision". Incidentally, individuals who would like to receive a copy of the basic pamphlet "Your Eyes and how they Function" need only send a request, together with a stamped self-addressed envelope to "Eye Health, P.O. Box 128, Brighton, Ma. 02135.

Plans continue to go forward for the observance of the 200th Anniversary of our state Constitution, and exciting and ambitious plans they are indeed. This document which is the oldest written constitution in use in the world today has been termed the most significant product of the American Revolution. It protects the freedom of the press and guarantees trial by jury in civil and criminal cases. It guarantees the right of assembly and establishes the separation of executive, legislative and judicial powers. The Constitution of the United States was modeled after it; and since Braintree-ite John Adams was the principal author of this superb document, and happened to represent our historic town in the House of Representatives even as I do, it is understandable that I should be proudly playing a part in the Constitution's Bicentennial by serving as a member of the Sub-Committee on Special Events. It promises to be a splendid bicentennial program indeed and a thrill to serve as one of its participants.

FEBRUARY 21, 1980

There is little to report from Beacon Hill other than the fact that the Budget hearings have begun in earnest, and that every committee hearing room is occupied daily. Gardner Auditorium was packed to the doors during a hearing on Proposition 2 and ½ and a number of other tax proposals This past week. Similarly the public came out in force in support of funding for the Pine Street Inn and a series of bills providing protection from abuse for our elderly citizens. Incidentally, what a sad commentary on the times that such legislation should be deemed necessary!

There was a spot of agitation at the revelation that the rising price of gold has pushed the value of our Golden Dome into the millions… "What steps are you taking to protect our State House treasure???" has been asked of me more than once. We haven't noticed any particular change in routine about the place. It's so very high…it should be quite safe, one might think…Actually that's not so. A couple of years back someone (or someones) climbed up during the night and affixed a banner to that historic spot, which our Capitol Police had to climb up and remove the following morning…

Incidentally a second rather significant problem has emerged relative to our famous Bulfinch building. For the past five of my six years in office a wonderful old 3,000 pound 6 and ½ foot tall bronze eagle had soared above a huge column in the center of our parking lot. It once commanded a view of the stately State House lawn beneath it, so we've been told. With "progress", however came the necessity for paving that carpet of green, and the huge bird stood guard instead over the cars of the members of the General Court. The eagle was hollow, and had a large square opening in the back, a feature which drew my attention more than once. WHY??? I wondered…With the snow and the rain filling its interior and remaining there winter and summer, wouldn't our lovely State House eagle eventually fall victim to deterioration??? Well, apparently it did just that, and a few months back we watched with a spot of sadness as the great bird was lowered, to come to rest on a waiting vehicle, thence to be transported to a Rockland metal crafts firm. Here the damage was to be repaired. The beautiful and historic State House eagle was to be returned to us as good as new. Well, like so many projects these days, the repair of the State House treasure turned out too much more than had been anticipated. The cost has soared to $50,000. The statue has "completely deteriorated", and its 100 bronze plates will require extensive surgery to return them to their original beauty. A budget appropriation will now have to be sought on Beacon Hill…Not an easy accomplishment in these days when every penny counts in trying to keep down the cost of government and return as much as possible in local aid to our beleaguered cities and towns…

Now a word or two on the current status of the observance of the 200th Anniversary of the Massachusetts Constitution. The slide show is in the works. A series of sixty second TV and radio announcements of Special Commission events and programs has been planned. The Bicentennial train is in the process of being planned, and having had a hand in bringing Mary Jo Daley to Braintree from the State House to present a proposal to our Board of Selectmen a couple of weeks back, we rejoice in the knowledge that our town will host this historic Bicentennial train during the most significant week of the year…the week that will include the July 4th weekend!!! It will be a happy and appropriate way in which to celebrate the 4th, and as a member of the Sub-Committee on Special Events, this legislator is particularly delighted at the prospect of participating so beautifully and fully in the Bicentennial festivities.

Locally we were privileged to be present at the lovely Mass of Thanksgiving and Awards Evening program of the South Shore Center for Brain Injured Children, the magnificent "raison d'etre" for that super human being, "Liz" Connors and her great group of volunteers. What daily miracles are performed by these intrepid "nurses" on behalf of our handicapped little ones; and what love and dedication was manifested by them in the slide program that was the highlight of the evening, portraying as it did the beauty of the relationship that exists between the Center's volunteers and the children who are the beneficiaries of their unending love and concern..

There was another significant and happy event for your L. of the H.….participation in the 75th Anniversary observance, by our Braintree Rotary Club, of the founding of

Rotary International, where it was a distinct privilege to present a Resolution from the House of Representatives, memorializing the event and serving as a permanent record on Beacon Hill and in our town of the significant and continuing contribution of these excellent organizations to the people of Braintree.

APRIL 3, 1980

The MBTA managed to dominate the news this past week. For the people I represent, the big issue was, of course the opening of the South Braintree station and its impact on the community. We had envisioned the Town of Braintree as one huge parking lot at the start of business on Monday morning. It just didn't happen. Whether people were scared off by all the preliminary publicity, or whether it was the high cost of garage parking $2.00 or the lack of adequate bus service, no one knows. At any rate, not only did the traffic move freely throughout the early morning hours, but the new rapid transit was only sparsely used by the residents of the South Shore.

And speaking of the inadequate bus service the people of Braintree have been given, we plan to request an immediate meeting with Chairman Foster on the issue. The East Braintree bus, which has been relied upon by the residents of Heritage Lane has been taken off completely; and the service on Independence Avenue has been curtailed as well. For the residents of Independence Manor and everyone else in that area, the trip to the South Shore Plaza now includes two bus changes and two fares…one trip to the MBTA station, with a change of bus for the Plaza. Our residents are decidedly annoyed.

A discussion of these issues and complaints with Mary MacInnis of the "T" provoked her statement that nothing can be done to change anything until the summer schedule is posted sometime in June. A further investigation, however has revealed that efforts will be made by the DPW and "T" to secure grant money for at least installing sidewalks on those sections of the routes where none exist and our school children are threatened. We hope to pursue further our other complaints when we meet with Chairman Foster.

And speaking of Chairman Foster and the "T", it was indeed shocking to learn from him at a Transportation Committee investigation this past week that he had "fibbed" on the size of the recent LRV settlement with Boeing Verton Company. He had overstated the value of the settlement by more than $5 million, he admitted, in an attempt to "put the best face on an already good situation", to quote him. His assessment of the settlement as a good situation," especially the fee paid to the attorney who arranged it, is not shared by many: and our Transportation Committee has been charged with the investigation of that $79-9,000 fee that was paid to Attorney William Schwartz, who we hope to bring before us in the very near future.

And again speaking of Mr. Foster, we were interested to read that he is urging employers in the Boston area to stagger their working hours. This is something we've been plugging for the past six years; and this course will undoubtedly have to be taken in the light of the increasing numbers of people who are using public transportation because of the staggering cost of gasoline and the current drive for conservation. Currently the people attempting to board buses at Quincy Square are packed like sardines. And when I join them I get showered with complaints. My membership in the Transportation Committee is too widely known. I have decided. I shall take that issue up also with Mr. Foster.

Of considerable interest also on the Hill are those daily commission hearing where payoffs in the awarding of state contracts are being revealed to the consternation and dismay of most of us. It must be difficult indeed for anyone in high office who has so betrayed the public trust and is waiting for the axe to fall and end a perhaps otherwise illustrious career. Certainly money is and always has been the root of all evil, to quote a quote…

Locally it was a happy experience to attend the "Spring Into Fashion" Show of the Archbishop Williams Guild; and on Sunday at St. Francis School Hall to present House Citations to six new Eagle Scouts, Paul N. Allen, Daniel S. Climo, Thomas G. Climo, Brian Gately, James F. Tobin and Harold A. Valencia, Jr. This significant achievement will stand these fine young men in good stead during their entire lifetimes, and we share their parents' pride in them.

A meeting with representatives of the South Shore Home Care Services, Inc. to discuss the problems of our elderly rounded out the week locally; and we now find ourselves one week closer to spring. It's exciting…

APRIL 24, 1980

The week just passed began on a truly happy note on a Sunday evening when it was fun to be part of a slice of Americana at its best…The Press Rehearsal of our town's Annual American Legion Show! "You would join the town officials in the show" my friend Olive and had said last year. "You're our rep. and you love to sing: You'd have a ball!"

She was referring of course, to the annual appearance of "The Statesman", the members of our Board of selectmen, and of the Town Clerk and the Town Assessor and the Superintendent of the Highway Department and a few others who have been singing their hearts out in solo performances for years. If the truth were known, I can't carry a tune in a basket, but I do love to sing. And so this year's show will include an additional trio-"Two Bobs and a Bibs", the two Bobs being Bob Bruynell and Bob Frazier, and the Bibs being your L. of the H.

It has been fun for this rep. who has loved being present at the rehearsals and watching our great Braintree families and friends of the Legionaires do their thing.

By the way, the lyrics that precede our performances, all written by clever Ruth Laffin are just great! We quote our own: her name is Bibs Metayer; she represents us all; And when she needs publicity, she merely takes a fall…And though HER voice is usually heard, her husband is no mouse…You'll hear him say "Elizabeth, I'm the Speaker of THIS house".

So we are having a ball, and though it's been difficult to tuck the show rehearsals into our very busy schedule, we've managed it and it was worth it…

Monday say our Transportation Committee dealing in Executive Session with the Resolve to investigate the MBTA payment of $799,000 to Attorney William Scwartz for the Boeing Vertol settlement. We found no impropriety or illegality in the awarding of negotiating specifically of the attorney's fee. We were however, most unhappy with the procedure for setting the fee, and are filing a bill as part of our report which will prevent in future the sloppy manner in which an agreement was reached between the "T" and the attorney they hired to protect their interests and try for a settlement with the firm responsible for delivery of those sad LRV's that have caused too much difficulty for all concerned…

Wednesday was a day of varied activity. It began with Joint Memorial Service in the House Chamber, for the victims of the Holocaust and of the Armenian Genocide, "two shameful and horrendous evidences of man's inhumanity to man" to quote our House Majority Leader George Keverian; "two of the darkest moments in modern history… featuring the darkest side of human behavior" to quote Governor King.

Come afternoon, we began deliberations on the State Budget…deliberations that were to go on from 1:00pm on Wednesday afternoon to 4:00 am on Thursday morning… to be resumed at 3:00pm on Thursday and to end at 8:00AM on Friday morning…a grueling pair of sessions that resulted in the House voting a 1981 budget which will now go to the Senate for their turn at bat.

Interspersed with our State House obligations were a delightful visit from a group of Braintree Cub Scouts with their Den Mother Anne Vail and several other "Moms"; and a picture-taking session with Braintree's own Dr. Phillip Nedelman, who is currently serving as President of the Massachusetts Association of Family Physicians and was present for the signing of the Governor's Proclamation naming the week of May 11-18 "Family Doctor Week".

We all but forgot one additional small happening. We met on Saturday (Yes, we mean Saturday: the Governor like your L. of the H. usually works seven days a week…) with Governor King in a meeting at an eerie darkened State House, in an attempt to secure his assistance in getting an amendment to the State Budget through the Senate. This legislator had succeeded in amending and so correcting a $1,463,961 inequity in Vocational Education Funding in the House Budget; our Blue Hills Regional School officials and I were on hand to seek executive support for my amendment as it will be dealt with in the Senate. In my opinion, voc ed is the best educational bargain we have these days; when the students graduate from a technical institute or even from a technical high school their jobs await them….

MAY 1, 1980

For the members of the House of Representatives all roads led to Committee Hearing Rooms this past week as having torn a leaf or two from the family calendar, we revealed the deadline date for bringing all bills out of Committee. In extreme emergencies, House action can extend a legislative proposal's life for an additional week or two, but by and large everything had to emerge favorably or otherwise; and another milestone in the legislative process had to come and go.

One again it was difficult to be in two places at once, namely Transportation and Health Care Hearings that, in this final stage as throughout the legislative year, managed to schedule their hearings simultaneously. Thanks Heavens for my super Aide, Suzanne, who can cover for me in one place while I am in another, and take such great notes that I can feel reasonably comfortable about missing the hearing itself…

The tempest and the shouting on the recently passed state budget seem to have died, to quote our friend Mr. Shakespeare, and this rep is now actively pursuing a follow-up course of action in the Senate to protect that very important House amendment I was able to add to the Budget, viz. to increase somewhat the inadequate Regional School District Aid for our Vocational Education Institutions. We have already secured the Governor's backing on this, and have requested a meeting with Senator Chester Atkins to defend our House action and to have a go at securing his support in the Upper Branch.

Locally, of course the event of the week was the American Legion Braintree Post 86's 1980 Edition of "Bring Back Those Minstrel Days," an Extravaganza of Americana in which this rep had the privilege and the fun of participating. It's a wonderful event as we were soon to learn…a family affair. With husbands and wives, sisters and sisters-in-law, children and grandchildren, all merrily participating and like any family affair, it proved to be rich in warmth, wonder and excitement as talent after talent appeared to develop before one's eyes…the timid to lose their shyness, and the less timid to grow more bold and imaginative with each succeeding show…And oh, those merry marvelous looneys of Endmen!!! Those beauteous babies of the Ballet Russe…those terrific Tambouriners… (Lucky things-wouldn't I love to be one of them…) and that great, happy, rollicking chorus!!!

What fun to find a husband and wife team-the Opies, Hugh and Barbara, serving as Show Interlocutor and Show Director…to find that everyone in the show with the single exception of a couple of members of the band represents local talent…And that even that band featured Braintree's own John Capavella, who was present at each and every show rehearsal, encouraging us and urging us on…

The peerless production staff of the show, which was staged and directed so happily and handily by Barbara Opie included such additional distinguished Braintree families as the Laffins…Susie, Tom and Ruth…(Ruth wrote those delightful lyrics that preceded the appearance of our town politicians…) The Bruynells, Bob and Oralee and Anne, a score of Currans, all related; and Brokmeiers, and Stevensons and Gorhams, and Mortons and Molloys and Leary's and Harts and Eisenhauers and Bucknams…and john and Mary Rooney…

The small fry stole the show, needless to say…those marvelous Irish Step Dancers, and those adorable Bunnies and Susettes and Susie Q's and Bojangles…

Altogether it was a super show, and we had a ball participating in it…

Saturday noon and we were off to participate in the opening ceremonies of the East Braintree Little League, where it was a fun experience to throw out the first ball and start the season, off obviously with a bang, for they tell me that Rich Snyder hit two home runs in observance of the happy occasion.

And now it is back to the House of Representatives for what could be a heavy week as those thousands of bills emerge from committee and appear before us.

My we all but forgot to mention Ann Vail and her nice young group of Cub Scouts whose visit to the State House we managed to share very briefly indeed this week between Roll Calls on the State Budget…

Well, at least that is behind us for now…the Budget, we mean, not the nice visit of Ann and her boys…That was great!

MAY 8, 1980

Hallelujah! The past week on Beacon Hill as elsewhere in the Commonwealth saw the return of our old friend, the SUN, with a consequent lifting of spirits all the way around the House of Representatives, the bills came pouring out of the various committees and our sessions lengthened as we strove to deal with them, and so it was more like business as usual under the Golden Dome. Securing an extension of time were a number of bills that appear to have serious problems and will require extensive redraft before they will accomplish what they were designed to do. That additional time was voted, in some instances after extensive debate.

The State Budget meanwhile is being dealt with in the Senate, where it usually takes three weeks before a finished product is returned to us, invariably for rejection and the appointing of a Conference Committee to iron out the differences between the House and Senate versions and come up with a compromise which we must then either accept of reject as is, with no further amendments possible. Naturally, with the state's fiscal year running out, this Conference Committee versions is accepted, though usually with some misgivings on the part of us…

The week contained a number of especially significant events for your L. of the H. Thursday was "Law Day" throughout the Commonwealth, and it was off to attend the 8.30 AM Law Day exercises at Quincy District Court where the Judge Albert Kramer's address was an inspiring one, and Judge Mulhall was honored in a special way to the apparent delight of many. A strange happening occurred, however during the outdoor exercises that precede the Court program. While Old Glory was being raised to half staff on the Court House lawn, the Quincy High School band literally FRACTURED the playing of "Our National Anthem." Why had it happened, I kept wondering. There were those who felt they simply had not rehearsed it. They were furious. I couldn't agree with them however. The band has been playing together all year. The totally discordant notes they played could not have been accidental to my way of thinking. The entire Anthem was off-key. Were they sending us some kind of message, I wondered. I still do; and am still very much disturbed by the occurrence. Friday morning and our long awaited Press Conference was held by the Special Commission on the 200th Anniversary of the Massachusetts Constitution. Once again we were treated to a showing of the marvelous slide show that so graphically illustrates the background of the Massachusetts Constitution and the struggle leading up to its adoption. This slide show will, of course be part of the exhibit in that exciting traveling train museum, the "Constitution Express" that will be here in Braintree from July 2nd through July 8th, 1980. And along with your L. of H., Braintree Committee members Bob Bruynell and Otis Oakman were on hand to applaud the efforts of our State Commission and witness the latest in their accomplishments for the Bicentennial Celebration.

From Beacon Hill it was off to Logan Airport where as Chairman of the Sub-Committee on Aviation of the Transportation Commission, I was to preside at a meeting which included the top executives of Eastern Airlines and U.S. Air and the residents of Jeffries Point in East Boston, in an attempt to bring all parties concerned to some form of compromise position on the towing of aircraft as a noise reduction measure. My next step will be to contact, on Monday, the Astronaut Frank Borman, who is now President of Eastern Airlines, and secure his reaction to a compromise position I seem to have worked out…

Friday evening and the week was to end on such a nice note…I had been invited to extend a note of welcome to members of the Massachusetts Traffic Policewomen's Association who were holding their Spring Meeting at Braintree High School with our Braintree ladies as their hosts. And what a bright, smartly uniformed, dedicated and delightful group of women they turned out to be. Eleanor Murch and her ladies naturally shone…their hospitality was of the highest order and what fun it was to be presented with a doll, fully dressed in a policewoman's uniform, which had been made by my friend Sally. These dolls were used as table centerpieces to add an especially festive note. A lovely time, and it was great to see so many of the Braintree ladies who protect in such a dedicated way the lives of our schoolchildren day in and day out, in all weathers and under all conditions. What a debt we parents and grandparents owe to them….

MAY 29, 1980

Monday morning of another week on Beacon Hill, and the arches of flowering Japanese cherry trees through which we walked the last fifty yards to the State House are gone with the wind. Their millions of petals lie like pink snow on the lawn and on the granite walkway. The weekend winds have carried them as far as Tremont Street, and so we find small pools of pink in the cracks and crevices of the sidewalk as we ascend the Park Street hill.

There's no doubt about the season on Boston Common. The vendors are out in force, and the early morning air is already punctuated with the sounds of more than one musical instrument…Monday noon, and it's off to the Senate President's dining room to attend a Coffee Hour hosted by my colleague, Senator Paul Harold, for a number of government and business leaders from the Arab nations of Egypt, Saudi Arabia, Jordan, the Sudan and Morocco. We had a lovely chat with a member of the National parliament of Morocco, a charming young man from who we learned that Morocco has 267 members in its National Parliament, and that there are 30 young men and NO WOMEN members….

Tuesday and it wasn't easy to tuck in at 2.15 PM the taping of a one minute "Access" message for Channel 7 in and attempt to change the Chapter 70 funding formula so as to more adequately compensate those Regional Vocational Technical schools that graduate skilled technicians. I was there at the request of our super Blue Hills Regional Vocational School, whose battles for funding I lead in the House. 80 percent of our Regional Vocational Schools, many of which are experiencing increased student enrollment, will not receive any additional state aid this year despite the fact that State Aid to Education will be increased by $83 million over last year. Unfortunately while I was at the R.K.O. General Building taping the segment for WBZ-TV with Arch MacDonald, there were fireworks in the House involving the extension of the life of the Corruption Commission for six months. I was consequently listed as "Not Voting" on this. Had I been present, I would most certainly have voted in support of efforts to bring out the Resolve.

We continue in our efforts to bring Senate 2048, the Rape Staircasing bill before us for debate. This legislation would divide the crime of rape into four categories according to their severity, making the penalty more appropriate to the crime. In our opinion having this kind of law on the books would create an atmosphere more conducive to making rape victims more willing to report the crime. It would also make it easier for the criminal to be convicted. It clearly defines the penalties for the various categories of rape and for a first and subsequent offense as well as for rape in connection with kidnapping, breaking and entering, possession of a dangerous weapon, assault by means of a dangerous weapon etc, etc.

Most womens' organizations throughout the state are supporting this bill, as well as the Massachusetts Chapter of the National Association of Social Workers. It's a national problem, dealing with the crime of rape on a wildly escalating scale, needless to say.

We are certain you are as horrified as ourself at the revelations of the "I TEAM" in regard to the situation with some of the hazardous private medical laboratories within the state. We wonder about the efficiency of our State Board of health if a situation like this is allowed to occur. Every day people's lives depend on the findings of medical laboratories. We plan to contact the DPH and urge a speed up of their inspection process in this area.

Rep John Finnegan's budget proposal for the reorganization of higher education was deleted from the Senate budget which was voted on this past week. Having it in the House budget did manage to accomplish one thing however. It forced the 20 member Special Commission on the Reorg of High Education to accelerate its pace. We attended a sub-committee meeting on Friday afternoon where it was decided to meet on Saturday all day and even on Sunday if necessary to try to come up with an acceptable proposal for the consolidation of some state colleges. At Friday's meeting the chairman of the sub-committee proposed the merger of Boston State College with the University of Massachusetts and the consolidation of Boston's three Community Colleges, as well as the placing of the Mass. College of Art under control of the U/Mass. Board of Trustees. We have not yet heard the outcome of those weekend meetings on the above proposals.

6-12-80

The highlight of the week was easily the signing into law by the Governor of that six months extension of time for the Commission currently dealing with corruption in state contracts. We had rushed it through the House; the Senate had done likewise; and speculation was rife in regard to the Governor's action on the measure. He had come through for us, however; the bill became law; and additional time is now theirs for completing the work the Corruption Committee had set out to do.

Meanwhile in the House, we had voted overwhelmingly to stay in session until the remaining Commission bills are dealt with, and so in that area at least all goes well on Beacon Hill...The saga of the "Tall Ships" had happily continued for your L. of the H. As an Honorary Member of the Constitution 200 Commission, I had been invited to a State House Reception for the Captains of those exciting and beautiful Tall Ships. Accordingly, we had gathered in the Governor's office, then marched through a cordon of Ancient and Honorables to the historic Hall of Flags. Incidentally it was exciting to learn that the newly installed captain of those Ancient and Honorables is none other than Braintree-ite Barry Driscoll. And how nice it was to stand in the Receiving line and shake his hand along with the hand of each of the Tall ship Captains, meeting each one as we did so, and having an opportunity to exchange pleasantries with him (and with her - there was one Lady among the group...) and to learn first hand how exciting it had been for our visitors to Boston as well as for those of us who welcomed them. An exciting experience, with a lovely luncheon to follow prepared by a Vocational Education School in Haverhill- and perfectly at that...

Another exciting experience...this time a local event...had been participation in the 35th Anniversary celebration of our Braintree Safety patrol program, with an opportunity to present a House Resolution in observance of the event. What a great group of youngsters were being honored that evening. And a great deal of credit goes to Doris Barry and others in charge of that outstanding program to insure the safety of our school children.

Thursday evening, and once again it was a privilege to be in Braintree, attending the Cocktail Party to celebrate the formation of Financial Planning Advocates Inc., an institution headed by my good friend Ernest J. Gotta. It is always especially heart warming to salute a new enterprise since it indicated another evidence of faith in the economy of the Commonwealth...

Thursday evening also, and after chairing a meeting of our Braintree Constitution 200 Committee, it was off with the group to South Station for a visit to that historic Museum Train that will be in Braintree from July 2 to July 8- the "Constitution Express." A most happy experience for all of us who went merrily off on the "T" to visit South Station after a considerable absence and to observe the metamorphosis that has occurred in the vicinity of that old railroad terminal...as well, of course and to view the train and to get an idea of what lies ahead for us.

It's an exciting prospect for all of us, the bringing before the people of the Commonwealth a realization of the importance of our constitution in their lives. "This exhibit has been created to give the citizens of Massachusetts and their guests a feeling for their Constitution" we read, "its history, its vitality, its great value - as much for ourselves as for our forefathers two centuries ago." We were interested also, we who work at government, in reading a quote of John Adams, "from the beginning I always expected we should have more difficulty and danger in our attempts to govern ourselves...than from all the fleets and armies of Great Britain."

7-10-80

What in the world do you actually mean by Prorogation anyhow? People keep asking that question and they learn that I am arriving home in the wee hours of the morning and heading back to a the State House in the afternoon rather than the normal morning hour...Well, we have decided to keep a running record of what could turn out to be the last week of the 1980 session of the Great and General Court. So, here goes...

It is now Monday morning and we begin the last week of the 1980 Legislative session. We have brought a change of clothing to the State House. The admonition of the Speaker to prepare to work day and night during the coming week had an ominous ring, and we shall be able to work much better if we are secure in the knowledge that we're socially acceptable and well groomed. We keep remembering old timers' tales of the "good old days" on Beacon Hill when prorogation proceedings went on for as long as 72 hours without interruption except for meals. Having been a Girl Scout, we plan to be prepared.

So now here it is Monday morning and we are in an 11:00 a.m. formal session. We have been assured by Speaker McGee that the Controversial Commission bill will come before the House as soon as the House Calendar is dealt with. It's a 132 page bill, and it is highly technical and we retire to the quiet of the lounge to digest it.

The day is a gray one. Rain falls intermittently. The skies are clear, however at a noon recess we walk down Park Street and across Tremont Street to Downtown Crossing to pick up a Guest Book for our Museum Train. Here is all gaiety and activity. Bands are playing; performers are doing their thing and passing the hat hopefully. It's a jubilant scene.

We return to the House Chamber and continue to work on the day's calendar. The afternoon wears on and a dinner hour is indicated. One of our most popular colleagues, Mrs. Ann Gannett is winding up her many years of membership in the House. We decide to take her to dinner as a farewell gesture. The idea mushrooms and there are 40 of us assembled for our evening meal in the "Last Hurrah" at Parker House. Ann will be sent off in high style.

And now it is back to work, and we commence debate upon the controversial Commission bill. The debate will go on until after 3:00 a.m. on Tuesday morning, but the Commission bill to reform the State's contract procedures will have been engrossed in the House and sent on its way to the Senate.

Boston is beautiful in the early morning as we head homeward, its streets devoid of people, its lighted skyline lying against the darkness like a sea of gold. The Expressway would seem more formidable were it not for the presence of my colleague and friend rep. Antone Aguiar, the Chairman of Banks and Banking, who follows immediately behind me all the way. It's a nice feeling, and an even nicer one to find myself safely back in Braintree at around 4:00 a.m., with the birds chirping, and dawn threatening to break.

Back to the State House at 2:00 p.m. on Tuesday afternoon, and we're at it again, this time dealing with a possible increase in the gasoline tax. We break at 3:00 p.m. for a farewell party for retiring Rep. Dick Demers; and again at 8:00 p.m. for dinner. Back again - to the State House and to the gasoline tax…the final vote on which is taken at 6:15 a.m. on Wednesday morning. This representative has not been able to vote for a 10 percent hike in the gasoline tax. In our opinion it is devious of the Administration to have tied it to fuel aid for the elderly. We could not allow our elderly to be cold this coming winter. We would vote the money without question under any circumstances, the gas tax increase however, which as the cost of gasoline increases will rise to large proportions, has actually been pushed through to fund the Highway fund and MBTA reorganization. We cannot and do not vote for it. It does win in the House however.

It is Wednesday afternoon and we are back under the Golden Dome, a bit on the weary side, (we haven't had much sleep) but prepared to work the long night through. Rumors have now slated Prorogation for the morning of July 4th.

It is expected that we shall deal with the MBTA reorganization bill this evening. It doesn't happen, however. We struggle through the night and the session is adjourned abruptly. Your L. of the H. has missed the sum total of those exciting night before the fourth Committee events that took place in Braintree this evening. She must be on hand for the July 4th Commemorative opening of the Mass. Constitution 200 Museum Train. She hopes and prays and the time goes on.

Bills are coming over from the Senate for final enactment in the House; and members who will not return to Beacon Hill are making farewell speeches; and the session continues. We engross and send to the Senate a Hazardous Waste bill, a major piece of controversial legislation which has been in the wind all year. It's a major piece of legislation and it gives the local community a real voice in the selection of a hazardous waste site. Had we had this law on the books when Recycling Industries attempted to come to Braintree we'd have been properly protected. Your L. of the H. has had a voice in the preparation of this bill and we rejoice to note that because of a lot of advance contacts it goes through the House without debate.

The hours wear on. It is apparent that I shall not be in Braintree for our Museum Train opening. Dawn breaks, and we are still at the State House. The Speaker sends out for coffee and doughnuts for us; he sends out for lunch for us; and still the hours go on. We have been in session 24 straight hours by now, with no relief in sight we are accomplishing things, however. The Commission's Inspector General bill is enacted… without the vote of your L. of the H. the gasoline tax is enacted.

There are still difficulties with the Ward Commission's main contracts bill however it remains in the Committee of Conference, both branches having failed to come to any sort of compromise on the aspects of the bill with which they have differed in passing to be engrossed.

Meanwhile the clock has kept ticking. As I write this column it is 10:00 p.m. and we have now been in session for 32 hours. A bill to finance Convention Centers within the Commonwealth has been debated for the past hour. We go from one subject to another. And the hands of the clock keep moving…

In spite of everything, we do manage to observe the Nation's Birthday. We observe the fireworks display from the Esplanade…from where? From the very top of the State House.

7-17-80

There are those among the media who feel that the 1980 session of the General Court was a productive one. And there are those who do not. It appears to be a matter of opinion. Actually as the Secretary of State officially brought the session to a close he announced a total of 379 bills and 3 resolves passed by the House and Senate and sent to the Governor for signing. 379 plus 3 out of the close to 9,000 bills that were filed during the course of the year. That's awful, you may be thinking. Actually this legislator doesn't see it that way at all. In my opinion we now have too many laws on the books that are not being enforced. Let's not add a plethora of new ones just to make an impression. There were, of course, some good bills that fell by the wayside unfortunately, but among the 379 laws that did make it to the Governor's desk for signing were a number of excellent ones.

There were, for instance, the bills filed by Governor Edward J. King calling for mandatory sentencing for heavy drug traffickers and car thieves. Your L. of the H. was on hand for the official signing of these significant bills which Governor King said "will make Massachusetts a safer place for its nearly 6 million residents by putting the drug dealer and the professional auto thief on notice that they may face mandatory jail sentences for their crimes." A discussion of the specifics of the new drug law would seem to be in order. For the dealer in Heroin, the law sets a mandatory prison term of from 5 to 15 years; for Cocaine trafficking a prison term of 3 to 10 years; and for Marihuana a prison term of 1 to 10 years, all based on the quantity involved. The law mandates sentencing for dealers of Heroin; 3 years in state prison for dealers of Class B drugs (cocaine, opium, PCP or angel dust, amphetamines, etc.) and 2 years in state prison for dealers of Class C drugs (valium, librium, psiloycbin, mescaline).

There's a 5 year mandated sentence for convicted drug dealers of Heroin; 3 years for convicted drug dealers of PCP, cocaine, opium and amphetamines; and 3 years for dealers in valium, librium, psiloycbin, mescaline.

In next week's column I shall elaborate upon the new auto theft laws; and in future columns on other significant bills that were signed into law in the waning hours of the legislature. To date the gasoline tax increase and the bill to permit the Secretary of Administration and Finance to increase the Commonwealth's fees are as yet unsigned. I could not bring myself to vote for either of these bills. My constituents, laboring under 100 percent valuation and the horrors of inflation are already bowed down by taxes, and I disapproved of tying the gasoline tax increase to fuel aid for our elderly. You may rest assured, and our elder citizens may rest assured that we would manage to fund that fuel aid from existing revenues, however we accomplished it. We would not allow our elderly to suffer from the cold next winter. And the open-ended gasoline tax increase is really designed to provide funding for the Highway Program and mass transit and other related projects.

Locally, of course, the big event in my life as Chairman of the Braintree Constitution 200 Committee was the week-long presence of the "Constitution Express" the Museum

Train on the J.L. Hammett Company property (thanks to the extraordinary cooperation of Mr. Joseph Faraca, the General Manager of that fine civic minded organization). Well, since that exciting happening was covered in beautiful detail by my good friend Pat Leonard in last week's issue of the "Star", I shall simply state that in our opinion the event was a smashing success. I certainly regretted my inability to be on hand for the Commemorative Ceremony on the afternoon of July 4th. I was there in spirit, you may be sure, though my physical presence was required under the Golden Dome where we struggled with Prorogation proceedings. I thoroughly enjoyed the balance of the program, however, along with a great many of our Braintree citizens. So Happy 200th Birthday, you beautiful Massachusetts Constitution, you! You've protected the rights of our citizens for a couple of centuries and you're still going strong…And we in Braintree just loved helping you celebrate the great event…

8-21-80

It was interesting to read the latest vital statistic report for the Commonwealth of Massachusetts for the year 1978, which happens to be the last recorded year…and to learn that each day during that year 188 live babies were born; two infant deaths occurred; 56 of our citizens died of heart disease and 33 of cancer; and there were 117 marriages and 44 divorces recorded.

During the year there was the lowest rate of infant and neonatal mortality ever recorded in Massachusetts; divorces had decreased slightly and marriages had increased slightly; and other for women in the 30 to 35 age group, the fertility rate had decreased dramatically.

It was interesting to note that of the 42,882 marriages, up from the previous years figure of 41,949, 77 percent had not been previously married; 20 percent had been divorced previously and 3 percent had been widowed.

Changing the subject, of great concern to the citizens of the Commonwealth is the rising cost of health care, and efforts are being made to deal with it, we're happy to report. Among the bills signed recently by the Governor was a law creating a 19 member special commission to study the hospital rate structures, while barring hospitals from raising their rates for private patients by anything more than 115 percent cap placed on them under the new law. The most recent figures we were able to obtain on this indicated that between the years 1975 and 1976 health care spending rose from $4.3 billion to close to $5 billion, representing an amount of $845 for each of the Commonwealth's residents. You may well imagine what the increase is now under today's inflationary conditions. Incidentally that 1975-76 figure was 30 percent above the national average, and hospital services consume the largest portion of our health care expenditures.

We're hopeful, therefore that the special commission can come up with some assists in controlling the rapidly rising cost of health care for all of us. Incidentally again, for those interested in securing more in-depth information on this subject, a booklet entitled "Major Health Problems in Massachusetts" may be obtained through the MPHA, 55 Dimock Street, Boston 02119 (442-2208). We had a most interesting meeting with a representative of the Boston Educational Marine Exchange at Lewis Wharf recently, in regard to current attempts being made by this group and the MDC to save Paddeck's Island, one of the most colourful and historic harbor islands. It was fascinating to learn the history of the island which is currently closed to the public but contains 26 fine turn-of-the-century brick buildings, all of which are rapidly deteriorating. It is naturally proposed to save them for posterity...

The island was first settled in 1622 by one Leonard Peddock, and there must have been fine pastureland there because history records that during the Revolution British raiders made off with 30 cattle and 500 sheep. It apparently developed into a summer resort during the 1800's, when a number of inns were built there. In 1897, however the U.S. Government purchased the islands East Head and built a mortar battery on the 88 acres it had acquired.

Between 1904 and 1915, Fort Andrews was built, and its 26 buildings still stand. They include a hospital, barracks, a guardhouse, a quarter-master storehouse, a church, a stable, a gymnasium and an administration building along with a bakery, a firehouse and a family residence. The brick buildings are reported to be quite handsome and rich in the period architectural detail.

Fort Andrews saw service through World War II when observation stations, anti-aircraft guns and prisons were located there. It was finally sold as surplus in 1958 and acquired by the Commonwealth in 1970, to become part of the Boston Harbor Islands State Park, which is managed by the MDC. Well, dealing as we do with this agency's budget, it was interesting to learn to what use it is proposed to put some of its funding in the future, and we approve...

8-28-80

It's the question of the hour on Beacon Hill these days. Shall a sufficient number of representatives and senators petition the Clerks of these governing bodies to call us back into session for a Constitutional Convention, particularly to deal with Proposition 2½??? (I have added my name to the growing list of legislators who have done just that). Or will the Governor call us back into special session for the same important reason? The lobbying groups have been active; the media has indicated wholehearted support for such a move. We have been told that it is our constitutional duty. And we all wait to see just what will develop on this very important issue.

Proposition 2½. It has been on the minds of all of us since the idea first saw the light of day a couple of years back. Will it solve the problem for our overburdened homeowners and real estate taxpayers? Will it decimate the municipalities' school systems, fire and police departments, and curtail or eliminate services of all kinds that we have been taught to take for granted? Or will it merely force our town and city officials to search for ways to spend our tax dollars more judiciously? Those are the questions that are being tossed about on Beacon Hill as well as the corridors and offices of our town halls. And the answers will only be known when our town officials inform us on the specifics of the effect Proposition 2½ will have on their departments, our schools, our fire departments, our police departments, our highway departments, etc…and these services that they have rendered to date but will be unable to render should Proposition 2½ prevail it should be clearly spelled out before our people are asked to vote on this vital issue come November.

At last Monday's meeting of the Board of Selectmen the Chairman of our Board of Assessors requested and secured an executive session for the discussion of "Classification, Revaluation and Proposition 2½." Your L. of the H. was on hand purposely to hear this discussion. She has formally requested the Board of Selectman to ask Mr. Mahoney to return and present the same discussion in an open meeting at their September 2 meeting. It is our feeling that everyone in town should be privy to all information that will affect our real estate taxes and the manner in which our assessors propose to deal with "Classification, Revaluation and Proposition 2½"…the answer we receive when questioning what was discussed in the executive session. We are happy to report that the formation of a Proposition 2½ committee will be announced at that same September 2 meeting. This committee will be charged with researching the possible ramifications, etc. etc. We want our people to be fully informed as possible when they go into the ballot box to vote for or against Proposition 2½; and the only way this can happen is to research and publish specifics prior to that November election. Well, we shall see.

Locally we've had a very happy week. Monday evening and we dashed home from the State House to attend the Selectmans Meeting and cover our weekly office hours at Town Hall. Tuesday evening and it was off to the Sheraton Tara to attend a meeting of the Board of Directors and Citizens Advisory Board of our stupendous Braintree Hospital, where we were to hear the exciting details of a new department which will have an extensive Audiology Department. Having filed the bill (and had it signed in to law) that requires and Audiologist's examination prior to the purchase of a Hearing Aid, this representative was delighted to hear the hospital's plans unfold. We had filed the bill after hearing from the countless people of the hearing aids that lay in their bureau drawers, of absolutely no use to them…and after learning of the small amount of training required for the dispensing of these appurtenances which are great if they work but do not always work for people with a hearing loss.

Friday evening and it was privilege to present a House of Representatives citation to the worlds dearest couple, Elaine and Joe Lally, on the occasion of their 25th Wedding Anniversary at a marvelous surprise dinner-dance planned and executed for them by their beautiful children. A truly lovely occasion. We still dash off to the State House most days, despite the Prorogation that indicates the end of our 1980 legislative session. With the economy in disarray these are a lot of constituent problems in Braintree these days… but isn't it wonderful to be able to help with most of them?

9-18-80

One more eventful week. It began with the presentation of House of Representative Citations to three distinguished Braintree-ites - to Sister Alice Donahoe on the occasion of her Golden Jubilee celebration as a Sister of the Order of St. Joseph and her 75th Birthday; and to my good friend John D. Callahan, Principal of the John W. McCormack Middle School upon his retirement after 33 years of dedication as a member of the faculty in the Boston Public Schools; and to Kimberly Ann Knave, an 8th grader at South Junior High, State Finalist in the "Miss Teen Massachusetts Pageant for 1980." Always a particularly happy experience for your L. of the H.

The week included participation as a member of my Braintree Point Women's Club in Ted O'Brien's "Weekday" program on Channel 7. A fun time when one of 14 club members I attended panel discussions on "Fashions" in the morning, and then in the afternoon on the more interesting topic of "Cops and Women." Here, through the eyes of wives of police officers, the author of the book "Cops and Women", and two very bright Boston Policewomen we were permitted a glimpse into to what to us is an alien world - the world of police officers and their relationships with their wives, the women criminals they encounter, and the police women with whom they work. We were to learn how an officers relationship with his wife will affect his attitude toward the women with whom he comes in contact during the course of his days work. A fascinating discussion, and the consensus seemed to focus on the necessity for psychological testing prior to hiring the officer who will be entrusted with our safety and the enforcement of the law.

It was pleasant to be present on that same afternoon at the swearing-in of a former colleague, Robert F. Larkin, Jr., of Needham as First Deputy Secretary of State; and to attend afterwards the Dinner and Preview Showing of the "Make it in Massachusetts" Campaign at Faneuil Hall. With Dick Flavin of Channel 4 in the role of Master of Ceremonies, you may well imagine what a fun evening that turned out to be, (as well as a productive one.) We wish our good friend Governor King all possible success with his latest campaign to improve the economy of the state since the condition of our state's economy has a direct bearing on every aspect of its ability to provide services for the people of the Commonwealth.

It was especially rewarding to learn during the past week that the project to install sidewalks on Route 37 from the "Village Pump" to the South Congregational Church will finally go out to bid on or about September 20th. We've been bugging the D.P.W. for years on this issue. The where with never seemed to be available. Hallelujah, at long last it apparently is! The highlight of the week personally was, of course my reception of the Old Colony Council Boy Scouts of America Distinguished Citizen Award on Friday evening at the Lantana in Randolph. What an affair that turned out to be! I had, of course anticipated receiving this prestigious award, and was thrilled to death at the thought of it.

We've always loved Scouting and have two nephews, Kevin Timmons and John Cogan achieve the rank of Eagle Scout. And of course, having served as Juliette Low Chairman for the town's Girl Scouts, we've come to know the value of this wonderful program for our girls as well as our boys. What was a surprise, however, was the number of additional awards that were to come my way from just about every organization in this wonderful town I have had the privilege of representing in the General Court.

We shall never be able to thank the people who engineered this marvelous event. John Shaughnessy, the Chairman unparalleled; Olive Laing, the most super of Secretaries; Ticket Chairman John Connors and Treasurer Lindsay Tait and Assistant Donald Olsen; Committee Members Joseph Avitable, Suzanne Bump, Dick Fry, Barbara Keefe, Stanley Komich, Elaine Lally and Sonny Shaw and of course the incomparable Bill Roberts of the Old Colony Council BSA.

9-25-80

The big news during the past week was, of course, the reconvening of the Constitutional Convention in order that we might address particularly Proposition 2½ and the death penalty. There are other issues before the Convention, 25 of them in all, however it is Proposition 2½ that really brought about the Governor's decision to recall us. So what have we accomplished to date in this joint Convention? Well, on Proposition 2½ Representative Cohen's bill which has secured the grudging support of those responsible for the 2½ proposal was substituted and passed overwhelmingly with both Democratic and Republican support. The proponents of 2½ had decided that their bill had little chance of passage and that the less stringent Cohen bill would undoubtedly process of limiting our state and local spending had to begin somewhere and that the Cohen bill at least a step in the right direction.

It limits increases in government spending to increases in the average personal income; and would bring the total tax burden of the state in line with the average of 17 states which will be chosen by a committee of state official, legislators, and representatives of business and labor. It sets local aid at its present level. The idea behind the 17-state aspect of the proposal is, of course, to keep Massachusetts competitive with other similar states.

It is not a particularly restrictive bill actually, since the average personal income increase has been in the range of 9 percent to 12 percent, and our state budget has not increased to anywhere near that level in the past several years. It is however a step in the right direction and we must now all wait until the people of Massachusetts make the actual decision on Proposition 2½ itself. They will vote for or against this much more restrictive proposal in November on what is a binding referendum question, and we will have to live with the result. In Braintree now as in most cities and towns a committee is hard at work determining the precise effect a mandates 2½ will have on our town and its services. Hopefully our people will therefore be voting in November from an informed point position and that is right. Legislators will have no more power than any other citizens in determining the fiscal future of the Commonwealth. We shall have our one vote on the issue like everyone else. Incidentally the Convention vote for Cohen's tax limitation was 170 to 9.

We're delighted to report that a bill which I have filed for the past several years, viz. Legislation banning on the state from mandating local programs without full state funding will also be on the November ballot as a result of Convention action. Outcries against mandating state programs without full funding have come our way since our first year in the House; and a great many people are hopeful that our Massachusetts citizens will vote to put an end to a practice that had profound effect on our local tax rates.

The death penalty also cleared its first hurdle, approved by a vote of 123 to 62. The measure must, of course be approved by a joint Convention next year and if that happens will go on the ballot in 1982.

A proposal to increase the state's representative districts by adding one for Dukes and Nantucket Counties failed; more successful however was one to provide that an emergency preamble may be added to a bill on a voice vote unless challenged by two Senate or five House members. A recess until Wednesday called a halt to the Convention, leaving more than 20 issues yet to be faced. Locally, the week had been a busy one, with attendance at the Selectmans Meeting on Monday evening; the Primary on Tuesday; and on Wednesday State House Meetings on the Displaced Homemaker issue, which is a program to get our women off welfare rolls and back into the world of work. And, of course on Friday morning it was off to the Lantana where the South Shore Chamber of Commerce held its breakfast meeting with Governor Edward J. King as Guest Speaker. We thought his speech was terrific. The gentleman in the corner office is a businessman rather than a politician, and as such we feel he should enjoy a certain amount of rapport with our Chamber members. Those at our table seemed to reflect that way of thinking. An enjoyable morning at the end of a most enjoyable week.

10-2-80

Congratulations are in order for the 13 percent of our Braintree voters who went to the polls on Primary Day, and wouldn't it be great if the remaining 87 percent were to join them on November 4th, crowding our polling places and exercising the privilege and responsibility of selecting those individuals who will play a part in charting the course of governmental action on the national as well as on the state level during the important years that lie just ahead?

You know, your vote DOES indeed make a difference. According to a most engaging piece of literature that was being given out by my good friend Ruth Langley Hill at Primary time, "History shows that one vote gave Oliver Cromwell control of England in 1645; gave America the English language instead of German in 1776; saved President Andrew Jackson from impeachment in 1868; gave Rutherford B. Hayes the Presidency in 1876; gave Adolph Hitler leadership of the Nazi Party in 1923 and retained the Selective Service System in 1941 - just 12 weeks before Pearl Harbor."

In light of these interesting facts, many of which were new to me, a realization of the importance of your vote must be seeping in, and we hope to see a lot more of the wonderful people I represent in the General Court on hand in November, eager and willing to exercise the all important voting privilege that enslaved people are fighting and dying for elsewhere in the world.

Congratulations are also in order for the very special gentleman who won last week's election as my counterpart in the Silver Haired Legislature - Edward Morrissey! I look forward now to working closely with him in behalf of our elderly citizens, or our "super citizens" as I call them; to filing his bills and to working for them on Beacon Hill.

We had good news during the past week on a project on which we've been working for a very long while - a project for which the D.P.W., involved so extensively financially elsewhere in the town, could not seem to find the funding. Bids will be received on October 7th for a sidewalk betterment project on Route 37 from the Village Pump to South Congregational Church. Persistence has paid off.

Very little action resulted from the second recalled Constitutional Convention. Efforts to assemble a quorum of members failed on Wednesday afternoon. We had sat awaiting their arrival from 4:00 to 9:00 p.m. when the Convention was recessed until Thursday, with no more success achieved. Apparently, a lot of our colleagues who are having difficult races decided to campaign rather than to come to the state House. We had, of course addressed the two major issues that actually brought us back the previous week, viz. Proposition 2½ and Capital Punishment. It was a tiring time for those of us who were on hand in the House Chamber, myself included, waiting and hoping. Senator Bulger, the Convention President, gave up finally and recessed the Convention until November 12 when it is hoped he will have no difficulty in assembling the quorum necessary to address the remaining issues on the Convention Calendar.

As a result of our Convention action, however, two additional proposals will appear on the November ballot-one to change from a majority vote to a 4 majority vote, the legislative procedure for adding an emergency preamble to the bill; and a proposal barring the Legislature from mandating programs on our cities and towns unless they are fully funded by the State (with a ⅔ vote of both Houses providing for an emergency situation).

A decidedly less restrictive tax limitation was substituted for Proposition 2½; and reestablishment of the death penalty was advanced. It must, of course, be approved again by the next Constitutional Convention, and if that action is taken, it will appear on the 1982 ballot.

Advanced also was a bill to ban persons convicted of "malfeasance or misfeasance" from holding further public office; and one to establish the "right of privacy" for all citizens.

With the sudden change in our New England weather, the need for fuel assistance can become real for many of our citizens, especially for our elderly; and information on the guidelines for qualification for assistance may be obtained by calling Mary Brelsford, Director of the Southwest Community Center at 471-0796. She is ready and willing to answer any questions you may have in this most important regard.

10-23-80

What a wonderful evening was provided recently for our "Super Citizens" - our Seniors-by the Braintree Legion Post 86! With Edward Sweeney at the helm as always, and the Ladies of the Legion in charge of a mid-evening buffet so lavish that it spilled over into "doggie bags" for all who wished them, the evening turned out to be a fabulously successful one. Dance music was provided again by that great Boston orchestra that each year volunteers its services to friend Ted Sweeney for his special event; and altogether, thanks to Ted and his Legionnaires and their Ladies everyone had a perfect ball.

At the State House the spotlight was on the M.B.T.A. as its maintenance service came under the gun following criticism of its repair records by the office of the State House Auditor. I attended a public hearing held by a Sub-Committee of the Legislative Post Audit and Oversight Committee, where circumstances surrounding those repair records were examined, in depth, only to reveal that although records have been kept on bus repair shop work since last spring, no one at the MBTA has ever examined them.

The reason given by John Toomey, deputy chief of the automotive maintenance department brought a gasp from those in attendance at the meeting. "The T" he said, "had not hired a clerk to collect the forms." Rep. Louis Nickinello whose bill to restructure the T has been around for the past several years (Our Transportation Committee aired it in Braintree and the Selectmen voted to support it a couple of years back) declared that under the present structure, the T is unmanageable. Its structure must be changed, he said. Deputy State Auditor Robert Ciolek did state that the present T administration is more receptive to the auditor's complaints, we're happy to report, and it was revealed that the Authority has budgeted $500,000 for a computerized system which will measure productivity and schedule repairs. Facts that came to light in the course of the meeting revealed that the T does not test its mechanics, and keeps them on probation for only 30 days.

There is, needless to say, grave disagreement between the union and management in the current contract negotiations. Rep. Gregory Sullivan, who chaired the sub-committee urged the T to use the 1978 arbitrator to consider the communities' ability to pay, and comparable salary levels. The Unions claim that law is in violation of the federal Urban Mass Transit Act and a suit on the issue is pending.

As a member of the Health Care Committee with a special interest in the nursing profession I attended the legislative breakfast of Mass/Plan (Mass. Political Leadership And Action In Nursing) on Thursday morning. It wasn't easy to be present at the 57 Park Plaza Hotel in Boston by 7:30 a.m. I managed it, however, and turned out to be the only State Representative who did so. (There was also one Senator present.) Our nurses will be pushing hard this year for legislation that would guarantee third party payment for their professional services. Their bill to accomplish this died in prorogation last year despite our committee support. The nurses plan to attempt to bring it before the General Court much earlier during the coming session so as to prevent a recurrence of that happening.

It was extremely interesting to learn form these professionals of the effect that our patients' rights bill is having upon medical care. Under the provisions of this law a patient has access to a great deal more information relative to his case, including possible side effects of medication proposed and alternative treatments, etc. The bill was apparently a step in the right direction.

Locally, the weekend was as hectic as always - hectic and enjoyable, with attendance on Friday evening at the annual dinner-dance for our Brain-injured Children's Building Fund, with "Liz" Conners doing her usual superb job in making the evening a memorable one; participation on Saturday evening in the 30th Wedding Anniversary celebration for our dear friends Frank and Ruth Reed, with a Citation in order for this charming couple; and on Sunday a couple of other interesting events. I was on hand at the Weymana for a Country Western Music presentation to benefit our Diane DeVanna Center for the combating of child abuse; and at the South Shore Plaza for a positively great cocktail party and entertainment to benefit our new Braintree Highlands Branch Library. So many happy and productive events tucked into one little old weekend! P.S. Don't forget to mark that calendar of yours for November 4 - Election Day! Your vote DOES count; and a lot of us are hoping to see you at the polls!

10-30-80

Unbelievable as it may seem to many of us, this will be my last Column before Election Day-that vital Tuesday, November 4, when we shall vote to place at the head of the most powerful nation on earth- our own - the man who will then possess the power to change the course of our history, and indeed of the history of others, for the next four years. I again urge you to go to the polls in untold numbers on that all-important day; to place your "X" next to a candidate for that all-important office, and of course next to candidates for the several additional offices that are to be filled.

Do I hear you say that you find it difficult to choose between the Presidential candidates? You're not particularly enamoured of any one of them??? We're hearing that sort of thing a lot these days, unfortunately, and it grieves me to no end, especially when it is accompanied by the remark, "I don't think I'll vote for any one of them. Anyhow, my vote doesn't make a difference!"

How wrong you are! Your vote does indeed make a difference. At the risk of being chided for repetition I find myself repeating from an earlier Column a few pertinent facts that came my way via good friend Ruth Langley Hill. "Does your vote count?" her handout had asked. "History shows that 1 vote: Gave Oliver Cromwell control of England in 1645; Gave America the English language instead of German in 1776; Saved President Andrew Jackson from impeachment in 1868; Gave Adolph Hitler leadership of the Nazi Party in 1923; and Retained the Selective Service in 1941 -just 12 weeks before Pearl Harbor…" That one vote of yours DOES count!

And supposing too any of you, having decided that your vote doesn't count, stay at home on November 4 - and no one of the three candidates carries enough states to come up with the 270 electoral college votes needed for victory??? Well, our national security and our domestic welfare might easily be in turmoil then while a number of decidedly unpalatable events could follow. The election having been thrown constitutionally into the House of Representatives, it could conceivable happen that no Presidential candidate would receive a majority of votes there - in which case the Vice-President elect (who would be chosen by the Senate) would act as President until a President succeeded in qualifying for the office.

Meanwhile, in the event of the failure of both a President and a Vice President to qualify, Congress could exercise its right to declare who shall perform the duties of President, or even to designate the manner in which one person shall preside until a President or Vice President shall have qualified for that powerful high office that during this time would be uncovered - with the nation adrift, perhaps, on what could be a most unquiet sea. Sounds complicated, doesn't it? And fraught with portent. It is both!

In dealing with a situation where a majority fails to be received by any Vice-Presidential candidates, the Senate could enter the picture, and it is entirely possible that we could end up with a President of one party and a Vice President of another; and wouldn't that be something???

I guess that what I am saying to you as you face the November 4 Election that now lies so close in time is, THINK HARD! And perhaps if you are a religious individual, PRAY HARD! But VOTE! Please go to the polls in record numbers and exercise this blessed privilege that is yours. Your VOTE is your only and real VOICE in the selection of those who will play a major role in determining the quality of life for each and every one of you.

Under the Golden Dome, it was comforting to learn from the Department of the Environment Quality Engineering that developing a successful hazardous waste management program is its first priority; that managing the generation; handling, treatment or disposal of hazardous waste at active or abandoned sites is recognized as the most demanding environmental challenge facing Massachusetts and that their energies will be directed toward those ends. It was also great to learn that the state has taken significant steps toward developing comprehensive regulations, strengthening the enforcement program, assessing improper disposal activities, and developing treatment storage and disposal facilities.

It was also interesting to learn that through the Mass. Industrial Finance Agency, the Grossman Companies/1515 Washington Street Braintree Trust has received approval for a $6 Million bond to purchase a 20 acre industrial complex at 1515 Washington Street, formerly occupied by the Walworth Company. The trust plans to convert the Building into a multi-tenant industrial research park.

Locally it was a privilege to present a Citation to one more fine young Eagle Scout, Thomas R. Bricknell, of Troop 17, Hope Lutheran Church. Congratulations are in order for young Thomas and the proud parents and family members who were on hand to share the honors with him.

11-13-80

May I begin by thanking from the bottom of a deeply grateful heart the 13,286 wonderful Braintree people whose vote I received on November 4-individuals who have paid me the supreme compliment of sending me back to Beacon Hill to represent them for another two years. I promise to continue to serve you all with dedication AND WITH DELIGHT during the additional two years that now lie ahead. My door will be open to each and every one of you. I and my office staff will be at your service. I am extremely humble and very proud indeed to have been so honored by the people of our town, (the only town in the United States that can boast the birth records of two Presidents incidentally). - the people of Braintree.

And may I say additionally that I noted with considerable pride the huge percentage of our voters who went to the polls on Tuesday last - more than 86 percent of them- and incidentally, isn't Town Clerk "Bob" Bruynell something??? His predictions are more accurate than Blackstone's. (The magician.) He hit our numbers right on the head as usual.

On Beacon Hill the referendum questions dominated the news as we returned to work, the election behind us. Having for the past several years filed legislation mandating full state funding for all state-mandated programs, I delighted particularly in the fact that Question 5 went so beautifully and so big. Funding of programs can represent a complex problem. Should the state accept federal funding it must take all the frustrating mandates that go with it; and should the cities and towns accept state and federal funding, they're in even greater difficulty for they must accept both state and federal mandates. And the state's happy habit of mandating programs upon those cities and towns and then leaving their taxpayers to pay for them has annoyed me no end from the first day I arrived on Beacon Hill. I'm delighted to learn that our taxpayers feel the same way.

It was good news to learn from the MBTA this past week that the number of arrests made by their Police officers has increased by more than 50 percent since the so-called "Operation Rainbow" program went into effect. Under this program undercover police decoys ride the trains and the buses, and are therefore right on hand to make arrests when crimes are committed. Uniformed MBTA officers are also assigned to foot patrols in a number of stations, and they have also made arrests on the scene, giving the offenders no opportunity to escape capture once they have transgressed. The "T" has instituted a monetary reward system well, under which cash awards of from $100 to $1,000 are made to individuals who furnish information leading to the arrest and conviction of vandals. This action was of course taken in the wake of the many stonings and other acts of vandalism that have been plaguing the Authority during the past few months. Here's hoping that the possibility of sharing a train ride with an undercover police officer will deter a great many potential criminals from selecting the "T" as a target area for their criminal pursuits.

And, speaking of the "T", on Friday afternoon I participated in the dedication ceremonies that were at last scheduled for our Braintree MBTA Station; and with Senator Paul Harold I had the pleasure of unveiling the dedication plaque. This was a happy occasion with a more moving one to follow when our Braintree Yard was dedicated and named for a very gallant gentleman, Mr. Raymond M. Caddigan. Mr. Caddigan was a long-time employee of the "T", retired because of illness some time ago. He was obviously a valued "T" employee and a much-loved fellow worker, for his fellow workers and friends turned out by the hundreds to be on hand for the occasion. A loyal and loving family was also present. It included ten proud and lovely grandchildren who were sharing a memory with their grandfather that will be theirs for always.

Autumn had given way to what felt like spring for this special occasion. The sun shone and the station sparkled, and MBTA officials were quick to note the lack of vandalism in the facility which has been operational now for several months. May it remain free of vandalism, sparkling and clean as it is today. It is now a generally accepted fact that the Braintree Station is the finest station of them all. It paid to demand the best the "T" was able to produce for us and for our town.

11-27-80

Another frustrating week in the House of Representatives as we continued quite futilely to deal with the monumental problem that is the MBTA! It's a multi-faceted problem as everyone knows. On the one hand, more than 200,000 people daily must use public transportation to get to work, to school, to hospitals and to doctor's offices and to a multiplicity of destinations-people who in many instances have absolutely no other form of transportation available to them. On the other hand, there's the massive deficit assessments that are being made on cities and towns already attempting to deal with the fiscal constraints imposed upon them by Proposition 22; and the $41 Million being sought by the "T"; however, it is addressed, will have a serious financial impact on each and every one of our communities.

All money bills originate in the House and do not go to the Senate for action until we have dealt with them; and the problem was a multi-faceted one for all House members but a particularly difficult one for those of us who are members of the Transportation Committee. And it was to our Transportation Committee that the Governor was to send his message on Monday last as we gathered at 1:00 PM. for another special session of the House. (It was to last until 5:00 A.M. on Tuesday morning.)

We were told that the Governor's message would include the basic elements of an MBTA reorganization bill that our Committee had been attempting unsuccessfully to put before the House for the past several years; and when that message arrived, our Committee held an executive session to vote on it.

It came in two sections. Appendix A dealt with the reorganization itself; and Appendix B with the Management Right's section of the proposal. It was generally agreed that unless management were given more leeway in dealing with the 29 MBTA unions, no reorganization bill could be of much help in dealing with the fiscal situation on the "T", so we demanded that it be dealt with first. Since it dealt with personnel issues, it was sent to the Public Service Committee, and we addressed the remainder of the bill. It did not contain all the provisions of our original reorg. bill, however as our Chairman said, "We get what we can". Essentially, it would permit cities and towns like Braintree those outside the original 14- to decide upon their own bus requirements and if they wished, to contract with a private carrier, excluding the high priced "T", and paying the entire bill for those services. Incidentally the current MBTA assessment upon the town would have been dropped entirely. For the core cities, the state would pay 25 percent of their bus costs. It would pay 100 percent for all commuter rail services outside the district for 1980 and 81, and, beginning in calendar year 1983, the state would pay for 100 percent of the express service deficits, with a limitation on the amount tied to the inflation factor. The power structure would, of course change, giving Boston and the other large cities less control of the "T"; and it seemed like a far better deal for towns like Braintree.

Under the proposal, because the state would be picking up a much larger share of the deficit, and because Boston, with its 58 votes out of 198 has always maintained tight control over the Advisory Board, the Governor or his designee would become a member of the Advisory Board with a vote equal to the largest city, which was, of course, Boston. This provision would therefore dilute the power of the Advisory Board. The bill was not perfect, of course, but it would provide a point of departure for dealing further with the MBTA.

There were, of course, other provisions, however the cost-sharing was the most important aspect of the proposal other than the management rights section, which to me was absolutely imperative. Happily the Public Service Committee not only voted endorsement of the Management Rights section of the Governor's bill, but substituted an even stronger one; so late in the day the bill came before us in the House and the debate began. (It never did come before the Senate.) The Management Rights section was voted overwhelmingly in the affirmative despite strong debate from our Boston colleagues - several hours of it. The bill itself, however, with the management rights appendix attached to it, went down to defeat; and it was obvious to me as it must have been to our Transportation Committee Chairman that our colleagues outside the "T" district entirely, especially those from the western part of the state will have no part in increasing the state's share of the deficit, however horrendous it may become for the rest of us.

The other proposal for restructuring the "T", viz. The Barrett-Cohen proposal, would have strengthened the power of the Advisory Board, with no additional power given to the Governor or his designee. It had the endorsement of the League of Women Voters and other groups who consistently favor the big cities; and though I would have voted for it as a second choice had I been given the opportunity, that opportunity never arrived. Not enough votes could be mustered AGAINST Prorogation, and so, with the problem unsolved and returned to the Courts, the House prorogued once more. Incidentally, once again I voted AGAINST Prorogation until the Supreme Judicial Court had addressed the issue at a hearing which had been scheduled for Saturday.

12-11-80

The "T" is back on track! We're still a bit worn about the edges, however, we who had to wrestle with the problem for hours on end, driving over the Expressway at 2:00 A.M., and 3:00 A.M. and even 3:45 A.M., night after weary night; at the end of day after weary day…

We were facing, of course a multi-faceted problem. There was so very much at stake. A shut-down transit system with its unbelievable financial impact upon the Commonwealth; and the more human aspect of its effect upon the 200,000 people who rely upon the "T" to get to work, to hospitals, to doctors' offices, to shop, etc. This aspect of the situation was grave. On the other hand, the taxpayers of the various communities we represent already have their backs to the wall; and in communities that even now are wrestling with the impact of Proposition 2½ upon their budgets…I rejoiced at the new

Management Rights section we had included in the House version of the bill, however I had to balk at the provision which would require those communities to pick up one-half of the current deficit. I therefore had to vote AGAINST the bill with that provision and for a proposed amendment to have the State take over 100 percent of the deficit, - reluctantly, I must add, for I feared that some of the funding would have to come from local aid, another dismal prospect.

At any rate, that amendment failed to pass. Legislators outside the T district voted against it, and they outnumbered those within it. And so the House version went to the Senate with the 50-50 funding section intact, where they promptly voted for 100 percent state assumption of the costs, along with a 4 percent cap upon our assessments and a number of other changes.

And now back to the House the bill came for concurrence, and the House having failed to do so, a Committee of Conference consisting of 3 House and 3 Senators was handed the bill with the task of ironing out the differences and coming up with a compromise. It was their deliberations, leading to an impasse on the question of the deficit funding that lead to the shut-down of the T and a crisis situation.

Meanwhile, we who would have to vote on the final version waited, and waited and waited. "I keep seeing you on T.V.", people were saying on Sunday. I was indeed present at all Conference Committee meetings, day and night, hoping and praying that somehow or other the impasse would be broken; and it was with considerable relief that on Saturday evening at 8:30, in a room crowded with legislators and media people, the long-awaited announcement was made. The Conferees had agreed on a 75-25 percent funding mechanism with the communities within the MBTA District on the shorter end of the amount involved.

Few voted happily for this compromise version, however we really had no alternative and so it sped back to the Senate and finally to the Governor for signing. It is anything but a perfect bill, to be sure. Few bills are perfect. The all-important Management Rights section of the legislation was left intact, however a 4 percent cap placed on future MBTA assessments; and these provisions should represent some safeguards against what has become a soaring T deficit with which we cannot live. For those things we can be thankful. And will these safeguards ultimately offset the amount we were forced to invest to keep the T running? We have been assured of this fact by our Ways and Means Chairman and the weary Conferees who incidentally failed even to enjoy the luxury of travelling over the Expressway in the wee small hours of each of those mornings but were locked into the situation, catching catnaps as they could. We pray with them and with you all that they are correct in this assumption.

There have been other important happenings on Beacon Hill this past week but for those of us on the Transportation Committee the MBTA crisis was definitely it! It seemed to blot out all else excepting of course for your L. of the H. the marriage Legislative Aide, Miss Suzanne Bump, who was, as we all knew she would be, the most regally beautiful bride to walk down a church aisle in many years. Untold happiness for this very special young woman who shares my life so perfectly on Beacon Hill.

1-8-81

We have not yet ceased to place "1980" on our correspondence and in our checkbook. It takes a while for the newer year to sink in. Actually it is difficult to believe that another year has gone by. How fleeting is time when one's life is filled to the brim with meaningful activity! And speaking of meaningful activity, by the time you read this column, we shall have been sworn into office by our esteemed Governor King, and a brand new session will lie ahead for those of us on Beacon Hill. What changes in our way of life will come about as a result of legislative action in the General Court, we wonder as we contemplate in prospect the multiplicity of issues to be raised via the close to 9,000 bills that have been filed by our 200 legislators???

There has naturally been very little action under the Golden Dome during the past holiday week. Things have appeared to be in suspended animation, although here and there a rumor would surface to the effect that we would be called into session once again prior to January 7th to deal with this issue or that problem. The date being January 3 as I write this column, there has obviously been little substance to those rumors, and we shall be dealing with a brand new session when we next meet as an official body in the House Chamber.

As is the case at the ending of any year as a House Member, we have been deluged with statistics on the twelve months just past, and on things in general. In the area of health insurance for one thing, it was interesting to me a strong supporter of the preventative medicine concepts of Health Maintenance Organizations to learn that HMO's enjoyed an annual growth rate of 38.8 percent during the years 1973-77 as opposed to a less than 20 percent growth rate among all of the other carriers. And as a supporter of childrens' services I was pleased to learn that in the 1982 state budget, out of the $2,927,248,913 (that's Billions, by the way) requested by the Executive Office of Human Services, 45.77 percent is for children's services despite the decline of the Massachusetts population age 0-22.

As a firm supporter of the theory that the state and private industry work best when they work together, I was pleased to learn of the success of a new state Administratively Necessary Days campaign which rewards our nursing homes for taking Medicaid patients who no longer need extensive hospital care but are still in the hospitals awaiting beds elsewhere. As of December 29, we learned, this campaign has moved 590 patients from those hospital beds into nursing homes, an action which represents an estimated annual savings to the Commonwealth of close to $2 Million. In the area of Crime, it was interesting to learn that Governor Kings proposed crime legislation will address seven areas he feels should be targeted by the Legislature during the coming session. We subscribe fully to the philosophy of his Committee on Criminal Justice that "victims of crimes should have rights similar if not better than the criminal defendants. "This legislation will deal with auto theft, bail reform, crimes against the elderly, juvenile crime, violent and serious crime, self-defense in the home and drug paraphernalia. Having filed a large number of bills dealing with many of these issues, I look forward to supporting the Governor in his attempt to get a handle on the issue of the escalating crime rate. Incidentally, as one who filed and fought consistently for auto theft legislation, it was great to learn that the Governor's assault on car thieves last year has apparently paid off. Statistics from the first 6 months of 1980 showed a 9.3 percent decrease in the motor vehicle theft rate. And by the way, we're the only major industrial state to report a decrease in this area. It was comforting also to learn last week from George Luciano, Secretary of the Executive Office of Public Safety that in 1980 crime in Braintree decreased by 1.7 percent over the previous year.

So as you read this column we shall have begun another legislative session on Beacon Hill. There are many vital issues to be addressed there. I ask your prayers for our guidance in the way we shall address those issues, so that the 1981 session of the General Court will be a productive one, with our legislators guided in their decisions by justice, prudence and a deep and abiding concern for the greater good of all citizens of the Commonwealth and for the citizens of the communities they are privileged to serve.

1-15-81

January 7, the first Wednesday of the New Year!!! Under the Golden Dome it was seeing exciting Swearing-In ceremonies for House and Senate members; however although merriment was the order of the day on Beacon Hill, at 33 Arthur Street back here in Braintree things weren't quite so jolly. It was a sad legislator indeed who, having suffered an accident two days after Christmas, had not been allowed to take the journey to Boston on that stormy morning and so was obliged to watch the proceedings on T.V. to learn only afterwards that she would be obliged to wait one full week before being sworn in by the Governor before the Governor's Council. (They meet only weekly, on Wednesdays.) It was deeply disturbing to have had to miss a number of roll calls during the lost week, but comforting to know that no Committee Hearings having been held, no issues of import to my constituents would have been raised.

The General Court as sworn included 22 new House members and 7 new Senators. House Speaker Thomas W. McGee and Senate President William M. Bulger, both of whom were re-elected without opposition, referred specifically in their remarks to the problems we shall be facing in dealing with budget restrictions and Proposition 2½.

This was the 172nd session of the General Court, and the pomp and circumstance that surrounded its commencement will soon be forgotten in the multiplicity of problems we shall undoubtedly be facing in the year ahead. Incidentally, your L. of the H. was not the only missing legislator on January 7th. Several others were out with the flu and so will also have had to face a private swearing in on Wednesday. And speaking of the flu, it appears to me that one way to avoid coming down with that horrid Bangkok could be to try hard to avoid the common cold…to keep well. I was the recipient of a lot of excellent advice on that score from my good friend Doctor Vincent Pattavina. It was he who introduced the Metayers to the beneficial effects of a humidifier that now reposes in the family dining area and enables us to live much more comfortably with the lower house temperatures that we-like most others - are having to handle.

The good doctor attributes many of our colds to the lowered humidity that results from fine heating systems in our homes and elsewhere. Our homes are usually kept very tight and very dry, he says, with the result that our nose and throat and bronchial tubes become dry and nature's defenses against a cold are therefore removed.

We are advised to lower our home temperatures to the mid 60s provided of course we have no other medical problems, and to wear heavier clothing, preferably in layers of lighter weight, loose clothing; and to include a liberal amount of fluid in our daily diet.

Dr. Pattavina suggests that until it becomes real (shall we ever face that happy situation again???) it is advisable to sleep in an unheated bedroom-with lots of blankets, of course; and to don thermal underwear around the house if all else fails.

We've been following our good friend's advice, and it's working beautifully, we are happy to report. And just think of the savings in energy that would result if all of us followed that advice, along with the lessening of our dependence on foreign oil - AND the beneficial effects that horrendous balance of payments deficit that is devastating our Country!

1-22-81

How good it feels to be back in the swim again, setting out daily for Beacon Hill, secure in the knowledge that the action has once more begun - action that will be translated into the addressing of those legislative issues that will have to be dealt with, initially in their appropriate committees, and eventually before the Great and General Court, in the 1981 session.

The week began auspiciously as members of the House and Senate gathered in the House Chamber to hear the "State of the State" speech delivered proudly by His Excellency, Governor Edward J. King. He appeared to have a lot to boast about…an additional 137,000 people in the Commonwealth's work force; the lowest unemployment rate of any of the industrial states; major initiatives in conservation of energy and in alternative energy sources; new crime control programs; and the reorganization of public higher education.

A record of the Administration's accomplishments went on! Approval of the largest housing program in the history of the State; revitalization of a number of areas of state government; a 15 percent increase in tourist revenue; increase support of the arts and libraries; and finally, and we quote the Governor himself, reversal of the "destructive rise in taxes…taxes which have stagnated our economy and discouraged personal initiatives."

In the last two years, individual income in Massachusetts has risen faster than the national average, Governor King told the state's lawmakers, stressing his policy of "fostering private sector expansion, replacing years of anti-business, no growth policies, and the notion that government can do it better."

He discussed the "Bay State Project", which is designed to encourage job training in high growth industries. The Governor outlined his comprehensive energy program which includes every form of energy conservation and the development of alternate source; and last but not by no means least, he promised to file "a major proposal relating to the fuel adjustment clause" which will "guarantee strict controls in the use of fuels by Massachusetts utilities."

Having been deluged each month with calls from constituents enraged over the enormity of the fuel charges they are being assessed by our Electric Light Department, I was especially pleased at that particular announcement. I have for the past two years filed legislation that would mandate the utilities to justify their enormous fuel charges. I have not, however been able to get this bill on the floor for debate. With the Governor's support, we hope to have better luck this year. And incidentally by the time you read this column, a threatened revolt may see a significant number of Braintree-ites refusing to pay this fuel charge, and placing the amount in an escrow account in an effort to combat what they feel to be excessive fuel charges levied by our municipal light plant. Shall these threats be translated into action??? We shall wait and see. Additionally I have been asked by several of these irate constituents to notify them when my bill comes up for a hearing. They plan to be on hand at the State House to support it.

Dealing with Proposition 2½ and the general tax picture, Governor King had this to say: "Taxes must and will be cut. We all know what the people have demanded... with stark, insistent, unmistakable clarity." "The Massachusetts Taxpayers Association recently concluded that after a seven year rise, this Administration cut state spending in constant dollars by 5 percent," he said. He promised to make further tax cuts.

An excellent speech we thought - well written and well delivered - with 29 interruptions for applause that rocked the House Chamber, and must have provided a measure of real satisfaction to the problem-ridden, harassed and hard-working gentleman in the corner office.

At any rate, the 1981 session of the General Court has begun in earnest. There are indeed a multiplicity of problems to be faced. We pray, as we face them, that the Governor's optimism may not be misplaced.

FEBRUARY 5, 1981

The highlight of the past week was, needless to say, the unveiling of the Governor's 1982 Budget. It was a record $6.39 Billion Budget. He declared upon its presentation that it reflected "the spirit of the times. It is frugal," he said. "It is lean." It contained no new taxes, however it represented an increase of 6.5 percent over the 1981 budget and an increase of only 2.8 percent for local aid despite the impact of proposition 2½…an amount of $37.6 which left the cities and towns irate to say the least.

The budget reflected to some extent the governor's philosophy, and to some extent the enormity of the demands that the Commonwealth's citizens are making on their state government. On their first statement, more money is being sought for the Corrections system. The Governor's concern for the rising crime rate in Massachusetts has been articulated since his election and is, I believe, shared by a majority of our citizens. We must take dangerous criminals off our streets and we must have places to put them, and that costs money, he insists.

In regard to the second statement articulated above, viz. the demands that the Commonwealth's citizens are making on their state government, it was noted that the 1982 budget contains an increase of $138 million in Medicaid alone, and yet provisions that seek to reduce this figure are already being challenged on all sides.

Efforts are to be made remove recipients from the Welfare rolls by expanding the sliding fee day care services being offered by the Commonwealth, and that would seem to be a good investment, though perhaps a costly one.

There was considerable dismay, however, when the local aid figure was announced. In the light of Proposition 2½, municipalities had apparently hoped the state would bail them out. It is at that stage difficult to predict what impact the hue and cry and lobbying that followed the low local aid figure will have on the final state budget. I am reasonably certain of one thing however. If an adjustment of this or any other budget amount is dependent upon increasing state taxes, the solution will have hard sledding on Beacon Hill. The people's overwhelming support of Proposition 2½ is very much on the minds of most of us regardless of how we may have felt individually on this tax-cutting measure. We "got the message!" Our citizens are overtaxed.

In other business on the Hill, our Caucus of Women Legislators met on Monday to set goals and determine priorities for the year ahead. There are now 15 women reps, and we decided to select five issues of major importance to women, and to concentrate our efforts on them. Since we are philosophically a most divergent group of women, it is not easy to work as an unit on too many issues, however we manage to settle on 5 or 6 each year, and we have had pretty good luck in getting our bills through the General Court.

Monday evening and it was off with my good fire fighter friends, Jim South, John Whelan and Bob Dryer to attend the annual Legislators Night of the Professional Fire Fighters of Massachusetts a delightful evening as always in the company of these fine young men.

Tuesday and our Transportation Committee held its organizational meeting and planned its scheduled committee hearings for the year; and Saturday morning I was privileged to be on hand when Braintree Girl Scouts held a most impressive ceremony in observance of the safe return of our 52 hostages. This group of lovely, bright eyed youngsters is to be commended for their concern and demonstrated interest in the hostage situation. The patriotic fervor with which their ceremonies were flavored was indeed heartwarming.

On the previous Sunday it was a privilege indeed to join Congressman Brian Donelly and Selectman Chairman Anthony Mollica in participating in the fourth annual Pro-Life Mass at St. Frances Church. This event which is sponsored by our Braintree Council number 1462, Knights of Columbus is always a beautiful and moving one, and Ted and I delight in being present for it. One more exciting week on Beacon Hill and in Braintree; and since the first of my bills will be heard before committee on Monday morning, February 2, I feel as though the 1981 session of the General Court has begun in earnest.

A most happy thought...

FEBRUARY 12, 1981

Hostage William Keogh came to the State House on Monday of this past week. He made quite an impression on us. "You don't know how serious I am when I say I am glad to be here today," he said as a prelude to a most impressive and beautiful address.

The representatives and the senators and just about everyone else in sight were all sporting yellow ribbons, and many of us waved "Welcome Home" pennants intermittently during his stay with us. I was among those selected by the Speaker to "proceed" to the Governor's office to notify him that "the House and Senate were in joint convention assembled" and so I had the pleasure of meeting Mr. Keough personally - all 6'9" and beautiful smile of him.

We had been invited to a Reception and picture-taking session afterwards in Doric Hall, and you can well imagine how badly I felt at having had to pass up that additional pleasure. The MBTA General Chairman Barry Locke was to appear before our Transportation Committee at the same time, however, and so it had to be back to the office for that all important hearing, duty coming before pleasure as it must always be.

Earlier in the day I had appeared before the Local Affairs Committee in defence of my bill to assist towns in holding and conveying property by increasing from 10 to 30 or 50 years the time during which property may be leased by a city or town. With Central Junior High on the block, this bill is mighty important to our town fathers, and Selectman Don Laing, who had asked me to file the bill and Selectman Saran Gillies were also on hand to defend it. Incidentally we're happy to report that it received a Favorable committee report, which represents a most important first step toward making it become law.

I had also defended before Urban Affairs a bill I had cosponsored with Senator Harold to petition the MDC to acquire land and construct and maintain baseball and little league fields in Braintree; (the MDC promised to study this) and before the Committee on Counties a bill which would authorize the Norfolk County Commissioners to borrow up to $950,000 for renovations to the Norfolk County Hospital. This excellent facility which was more than a million dollars in the red in 1976 is now self-sustaining and so deserves our support. And, of course I appeared before the Government Regulations Committee to express my outrage against the utilities companies for that horrendous fuel charge my constituents have been calling me about-but I'm sure I don't have to report that little incident since my remarks appear to have been carried in news stories from one end of the Commonwealth to the other, including on the UPI.

But to go back to Barry Locke's appearance before our Committee, we were all happy to learn that a productivity committee has been formed on the T. We hope for some improvement in that area, needless to say. We also learned that $25 Million of their funds have been spent in January with an estimated expenditure of $25 to $30 Million in February; also that a new General Manager is expected to be hired within 60 days.

Tuesday evening and it was off to the Parker House for the legislative meeting of the Mass. Association of Housing and Redevelopment; and later on to a legislative dinner meeting at the Sheraton-Boston, hosted by the Mass. Railroad Association. Wednesday and it was a pleasure to attend the kickoff reception for the League of Women Voters-mass. Teachers Association sponsored publication "You're in the Driver's Seat", a guide to government which should prove helpful in our school system. Thursday and I spent a happy evening with my good Braintree League friends Carol, Judie and Peggy discussing legislative issues of concern to all of us.

I presented three House Citations in the course of the week; one to my own cousin Helen Kelley, of whom I am inordinately proud. Helen was recognized during the recent WBZ-Radio Blood Brotherhood Week for having contributed 58 years of volunteer service to the Red Cross, and for having contributed 15 Gallons of Blood. What a lady! A second citation went to my good friend Cathy Conley, manager of the Braintree Forum for having won first prize for editorial writing excellence in the New England Press Association Annual Newspaper Contest, topping all New England weekly papers. And a third Citation went to John Fruth, the newest Eagle Scout in Troup 22, First Congregational Church. It was quite a week.

MARCH 26, 1981

Sure and begorrah, this week that housed St. Patrick's Day began on a wonderful note, with attendance as an invited guest at Senator William Bulger's St. Patrick's Day Breakfast/Luncheon at the South Boston Social Club on Sunday morning. Even the sun was smiling as a hundred others, not so fortunate as ourselves, crowed into the hall, indicating a willingness to stand, unfed, for a good three hours so as not to miss the fun. And what fun it was! The Irish songs, and the Irish wit, and the political fun poking and prodding…The quips and the tales…And over all the magnificent Irish Humor of that incredible son of South Boston, the president of the Massachusetts Senate, "Billy" Bulger.

The corn beef and cabbage was delicious, needless to say, but it was the happening itself that tickled palate. From the green carnations that adorned the long, politician-laden tables, to the merriment of our table companions, delightful people from all walks of life, the day was SUPER in every respect. With handsome Bridie O'Flaherty, the Lord Mayor of Galway seated at the head table; and "Miss Galway" herself not ten feet away, it was one great way to salute the Patron Saint of Old Ireland and we delighted in every minute of it.

And so it was off to the Senate House on Monday morning with the sound of Irish laughter still ringing in our ears, and memory beautifully awash over' us…to attend a Health Care Committee in the morning; and come afternoon to appear before the judiciary Committee in the morning in support of my bill to provide that suits for personal injuries or death arising out of exposure to radiation or hazardous wastes may be commenced within three years of the date when the injurious effects of such exposures are discovered, or should reasonably have been discovered. Current Mass. Law stipulates that tort action must be commenced within 3 years from the date of exposure to the hazard. This creates a most inequitable situation for those whose injuries do not become immediately apparent, I stated; for persons, for instance, who developed cancer later in life, or give birth to children with serious defects.

St. Patrick's Day was actually on Tuesday. It was also "Evacuation Day" for the residents of Suffolk County, who had a Holiday. I was included in the group; the State House lies in Suffolk County. I utilized the day by catching up on a lot of letter writing I haven't been able to tuck into these wildly busy State House days we've been enjoying of late. All roads lead now to that imminent April deadline date when everything must emerge from committee to be addressed in the General Court. The result is, needless to say, a succession of whirlwind days that tumble one upon the other to be followed by the customary spate of whirlwind evenings. One of these evenings included attendance at the MBTA meeting on bus service cuts that was held at Braintree Police Headquarters; another evening during the past week I appeared as Guest Speaker at a meeting of the American Association of University Women a delightful and challenging happening.

At the State House I appeared before the Judiciary Committee in support of a bill I had filed at the request of Dick McDermott, which would provide for the expeditious settlement (within 3 years) of civil suits involving those over 65. I also testified in support of a bill I had filed at the request of a young Quincy woman attorney. It would permit one accused of shoplifting to receive a copy of the document he signed before leaving the establishment where the alleged theft occurred.

I also appeared before Taxation in defence of a bill I had filed at the request of Braintree's Silver Haired Rep. Ed Morroney, which reduced by ½ the fees of elderly citizens for motor vehicle licenses and registrations. And I defended as well a bill filed at the request of Louise Caruso to allow the owner of an owner-occupied single-family dwelling to deduct home repairs from his income tax. And on a bill I had myself filed to increase the amount of non-taxable interest on savings accounts to $1000 for a single person and $2000 for a husband and wife filing jointly. All in all, it tuned out to be one more decidedly busy week for your Lady of the House.

APRIL 2, 1981

What a great way to begin a week! On Sunday morning, with spring in the air and robins dancing on the greening lawns. It didn't take Ted and I long to don our gardening attire and lock the front door behind us and head for the family garden; and for one long beautiful day to do such delightful things as pruning the rose bushes and uncovering the flower beds…And if a charley horse or two were to impede our progress a bit on Beacon Hill come Monday morning, who even gave it a thought? How beautiful is spring in New England!

And speaking of Beacon Hill, the week turned out to be busy one as usual. The advocates of quality day care for children were on hand in Garden Auditorium first thing Monday morning. Concern for the latest proposed changes in the funding mechanism for this service saw 1,000 or more day care center employees and welfare mothers on hand to lobby their legislators against the proposal. We are setting up a meeting with the agency to discuss several facets of the issue about which we are hearing conflicting stories. According to day care advocates, the proposal would reduce the amount of day care funding from $60 to $75 per child as it is at present (and we think that's rather a lot, to be honest) to a figure of $50 per month, which we think is low. There's a lot of confusion on this issue as there is on most new proposals that are coming our way in the light of Prop. 2½; and we must be fully informed on both sides of the issue before coming to a judgment on it, needless to say.

Wednesday morning and an estimated 6,000 municipal employees arrived on Beacon Hill to lobby for the Repeal of Proposition 2½. Most of us were unavailable for individual lobbying on that morning, however. We were attending a legislative luncheon seminar given jointly by the Mass. Assn of School Superintendents and Business Officials. I was a guest speaker of Braintree School Superintendents Dr. John Monbouquette.

And Blue Hills Regional Vocational School Superintendent Charles Brenan. From both of whom I was to learn first-hand of the problems they envision as a result of Prop 2½.

Thursday and it was a decided pleasure to host members of the council, The Conservation Department and the Public Affairs Department of the Mass. State Federation of Women's Clubs at a "Legislative Day at the State House" seminar. Led by the Federation's First Vice President, my good friend Beatrice Ahearn, the 30 or so ladies who participated had what they termed a "great day". It was a "walk through" the legislative process; attendance at an informal House session: and the enjoyment of three speakers we had arranged for them. Jane Malme, Chief of the Bureau of Local Assessments, Dept. Of Revenue discussed the state's role in implementing Prop 2½; Patty Brent, Executive Director of our Mass. Caucus of Women Legislators discussed women's issues; and finally, as the highlight of the whole day, the role of the media on Beacon Hill was discussed by that political reporter extraordinaire, "Bill" Harrington, of Channel 5. It turned out to be a great day for all of us.

Thursday afternoon, and I was on hand for a meeting between our town officials and house counsel Paul Menton for a further discussion of the bill I filed at the town's direction to deal with extension of the lease time for our closed school buildings.

Friday noon and how pleased I was to participate in and speak at a ceremony at Elihu White Nursing Home as this excellent facility received the prestigious "Star Award" of excellence from the Mss. Federation of Nursing Homes-one of only 24 nursing homes to have achieved this distinction during the past five years.

As an Honorary Co-Chairman of the event, I continue to work diligently in support of the Tony Quintilliani fund raising evening on May 3. Scheduled for from 4.00 to 8.00pm on that Sunday afternoon at the South Shore Plaza Mall, this promises to be an outstanding event indeed, and I have tickets which I would love to sell to you. The wonderful Quintilliani Family needs your help to contend with the results of the 4½ year illness of its breadwinner, Braintree's own Tony Quintilliani; and if only those Braintree-its who have reason to be personally grateful to Tony for his contribution to their children's welfare attend this event, there wouldn't be room enough to hold them. Please call me for the tickets at home, 843-5159 or at the State House office, 727-5374. They're $15....

APRIL 9, 1981

Since last week's column went to press on Friday afternoon, we shall have to address the events of the weekend that followed before going on to the happenings of the current week. Saturday morning and I was on hand at Braintree Town Hall were the Wampatuck Demolay placed a wreath at the veterans mall as part of their Demolay week.

Saturday evening and with enthusiasm I participated in the 30th anniversary Dinner of the South Shore Association for retarded citizens! It was a privilege indeed to present a House Citation to this distinguished group as well as to preside at the swearing in of its 1981-82 slate of officers, with my good friend Dick Frye going in as president.

Sunday afternoon, and not only Spring but summer accompanied us as what seemed like half the town arrived at the new Braintree Masonic Temple for its Open House. A House Citation highlighted the significant contribution of this distinguished organization to the town of Braintree. The new home of the Masons is beautiful indeed; and it was especially heartwarming to note the key role that was played by their "brothers" in the Knights of Columbus as the event progressed. And incidentally Chairman Morris Harrison made it a lively event indeed.

At the State House, the House Committee on Ways and Means is conducting its hearing on the vitally important 1982 state budget. Theirs is an especially difficult task this year. They are being faced with huge advocacy groups daily seeking additional funding, lobbying for those the original amounts requested by their agencies; and added to these are those lobbying for $300 million in additional aid to combat proposition 2½. We do not envy the members of this truly beleaguered committee. Providers of social services are turning out the recipients in very great numbers, and it will be very difficult for our committee members to refuse to act upon their requests, an action which they will probably have to take.

In both Health Care and Transportation Committee action, we raced to "exec" countless bills as the date for completion of our committee work nears; and since the cost of government must be kept down, a majority of them are going out with an OUGHT NOT TO PASS. We simply cannot afford to implement anything with a price tag on it. A negative committee vote may be challenged in the House or Senate, however this year not too many legislators are attempting to go this route. We are all too concerned with Proposition 2½ and the state budget that is in the wings.

On Friday morning I met with members of the medical professional and representatives from the emergency medical services to discuss further a bill I filed at the request of radio personality Neil Chayet. It would reorganize the delivery of emergency medical services. I am sure you will recall the emergency of the so-called "Ambulanced Law" a couple of years back. It saw Braintree, along with all other cities and towns within the Commonwealth providing a specified form of ambulance service for citizens. Our Police Department purchased ambulances, and E.M.T.s were trained in the rudiments of emergency care. It was all done under Chapter 111C of the General Laws. Well, as with most new laws, problems have surfaced. Life support services are being offered by some emergency care personnel, with no rules or regulations governing their conduct. My bill addresses this situation in a further effort to protect the Commonwealth's citizens. We shall meet again next Friday morning with D.P.H. Commissioner Frechette on hand, to respond to some aspects of our proposal and make recommendations of his own. The bill has little chance of becoming law this year, needless to say. It took 12 years for the Ambulance Law to be signed by the Governor. It will, however at the very least, highlight the need for action in this area and push the D.P.H. into action…

Friday was also Student Government Day at the State House and Braintree High School "Senator" Rick Higgins distinguished himself with an impassioned plea against gun control. You may well imagine his delight when his side of the issue won. We understand that the student House also voted down this and every other issue it tackled, a situation which we legislators found very interesting. It appeared to echo our own reluctance to sign into law many new proposals these days on Beacon Hill.

4-16-81

What turned out to be a most interesting week on Beacon Hill began on Sunday afternoon when the Randolph Lodge of Elks hosted our own newly organized Braintree Lodge No. 2622 during the installation ceremony. The outgoing Exalted Ruler, Paul W. Milward was feted and applauded for a job well done. His Citations included one from the Senate and my own from the House. Incoming exalted Ruler John P. Harrington's speech of acceptance augers well for the new lodge. He pledged to work toward bringing in 240 new members during the coming year, and I shouldn't be at all surprised if this dynamic individual did just that! I knew when I read its roster that his new organization would do things up brown. Its membership includes a lot of "movers and shakers", as I informed them on Sunday.

Monday's Health Care Committee hearing included special testimony form Neil Cheyet, the radio personality with whom I have filed a bill to reorganize that State's emergency medical services. This had turned out to be a complicated and controversial issue since the Department of Public Health is coming out with its own rules and regulations for emergency service, a fact of which I was unaware until the previous Friday. We shall be bringing all elements together, however before the final draft of the bill comes before us. The art of compromise, which is the cornerstone of government invariably comes into play when a bill of the magnitude of this one comes before the Legislature; and so what a learning experience this has been for all of us! We've loved it...

Tuesday, and in Doric Hall 60 state supervisors were graduated in a most impressive ceremony from a course in "Management Skills for Massachusetts Supervisors. The course was initiated as a result of the Governor's Task Force recommendations, and was funded by the Intergovernmental Personnel Act with matching State Funds; and as a result of it, successfully trained motivated employees are now equipped to return to their agencies and train other supervisors in leadership and productivity skills.

Wednesday, and we learned from the Independent Insurance Agents of Braintree and Quincy of some of their concerns at an early morning breakfast meeting in Quincy. Agents are apparently experiencing great difficulty in dealing with a most comprehensive arson application form for those seeking commercial insurance. It is referred to as "Fire Ap No. 2". We understand fully where it is coming from; arson for profit must be brought under control. Clients are objecting to the application's questions as an invasion of privacy, and so our insurance agents are experiencing great difficulty in dealing with it. Concern was also expressed over the Governor's new auto Insurance bill. We have asked that they analyze both the Governor's and their own proposals for auto insurance reform and present us with a summary of their differences so that we may come to a judgment on the issue from a more informed position. One particular aspect of the Governor's bill that came in for criticism was his penalizing of a driver for "accident involvement". They (and I must admit WE) felt it should read "at fault accident"..

The highlight of Thursday's happenings was easily the presentation of a House Citation to Braintree's own Ethel Swanson on her 91st Birthday! And Friday saw us meeting once more with members of the medical profession as well as with Commissioner Frechette of the D.P.H. to further study my proposed legislation to reorganize the emergency medical services. A number of decidedly controversial issues have surfaced, and so I shall probably recommend that the bill be placed in a study so that we may examine it more deeply and thoroughly before taking action on it as a Health Care Committee.

Saturday morning and it was off to Springfield for the State Democratic Committee's Issues Convention where the most liberal platform imaginable was adopted with complete disregard for those Democrats who have moved toward the middle in the light of today's inflationary situation and the financial burdens we are all carrying. A disappointing day for your L. of the H., the only bright spot on the horizon of which was the presentation on Saturday evening of House Citations to Natalie Shaughnessy, the Chairman of the Sacred Heart Community Theatre's "Show time 81", and to Father Brian Flatley for his ten years of dedication to the Showtime productions. A superb show, as always!! How do they manage to do it year after year after year???

4-30-81

On Beacon Hill these days we're eagerly awaiting the arrival of the Ways and Means Committee version of the State Budget. It is due to reach us on May 4, with the required seven day period for evaluation and study leading us up to May 11 when we shall begin debate on this vitally important aspect of life under Golden Dome. Only then shall we be in a position to determine where cuts can be made. Only then can we really begin to face that all important question of additional local aid for our cities and towns. The late-night and the all-night sessions will begin and the financing of our state government will be the consuming topic on the Hill.

Leading up to budget time, we've attended to a series of meetings with advocacy groups seeking to have their funding increased; and with individuals and organizations with programs they wish safeguarded and problems they wish help in solving.

Monday being a holiday, the week begun in earnest on Tuesday morning with all committee rooms seeing action. All bills had to be reported out by Wednesday, April 22 and so executive hearings went on all over the State House. In our Health Care Committee and in our Transportation Committee hearings we struggled madly to dispose of all remaining bills before the deadline. We did it!

Tuesday evening and it was off to Carney Hospital at six for a legislative dinner, the primary purpose of which was to acquaint us anew with the alleged disastrous effect of the Governor's Medicaid reform proposal on hospitals throughout the state. Off from

Carney to East Junior High School for a dress rehearsal for the fabulous Post 86 American Legion Show, "Bring Back those Minstrel Days".

Wednesday and at the State House, at the request of the President and Vice President of the Parents Association at Lakeville Hospital, I met with Governor King to protest a proposed transfer of 36 psychiatric geriatric patients from Tauton State Hospital. Lakeville currently houses the severely handicapped, with many young children among them and my assistance had been sought in preventing the transfer. I had arranged a meeting with the Governor to allow them to voice their objections. I have also arranged a meeting with Secretary Charles Mahoney for Tuesday of next week when I shall marshall a group of area legislators behind them. Wednesday afternoon and I met with representative from the Mass. Association of Insurance Women where I learned of their reaction to the proposed Auto Insurance Reform package.

Thursday began with an early morning legislative breakfast at the South Shore Council on Alcoholism headquarters in Quincy where I was appalled to learn of the extent of this problem in our area as elsewhere. The Council is seeking additional funding for an education program as well as for a counseling and referral service. Then on Thursday evening, "Bring Back Those Minstrel Days" was on for the first of the three evening performances. And what fun it was to participate in this happy family-oriented annual event where the world's nicest people manage to put together a super show in the sunniest and most congenial manner imaginable. Loved being involved in it! And we're proud to say it was a sell-out smash hit for all 3 nights! Because of my four-evening commitment to "Bring Back Those Minstrel Days", I was unable to be on hand for a series of Braintree events that would normally have demanded my presence. It was a pleasure, however to see that citations were presented in my name to a number of special Braintree-ites and organizations. On Saturday evening to the remarkably successful youth rehabilitation facility "Pilgrim Center for the Development of Life" on the occasion of its 10th Anniversary and to the incomparable Father Jack Curley who has been running the rehab program from its inception...and to the distinguished Braintree-ite Kenneth N. Ryan, on the occasion of his retirement after 3 years of super service as District Deputy, Knights of Columbus; and to the equally distinguished Joseph F. Cusick and Virginia Kelly, both of whom retired on Sunday as Commanders of the Braintree Post, D.A.V., and its Ladies Auxiliary.

Locally also there was the Opening Day Ceremony for the Babe Ruth League at French's Common on Sunday at noon, to be followed by a similar ceremony for the east Braintree Little League at Watson Park, where once again I was accorded the honor of throwing out the first ball - to a "Mr. Hanigan", (Hope we've spelled his name correctly), a handsome young Little Leaguer who caught it like a veteran. A happy week and a productive one...

5-21-81

It is mid-May as I write this column. All traces of the once pale pink and beautiful petals from our Japanese flowering cherry trees have been carefully removed from the State House walk. Now pale brown and "littery", they still line the sidewalks on park Street and are carried through the air on the swift seasonal breezes that are always with us on Beacon Hill.

The weather is generally mild and so the Common is swarming with hawkers, peddlers, flower sellers, musicians and of course Visitors. They climb the State House steps; and they "Oh!" and "Ah!" in the State House corridors as the beauty of our magnificent Capitol building is borne home to them. It's a special time of the year -Spring in Boston - and we revel in every single aspect of it. The week has been a busy one. It began on Sunday afternoon when the John Scott House Nursing Home observed "National Nursing Home Week" with a super parade. And what fun it was to ride as a participant in a 1926 Studebaker, a beautifully refinished antique car, along with its owners, Eugene and Helen Baker and their young son Mark. It was Mother's Day and it was rainy. Could people possibly be enticed out on this Sunday afternoon to watch our world go by?? People were indeed enticed out. And they received balloons and lolly pops from the humorously costumed employees of John Scott. And a very happy time was had by all.....Monday's State House activities included a meeting and picture-taking session with a group of young people from the Temple Christian Academy of Braintree. And Tuesday's happenings included a meeting with representatives from the Norfolk County Agricultural School, which is seeking to complete a building program. With an 82% upon graduation employment figure, it would seem that funds invested in this vocational institution are well spent...

Wednesday evening and I was privileged to be Guest Speaker at the Mass. Medical Society's Legislative seminar in Boston; and Thursday evening to participate in the Braintree Historical Society's gala in observance of its 50th birthday; 20th anniversary of its Thayer House School Program; and its salute to the remarkable Mary Bean Cunningham, founder of the school program and active participant in just about every facet of society activity. I was delighted to present my dear and long-time friend Mary with a House Resolution and the Society with House Citations. And on Thursday, how nice it was to receive a visit from a group of young people from St. Coletta's Braintree School.

At the State House, needless to say, all eyes (and ears) are attuned to the State Budget which, though we had expected it to arrive in the House on May 4 has yet to make its appearance. The arrival of a second budget proposal from the Governor has, needless to say, complicated things for our Ways and Means Committee members. We are all committed deeply to helping our cities and towns, but how we shall reconcile the cuts in the many budgets that have come our way is difficult to assess. So far we shall be dealing with the Ways and Means Budget, two Governors' Budgets, "The poor man's budget", and the "Better budget". Life is anything but easy on the Hill as we struggle with these assorted suggested ways of allocating the State's money while we deal with the countless advocacy groups that literally haunt the Capitol building, each group seeking to protect a particular piece of the pie. On Wednesday, for instance, in the middle of the House session and while we had turned toward the House gallery to acknowledge the presence of some schoolchildren, a group of individuals seated in the two front rows unfurled a long banner reading, "We Demand Action -Save Our Services." They were ushered out before we learned what services they wish us to save, however they'll be back…There is stormy weather ahead for everyone, it seems…for those of us who must make the cuts and for those whom the cuts will adversely affect. It is difficult indeed to make cuts in programs that people have been enjoying for may years and have come to expect as their right. It is especially difficult when one is torn between a desire to help our cities and a desire to provide for those who need our help. We're between a rock and a hard place, that's for sure…

6-11-81

It was three o'clock on Saturday morning, June 6th when a $6.5 Million State budget was finally engrossed in the House and sent to the Senate. The vote 117 to 39. We had debated it steadily for 10 days…for well over 100 hours. Our days in the House Chamber had begun at 10:00 a. m. and ended at 12:00 midnight day after day after weary day…We have, however ended with what in my opinion is a good budget - indeed this compromise document is easily the "BEST" Budget.

The Commonwealth has made major sacrifices. More than 1900 middle management state employees will be receiving the same kind of "pink slips" our municipal employees have received. An additional 1900 positions that were recommended will not be filled; and by the end of 1982, by virtue of attrition there will be 6,000 less people on state payroll.

The budget contains an additional $201.6 Million in local aid; and a result of adverse reaction in the House to the first Ways and Means budget with its level funded Human Services programs, those programs will be increased substantially to the tune of an additional $53.97 Million. The AFDC funding by an additional $15,600,000; with the retaining as AFDC recipients of 18 to 21 year old high school or vocational education students adding a additional $1,788,000; and the AFDDC clothing allowance an additional $11,700,000. Department of Mental Health Children's programs were upped an additional $1,200,000 and unserved adults $500,000. $13,771,467 was added to the fuel assistance funding; and $5,498,850 to the elderly home care program; and $1,930,000 to the food stamp program for S.S.I recipients…All these amounts in addition, of course, to the level funded amounts in the original Ways and Means Budget.

The debate on the 1982 budget was long and frequently tiresome. There were at times as many as 125 amendments waiting to be dealt with each one of which could generate unlimited debate; and to further complicate the situation, as fast as these amendments were disposed of they would surface again with a slight change in the wording or in the amount of the funding involved. The debate went on and on and on. As a matter of fact, we might easily be still at it as you read this column.

This delayed action could be extremely hazardous for all concerned, the July 1 deadline for reporting out a new annual budget being perilously close. It was decided finally to attempt CLOTURE, the shutting off of debate at a certain time, in this case at 1:00 a.m. on Saturday morning which was at that point in time eight hours away. Cloture happily prevailed.

And now a word or two about the necessity for haste in getting the 1982 state budget to the Governor's desk for signing. The current budget year ends on June 30; the 1982 budget applies as of July 1. If, however, there is no agreement on a state budget, we may have to come up with what is know as a 1/12 Budget, meaning that agencies will all be forced to operate at 1/12 of their 1981 budget funding. This is never a satisfactory situation since many of our agencies operate on a seasonal basis with their funding use decidedly variable at different times of the year. In this particular instance, however the result would be available to our cities and towns while the 1/12 budget prevailed. It is therefore crucial that in the three weeks of June that remain, the Senate will pass its version of the Budget; it will differ from the House version which will vote to "non-concur": a Conference Committee will hammer out those differences and come up with a compromise budget that is acceptable to all; and the Governor will sign it - all prior to the deadline date of July…Well now, so much for one more State Budget. What has been happening locally for your L. of the H. Well, on Wednesday, the House recessed while our Ways and Means Committee could come up with a revised budget that would meet the demands of those advocating the additional Human Services funding and so I was able to attend the 24th Anniversary Luncheon of the South Braintree Senior Citizens and to present a House Citation to their charming president, "L'il" Gibbons. On Friday, however, because we were in session on Beacon Hill, my House Citation had to be presented by my good friend John Rooney to the retiring Commander of Post 86, the American Legion, my good friend Jim Eisenhower. It was quite a week for the members of the House of Representatives and I must admit I'm mighty glad it's nicely behind us….

7-2-81

Once again it was the State Budget that dominated on Beacon Hill during the week just past. The Senate version of the budget had been passed with one dissenting vote at 7:00 or thereabouts on the previous Saturday morning; and now, bright and early on Monday we House members faced the decision on whether to concur or not concur with this decidedly different version from our own - this Senate budget.

It soon became obvious that an effort was afoot to push CONCURRENCE, an almost unheard of development in the budget process. There were press conferences and there was lobbying, and since the Senate budget included $300 Million in local aid as opposed to $200 Million in our own, there appeared to be considerable support for its acceptance in the House. It was to be Tuesday evening, however before the issue would come to a head. Concurrence fizzled. It secured a mere 46 votes, and both budgets were promptly transferred to other waiting hands of a committee of conference, where the issue still rests as I write this column on Sunday evening.

Shall the six member committee (3 from the House and 3 from the Senate) ever be able to reconcile the enormous differences between the two versions and come up with a vehicle that is acceptable to all? That is the question we ponder as we await the results of what must be around-the-clock deliberations on the conference committee's part. In our opinion they simply must do so, since the alternative to compromise - a $1/12$ budget- clearly represents a no-win game for all parties involved.

We had the budget by day and by night there were a host of other activities requiring the participation of L. of the H. On Tuesday evening it was off to the Wollaston Golf Club for the Second Annual summer part for Governor's Councillor Peter Eleey. And on Wednesday there was the most memorable evening ever at Boston Pops where the Ancient and Honorables "occupied" Symphony Hall and hosted an evening of patriotic fervor such as we have not witnessed in a very long while. As guests of our good friend Larry Warner, Suzanne (my Administrative Aide) and I had a perfect ball.

Thursday and after a day on the Hill it was off to the Viking club and the happy privilege of presenting a House Citation to my dear friends Arthur and Helen Peterson on the occasion of their 50th Wedding Anniversary; and on Friday evening joy and sadness seemed to be intermingled as Ted and I attended the "Last Hurrah" of the Watson School P.T.A., to present as part of the evening's events a House Citation to the very popular Edward M. Wells, the retiring principal of that wonderful neighborhood school which is closing its doors this year. The Ritter Country Club is a great place for a party and it was a great party indeed.

Sunday afternoon and we turned back the clock to Colonial Days, donned our colonial costume and departed for the annual Knights of Columbus Pancake Breakfast with its gathering of Captain Gordon Campbell's Militia, and the scheduled march to town Hall for the annual inspection ceremonies for our famous Time Capsule. Here as part of that inimitable "Time Capsule Team" of Pat Leonard, Mel Miller, Nancy Nicosia, Otis Oakman and Bob Bruynell, along of course, with our Militia captain Gordon Campbell, I had the usual fun time.

You will be pleased to know, incidentally that we found all to be tiptop with the Time Capsule; and we settled it down nicely for one more year (its sixth) in its place of honor on the village green before the seat of our local government, our historic Town Hall.

All in all, the past one was a banner week for your L. of the H. The July 4th weekend now lies ahead as we journey to Beacon Hill. Rumor has it that we shall be spending the day right there, still grappling with the state budget. Oh well, if we must we must.

7-9-81

Monday morning, and the State House is alive with rumors. There is a stalemate on the budget. We shall go to a 1/12 budget…a 3/12 budget…We shall have no budget at all…We wait and worry. Who is correct??? The differences between the House and Senate budgets are of course, enormous, however these differences could undoubtedly be addressed if the conferees set their minds to it. we feel, as we listen with considerable dismay to the rumors that fly unceasingly about. We worry because failure of the legislature to meet the July 1 deadline could leave our cities and towns out in the cold, to deal with the full impact of Prop 2½ on their own…

Tuesday, and our hopes are fading for the passage of a State Budget by tonight's deadline. Failure to act will result in devastation…payless paydays for our state employees; no money for our welfare recipients or for the agencies' various providers of services. We arrive at the State House early for the signing of a bill to permit the 25 year leasing of the Noah Torrey School by John Hancock. Attorney Robert S. Farrington, Jr., of the firms's Law Department is on hand for the signing, which goes off in great style as usual.

The day wears on. Conferees, we hope are meeting; they are, however, apparently getting nowhere, and at 6:30 p.m. we break until 9:30 p.m. for a dinner hour which four of us female legislators spend at Lerner's a gourmet German restaurant we have passed many times on our way to Quincy Market.

We have learned a number of things as the week progressed…that our own Norfolk County Hospital, which had a $1.2 Million deficit in 1976 will end the year in the black…that a new left-turn-on-red law went into effect on June 21. (It will permit a left turn only from or into a one-way street)…that Massachusetts bears the unique label "stolen car capital of the world"…

The House has given preliminary approval to a bill which would allow automobile dealers to sell used cars which are priced at $750 or less "as is" with no implied warrant. I had voted AGAINST it. I had also voted AGAINST permitting radio and T.V. coverage of all formal House sessions. Too many of our colleagues now play daily to the press gallery; we'd never get them off center stage if the T.V. cameras were rolling.

Legislation making it unlawful to transport open alcoholic beverages or to drink alcoholic beverages on MBTA vehicles or property has been signed into law and will take effect on August 19. We break at ten minutes before midnight; there is still no state budget.

Wednesday noon, and under the Golden Dome we attend the Governor's press conference. He proposes another budget of his own, the House and Senate conferees having reached an impasse. He hopes to step into the breach, and the day goes on and on and on…and ends still without a state budget.

Thursday, and the budget battle goes on. The conference committee cannot constitutionally accept the Governor's new budget proposal. The conferees continue to meet and to wrangle and the rest of us to wait here at the State House and hope…

Friday…and we debate the governor's newest message providing for an appropriation to pay our state workers, our pensioners, our welfare recipients, etc. After hours of debate, we vote to accept it. It is, of course, the night before the Fourth. Our fireworks however are of a different variety than those that will accompany that wonderful Overture on the Charles…an attempt had been made to tack on $300 Million in local aid; it failed. There has been no firm decision on just how much local aid we can send back without letting the state in for a tax increase. The bill goes to the Senate where $273 Million is added to it, for local aid to be sent back to our cities and towns. We who have been recessed subject to the call of the chair are notified that we shall address this Senate version on Monday morning at eleven. I am reasonably certain as I write this column on Sunday evening that we shall reject the Senate version. The battle of the State Budget will therefore continue…

7-16-81

The budget impasse continued as we passed from Monday to Tuesday to Wednesday to Thursday, to Friday, to Saturday and to Sunday…The House and Senate remained poles apart in their attempt to address the issue of a $1/12$ state budget to provide for our state workers' salaries, our elderly, our blind, our disabled and our welfare recipients. The Governor's proposals repeatedly called for this funding, and in the House we had repeatedly refused to add the $273 Million more local aid that had been demanded by the Senate as a condition for acceptance of the interim budget. Neither branch would retreat, and so the stalemate went on. In the House we see that $273 Million as a bailout for Boston and a prelude to an additional tax package later on. The Senate favors the Massachusetts Municipal Association formula by which those communities that have been managed well will be short-changed, while Boston, which community has had the worst possible fiscal management, will benefit with additional local aid that has been estimated to be as high as $52 Million.

As the week progressed, various other matters surfaced. Governor King signed into law a couple of measures designed to deal with our current crime situation. Under a new law it will now be legal for the police to make a warantless arrest of any individuals whose motor vehicles carry altered identification numbers. Additionally in a move to strengthen the state's gun laws, a penalty of up to five years may now be imposed for altering or counterfeiting a license to carry a firearm, or a state firearm identification card. The Governor's bill to permit the use of deadly force in the home also received initial House approval incidentally…But back to the issue of the 1982 State Budget. On Thursday we had been assured by the Speaker that the Conference Committee members had compromised on a flat figure of $265 Million in additional local aid…a middle ground having been reached between the House figure of $246 Million and the Senate Figure of $301 Million. No attempt was therefore made (for the first time; it had been proposed and had failed to receive a majority of the House votes on each of the two previous occasions during which we had voted a $1/12$ budget covering salaries and relief payments), to attach the local aid provision to this third attempt by the Governor to address the salary issue, the $255 Million budget figure that would be needed to avoid a strike on the part of our state workers and further demonstrations by welfare recipients. This third message of the Governor therefore sailed through the House with but two of our colleagues voting against it. It was, unfortunately not to have a similar experience in the Senate. On Thursday evening the "upper branch" was unable to secure a quorum. It was the $1/12$ budget we had passed and sent their way… and as midnight neared, our House speaker, deeply disappointed, recessed the House "subject to the call of the chair."

We awaited such a call throughout Friday, and Saturday, and Sunday. It came at 10:30 on Sunday evening; and as I write this column, I face a House session at 1:00 tomorrow (Monday) afternoon. According to the T.V. news, the Conference Committee is still at it on Beacon Hill and they are close to agreement on a majority of the issues at variance. Shall they agree on the $1/12$ budget that will avert the strike of 25,000 state workers that is scheduled for tomorrow unless action is taken to their overdue salaries??? That is the $64 dollar question as we head for Beacon Hill and another go at restoring order out of chaos in the legislative process. We shall see…

Being tied to the telephone awaiting the call of the Chair, I was unable to be present at the retirement party for my good friend Alfred Mauceri, however as has happened previously, my dear friend Olive Laing presented a House citation to the gentleman in my absence, along with my best wishes for happiness and health for him and his dear Lillian during the Leisure years that now lie ahead. Thank you, Olive…

7-23-81

The 1982 State Budget crisis on Beacon Hill came to an end at last around midnight on Wednesday evening. The Conference Committee's $6.3 Billion budget was accepted in the House with only 7 votes against it, and in the Senate on a 35-3 vote. There were many aspects of this highly controversial budget I found difficult to accept. My concerns deal to a great extent with the budget's "outside sections." As a matter of fact, the entire concept of changing the laws of the Commonwealth via the addition of outside sections leaves me uneasy. 299 of them were added to the 1982 state budget...an unprecedented number.

Most of these outside sections were, of course, added to the Senate version of the budget, and a majority of these were found to be intact when the Conference Committee's deliberations ended. The provision to permit the withdrawal from the transit system of 23 of the 70 cities and towns within the MBTA district shocked me. It originated, of course with Senate Ways and Means Committee Chairman Chester Atkins. A provision to permit his town of Maynard to withdraw from the "T" was expanded by the Conference Committee to include the 22 cities and towns of House members that fell into the same category. Many of us were outraged. This will add considerably to the assessments of the 56 remaining towns. A conference Committee budget however cannot be amended (It may be either voted up or down), and so there was really little or nothing we could do about this decidedly unfair move. With the current fiscal crisis facing the state, the budget simply had to reach the Governor's desk and speedily.

My principal concern with this relatively new scheme of things...the adding of outside sections to the budget lies in the fact that I perceive this as a path to the destruction of the system of checks and balances that was built into our Constitution. In the normal course of events, a bill filed to change a law requires a public hearing and takes a great many steps through the general court prior to its reaching the Governor's desk for signing. There can be unlimited debate on the issue; and ample opportunity is provided for citizen participation before any bill can become law. Not so with a law change contained in an outside section of the state budget, however. It requires NO public hearing; may be inserted by leadership at will; and there is even concern on Beacon Hill as to whether the Governor can legally veto it. I consider it a potentially dangerous development in lawmaking in Massachusetts.

My principal concern with this particular State Budget however lies in the fact that my community was short-changed in local aid. Although the quoted figure of $857,000 plus, in additional local aid for Braintree sounded like a sizable amount, the issue of the RELATIVE PERCENTAGES of aid to the 351 cities and towns never surfaced during the final Conference Committee budget debate. I was, therefore shocked to learn that Braintree, at 14% is at the bottom of the ladder, percentage-wise, and that many affluent towns benefited to a ridiculous extent under the lottery formula used. Amherst at the top of the ladder received in excess of pf 300% of its Prop 2½ tax loss. At fault, of course, is the use of that lottery formula. I have since been told that Braintree's high valuation is responsible for our failure to receive additional local aid. Are we then to be penalized for obeying the law and going to 100% valuation, I keep asking myself...This is the question I shall be asking of leadership tomorrow (Monday) on Beacon Hill. I shall also express my concern to the Governor whom I have been attempting unsuccessfully to reach by phone yesterday and today, despite the fact that I know he is at work in the State House. Among others he is meeting with a group of local officials on this very issue…

Tomorrow will see the start of another potentially wild week on Beacon Hill. Along with dealing with the Governor's vetoed items, we shall be facing the County budgets and a deficiency budget for 1981. I'm beginning to shudder at the very word…

8-13-81

Although we are in "recess" until next month-supposedly on vacation-the pot continues to boil on Beacon Hill. For one thing, a move is underway to abolish the Registry of Motor vehicles and to permit the cities and towns to handle the chores of issuing licenses and registering vehicles. The registry, even without this move to eliminate it, would appear to be in deep trouble anyway. The Legislature had cut $1.8 Million from its budget; and added to its woes in dealing with that cut is the fact that an additional $2.3 Million in negotiated pay raises must be absorbed. As many as 450 of its employees will face layoffs as attempts are made to reconcile the situation…and to keep the agency afloat…while on all sides efforts are being made to sink her…

The release of the "Cherry Sheet" figures made a few waves as well during the past week. I was pleased to note that Braintree received an additional $793,727 over last year's amount. That seems like a sizeable increase of itself, however we'll have much more if we can steer through the General Court that bill of ours to change the distribution formula for the additional $293.6 Million in local aid that was included in the 1982 state budget. We're working hard at it!!! Meanwhile it was mighty encouraging to learn despite that unfair distribution formula, Braintree had handled Prop 2½ so well that the town ended its fiscal year with a $1.2 Million surplus.

Day care providers and recipients descended en masse on the State House first thing Monday morning in an attempt to block the King administration's proposal to reduce Day care payments per child from the current $251 per month to $160 per month. The opponents of the plan claim it will decimate the Day Care program. Its supporters claim it will merely force providers to modify existent programs if they wish to continue operating. It's a highly emotional issue, and the members of our Women's Legislative Caucus are deeply involved in it. The plan was devised by Human Services Secretary Charles Mahoney who resigned from office during the past week, to be replaced by Welfare Commissioner William Hogan.

Actually Secretary Mahoney recommended a total reorganization of the state's human services program. His proposal to restructure the $1 Billion Medicaid program is also in the wind. Assistant Human Services Secretary Robert Murray will be heading the state's Medicaid program during the coming year, and we are awaiting this evaluation of the proposed changes in the program he will now be administering.

It was interesting to learn that Attorney General Francis X. Bellotti has involved himself in the current move to ban changing out state laws by means of the back door approach that was used so extensively by the Senate during this year's budget deliberations, when 300 "outside sections" were added to the state budget. Having served - more than a week ago - as one of the sponsors of a bill to do just that-BAN the use of outside sections - we're delighted to learn that should our bill fail to reach the Governor's desk, the Attorney General will support an initiative petition campaign to address this vitally important issue. Changing the laws via outside sections of the state budget totally prevents participation by the general public or by those who would be affected by such changes, it prevents a public hearing before an appropriate state committee. It is dictatorship and nothing else…

A probe of the Metropolitan District Commission was officially launched, with charges of wrong-doing in the top echelon as elsewhere being made by two of our colleagues during a press conference. The charges were followed by a flat denial from Commissioner Geoghegan. If, however, there were "payoffs in connection with the awarding of construction contracts" as is alleged, then a probe of the agency is definitely in order. These charges should be disproved or substantiated…

While in Secretary of Public Safety Luciano's office recently, I noticed on the wall a quote from our famous Braintree-ite John Adams (whose seat I occupy in the House). I simply had to jot it down. It reads: "I must study politics and war that my sons may have the liberty to study mathematics and philosophy…in order to give their children the right to study painting, poetry and music." We've plenty of both politics and war to study these days, have we not???

9-3-81

With the advent of what could easily be termed inclement weather for August… temperatures falling into the 40s at night…we begin to think, most reluctantly, I might add, of the winter that lies ahead. Thinking of winter can't help but bring to minds our staggering energy costs; and as we deal with the idea of staggering energy costs, how can we possibly fail to be angered anew by that ridiculous "fuel charge" we've all been raving against for the past few years???

It is comforting however to know that on August 6, Governor Edward J. King signed into law a bill that will set up a watchdog bureau to see to it that utilities purchase and burn the very cheapest fuel available. It's been a long struggle, this effort to place some controls on the way our utilities do business. They have been very reluctant indeed to accept the kinds of curbs that lie within this new law. They fought so hard against the idea last year that a similar bill was vetoed by the Governor. This year, however, in June, after about 50,000 consumers began to fulfill their pledges to withhold their fuel adjustment payments if the bill failed to reach the Governor's desk the action was taken. We shall now see how well it will work.

The state's new Human Services Secretary, William T. Hogan, Jr. went public this past week with his plans to tighten control over state spending for human services. Human services consume the greatest proportion of our state budget. As we understand it, the state's welfare system will be computerized. Pilot programs will be set up for the testing of that much publicized Medicaid fixed budget proposal. It has been stated that our $900 Million annual Medicaid costs could be reduced by close to 4 if the state substituted a prepaid fixed cost plan for the present opened billing system. A workfare program will be attempted once more. As we understand it, the proposal will mandate that certain welfare recipients take mandatory public service non-paying jobs. Areas such as child day care and home care for the elderly are under consideration as appropriate for this "workfare" employment. The new Human Services Secretary's proposal will also include an auditing division which will carefully monitor the contractors who have been engaged by the state to provide services to those in need of them.

We have also begun to learn of some of the effects of those massive cuts in state spending that are having to be made as a result of providing that additional $265 Million in local aid for our cities and towns. The picture is not a pretty one. The Department of Public Health, for instance, has had to lay off approximately 400 of its employees. That represents about 10% of its workforce. We have been told that the $5.3 Million reduction in its budget will result in the "modification of elimination of some programs and services." The Determination of Need program's workforce will be reduced by 50%, we were told. This is a program designed to keep down hospital costs by preventing unnecessary expansion programs. The licensing and certification of the state's health facilities and services will be cut by 40%; central DPH management services by 25%; the division of Food and Drugs by 18%; and the state's public health hospitals by 10%.

Necessitated cuts will include less on-site surveys of health care facilities; the halting of a three year effort to license and inspect the more than 700 private medical laboratories; and the halting also of a computerized personnel management information system. Only 4 sanitarians will be left to enforce the state sanitary code; and our state hospitals will be forced to close a number of currently functioning units. Tewksbury Hospital will be forced to freeze admissions and close a 60-bed chronic care unit, we have been told. Westfield's western Massachusetts Hospital will have to close its alcoholism unit and Lakeville Hospital its dialysis unit; and the Lemuel Shattuck Hospital will be capped at 140 patents, with its dialysis and research programs significantly reduced.

As a member of the Legislative committee on Health care, I cannot but be extremely concerned.

10-2-81

Another week to start off with a bang on Monday morning as the "Bottle Bill" came before us for House action. It was to generate a lot of debate, needless to say and the final vote was short of the ⅔ that will be necessary to override a gubernatorial veto should that situation arise. The bill WAS passed in the House, however; and as this column goes to press, it has received initial approval in the Senate. There also the vote of 21-12 cannot be relied upon to override that veto that so many of us fear will come from the corner office. We can only wait now, however, for what will follow when the bottle bill has reached its final stage of enactment in both branches of the General Court. The Civil Service Reform legislation also came before us and after endless debate - most of it on the "Veterans Preference" aspect of the bill, it received initial approval on a vote of 104 to 52. The decision to retain absolute veterans preference in civil service jobs was even higher. The vote was 130 to 25.

Meanwhile as the week progressed we began to learn of the devastating effect upon our state government of that $265 Million in additional local aid we'd had to come up with for our cities and towns. With a $9.5 Million shortage in the Department of Public Works budget for one, close to 1,000 employees have been or will shortly be laid off. An additional 1,000 plus employees have been or will be obliged to take a cut in pay that will average $40 per week. Several hundred DPW employees were on hand at the State House in a demonstration against a situation which has seen the salary of one of the traffic engineers present reduced by $113 weekly. A move is afoot to lessen the use of consultants in an effort to provide for additional in-house personnel.

James H. Fish, the State Librarian has submitted his resignation to Governor Edward J. King to become effective the first of the year. He has stated that his 1982 library budget will not provide the efficient operation of his facility, citing a figure of $561,000 which is $10,000 less that he spent last year and $125,000 short of his budget request. It's a real loss to the Commonwealth. Mr. Fish is extremely well qualified, and had great plans for the more efficient operation of the library we all use so extensively.

The members of our Women's Legislative Caucus met with Dr. Mary Jane England and with Secretary William Hogan to discuss the proposed changes in the day Care program which in its final stage appears to be much more palatable that we had at first expected.

State Transportation Secretary James Carlin met with our South Shore legislators and pledged his support for the inclusion of $20 Million in the state bond issue to prevent the termination of rail service from Braintree south. Many of our industries rely heavily on rail freight, including Proctor and Gamble. It is to be hoped that we members of the Transportation committee can be successful in bringing this about.

Here in Braintree I was delighted to read the School Committee has raised its reading and mathematics standards so that our students may pass the state's basic skills test. Having sponsored the legislation that mandated this state testing program, I am extremely interested in the upgrading of our scores since last year when students in grade 2 needed 42 percent; in grades 5, 46 percent; and in the important grade 8, 54 percent. Failure to pass the state test leads to enrollment in a remedial program.

Important local events included the swearing in of my wonderful family physician treasured friend Dr. Archie G. Keigan to an additional seven year term as Medical Examiner; attendance at a dynamic South Shore Chamber of Commerce Small Business Conference Breakfast where Governor Edward J. King was the featured speaker and what he said made a great deal of sense; and a most happy evening at the 10th Anniversary Dinner of RSVP, the Retired Seniors Volunteer Program and what a dynamic and handsome group of "Super Citizens" this organization embraces!!! The quoted figure of 80,000 hours of volunteer service on their part during the past year brought home forcibly the value of this great South Shore group to the Commonwealth of Massachusetts and its citizens. Happy Birthday, ladies and gentlemen of the R.S.V.P…and here's to your next ten years of super service.

10-9-81

October has arrived, that fateful month in which the extent of the federal budget cuts will be made known to the states, Massachusetts included. Here in the Commonwealth we have already wrestled with those agency cuts and reductions that have been necessitated by the return of that $265 Million in additional aid to our cities and towns. Our phones ring constantly. We are hearing from state employees within our community who have either been terminated or forced to take a salary cut. We are hearing from Welfare recipients, and the users of state-subsidized Day care. We receive calls reporting terminated programs and curtailed programs, and heavy workloads, and delays in receiving state services. All this is the result of STATE budget cuts. We shudder to think what lies ahead now that October is here and the burden of those FEDERAL cuts will be added. It is a sad and difficult time for a CARING legislator. And since the tax cut that came our way from Washington does little for the average taxpayer, we are finding it difficult to produce any kind of a silver lining for those with dark days.

The proposed Auto Insurance legislation was very much in the spotlight on the Hill during this past week as details of the plan were revealed to the general public as well as to members of the Legislature. Under it, the 24 auto insurance territories would be reorganized. A 7% cap would be placed on any increase to those whose territory reclassification would result in higher premium rates.

Hearings on this bill will commence on Monday. The requested industry increases average 24.5%; a 15.5% increase has been recommended by the Commonwealth's Rating Bureau, and from the Attorney General's Office comes a recommendation of 6.7% increase. (I like the last one best, although I would prefer no increase at all…)

Meanwhile under the proposed bill Braintree would move from Territory 8 to Territory 9, which would represent an increase in our premium costs. Need I tell you how hard the insurance industry is lobbying on this one???

The matter of hazardous waste disposal is very much in the forefront. Environmental Affairs Secretary John A. Bewick; in pleading for the siting of "tightly regulated" facilities within the Commonwealth, offers as the only alternatives, "shipment out of state" or a continuation of the "illegal midnight dumping" that has been going on for years; the results of which are now surfacing from one end of the state to the other..

Locally, we read of another fire at the hazardous waste treatment plant that was placed surreptitiously and in our opinion, illegally in Braintree. We pray that our town officials are keeping a close watch on this particular facility which was placed in one of the most densely settled areas of the town population-wise and industry wise.

The past week had begun on a marvelously festive note as on Saturday about 50 congressional and State legislators and their spouses gathered at Dunfey's in Hyannis Port to be transported to the Kennedy Compound for a most exciting day as guests of Senator "Ted" Kennedy.

We were greeted by the Senator and a host of handsome Kennedy grandchildren (from Rose's point of view); and to enjoy the exciting events he had planned for us… events that included a tour of the "President's Home", "the Ambassador's Home", with Mrs. Rose Kennedy's own home on Squaw Island, a couple of miles away. A sail down the harbor, with a band playing and the Senator circling our craft, "the Prudence', in his handsome sailboat; and a clambake were to complete the day on which, incidentally, the weatherman had certainly smiled. It was a gorgeous Fall day.

It was a memorable experience. It was like turning the pages of history as we went from room to room, particularly in the Ambassador's home whose walls were lined with literally hundreds of pictures of the Kennedy family under every circumstance imaginable…with all the rulers of the world for the past fifty years, or so it seemed…one of the fringe benefits obviously from the office that-thanks to the wonderful people of Braintree - I hold in the great and general Court.

10-16-81

The week began quite auspiciously from the point of view of your Lady of the House. We succeeded on Monday afternoon in sending to Third Reading by a vote of 91 to 61 a bill to redistribute local aid more equitably to our cities and towns. As one of the bills co-sponsors, I was elated.

Should we succeed in getting this bill signed into law, Braintree should receive an additional $756,698 which hopefully the town may be able to tuck away against next year's Prop. 2½ effects. The bill as passed would redistribute $221 Million of the total $2.1 Billion local aid figure. (Did you realize the towns received that much???) $14

Million of that money would be taken back from the 123 cities and towns that under the original distribution formula would receive more new state aid than they had lost under Prop. 2½. The 64 communities that suffered under that original formula would receive the $14 million. Under the bill additionally, no community would receive more than 100% of its Prop. 2½ losses, and no community would receive less than 30%.

In another first day event, Governor King called a meeting of his state agency heads to warn them that regardless of inflation and the costs of collective bargaining, next year's budget will have to be funded "as nearly as possible" to the 1982 budget figure of $6.3 Billion total. There are lean days ahead for State Government.

The Auto Insurance Rate hearings began in earnest before Insurance Commissioner Michael Sabbagh, who will ultimately set the rates for 1982. A proposal for turning over to the industry the responsibility for setting these rates on a competitive basis is currently being reviewed by the House Way and Means. We hear horrifying rumors of rate increases running as high as $85 per car. Among the bills signed into law by the Governor was one that will permit income to be attached in order to enforce support orders for a child or a spouse. There was no further Senate action on the Bottle Bill, which we're all watching very closely.

We passed and sent to the Senate the "campaign financing" bill. It limits contributions by special-interest groups to $2500 for candidates for state-wide offices and $1000 for those seeking other offices. Under existing law there is no limit whatsoever on the amount that may be contributed by Political Action Committees. It is therefore a large step in the right direction.

The House rejected an amendment which would have permitted taxpayers to designate $2.00 of their income tax PAYMENT for a financing fund to be used for all those seeking office. Under the law now, the $2.00 is assessed to the taxpayer and added to his tax refund if he elects to indicate his willingness to pursue this course of action when filing his state tax annually. With the State in dire straits fiscally, it did not seem like the right time to further drain the GENERAL FUND to provide up to several thousands of dollars for each of us seeking to secure public office or to hold onto an office we now hold. In the course of the House debate the procedure was referred to as "Welfare for Politicians". At any rate it failed in the House.

Locally, shall we ever in our lifetime forget the beautiful Month's Mind Memorial Mass which was offered as a gift to the Metayer family by its treasured family friend Rev. John Berube, the Pastor of St. Francis of Assisi parish in memory of our beloved grandson, Richard, who passed away a few weeks ago? Termed by the many friends who shared it with us "an unforgettable experience", it represented easily the most beautiful gift we shall ever in our lifetime receive.

The heartfelt thanks of our bereaved family go out to this cherished priest, and to all the many friends who shared in Liturgy with us and afterwards came to Father's Rectory Reception to offer their condolences and partake of the wonderful hospitality that was offered there.

As I state so many times on Beacon Hill, I represent the most beautiful people in the Commonwealth. My heart goes out to you for the hundreds of cards, notes, Spiritual Bouquets and flowers that have helped so enormously to assuage our loss; for the sympathy I receive on all sides in the supermarket and on the street and everywhere I find myself. It helps so very much to know that beautiful, caring people like the ones I represent on Beacon Hill share our grief…May God love and reward you all for your infinite kindness.

10-30-81

We had another go at the Civil Service Reform Bill when it came back to us for enactment in the House on Monday morning. An issue surfaced that had not been brought to our attention during previous debates…the inclusion of "sexual preference" in Civil Service in the "Reform" bill. And since a similar Gay Rights bill had been soundly defeated in the House earlier in the session, the inclusion of the issue in the Civil Service Reform legislation was viewed by many as being slightly on the devious side. An amendment, therefore, to exclude all reference to sexual preference was offered; and it prevailed quite handily. It is not always easy to absorb every word of an enormously long bill such as H-6500; and sometimes, as in this case, the mere inclusion of a few words in key places in the wording of a bill can bring other major change in the law that had previously been voted down by the members of the General Court.

In a day-long program dedicated to educating our law makers on the disease, Lupus Erythematosus, we learned a great deal about this disease which is of unknown cause and affects primarily women of child-bearing age; and which can cause the destruction of the skin and virtually all systems of the body. Governor King had declared the week of October 18-24 "Lupus Awareness Week", and it was shocking to learn that an estimated 20,000 people in the Commonwealth are afflicted with this disease and that many of them are not even aware of the fact. In the course of lectures provided by medical and other experts in the subject, we learned that symptoms include having a prominent rash on the cheeks for longer than a month; having one's skin break out after exposure to the sun; and having a rapid loss of hair. There are other symptoms, of course; and a copy of the screening questionnaire, along with information regarding lupus clinics, may be secured from the Lupus Foundation at 120 Tremont Street, Boston 02108. As a member of the Health care Committee, I am always interested in seeking and passing on information that can serve to safeguard my constituents' health.

We continue to express concern on the issue of controlling violent crime. It was horrifying to read during the past week in Senator Kennedy's "Report to Massachusetts" that "last year 23,044 Americans were murdered, 82,088 women were raped and 654,957 people were assaulted." In my opinion we must concentrate on preventing those guilty of violent crimes from being let out on bail to commit further crimes; and we must work toward the end that those committing violent crimes receive sentences commensurate with the category of their crimes. I find that I am still seething over the sentences handed down to those 5 rapists who admitted their guilt in the gang rape of a young woman.

12-4-81

The Tregor bill will have come before us as you read this column - a bailout bill for Boston that will allow the floating of a revenue bond issue and the creation of an excise tax on parking, hotel rooms and condominium conversions. It is indeed difficult for suburban legislators to accept one particular aspect of the bill, viz., the excise tax on parking. As it is, it costs those people who work in Boston from $5.00 to $6.00 and even higher to park their cars daily. It was, therefore, with some dismay that we learned originally that $11 Million of the required total amount was to come from that particular source. Now, however, with the elimination of the Boston Common Underground Garage and one other major Boston facility exempted from this tax, the anticipated revenue from that source has been reduced to $4 Million not too great a sum when one considers the total funding involved. We trust, therefore, that an attempt will be made to eliminate the excise tax on parking when the bill comes before us. This would make it more palatable for suburban legislators, your L. of the H. included....

There is no doubting the fact that suburbanites benefit from the city, which must be kept viable. We address this situation in countless ways annually - right now, however, through subsidies of all varieties, education reimbursements, local aid, transportation financing, etc. A classic example of indirect aid to Boston lay in the recent revelation that although the city's population has declined dramatically in recent years as well we know, Boston was permitted to use 1975 population figures in applying for its share of that $265 Million in increased local aid that was distributed to our cities and towns... Well, by the time you read this column, we should all know the fate of the Tregor Bill on Beacon Hill...

Disenchantment with the present system of sentencing criminals to "indeterminate" prison terms would be replaced with one requiring judges to set "determinate" sentences for specific crimes under a bill filed this past week by Governor Edward J. King. The bill which would go into effect in 1983 would, in addition to setting determinate sentences, requires individuals convicted of major crimes to serve ⅔ of their sentences prior to them becoming eligible for parole. Additionally, victims of their crimes would be permitted to present to the court statements on the impact of those crimes upon their lives; and those convicted of such crimes would be required to make full financial restitution to their victims.

There would appear to be considerable support within the state for this kind of "about face" in dealing with crime. Unfortunately, however, the implementation of his crime control proposal will cost money. It will add many inmates to our already overcrowded prisons; so once again the state's fiscal situation will have to enter the picture...

In House action we gave initial approval to legislation which would tighten regulations governing halfway houses for the mentally retarded...regulations that would be designed "to promote the deinstitutionalization of dependent persons in a manner consistent with the health, safety and welfare of residents" of those cities and towns where halfway houses are to be located.

It was horrifying to learn during this past week that Massachusetts has the strongest acid rain of any state in the nation. I was not surprised, however, at the findings of that National Wildlife Federation study on the subject of acid rain. It took the Metayers close to a week to restore the family pool to normal after the acid rain that fell during that historic downpour of last July 2. We were totally at a loss to understand what had happened to our normally clear and lovely pool water. It begins, they tell us, with those tall stacks of coal-burning power plants in the Ohio River Valley. Their sulfur dioxide gases are altered chemically as they travel our way to become sulfuric acids and sulfate particles when they reach our state. It's a frightening thought. It is comforting to know that by the use of coal we shall be lessening our dependence on foreign oil, however, are we to pay too great a price in other ways? How do you like this sudden cold weather? I had hoped that the good Lord planned to forget the winter season this year; guess not....

12-11-81

It's beginning to look a lot like Christmas in the capitol City. Cherry pickers are to be seen on Boston Common, stringing their holiday lights on the Common trees. There's a great shining star marking the entrance to "Downtown Crossing"; vendors are hawking their Christmas wares; and the Salvation Army bands are on the scene, their bells and kettles reminding us of those whom the greeting "Merry Christmas!" would be an empty phrase without the generosity of others.

On the Hill, the great bronze eagle that once soared above our parking lot is back again in time for the holidays; and carolers' voices are on the winds; and great scarlet poinsettias seem to be springing up hither and yon on office desks; and wreaths on doorways; and here and there a lighted Christmas tree twinkles merrily.

The past week began we thought, most appropriately for the blessed Christmas season with attendance on Sunday afternoon at the "Celebrity Fun Sunday" fundraiser for the Little Sisters of the Poor. These dedicated women are attempting to build a 27 apartment housing complex for the aged poor. My good friend Fred Galeazzo and his Braintree cohorts were in the forefront in running this happy event, and we had a great time. Hope it was financially successful…

On the Hill it was good to learn that the Boston Gas Company will comply promptly when the Governor signs our bill ordering the company to cease billing its customers for those extra cost incurred during last January's fuel emergency.

Governor Edward J. King's proposed Workfare Program is in the news. Massachusetts is one of 26 states attempting to implement their program, which has received the approval of the federal government.

The Tregor Bill continues to haunt us all. The issue has become confusing than ever with the reading of a number of recent news stories. There was, for instance the statement of Globe Columnist Ian Menzies to the effect that "Boston's Fire Department has been, per capita, the most heavily manned in the nation…62% above the cities' average". And Mayor White's statement, "I'm willing to go 85% above the city average, but not 107.5%, which is what the firemen want and what the Boston legislative delegation supports."…And then there is Police Commissioner Joseph Jordan's statement that he "needs a minimum of 1550 to 1650" and that "if all the officers fired this year are hired back, he'd have 1650 to 1700." Additionally we've the statement of Boston School Superintendent Robert R. Spillane that "Class size is not the problem…or the solution… in schools." We've faced a lot of difficult decisions of late on Beacon Hill, but this Tregor situation seems to top them all.

On voting level, it was a bitter disappointment to your L. of the H. when by a vote of 78 to 74, the so-called "Auto Insurance Reform" bill was engrossed in the House. Remembering that the insurance industry had this year sought a 25% increase in everyone's auto insurance; that the industry was granted a 7% increase; and that they took the issue to court (only to lose), it is frightening indeed to accept the fact that they will be given a free hand in determining our auto insurance rates under the proposed bill. We shall, of course, continue to fight against the bill at its enactment stage should the Senate see fit to follow the lead of the House. We shan't give up until the last gun has been fired, those of us who remember well what happened to the drivers in our communities under competitive bidding in 1977.

12-18-81

The week began with a stunning upset for the insurance industry when the Auto Insurance Bill went down to defeat in the Senate by a vote of 21 to 8. In the debate the Commercial Union Insurance Company, a British firm with a Boston subsidiary, was accused of spending $1 Million in lobbying to secure passage of the legislation. It was said that they used in their lobbying efforts a "front organization" which they named the

Coalition for Auto Insurance Reform. There's no doubt about the fact that we must have auto insurance REFORM; good drivers should not be penalized along with bad drivers; but giving the insurance industry carte blanche in setting their insurance rates did not seem to be the way to go in the opinion of many of us. Meanwhile, the state's Insurance Department is ruling that drivers who have merited surcharges will no longer have three years to pay them. Motorists with a first-time surcharge would not be penalized, but should a driver be convicted three or more times of driving under the influence, his surcharge - said to be in the amount of $657- would have to be paid in one year, as would the $150 surcharge of a driver who had been involved in and at-fault accident for the second time.

The Drug Paraphernalia bill, one of the Governor's priorities, which had passed in the House was also passed in the Senate, we're happy to report. This legislation is designed to outlaw "head shops" where drug paraphernalia has been made easily accessible to our young people.

The proposal to reduce the number of Massachusetts Congressional districts hit the Hill with all the force of a bombshell as it was learned that Democrat Barney Frank and Republican Margaret Heckler would be battling it out for the redesigned 4th District. We look for fireworks on that one in the week ahead.

Locally it was a busy week for your L. of the H. Thursday evening saw me rushing madly to Quincy after a late House session to attend the Christmas party of my good friend and colleague, Senator Paul Harold. Held at the Neighborhood Club, this was a fun time. The highlight of the evening was the "burning" (literally) of a note covering campaign borrowing from his last election.

Friday and I seemed to be moving in a whirlwind with a luncheon at noon at the home of my good friend, Ann Lyons of Quincy, where a group of Past Presidents of the Archbishop Williams H. S. Mothers Guild were to meet and to salute the Christmas season together, as is their custom. From Quincy it was off to Dorchester for the annual Christmas Party of The Boston Building Trades Council, a delightful affair that brings together labor leaders from throughout New England states.

From Dorchester it was back to Quincy where the South Shore Chamber of Commerce was hosting a Reception for my good friend, Martha Reardon. Martha, who has certainly served as one of the Chamber's spark plugs over the past several years, was sworn in at the State House on Thursday as a new Associate Commissioner of the Massachusetts Department of Public Works. What a happy and warm and loving occasion the party turned out to be as this very special lady was feted and saluted in song and story. Her farewell gifts, which were many and varied, included a PINK hardhat with D.P.W. on the front and a marvelous huge cartoon depicting Martha in the engineer's cab of a Conrail locomotive, poised on the edge of a cliff. "Madame Commissioner" was her title, plainly emblazoned on the side of this little train which was, of course, tied to the current Conrail situation we're facing on the South Shore.

The Commonwealth will certainly be the richer for the services of Martha Reardon. There is no area in the state with more transportation problems than the South Shore; and there are very few people in the state who know more about those problems than the lady whose work on transportation as the Chamber's Transportation Committee Chairman has led her to this new and challenging position with the Commonwealth of Massachusetts. We wish her enormous success; how nice it will be to have another friend at the top of Beacon Hill…

1-15-82

The week just past saw the wrap up of the 1981 session and the start of the new 1982 session of the General Court. The second year of our term of office lacks much of a ceremony of a brand new session. There is no swearing in of legislators; we are sworn in but once-at the beginning of our term. Nonetheless it was fun to have been elected as one of the committee members charged by the Speaker with notifying the Senate that the House was ready to proceed with the new year's work and to parade down the State House corridor on our official errand, and then again to have been part of the committee charged with notifying the Governor of the same fact. Here it was an added pleasure to greet David Bartley, the new Secretary of Administration and Finance and to wish him well in his new role as a sort of deputy to Governor Edward J. King.

Foremost on the minds of most of us during this past week has been, of course, the issue of dealing effectively with drunk drivers. We are all outraged by those holiday tragedies that saw innocent people wiped out by drunks at the wheel. The Governor's newly-appointed task force should have overwhelming support when it comes before the legislature with stern punitive measures for those caught driving under the influence…stern measures that by all accounts will include some time in jail with no exceptions….

We are still reeling from those auto insurance increases announced recently. What can be done about them?? We're really not sure. A sizeable group of representatives, myself included, have sent an urgent appeal for help to Attorney General Francis X. Bellotti. If you will remember, he advocated only a 7% rate increase; and in our opinion the 15% increase secured by the industry is outrageous. We shall see what, if anything, he can do.

Speaking of Attorney General Bellotti, I was delighted to read that in his opinion the Boston Gas Company and not its customers should be ordered to pay that $46.5 Million loss occasioned by last January's gas crisis. It's a consumer-oriented position and we trust that the state D.P.U. will react favorably to the excellent brief filed by Mr. Bellotti and State Energy Secretary Margaret St. Clair in defense of this stand on the issue of who should pay for utility mismanagement.

There has been a lot of action in the office of our Chief Executive these days. There was, for instance, his signing of the law that will place student members on the state's five boards of trustees- which, of course, control the state's 28 public colleges and universities. There was, his veto of the Primary Source bill and his veto of the bill to allow the sale of cars priced at $750 or less "as is". Since I had voted AGAINST both of those bills, I was delighted with his decision that they were not in the best interests of consumers.

A number of public hearings were held last month in order to receive public input on the proposed regulations on medical care. I was heavily involved in this issue last year as sponsor of a bill that among other things was designed to protect E.M.T.s who could be operating in violation of the controlled substance law by administering certain drugs in an emergency and who could also be charged with practicing medicine without a license. The bill turned out to be too comprehensive and too costly; however it served as a catalyst in making the Department of Public Health come up with the proposed regulations which among other things, seek to address those issues that have been troubling too many of our more conscientious emergency medical technicians. E.M.T.s can be mighty effective in saving lives, and we want them to have all the protection they need in handling emergency situations.

Boston's Tregor issue remains unresolved as we proceed into the 1982 session of the Great and General Court. It will undoubtedly represent our first major problem. We trust that somewhere along the way Mayor White and our Boston colleagues can come to a meeting of the minds…It's been a nightmare.

Locally it was a distinct pleasure, as always, to be able to present House Citations to four brand new Eagle Scouts from Troop 67, Boy Scouts of America which is sponsored by St. Francis of Assisi Parish. Laurence Gately, Stephen J. Climo, Stephen T. Valencia and Shawn P. White all received Scouting's highest award. We congratulate the boys, their families and those great volunteers who make scouting possible for our young men. It's a wonderful character-building program, and it is needed now like never before.

1-29-82

Our attention was centered on midweek as we gathered under the Golden Dome on Monday morning, for on Wednesday before a joint session of the House and Senate, the Governor's 1983 budget was to be unveiled. This represents the first step in the budget procedure. It will, of course, be promptly forwarded to both the House and Senate Committees on Ways and Means. Public hearings will then be scheduled, and an opportunity given to each of our state agencies to justify its budget request to the governor or to seek increased funding from either the House or Senate committee members. Incidentally, all public hearings are open to the general public whose input is also sought prior to the recommendations of either branch of the General Court. It's a long drawn out process, however a state budget must finally emerge. State government must go on....The week just past was a busy one as always. I was hard at work at the request of our Women's Caucus, seeking support for a state-wide program for "Displaced Homemakers." What precisely IS a displaced homemaker, you are undoubtedly asking. Well, it is a widow or divorcee who suddenly finds herself in the position of breadwinner for her family. She has two ways open to her-Welfare or Self-support. We who have to deal with our enormous welfare budget naturally prefer self-support. Our program is designed to make self-support possible. Since we are too late to enlist the support of Governor King for this displaced homemakers program and so we were unable to have him include its funding in his budget, we must rely on the Speaker and Senate President to include it in our versions of the budget which we shall be receiving on Wednesday. Accordingly, I spent a good part of the week lining up key people in support of our proposal...and I might add, with excellent results.

The program has been in effect for the past year at Quinsigamond Community College in Worcester and with phenomenal success. It works! It includes counseling and confidence building, along with skills and an educational aspect; and those employers whose assistance has been secured are pleased with the women who are being employed. They are becoming valuable employees.

They want to work...

Locally the week was the busiest in a long while. It began on Saturday evening with the attendance at the Wedding Reception for my good friend Elizabeth Hawes, followed by a mad dash to Canton for the Inaugural Ball of the Quincy and South Shore Board of Realtors where Braintree-ite Daniel Lauria was installed with due ceremony as this fine organization's president.

Sunday it was off to Hanson for a 75th birthday celebration for a most distinguished former Braintree-ite Clara Beard, with the occasion marked by a Citation from the House of Representatives. As the week progressed I found myself dashing home from the State House for one evening event after another. Tuesday and it was off to the Sheraton Tara for the 112th Annual Meeting of the Corporators of the Braintree Savings bank. Wednesday evening housed the first dance rehearsal for the 16 intrepid souls (myself included) who will "grace" the Braintree Historical Society's February 20th Ball with a performance of the Minuet.

Thursday evening and once again I found myself at the Tara, attending the "Legislative Buttonhole Session" of the South Shore Chamber of Commerce. I had planned to attend the Health Fair at Braintree Town Hall on Saturday morning. The weatherman wasn't too cooperative, however. The roads became increasingly hazardous as the snow descended, and so the Metayers decided that their health would be better served by remaining safely at home. The roads were in somewhat better condition on Sunday morning, we're happy to report, for it was possible for Ted and me to attend the beautiful Pro-life Mass at St. Francis of Assisi Church. This Mass, which is sponsored annually by our Braintree Knights of Columbus is a moving and memorable event, and Ted and I look forward always to participating in it.

There was one more House Citation to be presented before week's end…to my good friend Henry Galebach who retired from Armstrong's Braintree plant after 40 years of dedicated service. He's off to Florida like so many others we know, and we wish him the best of everything in his retirement.

THE COMMONWEALTH OF MASSACHUSETTS
EXECUTIVE DEPARTMENT
STATE HOUSE BOSTON 02133
EDWARD J. KING
GOVERNOR

9-1-82

Dear Elizabeth-

You are just a superb friend, so kind and helpful!

Bless you in every way always-Health, Energy and continued Love for, and interest in everything good and wholesome.

Ever grateful for your help and always willing to assist you and your people-

Best
Ed King

***

THE COMMONWEALTH OF MASSACHUSETTS
EXECUTIVE DEPARTMENT
OFFICE OF INTERGOVERMENTAL RELATIONS
STATE HOUSE BOSTON 02133
727-7238

EDWARD J. KING
GOVERNOR

GARY D. SULLIVAN
LEGISLATIVE SECRETARY

November 4, 1982

Representative Elizabeth N. Metayer

Room 446, state House
Boston MA 02133

Dear Representative Metayer:

Congratulations on your recent victory in the final election.

Your re-election means that the people in your district will benefit from two more years of responsive leadership. I am sure that it is gratifying to you to see your hard work rewarded in this manner.

My years as Governor have been the most enjoyable ones of my professional career. I have enjoyed working with you and I look forward to serving with you for the remainder of this session.

I wish you many future successes and once again want to extend my congratulations to you and your family.

Sincerely,
Edward J. King
Governor
EJK:ap

3-12-82

It was a busy, and in some respects a banner week on Beacon Hill. A conference with Chief Engineer Justin Radlo of the department of Public Works revealed the fact that the Ivory Street extension project will finally go to bid, with construction expected to begin in the Spring, and a targeted completion date of late 1983. Ivory Street will be extended from Pearl Street to Plain Street, and a series of improvements planned for the Plain, Hancock and Washington Street intersection will include a right-turn lane to accommodate northbound traffic.

I have been hounding the D.P.W. on a number of Braintree issues, and it's great to be getting results. The Elm and Commercial Street traffic signalization will also be begun shortly; we've worked very hard on that one. And the signalization at Five Corners is also being pushed to the forefront. According to Mr. Raldo, all of these problems that have plagued the people of Braintree for so long are finally to be addressed.

Additionally the dredging of the Fore River Basin is expected to begin shortly, and I opposed vehemently a Corps of Engineers' proposal to introduce all-night dredging into the schedule. Because of a number of difficulties to be encountered, such as the narrowness of the river with its inability to accommodate the dredging apparatus and the scow side by side…and the shallow depth of the river at certain points (a 15' depth with a scow that draws 14") an attempt was made to adjust the dredging hours in the interest of holding down project costs. I was appalled at the suggestion and let the Corps know definitely how I felt about their proposal. The entire project is to be completed before the end of June.

An announcement of MBTA plans to eliminate bus service to six Quincy public schools and six South Shore private schools has us most disturbed. The Sacred Heart High School, Weymouth-East Braintree is one of the six private schools targeted. Accordingly I sought out "T" Chairman James O'Leary for verification or explanation of the proposed move. I was slightly relieved to learn from him that he is meeting with the involved school principals prior to March 29 when the first of three

public hearings on the issue will be held in the Braintree Police Station. I shall definitely be there. The tempo has definitely increased in the House. The bills I have filed are being heard in a veritable flood before the appropriate committees. It has become a case of racing from one hearing room to another each morning in order to tuck in my testimony in defense of each of the bills I have sponsored.

Among those bills was one to mandate that "no recipient or vendor who shall have been CONVICTED of defrauding the department of Public welfare or the Commonwealth shall again be eligible to receive any payment from the Department of Public Welfare." Incidentally from all accounts there are as many guilty VENDORS as there are recipients in this area. In my opinion the Governor's Fraud Squad, which is doing a great job in rooting out welfare fraud, should have all possible assistance in their endeavors. My bill could at least act as a deterrent to those contemplating fraud were it to be signed into law.

Another of my bills would mandate that medical statements be made available to injured employees for use in Workman's Compensation decision appeals. Sadly enough some physicians consistently refuse to cooperate in this manner.

Another of my bills would require that any increase in compensation for members of the General Court must take effect only on January 1 following the next general election; and another bill would prohibit the Lottery Commission from being able to use slot machines. Most important of all perhaps is my bill to fix responsibility of persons releasing hazardous waste and oil into the environment. It was an unusually productive week. I was able to secure leadership support for funding the displaced homemakers program, which is perhaps the No. 1 priority of our Caucus of women Legislators.

Locally those evenings that follow my days under the Golden Dome continue to be numerous as ever. The highlight among them this week was easily my presentation of a House Resolution to my dear friends Liz and Jack Connors

3-19-82

Another busy week under the Golden Dome as the bills we filed on December 3 of last year came flooding out of the House Clerk's office and had to be defended before the appropriate committees.

Among them was my perennial "sunset legislation", a concept that was introduced when FDR was setting up agencies to deal with the great depression during which he was elected. At that time he was advised by Justice Douglas that he should include in every agency a provision to terminate that agency within ten years.

My bill would mandate a periodic review of state boards and agencies with a look at such things as whether or not they are protecting the best interests of the Commonwealth's citizens and whether they are duplicating the services of another board or agency etc. Effective agencies would be permitted to continue; ineffective ones would be terminated.

I also testified on a most important bill of mine which is designed to protect co-signers and guarantors of loans; and which had the support of Consumer Affairs Secretary Eileen Schell, the Mass. Consumers Council, the Federal Trade Commission and the Community Advocates Law Office. I succeeded in getting this bill through the House last year, however it died in Senate Third Reading. The bill limits the liability of co-signers, and requires that they be given a printed notice of their total liability as co-signers; the steps which the lender must follow before the co-signer can be held liable for the debt; and the actions a lender may take against the co-signer in recovering the debt.

Current law is clearly inadequate in protection of the co-signer, who is often a family member or a co-worker. I hope to get this bill to the Governor's desk for signing this year.

Another of my bills which came before the Taxation Committee would require the Local Aid be allocated to cities and towns according to a more equitable formula than was employed last year when Braintree received a mere 13% of its lost revenue under Prop 2½.

I was also busy testifying on a number of bills I had filed for individual constituents. We've a rather hectic schedule these days on the Hill, since, along with attending committee hearings for the purpose of testifying on our own bills, we must attend our own Committee hearings.

Additionally as the week passed a number of significant governmental happenings came to light. A statewide Cancer Registry began operation as part of the Dept. of Public Health's Division of Health Statistics and Research. Its function will be to collect information from hospitals on the frequency and types of cancer in the Commonwealth. The information will be used to identify areas of the state where cancer incidence is high and where early screening programs should be started, or investigation into possible environmental causes is warranted.

It was announced that the first Arts Lottery game had realized a profit in excess of a quarter of a million dollars. This money will be distributed this Summer to the local arts councils throughout the state to fund community arts. I was pleased to note that Braintree will receive $1,056 from this new Arts Lottery game..

As a member of the Health Care Committee I was also pleased to note that as of March 18 a law will go into effect amending that controversial 1980 law that kept confidential investigations of physicians by the Board of Registration in Medicine until the Board had come to a final decision on each case, a situation that could have taken many months or even years. Because of the wording of that original law, the Board could not under any circumstances comment on such an investigation. Now, however under the new law, such information is public record.

4-23-82

The week just past was "Water Conservation Week" in Braintree. The designation as "Water Conservation Week" had my complete approval, as does the prospect of having our Braintree school children educated on the importance of our water supply to their future and to the future of generations yet to come. It was with a great deal of pleasure, therefore, that I introduced a Resolution in the House of Representatives, commending the Town of Braintree, and the Water and School Departments, and all others responsible for this very novel idea, a Resolution which I presented to its originator Selectman Joe Cleggett.

On Beacon Hill, House sessions and committee hearings tumbled over one another as we raced to get all of our bills out of committee before the deadline date, no less than two weeks away; and by midnight on Thursday, after an all-day, late-night session, we were passing a supplementary budget and heading for home totally unaware of the nightmare that was to lie ahead with the MBTA strike on Friday morning.

Considerations of crime and criminal justice have seemed to dominate all else of late on Beacon Hill; and a host of bills designed to stiffen the penalties for drunk driving and vehicular homicide were heard before the new Criminal Justice Committee. My own bills on those crimes were to be included. Governor King also proposed his overhaul of the state's sentencing system, which would force judges to establish specific prison terms for individuals who are convicted of violent crimes. It would give prosecutors the authority to appeal sentences which they considered to be too lenient. Fixed sentences would be set for such crimes as aggravated assault, rape, arson, burglary; and an early parole would be made more difficult to obtain. Convicted criminals would be forced to serve at least ⅔ of their prison terms before being eligible for parole.

In action before our Transportation Committee, officials of the Bay Colony Transportation Company of Wareham came before us for further dialogue relative to their proposal to take over the rail freight service on the South Shore and Cape Cod. They appear to be the frontrunners in this attempt to provide the rail freight service that is shortly to be given up by Conrail.

The new "Workfare" program went into effect on Tuesday. Its intent is to reduce the welfare caseload in Massachusetts by assisting welfare recipients with children over 6, and new welfare applicants to acquire unsubsidized jobs in private industry.

According to the DPW, about 30,000 of the current 104,000 AFDC recipients will be eligible for the program. These recipients will not be obliged to accept employment at less than minimum wage; and after six weeks of unsuccessful job hunting they will be offered vocational education or high school equivalency courses or a volunteering opportunity as a means of gaining experience. We hope this Workfare program will work…

As a member of the Health Care Committee I was reminded anew of the seriousness of the current nursing shortage in Massachusetts upon learning that 80% of the nations hospitals have crucial problems in this area. Accordingly we voted favorably in committee on a bill calling for "an investigation and study by a special commission relative to the current nursing shortage in Mass." We pray that this group will come up with some innovative proposals to interest our young people in this important career.

The State House continues to be flooded with visitors. It was a special pleasure for me to greet on Thursday afternoon a number of most distinguished visitors from Egypt. They were guests of my good friend Jack Holzman, and having visited Egypt a couple of years ago I was delighted to chat with Mr. Abdel Monem Bahi EL-DIN, the country's General Director of Customs; and Mrs. Nahed Talat, Assistant Director of Traffic; and Mr. Youssef Helmy, the General Controller of Exemptions…all with the assistance of a Department of State Interpreter, Mr. Mohammed Shanin. It was such fun to happily reminisce with these distinguished individuals whom Jack and his friend Mel Montpelier, a Regional Operations Officer, accompanied on a tour of our beautiful State House. Jack Holzman is an American Customs Supervisor.

Guests continue to pour into the handsome Capitol building. During 1981 the state's Tours Division greeted 101,171 visitors, believe it or not - a 22% increase over the previous year…

5-7-82

The 1983 Budget dominated all else on Beacon Hill this past week as we members of the House (not the Senate, of course) sat day after wearying day in twelve-hour sessions during which we wrestled with the problems of state government as it is currently being affected by Prop 2½ and as it is destined to be affected by budget cuts that are on the way from Washington. A $6.86 Billion budget was to emerge finally at midnight on Friday, and we were to wind our way homeward with a feeling of elation if we had personally succeeded in funding programs that were important to us, or with a sense of disappointment if we were not so fortunate.

I was one of the lucky ones. I had succeeded in securing funding for two additional "displaced homemaker" programs - one in the western and one in the eastern part of the state. These programs represent a wonderfully economical way of getting new divorcees or widows into the workforce rather than on the welfare rolls. The one program we funded last year produced a fantastic number of success stories; and I was able to convince Speaker McGee and Ways and Means Chairman Creedon that the funding I was seeking would bring great and immediate returns. Additionally, I secured funding for a DES educational and screening program for those mothers for whom diethylstilbestrol was prescribed during pregnancy. This drug, which was widely prescribed by physicians during the later forties and early fifties, has been found to cause a form of cancer in the mothers and in their offspring. The cancer is treatable with early detection, but we must get the word out and see to it that those who are potentially menaced seek diagnostic evaluations if their physician detects any abnormalities.

And last but by no means least - I successfully introduced an amendment that was to result in securing an additional $3 Million in regional School Aid. Part of this money goes to our Vocational Education institutions, and I am their advocate in the House. I was, therefore, delighted to secure the additional $3 Million, and I am now working on having that amount increased in the Senate when the 1983 State Budget comes before them, hopefully within the next week or two.

This has been a wonderfully successful year for your L. of the H. The Monatiquot River is to be dredged; the Five Corners Signalization is under way; I have secured a favorable committee report on my Volunteerism Bill, both for the very first time; and now I have been successful with each one of my budgetary concerns for 1983. Additionally and most important- under the state budget we have just voted to adopt, Braintree will receive an additional $1,461,161 in local aid, which should solve most of the problems the Town will be facing in dealing with Prop 2½. There was another plus for our elderly citizens…our "super Citizens" as I call them…We voted additional real estate tax exemptions for them, and we shall lobby hard to keep these exemptions in the Senate version of the budget.

Extra curricular activities I was able to enjoy during the first part of the week (before we commenced those twelve-hour sessions and faced a "lock-in" situation in the House Chamber) included attendance as a Health Care Committee member at the Boston University School of Medicine. Legislators Luncheon on Tuesday noon; and at the meeting of the Hospital Auxiliaries volunteers at the State House on Wednesday.

Despite a budget session that had ended at midnight on Wednesday, I was on hand bright and early on Thursday morning at St. Thomas More Church as a participant in a marvelous Seminar that was sponsored by St. Colleta's day School. Our subject was "For the retarded after age 22, what then???" A strange and indeed a sad situation now faces those parents who elected to keep their retarded children at home rather than to institutionalize them. Under the court's Consent Decrees, and in connection with the state's Deinsitutional Program, those retarded citizens who were in our state's institutions and are in community residences now must be provided with educational and other programs for the remainder of their lives. They, and those judged "at risk" are therefore, being given priority in attending any and all existing programs as well as any new programs. The result is, of course, that those tax payers who have not cost the state anything for caring for their retarded children are being penalized. It represents a situation that must be addressed and we shall try to help. The bottom line is, of course, MONEY, but we shall work on it...

Saturday evening and it was off to the Sheraton-Regal in Hyannis where I was guest Speaker at the annual Convention Dinner of the Mass. Vocational Education Association. It was quite a week on Beacon Hill for your L. of the H.

5-14-82

Spring has come officially to Beacon Hill. The Japanese cherry trees are in full and beautiful bloom. We enter the Capitol building these days under an archway of purest Rose, the color lying like a poem against the gray of the old stone walkways and the wide stone steps. Another week, and the petals will commence to fall. They'll float above us in the soft Spring breeze, and lie in pale pink pools upon the gray. They'll be carried down Park Street upon the playful winds; and they'll be whispering to all who come their way that Spring has come officially to Beacon Hill...

There are other signs, of course. The flower vendors display their wares to passersby; and the street musicians are back. It's a happy place to be now that Spring is here, and Summer is not far behind.

The week under the Golden Dome was a busy and happy one. With the 1983 State Budget temporarily out of the House, our minds turned to other legislative doings.

Law Day 25 was held on Tuesday morning at Quincy District Court, and for one who has the honor of representing Braintree in the General Court it was a proud happening indeed. To begin with, my good friend Rose Mary Kirwin, President of D.O.V.E. (Domestic Violence Ended) was on hand to accept the South Shore Chamber of Commerce Award for the area's "Outstanding Community Organization." Then there was Braintree Patrolman Gary Connell receiving a plaque for having rescued two people from a burning building; and finally Braintree businessman Gerald M. Ridge doing likewise for his consistent support of the "Earn It Program", and being designated a "Special Citizens" for his civic involvement.

And finally, of course, it was great to see my good friend Arthur Tobin in his new role as Clerk-Magistrate of this prestigious court.

Wednesday, and a very busy legislative day had to be arranged so as to include attendance at the "Endangered Species Day" observance in the State House; and come evening, at the 9th Annual Meeting of the Construction Industries of Mass. as a guest of Mr. J. Barry Driscoll of Reynolds Bros. Inc. Thursday and a mad dash from the State House at 2 p.m. brought me to 376 Boylston Street for an Open house sponsored by the Mass. Nurses Assoc. in celebration of National Nurses Recognition Day.

Saturday evening, and it was off to Sons of Italy Hall for the Joint Installation of Officers of Braintree Ladies Lodge No. 1422 and Braintree Mens Lodge No. 760, Order Sons of Italy in America. It was a special pleasure for me to present a House Citation to my good friend, the outgoing Venerable Joanne Pistorino; and to wish Venerables Fred Leo and Margaret Pettricelli success and happiness during the terms that now lie ahead for them.

Sunday afternoon and it was off to Town Hall to participate in the Second Annual John Scott Nursing Home Kickoff Parade for National Nursing Home Week. A huge and exciting parade that drew a huge crowd despite the fact that it was Mothers Day. And incidentally we hope that Mothers everywhere had a great time on this, their special day…

Additionally there were House Citations for 96 year old Abbie Whitehouse, a Woodward School for Girls graduate and the eldest lady in Resthaven Nursing Home; and for 90 year old Louis Blum, the father of my good friend Ruth Collins. Two remarkable individuals who easily bear out the philosophic statement that age is a state of mind.

Legislatively, it was a week for tracking down and seeking to spring all the important bills that had lost the limelight to the state budget during the past two weeks; and so the hunting of the House Clerk and the Chairman of Ways and Means and Third Reading were definitely in order. And, of course, following into the Senate the course of the budget funding I had been successful in securing for my displaced homemaker Program, My DES Program and my Regional School Aid… "battening down the hatches', so to speak, lest we lose any of it as the Senate deliberations on the 1983 State Budget follow our own. Their budget, incidentally, could reach the Senate Chamber for debate the first of next week. It's great to know that we shall have no budget crisis this year. Unpaid state employees and unpaid welfare recipients can be difficult to deal with, and we can well understand why. All in all, it was a busy week on Beacon Hill, and a most productive one, we thought…

THE BRAINTREE STAR MAY 28, 1982

SMALL CLAIMS LAW REVISED

Legislation that increases from $750 to $1,200 the recovery limit for damages in small claims courts was signed into law recently by Gov. Edward J. King, Rep. Elizabeth N. Metayer reports. According to Mrs. Metayer the increases are necessitated by the increased costs of goods and services that have come about as a result of inflation. "People were finding themselves priced out of the small claims court," she said. "This avenue of redress must be kept open for the average citizens with a claim that may be small by comparison but represents a considerable investment for him or her."

THE BRAINTREE STAR MAY 28, 1982

ELDERLY CARE CHANGES RECOMMENDED

Legislation changing the MBTA fare system for the elderly has been reported favorably by the Committee on Transportation, reports Representative Elizabeth N. Metayer, a committee member and bill supporter.

The bill directs the MBTA to collect a ten cent cash fare from persons aged 65 years and over who possess an MBTA identification card. It puts an end to the system of charging full fare during peak travel hours and providing free service at off-peak times.

"This legislation recognizes the desire of the elderly to contribute as individuals to their mass transit service and eliminates the confusion surrounding peak and off-peak hours," according to representative Metayer. "It has the support of the Silver-Haired Legislature and of local associations of retired people. Since the MBTA does not project a decrease in revenues as a result of this bill, its passage is most likely."

THE BRAINTREE STAR MAY 28, 1982

DENTAL SERVICE FOR ELDERLY

Representative Elizabeth N. Metayer wishes to inform her constituents of the development of the Mass. Dental Society of a program of comprehensive dental care for financially disadvantaged elderly persons.

According to Mrs. Metayer the dental service will include cleanings, fillings, extractions, partial dentures, root canal and gum treatments.

The reduction in dental fees will be made available to elderly persons who are not on Medicaid or public assistance, are without dental insurance, and can meet the requirements of the Mass. Dental Society's "Consumer Full Denture Access Program."

Information on these requirements and on the program in general can be obtained by calling the toll-free number 1-800-342-8747 between the hours of 9:30 a. m. and 3 p.m. weekdays.

5-21-82

Business goes on as usual on Beacon Hill. In the back of the minds of most of us, however is the fact that the Senate Committee on Ways and Means is dealing with that 1983 State Budget we sent their way a couple of weeks ago. As individuals, we have items on that budget that must be protected; consequently, many little treks to the other branch punctuate our days. An increase in real estate tax exemption for our elderly, our widows and our veterans was included in the House budget; we certainly hope to see that increase retained in the Senate version as well.

The so-called Tregor Bill managed finally to find its way through the General Court and head for the Governor's desk. He has said he will veto it; and should he do so, it is doubtful if the required ⅔ vote to override can be secured either in the House or the Senate. We shall see, however…

The bill's final passage came about as we considered an alternative proposal to have the state purchase Boston's Hynes Auditorium and run it under a State Authority. The idea was decidedly not palatable to lawmakers disillusioned with the performance of the MBTA. At any rate, the fate of the Boston Bailout bill as it is called, now rests with the Governor.

Many of us have grave concerns about the 15% parking excise tax in the bill. In that context. we were pleased to note that a new commuter service is being made available for routes into. Boston. Caravan, which is a private non-profit Vanpool Corporation has announced a concentrated. campaign to coordinate commuters with their destinations in the Boston area.

Since it inception in 1979, Caravan has assisted individuals and employers in organizing 85 vanpools, serving more than 1300 Massachusetts riders. Now the organization has turned its resources to assist workers who drive into Boston daily. It will match commuters with vanpools that are being organized in the area. The Caravan staff will assist individuals in organizing a group. It will lease the group a van on a monthly basis and administer the program. It sounds like a great alternative for those among us who battle the Southeast Expressway on an individual basis each morning. It will also help on that 15% parking tax increase. Information about what is being called the "Boston Project" or any other Caravan route may be secured by contacting the Caravan office at 742-2655.

A Constitutional Convention which was called on Wednesday was adjourned abruptly via a series of parliamentary maneuverings on the part of Senator Jack Bachman. Reportedly he opposes capital punishment vehemently and took this means of avoiding a vote on the issue. Senate President William Bulger was in the chair. The Senate President always presides over a ConCon. We shall reconvene on June 12, when it is hoped we shall have an opportunity to vote on the capital punishment issue as well as the tax control issue on which Massachusetts residents secured the necessary signatures and on a number of other important issues that we must face in order to settle the question of whether or not they should appear on the ballot in the Fall.

It was interesting to note that a report issued by the Executive Office of Public Safety indicated a drop in serious crimes in Massachusetts last year with 300,487 cases in 1981 as compared with 329,308 serious crimes in 1980. Is this new trend toward placing criminals behind bars beginning to pay off??? We hope so.

Incidentally of the 198 homicides reported during 1981, 64 were by handgun, 16 by rifle-shotgun, 59 by knife, 20 by hands, fist or feet, 23 by other dangerous weapons and 16 by unknown weapons; 64 murders were related to a criminal act, 34 were committed during a domestic-type situation, 66 in civil situations and 34 in circumstances unknown.

Those among us who support presumptive sentencing and have been filing legislation to that effect for a number of years (of which your L. of the H. is definitely one) endorse Governor King's attempts to place criminals behind bars. He has joined us in our efforts, and we begin to see a ray of hope, especially as we read the crime statistics reported above.

There were the usual extra-curricular activities for your L. of the H. I had the privilege of appearing as Guest Speaker at the Braintree Catholic Women's Club on Wednesday evening; was on hand early on Thursday morning for a picture-taking session in connection with the insulation program currently underway at Heritage Lane; on Friday evening at the East Braintree Little League Dance at Elks Hall in Weymouth; on Sunday evening at the Joint Installation of Officers of Braintree Post No. 1702, V.F.W. and their Ladies Auxiliary, all of which took place in the newly-decorated Veterans Memorial Building that fell victim to such a disastrous fire less than a year ago, but has emerged more beautiful than ever- thanks to the generosity of the townspeople and the hard work of those amazing and indefatigable V.F.W. members. It was a distinct pleasure for me to present House Citations to the outgoing VFW. Commander William H. Colligan and to the Ladies Auxiliary President Gail Madera. What a pair of dynamos!

6-4-82

Another week without the appearance of the Senate version of the 1983 State Budget! We understand that the Ways and Means Committee of the other branch is having problems with it. We would hope that those problems are not so insurmountable as to bring about payless paydays for state workers and a cessation of checks for the state's welfare recipients - a situation that has occurred too many times in recent years. We in the House had hoped to avoid the nightmare of dealing early on with the 1983 state budget. Well, perhaps the week that lies ahead as I write this column will see the emergence of this vitally important piece of state government. We hope so…We Norfolk County legislators spent several hours on Tuesday and Wednesday of the past week dealing with the matter of whether or not to support a supplementary budget of close to ¾ million dollars for Norfolk County Hospital. The hospital's administration is being challenged to explain the unpaid bill situation that recently surfaced, and we legislators are naturally extremely concerned about this issue. We voted on Tuesday to have an independent audit done immediately. Meanwhile, of course, the proposal to sell Norfolk County Hospital and "get the County out of the hospital business" keeps surfacing. It is a most disturbing situation as the facility in question is an excellent one…one that renders respiratory care that to the best of my knowledge is being offered nowhere else in the Commonwealth.

I participated on Wednesday in a press conference to announce the beginning of the Department of Public Health's public education campaign on DES, which is short for Diethylstilbestrol, that dangerous drug that was given to an estimated 150,000 pregnant Massachusetts women during the forties and fifties and in some cases even beyond those years. Some of the mothers to whom the drug was given and their offspring - male and female are threatened with the abnormalities that could affect their reproductive processes, and even in some cases, with a form of cancer that is treatable with early detection. The campaign is designed to alert the mothers and their offspring to the potential menace they face and provide the necessary diagnostic evaluation clinics for those whose gynecologists find abnormalities or difficulties. The media will be used to alert DES individuals. It will also be used in conjunction with the Department of Public Health to alert physicians to the potential menace that faces those to whom the drug was administered so widely, especially in the forties, as a means of preventing miscarriages and of assuring an easier pregnancy. It has since been determined that the drug was of no real value at all in dealing with problem pregnancies, and a court case is currently underway against the drug's manufacturers.

Thursday morning and it was off to the Lantana for the South Shore Chamber of Commerce's 7:44 Breakfast where State Secretary of Transportation James Carlin discussed at length the transportation problems of the South Shore and asked for the Chamber's help in addressing them.

Saturday evening, and I was on hand at the Sheraton Tara to present two House Resolutions at the St. Coletta day School's Silver Anniversary Gala Ball - one to the school itself in observance of the occasion and in recognition of its tremendous contribution to the wellbeing of our handicapped young people and another to Sister M. Johnice Flanagan, its retiring Principal, whose inspiration and dedication have been responsible to such a very large extent for the outstanding record of accomplishment that was being highlighted on that very festive evening. And a festive evening it was, with Sister Johnice the Guest of Honor and Dr. Tom O'Connor the Master of Ceremonies - and the most exciting entertainment we've enjoyed in a very long while.

Sunday and I was on hand as always for the Annual Memorial Day Observance when we look back lovingly and gratefully upon those veterans whose blood was shed in defense of our freedom and extend our gratitude to those who survived the horrors of war and are standing with us in tribute to their fallen comrades. My good friend Don Laing was the featured speaker, and as always his remarks were appropriate and moving

7-2-82

The week just past began with the proverbial bang on Monday. Colonel Richard Cator, the newly appointed Post commander of Fort Devens was introduced in the House Chamber where he reported on the state of the Army in New England. His report of the training program currently handling 60,000 recruits was most encouraging. "The soldier of today is every bit as capable and well trained as the soldiers anywhere else in the world." He said. "We don't man equipment; we equip man…and that is why others hesitate to take us on." One received the distinct impression that this man would develop pride in their Army in the young men and women entrusted to his care. The Colonel left the Chamber, and the Constitutional Convention was immediately convened. We began debate on the first item on the Convention calendar - "a proposal for legislative amendment to the Constitution permitting the Commonwealth or its political subdivisions to extend aid to non-public school students within the limits of the United States Constitution." The proposal which would merely put Massachusetts laws on such aid in one with federal laws, passed on a roll call vote of 144 to 4. Since this proposal was approved during the 1980 Constitutional Convention as well, it will appear as a referendum on the November ballot. The vote, therefore, will of course merely serve to provide an opportunity to decide on whether or not to make the constitutional change.

With state aid to nonpublic schools out of the way, our attention went next to "an Initiative Amendment to the Constitution relative to limiting state and local taxation." The decision to address this question was put off until Monday however, since there appeared to be problems with a recent court decision involving a number of issues, including the size of the required vote, namely a majority vote versus a 50 member vote.

Capital punishment was next in line, and at 12:30 a.m. on Tuesday morning a final vote was taken with 145 legislators voting in favor and 62 against. And so the issue of whether or not to reinstate capital punishment will also go to voters for determination.

It was cool and beautiful as I arrived back home in Braintree in the early morning hours. The streets were deserted; and as I drove through the sleeping town I smiled to myself as I thought of those who term ours a "part-time job…"

Tuesday, we addressed the Conference Committee version of the 1983 State Budget. An anything but controversial issue this year, it was voted to accept it in the House with but 14 dissenting votes. Braintree fares beautifully under the Local Aid section of this 1983 budget. We shall be receiving an additional $1,461,160 over last year's local aid figure. $57,580 of this amount will come from the state lottery.

It was to be a week for addressing knotty problems. The Tregor Bill was next in line to be debated Wednesday, and again on Thursday until 4:00 a.m. on Friday morning. Dawn was breaking as I drove home on that truly beautiful morn, the Tregor bill having been voted affirmatively. I opened the car windows to admit the cooling breezes; and I delighted in the sleeping world about me. Tregor was at last behind us, I told myself happily. That thorny issue that had plagued the General Court for more than a year was to be laid to rest. No difficulty now was expected in Senate where after a mere two hours of debate the vote was 32 to 1. House debate had been long and acrimonious, but the issue had easily received the required ⅔ vote at debate's end. There were a couple of differences in the two versions, and so a Conference Committe had to be appointed, but the final compromise version passed as easily. What a shock it was to learn from Saturday's newspaper, therefore, that "a language change" would be necessary, and that we shall all have to enact the Tregor Bill one more time....

Locally the highlight of the week was easily the 25th Anniversary observance of the founding of our Braintree Senior Citizens, where I was pleased to present a House resolution tracing the history of this prestigious organization. Saturday morning and we had our annual South Braintree Board of Trade Sidewalk Sale, which was fun to attend; and on Sunday morning there was the annual Knights of Columbus Pancake Breakfast.

An eventful week and a fun weekend!

7-9-82

It was a week for late night sessions and it ended with a bang at 4:00 a.m. Friday morning as we adjourned to enjoy our Independence Day holiday with the rest of you. It was perhaps the first time in my 8 years as your representative that I was not in the State House on the night before the 4th. We are usually struggling to pass the annual State Budget at the last minute and so to prevent state government from coming to a halt. This year the State Budget process went smoothly for a change. There were but minor differences between the House and Senate versions, and these were easily ironed out by the Conference Committee. So - what were we doing during those hectic days and nights this past week??? Well, primarily we were dealing with bills that were particularly important to legislators...bills that had languished in Third Reading while their constitutionality was being checked, or in Ways and Means while it was determined whether or not the state could afford them.

On the controversial issues we were facing, most of the lobbying and soul searching had already been done by the time we were ready for debating them, and so it was a matter of following the complicated step-by-step process that leads to the Governor's desk.

At any rate the week ended on a happy note for most of us. Some of our problems still lie ahead, but many of them have been comfortably solved, and that is always good news.

It was great news also to learn that as of Thursday of this past week, strict hazardous waste regulations went into effect in the State. As of October, a computerized manifest system will be mandated for all companies that generate in excess of approximately one ton of waste per month. Generators of smaller amounts (between 20 and 100 kilograms monthly) will have a little more time. They will be required, however to file the mandated "cradle and grave" manifests by December 1. The company and the transporter must report to the state's Environmental Quality Engineering Department the amount and the type of hazardous material being removed. A report of the waste disposal will also be required. Our State regulations are far more stringent than the federal regulations, a fact for which I am personally grateful.

To date the drunken driving bill has failed to reach the Governor's desk. There is strong disagreement as to the use of mandatory or presumptive sentencing for those convicted of two or more violations. Although I shall certainly vote for the bill if it winds up with mandatory sentencing, I would personally prefer the presumptive sentencing approach. I have filed presumptive sentencing bills for the past several years.

Part of the lawmakers' reluctance on this issue lies with the fact that we have no place to put the offenders. With tougher sentences being handed out of late, our jails are filled to overflowing. On one thing we are all agreed, however. Too often the criminals serve far less than their minimum terms, and are back on the streets looking for more victims. The Hinckley case has focused additional attention on the issue at the State House as elsewhere, needless to say. As many of us see it, the verdict on that case represents an open invitation for any kook to go after any public official, and especially are our world leaders in additional danger as a result of it. I was personally especially outraged when reading of the newspaper interviews this criminal had managed to secure from the media that frequently neglects to cover fine individuals and their stories. Well, you may rest assured that the drunken driving issue anyhow will be faced in the not too distant future. Too many of us, myself included, had filed tough bills dealing with this furor over it.

I hope you all had a safe and sane 4th of July. I had a wonderful one. As a special guest of the Mass. Bay Yacht Clubs association, I was privileged to watch the turnaround of the U.S.S. Constitution from the pavilion at Anthony's Pier 4. and what a sight it was to see this grand old lady ride the waves amid the cheers of thousands and the salutes from the small ornamental cannon that was manned on our own particular ramparts by the "Cannoneer," no less, of the Yacht Clubs organization. A tour afterwards of the U.S.S. Yellowstone, the wonderful destroyer tender that lay close by; and another "Glorious Fourth" came to an end…a red, white and blue letter day, as always, for all Americans everywhere.

JULY 16, 1982

Although, according to the media, we in the General Court are on vacation during this month of July, one would not have known it had one visited the State House last week. Many of us were hard at work, on special summer committee assignments, work for our constituents and for our communities.

I was pleased to receive notes of thanks from several quarters for those two new Department of Public Works signs I was able to procure indicating the Washington Street exit from the Southeast Expressway; one on Route 3 Southbound and one on Route 128 Southbound. The DPW was prompt in handling my request for those vitally needed signs, and I was deeply appreciative of their response. I had heard from several townspeople who were experiencing great difficulty in negotiating the turnoff, especially at night. They tell me the signs work beautifully. They and I are pleased…

It is always a pleasure to remind out Senior Citizens (Super Citizens, I call them) of special services that are available to them from our state agencies. Among these services is the free notarization. of documents that is offered by staff member of the Secretary of State in the State House and in the McCormack Building in Boston, and at SOS in W. Springfield. Information on issues including retirement laws, pension plans, elderly property tax abatements, etc. is also being provided by calling the Citizen Information Service in Boston at 727-7030 or in Springfield at 1-800-393-6090. With our Seniors in mind, during this past week I checked on the contributions to their welfare that have been made by the Secretariat of Elder Affairs since its inception in 1973. It has certainly come a long way in the past decade. In the area of Home Care, for instance, a service which keeps people in their own homes and out of the more costly nursing homes, the appropriation has gone from zero in 1973 to a 1983 state budget figure of $71,694,866.00. The Elder Service Corps budget has risen from zero in 1973 to $791,540; the Councils on Aging Budget from $27,5000 in 1973 to $2,140,000.00. We're pleased to be able to report that the State of Massachusetts is treating its super citizens well.

We in the House are eagerly awaiting the arrival of a Senate-passed bill which is claimed by its sponsors to result in lower automobile insurance premiums for those drivers who have accident-free and violation-free driving records. Drivers whose records include repeated accidents, traffic violations and claims would have to pay surcharges. Bad drivers will also have difficulty, and will pay higher premiums, for such optional insurance as collision and fire and theft coverage. The bill repeals the present competitive rating law; the state insurance commissioner would continue to establish insurance rates for the Commonwealth's drivers.

It was good to learn that the Bay State Skills Corporation will shortly administer a $2 million job-training program geared to providing Massachusetts residents with skills for employment in the private sector. The program will be geared to unemployed 16 to 21 year olds, primarily from urban areas.

During the week ahead I shall be accompanying our town officials in appearing before the Committee on Public Service, testifying on two of the four bills we filed a couple of weeks back as a result of Town Meeting action. One bill would place the maintenance personnel of the Braintree School Department under the civil service law; the other would exempt from the civil service law the positions of Sealer and Deputy Sealer of Weights and Measures and Inspector and Deputy Inspector of Plumbing.

Current holders of these positions would be grandfathered in and retain their civil service status, of course…

Additionally during the coming week I shall be meeting with town officials, representatives of the state's DPW and several citizens from the River Street Bridge area who feel they have been aggrieved over situations that have resulted from the bridge replacement a couple of years back. I shall also be addressing the issue of a proposed expansion at Recycling Industries, a firm that is highly detrimental to the people of East Braintree in its present form, pays no taxes to the town since it rents its building from the Cities Service Oil Company, and in my opinion should not be allowed to expand in any sense of the word.

Hasn't the month of July been gorgeous to date? It almost makes one forget the month of June…Warm days and cool nights the norm…Who could ask for more????

JULY 23, 1982

A sweltering week on Beacon Hill as elsewhere…It began on Monday morning with an appearance before the Public Service Committee in defense of a couple of bills I had filed as a result of our recent Town Meeting action. House Bill 6534 would assure the civil service status of a number of maintenance employees in the Braintree public school system; and House Bill 6535 was filed to assure the exemption from civil service of the town's Sealer and Assistant Sealer of Weight and Measures, and our Inspector and Assistant Inspector of Plumbing. I was joined at the hearing by Bob Sherman and Bob Frazier, as well as two of the maintenance employees involved; and with the addition of a couple of minor amendments proposed by the Committee, the bills should have no difficulty in reaching the Governor's desk for signing. […]

Friday afternoon and I joined a number of our aggrieved residents in seeking a solution to the problems that have arisen in the wake of the River Street Bridge rebuilding project. On hand for the meeting were local and state officials including Bob Sherman, Jack Fehan and DPW project engineer Horace DelGrosso. It's a complicated situation since the town engaged the engineering firm that produced the project design; and the contractor who handled the job has gone bankrupt. In the several layoff sprees involving state workers, (primarily to provide more local aid to cities and towns), the DPW has lost 12000 employees. It is therefore difficult for them to provide manpower to deal with the repair of the riprap and fencing that, with the help of vandals, has fallen into the river, eroding the protecting bankings and cutting into the properties of the Pilgrim Center and the Nehiley family home particularly. Complaints that surfaced also […] to our good Highway Superintendent Bob Frazier, to see what in his opinion the town can do to alleviate the situation. We shall, needless to say, follow up on the issue, and we hope with those involved that somehow or other what is not only an eyesore but a source of danger as well, can be eventually remedied. Under the Golden Dome our efforts were directed principally toward seeing to it that those bills in which we have an interest…bills that managed to get to the Governor's desk…are signed into law by Governor Edward J. King. We were also directing our energies toward attempting to secure MDC summer employment for the five young Braintree men and women whose applications were filed in a timely manner and approved with our endorsement. I was appalled to learn that their failure to hear from the State was due to the fact that the money had run out. From what we have heard, it would appear that inner city kids were hired first. I have been assured, however, that another $500.000 will be sought from the Governor, and that if it is secured our kids will be among the first to be called. We hope so; and we'll certainly keep in touch with the "powers that be" on this one…

AUGUST 13, 1982

The Constitutional Convention was called to order on Monday afternoon as scheduled. It was to deal with but one agenda item, "An Initiative Amendment to the Constitution relative to limiting state and local taxation." It had been voted affirmatively at the last Constitutional Convention, which meant that should it receive a second affirmative vote, the issue would come before the voters of the Commonwealth as a referendum question.

There were pros and cons on the issue, which was one with potentially far-reaching consequences; and I found myself listening intently to the debate and trying hard to sort out in my mind the ramifications of all ten pages of the tax limitation proposal. It was complicated; it would be difficult to deal with; it wasn't the best piece of legislation I'd seen of late. Nonetheless, 60,000 of the Commonwealth's citizens had signed that petition to place tax limitation on the ballot as a referendum question. After considerable soul searching, I voted for it. It lost, however, by a vote of 78 to 111.

Strangely enough, several of the features encompassed in the "Cohen Amendment" as it has been called, were lifted from a tax limitation bill I had filed, along with Representatives Syd Conway and Bob Teahan a few years back. At any rate, the Con Com rejected the Cohen Amendment, and I am certain we shall be dealing with this issue again next year.

Tuesday and we faced the long awaited "Drunk Driving Bill." It received a unanimous vote, but only after hours of debate. On this issue I was reminded by my good friend Paul McDevitt that the issue of dealing with alcoholism dates all the way back to the year 1300 BC when the Hammurabi Code in Babylonia dealt, among other things, with the hours of operation of drinking establishments and the control of alcohol abuse.

Under House Bill 6621 penalties are increased. First offenders who have not been involved in an accident causing personal injury or death will be assigned to an ASAP (residential alcohol treatment facility) program at a cost of $400, and will lose a license to drive for thirty days.

An ineligible first offender will suffer a year's loss of license and be subject to fines of up to $1,000 and imprisonment up to two years.

A second offender will lose his license for two years, with a minimum mandatory incarceration/confinement for seven days.

For a third offender the loss of license will be for five years, with a mandatory jail sentence of sixty days.

The penalty for drunk driving after a license revocation will be a minimum of seven days. incarceration and the loss of a license for five years.

Vehicular homicide while under the influence will result in a fine of up to $5,000, imprisonment for not less than one year and not more than ten years and a ten-year license loss.

We hoped that this new law would be signed speedily by Governor Edward J. King as it sped through both branches of the Legislature to reach his desk in record time. We also hoped as we voted unanimously for it that it would make a sizeable dent in the number of drunk driving cases within the state.

Incidentally, an amendment mandating a one o'clock closing for liquor establishments went down to defeat along the way. Since Braintree now has a twelve midnight closing hour I was along those voting against it. I did not relish the thought of having a wave of one a.m. closing applications flooding the Selectmen's office.

The Hospital Cost Control Bill, S-2033, was engrossed in the House after considerable debate. It would appear to be acceptable to all parties concerned in its revised form…including those hospitals to stay within a rate of expenditures which is determined in advance…a step in the right direction obviously…

If the hospital remains below the pre-determined rate, it can keep the difference; if it exceeds the rate, it must itself absorb the loss.

A "productivity factor" will hold the rate of hospital expenditures at 7.5% of the rate of inflation for the next six years. The bill includes a 1983 reduction by 1.4% in the differential between what Blue Cross pays hospitals and other health insurers pay. "Financial hardship" hospitals will be provided with protection, and a more equitable approach to sharing the costs of "free care" is included. The legislation will take effect only if we receive from the federal government a Medicare waiver which will permit Medicare to participate in the new system of payments.

Tuesday turned out to be a long legislative day indeed. It was 4:30 a.m. when I drove over the Southeast Expressway enroute to Braintree on a lovely Wednesday morning with the sky bright and shining above me…

SEPTEMBER 20, 1982

Since we are in informal sessions these days in the General Court, with only non-controversial routine matters coming before the House, it seemed like a good time to focus on that beautiful State Capitol of ours, in the hope that more of my readers will take the time to explore its beauty.

The Bulfinch front of the Massachusetts State House dates back to 1798. As we now have it, it lacks only the original chimneys and side entrances which were removed in the mid-1880's. the dome also differs slightly in that it was originally coppered by Paul Revere in 1802; however, some seventy years later it was gilded with 23-carat gold leaf. During the Second World War it was painted black for protective reasons; and the gold leaf was restored in 1969 at a cost of $36,000. We wonder what it would cost in today's gold market...

Most of the wood used in the original bullfinch front came from Maine, which was a part of Massachusetts until 1820; and that pinecone at the top of the cupola above the dome symbolizes the importance of the lumber industry to the early New England economy.

Between 1889 and 1895 a large yellow brick extension was added to the back of the Bulfinch State House; and in 1917 two white marble wings were added to the east and west of the Capitol building.

The elegant interior of the State House makes extensive use of marble, wrought iron and carved wood paneling. It's a magnificent building indeed....

One enters the Capitol building at Doric Hall, named from the architectural style of its ten columns. These columns were originally carved from pine tree trunks with the work done on the front lawn of the building itself. Today's replacements columns are fashioned of practical iron and plaster. One climbs a fight of stairs at the end of Doric Hall to enter Nurses Hall, which features an imposing statue of an Army war nurse. Sculpted in 1914 by Bela Pratt, it was the first statue erected in honor of the women of the North after the Civil War. A series of murals depicting events crucial to the start of the American Revolution adorns the walls, with the central panel portraying the fiery orator James Otis pictured as he argues against the Writs of Assistance, the true beginning of the colonists' break with England.

One next enters the Hall of Flags. Here can be seen the original flags that had been given by Governor Andrew as the Massachusetts companies departed to fight in the Civil War, as well as flags that have been returned after duty in every war since then including the Spanish-American War, World Wars I and II, the Korean War, the Berlin emergency and the Vietnam War...over 300 of them in all. High above, in the stained glass skylight, can be seen the seals of the original thirteen colonies of the United States, with the Massachusetts seal in the center.

And so we come to the Chamber of the House of Representatives...Massachusetts became a Commonwealth in 1780 when it adopted its remarkable Constitution. It included a groundbreaking Declaration of Rights, and was a model for the Constitution of the United States. The oldest written constitution in effect in the world today, it has been amended more than 100 times. The room is paneled magnificently in Honduras mahogany. A series of five paintings by Albert Herter depict "Milestones on the Road to Freedom"; and it is significant that of the five murals, three contain the figures of Braintree men-a fact which I invariably point out to the Braintree children who visit our beautiful building.

The Senate Chamber lies directly below the gold dome. Its sunburst ceiling contains emblems symbolizing commerce, agriculture, war and peace. It was in this chamber that Angelina Grimke made political history when, in 1838, she gave a speech advocating the abolition of slavery. It was the first time that a woman had addressed a United States legislative body, and contrary to expectations she was rewarded with a standing ovation....

In the Governor's private waiting room can be found the portraits of the those who have preceded him in that high office; and in the Governor's office itself can be found stucco ornaments symbolizing the arts, liberty, justice and the executive powers. The gentleman in this corner office may select the portrait of a predecessor to be hung over the Connemara marble fireplace behind his desk. Governor Edward J. King has selected John Adams, a fact which delights your L. of the H. who occupies the seat of the illustrious American president in the House of Representatives, representing even as he did the people of Braintree.

It's a magnificent building, our Massachusetts State House. How I wish every resident of Braintree would have the pleasure of visiting it....

SEPTEMBER 17, 1982

By the time you read this column, the Massachusetts Primary election will be behind us. The hard-fought election will be over. Edward J. King will have been re-elected, or Mike Dukakis will be looking forward to four more years on Beacon Hill. Our efficient and great Town Clerk Bob Bruynell has forecast a 50% voter turnout, and he's never wrong. We would have liked a 100% turnout, but they tell me 50% is rather good. At any rate, one more primary election will have become history in this great Commonwealth of ours...an exciting and extremely important happening for its citizens.

[...]

Accordingly, having succeeded in pushing through legislation to provide for an educational and diagnostic screening program for those mothers and their offspring (sons as well as daughters) to whom diethylstilbestrol (known as DES) was prescribed during pregnancy; and having secured funding for this program in the 1983 state budget, we set out on Wednesday morning to visit the DES clinic at Children's Hospital. It was to be a most rewarding experience. Dr. Donald Goldstein, who is heading the program, turned out to be wonderfully sensitive to the entire issue. We left Children's Hospital confident in the knowledge that in that world-famous facility any young person facing the traumatic experience of finding herself (or himself) vulnerable in this area, would be guided with sensitivity and compassion through the trauma of coping.

Thursday morning and we were off again to visit the Beverly Birth Center. It is affiliated with Beverly Hospital and is situated in a lovely old home adjacent to that fine medical facility. The state Department of Public Health is currently in the process of promulgating the rules and regulations for this relatively new approach to the childbirth experience. We have been dealing with legislation relative to birth centers and home births for the past several years. Although the medical profession is pretty much united against this new wave, it is obviously here. Mothers are having their babies in birth centers and at home. Midwives are delivering those babies, and it seemed important for us to know how closely regulated these options must be in order to safeguard the health of our mothers and their babies. It was an extremely interesting visit, and certainly a revelation to many of us. As a member of the Joint Legislative Committee on Health Care, I was especially interested. This is a most emotional issue. I can recall committee hearings where literally hundreds of young mothers (and many fathers) and children arrived from all parts of the state, clamoring for state approval of home births. They brought their home-delivered babies with them, and the hearings were charged with emotion.

As you probably know, we are in informal House sessions, and a majority of legislators utilize the time in making the kind of on-site visits that are helpful in intelligently coming to grips with legislative issues that face us. We in the Women's Caucus have several more on-site visits planned for our Fridays (when we are not in session) during the coming months.

Locally it was an especially great privilege for me to present a House of Representatives Citation to my dear friends Vincent and Annette Coyle on the occasion of their fortieth wedding anniversary. Annette and I enjoy a friendship that spans most of our lives. She and her Vinnie are two very special people indeed, and I was pleased to have been included among the members of the lovely Coyle family and close friends who attended their Anniversary Mass and the renewal of their marriage vows.

Sunday and on the grounds of our lovely Thayer House, under a beautiful blue sky, I had the most happy time as guest of the Gardeners Guild of Braintree at their annual New Members Tea. A delightful group of young women, and it was fun to be with them.

NOVEMBER 26, 1982

The Massachusetts Caucus of Women Legislators operated in high gear during the past week. With a new legislative year ahead and a December 1st deadline date for filing our 1983 bills, there was much to be done about those women's issues which have not been addressed to date. As legislators, we represent both the men and the women of our communities and of the Commonwealth as a whole, and so our legislative concerns embrace an ever-widening area of responsibilities. As women legislators additionally, however, we must add to those other responsibilities the addressing of issues that affect the quality of life for women. You may well imagine, therefore, how busy and full are our days under the Golden Dome during this merry month of November...

Among the first set of my concerns is always to be found my ever-present interest in adequate funding for vocational education within the State. Accordingly, bright and early on Monday morning I met with Don DiFiore, the business Manager at the Blue Hills regional Vocational School and Technical Institute, to discuss proposed legislation to safeguard state funding for the Technical Institute. After a meeting with our competent House Counsel, and with his assistance, the bill was lined up to be put into correct legal language by his department. I shall then "have a go" at steering it through the General Court.

Tuesday, and as the Chair of the Women's Caucus, I presided at a welcoming reception for our seven new women representatives and two new women senators-a significant increase, incidentally, in our ranks. Our program included an in-depth discussion of the legislative process, with an opportunity provided for the airing of any concerns our new colleagues might have about the new role that lies ahead for them. House Speaker Thomas W. McGee was on hand to formally welcome the women; and, representing Senate President William Bulger who was vacationing in the British Isles, was Senator Sharon Pollard, who also warmly welcomed the newcomers to the General Court. Governor-elect Michael Dukakis' transition team members dropped by, and their chairman addressed the group. It was a new-and I thought a rather innovative way of establishing an early rapport with our new women colleagues, and it provided them with an early acquaintance with the functioning of the women's caucus. An extremely intensive orientation course will be provided for these new members, needless to say. Speaker McGee has always provided an excellent program. We felt, however, that a general overview of the legislative process would prove helpful as a prelude to this formal educational program.

Task force meetings had been set up for the remainder of the day on such issues as Divorce and Custody, and Domestic Violence; and our new members were invited to attend.

Wednesday saw us involved with task force seminars on Health, Criminal Justice and Pay Equity. The week was racing by with never enough hours in any of its days to accommodate those all-important in depth studies that had to precede the filing of remedying legislation for the problems that would surface as the issues were examined.

Thursday morning, and I met with a New Hampshire resident, Sam Langley, to discuss the possibility of extending train service to N.H. Sam is a railroad man and the son of Braintree's Ruth Langley Hill; and we discussed exchanging reports of any legislative action in either state that could affect such a change in railroad operations.

Locally the week was a busy one as well. On Tuesday evening I was on hand to attend what was truly a sensational South Shore Chamber of Commerce Business Fair at the Lantana in Randolph, with more than 700 exhibitors and hundreds of patrons milling around in an informal and highly Informative way. Not for nothing is our South Shore Chamber the largest Chamber in the country! They certainly do make things hum in this part of the state…And on Wednesday evening I had the pleasure of attending a most rewarding Open House at the new Adams Park Office Condominiums on Adams Street. Thursday evening and I was on the move again-attending a "Braintree Buttonhole Session" with the South Shore Chamber once more running the show.

Friday morning and it was off to the new Quincy Mental Health Center for an airing of their funding problems; and then to Boston for a very busy day under the Golden Dome. Saturday and there was the Health Fair at Town Hall to be visited and patronized-a great public service rendered by our Board of Health.

Sunday-and wonder of wonders-no local commitments! I was permitted to stay at home and prepare for that wonderful family Thanksgiving Dinner on Thursday, all of which reminds me to wish each and every one of you wonderful Braintree people your finest Thanksgiving Day ever! May you all have a lot to be thankful for…Among other things, I am thankful for the privilege of serving you in the Great and General Court!

AUGUST 27, 1982

While doing a spot of research in our beautiful State Library the other day, I came upon a document that to my way of thinking simply screamed to be shared with other residents of our Bay State. It was a list of "First in the Nation Legislation", and it was compiled by political scientist Jack L. Walker of the University of Michigan in a study of state governments for the American Political Science Review. It needs to be updated, for it ends at the year 1972. Incomplete as it may be, however, it makes for very exciting reading. I shall include as many of these "firsts" as I can tuck into this column, and continue to pass them along in subsequent columns since they should certainly be of interest to our young people as well as to the rest of us:

1630 The first session of the General Court was held October 17
1644 The first time the House of Deputies separated from the House of Magistrates
1676 First legislation for the care of the "insane"
1692 House of Deputies renamed House of Representatives (First time this name is ever used)
1764 First official census authorized by the General Court

1780 First General Court under the new Constitution-oldest written Constitution in use in the world-prototype for the Federal Constitution framed in 1787

1788 First state to outlaw African slave trade

1820 First amendment to the Constitution accepted granting voting privileges to all male citizens over twenty-one years of age

1821 First public high schools established

1836 First state to regulate investments by insurance companies

1837 First State Board of Education in the United States-Horace Mann, a former member of the Massachusetts House, appointed its first chairman

1841 First state to adopt a probation system

1842 First state to enact laws regulating child labor

1843 Pioneers in the treatment of the mentally retarded-led by Dorothea Dix and Dr. Samuel Woodward

1847 Cities and towns authorized to provide for adult education

1852 First mandatory school attendance law

1855 First Department of Insurance in the nation

1855 First bill prohibiting discrimination based on race, creed, color or religious opinion in establishing qualifications for admission into public schools

1864 First state to establish a Board of Health

1865 First state to create a law enforcement agency with police powers everywhere in the state, Department of Public Safety

1869 First to establish a Bureau of Labor Statistics to gather and compile information on the wage earners of the state

1885 Constitutional Amendment ratified granting the General Court the power to regulate elections

1888 First use of the reform-oriented "Australian Ballot" authorized by the General Court

1893 First State Highway Department in the nation

1900 First proposed motor vehicle legislation-requiring that automobiles be equipped with bumpers

1912 First state in the union to establish retirement system for Public employees

1912 First minimum wage law in the nation enacted June 4

1913 First law (Briggs law) in the U.S. to require psychiatrists for people accused of capital or repeated offences

1918 First public housing project in the nation completed in Lowell

1919 Designation of the responsibility for preparation of the budget to the Governor in an effort to modernize government

1923 First women elected to the Massachusetts House of Representatives

SEPTEMBER 24, 1982

[…]

From my own point of view, I cannot adequately express my gratitude to the great people I represent, for once more bringing me in at the top of the ticket. This fact is important to me only because it indicates that I am representing the majority of our Braintree residents as they wish to be represented as a full-time, hard-working legislator.

The Primary Election, needless to say, constituted the highlight of the week. Nonetheless, a number of significant events occurred that affected our town. We received word from the Governor's office that Braintree has been awarded a sizeable ($10,500) grant for a leak detection program for our Water Department, as well as a $8,782 grant for a system rehabilitation grant for pipe repair and replacement. Governor King has been wonderfully sensitive and responsive to the needs of the people of Braintree; I am hoping, of course, that Governor Dukakis will be equally sensitive and responsive to our needs…

Locally we had a number of interesting happenings designed to handle our evenings as well as other times of day. On Monday evening I was present for the ribbon-cutting ceremony for a new firm in our midst the South Shore business Brokers, Inc. Located at 400 Washington Street, this new business establishment would seem to be fulfilling a need in steering potential firms to the South Shore; and we wish Bill and Mike Trudeau well with their new Braintree venture.

The Braintree Garden Club celebrated its Golden Anniversary on Wednesday, and it was delightful to share the happy occasion with President Ethel Collier and her group of nice garden lovers. The favor for the occasion was a huge tulip bulb, appropriately wrapped in gold, with curling gold ribbons. It will be fun to plant it in a special place in one's garden to serve always as reminder of what was a festive and most happy occasion. Happiness and success and all that go with it for this great group for the next fifty years!

Thursday evening and it was off to Town Hall to attend a public hearing on the designation of the Cranberry Pond Watershed as an area of critical and environmental concern. The designation of this area by the state would mean that any proposed development would have to be approved by the Commonwealth. One of the most telling arguments used to support the nomination of the Cranberry Brook region was its tie-in to the water supply for Braintree, Holbrook and Randolph. At a time when throughout the state our cities and town are facing and dealing with horrendous water shortages, the protections of any watershed is uppermost in the minds of all of us. Thursday's public hearing was part of the selection process, and the state will have two months to decide if the Cranberry Pond Watershed will be designated and therefore protected from any form of development that would imperil this fragile section of our town.

Saturday, and the day dawned bright and beautiful, gladdening the hearts of a lot of our Braintree "super citizens" who had been invited by the members of the Braintree Yacht Club to enjoy a clam chowder luncheon and a sail down the harbor in one of the lovely boats belonging to club members. It was fun to be with them. "We Seniors have more fun than people," one of them said to me as echoes of laughter floated all about us during the luncheon. They do indeed. Our thanks to the members of the Braintree Yacht Club for this annual treat for our elderly. They love it....

I met on Friday afternoon with the gentlemen who will continue to serve as our Governor until the first of the year, His Excellency Edward J. King; and I was pleased to hear him say, "I'll be right here for the next three and a half months, [...]

OCTOBER 1ST, 1982

We returned to the formal House sessions on Beacon Hill this past week and it was good to find everyone present in the House Chamber once again, instead of in those offices we've been occupying lately as we handled our constituent issues and prepared the legislation we propose to file for next year.

Monday began in a most interesting fashion. As Chairperson of the Massachusetts Caucus of Women Legislators, I chaired an extremely informative meeting with Dr. Mary Jane England and Representative Joe DiNucci, where we discussed the matter of reporting or not reporting directly to the District Attorney-as well as the Department of Social Services all cases of child abuse. It is not a clear-cut issue, of course. Only about 20% of parents guilty of this heinous offense are sadistic individuals. In a majority of cases, counseling and help with family problems is indicated. We have, however, apparently swung a little too far to keep families together. Something must be done and the support of dual reporting would appear to be the legislative route to take.

Monday noon, and I cut the ribbon for our women on a newly renovated room: and thereafter. with my sister legislators, enjoyed a lovely luncheon as guest of House Speaker Thomas W. McGee, who is especially kind and considerate of our women, and we appreciate the fact.

Wednesday morning and I chaired a seminar on "Child Custody" and "Common Law versus Community Property." There is so much to be learned in regard to the complex issues we face daily as we legislate for the people of the state; and on Wednesday we ended, as usual, with the feeling that few issues are either black or white; it's those gray areas that confuse one...

Wednesday afternoon, and I was present in Nurses Hall at the State House for the celebration of the formation of the first 100 vanpools by the Caravan for Commuters; and, incidentally, it was announced that since the planning of the party, the number had swelled to 102. I have been a consistent supporter of vanpools as a means of reducing highway traffic and saving vital energy. I was, therefore, delighted to learn some great statistics…The use of those 100 vans over the past year has saved 576,000 gallons of gasoline; reduced air pollution by 26 tons; and eliminated 11,772 million vehicle miles. Every weekday, Caravan's fleet travels nearly 9500 miles, three times the distance between Boston and San Francisco. The average vanpooler in 1982 saved $860.

Thursday and it was off to an 8:30 a.m. breakfast at the Parker House where supporters of the Massachusetts Bottle Bill gathered to plan strategy for safeguarding that legislation and defeating Question 4 on the November ballot. A defeat of Question 4 will see the law implemented on January 1st; and the two remaining New England states can then be expected to fall into line, making it. easier for all of New England to handle the new law.

Saturday and it was off to the Thayer House where Braintree's own Massachusetts IX Regiment was holding an encampment, and displaying a handsome new cannon it hopes to purchase through the generosity of our fellow citizens. Captain Gordon Campbell and his intrepid band of militiamen offer honorary membership in the regiment in the exchange for a donation to the cannon fund. It was great to watch this dedicated group in their maneuvers; to watch them cooking their dinner over an outdoor fire; and to view their tents and the other accoutrements they had assembled for their three-day encampment behind Thayer House.

It was also a happy experience for my visiting sister Jeanne, as well as for me, to tour our beautiful Thayer House in the company of Don and Mary Cunningham. Unlike myself, Jeanne, who joined the Braintree Historical Society after our George Washington Ball, was seeing Thayer House for the first time, and she was enchanted…

Weather-wise, the week was nothing to boast of. Summer ended officially on Thursday, and Autumn arrived. Areas of gold and red began to appear in the neighborhood maple trees. The leaves commenced to fall. The evenings were crisp and cool, as were the mornings: but wasn't the weekend lovely!!!

OCTOBER 8, 1982

It was back to normal at the State House this past week, with happening after happening, and meeting after meeting; and formal House sessions each day. Tuesday morning I accompanied a delegation of Braintree-ites to a meeting with Justin Radlo, Chief Engineer of the DPW. We were there to request the restoration of the pedestrian light on Quincy Avenue at Dewey Road. It was removed a couple of months back. We were also seeking to preserve the light at Watson School. We secured a pledge from the DPW to look further into both situations. I shall keep my eye on things, needless to say…Those lights are needed…

Wednesday, and as Chair of the Caucus of Women Legislators I chaired a seminar on day care, a subject of vital concern to our working women. There are, of course, several kinds of day care; and since we in the Caucus must defend the huge budget appropriation for this state service, we were on hand to learn, from a dozen or so key people, of the various services offered. We heard the pros and cons of Family Day Care, with a report of a pilot project currently underway on the North Shore; and of employer supported day care. This segment of the program was presented by Miriam Kertzman of Stride Rite, and it was fascinating. The Voucher system was described, as was the program for after-school care. We had an update on the state's new Child Care Center in the McCormack building. We are now better informed by far…

Wednesday afternoon, and I met with a group of bankers and finance company executives to discuss my bill to afford an increased amount of protection to co-signers of loans. And Wednesday evening I attended a legislators' Unity meeting with Governor Mike Dukakis; after which it was a race to Braintree Town Hall for an appeals board hearing.

Wednesday also saw us dealing in the House with the Capital Outlay Budget, a $243.1 million document that contained in excess of $108 million for housing for the state's elderly and moderate-income residents. The package, which will be funded by the issuance of state revenue bonds, also contains funding for ten new judges that was added in an amendment. "Justice delayed is justice denied"; and with the new anti-crime laws we have enacted, our courts' calendars have become unmanageable. A recent study indicated that 21 additional judges are needed. The addition of 10 will help. Five are the Superior Court; three for Probate (1 in Plymouth, 1 in Middlesex and 1 in Suffolk Counties); one for the Boston Juvenile Court and one for the Boston Municipal Court. Thursday morning and I was delighted to participate in and to speak at the ribbon cutting […]

OCTOBER 29, 1982

Our week on Beacon Hill turned out to be the usual busy and productive one. Monday morning and I was on hand at Columbia Point for the dedication of the Commonwealth's new Archives Building…a momentous occasion for those among us who are concerned with the preservation of the rich historic heritage that is ours here in Massachusetts. Brrr! It was cold on that little old platform…the warmth of our hearts, however, seemed to make even the weather palatable. The new building will be located between the JFK Library and UMass/Boston, a most appropriate placement, we thought. The framers of our Constitution, aware of the value of historic records, carefully made provision for their preservation. The Archives collection has, however, outgrown its small quarters in the basement of the State House, and the new facility is scheduled to open in the Spring of 1985. It will house some truly remarkable documents. The treasured history of our past will be displayed there, of course. There will such interesting items as Queen Elizabeth's Royal Seal, a Bennington Drum and pictographic signatures on an

18thy century Indian Treaty. Every one of the Commonwealth's citizens should tuck in a visit there, along with those scholars who will be enabled to research the history of the state from its earliest times. It was wonderfully rewarding morning…

From Dorchester it was back to Braintree for another special occasion-the "dedication" of the new bus shelter at Highlands Green. It was a pleasure to honor the lady whose diligent efforts brought about this great benison for the residents of the handsome senior citizens complex, Ruth Langley Hill-to whom I presented a House of Representatives Citation with great pride and satisfaction.

Back to the State House for a conference with Suzanne, my great Administrative Assistant who was holding the fort there; and then it was off again from Beacon Hill at 6 p.m. to address the Suffolk County Chapter of the Massachusetts Association of Insurance Women at a lovely dinner meeting at Purcell's.

Tuesday morning, and as a member of the DES Advisory Board I was on hand at the headquarters of the Public Health Council for a meeting and update on the progress of our program to alert those mothers for whom the drug Diethylstilbestrol was prescribed during pregnancy, along with their offspring, all of whom are potentially menaced. We are currently educating the public and setting up diagnostic evaluation centers for the detection of any signs of this menace, which is easily treatable in the early stages but potentially dangerous without such treatment.

Turning from what we are doing on Beacon Hill to the Hill itself; there are a few real signs of approaching Winter in this part of the world. The street musicians are still performing daily on Boston Common. They're finding warm, sunny spots now for their performances, but they're there. The trees upon the 'Common are still as green as they were in July, and people still lie sprawled under them in the early evening as one makes one's way down Park Street. It is only the rather sharp wind that whips about the State House in the early morning that reminds us that soon all of the delightful Boston Common activity will cease to exist; that artists will cease to set up their easels before the Capitol building; and that the Summer's steady stream of State House visitors will dry to a trickle.

But to get back to those extracurricular activities of mine under the Golden Dome, I chaired on Wednesday morning a vitally interesting "Economic Literacy Workshop" where economists Pat Jerabek and Gail Shields addressed the issues of "women in the economy, Reagan administration policies, human services-problems and solutions." A fascinating program indeed. And on Friday afternoon I was on hand for the dedication of that wonderful new addition to our community-the Medical South Community Health Plan, a Health Maintenance Organization that represents an invitation to good health for the people of the South Shore.

As an eight-year member of the Legislative Committee on Health Care, I have become increasingly convinced that HMO's, as they are called, are the wave of the future. They stress preventive medicine, and it's a whole lot easier to keep people well than to make them well after they've become ill. Welcome Medical South!

NOVEMBER 12, 1982

[…]

I think we are all a bit relieved now to know that the 1982 election is behind us. The die is cast for the next few years. On the Hill a different administration will soon be taking over. I pray that I shall receive from Governor Michael Dukakis and his administration the same wonderful response to my concerns that I have always received from Governor Edward J. King and his administrative officials. Now, with Tuesday, that fateful election day over, life returned to normal on Beacon Hill. Wednesday saw my attendance at the second of the U.S. Trust Company's excellent two-day seminars on financial planning and tax strategies. I was among the 45 women statewide who were selected for this exciting program. It began with luncheon, and we were joined at our table by the bank president, Mr. James "Jack" Sidell, and by one of the extremely bright young women who were running the program; and it afforded me an excellent opportunity to discuss the economy, present and future, with an extremely knowledgeable banker. An exciting interlude in a very busy day on Beacon Hill.

Thursday, and we met with Susan Moulton, Executive Director of the Bay State Skills Corporation for an update on the "Displaced Homemakers" program which her organization is administering. This is the program designed to prevent newly divorced or widowed women from going on Welfare, by providing support services that will lead to employment. Since securing funding for this very important program was one of my Women's Caucus priorities, I was delighted to learn that it is alive and well and growing by leaps and bounds. Unfortunately it MUST grow. The number of divorces continues to grow, and the Commonwealth simply cannot afford to keep expanding its Welfare rolls. Besides, welfare can represent a destructive force for our women. Work, on the other hand, is of proven therapeutic value when the world crashes about one.

Friday morning, and I was on hand at Mount Saint Joseph Academy in Brighton as Guest Speaker on Career Selection for the members of the Senior Class who will soon be making that choice. My role was to describe the rewards of a career in pubic service-my favorite topic…Saturday morning and it was off to the Harborlight Mall to attend the Holiday Fair in which our Braintree Point Women's Club was to participate. An exciting prelude always to the holiday season that lies ahead; and how creative and talented are those club members of ours whose creations are annually offered for sale at this event? Saturday evening, and I was on hand at Braintree Sons of Italy Hall for the 46th Annual Banquet of the Braintree Ladies Lodge No. 1422, where Josephine M. Martino was to be named "Woman of the Year." A lovely event as always, and an excellent choice for this fine distinction. The lady was presented, of course, with a House of Representatives Citation. Sunday afternoon, and as a member of the Board of Trustees of the Woodward School for Girls, I was on hand at a reception honoring Miss Katherine Bacon on the occasion of her 90th birthday. Miss Bacon served as Headmistress of the school for some 43 years, and judging from the number of well wishers present, was a dearly loved lady who exerted a profound influence on the lives of the young women who attended that splendid school over the many years. A House Citation was also in order for this most distinguished former Headmistress.

A great week as always, and it's back to normal on Monday as the Legislature returns to formal sessions and we pick up and deal with a number of important issues that had to be shelved during the last weeks of the election campaign. I look forward to the renewed legislative activity.

JANUARY 14

It was an exciting and dramatic week on Beacon Hill as the Administration of Governor Edward J. King prepared to leave the Capitol building and the Administration of Governor-Elect Michael Dukakis prepared to come on board. The transfer of power went smoothly. Promptly on Thursday morning Governor King turned over to the incoming Chief Executive the worn state bible and the great brass key that have come to represent the transfer of executive authority. In the corridors, the personal effects of the outgoing governor and the incoming governor passed each other occasionally, to be viewed with sadness by the supporters of the loser and with glee by the supporters of the winner in what is, of course, the Commonwealth's most significant political campaign.

Promptly at eleven forty-five, Governor King began the long sad journey to the great central doors of the State House…those doors that are opened only for the visit of a United States President and the departure of a retiring governor. His friends lined the corridors and filled the Hall of Flags. They fill Doric Hall as well, and amid cheers and acclaim he made his way to the open doorway that lay ahead. Snow was falling softly; it turned to rain…the Governor reached out to shake the hands of his many friends as he moved along. "Governor, you have only four minutes," the Capitol Police Officer was heard to say. The Governor must have passed through the doorway by twelve noon. He made it. He walked through the wide doorway into the rain where thousands of the Commonwealth's citizens waited and cheered. Jody, his loyal wife, accompanied him, breaking with tradition. So did the various members of his Cabinet and several legislators who had been close to him during his term of office. He made his way down the great Capitol stairway to the street where a limousine awaited him…and he was off…Another page in the history of the Commonwealth had been turned…

Meanwhile, of course, up in the House Chamber, the incoming Governor had been greeted, seated, and was awaiting his Swearing-In by Senate President William Bulger, amid the cheers and applause of his followers. Government was to go on. Michael Dukakis took his Oath of Office, gave his Inaugural Address, and then repaired to the Hall of Flags for a reception that was equally wild. The lines of well wishers were long. A lot of happy people awaited an opportunity to greet their new Chief Executive. They were met by the now Governor Michael Dukakis and his Lieutenant Governor John Kerry. And the pomp and circumstance went on…to be followed as always by the inevitable Inaugural Balls and all the other festivities that go to make up that wonderful day in the life of an individual who has been chosen by the people of the Commonwealth to be their leader for the coming four years. We wish the new governor all possible success. His success as the state's Chief Executive will be reflected in the well-being of the Commonwealth citizens; and so, Michael Dukakis, here's to you! May you succeed in keeping each and every one of those promises you made in that stirring Inaugural Address of yours. We'll be praying for you….

Wednesday had been OUR day for the Swearing-In ceremonies, and it had all gone beautifully. The members of my wonderful family, led by my dear husband Ted, some treasured friends, a colleague and a couple of staff people from my office had joined me for the ceremony and for luncheon afterwards at Dini's. The luncheon was great; my guests warm and wonderful as always; the weather was superb; and another great day in my life came to an end, leaving in me the kind of rosy glow that comes from being on top of the world…

Tuesday for your L. of the H. had represented a wild prelude to that exciting day. I had raced up and down the marble stairways and back and forth along the marble corridors from nine in the morning until midnight, as I fought to get to the Governor's desk for signing a couple of vitally important remaining bills. I was weary as I left the State House at 2 a.m. (The session had ended at midnight but a few of my dear departing colleagues had made their farewell speeches…) Yes, I was indeed weary, but that rosy glow I talked about earlier in the column was in evidence at that point as well. I'd experienced success in everything I had undertaken; and so how great it had been to be able to walk into the "Corner Office" and participate in bill signings and picture takings with my good friend Governor Edward J. King…

And so we begin another session of the Great and General Court…May it be a productive and happy one. And how have we fared as a legislative body during the past year??? Have we performed??? I shall enumerate a number of our accomplishments in next week's column. I wanted to convey to you the exciting flavor of the past week's events in this one…

JANUARY 21, 1983

It was a busy week in the House of Representatives. In a series of late sessions, we managed to debate and hammer out the rules under which we shall operate during the next two years. Committee assignments were announced, and I was proud and pleased to have been appointed Vice-Chairman of the very important Committee on Health Care. A tremendous responsibility, since the health of the Commonwealth's citizens will rest within our hands at a period in time when the soaring costs of health care must be dealt with, while at the same time, medical services must be made available to those who need them.

It seems as though we hear nothing these days but a litany of our failures as a legislative body during the past year. Looking back over that 1982 legislative session, however, I feel that we can boast of a significant number of important accomplishments. In the area of Public Safety, for instance, laws were enacted to increase fines for the sale of alcoholic beverages to minors; and parole hearings are now mandated to include a representative of the victims of the crime involved. We allocated $30.5 million for the secure treatment and detention of DYS juveniles; and increased the penalties for drunk driving. We appropriated $100 million for new prison space; and reinstated the death penalty for specified capital crimes under specified circumstances. Requirements were increased for the mandatory reporting of suspected child abuse cases; and penalties were increased for persons involved in "Child Porn". Thanks to the notorious "Stoughton Case," we have enacted laws that give us more local control over the operation of "adult" bookstores. A $4.6 million appropriation in new safety funds will include allocations for creating 100 new State Police drug teams. So much for our action in the fight against crime, which is a high priority concern of just about everyone I know…

When it came to Local Aid and Taxes, we allocated $2.25 billion in local aid, an all-time high; and $3.2 million in increased aid for regional schools. $17.5 million was made available to our cities and towns for local off-street parking. $20 million was allocated for the preservation of our agricultural lands, along with $5 million for local parks and recreation. All this was done while at the same time providing for the state's taxpayers a $45 million tax cut in personal income taxes. A $45 million bonding authority assisted Boston in meeting court-ordered Tregor abatements. Many of you will disagree with our action on that issue. It must be kept in mind, however, that Boston is our Capitol city, and though we find it unpalatable at times to be forced to help solve its problems, those problems must be solved. The city must survive.

The elderly and our young people were well treated during the 1982 session of the General Court.

We allocated $415 million of record high aid to the State's public higher education system; $1.6 million to private schools assisting special needs school-age children and $1.5 million for urban youth job training. New sources of private-sector student loans were established; and the Massachusetts Technology Park Corporation was established for state-of-the-art training in semiconductor and microelectronics technologies. Legislation was signed into law that provided for third-party payment of Chapter 766 medical costs, as significant aid to local school budgets; and a new Adoption Subsidy Plan will now facilitate the adoption of children with "special needs." Our AFDC families received a 5% increase, with a $75 cash clothing grant. For our elderly, we had signed into law the protection of the privacy rights and the personal property protection of nursing home residents; and established a permanent 10 cent fare on the MBTA, with half-fare on bus and rail MBTA lines. We increased the abatement for the elderly-blind; and secured grandparents visitation rights to children of divorced or deceased parents. Additional accomplishments will be reviewed in next week's column. Many good things were accomplished in the 1982 session of the General Court.

FEBRUARY 4, 1983

We are beginning to feel at home in Room 130, Suzanne and I. It hasn't been an easy adjustment. I have left dearly loved friends in our 4th floor office. It does make sense, however, to have the Chairman and Vice Chairman of a Committee located in the same office; and we've good friends on the 1st floor as well, I'm happy to say-friends acquired during my eight year contact with the most dedicated and capable staff members of the Health Care Committee.

We have added our plants and our plaques to make the place look more like home. In one corner of the room is the gorgeous Bromillade that was a "Swearing In" gift of my dear friends Lainie, Ruth, Mary and Eileen. It lights up the office in a very special way because of its uniqueness, it arouses everyone's interest.

The Committee held its first organizational meeting bright and early on Monday morning and I'm convinced we shall have a wonderful year.

Not very much is doing as yet legislatively on the Hill. We are waiting for the thousands of bills we filed to be in print and assigned to various committees. The Transportation Committee will hold its first public hearing on Monday, and our Health Care Committee on the following Monday, so we are on the move. And, of course, our constituent work goes on as usual. That never ceases. Too many of our great Braintree people have problems, and we are always delighted to assist in their solution if we can.

It has really been an especially sad week for many of us here on the Hill. We have lost our beloved House Chaplain, the Reverend Monsignor George V. Kerr. He passed away and was buried on Thursday morning after having served as Chaplain of the House of Representatives for the past 24 years. Although a victim of cancer, Monsignor Kerr was on hand with his daily opening prayer for our House sessions almost to the end. His prayers were always inspirational and beautiful. I especially recall one of them. It was the opening prayer for our Monday, October 4th, 1982 House session, and I had found it especially appealing. I should like to share it with you all:

> "God bestows all the beauty and all the loveliness of this world upon saints and sinners alike. Even though we should have disobeyed Him, His hand still feeds us. Even should our hearts be tainted by imperfections, His stars look down upon us in tenderness and compassion.

Even though we should wander and forget Him, His sun would still shine, His rain would still fall upon us.

This world is too bright and fair to darken it with clouds of anger.

This world is too short to waste it in bearing that heaviest of all burdens-revenge.

Give us the wisdom, O Lord, to forgive and forget if we can; but to forgive anyway; and pray heartily and kindly for all, for thus only can we be truly called Your children on earth. Amen"

Returning to the Joint Legislative Committee on Health Care, of which I have been appointed Vice-Chairman, it originated in 1974. It provides a forum for medicine and politics to come together, and its function is to protect the health of the citizens of the Commonwealth a…vitally important function indeed. We shall hold our public hearings on the Monday and Wednesday mornings of each week at eleven o'clock; and both oral and written testimony will be accepted on all bills. A number of most important issues face us. We shall be dealing with the issue of permitting nurse practitioners and physicians' assistants to administer drugs in nursing homes. […] this as a measure of cost containment, needless to say. The implementation of Chapter 372 of the Acts of 1982 will be under close scrutiny. This attempt to control legislatively the incredibly high cost of hospital care, which is known as the "Hospital Cost Control Act", provides a "prospective" payment system designed to encourage hospital and health care economies. We pray that it will work. Hospital cost containment is vitally needed by people everywhere.

JANUARY 28, 1983

It was "Moving Day" at the State House on Monday of this past week, as those among us who had been assigned to different offices packed up and left, making way for others who would occupy those places that had grown near and dear to us by virtue of the people whose lives had touched our own there during previous years. In my own particular case, it was really difficult to say farewell to colleagues and staff people with whom I had spent five days a week for the past eight years-my colleagues located in the Committee on Transportation and those great staff people who work for it.

On the other hand, appointment as Vice Chairman of a very important committee is definitely a signal honor, and there was the ever-present knowledge that having been reappointed as well to the Transportation Committee, I would be with those friends at committee hearings, and for that fact I was glad.

The movers were to have been on hand at dawn to help us with the task of transporting what seemed like tons of "good stuff" from the fourth floor of the State House to our new first floor office. Well, it may have been the weather-that incredibly icy Monday that had followed that incredibly stormy Saturday and Sunday…or it may have been the number of people waiting to be moved…At any rate, Suzanne and I found ourselves toting one load after another along the State House corridors, and down in the elevator to room 130. Yes, the movers were on hand, we were told. There were just too many people to be helped. We would have to await our turn. We did just the opposite, needless to say. We moved ourselves with the help of some staff members, and were rather well settled as darkness fell on Beacon Hill.

Our new office is functional, but quite unlike the handsome office we had left behind us. The Committee on Transportation had undergone a wonderful renovation a couple of years back and it showed. The quarters of the committee on Health Care, however, more closely resemble the average committee rooms under the Golden Dome. Much renovation needs to be done in our State Capitol which, lovely as its great halls may be, is a very old building whose offices leave much to be desired.

The decree had come down from House Speaker Thomas W. McGee, however, that all Vice Chairmen were to be located with Chairmen in the appropriate offices, and so that's where we wound up-happily among good friends in Room 130 as well-since my eight year membership on the Health Care had permitted me to know, respect and indeed to love the great staff people assembled there. We shall have an organizational meeting on Monday morning, and our committee work will then begin in earnest. We face a year which would appear to be tied with many health-related issues and problems. It will certainly represent a challenge for this new Vice Chairman, and I welcome it…With critic's words ringing dismally in our ears as the 1982 session of the General Court ended, I included in last week's column a number of the ACCOMPLISHMENTS that were ours during that stormy session. I would like to add a few more of the same in this week's column.

As regards the environment, we stream-lined regulations to encourage alternative supply sources, and increased fines for illegal trash disposal. We allocated $200,000 to a study of the disposal of low-level radioactive waste; mandated deed recordation of waste dumping; and allocated $358 million for water quality programs. The State purchased the South Cape Beach at Mashpee, which is the only state beach on Cape Cod; and included various environmental protection programs within the Offstreet Parking Act. We modernized the State Banking Laws; and via a Massachusetts Housing Finance merger, we provided $200 million in new low-interest mortgage loans to an estimated 5,000 low and moderate-income first-time homebuyers. We increased the Inspector General's authority to include vendors' service contracts; and extended the "Middlesex Jury Procedures" (one day/one trial) throughout the state. $729 million was allocated to the Southwest Corridor (Boston) mass transit and community rehabilitation program; and a $75 million transportation bond issue included $60 million for local and state highways. And there were other significant accomplishments which I shall go into in my next column. The media, of course, could make reference occasionally to some of these worthwhile things we accomplished during the 1982 General Court session, but how often do you read or hear of the accomplishments of good teenagers? Apparently politicians fall into the same category.

FEBRUARY 25, 1983

    I thoroughly enjoyed my first public hearing as Vice Chairman of the Legislative Committee on Health Care during the past week. It was scheduled for Monday morning, and among issues to be addressed was a petition to limit the costs of health care attributable to capital construction by hospitals, and a bill to further amend the Determination of Need law and to establish a commission to study the cost impact of hospital capital expansion.

    Neither the issue of controlling capital constructions costs nor the DON law were addressed in Chapter 372, the Hospital Cost Control law we passed last year. The bills we were dealing with on Monday are companion pieces to chapter 372. they were filed by Senator Edward Burke, the Senate Chairman of our committee, and they elicited a couple of hours of testimony before our committee members. Very naturally, Blue Cross and the business community supported the bills, while the Massachusetts Hospital Association and labor opposed them, DON applications have been filed for $600 million in additional capital construction. If all of this capital construction were approved, it would result in an increase of $27 million in Medicaid costs and $63 million in the cost of Blue Cross an obviously heavy burden to be borne by the Commonwealth's citizens. This issue of hospital cost control would easily appear to be the most important issue we shall be facing in Health Care this year, and its effect upon our lives will be far reaching indeed.

    Monday evening saw your L. of the H. heading for the Long Wharf Marriot to attend the final segment of the 8th Boston Conference of the Savings Bank Association of Massachusetts. It was a beautiful evening, and looked forward as I always do to being in the company of our great Braintree Savings Bank executives. It was rather disconcerting, however, to learn from some of our legislators who had attended the entire daylong conference that feelers were being put out by the Administration and others for a possible tax increase this year. Is there, or is there not a $300 million shortfall facing the State this year as we prepare to deal with the 1984 budget??? That is one of the questions on which there were almost as many opinions as there were people involved. At any rate, I foresee considerable difficulty for anyone who attempts to get any kind of a tax increase through the General Court this year.

    February 15 was the 163rd anniversary of Susan B. Anthony's birthday, and we women legislators wore white carnations in her honor and presented a showing of her remarkable life story.

    The week raced by, with Health Care and Transportation Committee hearings scheduled for each of the first three days. Thursday seemed to come all too quickly, and we were back in the Transportation Committee hearing room once again, this time to discuss possible ways of alleviating the situation that will arise as of December, 1983 when the Expressway will face another drastic reconstruction program-a program that will go on for at least two years. I was assigned the task of attempting to expand the use of Flexitime among Boston businesses, along with consideration of adopting a four-day workweek. Since I have for the past eight years advocated Flexitime as a cure for our Expressway ills, I accepted the assignment gladly, and we are hard at work pursuing it.

Friday was an especially busy day. It was a happy occasion indeed for Senator Paul Harold and me to be hosted for a lovely luncheon meeting by the members of our Braintree League of Women Voters, and I enjoyed enormously the company of these bright young women. Late afternoon found me at Valle's where I attended a reception for Helen M. Walsh, a dearly loved lady who is retiring as Secretary at Police Headquarters. The party was given by the Patrolmen's Organization and it was a gala occasion indeed. I was pleased to present my dear friend Helen with a House of Representatives Citation. It was one of many tributes she received.

Citations were also in order on Friday evening for Lieutenant Richard Alley, who was named "Fire Officer of the Year" and Firefighter Kenneth McHugh, named "Firefighter of the Year" by the Braintree Firefighters at their annual Retirees Dinner Dance; and another happy evening was spent in the company of my good friends in the Braintree Fire Department.

MARCH 18TH, 1983

The past week was "Women's History Week," and under the Golden Dome we observed this historic occasion with a series of interesting events. Appropriate Resolutions were passed in the House and in the Senate. A series of films were shown daily. Sizeable audiences came to see "The American Woman-What Price Equality" and "The True Nature of Women, or Here We Go Again" and "How We Got the Vote" and "Women's Work America" or "The Artist was a Woman." Doric Hall housed attractive exhibits highlighting the lives of Deborah Sampson, that intrepid. South Shore heroine who disguised as a man-fought in the American Revolution, and of Dorothea Dix.

It was all sponsored by our Massachusetts Caucus of Women Legislators, needless to say. We held a press conference in mid-week where we presented our Women's Caucus legislative priorities. My priorities deal with calling for the expansion of the Displaced Homemakers Program which is working so well and keeping so many newly divorced or widowed women from falling into the welfare trap; and with a brand new bill filed for the first time this year, calling for occupational safeguards for employees resulting from the introduction and utilization of video display terminals. I had filed the bill at the request of Braintree's Frank Tolland, and it has already aroused considerable interest. At the conclusion of the press conference I was assured of the support of the "9 to 5" organization. Most VDT operators and programmers are women office workers. They do not belong to a union and, so it is felt by the AFL-CIO, which Mr. Toland represents, that this protection is necessary.

Other caucus priorities include legislation for the protection of victims of domestic violence, expansion of the rape shield law, the correction of insurance inequities as they relate to women, sexual harassment, etc.

A number of significant events occurred as the week progressed. A seminar and trade show in Nurses Hall featured Massachusetts agricultural products, and provided our state's farmers with an opportunity to illustrate that "Massachusetts Grown and Fresher Means Business." The Massachusetts Railroad Association held a legislative luncheon to acquaint us with the problems currently being faced by that segment of the population.

A reception honoring House Speaker Thomas W. McGee saw what appeared to be close to a thousand well-wishers gathered at Pier 4 on Wednesday evening, your L. of the H. among them. "DES Awareness Week" was observed with the signing of a Proclamation by Governor Michael S. Dukakis.

As Chairman of a Health Care Committee Sub-Committee I presided at a meeting of those involved in the several Nursing Home Ombudsman bills that have been filed this year. The establishment of a State Ombudsman program this year is a goal of the Department of Elder Affairs. Our sub-committee's goal is to come up with one that will serve the purpose of protecting our elderly nursing home residents while at the same time safeguarding the nursing home industry itself.

As a member of the Board of Trustees of Quincy's Woodward School for Girls, I attended a meeting where we learned that this fine institution is about to enter the age of computers, and like so many other fine institutions of learning, will be installing computers in the school in the very near future. That VDT legislation becomes more necessary every minute…

The week ended happily on Saturday morning with my appearance at the 65th Anniversary of Girl Scouting in Braintree observance at the Thayer Academy gym. At what was a lovely opening ceremony for a great Scouting Exhibition, I was privileged to present to Council a House of Representatives Citation in observance of what is truly a most significant birthday.

I continue to hear from Washington, D.C. in response to my letter of concern regarding the fate of our American POW's and MIA's. This week it was a letter from the Department of State, as well as a copy of an address on the subject which was given by the Assistant to the President for National Security Affairs. It is encouraging to know that the issue is being pursued once again…with moresuccess this time, we hope, than in the past…

MARCH 25, 1983

Any week that housed Saint Patrick's Day would have to be an especially colorful one on Beacon Hill. It was! The feast itself had to be observed on March 16th, of course. The official observance of the 17th of March is tied to Evacuation Day. That particular day is a holiday in Suffolk County; the State House is situated in Suffolk County; ergo the Irish (and those who wish they were) always observe their own special day on the day before. Shamrocks bloom on the office doorways, and just about everyone in sight wears a spot of green. Representative Michael Flaherty hosts his annual Saint Patrick's Day Party in the late afternoon, the fact that we are served Chinese food matters not an iota. Ah, 'tis a grand day indeed for all those under the Golden Dome…

So apart from the Saint Patrick's Day doings, what were the principal happenings on the Hill as the week progressed? We passed the long-awaited "Superfund Bill" and placed an eleven-cent floor on the gasoline tax. At our Health Care Committee Hearings we dealt with a number of issues involving our nursing homes and the quality of their care; and we voted for a study of Non-Institutional Care for the Elderly.

Elsewhere I appeared before the appropriate committee in defense of a bill I had filed for my good friend Pat Leonard. It would designate one Deborah Sampson as our state heroine, and set aside an annual day in her honor. This particular lady was so fired with patriotism and love of country that, under the name of Robert Shurtliff, she enlisted in the Continental Army during the Revolution. Deborah served with distinction until was wounded and her real identity revealed. Pat hand his friends were all on hand to add their own special eloquence to the matter at hand; and I am happy to report that the bill received a favorable report from the committee. That's a beginning and a good one for this bill that is so close to our Patrick's great heart.…

I was a participant in Senator Paul Harold's Palmer Institute Legislative Seminar on Wednesday morning, and with Senator John Parker, I discussed Government from the point of view of a member of the General Court; and I was on hand in the Governor's office later that day for the swearing in of my good friend former Representative Louis R. Nickinello as Assistant Secretary of Transportation. In my opinion, he and Secretary Fred Salvucci will make a great team.

Friday morning and I was off to Sons of Italy Hall where a statewide meeting of the Professional Firefighters of Massachusetts was hosted by our Braintree Fire Fighters; and Saturday morning found me participating in the annual Wreath Laying ceremony of the Wampatuck Chapter, Order of DeMolay. A driving rain drove us indoors, however the Town Hall ceremony lost nothing in its impressiveness. Representatives from our Veterans Council, and a contingent from the Aleppo Temple Minutemen added significantly to the solemnity of the occasion. It is always especially pleasing to me to find young people willing to publicly pay homage to the great men and women whose lifeblood was shed to assure for us the freedom we Americans enjoy so completely today. A highlight of the week was our attendance at the annual Dinner Dance of the South Shore Chamber of

Commerce on Friday evening at the Lantana. It was a gala occasion indeed. It always is. And in the company of our charming hosts, Braintree Savings Bank President Lindsay Tait and his Vice Presidents and their lovely wives, Ted and I had our usual great time. Honored as Statesman of the Year was my good friend Senator James R. McIntyre; and as Businessman of the Year the incomparable "Tom" Flatley. Well having decided to honor a couple of Irishmen on the 18th of March, it was inevitable that a dash of Saint Paddy's Day would find its way into the proceedings as the evening progressed, adding to the fun and providing a special flair to the occasion. Outgoing President Roundtree was also honored; and all three special guests were roasted and toasted and treated to the special brand of humor that characterizes all annual meeting celebrations of our South Shore Chamber of Commerce.

Legislatively things are beginning to hum in the House Chamber. Our committee hearings are producing results. Bills are being released to the House for action. A majority of these bills seem to be coming out unfavorably and I approve of the fact: we have too many laws on the books now that are impossible to implement or police. It begins to look as though it will be a good year legislatively on Beacon Hill…but of course, time will tell…

APRIL 8, 1983

The past week began with a bang on Monday morning. In our Health Care Committee hearing we learned first-hand of some of the problems that have surfaced since we passed Chapter 773 of the Acts of 1981, a law that removed from the Counties to the State what was alleged to have been a most unsatisfactory system for Medico-Legal Investigations. The Suffolk County Medical examiner and his staff have always operated independently, and Monday's bills were filed in an attempt to bring them into the new State system. It was interesting to learn from 1982 Suffolk County records that the Medical Examiner handled 4006 cases of sudden death, of which 437 cases required autopsies. We learned that the office of their Medical Examiner is located in Boston City Hospital, and that they have no security; they cannot block evidence from the outside world. The importance of the work of the Medical Examiner was brought home to us with the reading of a letter from the District Attorney of another county. It indicated that the actions of the gentleman testifying before our committee had been responsible for a conviction in major criminal case.

Defending a couple of my own bills had to be sandwiched between our public hearing and the formal House session. One bill had been filed for a constituent attempting to employ the Legislature as the "Court of last resort" in straightening out a number of retirement difficulties. Another bill called for the publication of juveniles' names.

The House session found me attempting to send to third reading a bill designed to make available to the hundreds of people awaiting it a supply of corneal tissue. It would allow-after an unsuccessful attempt to locate the next of kin-for the removal of a 1/25 of 1" thick wafer of corneal tissue from the eyes of a sudden death autopsy victim. This tissue would be sent to the Eye Bank and used to restore sight to one of the hundreds of people waiting and praying for this to happen. The bill was challenged, and so we shall attempt to bring this about in another way. Having heard the pleas of those in need of corneal tissue during the public hearing on the bill, I am determined to win on this issue, one way or another.

Monday afternoon I was asked to attend a meeting set up by Boston representatives where the issue of the MBTA Columbia Station reconstruction proposal was to be discussed and an update provided. I was responsible for the original proposal and for its revival, and so I continue to be extremely interested in every facet of the program. When this new station is built, South Shore residents using the Red Line to go to school at UMass/Boston and Boston College High School, and those visitors to the JFK Library, the new Archives Building and the new Exposition Center, will be able to leave the train at Columbia Station instead of having to go beyond it to Andrew and take a bus back to Columbia.

Tuesday morning, and at an 8:30 meeting at the Parker House, we members of the Transportation Committee received a briefing on the new U.S. Navy's Homeporting Project for the South Boston Army Base, and Massport's proposal to house it there. Boston is one of three cities bidding for it, and we read that Governor Dukakis and Mayor White approve the project, and so we shall probably wind up with it. It is proposed to house a "Surface Action Group" consisting of 5 ships and 3,300 personnel. The ships would include the Battleship USS Iowa, a guided missile cruiser, destroyer and two guided missile destroyers. The figure of $75 million annually in wages alone was mentioned in the course of the discussion of what was presented as a shot in the arm for the state's economy.

Well, we shall see...

As Chairman of our Health Care Committee's Sub-Committee on the issue, I continue to meet with all parties concerned in the drafting of an acceptable "Ombudsman Bill" for our Massachusetts nursing homes. It's a complicated issue, but one which the Department of Elder Affairs seems committed to deal with this year.

Tuesday was "Vietnam Era Veterans Day" at the State House. Marking the 10th anniversary of the Paris Peace Accords and the last major troop withdrawal, ceremonies were scheduled on an all-day basis. I attended the Proclamation signing and the Candle Light Service, both of which were held in the Hall of Flags.

In a late night session on Monday evening we dealt with the gasoline tax issue once again. A Conference Committee decision discarded the Senate version of 13 cents per gallon and restored the House-passed version of 11 cents which was the amount proposed in the Governor's bill. In a companion bill we voted for $15 million in additional funding for scholarship aid for higher education. Changing the subject of government, isn't it great to find those big, fat, red-breasted ROBINS frolicking on the lawns on these Spring-like mornings??? It's coming!!!

APRIL 22, 1983

A lot happened on Beacon Hill this past week. The Governor, the Speaker of the House and the President of the Senate announced a Local Aid agreement calling for $151.2 million in additional local aid for our cities and towns. It including $145 million in new aid; it provided $6.2 million to fully fund regional school transportation; and $2.5 million in new public library aid; and $4.1 million to reimburse those of the Commonwealth's cities and towns that are assessed by the MBTA but receive no service.

Braintree's share of the new local aid is a nice whopping $571,207. The figure delights me. We fared well last year, and, needless to say, I shall keep on top of the rest of the local aid picture as it develops, and work hard in support of that distribution formula which provides the greatest amount of aid for the people I represent.

There are some who criticize one provision of the new aid proposal. This provision would allow those communities that will have a levy loss in 1984 to spread that loss over two years by vote of Town Meeting or of the City Council-7.5% in each of the two years instead of the 15% called for this year under Prop. 2½. Eleven communities fall within that category. It is a bit difficult to accept the huge local aid increases that are going to the big cities, however, since Braintree fares so well under the proposal I can accept the rest.

In our Health Care Committee hearings we dealt with a number of substantive issues as usual. It's a challenging and vitally interesting committee to be "Vice Chair-ing."

Monday's hearing dealt with such important issues as state reimbursement for long-term care services, industrial accident cases and rates for chronic disease and rehabilitation hospitals. Health care cost containment becomes more of an issue daily. Its tremendous impact upon health insurance rates has everyone concerned. Businesses and industries that to date have absorbed all or a large percentage of health insurance costs are now thinking in terms of assessing employees for the amounts of any rate increases. Those on Medicaid have no real concern since their bills are paid for by the State. The wealthy have no real problems since they can absorb the increased costs of health insurance. There are enormous problems however for the "great middle class"-those who must pay their entire health insurance bills-young families with children to whom health insurance is almost as important as food and shelter. It's a complex and multi-faceted problem as are so many we face today. It's also an extremely difficult problem for those of us who are members of the Health Care Committee and so whose primary concern must be for the health of the Commonwealth's citizens.

Wednesday's hearings dealt with the Determination of Need program. We heard bills dealing with program thresholds. Health care facilities are now required to submit application to the DON program if projects for the installation of energy-saving devices involve expenditures of more than $600,000. An exemption would be made for projects unrelated to patient care that must be cost effective within five years. The facility could not, of course, recover its loss through patient charges.

Consumer representation on Hospital Boards was sought in another bill we heard that day, as was the issue of duplicate inspections of hospitals....

Tuesday afternoon we members of the Women's Legislative Caucus met with Governor Michael S. Dukakis to acquaint him with our Caucus priorities, and to seek his help in bringing them to fruition-help that we feel is to be forthcoming if at all possible. My concern lies with the Displaced Homemaker Program, and already Secretary Evelyn Murphy (bless her!) has indicated her support for our attempts to extend the program further within the state SINCE IT WORKS!!! It is keeping people from going on Welfare initially and it is taking people off the Welfare rolls.

Tuesday morning I chaired a final meeting on the proposed Nursing Home Ombudsman legislation; to race at noon to the Boston Park Plaza Hotel for a Legislative Reception sponsored by the Massachusetts Association of School Superintendents and the Massachusetts Association of Business Officials. Wednesday evening, and after a decidedly busy day it was off to the Great Hall at Quincy Market for a Legislators Reception hosted by the Massachusetts Cooperative Banks. Thursday morning and it was breakfast with the Quincy and South Shore Board of Realtors; and Sunday morning it was off to Randolph to attend a Testimonial Breakfast for a Braintree-ite Murray H. Krotman, retiring as Commander of the Massachusetts Jewish War Veterans. A Citation for Murray-as a matter of fact, three Citations for Murray, one from the Governor, one from Senator Harold and one from me...and it was off again to the South Shore Plaza for a demonstration of the marvelous "Jaws of Life" which we are seeking to purchase for our Fire Department. As a member of the "Jaws of Life" committee, I cannot urge you all too strongly to send a contribution for this great life-saving tool for our Braintree firefighters. Make checks payable to the "Jaws of Life Committee" and send them to the Braintree Savings Bank. The life that might be saved with the "Jaws of Life" could be your own, or that of someone you love...Let's make it easier for our brave firefighters to save lives in accident cases!

JUNE 17, 1983

Budget meetings! Budget meetings! Budget meetings! As we lobby the Speaker of the House and the Chairman of Ways and Means for additional funding for all of the priority issues of the Women's Caucus, as well as for the priority issues of the various Human Services agencies who have enlisted our assistance in attempting to reach what seems to be the goal of everyone under the sun, more and more of those scarce state dollars that seem to have to go further become fewer each year.

The die is, of course, already pretty much cast; and we shall begin debating the 1984 State Budget on Monday in a series of 10 a.m. to at least 10 p.m. (this hour can be extended by vote of the House members) sessions that will last until the last item on that multi-billion dollar budget will have been debated.

It was a busy week, as usual. I met with the Committee on Post Audit and a representative from the Inspector General's office for further discussion of why all the MDC flood control money went to deal with Quincy's flooding problems and our Braintree Dam problems simply were not addressed. The original money appropriated to deal with this issue had clearly spelled out its commitment to addressing our town's problems. I had personally brought them to the attention of the Corps of Engineers as well as to the MDC a great many times.

In Health Care we held a public hearing on a bill to further clarify the issue of emergency medical care. Conditions currently vary from town to town in regard to the kinds and quality of ambulance service that can be rendered by the community's ambulance technicians. A group of emergency physicians was on hand to point out the problems that could be attendant upon the current uniform state regulations. The bill calls for certain changes in those regs to make them more compatible with the kind of service our greatly differing cities and towns can and need to offer. The doctors feel they should have had input in setting up the regulations.

Thursday and at a noon meeting at the Sheraton Boston we heard from Massport's Executive Director David Davis that the Port Authority endorses the joint widening and depressing of the Southern Artery and the building of a Third Harbor Tunnel from a point in South Boston to the airport. The Boston Chamber of Commerce had arranged the meeting. An Environmental Impact Study encompassing both proposals must be in the hands of the Federal Government by September 30th in order to qualify for consideration as a 90% federally funded transportation project. It will be a tight squeeze but somehow I feel that with the Administration backing the proposal 100% and Massport sharing the cost of the EIS, it will be done on time.

I had begun the day Thursday as a member of a panel brought together to discuss before several hundred interested medical and business people the pros and cons of Chapter 372, the new Hospital Cost Control law. My being there was quite unexpected. The Health Care Committee Chairman was taken ill on Wednesday afternoon; he was scheduled to be one of the panelists. Well, at 5 pm I was asked to fill in for him. It was a challenge to be sure. All went well, however, I am happy to say; and after my own fifteen or twenty minutes of fame, I thoroughly enjoyed hearing from the other knowledgeable people present of their experiences with the new law and their recommendations on how it can be dealt with.

Thursday evening and it was off to Town Hall to support the members of our Braintree Conservation Commission and their Holbrook counterparts in their attempt to safeguard the Cranberry Brook Watershed by placing it under the protection of the state as an area of critical environmental concern.

Friday morning was easily the nicest day of the week. I presented diplomas to a group of small boys and girls at the annual Watson Park Library "Library School" graduation. A fun time, as always. Braintree Point Woman's Club member Ethel Spano and her dedicated assistants continue to do a beautiful job with the 60 to 70 3½ to 5 year olds who attend their Story Hour program each Friday morning. Thanks, Ethel!

Sunday was a busy day. There was the Braintree Fire Fighters Memorial Mass at Saint Francis Church at 8:15 a.m., a flying trip to Connecticut and back again to attend the 40th Wedding Anniversary celebration for my good friends Tony and Alice Mollica… and a House citation for them, needless to say…

JULY 8, 1983

It was quite a week for all of us on Beacon Hill. A bill tightening the law on the reporting of Child Abuse cases went rapidly through the Senate after having made it easily through the House. It would mandate that Massachusetts social workers report to the District Attorney any child abuse cases involving serious injury, rape or sexual exploitation.

An acid rain monitoring project, spearheaded by the Governor, turned up the fact that samples from 1173 of the state's lakes, ponds, rivers, etc. showed 80% plus of those tested are threatened by acid rain. Governor Michael S. Dukakis has joined other New England governors in seeking federal programs to offset this sad situation.

The state's homeless came in for further help as nine additional shelters were ordered for Hyannis, Worcester, Lowell, Brockton, Holyoke and Fitchburg.

The Senate followed the House in approving a new "Lemon Law" which will require the manufacturers to refund or replace a severely defective new car whose problems still remain after three attempts to rectify it. Any new car, truck or motorcycle would come under the bill if defects surfaced during the first year or within 15,000 miles of use.

My bill to designate Deborah Sampson as the Official Heroine of Massachusetts was approved in the House without debate and went on to the other branch for further action. It also calls for an annual Governor's Proclamation in observance of the May 23rd date on which Deborah Sampson disguised as a man, enlisted in the Revolutionary War. As Robert Shurtliff, the lady fought with distinction. During one battle, she received a head injury and a musket ball in the leg. She permitted a doctor to treat the head wound; however, as a precaution against discovery, this intrepid lady hid in the woods and herself removed the musket ball with her knife. I had filed the bill at the request of my good friend Patrick L. Leonard. Sr.

An auto insurance bill was approved in the Senate and in the House. It would set up a "not safe driver" classification for those drivers who have been responsible for four or more accidents within a period of three years, or who file more than two fire or theft claims within three years. Drivers convicted of vehicular homicide, car theft or insurance fraud would also be placed in this category. The bill would eliminate the Massachusetts Motor Vehicle Reinsurance Facility or high-risk pool and replace it with a Commonwealth Auto Reinsurers pool where good drivers would not be forced to pay the higher rates assessed against bad drivers. It would also repeal the current "take all comers" law. A "fraud squad" would be established in the high-risk pool and insurance companies would be required to return policy holders profits in excess of 9%.

Wednesday's deliberations on the Governor's revenue enhancement protection, or REAP plan, were interrupted along the way by a bomb threat in the House Chamber. It had to be evacuated for one-half hour while the search for the bomb went on. Thankfully the search revealed nothing. The REAP bill went down to defeat on an 85-69 vote at seven o'clock that evening. It was reconsidered on Thursday and was signed into law by the Governor after a reversal of the vote at 1:30 a.m. on Friday morning.

My own week in the State House was among the wildest on record. Evening sessions prevented my involvement in anything happening in Braintree; however, under the Golden Dome I could have used roller skates. On Thursday, for instance (and that was just one out of four of these hectic days), I attended a meeting on Joint Custody of minor children in cases of divorce; a Transportation Committee Hearing where MBTA General Manager James O'Leary discussed the Authority's funding requests in the Transportation Bond legislation; a Health Care Committee "Informational Public Hearing" on mandated health benefits. I also managed to speak on the legislative process to a group of Juniors and Seniors from Belmont High School (its Political Science class). Sandwiched in between a couple of these happenings was the most important happening of all-a meeting with House Speaker Thomas W. McGee and Governor Dukakis to secure immediate emergency funding for water quality testing of the Richardi Reservoir. Our great Water Commission Chairman, my good friend Joe Cleggett, needs all the help he can get in his untiring efforts to protect the town's water supply, and we were happy to have been able to lend him and our citizens a helping hand at the State House.

JULY 22, 1983

Summer was in full swing on Beacon Hill. We who come daily to the State House find we must wrestle the tourists for walking space in the marble corridors…and we're eating our lunch standing up in one decidedly overcrowded lunch room…

On Boston Common one may purchase just about anything grown, created or manufactured from stands, barrows, bicycles and vans. The music of many lands and as many instruments flows in a sometimes discordant but always interesting symphony upon the summer air. On Park Street, enroute to the Capitol building, one walks over a magnificent portrait of Paul Revere, the work of Boston's talented sidewalk artist "Sidewalk Sam."

Within the State House itself during the past week government was also in full swing. It was check and double check for all of us, on those particular items we favored in either the House or the Senate versions of the state budget, still in the hands of the Conference Committee. It emerged finally on Wednesday morning, and our lobbying went on until we saw the final document in print, and realized that the die was cast and the 1984 State Budget was just about cast in stone.

Surprisingly enough, it generated considerably less debate than had been anticipated. The morning had been spent in a briefing session held by the House Chairman of Ways and Means, Representative Michael Creedon of Brockton, and Frank Keefe, the Governor's Secretary of Administration and Finance. We House members had been invited to attend and to ask our questions on the budget's content. We did just that, with the result that most of our concerns had been addressed. The budget therefore, went through the House almost smoothly.

Actually it is a very good budget, and it was accepted on a 129-23 vote. Under it, our cities and towns will receive an additional $159 million to assist them in dealing with the third year of Prop 2½. The State Revenue Department will have an additional 250 employees to assist in its efforts to function more effectively and to carry out the fraud control policies contained in the so-called REAP law.

A 3% cost of living increase for those state and local pensions has been provided for, along with a $125 per child Winter clothing allowance for AFDC families. And under the budget, the Administration must report tax collections on a quarterly basis; and should those collections fall below the estimated receipts for two consecutive three-month periods, the Governor will be obliged to cut the budget or propose additional sources of revenue.

The budget debate enjoyed an added dimension this year. Representatives from WGBH-TV (Channel 2) were on hand, conducting a series of tests in the House Chamber to determine the kind of lighting and cameras that will be required for its "gavel to gavel" coverage of our House sessions come January.

…the Parker House where we attended an "Appreciation Breakfast" planned for members of the General Court by the Boston Building and Construction Trades Council in gratitude for our "overwhelming support in the defeat of recent legislation to do away with Chapter 149, the Prevailing Wage Law in Massachusetts." Anticipating what was expected to be a late-night session, it wasn't easy to be up and at it at the Parker House at that early hour. Nonetheless we made it, and enjoyed both the breakfast and our labor-oriented breakfast companions.

Wednesday afternoon had to include, in addition to a number of other obligations, a Transportation Committee hearing where we voted unanimously in support of the

Transportation Bond Issue which will cover MBTA, MDC and DPW and railroad capital construction funding for the next two years. We anticipate no real difficulty with this one either.

The week ended with a bang legislatively at 2:20 a.m. Friday morning (we had been in session since 1 p.m. the previous day) and for perhaps the first time in my eight and one-half years under the Golden Dome, we went into a sort of Summer recess. Unless an emergency arises, only informal House sessions will be held from now until September. Our committee work and our constituent work will go on as usual, needless to say. Either my Administrative Assistant Suzanne Bump or I will be on hand at our State House office daily to assist with our constituents' problems, and so feel free to continue to contact us. Lawmaking only will come to a standstill on Beacon Hill this summer.

OCTOBER 7, 1983

A productive week under the Golden Dome…The two-year $1.2 billion Transportation Bond legislation was engrossed in the House on Tuesday. There was no debate on the bill at this final stage. It had been redrafted to place strict controls upon the Metropolitan District Commission's handling of its funding, there being considerable controversy at present between the agency and the Inspector General about past performance at the MDC.

$500 million of the bond issue would be paid for by state funding, supplied by the sale of bonds; with $700 million of federal money involved.

The spending proposal provides additional money for critically needed bridge repairs within the Commonwealth; a transit program for the elderly and handicapped; millions for mass transit; and funding for passenger rail improvements for the inland route to New York. Of special interest to your L. of the H. was the $60 million to $80 million allocation for the reconstruction of the Southeast Expressway, this particular project promising to have such an impact upon the residents of Braintree.

Funding for the completion of Routes 195 and 146 is included; and $40 million in grant money will be awarded to cities and towns for local road projects. The legislation includes funding for the hiring of 100 new junior civil engineers for the Department of Public Works, an agency devastated by cutbacks during the past few years.

Money is provided for the acquisition of 58 new MBTA Red Line cars, and some new buses, along with some station improvements.

This bonding bill will provide for transportation spending for the next two years, and it went through the House with ease, plenty of supportive information having been provided by our most efficient Transportation Committee staff members. We anticipate no problems with the bill in the Senate, and as a member of the Transportation

Committee, I am hopeful that the legislation will soon find its way to the Governor's desk for signing.

The so-called "Lemon Law" legislation reached the Governor's desk this past week. It applies to any new car, truck or motorcycle purchased for personal use. Should a new car continue to have a problem after 4 attempts to repair it, the consumer would be entitled to a refund or a car replacement within 30 days. A refund will include sales tax, registration fees and finance charges. There is happily a general feeling that the Governor will sign the lemon law bill without delay. We hope so. We've had a significant number of new car horror stories come our way during the past nine years on Beacon Hill; and we've not always been able to help the unfortunate car buyers in their quest for justice.

As we bade farewell to Summer, and thoughts of those unpopular heating bills began to loom upon the financial horizon, it was interesting to learn that the Commonwealth is offering its citizens an opportunity to purchase firewood for $10 a cord. It must be cut, split and hauled away, of course, by the purchaser. The wood is in our state parks, among them the Wompatuck State Park in Hingham. The program will be administered under the Home Fuel Wood program, and there is a $1 filing fee for each bid submitted. Anyone interested in the program is asked to call forester Austin Mason at the Miles Standish Forest in Plymouth for more information.

As the week progressed we learned that Governor Michael S. Dukakis has endorsed the proposed plans to widen the Central Artery and to build a third harbor tunnel. Having been caught more than once in the massive traffic jams that will be eased by the proposed highway construction projects, we rejoice at the willingness, indeed the far-sightedness of our Chief Executive in endorsing the proposed Central Artery Third Harbor Tunnel project. We've built too many highways in the past that proved to be obsolete almost before they were completed…Take the Southeast Expressway for example-built to accommodate 75,000 cars and within 25 years it is handling twice as many. Let's look ahead and plan on a sufficiently large scale to deal with Boston's traffic problems…

NOVEMBER 11, 1983

The week began for me on Sunday when I participated in a ceremony dedicating a lovely dogwood tree to the memory of my dear friend Doris Canavan. Situated on the lawn of the Watson Park Branch Library, this handsome living tree will serve for all time as a reminder of a very remarkable lady who spent her lifetime in the service of others in Braintree.

Monday morning and I met with MDC Commissioner William Geary to discuss further the alleviation of the flooding problems in the area adjacent to Braintree Dam. It was I who nine years ago brought together the MDC, the DPW and the Army Corps of Engineers seeking their assistance in solving Braintree's problems. The dam, which is owned by Quincy but located in Braintree, is an earthen dam. The flow of water from the basin is controlled by valves. (It may even be a single valve; I have heard that the second valve is out of commission.)

At any rate, during unusually heavy rainstorms our town highway superintendent Bob Frazier is called upon to babysit the facility, opening the valve when needed to keep the water level under control. Failure to keep a close watch on Braintree Dam could result in the kind of flooding that devastated the area a few years back and almost caused the drowning of young child who was enroute to Lakeside School. I had secured the initial funding for the state's share of the project and additional funding was secured from time to time since then. To date, however, only Quincy has profited by the deal. Its flooding problems were, of course, exacerbated by the building of the new T station and the projected development of the Old Colony Crushed Stone land. The argument we heard was that addressing the problem at our end would only increase the problem downstream. I simply cannot buy that. I asked that Braintree's culverts be rebuilt adequately, not in the future, but now. The Commissioner appeared to be convinced of the validity of our case, and I shall attempt, via the capital outlay budget we are currently considering on Beacon Hill, to assure the state funding for the project. Monday afternoon and we held a Health Care Committee hearing on a bill filed by my Chairman and friend Representative Richard Voke which would authorize the Department of Public Welfare to establish a statewide system of long-term health care pre-screening teams. This being potentially a complicated issue, we elected to place it in a study. Tuesday morning found me on hand in the State Senate for a memorial program honoring Humberto Cardinal Medieros. The ceremony highlighted the role of the Gerontology program CPCS UMass/Boston, the Archdiocese of Boston and the Commonwealth of Massachusetts in serving the elderly within the inspired vision of Cardinal Medieros. Tuesday evening and it was off to the Quincy Neighborhood Club for the Friends of the South Shore Rehab Center's annual Cocktail Party and Awards Night, where my good friend Senator Paul Harold was among the award recipients. Wednesday was a red letter day for your L. of the H. as I debated at length against strong opposition (and won by a vote of 96 to 53) my bill to open up a new source of corneal tissue to provide sight to the more than 200 Massachusetts residents awaiting this thin wafer, 1/25th of an inch thick and as big around as a lead pencil, that will lead to the gift of sight.

The day had begun with a meeting of the Rules Committee of which I am a member, where the proposed rules changes were considered. It was moved and speedily seconded to appoint a committee of five persons to consider the rules changes and report back to the floor of the House by November 14.

Thursday held a formal House session and began when we members of the Massachusetts Caucus of Women Legislators met with the House Speaker, the Hon. Thomas W. McGee, to outline our legislative priorities for this year and to seek his assistance in bringing our important bills to the floor of the House. I felt that we were quite successful in our quest for his support. Speaker McGee is extremely supportive of women's issues and we have had phenomenal success with our priorities during the past few years as high as 95%…

Saturday evening and I was pleased to present a House Resolution to Joan Giglio, this year's "Woman of the Year" for our Braintree Ladies Lodge No. 1422, Order Sons of Italy. Sunday morning and my week's work went on. I was on hand at Beth Israel Synagogue for the 33rd annual breakfast of the Jewish War Veterans Post 193 where my good friend Senator Harold was honored once more, this time as the Post's "Citizen of the Year". A full week and a good one….

NOVEMBER 25, 1983

A Happy Thanksgiving to each and every one of my readers! May you have much to be thankful for. High on the priority list of my reasons to be thankful is enjoying the privilege of representing 38,000 wonderful people of Braintree in the House of Representatives.

We've had a series of late night sessions and so we will now be facing no formal House sessions during the three days prior to Thanksgiving Day…all of which sounds like a nice spot of vacation time for Massachusetts legislators. It won't be…although we shall be spending no time in the House Chamber, we'll be on hand at the State House as always, handling our other responsibilities, doing such things as working on the bills we have filed for next year and attempting to solve the many problems that seem to beset our constituents; and, of course, attending those home town and other evening events that seem to abound as the legislative year winds down.

We have just concluded a very busy week. We voted in a series of reforms that will affect the running of the House, we approved a revised condominium conversion bill that will force real estate agents to give tenants a one-year notice and a moving allowance of up to $1,000 prior to converting to condos. A longer notice must be given to the handicapped, the elderly and the low-income tenants. The voice-vote by which this bill was accepted in the house represented a significant victory for Massachusetts tenants, representatives of whose organization had haunted the State House during the past few weeks.

I succeeded in getting engrossed in the House a bill which would establish a Nursing Home Ombudsman program throughout the State. Having chaired the sub-committee that worked out with all parties involved (including the Massachusetts Federation of Nursing Homes) an acceptable compromise version of a bill that has had no success on the Hill for the past six years, I felt a definite sense of accomplishment as I now prepared to steer it through the Governor's legislative office. The signing of this bill into law will make a great many people happy, and have a distinct impact upon the kind of care our elderly receive in the state's nursing homes.

I haven't been using the Red Line much of late. We've had a superfluity of late night sessions in the House and so I've been driving the Xway (Heaven help me). I was therefore, blissfully unaware of its latest difficulties. I was interested to learn that the MBTA is currently spending about $300,000 to replace the rail supports on the Red Line's Quincy-Braintree extension. The T is anything but happy at the prospect of having to replace these rail supports which are but three years old. They feel they should have lasted "almost indefinitely" and plan to determine who is liable for their failure...a failure that has caused considerable difficulty on the Red Line of late. Insulator problems, as well, are causing trouble. According to the T's Operations Manager William Stead, 10% of the 3400 insulators supporting the electrified third rails have failed. If ever there was an ill-fated project, the Quincy-Braintree rapid transit extension is it...

Extracurricular activities as the week progressed included a meeting with representatives of the Massachusetts Municipal Wholesale Electric Company, where we were given an overview of the MMWEC's energy program and a preview of our energy needs in the decades ahead. Since Braintree has its own municipal light department. I thought it wise to be on hand so as to keep abreast of energy developments within the State.

I was on hand for a briefing by Administration and Finance Secretary Frank T. Keefe on the proposed "Massbank" which would appear to provide for our cities and towns an additional mechanism for securing low-cost loans for the repair and maintenance of their public buildings, etc.

I attended a Legislative Breakfast at the South Shore Hospital where we heard anew the problems the hospital is facing in attempts to secure Certificate of Need for the renovations and expansion it feels are essential to its operation.

DECEMBER 9, 1983

The days could use an extra eight hours at least, as rumors of Prorogation float about the State House these days, and each and every one of us springs into action, tracking down and seeking to bring to the floor of the House for action those pet bills that for one reason or other (usually their questionable constitutionality or their price tag) languish in Third Reading or Ways and Means. As the week began, I was invited to speak at a Legislative Reception held at the State House by the Massachusetts Association of Home Care Programs/Area Agencies on Aging, and the Massachusetts Council for Homemaker-Home Health Aide Services. The organizations had elected to jointly observe National Home Care Week in this manner, and I was pleased to help them do so. The highlight of the week occurred for me on Tuesday afternoon when the Governor officially signed the Cornea Transplant Bill, legislation that, as the primary House sponsor, I had steered through the House after extensive debate. Since this bill had taken 4 years to reach the

Governor's desk, you may well imagine my elation when it was signed into law with picture taking and much ceremony, and indeed with general rejoicing.

Another equally exciting personal triumph was mine on Tuesday as the Nursing Home Ombudsman Bill was finally enacted in the House and sent to the Governor for signing-a ceremony which has been scheduled for next Friday morning at a North End Nursing Home. I had chaired the Sub-committee that had finally succeeded in working out a bill acceptable to all parties involved, including the Mass. Federation of Nursing Homes, accomplishing a feat that had been attempted for the past 8 years, believe it or not. You may well imagine my pride in that one also! Thursday was a rather interesting day. The West Suburban YMCA of Framingham held its annual Leader Luncheon, honoring women of achievement in business and industry at the Chateau de Ville in Framingham. This Leader Luncheon is sponsored annually by major corporations in the Greater Boston area; and this year, for the first time, women at the highest levels of Massachusetts government were invited to join the group and "be recognized for their contributions in the public sector." It was an extremely interesting event. It is always a delight to me to see women achieve the highest levels of employment in business and industry. The principal speaker was Evelyn Murphy, Secretary of Economic Affairs for the Commonwealth; and I was personally delighted when she plugged the Displaced Homemaker Program which has been my Women's Caucus priority issue since its inception, and which has proved to be wonderfully cost effective and successful as I had forecast when seeking appropriations. In other action, as a member of the House Caucus of Environmentalists, I attended an updated meeting on Acid Rain, a problem that is besetting Massachusetts to a very great extent, and with which we are trying to cope through governmental action both on a federal and on a state level. The Condominium Conversion bill was signed into law and the Department of Public Welfare began issuing photo ID's for recipients of food stamps. For several years I had filed legislation to mandate the use of ID photos for all public assistance recipients in an effort to cut down on fraud and abuse; and why not I would ask of Human Services Committee members who always voted it down…ID photos are required on our automobile licenses; and they are required when the elderly seek reduced fare on the MBTA. I could not see the issue as one of discrimination. Now the DPW is about to use my idea. On some issues it takes longer to win…

The Housing bill went through the House on a 145-0 roll call vote. It would provide $196 million in subsidies for the construction of housing for the elderly and for handicapped and low and middle-income individuals.

The MBTA proposed to run fewer trains on the Red Line during off-peak hours and additional trains during peak hours, as a means of improving its rapid transit service. We trust it will help the present situation, which is anything but good at present.

It's beginning to look like Christmas on Beacon Hill. 30,000 lights are in place on Boston Common, and by the time you read this column, the trees will be alight. Christmas music from the Carillon of the Park Street Church comes our way each evening as we open the huge State House doors and descend the great stone steps. It's easily my favorite time of year. How I love the beautiful feast of Christmas.

DECEMBER 16, 1983

"THAT WAS THE WEEK THAT WAS" -the title of a very popular TV program a few years back- it could certainly be applied to the week just past on Beacon Hill as all and sundry began their mad attempts to spring their all-important bills before the 1983 session of the General Court would be brought to close.

The one remaining piece of legislation that I absolutely had to get to the Governor's desk was my "Displaced Homemaker" bill. The bill wore no price tag whatsoever, but was of vital importance to the continuity of a program that is working beautifully under current management. H-6880 would provide the statutory framework for the establishment of a network of Displaced Homemaker programs already in place through the Bay State Skills Corporation.

The Displaced Homemaker program has been my priority issue with the Women's Caucus from its inception, and over the past 3 years of heavy action I have succeeded in having it funded adequately and extended into areas of need. Its permanent existence had to be assured statutorily, and that was my aim on Friday-the last day of real action in the General Court.

I had succeeded in getting it through the House. The tie-up was in the Senate, and so I madly lobbied every Senator numbered among my friends, including the Senate President, and then began what turned out to be an all-night vigil to spring the bill form a pile of hundreds of important pieces of legislation that had found their way to the Senate Clerk for action during this end-of-the-year session.

It was all rather exciting. I positioned myself in the rear of the Senate Chamber, in full view of those friendly Senators, all of whom knew for what reason I was there. Interspersed with this Senate vigil were the more than 40 dashes to the House Chamber for roll call votes on the bills that were coming through my own branch of government at the same time. What a moment of triumph I enjoyed, however, as my bill finally made it in the Senate the motion to suspend the rules for its engrossment having been made by no less a personage than Senate President William M. Bulger. The bill had then to return to the House for enactment before being sent to the Governor's desk for signing into law. And so, secure in the knowledge that it was now reasonably safe, at 10 a.m. I left the Senate Chamber a happy legislator indeed.

It had been a busy week in other respects for your L. of the H. On Monday evening I had enjoyed attending the annual Christmas Party of the newly reorganized Braintree Business and Professional Association. It was a gala occasion indeed; and with my good friend Mary Medico very much in the forefront, a happy happening was assured for all those who had gathered in the handsome VFW hall on Washington Street.

On Thursday afternoon I had been very proudly on hand at the North End Community Nursing Home when His Excellency Governor Michael S. Dukakis signed into law, with due ceremony, the long-awaited Nursing Home Ombudsman bill. I had chaired the sub-committee that, after 8 years of frustrated endeavor to bring this about, had produced a bill that was acceptable to all parties involved in the issue, including the Massachusetts Federation of Nursing Homes. It was, therefore, a happy and indeed a triumphant moment for me when Governor Dukakis placed his all-important signature on this all-important piece of legislation…

Signs of the Christmas season are everywhere, needless to say, on Beacon Hill. The State House itself is alive with strings of white lights and with a white star atop its Golden Dome. Situated as it is at the top of Beacon Hill it is visible from all parts of Boston. Additionally 30,000 white lights are strung from the trees on Boston Common, and a huge white lighted star adorns the entrance to Downtown Crossing. There is seasonal beauty everywhere, and how enjoyable it was for our group of legislators returning to the State House after the dinner break that punctuated those 10 a.m. to 10 p.m. sessions we labored under during the past week. We would be steeped in the Christmas spirit as we walked up Park Street on our return trip to the State House for another go-around on legislative priorities.

Well, now, after a final 24 consecutive hours of formal legislative action, my own most successful year in the House of Representatives has come to a close. We'll be in the State House during parts of this week and next. However, it will not be for formal House action, but just for meetings and constituent responsibilities, etc. What an eventful year it has been, but then, haven't they all been eventful years for this legislator??? And haven't I loved them all???

FEBRUARY 3, 1984

It was an interesting week. My announced impending retirement has been a bit of a shock to a great many people on Beacon Hill. "YOU, of all people…Why in the world??? You, who LOVE the place so much…What will you do with that amazing energy of yours???" etc. etc. etc. It was difficult to get anything done. The shortest sortie outside the confines of my office turned into a time consuming trip as I encountered one after another of the great people who share my days under the Golden Dome. I guess I never really know how many friends I had there. Suffice to say it is a beautiful feeling to know that after ten years I shall be leaving that historic place unable really to identify a single enemy. That was my goal ten years ago when I took my first oath of office and I seem to have achieved it. That lump in my throat that has been present since I announced, seems to remain, however. Oh well, ten years is a nice long slice of happiness and fulfillment, wouldn't you say???

So what about the week itself…How did it go? Legislatively we are still awaiting the assignment of committee hearing dates for those bills we have filed or which our committees will be hearing, or in which we are especially interested. Legislatively, therefore, the action went on pretty much behind the scenes. There was, nonetheless, considerable action…Monday evening, and it was off to Pier 3 where the Massachusetts Association for Mental Health sponsored a Testimonial tribute to Speaker Thomas W. McGee in recognition of his unending contributions to the people of the Commonwealth during his twenty years of public service, the past nine years as Speaker of the House of Representatives. He received tributes from Human Services advocates and state officials alike, and was presented with a handsome framed portrait done in most appropriate setting; surrounded by the poor and the needy, and including his famous quote: "If you can say at the end of the day that you have been able to help at least one person…you've done a good job…you've had a good day…" The evening's most heartwarming remarks came from Governor Michael S. Dukakis. "When Prop 2½ threatened our cities and towns and we were called upon for massive amounts of aid for them it was speaker McGee who insisted there should be no decimation of the state's Human Services program to bring this about," he said. Tuesday, and as a guest of Stone and Webster Engineering Corporation, I was back at Pier 4 to attend a seminar held by the Massachusetts Association of Civil Engineers, where former Governor John Volpe was honored and our top state officials were on hand (from the Governor on down) to outline the Commonwealth's construction needs for the years ahead. I had raced to Pier 4 from a press conference at Quincy Junior College where through my efforts anew displaced area homemaker program was to be instituted. A nice assist for those area women who find themselves thrust suddenly into the role of family breadwinner and who need their confidence shored up, their skills upgraded, and a job to go to. Wednesday evening and I was on hand at Braintree High School, sharing the platform with Pam Wolfe, the Community Coordinator for the Southeast Expressway reconstruction project and her assistant Terry Murray, along with Braintree Selectmen Chairman Joe Cleggett. Despite the clamor that surrounds this forthcoming nightmare, only eight Braintree townspeople were on hand to express their concerns and to seek answers to their questions. Senator Paul Harold, Selectman Sarah Gillies and school Committeeman Paul Agnew were there to represent the town additionally, but the turnout was indeed disappointing. We had a briefing session that morning on the Governor's 1985 State Budget. It pretty much reflects the priorities of the House, however after I finish digesting the three-volume budget I shall be better able to evaluate it.

Thursday evening and it was off to the Sheraton Tara for the 6th annual "Legislative Buttonhole Session" of the South Shore Chamber of Commerce where I was pleased to have been invited to address this prestigious group that to such an outstanding extent protects the best interests of our South Shore business and industry.

I also had the pleasure of preparing House Citations for three new Eagle Scouts from Troop 138, Parish of Saint Clare. Robert Comption II, Douglas Foley and Robert Walsh are deserving of our congratulations and best wished on this most significant achievement.

MARCH 10, 1984

Uppermost in the mind of your L. of the H. during the past week was indignation at the proposal of the Norfolk County Commissioners survey team to place a jail at the Norfolk County Hospital. This indignation I expressed promptly in a letter to Chairman James Collins. It was followed by the drafting of a bill which I planned to file to prevent the placing of any facility to house prisoners in Braintree only to learn with considerable satisfaction that our Braintree Board of Selectmen proposed to do just that. I promptly shelved my own piece and filed their bill on receipt of it.

We had all been told meanwhile that two of the three commissioners opposed the choice, and that was good news, however let's not be lulled. Let's all keep up the pressure against what is clearly a reprehensible suggestion.

On our Health Care Committee we heard bills designed to weaken the lead paint law we now have on the books. Lead paint is a source of major poisoning in children under 6 who are inclined to lick any surface they can reach, especially windowsills, railings, etc. Most older homes have lead paint. Lead has a sweet taste which comes through any number of coats of unleaded paint, which is why children lick it. Ingested in sufficient quantities it can cause brain damage and even death. As the law now stands, pediatricians and clinics must test small children for lead paint, and its detection triggers a process that calls for the de-leading of a home or apartment.

On hand at our hearing were realtors and homeowners who have legitimate difficulty in selling single-family homes under the existing law. Our committee will be studying this issue in depth during the coming week.

My perennial bill to keep Five Corners Signalization project alive came before the Transportation Committee on Tuesday. The plans are 80 per cent complete and await the acceptance of the Selectmen Sadly, however, we may have hit a snag. An assessment is currently being made on the impact that construction will make on the Southeast Expressway reconstruction which will commence on March 19. I am keeping in touch with the DPW on this issue, needless to say.

On March 1, at my request, the Governor issued a Proclamation naming the month of March "Selective Service Awareness Month", and I was on hand with Colonel Bob Levine and national Aide-de-Camp Danny Wambolt for the signing of the Proclamation, Friday was a busy day. As a member of the Legislative Committee on International Trade and Foreign Investment, I was present at a meeting of the South Shore Chamber of

Commerce Foreign Business Council. Our staff director, Kathleen O'Donnell was present to offer the services of our committee in developing foreign trade. The Chamber's Public Affairs Director David Knight had arranged the meeting; and we hope to be able to work closely with the South Shore Chamber of Commerce to help in expanding our South Shore economy via exports to the developing nations in Africa (which need just about everything), China and Central America. The balance of payments situation has us worried; and the Chamber hopes to promote opportunities for exporters and would be exporters among its membership. And what a distinguished group of officials, bankers, and businessmen Dave Knight had brought together for that meeting! The Chamber gets things done…

Friday evening and it was off to Sons of Italy Hall to attend our Annual Fire Fighters Retirement and Awards Dinner, an event run flawlessly by its Union President, my good friend Jerry Kenney. I presented House Citations to Lt. A Parker Nadeau, "Officer of the Year," and to David Linscott, "Fire Fighter of the Year," for dedication and service beyond the call of duty. I also was in for a surprise. I was presented with a gorgeous silver tray in recognition of my support of our fire fighters. It is beautifully inscribed and comes from our Braintree Fire Fighters Association and the professional Fire Fighters of Massachusetts. How wonderful of them!

Saturday evening and Ted and I were enroute to Dedham to present a House Citation to my good friend Braintree Legionnaire Sam Caravella on the occasion of his retirement as Norfolk County Commander of the American Legion. A great testimonial dinner, and a fun time…

Another happy happening during this week. I was on hand to speak at Nurses Hall, expressing my thanks for a nice hefty tourism grant received by our Norfolk County. Tourism is big business and Massachusetts needs it…

MARCH 16, 1984

Local aid!!! It was the one issue that dominated all other news under the Golden Dome this past week. Like all of my colleagues, I headed for Gardner Auditorium on Thursday morning with a keen sense of anticipation. It was, happily enough, realized. Braintree, for the second year in a row, was to fare beautifully. We shall be receiving $742,589 more in estimated net State Aid for FY85 than for FY84. This, needless to say, is good news for the community I represent so proudly. Additional specifics on the local aid issue were promised for Monday, after which we should have the whole Cherry Sheet picture in plenty of time for Town Meeting action…a situation that has occurred for the first time within the memory of most everyone on the Hill.

Equally important, if not more important, was the stated decision of the Norfolk County Commissioners James Collins and George McDonald, along with Sheriff Clifford Marshall AGAINST placing a jail on the grounds of Norfolk County Hospital. They were on hand Tuesday evening at East Junior High School for a meeting that had been arranged by Norman Davis and Bob Kendall…a meeting that saw hundreds of Braintree residents on hand to fight the proposed Braintree jail.

By a strange set of fortuitous circumstances on that very morning, a bill was being heard before the Committee on Counties that dealt with the Norfolk County jail issue. It had been filed in a timely fashion last November by my good friend and colleague Representative M. Joseph Manning of Milton. It called for the prohibition of a jail at the Wollaston Recreational Facility in Quincy; and Representative Manning graciously allowed me to propose an amended version to the committee which would not only bring the Norfolk County Hospital site under the prohibition, but additionally spell out the "temporary or permanent" aspect of the situation. (We are all wary of that word "temporary".) I was pleased to make this announcement at the Tuesday evening meeting; and Representative Manning and Robert Emmet Hayes of Whitman were on hand to join us in our fight against the unwholesome proposal for a Braintree jail. Additionally, I was pleased to have been successful in releasing from the Joint Committee on Rules a late-filed bill I had filed for our Braintree Selectmen, also designed to prevent the construction of the jail. Having been accepted in the House, it will now go to the Committee on Counties for a hearing. I was also pleased to have been notified by DPW Commissioner Robert Tierney that the State will pay for additional police and crossing guards, at least for the first few weeks, during the Southeast Xway reconstruction.

The Mass. Convention Center Authority made its formal debut at the State House on Thursday morning, and I was there. Offices designed to lure tourism to Massachusetts will be opened in three cities; Washington, D.C.; New York; and Chicago. These three cities are headquarters for more than 847,000 group meetings and conventions annually, we were told; and in his official acceptance of the final report with its key provision of rebuilding the Hynes Auditorium, His Excellency Governor Michael S. Dukakis stressed again and again the fact (and it IS a fact) that Massachusetts has more to offer the tourist than any other state in the country. His proposal to put Massachusetts on the map as a Convention Center bids fair to rival the "I Love New York" campaign of our neighbor state. It was "Save Your Vision Week" in Massachusetts, and "Optometry Day" included a walk-in clinic where we were invited by the Commonwealth's Optometrists to receive vision and glaucoma screening. It was an interesting day.

My good friend of long standing, Janet Sullivan, retired in the course of the week, and I was pleased to present her with a House Citation in acknowledgement of her 24 years of dedication to the DPW as a Financial Assistance Social Worker.

The week ended on a high note indeed. Daughter Gael and I were on hand at the Bayside Club on Sunday morning to share and enjoy Senate President William Bulger's Saint Patrick's Day Corned Beef and Cabbage Gala and political roast. It's easily the most fun of anything we do in the course of the year, and we had a ball, as usual. I'll miss being part of these exciting happenings…

MARCH 23, 1984

It was to have been one of the busiest weeks on record…and, wouldn't you know??? your L. of the H. came down with the flu, and was immobilized for much of it. A high temperature and the bark of a trained seal are not very conducive to a first-rate legislative performance, and so I was obliged to forego many of the meetings and events I had pledged to attend. I trust I shall be forgiven by those in charge. I simply could not pull myself together, and incidentally this has been the first year in my nine-plus when an attack of flu has really laid me low enough to prevent the discharge of my legislative duties…Shouldn't complain, I suppose, with that record.

I did manage, however to be on hand, lightheaded though I was, for a couple of very important Wednesday happenings…at 10 a.m. for the 9 to 5 Press Conference on the VDT legislation, and afterwards in Gardner Auditorium I was on hand to defend my own VDT bill which, in my opinion, is easily the best of the eight or so that have been filed for this session.

This is the second year for filing my VDT bill, H-4537. It had been drafted by the AFL-CIO last year, and I had been asked to file it by my good friend and constituent Frank Toland. It went into a Commerce and Labor Committee study, and I instructed my office to participate. On the basis then of a number of what I considered to be legitimate concerns on the part of the business community. I amended the original bill, making it more palatable to business, while at the same time affording the kind of protection the state's computer operators are seeking and need so badly. H-4537 was the result; and I defended it well, I thought, on Wednesday.

H-4537 does not apply to all offices with a VDT, nor does it cover all employees who may have access to one in the course of their employment. It applies only to offices with employees whose primary duties require VDT use. It does not require immediate office refurbishing. It ties updating of the office environment with updating of automated office systems. It does not represent intrusion in to an area normally the subject of collective bargaining since only a small percentage of VDT operators are unionized. Most are at-will female employees, with no control over their jobs or working conditions.

What H-4537 does do is direct the Department of Labor and Industries to establish regulations to protect VDT operators from the health and safety hazards arising from their working conditions. It calls for: advance notice of office automation; flexibility and adjustability of VDT units and office furnishings to suit users and prevent muscle strain; reduction of glare and provision of proper lighting to minimize eye strain; employer provided annual eye examinations for VDT operators and eyewear necessary for VDT work; periodic breaks for VDT operators; alternative employment for pregnant operators; and establishment of medical advisory group to monitor the vision and health of VDT operators.

In defending my bill before the Commerce and Labor Committee, I reminded them of the asbestos problem with which we are dealing today, and about which Paul

Eustace, Secretary of Labor had just finished speaking. "Let us not make the same kind of mistake we made on asbestos," I pleaded. "Warnings were issued on this menace almost a century ago. They were ignored; and hundreds of thousands of people have died of cancer…"

On hand among the many testifying were countless VDT operators, wearing as a result of my suggestion neat VDT badges, Dr. Arnold Zide, a distinguished optometrist, who apparently agreed with me that my bill is the best, for he recorded himself in strong support of H-4537, discussing as he did so the potential vision and muscle problems that could result from unrelieved hours before a computer terminal.

Governor Michael S. Dukakis, through Philip W. Johnston, the Director of his Office of Human Resources, announced the commissioning of a "third party expert" to prepare a full report on the status of current research on the VDT question. He urged employers to voluntarily take steps to reduce the risk for the VDT user. He announced his intention to "work with manufacturers, employees and employers to provide education and information." I was disappointed. I had hoped for more. Oh well…

APRIL 13, 1984

A busy week as we approach the deadline date for reporting out all bills from committee. We seem to be in a constant flurry of activity. It has been a productive year for our Health Care Committee which, in my opinion, is the most important of them all. If we err in judgment on State Administration or Transportation, the issue can be straightened out. If we err on a matter that affects the health of our citizens, however, we may well have placed someone in real danger. Ours is, therefore, a dedicated, hard working group.

The week had begun on a sad note as we headed for Bourne to attend the funeral of a colleague, Representative Jerry Cahir. His passing was unexpected, and so a number of scheduled events had to be postponed. Tuesday was, therefore, a wildly busy time. We did manage to lunch with the Massachusetts Association of School Superintendents and the Massachusetts Association of School Business Officials always a happy occasion in the company of two of my special friends, Braintree School Superintendent John Monbouquette and Blue Hills Regional Technical School Superintendent Charles Brennan.

Tuesday afternoon and at 2:20 p.m. I was on hand in the Governor's office for the signing of the Braintree Sewer Department bill that will give the town the authority to penalize those who dump illegally, via a sump pump or otherwise, into the town's sewer system. My good friends Superintendent Joseph Toma and Selectman Carl Johnson were also on hand for the official signing. We "stayed put" in the Governor's office for our next scheduled event when, along with Representatives M. Joseph Manning of Milton and Robert Emmet Hayes of Whitman and Senator Paul Harold, I joined my good friends Bob Kimball, Richard Mazzola and Bob Gimble in presenting to His Excellency a petition (signed by thousands of Braintree-ites) against the Norfolk County Hospital Jail proposal. Governor Michael S. Dukakis appeared responsive to our pleas; we trust he shares our views on this issue. A jail does not belong in Braintree…

A meeting of our Legislative Foreign Trade Committee at 3 p.m. rounded out that particular afternoon under the Golden Dome. I'm a member, of course.

Wednesday, and at 10 a.m. I was on hand in Nurses Hall to support our "Super Citizens" (seniors) at a press conference designed to improve chances for passing an Act to Eliminate Mandatory Retirement. I'm a co-sponsor of the bill. At 11 a.m. we had a Health Care Committee hearing, followed by a Transportation Committee Executive Session and a luncheon as guests of our great Senate Chairman Joseph Walsh.

The highlight of that particular day, however, was my presence in the Governor's office for the swearing-in of Braintree's own Medal of Honor winner Charles MacGillivary as a member of the Governor's Advisory Committee on Veterans Affairs.

And-SPEAKING OF HIGHLIGHTS-that particular day housed another one, the crowning of my efforts to protect the health and safety of the state's computer operators via my famous VDT bill. With Representative Timothy Bassett, Chairman of Commerce and Labor, Representative Robert Ambler, Vice Chairman of Ways and Means; and Arthur Osborne, President of the Massachusetts Labor Council, AFL-CIO. I met with House Speaker Thomas W. McGee to discuss funding for the implementation of the key elements of my bill, along with an in-depth study of the entire issue by the Labor and Industries' State Division of Occupational Hygiene. We were successful in securing the promise that adequate funding will be included in the upcoming State Budget. My bill can therefore be put on the back burner. "The sweet smell of success!" There was to be one more important happening on Wednesday evening-my attendance at a meeting of the Braintree Five Corners Study Committee which is certainly keeping its fingers on the pulse of the DPW on this issue.

Friday was Student Government Day on the Hill, and I was pleased to meet with the fine young man who occupied my seat on that morning, Braintree High School's William Manley. He seemed to be enjoying himself immensely in that new role.

Friday afternoon and I chaired a second meeting of my sub-committee established to address the problems of the multiply handicapped young adults who at 22 are no longer eligible for Chapter 766 funding.

My goal was to emerge with a bill that the Administration, state agencies, pediatric nursing home owners and parents groups would all accept, and I did just that. Now to get it through the House and Senate and on to the Governor's desk for signing.

Friday evening, and I had the pleasure of presenting a House Resolution to my good friend, Braintree's Town Moderator Gerald Walsh, at a Testimonial Dinner marking his retirement from the New England Telephone Company.

Saturday afternoon, and I shared in the Dedication Ceremony for Quincy's new commuter boat service at Marina Bay; and on Sunday evening it was off to Monatiquot

Village to attend the installation of my good friend David Shaw as Exalted Ruler of Braintree Lodge of Elks No. 2622; and to present a House Citation to the outgoing Exalted Ruler Robert C. Smith.

APRIL 27, 1984

There was a lull of sorts on Beacon Hill this past week. It began on Monday with that 19th of April holiday for Suffolk County; and was followed on Tuesday by the commencement of the Feast of Passover and the Holy Week observance. For your L. of the H. however, there was plenty to do; and I was hard at work daily in Room 130 attending to the many duties that are mine as I represent the people of Braintree, along with my function as our Health Care Committee's Vice Chairman.

We are now facing a deadline date of April 25 for bringing all bills out of committee. We have been holding for further study a number of bills dealing with health issues; we must now reassess these bills and come to a decision on their merits.

Apropos the many obligations of my favorite committee work, we members, like most of you, have been concerned with the frightening implications of that recently highlighted disease AIDS When it was first brought to our attention it was presumed only to affect gay males. At a hearing we held on the issue during the past week, however, a decidedly different picture of the dimensions of the disease emerged.

From a panel of medical experts on the subject, we learned the following: it is a death sentence. Many victims die within a year, and many live for two years; no one has survived beyond three years. It is transmitted sexually, or via infected needles among drug addicts, or BY BLOOD TRANSFUSIONS and it was upon learning of that last means of contracting AIDS that our horror grew.

Our questions revealed a startling fact. There is NO TEST THAT CAN BE APPLIED to a blood donor to determine if he has the Acquired Immune Deficiency Disease, AIDS. As a consequence, a blood donor with the disease can infect any one of us or a loved one who will undergo surgery and require blood transfusion.

Hemophiliacs are especially vulnerable. A liver transplant operation calls for 400 units (not pints) of blood. With that amount of potential exposure a patient will be facing a risky situation indeed. The federal government is involved in research to develop this vitally important test for potential blood donors. The mills of our federal government, however, grind slowly as we know. We were horrified also to learn of the cost of caring for an AIDS victim-between $150,00 and $200,000 per year, so terrible is the disease to live with.

"If we could secure state funding for a crash program to develop a test to determine the presence of AIDS in a blood donor, I feel we could come up with that test within a year."

Doctor Flumara of the State Department of Public Health told us. "A crash program could be mounted in the state laboratory and in the hospitals where research is currently under way." "How much would you need to spearhead such a crash program?" He was asked. His reply: $1.5 million. And so during the coming week I shall be working to add $1.5 million to the 1985 state budget so as to fund this crash endeavor. Our goal will, of course, be to develop a test that could prove to protect each and every one of us from the horrors of this devastating disease. We're all in this together. In the sixties a similar situation arose with an epidemic of hepatitis. With a similar crash program of research a test was developed in time to put a halt to this epidemic by screening out hepatitis carriers among blood donors. We hope we can accomplish the same goal with AIDS.

JUNE 8, 1984

Monday being the Memorial Day holiday, our legislative week began officially on Tuesday, when a number of bills to control the sale and possession of short-barreled handguns once again went down to defeat. It is felt generally that gun control can only really be handled on a federal level since differing laws in different states would prove unworkable in law enforcement. One bill under consideration would permit local ordinances on the issue which would be even more difficult to live with…And so, although many of us believe firmly in gun control, when it comes to legislating the issue we find ourselves facing gray area. It's not black or white.

Another bill that won initial House approval would prohibit the MDC from accepting any additional communities in its sewer system. This bill was, of course, prompted by the problems the MDC has been having with its Nut Island and Deer Island treatments plants.

This week just past was "Massachusetts Tourism Week", and the event was observed with due ceremony on Wednesday at the State House. "Join the Pilgrims…the Minutemen…the skiers…the whalers…the beachcombers…the villagers…the artists…and the armored knights" our invitation to the event read. "Let Massachusetts entertain you…enjoy a taste of the Bay State." It was all part of the "Spirit of Massachusetts" TV and radio spots we're using these days? I think they're great. That "Spirit of Massachusetts" jingle seems to run through my head quite frequently and in my opinion the Massachusetts scenes that accompany it are great. Ours IS a wonderful state to visit, and tourism is a great plus for the state's economy…Like so many of you, I was disappointed with the weather that managed to cause Saturday's postponement of the Parade of Tall Ships. I had had difficulty deciding which of two invitations to accept to the event. Should it be Castle Island or the Boston Marine Industrial Park? With non-transferable invitations, the decision had to be made, and it wasn't easy. As it turned out, however, with nature taking a hand in things, no decision had to be made…And since Sunday is family day at the Metayers, we had to skip the entire exciting show…

A couple of columns back, I promised you some information on the latest Braintree profile, which was based on the 1980 census and just released in print. Here goes. We can expect a 1988 projected population of 38,315, with the largest increase in the 65 plus age group. The average household size as of 1980 was 3.07. 63.9% of our people were white-collar workers; 29.6% professional/manger, and 13.8% service employees. In the area of housing, the number of condominiums rose from 6 in 1970 to 250 in 1980. 43.7% of our housing in 1980 was valued between $30,00 and $50,000; and 40.9% between $50,000 and $80,000. Wonder what those values would like in 1984…(The next census should see quite a change in many of these areas.) Home values had doubled in those ten years from 1970 to 80 as did rental costs in Braintree. None of the above was very surprising. We all knew that Braintree was growing and changing. What WILL be revealed about this town of ours as a result of the 1985 federal census from which these figures were taken five years ago???

A couple things happened during the past week. A group of students from the Woodward School arrived at the State House with the school's director Carol Block. They enjoyed a tour of our historic building and Representative Thomas Brownell and I had a great time addressing them in the House Chamber which happened to not to be in use when they were present. Additionally I met with Martha Reardon, formerly with the South Shore Chamber of Commerce if you will recall, now as Assistant Commissioner with the Department of Public Works. Martha had assembled a group of high-ranking DPW officials for a discussion of proposed landscaping for that Abigail Adams Gateway marker we're planning to place in the vicinity of the Quincy Adams MBTA Station. Having filed the bill which was signed into law and brought about the proposal to honor this great American patriot, I am delighted with the interest and response of the state's DPW. I have always enjoyed a fine relationship with this state agency, which is to a great extent why Braintree seems to receive a great deal of cooperation from those in charge. Can't wait for the "Abigail Adams Gateway" to become a reality…

JULY 13, 1984 JULY 6TH COLUMN

America's Independence Day, the Fourth of July, lies dead ahead as I write this column on a rather dark and gloomy Sunday evening. We have just come in from watering the lawns and gardens. Those showers we were promised have not materialized; they'll probably arrive during the night and we shall have wasted our efforts, of course…

It is not obvious that as usual I shall have to miss the town's July 4 festivities. On the night before the Fourth I shall be on Beacon Hill, dealing with the Conference Committee version of the State Budget. It will not be all bad, however. We usually manage to dash up to the top of the State House now and then while one of our more longwinded debaters is on the floor. From there it is out the window to the parapet from which we can hear the music from the Boston Pops and if we can tuck it in, See the fireworks-a spectacular sight.

Legislatively the most important happening this past week was the House vote on Mayor Ray Flynn's bill calling for an excise parking tax. Much as I admire Mayor Flynn, and I do, I simply could not bring myself to vote for this discriminatory tax. In my opinion we are already gouged by Boston's parking people, and those workers who must use their parking facilities are already overpaying. The bill lost by a 72 to 80 vote, however we understand that the Boston Mayor will soon be back with another try at securing additional revenue for the Capitol City.

On the PLUS side during the past week was the resumption of summer passenger rail service to Cape Cod; and it was great to be on hand at the Braintree MBTA Station on Friday morning for the ribbon-cutting ceremony that saw the service off to a good start. The handsome train left Braintree with a distinguished group of passengers on board. I had planned to be among them. Duty called, however. We were in formal House session on Friday and so racing back to the State House had to be the order of the day… after I had been privileged to make a few welcoming remarks to those assembled for the great occasion.

I had met with Dr. M. Meyer and a number of MBTA representatives on Monday morning to discuss the oncoming rail service and to hear a progress report on the Southeast Expressway reconstruction. We were chagrinned to learn that 22 of the 35 state-subsidized private bus carrier runs were being cancelled for lack of ridership. The state subsidies were running from $2 plus to as much as $68 per rider, and naturally the state simply could not afford to finance these subsidies for the life of the Expressway project. Things are otherwise going well, Dr. Meyer said. Speeding has become a problem we were told; however additional police enforcement is in the works.

Tuesday and again I found myself meeting with representatives from the "T", including its General Manager Jim O'Leary, for an update on the progress of the Red Line's Columbia Station reconstruction project. It was ten years ago that I filed for the first time a bill calling for a Red Line stop at Columbia Station to eliminate the necessity of having to ride the Red to Andrew Station and then cross over and return to Columbia on the Ashmont line. Now at last we are about to get this additional station. (Of course I have filed the bill each year since that time…) Final design will be ready by Spring of 1985, Mr. O'Leary told us, and twelve to fifteen months later the station should be completed. The mills of government, like the mills of God, grind slowly. If, however, one is as persistent as this Representative, and as patient, they just may grind in the end. This has happened with the Columbia Station stop.

Locally it was interesting to attend a meeting at Braintree Town Hall on Tuesday evening when representatives from the MBTA and the Central Transportation Planning Staff were on hand to discuss possible additional bus service to Braintree Station; and, like a host of other Braintree-ites, I thoroughly enjoyed the Knights of Columbus Pancake Breakfast on Sunday morning. This has always signaled the beginning of our

Braintree Fourth of July festivities, and it is always a happy occasion. I shall certainly be sorry, however, to have to miss the annual inspection of our Braintree Time Capsule. It has been scheduled for the day before the Fourth at four in the afternoon, and of course I shall be busily engaged in debating in the 1985 State Budget at that hour. Oh, well, next year I'll be able to participate in everything. I'll be a retired state representative; and in case you're interested let me assure you that my heart will be under the golden Dome with those former colleagues of mine who will undoubtedly be once again missing the July 4th activities in their own hometowns as they debate…you guessed it…the 1986 State Budget..

JULY 13TH COLUMN

It was a typical "Nite Before the Fourth" on Beacon Hill…With before us the spectre of adjournment until after the primaries, we were concerned with getting through the House and Senate those bills which were deemed essential either to our communities or to our legislative committees. My own priority rested with two bills, either of which would permit the Town of Braintree to send out estimated tax bills. One bill had been held in Third Reading because, at my request, an "emergency preamble" had been put on it in the Senate. The second bill was also being held up in Third Reading, which was a scene of organized chaos as every one of our 160 representatives sought to spring their pet bills from this most important committee. The emergency preamble I had sought would permit the law to function immediately. In the normal course of events, a bill becomes law only ninety days after its signing by the Governor.

I appeared to be chief "pest" among those 160 Representatives as I raced back and forth between Third Reading and the House Chamber, following the bills to House engrossment, then trailing them to the Senate for engrossment…then back to the House and Senate for enactment, from which stage they could proceed to the Governor's desk for signing. It's a complicated process, this lawmaking…

Debate on the 1985 State Budget meanwhile droned on. By this time, needless to say, each and every one of us had decided whether to vote the budget up or down, but with the TV cameras rolling our die-hard debaters were determined to run their full course before allowing the issue to come to a vote. The vote was, as expected, overwhelmingly in favor of adopting the State Budget. It always is…It had been reported out by the Conference Committee an amended version that reconciled the differences between the House and Senate versions. I was personally delighted with the Conference Committee report. Each one of the amendments I had added were retained. I had gotten "the whole ball of wax, to quote our House Ways and Means Chairman when I questioned him. The Speaker had hoped to keep us in session on July 3 until the decks were cleared of everything important, regardless of the hour. It was not to be, however. At around 11 p.m. -with the Senate yet to face the issue of the 1985 State Budget-and our expectations that the Senate debate could be as endless as our own-the House voted to adjourn. We shall, therefore, be back in formal session on Monday where we may or may not lay the budget to rest once and for all. The Senate does not ordinarilty meet on Monday, and should they be out until Tuesday, we shall be unable to settle the budget issue until then. Meanwhile, thankfully, a 1984 surplus is permitting checks to be issued for state workers and recipients of public assistance. It is always a crunch to get the State Budget on the books by July 1. I can't help but wonder why....

I was delighted to learn that SCA (or Recycling Industries as I continue to refer to it) was fined by the Environmental Protection Agency for regulatory violations that were revealed after that March fire at the plant; and for failure to comply with EPA rules when applying for an operating permit. I have met recently with representatives from both the EPA and the state's Department Environmental Quality Engineering relative to that pending permit application, on which I am keeping an eagle eye. These individuals claim to be pleased with Braintree's hiring of a consultant to protect the town's interests in living with the hazardous waste treatment plant that is easily the bane of our existence in East Braintree. They know we're watching them and that, in my book, is mighty good. I was pleased to have been asked to secure a House of Representatives Citation for two fine Braintree couples who are currently celebrating their 50th Wedding Anniversary. My own personal best wishes go with these Citations to May and Larry Jenkins and to David and Gladys Blunt. A Golden Wedding is a wonderful milestone in people's lives, and I am always pleased when family members call the occasion to my attention so that I may extend to these happy people the best wishes of the members of their House of Representatives.

A great many people were delighted with the news that as of June 30 the Cape Cod and Hyannis Railroad will provide rail service from Braintree to the Cape. The announcement of the resumption of this rail service after a 25-year lapse, was made by Transportation Secretary Fred Salvucci at a meeting on Friday morning.

JULY 27, 1984

Our Health Care Committee activities still go on. Of major importance during the past week was the public hearing we held on S-2243 which would ban the "balance billing" of elderly Medex patients. Half a million Massachusetts seniors would be affected by this bill, which will offer the same protection from doctors' overcharges that were granted to younger Blue Cross/Blue Shield subscribers by the bill Governor Dukakis signed into law last week.

The hearing attracted a great many activists for the elderly and we committee members were pleased to give the bill a favorable committee report, with a couple of minor changes to be worked out between our staff members and the elderly advocates.

The sub-committee I chair is still working with members of the Massachusetts Nurses Associations to come up with some form of legislation that will address what they claim is an inequitable financial burden being placed on nurses as hospitals attempt to deal with the fiscal constraints of Chapter 672, the hospital cost control law. There was much ado on Beacon Hill when President Reagan signed into law a bill requiring the states to enact a 21-year-old drinking law within two years or lose federal highway construction funding. The loss represents 5% in fiscal 1987-for an estimated $10 million, and 10% in fiscal 1988-for an estimated $20 million. States that impose mandatory jail terms and the revocation of licenses for drunken driving convictions could however be eligible for a 5% bonus in federal highway safety grants.

According to federal safety statistics, drivers between the ages of 18 and 20 are more than twice as likely as other drivers to be involved in crashes related to alcohol. We shall of course, be subjected to considerable lobbying on the part of our student population, many of whom are irate at the prospect of the state's enacting such a law. An interesting time now lies ahead on that issue. I can already in my mind's eye see the busses roaring down from UMass/Amherst and elsewhere…Speaking of bills in the offing, we shall be dealing in the Fall with one I co-sponsored that directs the Executive Office of Transportation and Construction and the Department of Public Works to prepare a study plan for the timely and expeditious movement of traffic on the Southeast Expressway and Route 3 starting in November 1985 when the present reconstruction is complete. The study plan will consider among other things provision for permanent year-round reversible express lanes; a "contra-flow" lane for busses, vanpools and carpools; and restrictions on trucks-limited them to certain lanes or certain hours, and enforcement thereof. The plan is to be filed with the Clerk of the House on or before the first Wednesday in June, 1985. Darn it, I shan't be around when that important date for our South Shore commuters rolls around.

Easily the most exciting local happening for your L. of the H. was getting photographed with "Metayer's Marauders", that intrepid and truly beautiful girls softball team that achieved a distinctive record never before attained in East Braintree. I am privileged to sponsor "Metayer's Marauders" and MY team won eighteen games with NO LOSSES. My girls won the National League Championship and the Division Championship. They swept the championship series without a single loss. "The first time this has ever happened," announced their coach, "Skip" Romano, his face alight with pride. Mine, too! Hats off, and the congratulations of the entire House of Representatives to Kristy Romano, Mary Clarke, Rene Reeves, Alice Perniola, Jackie Cozzatti, Meredith Brown, Kara Genevich, Pam Smith, Terri Puliafico, Franny Pedersen, Michelle Hartnet, Cheryl Lepro, Lisa Devlin and Noreen Clarke-all members of this unusually beautiful as well as capable team. And three cheers for their coaching staff, "Skip" Romano and his lovely Donna Hutchinson. Am I ever proud of the entire bunch!

***

The Commonwealth of Massachusetts
House of Representatives
Assistant Majority Leader
State House, Boston
Elizabeth N. Metayer
5th Norfolk District
Committees on Health Care, Vice Chairman Rules, Transportation
Room 130, State House

In a way, I made my farewell speech a couple of weeks back, when Representative Marie Parente, Chair of the Women's Caucus, acknowledged the imminent retirement of Representative Doris Bunte and myself from the House of Representatives.

My Farewell Speech to the House of Representatives

On that occasion, however, I must admit I had not expected to be asked to speak, and I was really not prepared. I shall not today repeat the thoughts I expressed to you on that occasion. You all must know by now of my love for the House of Representatives, and for the Colleagues, past and present, with whom I have served here. Like Speaker McGee, I consider you "the finest deliberative body anywhere in the world," and the NICEST. You can never know how much I shall miss you. I shall be leaving a bit of my heart here with you under the Golden Dome.

This evening, however, I would like to amplify my earlier remarks by thanking some of the people who have made my life such a happy and fulfilled one here on Beacon Hill. I want to thank initially the great people of Braintree for having sent me to represent them for the past 10 years. And then, of course, my very dear and treasured friend Speaker Thomas W. McGee, whose large compassionate heart has, whenever it was humanly possible for him, responded to any plea I might have made for help for the people of Braintree, or for a particular segment of the Commonwealth's people whom I felt to be in need of help…help that I wanted to bring them. His shared concern, particularly on women's issues, has been unfailing; and I thank him. And I thank the great leadership teams he has assembled over the past ten years. I thank our Chaplain, Father Robert Quinn, for his daily inspirational prayers. We needed them…I thank our fabulous House clerks, Wally and Bob and Bart and Steve, and behind the scenes, Katie and Scottie and the rest…

I thank those in the office of the House Counsel, most particularly John Donovan, Paul Menton, and Charlie Martell…and Bruce, who has written so many wonderful House Resolutions for me. I thank the great people on the Speaker's staff…Jack and Mary and Al and Tim and the rest…I thank Jack and Bob in the Treasurer's office. They always seemed to have my check when I needed it…

I thank the Court officers who take such good care of us; and the Capitol Police, with the presence of whom I and the Capitol's priceless treasures are safe…

I thank all of the great people who work here under the Golden Dome, and whose friendship I have come to enjoy…

I thank the outstanding Chairmen, past and present, of all of our House Committees and of those Committees especially on whom I have been privileged to serve, not forgetting Ray Rourke and Lou Nickinello of the Transportation Committee, and all of that committee's super chairmen…

And the many Chairmen under whom I have served on the Health Care Committee, especially our present Chairman, my dear friend Richie Voke, and I thank you, Mr. Speaker, for having appointed me his Vice Chairman. It's been GREAT!

I shall miss you all…each and every one of you, my dear colleagues and friends, but especially I shall miss my seatmates (if that is what one calls them) Marie Louise and Fran…and before them

Tony Aguiar, now Judge Aguiar, and the late Paul Goulston…and Dee Corcoran…

House seat 102…formerly 104…has been a happy place to be, with good friends and fun people seated all around me…

Mr. Speaker, and members of the House, my life is the richer for the wonderful experience I have shared here with you all under the Golden Dome, in the beautiful Chamber and everywhere else in the House of Representatives.

As I stated before, "You have touched me; I have grown…"

May God love and keep you all…and may I wish you, along with my farewell thanks, a happy and holy Christmas season and the brightest New Year on record. Thank you…

BRAINTREE FORUM AND OBSERVER

Volume 107 No. 50
A Mariner newspaper
Wednesday, December 5, 1984

A WOMAN OF SUBSTANCE
BY OLIVE LAING

They came from all walks of life, more than 500 strong, colleagues on Beacon Hill, public officials at all levels of government, business men and women, family and friends.

They filled the main ballroom of the Sheraton-Tara Hotel. They wanted to show Elizabeth "Bibs" Metayer the affection in which they hold her and the appreciation they have, not only for her 10 years as State Representative, but also for long years of service as a leader and as a caring person.

Bibs is retiring at the end of this year.

While the tribute itself was not a surprise, its dimensions were. Details of the evening were kept secret. When Bibs, radiant in a long coral gown with corsage of blush roses, entered the ballroom and saw the standing throng waiting to greet her, a look of incredulity crossed her face. She was flabbergasted.

Toastmaster Gerald Walsh who kept the proceedings moving briskly, injecting humorous anecdotes, introduced the Rev. John Berube, pastor of Saint Francis of Assisi Parish, who offered the invocation. The décor was State House blue and white carried out at the tables and in the fresh flower centerpieces. Programs at each place with an impressive tribute by Linda Chase, a committee member, were also in blue and carried a characteristic picture of Bibs and the subtitle, "A Woman of Substance."

The parade to the podium by people wishing to offer presentations either as individuals or as representatives of organizations seemed unending. Their sincerity was obvious and their enthusiasm a marvel.

Honorary Chairman Thomas Flatley, a head table guest, gifted Bibs with a check of $1000 sent in her name to the Oxfam fund for the starving children of Ethiopia. Also a gift from Flatley was two round-trip flight tickets from Boston to Fort Lauderdale where arrangements have been made for a sojourn at the Sheraton for Bibs and her husband Ted. The only sad note to the joyous evening was the absence of Ted, who was unable to attend because of recent knee surgery. He was mentioned often during the evening.

Grand Knight Gerard Tobin presented a plaque from the Braintree Knights of Columbus as did Frank DeFrancesco, Braintree Legion Post commander. A token of appreciation was presented by Denise Polli, president of the Braintree Junior Philergians. Joanne Pistorino, vice president of the Braintree Catholic Women's Club, made a presentation for that group and one also for members of the Ladies Lodge, Sons of Italy.

Also making presentations were John Flood, president, Braintree Business and Professional Association; Charles Graziano, for the Braintree Sons of Italy Lodge. Representing the Massachusetts Federation of Nursing Homes, Kathy Warner said Bibs was "one of the ablest, most responsible and most responsive legislators on Beacon Hill."

For the Braintree League of Women Voters Judie Williams made a presentation in recognition of Bibs as founding president and read an original poem in tribute to her.

Joseph Aiello presented a beautiful heirloom jewel box containing a gold pin with cultured pearls, a gift from the South Braintree Board of Trade and Claire Devaney and Marjorie Smith spoke for the residents of Independence Manor thanking Bibs "for all the support you have given to the elderly."

Ned Wynot, chairman, Board of Selectmen, read a special letter to "Braintree's Gracious Lady." Speaker of the House Thomas W. McGee, a head table guest, told the crowd that in 30 years of public life, "I don't think I have ever met a finer, more dedicated, more wonderful person than Bibs Metayer."

He said he brought with him the longest resolution ever to come out of the House of Representatives and read excerpts from it which lauded the retiring Representative as a public official and as a person.

Father Berube, with his usual wonderful humor, added a light touch when he turned to McGee and said, "It's wonderful to see you in the flesh. I have heard your name so many times over the last 10 years on all those citations offered by Bibs." He spoke of her gift of reaching out, of giving so much of herself to others. His gift was a beautiful painting of hands breaking the bread.

For her support and contributions to public education, Bob Zanca, chairman of the School Committee, made a presentation.

Norfolk County Sheriff Clifford Marshall called Bibs a "legend in her time" and presented her a certificate of merit. She had already been made an honorary sheriff.

Calling it "a privilege" to participate in the "wonderful tribute," Senator Paul Harold said everyone on Beacon Hill hates to see Bibs leave. He referred to her as the most prominent woman in Braintree since Abigail Adams and got a great laugh when he said for the past six years of his term as Senator, Bibs often called him "lambie pie."

Harold made three presentations, the first a framed State House print surrounded by the original signatures of 159 members of the House. The second was a remembrance from Mayor Frank McCauley of Quincy for "the help she gave on issues of regional concern." The third was an autographed picture of Gary Hart who said, "We are saving a place on the ticket in '88 for you." Fire Chief Carl Vitagliano brought to Bibs a handsome plaque from his department and William Finn, president of the Braintree Police Club, announced Bibs had been named Braintree's first woman patrolman, presenting a gold badge.

Town board of water commissioners, expressed thanks to Bibs on behalf of the commissioners, and Braintree Star publisher Charles Knowles presented a framed page the Star on which appeared an advance story about the tribute and her "Lady of the House" column. A letter of congratulations and praise was read from Blue Hills Regional School.

Congressman Brian Donnelly told the gathering he has never met anyone like Bibs Metayer. He spoke of her qualities of caring and understanding, not only in her legislative work but in dealing with people on a day to day basis. On behalf of his wife, Ginny, and himself, Donnelly presented a beautiful framed seal of the United States. Representative Richard Voke, chairman of the Committee of Health Care of which Bibs is vice chairman, said he "watched her seek out those people who have no one to speak for them, people who had no lobbyist, no group." And he said she was a "dear and a love" and he added with a laugh that Bibs called him "pork chop" at times, but never "lambie pie."

Her family was on hand in force-her daughter, Gael; her son, Richard and his wife, Dolores; her sister, Jean and her grandchildren, Franklin Metayer and Byrne and Gregory Corbin. Her fourth grandson, James Corbin, is a meteorologist in Maine and was on broadcasting duty and unable to attend. As tokens of their love and admiration,

Richard and Dolores gifted Bibs with an elegant sterling lighted mirror. Gift from Gael and her family was an exquisite diamond and sapphire pendant on a gold chain.

Co-chairman John Shaughnessy added another light touch to the evening with funny asides to the toastmaster. On behalf of those attending, he presented a check representing the proceeds of the evening.

Elizabeth Laing, who with John Shaughnessy was co-chairman for the tribute. "We respect her, we admire her, we love her, but most important of all, we like her" was her theme, tracing the lovable characteristics of Bibs which have endeared her to all.

After a long standing ovation, Bibs, choking back emotion and struggling to hold back tears, told the audience "I am the richest women in the world."

"My wealth lies before me here this evening in my wonderful family and in my wonderful friends."

"I can't possibly put into words what it has meant to me to be able to serve the beautiful people of Braintree and to walk with and work with the beautiful people on Beacon Hill during the past 10 years."

"I have loved every day of my life under the Golden Dome."

Thanking the committee who planned the tribute and all those who attended, she said, "This is the happiest night of my life and I will remember it always."

Committee members, in addition to those already mentioned, were Bob Bruynell, ticket chairman; Donald Olson, treasurer and Olive Laing, publicity chairman.

As part of her gift from those attending, Bibs will be presented with an album of colored photos taken by committee arrangement by Charles Flagg, which, as John Shaughnessy told her, will be a memento of her tribute which she and Ted can enjoy in days to come.

Representative Metayer chokes back a tear as her town warmly pays tribute to her.

Senator Paul D. Harold show Representative Metayer State House print surrounded by signatures of 159 members.

Former Governor Edward King greets Representative Metayer at her tribute.

The head table gets a chuckle from the words of Rev. John Berube. They are (from left) Elizabeth E. Laing, House Speaker Thomas McGee and Representative Metayer.

In photo at right, the planners of the Metayer tribute flank the retiring State Representative: (from left) Thomas Flatley, Gerald Walsh, Elizabeth Laing, (Metayer)

[...]

Reprint with permission from the Patriot Ledger
The Patriot Ledger, Friday, December 14, 1984

"BIBS" LOVED EVERY MINUTE OF 40 YEARS' SERVICE

By Mark S. Morrow
Patriot Ledger Staff

Braintree When Elizabeth N. "Bibs" Metayer was a schoolgirl growing up in Malden, her mother told her always to keep a scrapbook "because you will lead a very active life."

What an understatement.

Metayer, who moved to Braintree in 1946, will cap nearly four decades of community service this month when she retires after 10 years as Braintree's state representative-the first woman ever to hold the post. Her successor is also a woman: Metayer's former aide, Suzanne Bump.

"My mother was right, of course," she said during an interview between roll call votes at the State House. "I have had a wonderfully active time of it, and I must have 40 volumes of scrapbooks recording every step of the way. I have been a glutton for punishment when it comes to service, and I have loved every minute of it."

Metayer, 73, decided to leave office this year at the behest of her husband, Ted, who had grown lonely holding down the fort at the family's home on Arthur Street while she worked late on legislative business.

"I have really had a remarkable man for a husband. He was always supportive of me, and he has always approved of women in politics," she said. "But we always had a perfectly clear understanding that when Ted finally said 'I've had it,' that I would leave."

Still, the pain of separation from her friends in state government is something Metayer admits will be hard to overcome.

"I really don't know what I'm going to do. I feel like I'm leaving my home," she said, looking wistfully around a conference room in the House lobby. "But I'll keep active somehow, I know I will.'

Elizabeth Metayer always wanted to live in Braintree, the Colonial-era hometown of her childhood hero, Abigail Adams.

And when she finally got here at age 35, she lost no time immersing herself in the political and social swirl of the community. To this day, she recalls her early battles with zest and an encyclopedic command of detail.

First, in the early 1950's, she founded the Northeast Braintree Civic Association- "the grandfather of the towns' civic associations"-and used it as a vehicle to fight plans to build a large trash incinerator in East Braintree.

"I fought them to a standstill," she said. "I remember at one point one of the selectmen telling me the plant would be beautiful. He said there is one of these that is "so beautiful and clean that they have banquets in it."

"Well, I called their bluff and went to see that plant. I saw the mountains of trash; I saw the rats; I saw the black smoke…With that information, I persuaded the board of health to rescind their approval," she said..

In the years following that victory, Metayer was elected to town meeting-a position she held for 20 years and become renowned as one of Braintree's busiest women. A 1957 Patriot Ledger clipping lists 18 civic and religious groups in which she played a leading role.

But, through all her activism, she remembered the condescending way she had been treated when she stood up to the political insiders planning the incinerator. She decided it was time for organized oversight of town affairs, and so, with some likeminded friends, she founded the Braintree League of Women Voters. "I decided that after we got that treatment," she recalls, "that Braintree needed a watchdog." Metayer, the League's first president, went on to play a key role in the extension of the MBTA Red Line to South Braintree. She was chairman of the Technical Advisory Committee of citizens that worked to make the station compatible with the town.

"I fought tooth and nail to get the best possible station…Do you realize they originally planned to bring an elevated structure right through the middle of town?" she said.

In the flush of her involvement with the MBTA issue, Metayer ran for state representative in 1966 and narrowly lost in the Democratic primary. Then came her successful move directly into the political arena.

"A group of us decided that the old guard then dominating the Democratic Town Committee could be unseated," she said. "And then the most remarkable thing happened; in the balloting for chairman, I ended up getting the votes of both the old and the new factions."

A political star was born.

Two young activists approached her and volunteered to manage her campaign, if she would run for representative.

"I was 62 at the time and I replied, "That's crazy. No one will elect someone at my age, but I ran and the support poured in from all the people whose lives I had touched over the years."

She was faced off against incumbent Democrat William Dignan in a primary campaign highlighted by a dramatic confrontation at a town hall candidates' forum.

Dignan shocked the gathering when he sought to capitalize on Metayer's status as a political neophyte by charging that her campaign had failed to obey finance laws. Metayer didn't do the expected. "I didn't dissolve into tears."

Instead, in a confident voice, she said she was mortified at the thought that her campaign committee had erred on some technicalities, and she hoped the penalty would not be so severe as Dignan alleged.

"I'd certainly hate to be in jail when I'm elected on Tuesday," she said to deafening applause. She went on to trounce Dignan by 1,000 votes in the primary. And with no Republican opposition in November (she had none in four of her five campaigns), Metayer never looked back.

It is the end of the 1984 legislative session. Members mill about, chatting and laughing. House Speaker Thomas McGee gavels fruitlessly for order. At the podium, a Boston representative is making a florid speech, but no one is listening.

No one, that is, except for Representative Metayer, who is poised at her desk with Catholic schoolgirl-perfect posture, the picture of attentiveness.

The hubbub, she says, is her tonic.

"I absolutely thrive on the excitement," she said. "I have to force myself to leave at the end of each day."

Looking back on her five-term career, Metayer has no trouble naming several dozen major achievements. She is proud to have:

Secured funding for the Ivory Street extension that relieves commuter traffic congestion in South Braintree Square.

Helped push along plans for improvements to the Five Corners intersection.

Fought, as a member of the transportation committee, for construction of a Columbia Street station on the MBTA Red line.

Pushed through an agreement that enabled the Massachusetts Port Authority to establish a second container port in the harbor.

Fought for vocational education funding. "Voke-ed was a stepchild in the state budget, until I arrived," she said.

Passed, as a member and then vice chairman of the health care committee, legislation establishing a corneal transplant tissue bank; creating the post of nursing home ombudsman to field complaints about service to the elderly; establishing the state's first pediatric nursing home; funding research on the disease AIDS; and perhaps Metayer's favorite creating a displaced homemakers program for the state.

"I became aware of the rising number of people getting divorced or widowed, and being faced all of a sudden with life alone with a family. Mothers were increasingly facing the fate of falling into the welfare trap, which is so hard to get out of. Why not instead give them the skills, and the motivation to help them pull themselves up?" she said. "The program has been marvelously successful." Metayer sees her whole career as a legislator as rooted in her people-oriented compassion, and her instincts for forging coalitions out of the conflicting interests that often stymie action in state government.

"My committee chairmen have been wonderful, because they've had the sense to see that I'm a person who likes to be given my head. They know that once I get my hands on a problem, I have the persistence to see it through to a conclusion," she said.

As she prepares to leave her position, Metayer is saddened by the divisive battle for the House speaker's post being waged by McGee and his former political lieutenant, George Keverian, D-Everett.

"I am very sad about it because Speaker McGee has been wonderful to me and to Braintree…and because I really love all my colleagues, every one of them, and hate to see them at odds with one another."

The last day on which I shall enter the State House as Braintree's State Representative. I begin my "last mile"…

The Park Street Carillon is playing "Joy to the World". Normally it would make my spirits soar. Today it doesn't.

I raise my eyes to the great Golden Dome that has been another roof over my head for the past ten happy years. How beautifully it shines against the blue of sky.

I enter the Capitol Building, and decide to walk its graceful corridors just one more time…Doric Hall, and Nurses Hall, and the Hall of Flags-how beautiful they are…Up the giant stairway where I have posed with so many of our Braintree schoolchildren; and on for one last look at my beloved House Chamber. On to the Senate Chamber with its magnificent view of historic Boston Common…

A phone call from the Governor's office has brought me to the Chief Executive for a farewell chat. Governor Dukakis is warm and cordial. It is difficult to say goodbye.

I leave the office of the Chief Executive to pause at the balcony for still one more look at the splendor of the high vaulted ceiling and the historic murals that lie beneath it. "The most beautiful seat of government in the world," I whisper, and there's a catch in my voice.

I approach the door leading out under the Arch, from where I shall proceed to the garage to pick up the family car from its special place under my H-102 sign. (My House seat number), for the very last time.

"Bibs!" calls a voice from above. It belongs to a colleague from the western part of the State. He flies down the stairs. He hugs me, and then plants a kiss firmly on my cheek. "Happy New Year!" he says; and then hugs me again. "Luv ya!" he adds…

How can I bear to leave? How much love I have found under the Golden Dome during the past ten wonderful years.

BRAINTREE GAZETTE

Your Hometown Newspaper
Wednesday, November 7, 1984
Metayer reflects on years as State Representative.
By Nancy E. Welch

Braintree-In 1973 Elizabeth Metayer was approached by two men who had the idea of running her for state representative. Metayer replied, "I couldn't possibly run. I'm 62 years old."

Ten years and five consecutive terms later, State Representative Metayer is retiring from a career in state government that she said has proved "the highlight of my entire life."

Prior to entering public life, Metayer worked as a volunteer in Braintree church and civic organizations for nearly 25 years. Among her activities, Metayer was a member of the Council on Aging, first president of Braintree's League of Women Voters, and town meeting member. Metayer also chaired the Town's Technical Advisory Committee on Transportation, working with the Massachusetts Bay Transit Authority in planning the Braintree station.

When Metayer announced her plans to seek the House seat, she found her volunteer work had won her supporters.

"All of the people for whom I had done things, all of the people whom I had helped, all of the people whose paths had crossed mine were ready to help me," Metayer said. "And then a funny thing happened: I won."

Throughout her career as a state representative, Metayer feels she has always worked for Braintree's best interests. As a 10-year member of the House Transportation Committee, she helped bring to Town "the kind of (MBTA) station we could live with." Metayer also worked on the completion of the Ivory Street Extension, which diverted MBTA commuter traffic from the center of town.

She played a key role in a number of projects with the Department of Public Works that resulted in signalization improvements in such locations as Five Corners and the South Shore Plaza. "I had a fine relationship with the Department of Public Works," Metayer said.

Metayer is Vice Chairman of the Health Care Committee and chaired a sub committee that was responsible for getting the Nursing Home Ombudsman Bill signed into law. The purpose of his bill, which took eight years to pass, is to protect the interests of nursing home patients.

In addition, Metayer worked on legislation to help the blind in need of corneal tissue. The Corneal Transplant Bill called for removing corneal tissues from deceased and unidentified persons during autopsy for the purpose of bringing sight to others. The result of the legislation, according to Metayer, is that a waiting list of 500 names for this tissue has been considerably reduced.

The Displaced Homemaker's Program is another program Metayer worked to establish. This program helps widowed and divorce women to support themselves through counseling, training, and job placement. The program, she said, is being copied throughout the country.

Running for federal office has not been one of Metayer's goals. "I never wanted to be anything but a state representative. I'm close to the people of Braintree, and they're wonderful people," Metayer said. "They've always felt free to call me with their problems."

Although she is now leaving office, Metayer said she would continue to fight to see no further PCB spills occur or go unreported.

"Town officials have been alerted and are very much in tune to what is going on. I would hope that they would monitor SCA very carefully and bring it up short on anything that goes on," Metayer said. A fine for hazardous waste spills is not sufficient, she said, adding that the plant should be closed down for a period of time if any further violations occur.

Metayer said she is pleased that the town is fighting the use of Norfolk County Hospital as a temporary jail and feels Braintree will be successful. Metayer would advocate town legislation that would prohibit use of the prison for terms longer than 30 to 60 days.

On Braintree's growth, Metayer said, "The Town has lost its small-town flavor. We have become more urbanized." People need to realize this as fact, and she said explaining that the key to controlling the Town's growth is zoning.

Metayer cited her marriage as the reason for retirement. "It's very difficult to be married to a State Representative," she explained. "I promised (my husband) that when the time came that he asked me to give it up, to be at home with him, to continue our travels, I would do so…I feel very noble and very sad."

Executive Secretary Robert Sherman said Metayer would be greatly missed by the Board. "She is a very gracious lady who has always been responsive to our requests and there have been many," Sherman said. "We'll probably get her involved in the town government before we're through." Metayer plans to remain involved in local affairs as a volunteer and has accepted chairmanship of the Displaced Homemaker's Program. "I should be terribly interested in everything that happens in Braintree," Metayer said. She said she does not know if she will run for local office and said she would first consult her husband before considering any plans to seek election.

"I feel that I am leaving the Commonwealth of Massachusetts and its citizens and the Town of Braintree and its citizens better for having served my ten years on Beacon Hill. And that's a very comfortable feeling to be leaving with," Metayer said.

BRAINTREE STAR

"Braintree's Own Newspaper"
November 16, 1984 Braintree, Massachusetts 02184 Est. 1966
"I Have Loved Every Day of It!"

In an interview with Star Editor Charles Knowles, Representative Elizabeth N. Metayer discussed her ten years under the Golden Dome as Braintree's State Representative. Mrs. Metayer is retiring at the end of the year.

"I have loved every day of it," she said, "and in leaving I am comforted somewhat by the fact that I am being assured on the Hill that I am leaving my constituents and the Commonwealth's citizens the better for my having served there."

Representative Metayer discussed the highlights of her ten years as a member of the Transportation Committee. "There was the key role I played in securing for Braintree an MBTA station we can live with, together with the construction of Ivory Street," she said; "and of reaching a solution to the Braintree Five Corners situation which should go out to bid soon." Metayer filed the legislation to have the MBTA construct a Columbia Station stop on the Red Line. "That one wasn't easy," she said, "but I persevered, and the station will soon go out to bid." She discussed her rapport with the State Department of Public Works, a situation which she claimed has helped to bring to fruition many town projects over the past ten years.

As the Vice Chairman of the Transportation Committee's Sub-Committee on the Port Authority, Mrs. Metayer played a key role in bringing Massport and the City of Boston together and paving the way for a badly needed second Containerport in Boston Harbor. "That was an achievement whose spin-off effects will benefit the economy of the Commonwealth for all time," she said.

As a member and past Chairman of the Massachusetts Caucus of Women Legislators, Mrs. Metayer worked extensively on issues benefiting women. Chief among these was her early support of the Displaced Homemaker Program, a program that functions to keep divorcees, widows and other single parents from "falling into the welfare trap" to quote the Representative. It provides counseling, self-confidence, the upgrading of skills and self-sustaining employment. Representative Metayer has been responsible for initially securing and annually increasing funding for this program in the State Budget. She will serve during the next year as Chairman of the statewide Displaced Homemaker Advisory Board. The program has now been successfully expanded to include AFCD mothers, and is being used as a model in many other states, Metayer said.

As ten-year member and vice Chairman of the Health Care Committee, she chaired the sub-committee that was responsible for the signing into law of the Nursing Home Ombudsman Bill. This law established a State Ombudsman and provided for access to nursing homes by certified ombudsman who may visit patients during reasonable hours, overseeing the quality of care they are receiving. She successfully pushed through the House a bill that has freed up a supply of corneal tissue for transplant to the more than 500 sightless people who had been on medical waiting lists, in need of corneal transplants.

Mrs. Metayer pointed to her "responsive" record as Braintree's State Representative. "I have never knowingly left a telephone call unreturned, or a letter unanswered," she said. She expressed gratitude for the "hundred or so" letters and cards she has received from constituents since she announced her impending retirement. "One of my more politically savvy friends called me "A citizen representative" she said, "meaning that I was close to the people I represent, and I had no other ambitions but to serve them well. I was delighted." Mrs. Metayer recently received an award from the AFL/CIO for her support of working people.

She also recently received awards from the Massachusetts and Braintree Fire Fighters and Police Departments, the nursing home industry, 9 to 5, and the Bay State Skills Corporation.

When asked to sum up her feelings about her decade of service as Braintree's State Representative, Mrs. Metayer said, "I have loved serving the wonderful people of

Braintree on Beacon Hill; and I have loved the wonderful people I have known there, the colleagues with whom I served; the people in our state agencies; the employees whose mission it is to smooth the paths of all of us in government; everyone in all three branches. They've been great to me. Altogether," she added, "the past ten years have represented the frosting on the decidedly beautiful cake that has been my life."

LOCAL
THE PATRIOT LEDGER, SATURDAY, DECEMBER 1, 1984

BRAINTREE 'LEGEND' PRAISED
honor Metayer
by Jody Feinbery
Patriot Ledger Staff

Braintree-Elizabeth Metayer radiantly kissed everyone who rose to honor her years in the State legislature. "One thing I've noticed," quipped Gerald Walsh, the master of ceremonies for the Thursday night tribute, "she's never missed the opportunity to kiss somebody."

More the 560 people bought tickets to the retirement banquet held in the Sheraton Tara. Officials and citizens, encouraged and inspired by "Bibs," called her a "legend" and "the most prominent woman in Braintree since Abigail Adams."

Metayer, 73, looked spryly regal in a peach-colored gown, the shawl of which unfolded around her like an open fan.

"I have never met anyone like Bibs Metayer," said Congressman Brian Donnelly, D-Quincy, "…(she) has the special quality of caring and understanding…not just in her legislative work, but in dealing with people on a day-to-day basis."

In her five legislative terms, people became used to being called "darling" and to seeing legislation which helped displaced homemakers, the elderly and commuters.

"She is respected by every one of her colleagues," said Speaker of the House of Representatives Thomas McGee, D-Lynne, who sat next to Metayer at the head table. "This is really what it's all about. The people that you work with are truly the ones who can judge."

Elizabeth Laing, co-chairman of the tribute along with John Shaughnessy, extolled the spirit of Metayer.

"There will never be another Bibs," Laing said. "We like her because she never turned her back on anyone who asked her for help…because she always makes us feel we are the most important person she's met that day…because she is always so colorful, her dress and personality dramatic." Developer Thomas Flatley chose to speak through gifts, rather than words. His gifts acknowledged the humanitarianism Metayer will continue during the more leisurely life she will be leading. Flatley gave a $1000 donation in her name to Oxfam America for famine relief in Ethiopia, plus two airplane tickets from Boston to Fort Lauderdale and reservations to stay at a Sheraton Hotel in Florida. There were presentations from Braintree's fraternal, women's, business and health organizations, the selectmen and the school committee. Metayer was feted with medals, plaques and gifts, including a commemorative seal of the Great Seal of the U.S. Congress from Donelly, an antique print signed by 159 state legislators from state Senator Paul Harold, D-Quincy, and a brightly polished police badge from the Braintree Patrolmen's Club.

When the crowd stood and applauded at the end of the 26th presentation, Metayer spoke. "When one reaches my age, one's riches…are measured by the amount of friends and love one has been able to garner over the years. My wealth lies before me this evening."

Then, with a slight quiver in her voice, "Lonely days are bound to lie ahead, but whenever my mouth begins to turn down at the corners, I shall bring to mind the memory of this evening and it will warm my heart and turn up the corners of my mouth."

STATE REPRESENTATIVE ELIZABETH N. METAYER TRIBUTE

Held at Sheraton Tara Hotel, Braintree, Massachusetts
November 29, 1984
Speech given by Elizabeth Laing, Attorney at Law, Guest Speaker

We respect her.
We admire her.
We love her.
But I think most important of all, we LIKE her.

We like her because she never turned her back on anyone who asked for help. She never received a phone call or letter that she did not answer.

We like her because after an exhausting day tending to State House business, she always answered her phone with that inimitable "H-E-L-L-O" (sing it.)

We like her because she is always so colorful, her dress and personality dramatic. She always has interesting stories to tell.

We like her because she is a loving wife, who in fact gave up her seat in the House of Representatives because she wanted to be with her beloved Ted who for all those 10 years had been her greatest supporter, fielding those phone calls when she was not at home and making her life comfortable. And who loves her dearly.

We like her because she is a loving mother to her daughter Gael and her son Richard.

We like her because she rejoices with her grandchildren, sharing their achievements, commiserating with them in their disappointments.

We like her because of the way she greets you and me always joyful, making us feel we are the most important person she met that day.

We like her for the way she calls us "dear" and means it-for we ARE all dear to her. And the way she tips her head and raises her shoulders to make a point.

We like her for the way she never complains or even mentions problems besetting her. And for the deep faith she has in God.

We like her for her unfailing loyalty to her friends, to those she believes in. (When I was six years old, Bibs came to my ballet recital. There were 12 of us; 11 were pointing right and 1 was pointing left. As we did our pas de deux and our pirouettes, she turned to my mother and said, "Look at that, Elizabeth is the only one in step.) She has never lost those stars in her eyes.

We like her for her gratitude for the smallest kindness done for her, and for her great generosity. We like her for her humility, the humble way she accepts any tribute paid to her.

We like her for her youthfulness, her bounce, her enthusiasm, her zest for life, the example she sets for her SUPER citizens.

We like her for her courage-when she took positions which were not popular but in which she believed.

We like her because we know how much she loves her town, and we recognize the years she gave to her town, long beyond her 10 years as State Representative.

There will never be another Bibs..

No one will ever match this woman, or enjoy the affection, the esteem, the love she has earned-which, at this tribute, we are showing her tonight.

Our wish tonight is for a long and happy life in her new leisure, great joy-and we offer the hope she and her dear Ted will now reap the rewards of their many years of selflessness of giving. With love, we salute them both, Braintree's WONDER COUPLE.

I present BIBS METAYER.

MY SPEECH AT MY TESTIMONIAL DINNER At Sheraton Tara, 11-29-84

I am the richest woman in the world…

When one reaches my age, one's riches are measured not by the amount of wealth one might have accumulated, but by the amount of friendship and love one has garnered over the years…

[Introduce the members of my family]

My wealth lies before me here this evening-in my wonderful family and my wonderful friends…

How can I possibly put into words what it has meant to me to serve the beautiful people of Braintree; and to walk with and work with the beautiful people on Beacon Hill during the past 10 years???

Truthfully I have LOVED every day under the Golden Dome…The past ten years have been the greatest years of my life…the frosting on the cake of what-thanks to a very special husband who because of knee surgery cannot be with us; and two very special children, and the wife of one of them; and five very special grandchildren, -has been a very happy life…

In sending me to Beacon Hill, the people of Braintree added to that happy life by providing for me all that makes life worthwhile--a job to do…good friends to make the doing of that job easier…the opportunity to be of service to others…the richness and warmth of a full and busy life…

I have served for 9-½ of my 10 years under a great Speaker, my good friend the Hon. Thomas W. McGee, a Speaker who has supported me 100% in everything I attempted to do both for my community and in a larger sense for the people of the Commonwealth. I always had to substantiate my requests. Speaker McGee was no easy mark…But once I had defended my bill or my stand and he had promised to help, I always could rely on his word.

I have served under great committee Chairmen, who allowed me to develop my potential and to share in all aspects of the committee work.

As Vice Chairman of the Health Care Committee I have been privileged to share totally in the workings of that committee with my good friend, Chairman Representative Richard Voke. We've literally become a TEAM..

I have loved my colleagues in government in the House and Senate. They're GREAT people. And I have loved all those who work so hard for us under the Golden Dome…our staff people and others. They have been friends as well as co-workers. How I shall miss you all!

As for this evening's Testimonial…this wonderful manifestation of your friendship and kindness, much of which I honestly feel is undeserved, WHAT CAN I SAY???

My heart is overflowing with gratitude to you all. I shall treasure the memory of this evening for all the days of my life…

I shall soon be closing the book on what has easily been the most exciting Chapter of that life. Lonely days are bound to lie ahead, but whenever my mouth begins to turn downward at the corners, I shall bring to mind that fantastic Thursday evening; and the memory of the friendship I found there…and indeed the love…will warm my heart and turn the corners of my mouth back up….

I particularly want to thank those who have worked so hard to make this evening such a success.

[Name committee members including Arthur Logan and Limousine]

Thank you and God love you. I do…

***

Braintree Forum and Observer
Volume 107 No. 50 A Mariner Newspaper
Wednesday, December 5, 1984

[handwritten comment]

November 29, 1984

Dear Bibs,

You will receive your gift from all your friends on hand to honor you tonight, as soon as possible.

As you know, included will be an album of photos in color of this evening's events, so you can recall to mind the tribute paid to you.

With love,
The Committee

THE MASSACHUSETTS POLITICAL ALMANAC

House of Representatives

Elizabeth N. Metayer (D)

33 Arthur Street, Braintree, Massachusetts 02184

(H) 617 843 5159

5ht Norfolk (5th Term)

Braintree

State House-Room 130 Phone 617 722 2130

Administrative Assistant-Suzanne Bump

Committees: (Vice Chair) Health Care; Rules; Transportation

Born: Boston, Massachusetts

Profession: Legislator

Personal: Married (Edward), 2 children; Roman Catholic

Interests: Gardening; Reading; Swimming; and especially my grandchildren

Education: Girls Catholic High School, Malden (29); Hickox Secretarial School; Attended Harvard University

Political Offices: Town Meeting Member (25 years); (Chair) Braintree Technical Advisory Committee on Transportation

Organizations: (Pres.) Braintree Point Women's Club ('54-'56 & '69-'71); (Chair) Division of Drama, Mass. State Federation on Women's Clubs; (Pres.) Second District Past Presidents Club, M.S.F.W.C.; (Chair) Division of International Affairs Club, M.S.F.W.C.; (Pres.) Quincy Deanery, Archdiocesan Council of Catholic Women; (Founder & First Pres.) Braintree League of Women Voters; (Pres.) Mothers Guild, Archbishop Williams High School

Election Results:

1982 Primary Metayer (D) 7468/ All others 1/Blanks 2067/Total votes 9506.

1982 General Metayer (D) 12271/ All others 6/ Blanks 3047 Total Votes 15324

Group Ratings: ADA 41%, AFL?CIO 38%, CLT 40%, CLUM 8%, CPPAX 39%, MLCV 50%, MTA 55%

Priorities: Displaced Homemaker Program, Legislation to increase funding and provide for expansion of program throughout Massachusetts; Hospital Cost and General Health Care Cost Containment, legislation designed to facilitate acceptance and application of Chapter 372; Eye Bank Legislation, legislation to enable corneas from unclaimed accident and other victims to be used to provide sight, cornea transplants.

KEY VOTES OF 1981-1982 SESSIONS:

FOR	1. Campaign Finance Regulation
AGAINST	2. Gay Rights
AGAINST	3. Auto Insurance Deregulation
FOR	4. Bottle Bill (Override)
AGAINST	5. Republican Budget
AGAINST	6. Motorcyclist Headgear
FOR	7. Prohibition of Abortion
FOR	8. Ad/Non-public Schools
FOR	9. Death Penalty
AGAINST	10. Nuclear Power Plant Moratorium
N/V	11. Handgun Control

| AGAINST | 12. Sunday Openings |
| AGAINST | 13. Living Will |

PATRIOT LEDGER

Saturday, December 15, 1984
Two Braintree Schools Share in Arts Grants

Braintree Two Braintree schools will share $1,625 in grants form the Institute for the Arts of the Cultural Education Collaborative, Representative Elizabeth N. Metayer, D-Braintree, has announced.

The grants will help finance programs by the Berkshire Ballet and poet Kate Rushkin at the Highlands Elementary School, and programs by the Boston Arts Group and the Old Jazz Ensemble at the Liberty Elementary School.

THE BRAINTREE FORUM

Wednesday, December 12, 1984
From our files
25 years ago, December 11, 1959

This year marks the 60th anniversary of the Braintree Philergians. "The Philergians Story," a colorful pageant written and directed by Mrs. Edward Metayer, a club member and chairman of the Massachusetts State Federation of Women's Clubs, will portray the history of the club, from its organization in 1899 with only seven members, to the present day, with the membership limit at four hundred.

The Commonwealth of Massachusetts
House of Representatives
Assistant Majority Leader
State House, Boston
Committee on Health Care, Vice-Chairman Rules, Transportation
Room 130, State House
December 13, 1984
Elizabeth N. Metayer
5th Norfolk District
Dr. Salvatore Mangano, Chairman Board of Registration in Medicine
100 Cambridge Street
Boston, Massachusetts 02202

The Candid Idylls of a State Representative | 443

***

TESTIMONY OF REPRESENTATIVE ELIZABETH N. METAYER: IN OPPOSITION TO PROPOSED REGULATIONS OF THE BOARD OF REGISTRATION IN MEDICINE REGARDING PHYSICIAN ASSISTANT AND NURSE-PRACTIONERS (243 cmr 3.01 and 4.01).

Dear Chairman Mangano and Members of the Board of Registration in Medicine,

I appreciate this opportunity to testify before you today on the proposed regulations regarding physician assistants and nurse practitioners. As Vice-Chairman of the Legislative Committee on Health Care, I am deeply concerned with the proposed regulations and urge the Board to reconsider them.

As you know, last year the Legislature enacted and the Governor signed Chapter 565, An Act Relative to Health Care Services for Certain Patients in Nursing Homes. Through the enactment of this legislation, it was the intent of the Legislature to expand the prescriptive privileges of physician assistants and nurse practitioners for patients in nursing homes and for other chronically ill patients in danger of institutionalization. Also, it was the intent of the Legislature to include adequate safeguards in the law, through the provision that the nurse practitioner's and physician assistant's prescriptions include the name of the supervising physician. The Legislature further intended that the details of implementing the law be coordinated by the appropriate executive agencies and boards,

In sum, last year the Legislature acted to improve the quality of life for thousands of the Commonwealth's neediest citizens. Through Chapter 565, we hoped to assist nursing homes and chronically ill patients to obtain access to appropriate primary care services. It is my sincere hope that the Board of Registration in Medicine will reconsider its proposed regulations regarding physician assistants and nurse practitioners and work towards developing guidelines more consistent with the Legislative intent of the law.

Sincerely,
ELIZABETH N. METAYER
Vice Chairman
Committee on Health Care

BRAINTREE FORUM AND OBSERVER

Volume 108 No. 37 A Mariner Newspaper
Wednesday, September 11, 1985

In less than three weeks, Braintree's "Woman of Substance," former Representative Elizabeth "Bibs" Metayer, and her husband, Ted, will say a final farewell to the town which has been their home for 38 years…They will head for Pompano Beach, Florida and a penthouse condominium, their new home…And Braintree will never be the quite the same…

Bibs Metayer is gifted in many ways…Not the least of these gifts certainly is an incredible personality…She is the kind of person who, when you meet her, makes you feel you are just the person she wanted to see that day. She is never too busy to stop and chat, to make a telephone call or to write a letter of recommendation…Her enthusiasm about everything is catching…Her sensitivity, her caring, are touching…

For 10 years she served the people of Braintree in the State Legislature and no one doubted she would be returned to office this year had she chosen to run for a sixth term…She opted to retire so she could spend time with her ailing husband…

Ted has undergone knee surgery and while his health has improved, he is incapacitated to some degree…The lovely house on Arthur Street they both dearly love became too much for Bibs to handle alone…The grounds, the shrubs, the flowers, the pool, all the things they tended with such loving care, were overwhelming to Bibs…And so they decided to buy the condominium at Pompano Beach…Summers will be spent on Cape Cod…

Bibs sits in her beautiful Ethan Allen Barnstable Rocker, a replica of the one owned by President Kennedy, and says, "This was the most difficult decision I ever made…I hope I will have no regrets…I hope I have made the right decision".

Everywhere she looks, everything she touches, conjures up precious memories…

She was an advocate for vocational education when she served in the State House…Her rocking chair was a gift from the Blue Hills District School Committee…It bears a plaque which reads: "Presented to Representative Elizabeth N. Metayer on her retirement from the legislature in recognition of her many years of dedication and devotion to the Blue Hills Regional School District, December 18, 1984"…

The culinary arts Department prepared the Christmas tea when the presentations were made…The sheet metal shop people presented her a handsome fireplace tool set, the wood working shop presented her a mirror and the nursing class presented pretty placemats…

She will take with her to Florida all her treasured mementos and memorabilia…More than 75 plaques, given to her over the years by appreciative groups, will find a home on the walls of her new home, along with countless citations.

"We have a den and there is a long hallway leading to it," she says, and she has already staked out that area for her display…Three lovely clocks with plaques are making the trip south along with a special seal of the United States, given to her by Congressman Brian Donnelly…

She points to a large silver tray, already in its packing box, a gift from the Massachusetts and Braintree Firefighters Associations..

"My magnificent spruce tree on the side lawn," she says wistfully as tears well up, "how can I leave that behind?"…

The tree was given to her by Braintree Rotary when she was recovering from a broken hip after a fall in her home…

"The Rotarians brought it into my home," she says, "and we decorated it for Christmas…After the holidays, the Rotary Club commissioned Mento Landscaping Co. to plant it…And we've strung it with lights every year since"…

Her eyes travel around the nearly empty living room (she has divested herself of just about all the furniture and she has scheduled a yard sale for this coming Saturday) and almost as though she needs to think of something bright and happy quickly to fend off her sad feelings, she talks about their new condo..

"We're on the 15th floor, high above the world," she says…

"It fronts on the ocean just a block away and backs onto the intracoastal waterway… And adjacent to the condo property is the 14th causeway drawbridge which opens twice an hour and all the sailboats and yachts wait beneath our balcony for the drawbridge to open"..

"Across from the waterway there is a huge park which will never be built upon, so at night we have the magnificent view of the lights of three communities, Margate, Fort Lauderdale and Pompano Beach…It's just breathtaking"…

It will be all new everything for Bibs and Ted…New home, new friends, new life… And there'll be all new furniture…

"Everything will be French Provincial…We've done all the rooms in melon, white and green…It is just beautiful"…

Before she packed all her fine china, lovely linens and crystal, she and Ted hosted one final Sunday evening formal dinner for her family and her grandchildren…The Sunday dinners have been a tradition of the Metayers for many years…

"The most difficult part is leaving everybody I love…My grandsons, my sister Jean, my friends, my neighbors and the people of Braintree"…

"I have always been so close to the people of Braintree…I loved going to the supermarket and having people I didn't know come up and wish me well and tell me I was doing a good job…I know so many people in Braintree…Wherever I go, I find friends…That will be different in Florida". "I'll miss the lilacs and the forsythia and watching for the first tulip to poke through the earth and all the flowering shrubs you don't see in Florida…I'll miss going to Town Hall where I know everyone, the policemen who wave to me along the route and the firefighters who would come to me in a minute if I needed them…I'll miss all the people who have been so good to me over 10 years…Oh it was such a tough decision to make…

"The balcony at the condo has two sections…I'm going to place two huge containers with white geraniums in one section and Ted is going to put a tomato plant in a pot in the other, because he always loved his garden tomatoes…

"It's so hard to leave a place you love and go to a place where you don't know a soul"

"It wasn't so bad when it was June…But now it's September.

"I haven't even reached there and I'm already secretary to the board of directors of the Condo Association…It's rumored I will be the next president," she says with a smile…

That's all right though…We have a bit of a problem at the beach with the coral sweeping in when there is a storm…I plan to get in touch with the State Representative from our area the minute I get there and I'll offer to help her or him…They may be having the same problems in Florida that we handled in the legislature here and there may be things I can help with in a volunteer way if I establish a rapport with the Representative"…

"I keep meeting people and I think this is the last time I'll ever see this one or that one"…

"It's difficult for Ted, too…He is leaving his buddies Arthur Peterson and John Ghiorse to whom he's been so close through the years…Our families grew up together and they did a lot of things together over the years…

Bibs has already made one friend, a librarian who is a retired teacher and as she puts it, "a fun person"…

"I plan to take my easel and start painting again…I'll have the ocean to paint…And I will join the women's club…I'm an active person…I have to do things to fill my life…I'll do volunteer work…I'll find things to fill my days…"

Yes, she has missed the legislature terribly…

"I had a three-hour lunch at the Parker House last week with Representative Frances Alexander of Beverly and Representative Marie-Louise Kehoe from Dedham…They were my seat mates in the House and we had a wonderful relationship…They promised to schedule a long weekend and visit me"….

The "Tribute to Representative Elizabeth Metayer" last November at the Sheraton Tara shines as the highlight of her life…

"I just couldn't believe it," she says as she recalls the capacity crowd in the main ballroom… "I never expected anything like that, not only the number of people but the gifts, the presentations, the words spoken…It was just unbelievable"…

"Dear me," Bibs says thoughtfully…

"I will leave a part of my heart in Braintree and another part in the State House"…

"And it's only what is left that will go to Florida."

THE COMMONWEALTH OF MASSACHUSETTS

Executive Office of Human Services
Department of Public Health
150 Fremont Street, Boston 02111

June 20, 1986

Representative Elizabeth Metayer
The Waterbury, Unit 1505 1401 North Riverside Drive
Pompano Beach, FL 33062

Dear Representative Metayer.

On my recommendation and in consultation with the Governor's Task Force on AIDS, Governor Michael S. Dukakis has chosen to recognize that outstanding contributions you have made to the Commonwealth's efforts in actively addressing AIDS in Massachusetts.

A reception honoring all recipients of the Governor's Recognition Award (see enclosed list) will be held on Tuesday, July 15th, 1986 from 4:00 to 5:00 p.m. in Doric Hall, State House, Boston. Please R.S.V.P. to Ken Schulman at 617 727 0049.

Many thanks for your dedicated efforts. We look forward to continuing to work with you.

Sincerely,
Bailus Walker, Jr. Ph.D., M.P.H.
Commissioner

Recipients of Governor's AIDS Recognition Award

Researchers: The Massachusetts AIDS Research Group
(Principal Investigators)

Donald E. Craven, M.D.
Boston Department of Health and Hospitals
Clyde Crumpacker, M.D.
Beth Israel Hospital

Martin Hirsch, M.D.
Massachusetts General Hospital
William A. Haseltine, Ph.D.
"Dana Farber Cancer Institute

Norman L. Letvin, M.D.
New England Regional Primate Research Center

Kenneth H. Mayer, M.D.
Fenway Community Health Center

Carel Mulder, D. Phil.
University of Massachusetts Medical School

James Mullins, Ph.D.
Harvard School of Public Health

Peter L. Page, M.D.
American Red Cross Blood Service
Ruth Margrit Ruprecht, M.D., Ph.D.
Dana Farber Cancer Institute

George R. Seage, III
Boston Department of Health and Hospitals

John Sullivan, M.D.
University of Massachusetts Medical School

Media:
The Boston Globe medical writers (Richard Knox, Judy Foreman and Richard Saltus), and Loretta McLaughlin, Deputy Editor of the Editorial Page and former media news reporter

Stan Freeman, science/health reporter for the Springfield Morning Union
Jeanne Blake, medical reporter, WBZ-TV Boston

Neil Miller, reporter, The Boston Phoenix
The editorial staff of the Patriot Ledger

Community Organization: AIDS Action Committee

Special Recognition: Swansea Public Schools-John McCarthy, Superintendent

Harold Devine, Jr., Principal of Joseph Case Junior High School

State Employee: George Grady, M.D., State Epidemiologist

State Legislators: Representative Richard Voke and former State Representative Elizabeth Metayer

BEACON HILL BY RENEE LOTH

In the rigorous pecking order of the Massachusetts Legislature, where power and influence are measured by the size of one's budget for paper clips, most first term representatives are assigned offices so tine and drab that they would find a phone booth liberating. And within the House chamber, where majority rule is revered as absolute truth, the pitiful minority of women legislators (fewer of them even than Republicans!) for years lacked the clout even to command its own restroom.

Survival Strategies
Playing the game: Part One

Elizabeth "Bibs" Metayer (D-Braintree) was 72 when she retired from the Legislature in 1983. Metayer was everybody's favorite aunt. Founder of a local League of Women Voters chapter, active in church committees, a graduate of secretarial school for whom public office was her first paying job, Metayer had a decidedly low profile in the Legislature. Soft-spoken and deferential, she once told a reporter her secret to success in the Legislature "is not to compete with the men but to cooperate with them."

One of Metayer biggest fans was Representative Richard Voke (D-Chelsea). Voke-though 37 years her junior and possessing many years' less seniority-had been Metayer's chairman on the health care committee until he was promoted to chair the omnipotent Ways and Means Committee when his poker partner Keverian became speaker. State House lore has it that on the day of Metayer's last committee hearing, Voke brought her a bouquet of flowers and handed her the gavel so that she could chair the meeting. And Voke gave Metayer a more substantive retirement gift: He shepherded through the Legislature one of her most important causes-$1.2 million for AIDS counseling and research. Metayer knew that's often the way it is with public policy: The press of events made funding for AIDS research a priority, but it took a personal favor to make it law.

BRAINTREE FORUM AND OBSERVER

Wednesday, July 16, 1986
Metayer honored for initial efforts in battling AIDS

Former Representative Elizabeth N. Metayer and Representative Richard Voke, chairman of the House ways and means committee, have received the Governor's Recognition Award for their contributions to the Commonwealth's efforts in addressing AIDS.

When the problem of AIDS first surfaced, Metayer was vice chairman of the Health Care Committee. A special meeting on the subject was held to which were invited the commissioner of Public Health and various members of medical profession to provide information on the medical dangers involved in the disease.

Among the causes listed for the spread of AIDS was the infected blood donors.

"It was stated that a crash program of research was needed to develop a test for screening out carriers of the disease," Metayer says.

"The Red Cross representative especially was concerned and it was revealed that many blood banks were located in areas were donors were frequently in dire straits and were selling blood for liquor, etc. The menace was great," the former Representative added.

Metayer asked Commissioner Bailus, Jr. of the Department of Public Health how much money they would need from the state to fund this crash program and after consultation she was told $1,500,000.

"It was budget time and I sought to have that large amount added. I defended it on the floor of the House and won," Metayer says.

"The million and a half was added and the research programs were instituted. Then last year Representative Voke added a million to the budget to continue the research."

The test is now a reality.

The letter from Commissioner Walker informed Metayer that "On my recommendation and in consultation with the Governor's task force on AIDS, Governor Michael S. Dukakis has chosen to recognize the outstanding contributions you have made to the Commonwealth's efforts in actively addressing AIDS in Massachusetts."

A reception honoring all recipients of the Governor's Recognition Award was held yesterday (Tuesday) in Doric Hall, State House.

Included were members of the media, AIDS Action Committee, researchers, Dr. George Grady, state epidemiologist and two school representatives.

AIDS TEST REPORTED SUCCESSFUL

The Associated Press Washington-Results of the first year of screening blood supplies for signs of AIDS indicate it has almost stopped the spread of the disease through transfusion, but more precise tests are still needed, experts say.

Because of the tests, which look for evidence of antibodies to the virus which causes acquired immune deficiency syndrome, and screening out high-risk donors, blood supplies are much safer than they were a year ago, specialists said Monday.

"The test have performed remarkably well," said Dr. S. Gerald Sandler of the American Red Cross. "In a short time, we were able to halt the spread of the AIDS virus through blood supplies." However, Sandler and other specialists told a panel of experts convened at the National Institutes of Health that despite the positive results achieved by the first-generation tests, more precise methods were needed to screen blood donors.

After considering the latest information on AIDS blood testing, the panel is to draft recommendations on how to properly use and interpret the test, as well as on future directions of research into better tests.

About 2 percent of AIDS cases have been associated with transfusions of blood and blood products contaminated with the AIDS virus. While screening has markedly reduced chances of getting infected blood today, federal health authorities say the numbers of transfusion related cases are expected to rise for several years because of blood received before there was routine testing. AIDS, an incurable and fatal condition that results in destruction of the body's infection-fighting immune system, had been diagnosed in more that 22,000 Americans, half of whom have died.

THE BOSTON GLOBE MAGAZINE

[handwritten note]

March 2nd, 1987

Dear Bibs,

I hope the winter in Florida was fun and productive for you. I'm sorry it has taken me so long to answer this letter, but between work and extra work, I have been hopping all over. You will be happy to hear that I did win a major international award for my pictures of the space shuttle. Now I am working full time for the Globe Sunday magazine-thus the article. I hope you find it interesting. Within the next few days I'll send the calendar to your. Your picture with the girls' softball team was included. Thanks again for the letter with all the news.

Best wishes to you and your family-
Janet

BIBS FEELS A WARM GLOW ABOUT THE REUNION OF BRAINTREE-ITES

To the Editor:

I keep feeling a warm glow as I look back upon the sixth annual reunion of our Braintree-ites, "expatriated" and otherwise. It was like a little corner of Braintree had been lifted up and set down in sunny Florida. (And it was sunny; the weatherman cooperated beautifully in that tinsel town that is Kissimmee.)

It was my first experience with this annual affair which this year attracted a total of 225, up considerably from that original Braintree High School Class of 11 that started the affair just six years ago.

The place was awash with memories for this "expatriate" for whom Braintree-ites have always been second to none. Ted and I and Gael and Paul and his two sisters, Clarice Sweezey Holmes and Ethel Sweezey Monti had arrived the day before, and were staying at the Hilton where the luncheon observance was scheduled to take place.

We promptly repaired to the lounge in the hope of meeting some of our friends ahead of time. We did just that! Enroute we found Bob and Mary Frazier, Jack and Mary Curran, and George and Helen Brown. The girls, having spent the day at Disney World, were tired, and so were off to bed. We promptly corralled the gentlemen, and all headed for the Entertainment Center where we had a ball! As part of the Braintree scene we were permitted to select the songs and join in lustily with the two performers, one of whom just happened to be from Massachusetts by the way.

Did I say that the place was awash with memories? The sight of my good friend Bob Frazier, with whom I had a delightful chat, brought visibly to mind the many times our paths had crossed in the service of the town..

I looked way back over the years and remembered his defense as a Selectman of my demand for the creation of a Blue Ribbon Committee to deal with the MBTA's coming to Braintree. He had joined me in shooting down every objection of his colleagues. The committee was formed and what a great committee it had proved to be!

A big hug from Bob Dawes, and I was remembered his ceaseless journeying around town as its dedicated Dog Officer. He was personally acquainted with every canine in Braintree; and no complaint went unanswered under our Officer Bob.

Another hug! This time from Marion Keigan Amann, and I found myself wishing that she had been accompanied not only by her dear Roger, but by my treasured friends Dr. Archie Keigan and his dear Dorothy. What a hit would have made…this man whom everybody in Braintree loves. He'd have been the Star of the Show. As a matter of fact, promptly dropped the good Doctor a line and urged him to come next year…

Morris Harrison's hug, and I was recalling fondly the occasion of the grand opening of the new Masonic Temple when I was escorted by him in a march about the Lodge Room, a distinction normally reserved for GENTLEMEN members only.

And a warm greeting from my dear friends Dot and Frank Lyons, and my mind went back to my very earliest days in Braintree when the lovely young Dot Hennebury campaigned with Carl Johnson (of happy memory). They were the first distinguished Democrats to cross my path.

It was fun to watch the various Braintree High School classes lining up for picture taking. We were seated close enough to see it all, and I found myself sporting an occasional tear or two as someone special passed our way enroute to the camera. How thrilled I was when so many of those dear Braintree-ites appeared as happy to see me as I was to see them.

The Candid Idylls of a State Representative | 453

Naturally the world's greatest Social Editor, my very treasured friend Olive Laing, with her dear Don, was on hand to photograph and record the event, despite a couple of hundred mile detour from their original destination which was the Palm Beach Airport to meet son Dee, his wife Annette and the adored Laing granddaughter, Andrea, who were arriving for a stay in sunny Florida. And returning to the subject of memories-how many golden memories indeed we share always with these two special people, Olive and Don Laing…30 years of memories, for our lives seem to have become entwined almost from the first day we arrived in Braintree 42 years ago.

May God love and keep you all…

Most fondly,
Elizabeth "Bibs" Metayer
1401 N. Riverside Drive
Pompano Beach, Florida 33062

PHILERGIANS-90 YEARS OLD AND STILL GOING STRONG

Your Braintree Observer
Olive Laing

Certainly one of the highlights of the year for members of the Philergians, the town's oldest Federated women's club, will be the celebration of the 90th anniversary of the club's founding. A tea is planned for Tuesday, October 17, in Emmanuel Parish Hall to mark the important milestone. The 70th anniversary of the Philergians, celebrated in 1969 and 1970, featured the most thorough history of the organization ever written. Compiled by Bibs Metayer, the series of articles, "The Philergian Story-Seventy Years of Splendor," ran for several weeks in the Observer and featured many of the club's achievements including the founding of a "Golden Agers Program," the beginning of today's senior citizens' groups, contributions of service to the establishment of the Gen. Sylvanus Thayer Birthplace, an historic landmark, and other services to the town.

In 1970 the club published "Braintree, Our Town," with Bibs Metayer writing the final text.

***

[hand written letter]

Archie G. Kiegan, M.D.
278 Quincy Avenue

East Braintree, Massachusetts 02184

4 December, 1989

Dear Ted and Bibs,

Now that my Shakespeare courses are coming to an unwanted close, it is time to keep you up to date. Dorothy has designated me as Christmas Card Signer. I was assigned your address. Rather [than] a card, I thought a letter would be better.

The present frigid weather keeps us indoors and occasions us time to catch up on much neglected correspondence.

Needless to say your last letter was much appreciated and read and re-read many times. Since retirement, which I most enjoy, my days have been quite full.

Up each morning at four o'clock and down to the horse farm in East Bridgewater for four to five hours seven days a week. The duties are as you would expect-emptying, cleaning and carrying water buckets, cleaning stalls, pushing wheel barrows, wrestling with the thoroughbreds and any other tasks associated with a barn full of horses. The deal is: I'll give your business thirty-four hours a week, you take care of all my horses' expenses. It is physically trying but fun for me. On 12 December 89 I will complete my fourth semester in Shakespeare-one semester at the University of Massachusetts in Boston, two semesters at Boston University and finally the fourth at Boston College. It has required a lot of study, reading, papers and examinations. I love it and am sorry when each semester comes to a close. It has proven to be honest incentive for idle hours. Thus far my grades have fluctuated between an A- to B+ so I hope you are proud.

The family is now within a two and a half hour drive from the homestead. Margot is in Newport New Hampshire with her husband, Phil, a stockbroker and their two-year-old son, Tommy. David is in Greenfield, New Hampshire running the Otter Lake Conservation Camp with Terri, his wife, Matthew, his twelve year old stepson and two young daughters Cassi (3 yrs), Ashley (1½ yrs) and recently, Christian (3 months).

Rory had an apartment in Quincy and Bobby is living at home. So, Dorothy and I are happy with their proximity. We catch your grandson on the Rhode Island TV station frequently. Our reaction, of course, is "Hey, we know that guy!"

If you have been reading or hearing anything about the state of affairs in our beloved Commonwealth, I presume you go to Mass every morning to thank the Lord you are living in Florida.

Again, apologies for enforced tardiness! I certainly hope you are both enjoying good health and happiness. Best wishes for a very Merry Christmas and a Happy New Year!

Dorothy sends her regards!

Sincerely,
Archie Keigan

[handwritten note: I filed this Legislation annually and followed it through to fruition.]

BRAINTREE FORUM AND OBSERVER

December 6-8, 1988
THE DIRECT LINE TO JFK STATION
By Marilyn Jackson
South Look staff

South Shore commuters on the MBTA's Red Line will be able to travel directly from Braintree to the JFK/UMass subway station beginning Monday, December 12.

The $13.7 million project at the station once called Columbia will be completed in the spring, according to MBTA spokesman Peter Dimond.

But the additional platform will be opened Monday.

Dimond said MBTA undertook the two-year project after passengers demanded direct connection with that station..

"There are many institutions there in addition to U/Mass-the John F. Kennedy Library, the State Archives and other businesses," said Dimond.

It was cumbersome for passengers to go first to Andrew Station, transfer and then head southbound, he said.

When the South Shore extension was in its earliest planning stages nearly 25 years ago, local politicians asked to have the trains stop at the Columbia station, but the design, engineering and construction costs at that time appeared to be prohibitive.

Dimond said the modernization of the station includes the construction of an overhead bridge to link the two platforms and an enclosed waiting room for bus passengers.

A signal system also was installed to alert passengers at which platform the next inbound train will stop.

Also to be built near the JFK/UMass station is a larger MBTA police station to replace the existing facility at the Cabot yards on Dorchester Avenue in South Boston.

It is presently under design, and construction could begin at the earliest in late 1989, said Dimond.

"We've spent more than $200 million on the Red Line," he continued, purchasing vehicles, rebuilding the entire track system from Harvard to the Andrew tunnel portal and rebuilding the JFK/UMass station.

During the past six years, the MBTA has spent nearly $2 billion in construction and $400 million in purchasing vehicles.

During 1988 alone, some 58 new Red Line vehicles were put into service, and an additional 42 Red Line vehicles, 24 Orange Line cars and 12 Blue Line vehicles have been ordered.

Also, the MBTA purchased 200 new buses, all equipped with wheelchair lifts.

The T has added a lot of new train equipment-26 new locomotives and 107 coaches and ordered 56 more coaches which will start arriving next summer.

Some of this equipment purchase is in anticipation of service for the Old Colony lines, he said. The environmental impact record for the proposed restoration of the three lines to Greenbush, Plymouth and Middleboro is expected to be completed by the end of the year or early 1989, at which time it will be circulated for public comment.

Dimond said the MBTA also has received proposals from manufacturers to build 75 double-deck coaches with the option for 70 more which would be put in use on the present commuter rail lines. Millions of dollars are being spent in capital projects for the MBTA, said Dimond. "I like to say, "the oldest subway system in the country is fast becoming the most modern."

Design work is under way for a $34 million maintenance and inspection facility for commuter rail to be constructed near South Station.

This facility will be used for the upkeep for all trains on the south side of the city. "It will be able to handle the equipment for the Old Colony lines."

The first phase of the modernization of South Station into a transportation center is winding down.

At a cost of about $49 million, the terminal building was refurbished, and 11 new tracks, with six high-level platforms, were constructed.

The station includes five levels of office space which are fully leased, and in the spring, retail shops and food concessions will open in the lobby.

The second phase of the project-which will cost an estimated $70 million-is under design and calls for constructing a bus terminal for the commuter buses and a two-level parking facility above the tracks.

Ramps from the expressway would provide a direct link into the station, he said.

The third phase of the project is under construction. It is an underground passageway between the South Station Red Line stop and the train station.

The Boston Redevelopment Authority will oversee the fourth phase of the development, Dimond said.

Portland, Maine, Press Herald, Thursday, January 5, 1989

Wednesday, December 21, 1988

FROM OUR FILES
JFK Station

I joined with MBTA manager, James O'Leary, at the dedication of the new JFK/Columbia station.

As a result of the new design, South Shore riders will now be able to get off at JFK without having to go on to Andrew, then doubling back.

This plan has been in the works since 1976 when then Representative Elizabeth Metayer pushed for the access for students going to B.C. High and UMass Boston.

***

The Commonwealth of Massachusetts
House of Representatives
Committee on Ways and Means
State House, Boston 02133

May 29, 1990

Ms. Elizabeth Metayer
1401 North Riverside Drive
Pompano Beach, Florida 33062

Dear Elizabeth,

    I am writing to say that it was wonderful to see you upon your recent visit to Boston, and to thank you for stopping by my office for our luncheon gathering. Throughout my years on Beacon Hill there have been many friends, and wonderful memories of the times that have been had by so many good people. However, as you know, there are always those that command a special place in one's heart, a special person cared for and respected by all the membership and staff alike.

    You have always stood out as one of these very special individuals. I have long admired your ability to match the professionalism and competence of a fine legislator with your own unique, caring compassion and truth to heart. Upon your departure, and throughout the remainder of the day, I was continuously reminded by those present at our gathering of how much you are missed by everyone on the Hill.

    I have enclosed a copy of the photo taken of all those gathered in my office to greet you upon your visit. I hope that the photo will serve as a memento of the fondness felt by all of us for you. Also, please continue to do all that has brought you so much success, and please accept my best wishes for health and happiness.

Very truly yours,
Richard A. Voke
State Representative
RAV/jf

***

The Commonwealth of Massachusetts
House of Representatives
Committee on Ways and Means
State House, Boston 02133

December 4, 1990

Ms. Elizabeth Metayer
1401 North Riverside Drive
Pompano Beach, Florida 33062

Dear Mrs. Metayer,

As the end of our session nears and I begin clearing off my desk to prepare for my next assignment, I came across the enclosed video tape of your visit to the House Chamber on May 14th. As I watched with great interest, fond memories of your recent visit and our service together before that came to mind. I always look back on my days in Health Care with great pride and special reverence. I am sure this has a lot to do with you. I hope you get an opportunity to view the tape and enjoy some of the same memories that it produced in me.

Legislators and others alike are waiting with great anticipation for the opening of the new session. With a Republican Administration set to take charge in the Executive Branch, Charlie Flaherty ready to begin his reign as Speaker and 16 Republicans now in the Senate, business on the Hill will certainly be different. I cannot wait to see the results these new wrinkles will bring to the system of running state government.

I hope Florida is still agreeing with you and Ted. During this holiday season, I wish for the two of you all the happiness you have brought into the lives of many others over your fine years of service to the Commonwealth and its people. Believe me when I say that hardly a session goes by without a former colleague of yours thinking of you.

Very truly yours,
Richard A. Voke
State Representative [handwritten note on this letter]

You are the Best! Wednesday, January 9, 1985

YOUR BRAINTREE OBSERVER
Olive Laing

The committee who planned the Tribute to Representative Elizabeth Metayer met for a lunch last week at Valle's with Bibs as special guest. Purpose of this final reunion was to present Bibs with a gold embossed leather album of photographs in color taken at the Tribute. Some 72 pictures were taken by Charlie Flagg which will be a permanent memento of the event.

Ah, but Bibs will not be absent from government long. After the luncheon, she went to Town Hall and took out papers for election as Town Meeting Member from Precinct 7. She had served as Town Meeting member for many years but did not seek re-election a few years ago when her schedule At the State House became so heavy, especially with night sessions, that she could not attend the meetings.

She describes her last day as Braintree's State Representative: "The Park Street carillon was playing Joy to the World," she recalls. "Normally, it would make my spirits soar... that day it didn't." She talked about looking up at the great Golden Dome, "another roof over my head for the past 10 happy years," which shone so beautifully against the blue of the sky.

"I entered the Capitol building and decided to walk the marble corridors just one more time...Doric Hall and Nurses Hall and the Hall of Flags...How beautiful...Up the great stairway where I have posed so many times with our Braintree school children... And then one last look at my beloved House Chamber"...

"A phone call from the Governor's office brought me to the Chief Executive for a farewell chat...Governor Dukakis was warm and cordial...It was difficult to say goodbye"...

"I left his office and paused at the balcony for one more look at the splendor of the high-vaulted ceiling and the historic murals that lie beneath it"...

"The most beautiful seat of government in the world," she whispers, and there's a catch in her voice.

HERITAGE WEEK

Saturday, May 12
10 a.m. Dedication of Heritage Memorial, Elizabeth Metayer, guest speaker

DELIGHTS IN FORUM'S HONOR

To the Editor:

I join in the pride of the Forum's achievement in producing the editorial and story that enabled our favorite newspaper to win first prize in the special award category for a feature, editorial and follow-up on the story of Linwood Tower, the Braintree veteran who was denied his dying request for a military funeral.

The story and editorial were poignant and beautifully written. I can recall the entire story vividly can still see the photos by your staff photographer Jim Wiltraut.

The editorials are always beautifully thought out and crafted and I am delighted that the judges of the "largest newspaper contest in New England" had the sagacity to recognize your outstanding work. Congratulations also for having received an honorable mention in the best front-page category.

It is indeed an outstanding accomplishment to have received such recognition in a newspaper contest that involved 200 papers from throughout New England, and as many as 3,500 entries, we're mighty proud.

Continued success to our favorite newspaper, its splendid editor and to all of its first class staff. I await its weekly arrival here in Florida as eagerly as I did in Braintree.

Elizabeth N. "Bibs" Metayer
Pompano Beach, Florida
350th Anniversary Committee
Town of Braintree

***

Mrs. Elizabeth N. Metayer

1401 North Riverside Drive Suite 1505
Pompano Beach, Florida 33062

Dear Bibs:

It was such a pleasure for all of us to have you share in our 350th Anniversary celebration.

It is difficult to determine whether you or your friends here in Braintree were more delighted at your return to Braintree and taking part in our festivities.

Thank you for your usual eloquent address to all in attendance at the Dedication of Braintree Heritage Rock on Saturday morning. Everyone one was so happy for the opportunity to speak with you.

You looked as lovely as ever in your beautiful ball costume gown. We hope that your accommodations at the Tara were satisfactory.

Do hope that you enjoy the commemorative mementos that I was late in presenting them to you. I did manage to catch up at the ball, however.

We were pleased that Gael was able to be with you and that you got to visit with your other family members.

Sorry that some of us never had the opportunity to wish you "Safe Journey" before your departure.

Together we have provided observances truly worth of Our Heritage of 350 Years in a meaningful and memorable way.

Most sincerely,
Nancy G. Nicosia, Co-Chairman
350th Anniversary Committee

CHALLENGES OF 1985

The Braintree Forum Wednesday, January 2, 1985
OFFICIALS COMMENT ON '85

The Forum asked several town officials their views of the greatest challenges the town will face in 1985. Here are their responses.

State Representative Elizabeth N. Metayer

Heading the list of challenges Braintree will face during the coming year will be dealing with the second year of the S.E. Expressway reconstruction. The first year has gone reasonably well, however the town has been impacted in various ways. Ridership on the Red Line will continue to increase with a consequent decrease in the number of parking garage spaces for Braintree residents. Our local streets will continue to bear the brunt of increased traffic as commuters seek to avoid congested areas.

With the state's acceptance of Braintree's revaluation figures, the issue of classification will have to be addressed. Shall there be separate classifications for business and industry and residential property? That's the $64 question…

The matter of placing a jail in the nurses' quarters at Norfolk County Hospital will undoubtedly come to a head in 1985. Occupants of the desired building, who have been ordered to vacate by January 31, have vowed to stay put. We hope they will be successful in preventing the establishment of a jail in our town.

If not, however, the town fathers must stand firm and demand IN WRITING from the county and from the state, safeguards that will prevent any but the most harmless kind of criminals from being placed so close to our Braintree Highlands residents.

The matter of the adequacy of our fire protection will have to be addressed. A new Braintree Highlands station is a must, and the adequacy of our manpower must be carefully looked into. Traffic problems will still be with us in 1985, and with construction projects lying ahead in several sections of the town, those problems are bound to increase. It will be difficult to wend one's way down any of our main streets during high volume times of day. The police department will have to be on its toes.

The availability of subsidized housing for our low and moderate income people will continue to represent a serious problem for our housing authority members. And we shall continue to shudder as we park the family car at the South Shore Plaza, for fear it will not be there upon our return from the shopping expedition upon which we must embark. (And where better to do one's shopping than the South Shore Plaza???) Crime is down in Braintree, however they are still merrily stealing cars at the South Shore Plaza despite the elaborate security system that has been set up there.

Here's to a good and prosperous 1985 for the great town of Braintree, and for the great people who reside here. May all of the problems and challenges we envision as we tear off the last page of that little old 1984 calendar and look ahead to a brand new year, be solved beautifully and permanently by the good people who have elected to hold office within the "Capital of the South Shore." And may I take this opportunity to thank those great people of Braintree for having accorded me the honor of representing them on Beacon Hill during the past great ten years…

THE BRAINTREE STAR LADY OF THE HOUSE

BY STATE REPRESENTATIVE ELIZABETH N. METAYER
AUGUST 3, 1984

The week just past began with a bang when on Monday evening I attended the Selectmen's meeting prepared to hear SCA Chemical Services Inc. defend its action in failing to report either to Braintree, DEQE or EPA the recent plant accident when 150 or more gallons of polychlorinated biphenyls (PCB's) spilled from a transformer at their dock. The resultant mess was cleaned up by the SCA and never reported to anyone. It was brought to the attention of the town fire department via an anonymous phone call, and the residents of East Braintree are understandably outraged. I am as outraged as any….

Lou DiBernandinis, a consultant hired by the town in April, stated that the facility "presents no acute danger." To the people of East Braintree, however, its presence among us represents a very real danger and we were there to inform the representatives of this most unwelcome neighbor just how we felt about it all. I exhorted the Selectmen to seek to prevent Citgo from continuing to permit SCA to operate on their permit which was issued many years ago to Citgo and does not cover the kinds of chemicals SCA is handling.

There was a great deal of action on Beacon Hill, not all of it pleasant. The State's Department of Personnel Administration announced that effective October 1, a $10 application fee will be required from all applicants for open competitive and open continuous Civil Service examinations.

The State Department of Elder Affairs released information on the home care program. We learned that 43,200 elderly in need of in-home services receive those home care services each month. Services include homemaker, case management, chore, transportation, laundry and home-delivered meals. The State Auditor unearthed a couple of major deficiencies in the system... "failure to solicit competitive bids for home care services; and weaknesses in DEA's fiscal monitoring of Home Care Corporations." These deficiencies will be addressed...

All in all, the Massachusetts elderly had a good year on the Hill. The Medex increase was modified significantly. The ban on "Balance Billing" by doctors was signed into law. The legislation eliminating mandatory retirement is due to pass without too much difficulty; and the Medicare Policy Posting bill has passed the Senate and is currently in House Ways and Means. It would require physicians to post and to inform patients of their Medicare policies.

We received the encouraging results of the Commonwealth's new employment and training program, which is a nationwide model. More than 6,000 welfare recipients have been placed in full or part time jobs during the program's first nine months. Governor Dukakis has estimated that the program will save our Massachusetts taxpayers in excess of $100 million over the next five years. That's good news.

It was shocking to us all to learn of last week's theft of the state's 355-year-old colonial charter. I personally came long ago to the conclusion that our historic documents are anything but safe in their current State House location. I have wandered through the Archives many times, with no sign of security anywhere-which probably explains why I so strongly supported funding for the new Archives Building under construction at Columbia Point. Upon reading a few years back of the potential menace to our historic documents in their State House location, I had asked to meet with the Archivist to discuss the situation in depth and to see how I might help to remedy it.

It turned out to be an exciting and indeed a memorable experience for this history buff. The distinguished gentlemen in charge opened the vaults for my inspection and I saw the history of the Commonwealth spread out before me. It represented an all-time thrill for me; and I worked hard from that day forward in support of efforts to secure a new Archives building. I was consequently invited to be present on a cold blustery day last year for the groundbreaking ceremonies for this all-important facility.

We are praying along with the police that fingerprints and descriptions will lead to the apprehension of the thief (or thieves) and the return of the precious first page of the Winship Charter that dates back to 1629. Also stolen was the wax seal of King

Charles I of England. It rested beside the Charter in the glass case from which the document was removed. As a later follow-up to the SCA and Attorney General Bellotti are bringing action against the hazardous waste facility for their failure to file proper notification of the recent PCB spill. We'll continue to keep after things at the plant, needless to say.

THE BRAINTREE STAR LADY OF THE HOUSE

OCTOBER 5, 1984
BY STATE REPRESENTATIVE ELIZABETH N. METAYER

There is little I can tell you about what went on at the State House during the past week since Ted and I managed to bring about what I have been trying all summer to tuck into my busy schedule-a week at Pompano Beach, Florida. As a matter of fact it was only the Testimonial Roast and Toast for our dear friend and family physician, Dr. Archie G. Keigan that brought us back in the wee hours of Thursday morning so as to be on hand for that wonderful 1100 participant "Evening of Love" that was to honor our beloved East Braintree-ite on Thursday evening.

At any rate, our stay in Florida was the nearest thing to Heaven I can currently contemplate. With a sweeping view of the gorgeous Florida coastline, waves and all, from the front windows of our 12th floor Condominium, and the exciting Intracoastal Waterway lying directly beneath our balcony to the rear of the Condo, you may well imagine the kind of dreamy days we spent under the Florida sun.

It was off to the nearby beach each sun-washed morning, for a romp in the waves that had followed a couple of nighttime storms that had swept over the Atlantic…with a mile-long walk along the golden sands to the towering lighthouse and back…with a couple of lazy hours in the company of seagulls and sandpipers, both of which species seemed intent upon amusing and entertaining us with their antics.

Afternoons, and we had a wonderful choice. Should we swim in the heated pool that was part of this handsome Condominium facility??? Or play at the shuffleboard court??? Or chat with our Condo neighbors under the handsome umbrellas that would shade us as we sat beside that heated pool and watched the yachts go by beside us on the inland waterway??? Or-should we settle ourselves quietly and comfortably on the balcony above, and watch the aquatic parade from twelve floors up??? What a way to live, even for a vacation. Is this the kind of afterlife that will lie ahead for us during the winter of '85??? At present our plans include just that, and if so, I shall be better able to cope with the traumatic experience of leaving my many friends on Beacon Hill and surrendering a life of excitement and accomplishment for a life of leisure…

While I was sunning myself in Florida, there were dire happenings in my beloved town of Braintree. I was stricken when upon catching up with my backdated newspapers, I learned that a majority of the County Commissioners had voted to place a jail in the nurses quarters at our Norfolk County Hospital. Governor Dukakis had promised me that he would meet with our legislators when the plan was presented; and while wading through my State House mail on Thursday morning I had found a note from his appointments secretary indicating that he would indeed have met with us Tuesday last. It would obviously have been too late to effect any change in the Commissioners' decision, however. The die had been cast. Nonetheless I shall have another go at arranging such a meeting tomorrow morning (Monday, October 1). He must realize how irate we all are at the decision to place a jail in a fine residential section, adjacent to a hospital that cares for 86 respiratory patients, and Highlands Green, our latest senior citizen complex. It is indeed too bad that the constitutional rights of law-abiding, tax-paying citizens. Well, we shan't give up the ship on this. We'll keep on fighting against this highly unacceptable proposal until the last gun is fired… It's too bad the Governor was not at home when our protestors arrived in Brookline. I was with them in my thoughts…

Returning once again to the magnificent tribute that was paid on Thursday evening to our very treasured friend, Dr. Keigan…From the moment of his arrival with his beautiful wife Dorothy, when the standing ovation went on and on and on… to the last of the roasts and toasts that so totally portrayed him as the "Number One Citizen of East Braintree" and the Number One person in 1100 hearts, it was an outpouring of love….

Dr. Archie Graham Keigan is one of the "special" people we meet once or twice in a lifetime. An awful lot of people took the opportunity on Thursday evening to let him know this very definite fact…

THE BRAINTREE STAR LADY OF THE HOUSE

BY STATE REPRESENTATIVE ELIZABETH N. METAYER OCTOBER 12 1984

The House Chamber was a happy place on Monday. We were meeting in FORMAL session for the first time since the Primary Election. We've been privately at work in our own offices during the past weeks, and it was great to be greeting one another en masse once again. We're a rather close-knit group, you know…

We were there to deal with the Governor's veto of a $600 Million tax cut and a $31 Million local aid item, both from the 1985 State Budget.

The $600 million tax cut would be totally effective in four years.

Under it, the personal income exemption would be increased by $200, which would save the average taxpayer $10.75 in 1985. Non-wage earning spouses would have their exemption increased by $1400 by the year 1988, with a four-year savings of approximately $75.00. The elderly would be exempted for the first $6000 from the 10 percent surtax on investment income. One of the flaws in the tax cut was the exemption from taxes on any interest paid to the elderly on accounts in banks outside Massachusetts.

There was great support for the Governor's stand on this issue. The elderly groups opposed it since few of their number would qualify for the $6000 exemption. The bankers feared an exodus of savings accounts to out-of-state-banks. The Massachusetts Municipal Association and the Massachusetts Taxpayers Foundation lobbied against it, along with a dozen other pressure groups; and the Governor's veto prevailed with a vote of 86 to 63. (A ⅔ vote was necessary.)

Governor Dukakis' local aid veto was also upheld. The distribution formula was, in the opinion of many of us, hopelessly flawed. It would have provided for a $35 per student local aid payment to each of our cities and towns, regardless of their affluence or of their need. Actually our cities and towns fared very well this year. They received a $252 million increase in local aid. A $29 million surplus is projected for 1985, and the Governor would like to delay any plans for utilizing this surplus until the fate of his Education Reform, Massachusetts Bank and Water and Sewer Authority bills is determined in the General Court. Incidentally a resolution on the Mass Bank issue was sent to the SJC on Monday before the House adjourned.

There were other events on Beacon Hill. The Centennial of Eleanor Roosevelt was observed at a Reception in Nurses' Hall at the State House; and your L. of the H., along with Secretary of Labor Paul Eustace and Secretary of Consumer Affairs Paula Gold, received an award from the AFL/CIO at their 27th Annual Convention on Friday morning…mine included a beautiful Paul Revere bowl, suitably inscribed.

From my point of view, however, the most important event involved Braintree's continuing determination to fight against the establishment of a jail in the Nurses building at Norfolk County Hospital. I was able to arrange a meeting with the Governor on Tuesday afternoon, and our Selectmen, and Braintree Highlands Civic Association heads joined me in an attempt to convince His Excellency of the unsuitability of the Norfolk County Hospital area. We were outspoken in our bitterness, however we seemed not to have made much of an impact on the powers that be.

It seems to me extremely sad that the constitutional rights of criminals, law breakers who will be incarcerated for short periods of time-30 or 60 days-would be protected at the expense of the constitutional right of the law abiding, tax paying citizens in the area, along with the unfortunate hospital patients and the residents of Highlands Green. I make this statement publicly at every opportunity, however little or no credence seems to be given to it by those making the decisions. We'll keep on saying it, however, you may be sure. A couple of days later we were meeting with Greg Torres, the state's Deputy Commissioner of Corrections, where I made the same statement and a lot of others. So did Bob Kimball, and Dick Mazzola. Did we really get anywhere??? I didn't feel that we did, however we'll keep on keeping on. We haven't given up the ship, any of us. And perhaps the courts will help us in our fight. We hope so…

THE BRAINTREE STAR LADY OF THE HOUSE

BY STATE REPRESENTATIVE ELIZABETH N. METAYER NOVEMBER 9, 1984

This past week began with an executive briefing on the Education Bill which is one of the Governor's top priorities for this legislative session. We were informed that our cities and towns would maintain control over their schools under this four-year plan to upgrade public education within the Commonwealth. Governor Dukakis has placed a $545 million price tag on the legislation. The plan as currently proposed differs in some respects from the original bill filed by the Joint Education Committee. Instead of a mandatory class size, it would now recommend pupil-teacher ratios. New Equal Educational Opportunity grants would assist poor school districts in meeting the per-pupil spending within four years. Under the current law, all school districts must spend at least 85 percent of the statewide average that is spent per child. Currently this yearly per pupil average is $2,600. 130 of the Commonwealth's 430 school districts will be affected by this law. Minimum teachers' salaries would be raised to $18,000 over three years under this education proposal. Statewide testing of students in grades 3,5 and 7 would also be required; as would evaluations of teachers and administrators every two years. Course requirements for High School graduates would be set and a disciplinary code mandated for all public schools.

At a transportation committee meeting, DPW Commissioner Robert Tierney gave us an informational briefing on the Plymouth/Bourne Route 25 Project. We learned that this 4½ mile stretch of highway will be constructed in three sections, the lower section hopefully going to bid this month; the upper section in December; and the middle section delayed until a number of local requirements can be met. This is good news for the many who find their way to our beloved Cape Cod during vacation time. Believe it or not. This project has been in the works since 1968.

Many environmental issues had to be addressed. It looks like all will be well now, however, and we Transportation Committee members who have been keyed into the proposal for years were delighted to learn that this vitally important stretch of highway is to be built at last.

Locally it was interesting to receive from Michael Oman of Connery Associates a preview of the Master Plan update that is currently being prepared for our town. The briefing had been arranged for Braintree Business Council members by their President Lindsay L. Tait. Concerns were expressed about some aspects of the proposed recommendations; and questions were asked in regard to the manner in which zoning changes will be handled by the Town Meeting.

Mr. Oman stressed the importance of using a regulatory method of making additions to the zoning districts "to make future commercial uses more compatible with surrounding land uses and the growth policies of the community."

Another Halloween has come and gone thankfully without incident in Braintree. I must admit I thoroughly enjoy seeing the little ones in their Halloween costumes; and what pains their mothers and dads seemed to take this year in costuming the small fry for what is a very special occasion for them the evening of "Trick or Treat." We had our share of tiny angels, clowns, Cinderellas, Fairy godmothers, ghosts and goblins, witches and whatnots. Happily our little ones were very well chaperoned, with Dads more often than Moms waiting at the end of the walkway while their angels trotted down the steps with their bags of treats-to be escorted on further to the next dispenser of candy bars and lollipops. It seems like yesterday when the Metayer grandchildren arrived with their huge plastic pumpkins or Halloween-decorated bags for the special "treat" that Grandma always had waiting for them. As a matter of fact it feels like only the day before yesterday when the Metayer children trotted off, costumed and happy to return with their bags full of Halloween goodies. Unfortunately, since the Metayer children were extremely fussy about the kinds of candy they liked, it fell to Mother's lot to consume most of the loot, a situation which she thoroughly enjoyed, despite the fact that she was always (and still is) on that perennial diet of hers. Well, at any rate, it was a fun evening, and as always, I thoroughly enjoyed it.

THE BRAINTREE STAR LADY OF THE HOUSE

BY STATE REPRESENTATIVE ELIZABETH N. METAYER OCTOBER 19, 1984

As we usually do, our Massachusetts Caucus of Women Legislators is utilizing this period of INFORMAL House sessions to a very great extent with a series of hands-on experiences. On Wednesday we were off on the Massport fireboat for a look-see at the great Port of Boston. And what a busy place it is, with development going on all sides! That historic landmark, the Commonwealth Pier, for one place, is undergoing quite a metamorphosis. It's in the final stages of being transformed into a $100 million computer exhibition and marketing showplace called BOSCOM, our Massport guide told us. And of course it will continue to serve as New England's only passenger ship terminal for cruise ships bound for Europe and Bermuda and the Caribbean Ports.

The Boston Fish Pier is having a $19 million face lift, which should lead to new growth for the New England fishing industry.

The Massport Marine Terminal is progressing nicely as is the Conley Terminal at Castle Island. As Chairman of the Transportation Committee's Sub-committee on the Port Authority, I played a major role in developing these modern container facilities, and it is therefore a decided thrill for me to watch development.

Our sail around the harbor had been preceded by an enlightening, and indeed an exciting report from Massport's Executive Director David Davis. It is helpful indeed for legislators to be kept abreast of developments within a state Authority, and of course Massport and Mr. Davis are noted for their cooperation in this respect.

Wednesday was an important day in other respects. It was the birthday of "Christoforo Columbo", and the Governor held a special State House reception in his honor.

It was also the effective date for Chapter 207 of the Acts of '84. "An Act to Establish a Privilege of Certain Communication Between Rape Counselors and the Victims." The importance of this piece of legislation was brought home forcibly on the following day when we met with members of the Massachusetts Coalition of Battered Women Service Groups. "The Burning Bed" had horrified you all on the previous evening. It had highlighted in a frighteningly dramatic way the plight of battered women; and it was equally horrifying to hear from those who run our battered women and children's' shelters that the experience of Mrs. Hughes (with the exception of the burning bed incident) is happening daily in enormous numbers within the Commonwealth of Massachusetts. It is apparently a problem of enormous proportions. We were told that the Cambridge shelter received 150 calls from battered women following the program; and that the Boston shelter was similarly besieged. There are many aspects of the problem to be addressed however, we were reminded. There is housing and employment and financing, etc. So often there are also psychological problems to be dealt with affecting both mother and child. "The Burning Bed" haunted me for days, and knowing now that this battered woman is one of so many battered women, has increased my concern a hundredfold. We must address the problem and do it speedily.

Once again our great Braintree Legionnaires and their wonderful wives hosted the town's "super citizens" during the past week. Their Wednesday evening party was as always a happy occasion for a lot of appreciative elders. The band was great; the entertainment terrific, and the buffet delectable as always. Thanks, Legionnaires and your Ladies…

Pond Meadow was cold but lovely on Sunday afternoon. I was on hand for the traditional "ribbon cutting" ceremony highlighted the opening of a new and exciting bicycle path. How that recreational facility has grown! I recall vividly the day we opened the facility itself with a similar ribbon cutting ceremony.

One more important happening occurred last week. It housed the 100th Birthday of Eleanor Roosevelt, and her Centennial was observed throughout the world. This remarkable lady's life reflected a concern for all mankind in its struggle for social, economic and political justice. I was privileged to participate in the Centennial ceremonies.

THE BRAINTREE STAR LADY OF THE HOUSE

BY STATE REPRESENTATIVE ELIZABETH N. METAYER NOVEMBER 16, 1984

As I write this column, we are preparing to return to formal House sessions on Beacon Hill, with many important issues lying ahead for us. We shall be faced with the Education Reform bill; the Water and Sewer Authority legislation; Massbank (should it be released by the SJC in time); and others.

We met on Thursday with Arthur R. Osborn, President of the Massachusetts, AFL/CIO, and the presidents of the Brockton and Norfolk County Labor Councils to discuss one of the impending issues, -the proposed Workmen's Compensation Bill that is being sponsored by Representative Timothy Bassett, Chairman of the Joint Legislative Committee on Commerce and Labor. Representative Bassett discussed his proposed 150-page bill in detail. Incidentally an Executive Task Force has been working for the past several years to come up with a solution to the present system which, according to Representative Bassett is out of control and has failed entirely to address the problems, both for our Massachusetts workers and their employers. The task force still fails to come up with a bill agreed upon by all parties involved.

The system was established in 1911. Its goal was to provide swift relief to those workers who were injured in industrial accidents, while at the same time protecting employers against personal injury suits. We were told that it currently costs business $600-700 million annually. It takes on average, 10.1 months to resolve a claim; it fails to rehabilitate injured workers and to return them to work. Its benefits have no cost-of-living adjustments; and its ratemaking system has limited power to control insurance premiums. The bill would include an expedited claim process; rehabilitation provisions, benefit adjustments and ratemaking reform.

According to our informants, those who benefit most are some lawyers who frequently drag out the cases and encourage the workers to accept a lump-sum settlement, of which, of course, they will take one-third. Instead of being rehabilitated and returned to work in most cases the workers go on Welfare when the lump-sum settlement money is exhausted. Massachusetts has ten times as many injured workers on Welfare and Medicaid than other states, we were told. Our manufacturers are at the mercy of the insurance companies, and the injured workers are at the mercy of the lawyers. This is sure to be a controversial bill, and we welcomed an opportunity to have our questions answered and our concerns addressed by the bill's sponsors. The Workmen's Compensation Reform Bill is one of many that will come before us as our 1984 legislation session winds up. Veterans Day was observed on Sunday with a memorable ceremony at the Blue Hill Cemetery's Garden of Honor. Cdr. Frank Drogo of the Disabled American Veterans served as officer of the day and conducted the ceremony with appropriate solemnity. Senator Paul Harold gave a memorable address. The weather was ideal, for a change. We usually freeze to death or are rained upon. It Is indeed fitting that we remember on this all-important national holiday those brave men and women who gave their lives for us, along with those whose lives were spared, to keep alight the torch of remembrance for their fallen brothers and sisters in arms. The Braintree Choral Society added its lovely musical note, as always, to the solemn proceedings; and the luncheon that followed in DAV Hall afforded Braintree Cemetery Commission Chairman John Shaughnessy and I an opportunity to greet our great Braintree veterans in person on their special day. Mr. Shaughnessy is, of course, himself a distinguished veteran who is always on hand for this impressive Veterans Day ceremony.

Sunday also housed the observance of the 75th Anniversary of Braintree's Emmanuel Episcopal Church. Unfortunately the service and reception featuring this important event were scheduled at the same time as the Veterans Day observance and so we had to miss them. I was pleased, however, to prepare a House of Representatives Citation in acknowledgement of this important milestone in the Church's and indeed in the town's history. It was presented by my good friend Mary Bean Cunningham; and it read "In recognition of the 75th Anniversary of the Institution of the Episcopal Church in Braintree, Massachusetts; and of its outstanding contribution to the spiritual welfare of the residents of the community."

I have since heard à rumor that the Reception may have been delayed in order to accommodate those officials who wished to attend. If this was so, I was unfortunately not privy to the information. Had I known it, I would certainly have been on hand to personally salute my many friends among the Emmanuel Church parishioners on this happy milestone in their history.

THE BRAINTREE STAR LADY OF THE HOUSE

BY STATE REPRESENTATIVE ELIZABETH N. METAYER DECEMBER 7, 1984

The week of November 26 was a "Red Letter" 7 days for your L. of the H. For one thing, the long-awaited Presumptive Sentencing Bill came before us for House action. It is a bill in which I am are particularly interested. I myself filed legislation for presumptive sentencing for most of my 10 years on Beacon Hill.

I can remember distinctly when my interest in this issue began. I had reacted with outrage when reading of trials in which the criminal involved had a previous record a mile long. I had discussed court action with a number of "Braintree's Finest". They had agreed with me that the Courts were soft on criminals. In order to make sure of my stand on this issue, however, I had persuaded Ted to accompany me to a number of court trials. They confirmed my feeling that our courts were bending over backwards to protect the rights of criminals and showing little regard for the rights of the victims of crime.

Presumptive sentencing seemed to represent an answer to this situation, I had decided. Let the criminal know in advance of the sentence awaiting him upon the commission of a crime. Place parameters on the judicial decision-making process. It could work, I thought. At any rate, it was worth a try. There were those on the Legislative Judiciary Committee who agreed with me, Representative W. Paul White of Dorchester among them. He formed a subcommittee which literally spent years researching all elements of the proposed legislation. The one we debated in the House last week was the result of his work and that of the Governor's task force.

It refers specifically by category to the various levels of violent crime; and calls for a graded sentence structure covering each level. A judge who deviates from the proposed sentence must include his rationale in the court records of the case in question. It's a good bill. It will hopefully serve to deter criminals from contemplated crimes; and it will hopefully offer a shade a more protection for the victims of violent crime.

There was considerable debate on the bill. Our liberal colleagues opposed it strenuously. We trust, however, that we shall see it signed into law before year's end. One more of my pet bills to make it before I pack up my things and leave Beacon Hill…

And-speaking of packing up my things and leaving the Hill, I am still on Cloud Nine after my wonderful Testimonial on Thursday evening at the Sheraton Tara. The occasion was flawless; and, to say that I was surprised to enter the huge Tara Ballroom and find every corner of it occupied by a Colleague or a Friend, is the understatement of the century. I was stunned!

As I told the close to 600 dear people gathered there, I felt like the richest woman in the world! At my age, one does not measure riches by the wealth one has been able to amass, but by the amount of friendship and love one has been able to garner over the years. My wealth lay before me Thursday evening! My heart and my love…and my prayers…go out to each and every one of you who were present.

As you know, I shall soon close the most exciting chapter of the book that is my life. Lonely hours will lie ahead, for I shall miss more than I can say my daily contacts with the wonderful people of Braintree, and the wonderful people on Beacon Hill. But whenever my mouth begins to turn. downward at the corners, I shall bring to mind that fantastic Thursday evening; and the memory of my mouth back up…the friendship I found there…and indeed the love…will warm my heart and turn the corners of I owe so very much to the dear and treasured friends who planned and executed that flawless "Metayer Tribute". To Thomas Flatley, the event's Honorary Chairman; to Elizabeth Laing and John Shaughnessy, Co-Chairmen; to Town Moderator Gerald Walsh, the Toastmaster; to Robert Bruynell, the Ticket Chairman; to Donald Olson, the Committee Treasurer; to Linda Chase, who handled the Program; an to Olive Laing, who was responsible for the Publicity (and, judging by the size of the sell-out crowd, must have done her work well…) And-last, but not least, my thanks go out to my good friend Arthur Logan who provided for the "Guest of Honor" limousine service to and from the event. Riding in such splendor, I felt like a one-day participant in an episode from "Dynasty" or "Dallas"…

My thanks go out also to the wonderful people who showered me with Awards and gifts on that matchless evening-not the least of which was the lovely framed front page of this fine newspaper, the "Braintree Star"-the gift of editor, my good friend "Charlie" Knowles…AND that gift from the Honorary Chairman, Mr. Flatley, a $1,000 check which I shall present this week to Oxfam for the relief of the starving people of Ethiopia, from Mr. Flatley, in my name. How wonderful to be able to share my memorable evening with people to whom this gift could represent the meaning between life and death…What a superb ending for what will always be my finest hour!

1-04-85

This is the 'Lady of the House' column, by Representative Metayer, prepared for the last issue of 1984, which would have been dated 12-28-84. Traditionally we close between the holidays and, thus, publish this column in the first issue of 1985.

How can I possibly put into words what it has meant to me to represent the wonderful people of Braintree, and to walk with and work with the wonderful people on Beacon Hill during the past ten years? I have loved every day of it, and my heart is heavy indeed as I face the prospect of bidding farewell to our exquisite State Capital and the countless friends I shall be leaving there under the Golden Dome. This will be my very last weekly column as your "Lady of the House," and it's a difficult one to write.

It is an especially sad time of year to be leaving the State House since it has never been lovelier nor the indoor tree more lavishly decorated, dominating the House lobby. It is a real tree, and its fragrance drifts gently into the House Chamber, whispering, "'Tis Christmastime" to those of us who are in session there. There are daily concerts on the wide Main Stairway, and music, Christmas and otherwise, fills the great halls and sets the heart soaring.

Doric Hall houses another great Yuletide tree. It was lighted by Governor and Mrs. Michael S. Dukakis on December 10 with due ceremony, and it's a handsome sight indeed. Lighted also on that festive evening were the two huge trees on the State House balcony, and the shining star atop the Golden Dome, and the myriad window candles that spill their gold upon the State House lawn. From the balcony one's holiday heart quickens and sings anew at sight of Boston Common, a kaleidoscope of color, white and gold and red and green, with the hundreds of bright shining lights that dance in the evening breeze and provide a backdrop for one more stately decorated Christmas tree and for the lovely Creche that is the reason for all the Christmas grandeur…the Creche that seems a lonely place as I stand beside it, even as that stable in the Bethlehem hills so long ago was lonely ere the tiny Prince of Peace was born and joy came to the waiting world…

A great six-pointed star leads one to Downtown Crossing where the merchants seem to have outdone themselves in Christmas decorating this Christmas season, and where the pleading bell of the Salvation Army Lassie is all but lost in the symphony sources, causing one to quicken one's step, and filling one's heart with that special kind of gladness that is everywhere during this blessed and beautiful time of year.

I find myself turning the pages of the Daily Calendar that was in my morning's mail, and making a notation for the first week of December 1986. "Visit Boston and the State House one evening soon."

I look sadly upon this Daily Calendar I have before me. It is a pocket calendar. For the past ten years it has had to give way to the huge version I have purchased at Barker's, a Daily Calendar large enough to accommodate the countless engagements that would lie ahead for me. This year, the small daily calendar that was in my morning mail will easily suffice, and I am sad as I contemplate the fact that the busiest and most exciting decade of my life is now all but over. A few more days and my career as Braintree's State Representative will be but history.

And so I say again, how can I possibly put into words what it has meant to me to represent the beautiful people of Braintree, and to walk with and work with the beautiful people on Beacon Hill during the past ten years???? It has been a privilege, a joy, and the avenue to a bright, new and exciting world for me. I shall never cease to be grateful to the wonderful people of Braintree for having chosen me to represent them.

It is Christmas Eve as I write this column. The birthday of the little Christ Child lies dead ahead. On this day of days, may I wish for you all the brightest and most blessed joys of the holiday season, and may the brand new year that will soon be ours bring to each and every one of you, my dear readers, the fulfillment of every dream that lies closest to your hearts. May God love you all.

I do…

Bibs hosts Federation Day at the State House March 24, 1983
introducing Governor Michael S. Dukakis

Bibs hosts Federation Day at the State House March 24,1983
Governor Michael S. Dukakis signs Proclamation

The Candid Idylls of a State Representative | 477

Bibs with House Speaker Thomas McGee and Candidate for President Fritz Mondale 1984

Bibs with State House Photographer Jack Leonard 1983

Printed in the USA
CPSIA information can be obtained
at www.ICGtesting.com
JSHW072005111024
71422JS00020B/78

9 781961 358980